SIGNALS and PERCEPTION

THE FUNDAMENTALS OF HUMAN SENSATION

Edited by David Roberts

The Open University

Edited, designed and typeset by The Open University.

Printed in the United Kingdom by The Alden Group, Oxford.

First published 2002 by
PALGRAVE MACMILLAN
Houndmills, Basingstoke, Hampshire RG21 6XS and
175 Fifth Avenue, New York, N.Y. 10010
Companies and representatives throughout the world.

PALGRAVE MACMILLAN is the global academic imprint of the Palgrave Macmillan division of St Martin's Press, LLC and of Palgrave Macmillan Ltd. Macmillan® is a registered trademark in the United States, United Kingdom and other countries. Palgrave is a registered trademark in the European Union and other countries.

ISBN 0-333-99364-0 (paperback)

This publication forms part of an Open University course, *SD329 Signals and Perception: the science of the senses*. Details of this and other Open University courses can be obtained from the Call Centre, PO Box 724, The Open University, Milton Keynes MK7 6ZS, United Kingdom: tel. +44 (0)1908 653231, e-mail ces-gen@open.ac.uk

Alternatively, you may visit the Open University website at http://www.open.ac.uk where you can learn more about the wide range of courses and packs offered at all levels by The Open University.

This book is printed on paper suitable for recycling and made from fully managed and sustained forest sources.

A catalogue record for this book is available from the British Library.

10   9   8   7   6   5   4   3   2   1
11   10   09   08   07   06   05   04   03   02

1.1

Contents

Preface

This volume is a constituent part of an Open University course *Signals and Perception: the science of the senses*. While it is designed to complement the other course materials (or to be used in tandem with other texts on sensation and perception for courses elsewhere) and as such is not intended to be entirely comprehensive in its coverage, it is also suitable as a standalone book about the human senses. Presenting the latest advances, it provides a coherent survey of our current understanding of how we interact with the environment via our senses. The book is divided into five parts: *Hearing and Balance*, *Vision*, *Touch and Pain*, *Smell and Taste*, and *Integrating the Senses*. For each of the senses, we have taken a consistent approach, following the path of the appropriate signal to the receptor, the transduction process, transmission of the resulting electrical signals to the brain, and the processing that gives rise to our various perceptions.

We have endeavoured to take a more balanced view of sensation and perception than is generally the case by covering in depth both the neuroscience and the psychology of sensation and perception. We have also taken a more interdisciplinary approach than is traditional, which accounts for the inclusion of some of the chapter topics, for example Chapter 8 *Colour science*, Chapter 9 *The cornea*, and Chapter 29 *Perceiving, misperceiving and hypnotic hallucinations*. The inclusion of Chapter 4 *Imaging central auditory function* and Chapter 13 *Functional imaging of the human visual system* is recognition of the huge impact that functional imaging has had on our understanding of the neurophysiological processes that underlie perception.

Each chapter was commissioned from an expert in the relevant field in order to ensure as contemporary an account as possible, a feature particularly necessary in areas such as taste and smell that are so fast-moving at the present time. It also provides an authority that is not always present in textbooks written by single or a few authors. The order of topics chosen seemed to us to be the most logical and provides a gradation in concept difficulty. Doubtless, others may have different views. However, the modular nature of the book means that the chapters could easily be studied in an alternative sequence.

Open University courses are produced by course teams, and the production of this volume is no exception. Accordingly, in addition to expressing my gratitude to our long-suffering authors for agreeing to contribute, I also wish to thank my numerous colleagues for their various contributions: academics Heather McLannahan, Mandy Dyson, Liz Parvin, Jim Iley, Peter Naish, Michael Mortimer, Eleanor Crabb, and Mike Harris (University of Birmingham); course manager Yvonne Ashmore; course team assistant Margaret Careford; publishing editors Gilly Riley and Val Russell; designer Jenny Nockles; graphic artists Andrew Whitehead and Roger Courthold; picture researcher Lydia Eaton; rights executive Christine Brady; indexer Jean Macqueen; the Deputy Manager OU Copublishing Department Giles Clark; and the external course assessors Professor George Mather (University of Sussex) and Professor John Mellerio (University of Westminster). Without their joint efforts this book would not have seen the light of day.

David Roberts

Chemistry Department
Open University, Milton Keynes

April 2002

Contributors

Jonathan Ashmore is in the Department of Physiology and Centre for Auditory Research at University College London, where he is Professor of Biophysics. His research on the cellular basis of hearing uses a variety of different approaches that draw on techniques both from biology and from physics. He has recently contributed to the *Human Body* television series, and large scale format film.

David Baguley is Head of Audiology at Addenbrooke's Hospital, Cambridge. His main clinical interests include tinnitus and diagnostic strategies in audiology. David was the Editor of the *British Journal of Audiology* from 1995–2000.

Stanley Bolanowski is Professor in the Department of Bioengineering and Neuroscience and the Institute for Sensory Research at Syracuse University, USA, specializing in general neuroscience, psychology and behaviour, sensory systems, vision, and somatosensation. His current research interests focus on tactile psychophysics, tactile physiology, tactile anatomy, general neuroscience, and vision psychophysics.

Jim Bowmaker is in the Department of Visual Science, Institute of Ophthalmology, University College London where he is Professor of Vision Research. His research centres on comparative aspects of colour vision in vertebrates, with specific interests in the evolution of colour vision and the molecular basis for the spectral tuning of visual pigments. He has recently contributed to a series *The Eye of Nature* on BBC Radio 4.

Peter Cahusac is a Lecturer in the Psychology Department at the University of Stirling. His research interests include somatosensory physiology and the neural mechanisms of cortical function.

Chris Darwin is Professor of Experimental Psychology at the University of Sussex. He carries out research in auditory perception and speech perception. The particular problem that intrigues him is how the brain can sort out the mixture of sounds that arrives at the two ears into separate sound sources. His time spent playing chamber music provides ample sound for thought on this problem.

Andrew Derrington is Professor of Psychology at the University of Nottingham. In his research on the mechanisms of visual perception he investigates how physiological processes determine the visual capabilities of humans and of non-human primates, which he also studies in behavioural experiments. In the future, he plans to integrate behavioural and physiological measurements more closely and to study how visual memory influences the physiological processes underlying vision. He also works as a freelance science journalist and has written articles for the *Financial Times* on scientific topics ranging from psychotherapy to astrophysics.

Robert Fettiplace is the Steenbock Professor of Neuroscience in the Department of Physiology at the University of Wisconsin-Madison, USA. He was formerly a Royal Society Senior Research Fellow at Cambridge University. His research over the last 25 years has been concerned with studying the ion channels underlying transduction and frequency tuning in auditory hair cells.

David Furness is Reader in Cochlear Cell Biology in the MacKay Institute of Communication and Neuroscience at Keele University. His main research interests are in the structure and function of sensory hair cells and he has published numerous journal articles in the field of auditory research.

Carole Hackney is Professor of Auditory Neuroscience in the MacKay Institute of Communication and Neuroscience at Keele University where she also heads the School of Life Sciences. Her research interests are in the structure and function of the auditory pathway, especially the inner ear and auditory brain stem. She has written many papers and articles in this area, including recent reviews for periodicals such as *Trends in Neuroscience*.

Debbie Hall is a Research Scientist at the MRC Institute of Hearing Research in Nottingham. Her main areas of research include methodological issues in auditory fMRI and in mapping the functional anatomy of the auditory cortex.

Mike Harris is a Senior Lecturer in Psychology at the University of Birmingham. His research focuses on human motion vision, and particularly on the ways that people use retinal motion to control and time their movements about the world. He is the founding, and only, member of the British Society for the Conservation of Gravity.

Anya Hurlbert is Reader in Visual Neuroscience at the Medical School, University of Newcastle upon Tyne. Her research into visual perception began with the study of computational vision at MIT, with the particular problem of how vision machines might attain colour constancy. She now studies the human visual system, using the tools of psychophysics, computational modelling, electroencephalography and magnetoencephalography, and is especially interested in how the human brain integrates colour perception with the perception of other object attributes, such as motion and shape. She is also interested in interactions between the senses, such as vision and hearing, and has been involved in several major efforts to integrate vision science and art.

Tim Jacob is Professor in the School of Biosciences at Cardiff University. His research into the sense of smell focuses on the physiological effects of odour, studying olfactory receptor potentials and event-related potentials. In addition he is interested in the relationship between the physiological and psychological responses to odour and how the brain discriminates between good and bad smells. At a more fundamental level, he also studies cell volume regulation, a better understanding of which may lead to new therapies for diseases such as cataract, glaucoma, diabetes and cancer.

Tyler Lorig is Professor of Psychology and Chair of the Neuroscience Program at Washington and Lee University, Lexington, Virginia, USA. His research is concerned with understanding the neurophysiological basis of cognition and its evolution. The primitive nature of the olfactory system provides an interesting avenue into this topic. Most of his research involves recording human brain electrical activity as subjects detect or label odours. He also has strong interests in the analysis and visualization of brain activity.

Ian Lyon was at the Medical Research Council's Human Movement and Balance Unit.

Don McFerran is a Consultant Otorhinolaryngologist in Colchester. His main areas of interest include sensorineural hearing loss, tinnitus and vertigo. He has published widely in these fields and is one of the editors of the *Oxford Concise Medical Dictionary*.

Keith Meek is Professor of Biophysics in the Department of Optometry and Vision Sciences at Cardiff University. His research centres on the structure of eye tissues, particularly the cornea and lens. He is particularly fascinated by the cornea, why it is transparent, and why transparency is lost in pathological conditions or following surgery. He is also interested in the relationship between the shape (and hence the optical characteristics of the cornea) and the arrangement of the various molecules that make up the tissue. In his spare time he relaxes by listening to all kinds of music whilst studying the behaviour of his tropical fish.

Tim Meese is a Lecturer in Vision Sciences in the Neurosciences Research Institute at Aston University. His background is in electronics engineering, computer science and psychology and his research interests are in the function and organisation of early visual processing in humans. His specialisms include psychophysical investigation and computational modelling of spatial vision and complex motion.

Julian Millar studied for his PhD with Professor Pat Wall and has been interested in pain pathways ever since. He now works at the Medical School of St. Bartholomew's and the Royal London Hospitals, investigating neurotransmitter actions in the spinal cord. His hobbies include attempting to grow plants on the chalk cliff-face that he laughingly calls his garden.

Peter Naish is a Lecturer in Psychology at the Open University. He obtained his doctorate in the Department of Experimental Psychology at the University of Oxford, where he researched the mechanisms by which reading takes place. Since then, a good deal of his research has been in the field of hypnosis. He was a member of the Advisory Group set up by the British Psychological Society to produce guidelines on the ethical use of hypnosis, and he has served as an expert witness in court cases addressing the alleged misuse of hypnosis.

Robin Orchardson is a Senior Lecturer in the Institute of Biomedical and Life Sciences at the University of Glasgow. His research centres on sensory and motor functions of the mouth and related structures. His main interest is dental pain, with particular reference to dentine hypersensitivity. He is president-elect of the Pulp Biology Group of the International Association for Dental Research and in recent years was an Associate Editor of *Archives of Oral Biology*.

Alan Palmer is head of the Neurophysiology Section at the MRC Institute of Hearing Research in Nottingham and is a Special Professor of Neuroscience in the School of Biomedical Sciences of the University of Nottingham. His research interests centre on the neural encoding of sounds in the central auditory system, but embrace psychophysical and imaging studies of auditory function.

Krish Singh is a Senior Lecturer in the Neurosciences Research Institute at Aston University. His research interests are in non-invasive functional imaging of human brain function, with a specific interest in studies of the human visual system. In his research he uses two functional imaging technologies: functional magnetic resonance imaging, which measures changes in blood oxygenation in active areas of the brain, and magnetoencephalography, which measures the very weak external magnetic fields generated by neuronal activity.

Charles Spence is a Lecturer in Experimental Psychology at the University of Oxford. His research concerns any situation in which people are required to respond to information from more than one sensory modality. A current objective is the identification of fundamental limits on our ability to process multimodal information, of ever-increasing importance for the design of multimodal user interfaces, such as aircraft cockpits. He also has a keen interest in the dissemination of current psychological research findings to the general public.

Rollin Stott qualified in medicine from Cambridge University in 1963 and later studied engineering applied to medicine at Imperial College. He has worked for the past 20 years in the subject of aviation medicine, initially at the Royal Air Force Institute of Aviation Medicine, and latterly at the Defence Evaluation and Research Agency (DERA) and its successor organisation, QinetiQ. His particular interests have been in the physiology of the vestibular system and the related aviation problems of spatial disorientation in flight, airsickness and the effects of whole body vibration.

Steve Van Toller is Emeritus Reader in the Department of Psychology at Warwick University. In the early 1980s, he founded the Warwick Olfaction Research Group. His research focuses on the senses of smell and taste, especially olfaction and emotion, olfactory memory, electroencephalography and evoked potentials, neurochemistry and sensory evaluation.

Stephen Westland is Reader in Colour Imaging at the Colour and Imaging Institute of the University of Derby. His research interests include colour measurement, colour and spatial vision, image processing, and transparency perception. He is a member of the Applied Vision Association, the Colour Group (UK) Committee, the Colour Measurement Committee of the Society of Dyers and Colourists, and a member of the International Editorial Board of the Journal of Coloration Technology.

PART ONE

HEARING AND BALANCE

The mechanics of hearing

Jonathan Ashmore

1 Introduction

When we think of the ears, we think of the flaps that stick out from either side of our head. However these are only part of a complex physiological apparatus that enables us to hear all sorts of sounds and, more importantly, to respond appropriately. The most visible part of the ear is the **outer ear**, also sometimes called the **external ear** (Figure 1). The rest of the hearing organ, comprising the **middle ear** and the **inner ear**, is buried within the temporal bone on either side of the skull. The temporal bone can be felt just behind the outer ear. The inaccessibility of the structural components of hearing and, as we shall see, the small size of the important structures, makes the study of hearing particularly challenging.

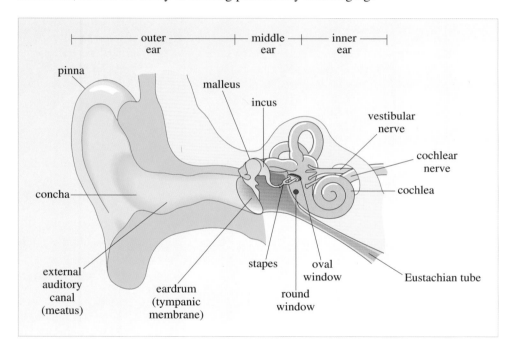

Figure 1 A cross section of the human ear.

We can hear because a precise sequence of events takes place in the ear. We shall explore these events in this and succeeding chapters. In this chapter, we shall trace the sequence of events from initial receipt of the signal to the stimulation of the cochlea. We use the word 'ear' as the collective description of all the structures and not just the outer ear. Normally when we hear a sound it is as a result of a physical disturbance transmitted through air, through the external auditory canal, through the middle ear and into the inner ear structures where it may be detected, if it is intense enough and of the right frequency. If you tap the temporal bone with your finger you can hear the percussive sound transmitted directly to the inner ear. In this case sound is said to be transmitted by **bone conduction**. This simple test is one of those used to identify whether hearing losses come about because sound is not being transmitted properly through the external and middle ear to the hearing organ of the inner ear or whether it is the inner ear itself that is working incorrectly.

2 The sensitivity of the ear

It is usually most convenient to describe the sensitivity of the ear in terms of a **threshold**. This threshold is the amplitude of a sound pressure wave that can just be heard when presented to a listener. To determine such a threshold it is important that the sound is delivered in completely quiet surroundings as any background sound can interfere with the measurement.

Experiments have shown that the minimum amplitude of a sound wave that can be detected under optimal conditions for a normally-hearing individual is $20\,\mu\text{Pa}$ (micropascals). For comparison, atmospheric pressure is approximately $100\,\text{kPa}$, and hence a disturbance 2×10^{-10} times atmospheric pressure is detectable by the ear. An equivalent comparison is to consider the situation where you blow up a normal party balloon and then start pushing the tip of a pencil into the side. When the pencil indents the side by 1 mm, the pressure inside will have increased by about $20\,\mu\text{Pa}$.

Our ears, like microphones, are sensitive to sound pressure. A sound stimulus can be determined by physical measurements of the sound wave at the entrance to the external auditory canal using calibrated probe microphones. Sound is measured in units of decibels (dB SPL) where **SPL** stands for **sound pressure level**, and is defined as follows using a logarithmic scale:

$$\text{sound stimulus (in dB SPL)} = 20\log_{10}(P/P_{\text{ref}})$$

where $P_{\text{ref}} = 20\,\mu\text{Pa}$.

This particular definition means that each increment of the sound wave amplitude by a factor of 10 will increment the sound level by 20 on the decibel scale. The definition is a consequence of sound energy being proportional to the square of the sound wave amplitude. The logarithmic scale is useful because of the very wide range of human hearing, where the amplitude of the sound varies by more than a million times, from the very softest that can be heard to the loudest, which can begin to produce damage. The energy per unit area (referred to as intensity) that passes into the ear from a sound wave with amplitude P is proportional to P^2 and has units of W m^{-2}. In air the threshold of hearing corresponds to $10^{-12}\,\text{W m}^{-2}$.

The threshold sound stimulus depends on the frequency. Figure 2 shows the auditory threshold curve (or **audiogram**) for a normal subject. The threshold rises at both lower and higher frequencies. Below about $20\,\text{Hz}$, the sound has to be so intense that it is possible to say that there is no hearing below this frequency. Depending on the history and age of the individual, the auditory threshold also rises at higher frequencies. The range over which we hear is, optimally, $20\,\text{Hz}$ to $20\,\text{kHz}$, but can be very different from individual to individual. In particular, the upper limit of hearing is severely reduced in age-related deafness. The manner in which the measured threshold curve differs from the curve obtained from a population of normally-hearing individuals is thus a measure of auditory performance.

3 Components of the ear: overall considerations

Figure 3 shows the sequence of sound processing components in the ear. As a functional entity, these components constitute the **peripheral auditory system**. The function of the outer and middle ear is to transform sound from a wave travelling in air to one travelling in the fluids of the inner ear. This idea was first developed by the German scientist Hermann von Helmholtz in 1877 (Figure 4).

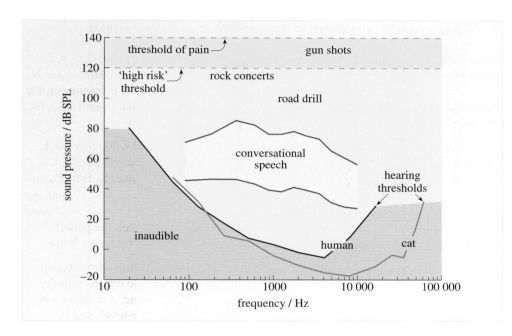

Figure 2   Auditory threshold curve for a healthy young normally-hearing subject. With age, the threshold rises at the higher frequencies. The auditory threshold curve for a cat is shown for comparison.

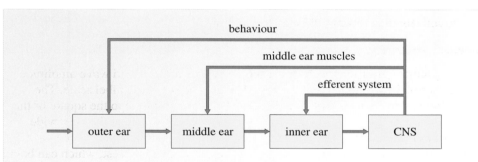

Figure 3   Block diagram of the mammalian ear and its components, and its relation to the central nervous system (CNS).

Figure 4   Hermann von Helmholtz (1821–1894). Helmholtz trained as a medical doctor before ultimately taking up the Chair of Physics in Berlin. He made many substantial contributions to physiology, and his book *On the Sensation of Tone* contains the first theoretical analysis of the process of hearing.

The effectiveness of the transmission in each structure of the ear is under central nervous system control. The outer ear can be oriented towards (or away from) a sound by movement of the head, and thus the intensity of sound entering each ear can be controlled. The middle ear, responsible for transmitting sound to the inner ear, contains two muscles that control the sound passing through. The inner ear itself is the target of a neural pathway (the efferent system) that can control the sensitivity of the sensorineural cells. Together these three subsystems determine the codes sent along the auditory nerve to the first relay nuclei of the auditory pathway. The descending control from the higher central nervous system therefore acts both to limit and, if necessary, to enhance the sound stimulus reaching the sensory structures of the inner ear and shows the importance of maintaining the correct level of stimulus.

4 The outer ear

The outer ear includes the visible flap (**pinna**), the funnel-like inner portion (**concha**) and the **external auditory canal** (**meatus**) (Figure 1). The shape of our outer ears (and those of many mammals) is approximately that of a tapered tube with the larger end open to the outside of the head. The consequence of this shape is that sound is less effectively transmitted at frequencies below a critical frequency that depends on the length and cross-sectional areas of the meatus and concha. For the human ear this frequency is near 1–2 kHz. In addition, there is sometimes a slight sympathetic vibration in the canal itself near 5–7 kHz, when the canal behaves like an organ pipe and slightly increases acoustic transmission at these frequencies. Some animals can move their pinnae to orientate them towards a sound. In humans, with a relatively static pinna, the acoustic shielding effect of the head between the two ears and the diffraction of the sound around the head provides the major clue for the brain to work out where a sound is coming from. Clues about the elevation of a sound source are also provided by the reflection of sounds from the curved surfaces of individual pinnae, which we learn to use by processing the auditory signals.

5 The middle ear

The middle ear is a cavity interposed between the eardrum (the **tympanic membrane** that closes off the ear canal), and the membranous **oval window** that opens into the cochlea of the inner ear but retains the fluid within it (Figure 1). In construction, the middle ear on each side of the head contains the ossicular chain of three bones (the **malleus**, the **incus**, and the **stapes**, collectively called the **ossicles**), that connect the external and inner ear structures (Figure 5). The middle ear contains (moist) air: its communication with the pharynx through the **Eustachian tube** allows the pressure on either side of the eardrum to be equalized to atmospheric pressure, as most airline passengers know.

The middle ear acts, functionally, as a device that matches the **acoustic impedance** of the medium through which sound travels to the fluid in the inner ear (see Box 1, p. 9). This **transformer action** allows a sound wave travelling in air (in the outer ear) to become a sound wave travelling in fluid (in the inner ear) without reflection at the interface. The transformer action of the middle ear allows more than 60% of the incident sound energy reaching the eardrum to be transmitted faithfully to the inner ear structures. Without the middle ear, the efficiency of sound transmission into the inner ear would drop and the sensitivity to sound would be reduced more than thirty

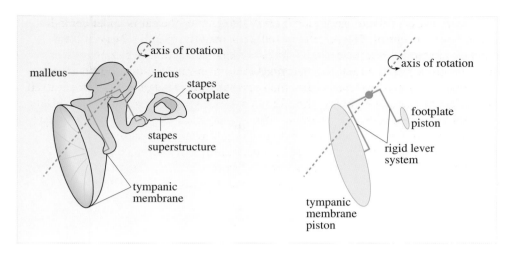

Figure 5   Structure of the middle ear. The diagram shows the eardrum, and the ossicular chain (stapes, malleus and incus). The axis of rotation of the ossicles is shown.

times. This situation occurs when the middle ear is prevented from working properly, for example, when it becomes filled with mucous fluid during an infection.

There are two main mechanisms that allow the middle ear to match acoustic impedance.

1 Area ratios

The area of the eardrum in the human ear is 17 times that of the stapes footplate, the region of the stapes in contact with the oval window of the cochlea in the inner ear. This allows the middle ear to act as a pneumatic lever: the pressure and flow velocity at the tympanic membrane is converted to a larger pressure (but a smaller flow velocity) at the cochlea:

$$\frac{pressure\ at\ cochlea}{pressure\ at\ eardrum} = \frac{area\ of\ tympanum}{area\ of\ stapes\ footplate} = 17$$

2 Ossicular lever

The three small bones of the middle ear, the malleus (Latin for 'hammer'), the incus ('anvil') and the stapes ('stirrup') link the eardrum to the flexible membranous oval window of the cochlea, which contains the fluid of the inner ear. These small bones are attached together by cartilage, but essentially move as a single unit. The axis of rotation of the ossicles runs through the point where the malleus and incus are fused together. Thus the ossicles behave like a lever system:

$$\frac{force\ at\ cochlea}{force\ at\ eardrum} = \frac{length\ of\ incus}{length\ of\ malleus} = 1.2$$

At higher frequencies the motion is more complicated than a simple lever mechanism. More complex modes of vibration occur. The pneumatic lever and the ossicular lever schemes provide the simple basic theoretical framework for understanding how the middle ear operates. Taken together, the two mechanisms should enhance, (as an ideal transformer), the sound pressure at the cochlea (P_C) over that of the eardrum (P_T) by a factor of 20, independent of frequency.

$$P_C/P_T = 17 \times 1.2 = 20$$

This figure is hard to verify precisely in humans, but can be studied in animals. Figure 6 (overleaf) shows the data for the middle ear of the cat where, because of the small differences in anatomy, the prediction for the sound pressure ratio P_C/P_T is that it would be enhanced by a factor of 80 (equivalent to 38 dB). The real data show, however, that this theoretically predicted value is too high by about 8 dB. It also shows that the middle ear transformer action is frequency-dependent. The ratio falls to 1 at low frequencies and also falls off at frequencies above 10 kHz.

Figure 6 Middle ear transfer function. The data show the measured ratio of the pressure at the entrance to the cochlea (P_C) to that at the tympanum (P_T) over the audible frequency range for the cat. The ideal transformer ratio would be about 80 on the basis of the measured anatomy of the cat's middle ear.

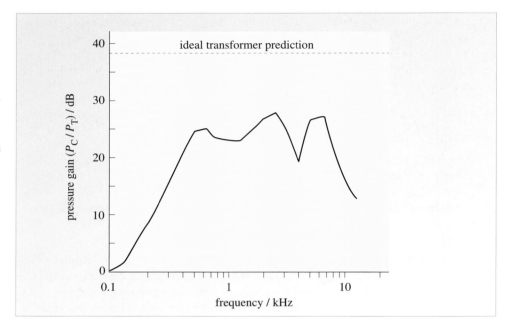

The reasons why the transformer ratio is frequency-dependent are complex. The following factors are thought to be critical:

1   The linkage between the ossicular bones is flexible. At low frequencies the coupling between the malleus and incus and between the incus and the stapes becomes imperfect. Thus at low frequencies the pressure gain (P_C / P_T) will fall towards the value of 0 dB which would be expected if no middle ear structures were present.

2   The ossicles have a finite mass. At higher frequencies the inertial mass of the ossicular chain (and of the eardrum) become significant and the ossicles will not follow rapid changes in sound pressure faithfully. In this regime also, P_C / P_T will therefore be reduced.

It is worth considering why, when we move our head, the ossicles do not move and produce a sensation indistinguishable from sound. A possible explanation is that the centre of gravity of the ossicular chain is close to the axis of rotation and so head movements would not move the ossicles relative to the middle ear to any appreciable extent.

The middle ear transformer ratio is also determined by the activity of two small muscles found within the middle ear cavity. The **tensor tympani muscle** is attached to the malleus near the centre of the eardrum. When the tensor tympani contracts, it pulls inwards on the eardrum and reduces the motion of the membrane to sound stimulation. The second muscle is the **stapedius muscle**, which is attached to the stapes near the attachment to the incus. When the stapedius muscle contracts it pulls the stapes towards the eardrum. Although the muscles are innervated by separate nerves, the effect of their simultaneous contraction is to lock the ossicular chain and prevent free movement of the middle ear mechanics. The functional effect is therefore to remove any impedance-matching advantage of the middle ear and to reduce the transfer of sound energy to the inner ear. Activation of the middle ear muscles occurs by a reflex pathway and constitutes the **middle ear reflex**. Activation certainly occurs when loud sounds are presented to the ear (i.e. when sound levels exceed about 70 dB SPL). The middle ear muscle reflex thus protects against loud sounds, although because of the time taken to contract the muscles (typically at least 40 ms), the middle ear reflex will not protect against short percussive stimuli such as gunshot noises. There is some evidence that the middle ear reflex is also activated during speaking and other vocalization. This prevents you being deafened by the sound of your own voice.

Box 1   Acoustic impedance

If we had no outer or middle ear and the oval window of the inner ear were directly exposed to sound waves transmitted through the air, only 0.1% of the sound energy would be transmitted through to the cochlea and the other 99.9% would be reflected. As a consequence, our hearing would be less sensitive by about 30 dB. The reason is that the inner ear is filled with fluid and consequently it has a much greater acoustic impedance than air.

Acoustic impedance is a measure of how readily the particles of the conducting medium can be displaced by the sound waves, which is much more difficult for water than for air. The acoustic impedance is equal to the ratio of the sound pressure to the flow velocity of the particles of the transmitting medium. (It is analogous to electrical impedance, which is the ratio of voltage to current flow.)

At an interface between one medium and another the amount of sound reflected, and hence the amount transmitted, is determined by the difference between the two acoustic impedances. The larger the difference, the greater the proportion reflected. The acoustic impedance of water is a factor of around 3750 times that of air, which is why 99.9% of the sound energy is reflected, and only 0.1% transmitted. This explains why, when swimming underwater in a swimming pool, you can only hear ambient sounds very faintly.

The main function of the middle ear is to act as an impedance-matching device to counteract this large difference in acoustic impedances, which it does by the two mechanisms described in the text.

---

6 The inner ear

The inner ear is a structured fluid-filled cavity within the temporal bone. It contains the organs of hearing and of balance. In this chapter we shall consider only that portion which is concerned with hearing. This is the **cochlea** (Latin for 'snail'), the organ of hearing (Figure 1). The cochlea is the site where sound is converted into a neural signal.

6.1 Overall organization of the cochlea

The cochlea is a fluid-filled tube that forms a part of the 'bony labyrinth'. The term labyrinth emphasizes the nature of the inner ear as a series of convoluted compartments *within* the bone, even though we tend to think of the structure dissected out from the surrounding hard tissue. The cochlea is coiled to save space.

Were the coiled turns straightened out, the tube would be about 34 mm long. In
other mammals, the uncoiled length varies from about 10 mm in a mouse to about
60 mm in some whales.

The cochlear tube (or duct) is closed at one end. This end is termed the apical
cochlea. The other end, the basal cochlea, is linked to other compartments of the
inner ear allowing fluid continuity. The basal end of the cochlea contains two
flexible membranes, the oval window, on which the stapes sits, and the **round
window**, which acts like a pressure release surface. The main structural feature of
the cochlea is the **basilar membrane** (Figure 7). The basilar membrane is an
acellular membrane mainly composed of radially-oriented collagen fibres, and
provides the support membrane for the sensory cells of the inner ear. The basilar
membrane divides the cochlear tube into an upper and a lower compartment, the
scala vestibuli and **scala tympani** respectively. The two are freely connected at the
cochlear apex by the **helicotrema**, an opening that allows the pressures in the two
scalae to equalize readily. Therefore, only rapid pressure changes produced in the
scala vestibuli by movement of the stapes footplate act across the basilar membrane.

The cochlear tube contains a third compartment, the **scala media**. The scala media is
a sub-compartment of the scala vestibuli and is bounded on one side by the basilar
membrane. It runs the full length of the cochlear duct, and provides a special
environment for the **organ of Corti**, the structure that contains the sensory cells of
the cochlea (see below). The scala media moves with the basilar membrane so does
not contribute essentially to the mechanics of the cochlea.

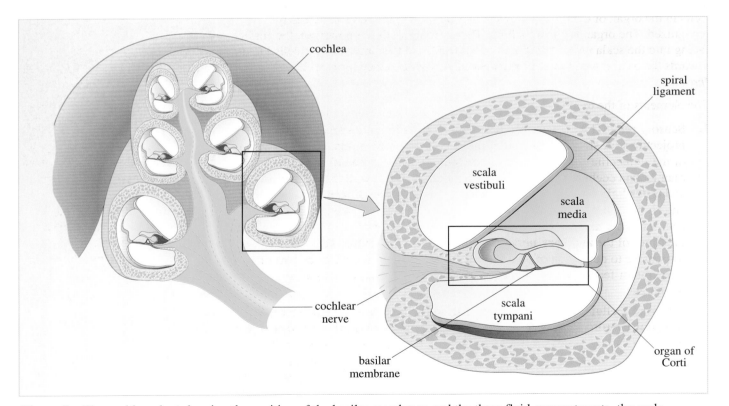

Figure 7   The cochlear duct showing the position of the basilar membrane and the three fluid compartments, the scala
vestibuli, the scala tympani and the scala media. Uncoiled, the duct would be a tube about 34 mm long, with the basilar
membrane dividing it along its length.

6.2 Cochlear fluids

The fluids within the inner ear are critical in maintaining the correct physiological state of the cells of the cochlea. However, for the physics of sound propagation they can be considered to have the physical properties of pure water. The fluid in the two major scalae of the cochlear duct is termed **perilymph**. This is a solution with the same composition as cerebrospinal fluid (CSF) and is the solution generally found outside cells (extracellular solution). The principal ion it contains is Na^+. Perilymph arises from the capillary circulation around the cochlea.

The fluid within the scala media is different in composition. This fluid is termed **endolymph**. The principal ion is K^+ but the solution also contains low Ca^{2+} concentrations (typically $30 \mu M$). Endolymph is closer in composition to intracellular solution. The source of the endolymph in the scala media is a transport epithelium, the **stria vascularis**, located on the lateral wall of the cochlear duct. The surfaces of the cells that surround and face into the scala media are linked by cell–cell tight junctions, preventing fluid within the scala media from readily diffusing out. The stria vascularis (as its name suggests) has a rich vascular blood supply that is responsible for supplying the high metabolic demands of the epithelium.

6.3 The organ of Corti

The organ of Corti (Figures 7, 8 and 9) is a structure that runs the length of the cochlear tube. It contains the sensory and non-sensory cells responsible for encoding the small movements induced by sound in the inner ear. Sited on the basilar membrane it moves with the motion of the basilar membrane as described below. Cells in the organ of Corti have very distinct morphologies and can be easily recognized. The organ is an epithelium. Therefore the cells are polarized, the surface facing into the scala media being termed '*apical*', and the surface of the cells facing towards the basilar membrane surrounded by perilymph being termed '*basal*' or '*basolateral*'.

The elements of the organ of Corti are:

Figure 8   Alfonso Corti (1822–1888). Corti was an Italian anatomist who discovered the organ that bears his name while he was studying medicine at Wurzberg in Germany.

1   Sensory cells. These are termed **hair cells**. The name comes from the short projections (or **stereocilia**) protruding from their apical surface. The deflection of the stereocilia is the first step in **mechano-electrical transduction**. In the mammalian cochlea, there are two distinct types of hair cell, **inner hair cells** and **outer hair cells**. The human cochlea contains about 3500 inner hair cells and about 12 000 outer hair cells, distributed in rows along the length of the cochlea. Inner hair cells are the primary sensory cells, and form synapses with the fibres of the **auditory nerve** (**cochlear nerve**). Outer hair cells are also responsive to deflection of their stereocilia but are now known to be part of a fast motor feedback system that modifies the mechanics of the basilar membrane.

2   A second acellular matrix of collagen and specialized protein fibrils, termed the **tectorial membrane**. The tectorial membrane lies over the apical surface of the organ of Corti and makes mechanical contact with the tips of the hair cell stereocilia. It is extruded from the inner spiral region of the cochlea during development. Computational experiments with cochlear models suggest that the tectorial membrane flexes around a point on the inner side of the organ of Corti. As each section of the basilar membrane moves up and down, the corresponding section of tectorial membrane will therefore slide radially over both the inner and outer hair cells, and deflect their stereocilia.

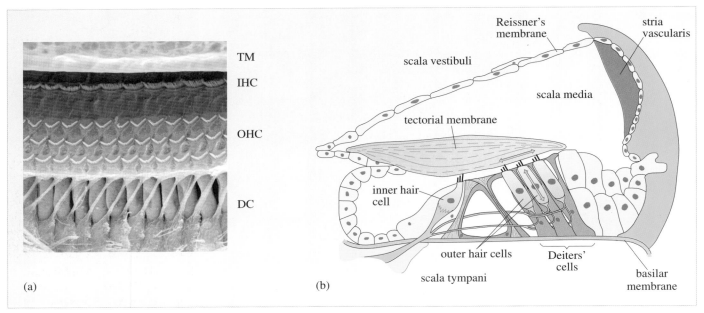

Figure 9　The organ of Corti. (a) A scanning electron micrograph of a section, with the view taken looking radially from the lateral side towards the spiral centre. The three rows of V-shaped stereocilia of the outer hair cells (OHC) and the single row of stereocilia of the inner hair cells (IHC) are apparent. The micrograph also shows the overlying tectorial membrane (TM) and non-sensory cells (Deiters' cells, DC). The hair cell bodies, beneath the stereocilia, are 10 μm wide. (b) A diagrammatic representation showing the basilar membrane, the hair cells and the overlying tectorial membrane. The non-sensory cells maintain the physiology of the organ.

6.4 Basilar membrane mechanics

The key element in the design of the mammalian cochlea is the basilar membrane. Through its mechanical design it responds to sounds by vibrating in a pattern that depends uniquely on the intensity and frequency of the incoming sound. The inner hair cells relay the information about this pattern to the auditory nerve and to the auditory brainstem. It is clear that more intense (i.e. louder) sounds will produce a larger pressure difference across the basilar membrane. Therefore the displacements of the hair cell stereocilia will be greater. How different tones are encoded within the whole auditory nerve is less obvious.

The fundamental property of the cochlea that enables us to hear fine differences in frequency depends on the specialized mechanics of the basilar membrane. In summary the cochlea behaves like a **mechanical spectrum analyser**. Different frequencies excite different populations of hair cells along the length of the organ of Corti. The design of the cochlea ensures that each tone within the auditory range selectively excites only a subpopulation of hair cells along the cochlear duct. The frequencies are spread so that high frequencies excite cells at the basal end of the cochlea near the stapes, and frequencies at the low end of the auditory range excite cells at the apical end of the cochlea nearest the helicotrema. The conversion of sound frequency to coding as position of excitation is referred to as a **tonotopic mapping** (from the Greek, τονοσ = sound, τοποσ = place) (Figure 10).

How do the mechanics of the basilar membrane determine the tonotopic map? The main experimental observation was made by the Hungarian-American Georg von Békésy (Figure 11) in the 1930s. He observed that the basilar membrane presents mechanical stiffness to a probe placed perpendicularly against it, the stiffness being

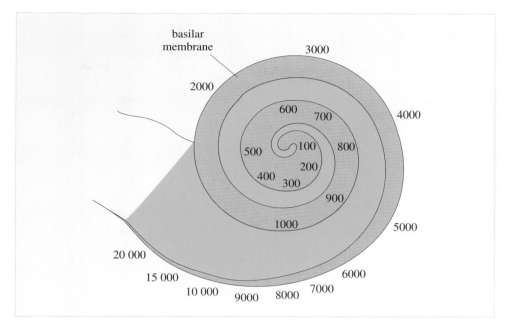

Figure 10   The basilar membrane showing where frequencies are mapped. Only the first 2.5 turns are drawn to scale. Note that approximately equal distances are assigned to each octave (i.e. doubling of frequency) of the auditory range.

Figure 11   Georg von Békésy (1899–1972). Békésy was employed by the Hungarian telephone industry before moving to the USA in 1949. His experimental work on the cochlea developed the idea of the cochlear travelling wave, for which he was awarded the 1961 Nobel Prize in Physiology or Medicine.

greater at the middle-ear end of the cochlea than at the helicotrema end. The stiffness is graded monotonically along the duct and as a result distinct sound frequencies cause vibration of distinct sections of the basilar membrane.[*]

The mechanical coupling between each section of cochlea depends both on the surrounding fluid and on the cellular components of the organ of Corti. When the pressure wave enters the cochlea from the middle ear, the sound wave will propagate through the fluids of the duct. Each component of the basilar membrane will start to respond, but only those 'tuned' to the appropriate frequencies will vibrate maximally. The net effect is that a wave of mechanical motion (the **travelling wave**) propagates along the basilar membrane and reaches a peak at the position where the frequency of the sound wave and the place frequency correspond. The estimated velocity of the cochlear travelling wave is approximately 15 m s^{-1}, considerably slower than the velocity of sound in water. The wave carries the information about the frequency, intensity and temporal envelope of the sound.

6.5 The cochlear amplifier

A cochlea constructed as described would lack sensitivity and be unable to separate frequencies in an input sound. The existence of the travelling wave was deduced by Békésy from measurements made on cadaver cochleas at sound levels high enough to produce visibly detectable movements. However, scaling down to the expected displacement of the basilar membrane at the threshold of hearing produced a value that was much too small. Békésy's data indicated that at threshold the displacement

---

[*] A similar conclusion, but for different reasons, was reached by Helmholtz in the mid-nineteenth century. He studied the early anatomical measurements of the cochlea made by Corti and others and thought that the basilar membrane resembled a set of piano strings, with the shorter, more tensioned treble strings at the basal end of cochlea.

of the basilar membrane might only be 1 pm ($= 10^{-12}$ m). High sensitivity measurements of the motion in *living* cochleas became possible in the early 1980s with the use, for example, of laser interferometers. The currently accepted threshold displacement of the basilar membrane is close to 0.2 nm ($= 2 \times 10^{-10}$ m), or about 2 hydrogen atom diameters. The mechanism in living animals that boosts the movement of the basilar membrane about 100 times (equivalent to 40 dB) is known as the **cochlear amplifier** (Figure 12).

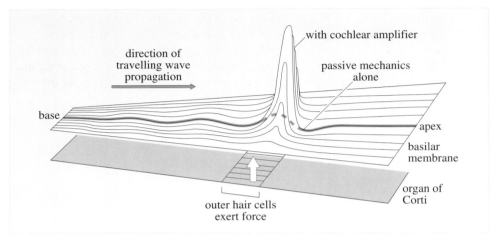

Figure 12   The movement of the basilar membrane with and without the cochlear amplifier in operation. The basilar membrane has been uncoiled, and shown stretched out along its axis. Its length in humans would be about 34 mm, but the vibration amplitude would be measured in nanometres. Here this displacement has been considerably distorted to show the small, but critical, enhancements.

As well as amplifying the motion, the living (as opposed to cadaver) cochlea, has a peak amplitude of the travelling wave that is much more localized. Thus two tones that differ by 1% or less will excite distinct populations of hair cells. We know from psychophysical experiments that the just noticeable difference (JND) for frequencies around 1000 Hz is 0.3% (that is, we can separate a tone of 1000 Hz from one of 1003 Hz). When hearing begins to fail, not only does sensitivity begin to decrease, but the ability to make accurate pitch discriminations begins to deteriorate as well. Thus within the inner ear, the cochlear amplifier is like a 'biological hearing aid' that is part of the normal physiology of the cochlea.

The cellular mechanism responsible for cochlear amplification depends on the outer hair cells. Transducing channels in the stereocilia of the outer hair cells detect motion of the tectorial membrane when sound enters the cochlea. They generate forces along their axis in response to changes in membrane potential, which oppose the viscous forces (due to the surrounding fluid and cells of the organ of Corti) that act on the cochlear partition. These viscous forces tend to damp down local excitation of the partition. With viscous forces removed, each section of the cochlear duct can act as a virtually undamped resonator, with a larger and more frequency-specific response to an appropriately matched tone. Undamping viscous forces requires energy. The energy source for the cochlear amplifier can ultimately be traced to the metabolism of the stria vascularis. For this reason, the physiologically normal cochlea is sometimes referred to as having 'active' mechanics.

7 Summary

Sound stimuli entering the ear are transformed by the peripheral auditory system into a series of signals sent along the fibres of the auditory nerve. The minimum detectable level of sound corresponds to an energy flow (or intensity) of 10^{-12} W m^{-2} in a sound pressure wave. The outer ear and middle ear structures ensure that sound energy is delivered to the inner ear where it causes a pressure wave to propagate in the fluids of the cochlea. The sound wave causes the basilar membrane stretched along the cochlear duct to vibrate and the many frequencies in a complex sound can be separated out as a result of this membrane's mechanical properties. The vibrations at each site along the membrane deflect the stereocilia of the sensory hair cells of the organ of Corti, and lead to the signals sent to the brain. A sub-population of hair cells in the cochlea is also responsible for mechanically amplifying the movement of the basilar membrane.

The transformation of sound stimuli into electrical signals

Robert Fettiplace

1 Introduction

Our sense of hearing depends on the correct performance of about 15 000 hair cells in each cochlea that serve as an interface between the mechanical vibrations of speech, music and other sounds and the electrical signals of the brain. Hair cells can detect vibrations of atomic dimensions down to 0.2 nm, and can respond more than 20 000 times a second. These cells cannot regenerate, so their atrophy in old age or destruction by loud sounds or drugs like streptomycin causes permanent deafness. Loss of sensation is often restricted to higher frequencies, and is linked to degeneration of hair cells near one end of the cochlea. This chapter explains how acoustic stimuli are detected by the hair cells and converted into a stream of electrical impulses that are relayed to the brain. It also describes the mechanisms by which each cell is affiliated with certain input frequencies.

2 Hair cells and their mode of stimulation

Hair cells are the sensory receptors for all components of the inner ear, including the organ of hearing, the cochlea, and those of balance – three semicircular canals, a saccule and utricle (see Chapter 7, *The vestibular system*). In each of these the hair cells are tightly anchored to non-sensory supporting cells in an epithelial sheet. In the cochlea, this sheet of cells, known as the organ of Corti, rests on a freely moveable basilar membrane (Figure 1a overleaf). The mechanically sensitive **hair bundles** project above the epithelial surface and the majority contact a gelatinous flap known as the tectorial membrane. The hair cells have no axons, but make synaptic contact with the endings of **afferent** and **efferent nerve fibres** that travel in the VIIIth cranial nerve (Figure 1b). The afferent fibres, bipolar neurons with cell bodies in the spiral ganglion, transmit the auditory message to the brain, whereas the efferent axons send signals back to the cochlea from the brain to influence hair cell sensitivity. The cochleas of mammals (and birds) contain two types of sensory cell, outer hair cells and inner hair cells, which have different function and innervation. While the majority of afferents emanate from the inner hair cells, only the outer hair cells receive synaptic contact with efferent fibres.

Sound stimuli reaching the cochlea produce vibrations of the basilar and tectorial membranes. The relative movements of the two membranes excite the hair cells by bending their hair bundles relative to the rigid epithelial surface. The mechanically sensitive hair bundle is composed of about 50 to 100 modified microvilli called stereocilia (Figures 2 and 3 overleaf). These are cylindrical projections, measuring a few tenths of a micron in diameter and 1 to 10 µm in height, which taper at the bottom where they fuse to the cell body. Each stereocilium is packed with actin filaments running along its length, but only a small fraction of the filaments traverse the narrow bottom to be anchored in the cytoskeleton of the cell body. Actin is a specialized protein also found in muscle tissue. The reduced number of actin filaments at the stereociliary base makes it the weakest mechanical point about which the stereocilium bends. The hair bundle superficially resembles the bristles of a hairbrush but when deflected its motion differs from the brush in several important

Figure 1   The mammalian cochlea contains two types of sensory cell embedded in a matrix of supporting cells. A single row of inner hair cells contacts auditory afferent fibres, whereas three rows of outer hair cells receive synaptic contact from efferent nerves from the brain. Sound stimuli vibrate the basilar membrane causing to-and-fro motion of the sensory hair bundles relative to the overlying tectorial membrane. The red arrows show excitatory motion that bends the hair bundles towards their taller edge.

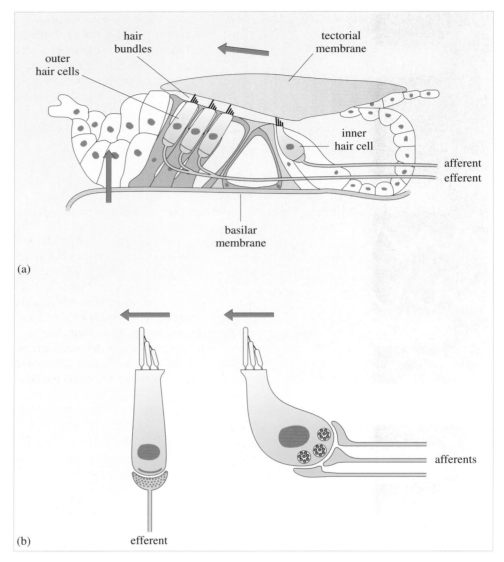

respects. Firstly, the stereocilia do not flex but behave as stiff rods pivoting around their base. Secondly, because the stereocilia are interconnected by fine extracellular strands they all move together when displaced.

An important feature of the hair bundle is its asymmetric bevelled form, reflecting the progressive increase in height of sequential ranks of stereocilia across the bundle (Figure 3). As a consequence, the hair bundle is morphologically polarized with an axis of symmetry bisecting it from the shortest to tallest edge. Only those movements of the bundle along the axis of symmetry (towards or away from the tallest stereociliary rank) are detected, whereas movements at right angles to this axis are not. In the cochlea, all hair bundles are oriented so that they sense only transverse motion of the overlying tectorial membrane (Figure 1). In the vestibular organs and in the developing cochlea, the hair bundle also possesses a single kinocilium. The role of the kinocilium is unknown, but it is not required for transduction and disappears in the adult cochlea.

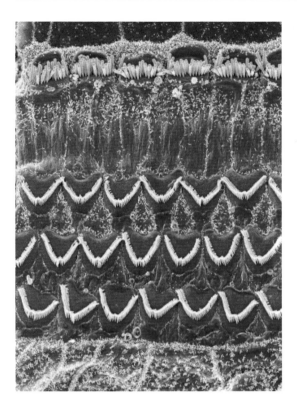

Figure 2 A scanning electron micrograph of the surface of the organ of Corti shows three rows of V-shaped outer hair cell hair bundles at the bottom and a single row of inner hair cell bundles at the top. The hair cells are excited by deflections of the hair bundles towards the point of the 'V'.

▼ **Figure 3** (a) A hair cell from the turtle cochlea. (b) The hair cell layer separates fluids of different ionic composition, the K^+-rich endolymph enveloping the hair bundles and the perilymph, which contains higher concentrations of Na^+ and Ca^{2+}. Displacements of the hair bundle activate mechanosensitive channels (C_{MT}) allowing influx of cations. Synaptic transmission depends on the influx of calcium ions through voltage-dependent calcium channels (Ca_V) to liberate neurotransmitter. An efferent axon releases acetylcholine, which binds to the nAChR receptor on the hair cell. Most hair cells also possess potassium channels activated by changes in membrane voltage (K_V) or intracellular calcium (K_{Ca}).

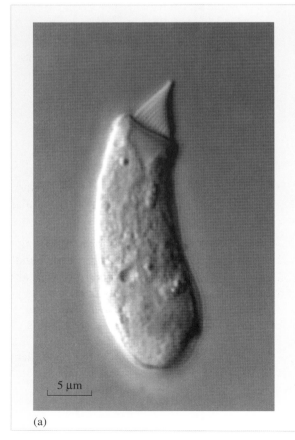

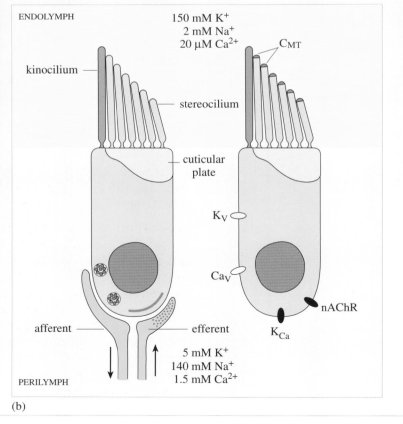

(a) (b)

3 Mechano-electrical transduction and generation of the receptor potential

Mechano-electrical transduction refers to the conversion of the mechanical stimulus into an electrical signal called the **receptor potential**. The mechanism underlying transduction has been studied using isolated preparations of hair cell epithelia, where the electrical response of the hair cells can be recorded while manipulating the hair bundle. Because of the fragility of the mammalian cochlea, much evidence about mechano-electrical transduction comes from experiments on hair cells of sub-mammalian vertebrates like frogs and turtles (Figure 3a). In those preparations, rotation of the bundle towards its taller edge was first shown to open specialized **mechanosensitive ion channels**. This allows entry of small positively charged ions, depolarizing the hair cell from its resting potential of approximately -50 mV (Figure 4). A small proportion (about 10%) of the mechanosensitive channels are normally open at rest, and rotation of the bundle towards its shorter edge closes those channels already open and hyperpolarizes the cell. Thus sinusoidal motion of the hair bundle about its resting position, as might be produced by a pure tone, generates a receptor potential oscillating around rest. As the magnitude of the stimulus is increased, the receptor potential grows in size and eventually saturates, reaching the greatest amplitude for hair bundle displacements of only $0.5\,\mu m$. The maximal stimulus transduced is therefore comparable to the diameter of a stereocilium. At auditory threshold, the smallest displacement of the hair bundle detectable is 1000 times less than this, and is estimated to produce a receptor potential of 0.1 mV. At threshold, the hair bundle motion is comparable to the size of a hydrogen atom, testifying to the extraordinary sensitivity of the mechanotransduction process.

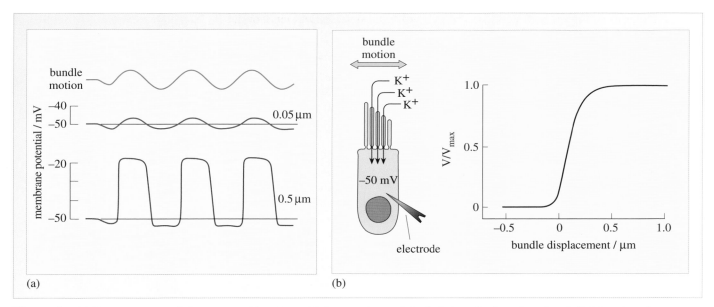

(a)   (b)

Figure 4   (a) Receptor potentials generated by sinusoidal excursions of the hair bundle for a low-level ($0.05\,\mu m$) and a high-level ($0.5\,\mu m$) stimulus. On the positive part of the stimulus cycle, the bundle moves towards its taller edge, opening mechanosensitive channels, which depolarizes the cell. On the negative half of the cycle, the bundle is deflected towards its shorter edge, closing channels and hyperpolarizing the cell. For low-level stimuli the response is sinusoidal, for higher-level stimuli it becomes square. (b) A plot of the receptor potential against hair bundle displacement is asymmetric about the hair bundle's resting position. The receptor potential, V, is scaled to a V_{max}, of 35 mV.

Hair cells do not themselves generate action potentials since they lack the requisite voltage-dependent sodium channels present in the axon; action potentials are first produced in the afferent nerve fibres for signalling to the brain. However, the performance of the hair cells, the encoding and transmission of the auditory message, depends on the operation of several other kinds of ion channels (Figure 3b). Motion of the hair bundle is transduced into changes in membrane potential by the mechanosensitive channels. The receptor potential is then shaped by the operation of several types of potassium channel that are activated by depolarization or a rise in intracellular calcium. Besides determining the resting potential, potassium channels may also modify the time course and amplitude of the receptor potential. In sub-mammalian vertebrates, **calcium-activated potassium channels** generate oscillations in the membrane potential and play a role in the hair cell's frequency tuning. Finally, release of neurotransmitter at the synapse is triggered by calcium influx through voltage-dependent calcium channels clustered around the base of the hair cell beneath the synaptic endings.

The mechanosensitive channels, like other ion channels, are thought to be protein pores spanning the plasma membrane. These channels, when opened by bundle deflection, allow the passage of small monovalent ions like sodium and potassium. The mechanosensitive channels are also permeable to calcium ions, which traverses them even more readily than potassium. The protein pore may therefore be lined with negative charges for calcium ions to interact with in transit. However, some larger positively-charged molecules can occlude the open channel thereby blocking the ionic flux. Blocking compounds of medical importance are the aminoglycoside antibiotics like streptomycin. Prolonged exposure to these antibiotics can cause deafness due to destruction of the cochlear hair cells. This pathological effect develops over the course of several days, and may require the antibiotic to gain access to the hair cell interior and interfere with the cell's energy supply from the mitochondria.

To understand the flow of ions through mechanosensitive channels in the intact cochlea, it is necessary to take into account the hair bundle's ionic environment. The layer of hair cells and supporting cells forms a tight epithelium separating two extracellular fluids of quite different ionic composition (Figure 3b). The base of the hair cells and the afferent nerve dendrites are bathed in perilymph, which has a composition the same as extracellular fluids elsewhere in the body. Perilymph has a normal sodium concentration in order to sustain action potentials in the afferent axons. In contrast, the hair bundles are immersed in an unusual solution known as endolymph, which is rich in potassium. Thus potassium will be the major ion flowing through the mechanosensitive channels *in vivo*. Because the concentration of potassium in endolymph is similar to its concentration in intracellular fluid, potassium ions will be forced through the mechanosensitive channels by the potential difference across the hair bundle membrane. This will be the sum of the negative resting potential of -50 mV and an endocochlear potential of 80 mV that exists between the endolymph bathing the hair bundle and the perilymph. The **endocochlear potential** increases the driving force on potassium influx and enhances the sensitivity of mechano-electrical transduction.

4 The site of transduction

The coupling of motion of the hair bundle to opening of the mechanosensitive channels must be rapid if the cells are to encode the waveform of the sound stimulus. Human hearing extends to frequencies near 20 000 Hz, where each cycle of the sound pressure waveform lasts only $50\,\mu s$! Such rapid temporal performance is incompatible with a mechanism that involves intermediate metabolism of second messengers, such as the cyclic nucleotides that mediate transduction in the sensory receptors for vision and smell. It is more likely that deformation of the hair bundle stretches mechanical linkages that directly open the channel (Figure 5). This is referred to as the 'bath-plug mechanism', where pulling on the chain removes a plug from the channel permitting ions to enter the cell. To establish this mechanism, it is necessary to define the location of the plug and identify the chain. Several pieces of evidence suggest that the mechanosensitive channels are concentrated towards the tops of the stereocilia. For example, it has been demonstrated (by filling the hair cell with a dye whose fluorescence changes after binding calcium ions) that deflection of the hair bundle causes an initial rise in intracellular calcium near the stereociliary tips. The additional calcium ions are assumed to have entered via the mechanosensitive channels. It has also been proposed that the channels are stimulated by **tip links**, fine extracellular filaments that pass from the tips of the shorter stereocilia to the sides of the taller row in front (Figure 5). Such tip links are visible in high-resolution electron micrographs where they appear to run approximately parallel to the bundle's plane of symmetry.

The 'tip link' hypothesis is attractive because it explains the directionality of transduction and the ubiquitous gradation of stereociliary heights in hair bundles. Thus rotation of the bundle towards its taller edge will result in a vertical shear between adjacent rows of stereocilia, and will stretch the tip links to open the channels. Conversely, rotation towards the shorter edge will slacken the links and close the channels. It has not yet been possible to identify the molecular composition of the mechanosensitive channels or the tip links. Part of the difficulty stems from the small amount of protein available, which is an obstacle to biochemical purification

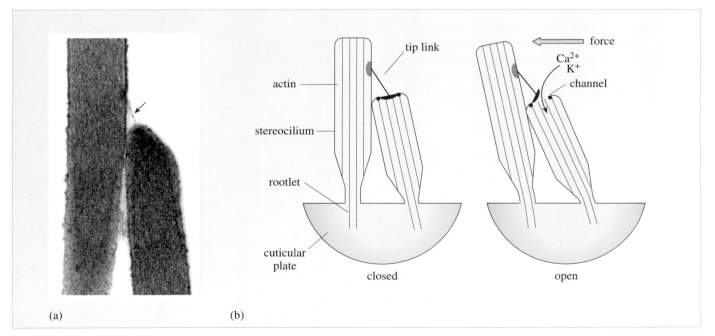

(a)   (b)

Figure 5   (a) Transmission electron micrograph of a pair of stereocilia showing the tip link (arrow) proposed to deliver force to the mechanosensitive channels. (b) The stereocilia are filled with actin filaments that flex where their rootlets enter the actin meshwork of the cuticular plate. The mechanosensitive channel may be located at the tip of the stereocilium and opened by force transmitted via the tip link.

of the channel. For example, it has been estimated that there are only a few hundred channels per hair bundle, or just a few per stereocilium. Characterization of the mechanosensitive channel is an important goal of cochlear research because the channel may be a prime site for hair cell malfunction in certain kinds of deafness.

5 Adaptation

The **activation curve** for the mechanosensitive channels, the relationship between the number of channels open and bundle displacement, is S-shaped with about 10% of channels being activated when the bundle is unperturbed. At this bundle position, the activation curve has the steepest slope so that the cell is maximally sensitive for the small perturbations. To preserve high sensitivity in the face of drifts in bundle position, an **adaptation** mechanism exists to keep the channels within a narrow operating range (Figure 6). For a maintained deflection of the hair bundle, the channels first open but then close again over a time period of 1 to 100 ms, depending on the conditions. Such adaptation does not represent inactivation of the transducer channels, but rather a shift of the activation curve to a new working point. This may be a way of ensuring that the sensitivity is always maximal close to the resting position of the bundle. Adaptation is mediated by calcium ions that enter the cell through the mechanosensitive channels to reset their mechanical sensitivity.

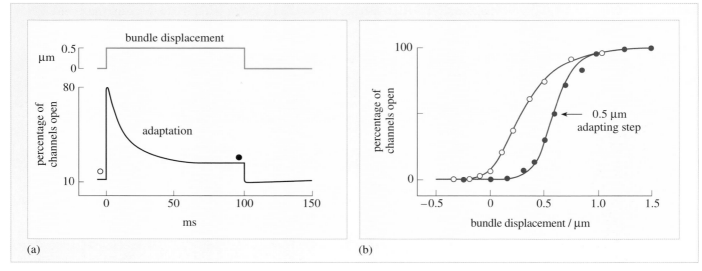

(a)   (b)

Figure 6   (a) During a prolonged displacement of the hair bundle, the mechanosensitive channels first open (open circle) but then close again (filled circle) in a process of adaptation. (b) The activation curve for the channels was determined from a set of brief displacements of the bundle presented prior to (open circles) or at the end of (filled circles) the adapting step. The results show that adaptation is due to a shift in the activation curve.

Two mechanisms have been suggested to account for adaptation. In one mechanism, calcium binds directly to the mechanosensitive channels and closes them. This process can occur very rapidly, within a millisecond, which may be important for the channel's operation at high frequencies. A slower mechanism may regulate the mechanical input to the channels by moving the upper attachment of the tip link along the side of the stereocilium. It has been proposed that this motion is driven by the climbing and slipping of myosin along the actin backbone of the stereocilium. Myosin is a specialized protein that interacts with actin to produce muscle contraction or cell movements. Calcium entering the stereocilia through the mechanosensitive channels is thought to control both types of adaptation. For such a control mechanism, it is important for the mechanosensitive channels to have a high permeability to calcium. Because calcium ions easily traverse the mechanosensitive channels, sufficient calcium can enter the cell to promote adaptation even at the low calcium concentration in endolymph.

6 The afferent synapse and the auditory nerve response

The receptor potential is a modulation in the resting potential of the hair cell that reflects the acoustic waveform. The receptor potential controls the release of chemical transmitter onto the afferent dendrite, where the signal is then converted into a train of action potentials. The synapse resembles other excitatory synapses in the brain by using the amino acid glutamate as the transmitter. However, unlike central synapses where each presynaptic action potential delivers a pulse of glutamate, the amount of glutamate released from the hair cell is graded with the membrane potential. Some transmitter leaks out in the absence of a stimulus and causes spontaneous firing of action potentials in the afferent dendrite. During a stimulus, depolarization of the hair cell releases more glutamate and increases the action potential firing rate. Conversely, hyperpolarization decreases the resting glutamate release and shuts off the spontaneous activity. Thus a pure tone of low frequency produces a sinusoidal receptor potential that modulates the firing of the afferent neuron in synchrony with the sound waveform. This is known as **phase locking** as the action potentials occur preferentially on one phase of the cycle.

In theory, the intervals between bursts of phase-locked action potentials can inform the brain about the frequency of the sound stimulus, but only if the frequency is less than 1000 Hz. At higher frequencies, phase locking is lost because the maximum rate of action potential firing in the auditory nerve fibres is exceeded. Furthermore, there are temporal limits imposed by the intrinsic properties of the hair cell and its transmitter release mechanism. At frequencies above 1000 Hz, the periodic receptor potential is transformed into a sustained depolarization of the hair cell known as the **summating potential** (Figure 7). The summating potential will augment transmitter release and cause a sustained increase in firing of action potentials throughout the stimulus.

The number of action potentials occurring during the sound stimulus depends on the intensity or loudness of that stimulus (Figure 8). For the lowest sound intensities, there is a small but reproducible increase in the mean firing rate over the spontaneous rate. The sound intensity at which this occurs is known as the neuron's **acoustic threshold**. As the sound intensity is raised above threshold, the action potential firing rate increases (Figure 8), but at the highest intensities it eventually saturates. The relationship between the action potential firing rate and sound level is thus S-shaped, similar to the hair cell's activation curve (Figure 4b and Figure 6b). However, different afferent neurons that synapse on the same inner hair cell have different thresholds. Some afferent fibres respond at the lowest sound pressure levels that are audible, but others are not recruited unless the sound pressure level is made 30-fold greater. The mechanism underlying this threshold variation is probably a difference in the sensitivity of the synapse connecting the hair cell to the afferent dendrite. The variation may enable the intensity of the sound to be represented over a wide dynamic range in terms of the firing rates in the population of afferent fibres.

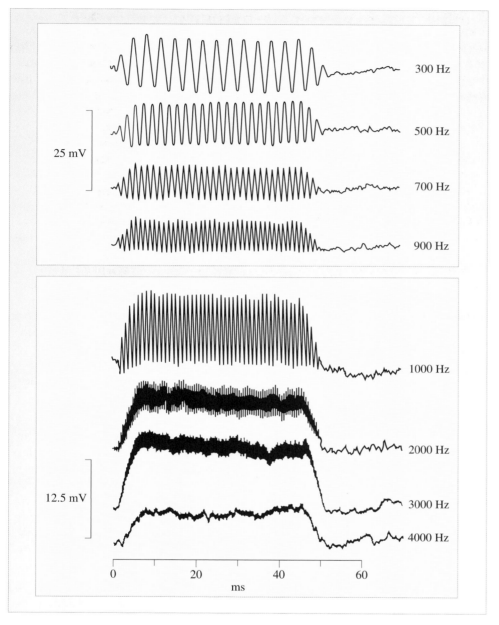

Figure 7   As the sound frequency is increased from 300 Hz to 4000 Hz, the hair cell receptor potential changes from a periodic to a sustained depolarization. The latter arises from the asymmetry of the activation curve of the mechanosensitive channel (Figure 4b).

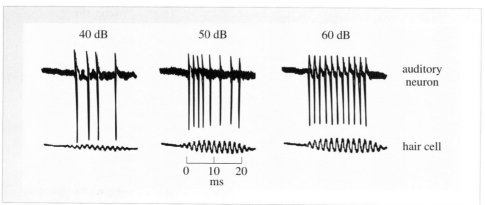

Figure 8   The timing of action potentials in an auditory neuron is synchronized to the cycles of a 500 Hz sound stimulus. The sound level in decibels (dB) increases from left to right.

7 Hair cell frequency selectivity

Besides converting the acoustic waveform into an electrical signal, the cochlea also analyses the frequency composition of the sound stimulus. The relative proportions of the different frequency components can then be used by the brain to recognize the sound. For example different vowel sounds can be distinguished by the relative intensities of their constituent frequency bands or formants (see Chapter 5, *Hearing the world*). As already noted, low frequencies can be derived from the timing of action potentials phase-locked to the cycles of the sound. A more general method is the **place principle**, where each frequency is associated with a particular cochlear location. Such frequency analysis arises in part because the vibrations of the basilar membrane are tuned and, for a given frequency, are largest at one place. With progressively higher frequencies, the place of maximal vibration shifts systematically towards the base of the cochlea (see Chapter 1, *The mechanics of hearing*). The frequency components in a complex sound are thus segregated along the basilar membrane, and individual hair cells (and their associated auditory nerve fibres) are excited by stimuli containing only a small range of frequencies (Figure 9).

Although such frequency analysis appears at first sight to be caused by passive tuning of the basilar membrane (like the response of a guitar string), such passive tuning alone would be insufficient to generate the narrow frequency selectivity observed. It is believed that the outer hair cells play an active role in the process by supplying extra energy to reinforce the vibrations of the membrane. The effect of each outer hair cell is to amplify the vibrations of the basilar membrane locally, and as a consequence increase its frequency selectivity. The process is similar to augmenting the excursions of a child's swing by supplying appropriately timed pushes. Several lines of evidence support this idea. Electrical stimulation of the efferent nerve fibres damps the outer hair cell responses, which can diminish the frequency selectivity of the inner hair cells. Furthermore, preferential destruction of the outer hair cells by loud sounds or by aminoglycoside antibiotics degrades the frequency discrimination of the inner hair cells (Figure 9). These results are explained by proposing that outer hair cells can influence the relative motion of the basilar and tectorial membranes and thus govern the stimulus to the inner hair cells. This requires outer hair cells to possess an intrinsic force-generating mechanism.

Figure 9 Frequency tuning curves in three auditory neurons, where the threshold sound level that just excites the neuron is plotted against sound frequency. Each neuron has a characteristic frequency where its threshold is a minimum. With destruction of outer hair cells (OHC loss), sound threshold is greatly elevated and frequency tuning deteriorates, as illustrated here for the neuron with the highest frequency.

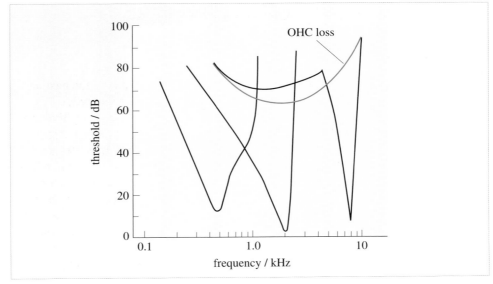

Evidence supporting the outer hair cells' role in cochlear amplification comes from the observation that *in vitro* they can contract like muscle fibres when electrically stimulated. Depolarization shortens them and hyperpolarization elongates them. Transduction in outer hair cells is therefore bidirectional. Motion of the hair bundle is converted into a receptor potential, but a change in membrane potential can itself produce a mechanical response from the cell. The electromechanical performance of outer hair cells does not employ the same actin–myosin mechanism used to produce muscle contraction, but entails a special motor protein present at high density in the outer hair cell's lateral wall. It has been suggested that changes in membrane potential modify the shape of each motor protein, the net effect summed over all motors being to alter the surface area and hence length of the cell.

8 The tonotopic map

Each hair cell responds best to one particular sound frequency known as its **characteristic frequency** (Figure 9), which changes progressively with the distance of the cell along the basilar membrane. Cells at the base of the cochlea have the highest characteristic frequency, whereas cells at the apex have the lowest (Figure 10 overleaf). The projection of sound frequency on to cochlear location is known as the tonotopic map (see Chapter 1, *The mechanics of hearing*). The existence of a tonotopic map implies that the properties of the cochlea are not homogeneous along its length. A variation in the stiffness of the basilar membrane contributes to its tuning properties. The hair cells also exhibit diversity in both structure and biochemistry as a function of location. For example, in progressing from the low-frequency to high-frequency end of the cochlea, there is a three- to five-fold reduction in the length of the outer hair cell body and the height of the hair bundle. Such variations may be important for optimizing the outer hair cell's electromechanical performance. There are also gradients in the hair cell's complement of ion channels. Both the numbers and types of potassium channels in hair cells are quite different at the two ends of the cochlea. Hair cells responsive to high-frequency sounds may also have more mechanosensitive ion channels. These ion-channel gradients, though not fully understood, may be related to the differential sensitivity of the hair cells. High-frequency hair cells are more likely to be lost in old age or destroyed by loud sounds. Fathoming the origin of their vulnerability may provide a strategy for treating this significant medical problem.

9 Summary

The cochlea employs hair cells to convert sound-induced vibrations of the basilar membrane into electrical signals via deflection of their stereociliary bundles. Displacement of the bundle towards its tallest edge activates mechanosensitive ion channels located near the tips of the stereocilia, and allows potassium and calcium ions from the endolymph to enter the cell. The influx of these ions generates a receptor potential across the hair cell membrane, which in turn modulates the release of a chemical transmitter, most likely glutamate, onto the auditory afferent neurons. The sound intensity is represented by the size of the receptor potential in the hair cell, and the rate of firing of action potentials in the afferent neurons. Each hair cell responds preferentially, or is tuned, to a narrow band of sound frequencies, which change progressively with the cell's position along the cochlea. Such frequency selectivity is due to a mechanical tuning of the basilar membrane assisted by local amplification by a motor protein in the outer hair cells.

Figure 10   (a) A high frequency sound causes the largest excursion of the basilar membrane near the base of the cochlea. (b) The vibration pattern shifts towards the apex for a low-frequency sound. (c) When the outer hair cells are destroyed (OHC loss), the vibration amplitude for the same stimulus as in (b) is reduced, indicating that the outer hair cells contribute to cochlear amplification.

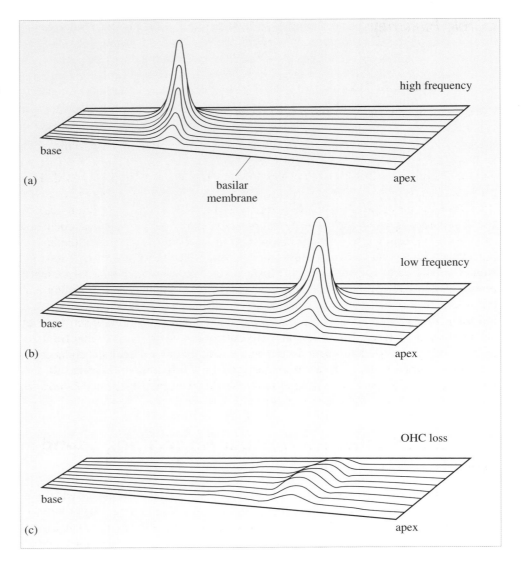

Further reading

Dallos, P., Popper, A. and Fay, R. (eds) (1996) *Handbook of Auditory Research,* Volume 8 *The Cochlea*, Springer-Verlag, Berlin.

Fettiplace, R. and Fuchs, P. A. (1999) Mechanisms of hair cell tuning, *Annual Reviews of Physiology*, **61**, pp. 809–834.

Hudspeth, A. J. (1984) How the ear's works work, *Nature*, **341**, pp. 397–404.

Kiang, N. Y. S. (1984) Peripheral neural processing of auditory information, in *Handbook of Sensory Physiology*, Section 1, Vol. II, Part 2, Darian Smith (ed.), American Physiological Society, Bethesda MD.

Kiang, N. Y. S., Liberman, M. C., Sewell, W. F. and Guinan, J. J. (1986) Single unit clues to cochlear mechanisms, *Hearing Research*, **22**, pp. 171–182.

From cochlea to cortex

Carole Hackney

1 Introduction

Once the sound picked up by the outer ear has been transformed by the middle ear, it is converted by the hair cells of the cochlea into electrical, or neural, signals. The **intensity** is represented by the rate of firing of neurons of different sensitivities in the auditory nerve (Chapter 2, *The transformation of sound stimuli into electrical signals*), and the **frequency** is also coded. For low frequencies, temporal coding is used. This relies on the fact that the neurons fire at a particular phase of the sound wave, a property known as phase locking. In addition, place coding is used, which relies on the fact that the sensory hair cells at different positions along the length of the cochlea are excited by different frequencies, from low ones at its apex to high ones at the base (Chapter 1, *The mechanics of hearing* and Chapter 2, *The transformation of sound stimuli into electrical signals*). In this chapter, we shall examine how this systematic representation of frequencies is maintained as a series of tonotopic maps throughout the ascending auditory pathway and how temporal and spatial information is represented. Complex sounds produce distinct spatial patterns of neural activity that can be used to analyse *what* the sound represents; *where* a sound is coming from is determined by comparing signals from the two ears. Extensive feedback connections between different levels of the auditory pathway, and with other brain areas, allow hearing to be integrated with our other senses so that we can differentiate *behaviourally relevant* sounds from others in the acoustic scene.

2 The vestibulocochlear nerve: carrying sound signals to the brain

Acoustic information from the sensory hair cells of the cochlea is transferred by the vestibulocochlear nerve (which also carries information from the balance or vestibular organs in the inner ear; see Chapter 7, *The vestibular system*) to the **cochlear nuclear complex** in the brainstem (Figure 1 overleaf). This is the first station of the central auditory pathway and it begins to process the signals set up by sound in the cochlear nerve and to extract different features to send on to higher centres in the brain.

The vestibulocochlear nerve is the VIIIth cranial nerve. Its cochlear portion contains two major sets of afferent fibres or axons that arise from nerve cell bodies in the **spiral ganglion** located within the central core (**modiolus**) of the cochlea. Dendrites from these spiral ganglion cells contact the hair cells. Type I cells have dendrites called **radial fibres** that contact the inner hair cells and Type II cells have dendrites called **outer spiral fibres** that contact the outer hair cells. Each inner hair cell synapses with many radial fibres (up to 20) whilst each outer spiral fibre contacts up to 10 outer hair cells. This innervation pattern means that the vast majority of the afferent fibres (up to 95%) in the cochlear nerve carry signals from the inner rather than the outer hair cells (Figure 2).

The axons from both types of spiral ganglion cell run down the centre of the cochlea within the bony modiolus. Nerve fibres from hair cells at the apex of the cochlea that respond best to low frequencies run in the centre of the bundle whilst those from hair cells towards the base of the cochlea that respond best to high frequencies, run down the outside (Figure 3). The axons of the Type I spiral ganglion cells that contact the inner hair cells are thicker and myelinated and are the ones from which microelectrode

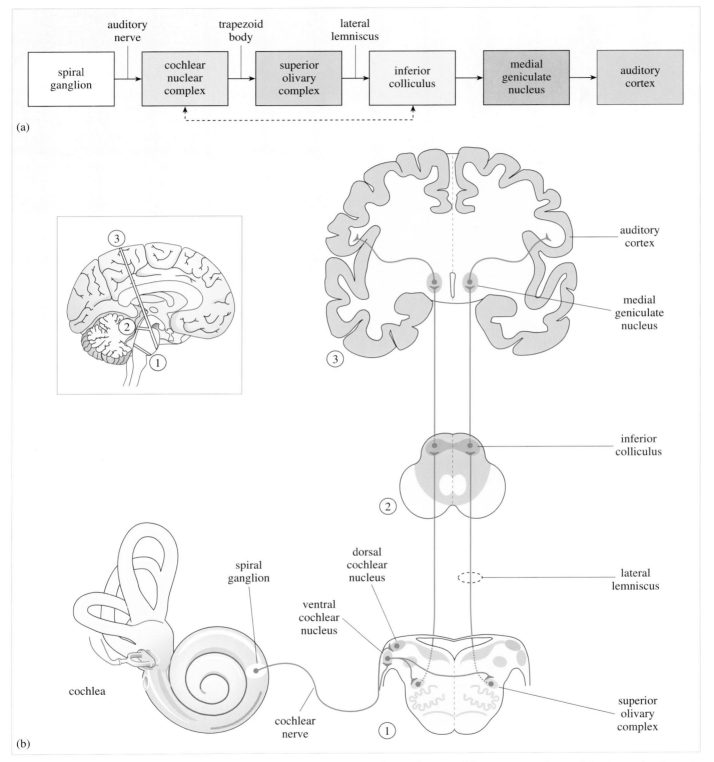

Figure 1   The main anatomical stages in the ascending auditory pathway from cochlea to cortex shown (a) schematically and (b) through brain cross-sections.

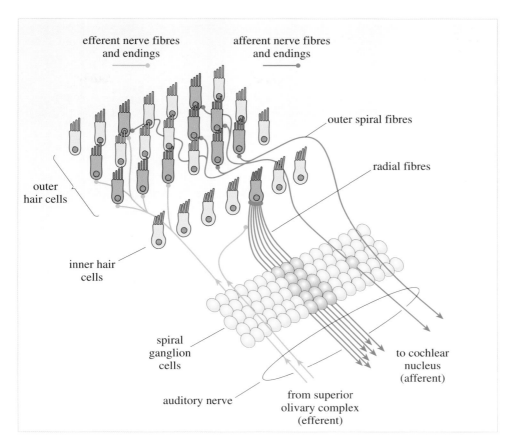

efferent nerve fibres
and endings

afferent nerve fibres
and endings

outer spiral fibres

radial fibres

outer
hair cells

inner hair
cells

spiral
ganglion
cells

to cochlear
nucleus
(afferent)

auditory nerve

from superior
olivary complex
(efferent)

Figure 2 Three-dimensional representation of the general innervation pattern of the organ of Corti. The afferent terminals of the radial fibres from the inner hair cells and the outer spiral fibres from the outer hair cells are shown in red; the efferent terminals from the olivocochlear bundle, yellow. The nerve fibres pass through openings in the central core of the cochlea.

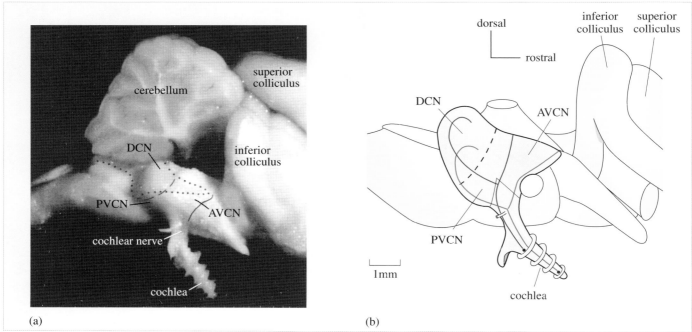

(a)

cerebellum

superior
colliculus

DCN

inferior
colliculus

PVCN

AVCN

cochlear nerve

cochlea

(b)

dorsal

rostral

inferior
colliculus

superior
colliculus

DCN

AVCN

PVCN

1mm

cochlea

Figure 3 (a) Lateral view of the cochlear nuclear complex and adjacent brainstem and mid-brain structures in a rodent brain after removal of the right half of the cerebellum. (b) Diagram of the same view showing how the projection of cochlear nerve fibres from the base and the apex of the cochlea (blue = high frequency; red = low frequency) conserves the original tonotopic representation set up in the cochlea. (AVCN, anteroventral cochlear nucleus; DCN, dorsal cochlear nucleus; PVCN, posteroventral cochlear nucleus.)

recordings are usually obtained. In fact, very little is known about what the unmyelinated axons of the Type II cells signal to the brain because it is so difficult to record from them. The only recordings that have been made suggest that they only respond to very loud sounds.

In addition to carrying afferent fibres *to* the brainstem, the cochlear nerve also contains efferent axons running *from* it to the cochlea (Figure 4). These efferent nerve fibres come from nerve cells around the outside of the superior olivary complex and form the **olivocochlear bundle**. Most of the axons in this bundle contact the outer hair cells but the bundle also contains some that innervate the Type I dendrites rather than the inner hair cells themselves (Figure 2). Only 10% or so of the axons in the cochlear nerve are efferents but they are important for auditory discrimination in noise. Stimulation of the olivocochlear bundle reduces firing in the cochlear nerve mainly by dampening the amplification produced by the outer hair cells. In other words, sound signals in the cochlear nerve result in feedback via the olivocochlear bundle, which reduces cochlear sensitivity in a frequency-specific way. This feedback loop probably helps to protect the ear from very loud sounds but takes several milliseconds to operate because several synapses are involved.

Figure 4 Diagrammatic cross-section of a cat brainstem indicating the paths of the uncrossed and crossed olivocochlear bundles and showing how the cochlear efferent supply arises in the region of the superior olivary complex. The olivocochlear fibres leave the brainstem in the vestibular portion of the vestibulocochlear nerve but cross over into the cochlear portion as it reaches the inner ear. (LSO, lateral superior olivary nucleus; MSO, medial superior olivary nucleus.)

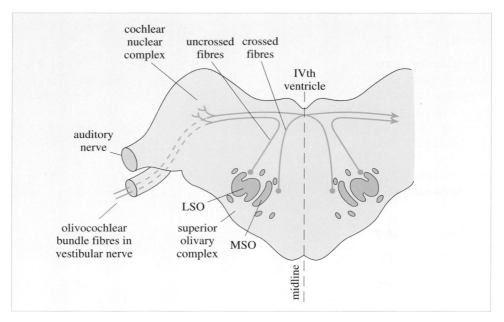

3 The cochlear nuclear complex: splitting up sounds

Each cochlear nerve fibre divides into two main branches as it enters the brainstem (Figure 3). Low-frequency fibres divide ventrally and high-frequency fibres divide dorsally maintaining the tonotopic map set up in the cochlea in all divisions of the cochlear nuclear complex. The nerve fibres innervate a number of different neuronal types, each of which sends their axons along specific ascending pathways to higher auditory centres in the brainstem and midbrain. In fact, the 50 000 or so afferent axons in the human cochlear nerve project to a much larger number of neurons in the cochlear nuclear complex and the number of ascending fibres leaving the complex exceeds that in the cochlear nerve. This suggests the separation here of different features from incoming sounds for further analysis higher up the pathway.

In the **anteroventral cochlear nucleus** (Figure 3), each Type I afferent terminates in one of the largest excitatory terminals in the brain, the **end-bulb of Held** (Figure 5). The end-bulbs ensure rapid and precise transmission of every action potential that passes along the nerve fibre to the **spherical bushy cells** (Figures 5 and 6 overleaf). These neurons send their axons via the trapezoid body to the superior olivary complex, the brainstem region responsible for comparing the signals from the two ears.

In contrast to the one of two end-bulbs that the spherical bushy cells receive, **multipolar** or **stellate cells** (Figure 6) in the **posteroventral cochlear nucleus** and central region of the **dorsal cochlear nucleus** (Figure 3) receive inputs from several cochlear nerve fibres. This means that they can compare signals from a large number of hair cells and analyse the pattern of frequencies found in complex sounds or determine their intensity. Indeed, some of the nerve cells found in the posteroventral cochlear nucleus respond to a much wider range of intensities than any individual cochlear nerve fibre. Another group of neurons in the posteroventral cochlear nucleus, the **octopus cells**, have especially thick dendrites that lie across the path of the incoming cochlear fibres, as well as thick axons (Figure 6). They respond rapidly to a wide range of frequencies and send branches to brainstem and midbrain auditory nuclei involved in motor reactions to sound. For this reason, it has been suggested that they may be involved in acoustic startle responses as well as in determining the precise arrival time of sounds.

In both the dorsal and the ventral cochlear nucleus, neural responses are found that are more complex than those seen in the cochlear nerve fibres. This is not just a result of the different patterns of afferent input to the different types of neuron but because inhibitory inputs from other types of neurons within the complex or from higher up the pathway influence their responses. Several different firing patterns are found to occur in response to the same tonal stimulus as a result of this interplay between excitation and inhibition (Figure 6). Complex neural responses have been recorded from dorsal cochlear nuclear neurons in particular, leading to the suggestion that the dorsal cochlear nucleus is important in determining what sounds are.

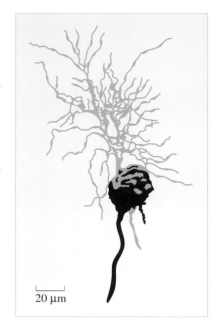

Figure 5   Drawing of a spherical bushy cell (red) with its cell body cupped by an end-bulb of Held (black), the final terminal made by each Type I cochlear afferent in the anteroventral cochlear nucleus. The dendrites of the spherical bushy cell are shown above the cell body and its axon, which goes to the superior olivary complex, can be seen below it.

4 The superior olivary complex: sound localization

The auditory pathway divides as it leaves the cochlear nuclear complex (Figure 1). One branch runs dorsally to the inferior colliculus in the mid-brain, the other ventrally to the **superior olivary complex** in the middle of the brainstem (Figure 4). This is where binaural comparisons are made of signals from each ear so that sounds can be located in space.

In humans, the main olivary nuclei are a pair of disc-shaped medial superior olivary nuclei and a pair of S-shaped lateral superior olivary nuclei. These nuclei use different methods to compare the inputs resulting from a sound entering the ear on the same side of the head with those resulting from the sound entering the ear on the opposite side. Neurons that detect **interaural time delays** are located in the medial superior olivary nuclei. Axons from spherical bushy cells in both the left and the right cochlear nucleus make contact with neurons in both the left and the right medial superior olivary nucleus. A sound from a source nearer to one ear than the other arrives at one medial superior olivary nucleus before the other. Neurons receiving inputs from both sides detect the time of first arrival of a sound at both ears by summing these responses (Figure 7a). However, this method cannot be used

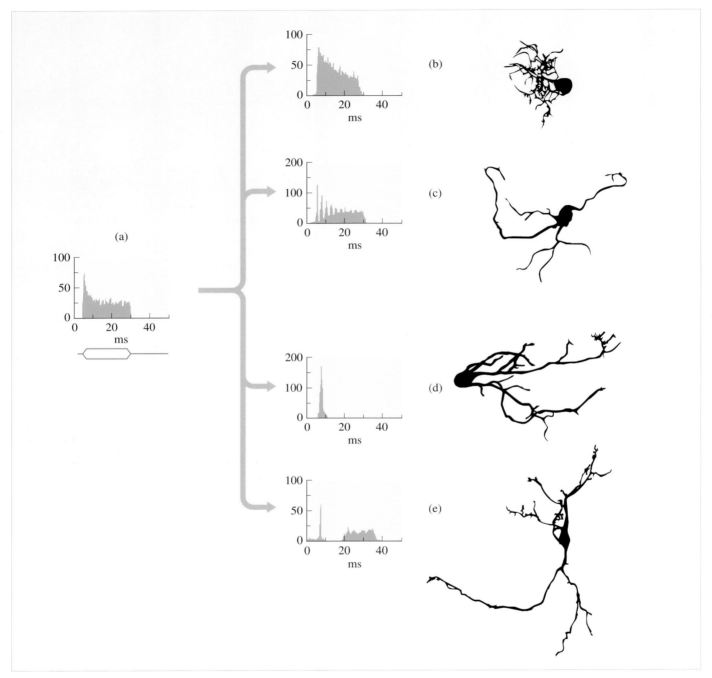

Figure 6 Types of responses obtained from cochlear nerve fibres and the cochlear nuclear complex in response to a tone burst. The vertical axis indicates the number of spikes recorded over time, and to the right of each histogram is a representative drawing of the cell type from which the recording was made. The time course of the tone burst (25 ms) is shown beneath the first histogram. (a) Only one type of response is recorded from cochlear nerve fibres, the so-called primary response. (b) Primary-like responses are recorded from the spherical bushy cells in the anteroventral cochlear nucleus and (c) chopper responses from multipolar cells in the posteroventral and dorsal cochlear nuclei. (d) Onset responses are recorded from the octopus cells in the posteroventral cochlear nucleus. These display a burst of firing at the beginning of a sound. (e) Pauser responses can be recorded from pyramidal cells in the dorsal cochlear nucleus. These show a reduction in firing after the initial burst and then a subsequent build-up.

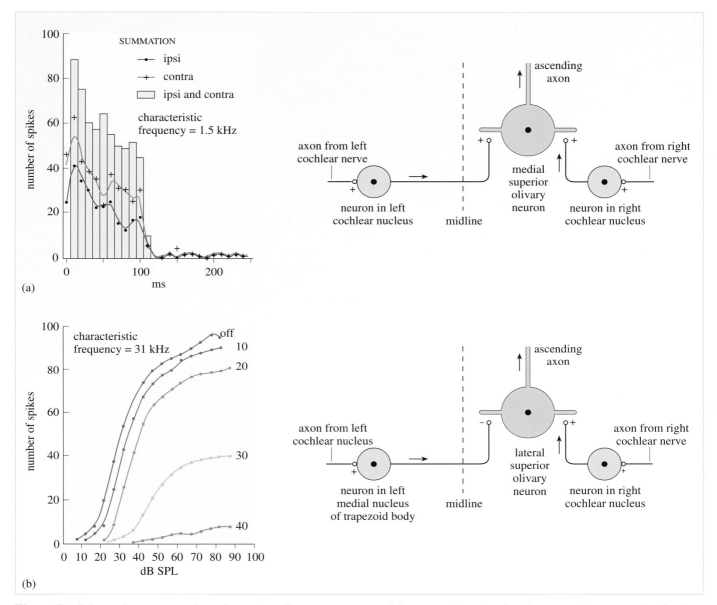

Figure 7 Schematic representation of superior olivary neurons receiving synaptic activation from sounds presented to both ears (+ = excitation; − = inhibition) and graphs showing the types of neural responses that may be obtained. (a) Response histogram and model of neural connections in the right medial superior olivary nucleus showing binaural excitation. The response adds together when the two ears are receiving stimulation at the same time as each other but is reduced if they are not. (b) Graph of binaural output from a neuron in the right lateral superior olivary nucleus that is excited by input from the same (right) side and inhibited by input from the left side. If the intensity is held constant in the left ear at 10, 20, 30 and 40 dB and gradually raised in the right ear, the firing rate increases at first but eventually levels off.

for detecting the location of a continuous tone. Instead, the arrival time of the same point in the sound wave (e.g. the peak or trough) at the two ears must be compared. For this, different points in the cycle are signalled by the process known as phase locking in the cochlear nerve. However, the wavelengths must not be smaller than the distance between the two ears; if they are, the same point but several cycles further along might be inadvertently compared. For this reason, comparisons of interaural time delays can only be made for continuous tones at relatively low frequencies in humans, in the range of 20–1500 Hz. For high frequencies (2000–15 000 Hz), we have to use another mechanism to locate sounds, the difference in **interaural intensity**.

Neurons that detect binaural differences in loudness are located in each of the lateral superior olivary nuclei. Most receive an excitatory input as a result of sounds on the same side of the head as each nucleus, but are inhibited by sounds on the other (Figure 7b). This results in the response being strongest when the sound is loudest in the ear on the same side and weakest when the intensity is the same in both ears as happens, for instance, when the sound is situated along the mid-line. This cannot be the only mechanism we use for locating high-frequency sounds in the horizontal or vertical plane, however, because we could not use it to determine whether a sound was directly in front, behind or overhead. In fact, the shape of our pinnae produces reflections that are delayed in comparison with the direct sound and which are also used in sound localization.

5 The inferior colliculus: mapping sounds

The **inferior colliculi** (Figures 1 and 3), which are involved in hearing, are the rear pair of four bumps located on the dorsal surface of the midbrain, the front pair being the **superior colliculi** (Figures 3 and 8) which are involved in vision. Neural connections between the two pairs of colliculi underlie some important behavioural responses that coordinate audition and vision.

Axons from the auditory brainstem nuclei travel to the inferior colliculi via the **lateral lemniscus** (Figure 1). Each inferior colliculus consists of a central nucleus and an external region composed of a dorsal cortex and a lateral nucleus (Figure 9).

In the inferior colliculus, the sound localization pathway from the superior olivary complex rejoins the one from the cochlear nuclear complex and further analysis of *what* a sound might be takes place. By this stage, a number of more complex aspects of the sound signal are processed as further features are extracted and mapped.

The central nucleus of the inferior colliculus has bands of cells with flattened dendritic fields forming **isofrequency layers** in which the neurons are sharply tuned to the same frequency (Figure 9a). High-frequency layers are found towards the mid-line and low ones towards the outside, again producing a tonotopic map. Superimposed on this map is another relating to sound intensity. Neurons in the centre of each isofrequency layer are the most sensitive, with concentric rings of neurons with similar thresholds and decreasing sensitivities occurring towards the edges (Figure 9b). This means that sound intensity can be related to the spread of excitation. Many neurons in the inferior colliculus also follow time-varying signals when either the frequency or intensity is being modulated. Different neurons respond best to different rates or amplitudes of modulation and these responses also appear to be mapped, approximately from the front to the back of each inferior colliculus.

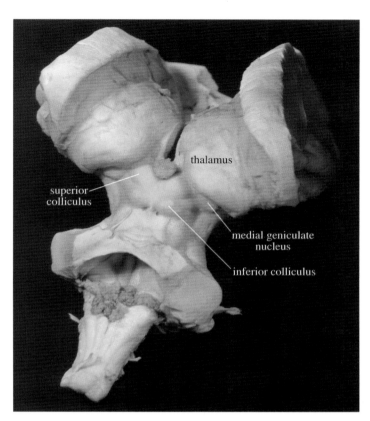

Figure 8 A dissection of the human brainstem and diencephalon viewed from the dorsal surface to show the locations of the inferior and superior colliculi and medial geniculate nucleus in relation to the thalamus.

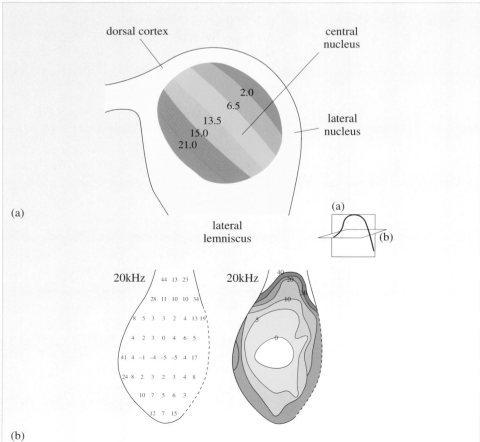

Figure 9 (a) Isofrequency layers in the inferior colliculus of a cat. (b) Two representations of the tone-response thresholds found in the 20 kHz isofrequency plane from the inferior colliculus of a mouse. The numbers on the left indicate the thresholds in dB SPL; the lighter colours indicate neurons with lower thresholds in the contour map on the right. The inset shows the plane of the sections seen in (a) and (b).

The maps described here are only some of those found so far but are useful for illustrating that precise patterns of activity are set up in response to a particular complex sound. This results in a pattern of neural output being sent on to the next stage of the pathway that relates specifically to that sound; in fact, in the medial geniculate nucleus, neurons have been found that respond only to particular complex sounds such as the mew of a kitten. It seems therefore that the intersecting maps in the inferior colliculus extract the features required for sound pattern categorization by the forebrain.

Neurons in the inferior colliculus also make responses relating to the position of sounds in space. In barn owls, a three-dimensional space map for sound location has been found in the avian equivalent of the inferior colliculus. In mammals, however, the signals are sent on to the superior colliculus (Figure 8) where the visual space map appears to align the auditory space map. The inferior colliculi are directly involved in a number of other sound-related behaviours, particularly auditory-motor responses such as those which change the tension of the middle ear muscles to protect the inner ear from loud sound. They also send projections to motor nuclei in the pons and cerebellum which contribute to turning the head and eyes in response to sounds. The inferior colliculi are also the origin of descending pathways to the periolivary region and the cochlear nuclei, and can affect cochlear responses by influencing the olivocochlear feedback loop.

6 The medial geniculate nucleus and auditory cortex: extracting behaviourally relevant features from sounds

Each **medial geniculate nucleus** is a rounded protruberance on the surface of the thalamus (Figures 1 and 8). It has three major divisions. The ventral one is organized tonotopically. Within each isofrequency layer, there is an ordered mapping of many different types of neural responses to different features of sound. The dorsal division is not tonotopically organized; the cells within it respond to a broad range of frequencies, many only to complex sounds. The medial division receives inputs from somatosensory, vestibular and visual sources, including the superior colliculus, as well as the inferior colliculus, and the neurons within it respond to one or more of these sensory modalities. Interestingly, learning can modify these responses.

The ventral division of the medial geniculate nucleus projects primarily to the **primary auditory cortex, A1** (Figures 1 and 10). The dorsal division projects to the non-primary auditory areas that surround the primary auditory cortex whilst the medial division projects diffusely to auditory areas of the cortex and to adjacent cortical fields. In humans, A1 is situated mostly within the **lateral fissure** of the **temporal lobe** in Brodmann's area 41.

Most cells within A1 respond to binaural stimulation. In fact, neurons in A1 show two types of binaural interaction: the first is summation with cells being excited by stimuli to both ears, the second is suppression with cells being excited by sounds in one ear but inhibited by sounds in the other. Bands of cells that show excitation–excitation responses alternate with bands showing excitation–inhibition responses and run approximately at right angles to the isofrequency layers (Figure 11). The firing pattern of these neurons appears to be important in encoding the locations of sounds in the cortex. In fact, sound localization may be the main purpose of A1.

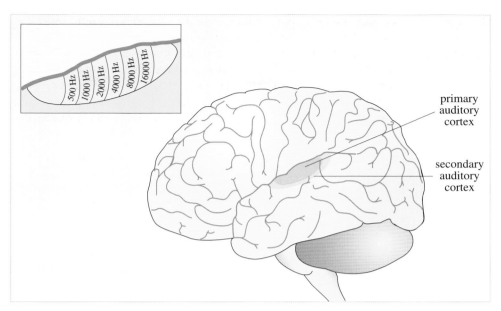

Figure 10   A dissection of the human brain in lateral view showing the approximate position of the primary auditory cortex (A1) (coloured purple) and surrounding auditory association areas (coloured yellow). The inset gives an indication of the tonotopic organization of the primary auditory cortex showing the position of isofrequency bands responding to different characteristic frequencies.

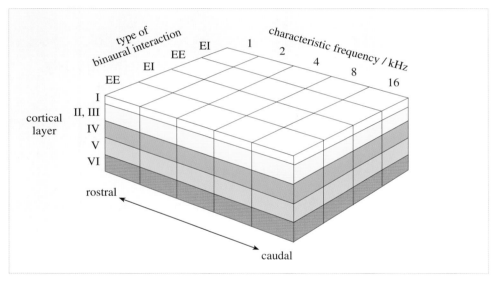

Figure 11   Model of a block of auditory cortex from area A1 showing how the isofrequency bands and alternating bands of binaural excitation–excitation (EE) and excitation–inhibition (EI) cells run at right angles to one another.

Auditory responses can also be obtained from the cortical fields that surround A1 (Figure 10). Some of these non-primary auditory areas extract complex features from sounds such as specific delays between significant parts of the acoustic signal, and the simultaneous occurrence of harmonically-related frequencies. It is likely that these mechanisms are important for analysing time-varying signals such as human speech.

The auditory cortex makes descending projections to the medial geniculate nuclei, the inferior colliculi and even the brainstem auditory nuclei. This **descending auditory pathway** modulates signal processing from the cortex right down to the cochlea. It has been suggested that the cortex can make the thalamus function as an adaptive filter, favouring the transmission of some signals over others. Attention level and anticipation of signals can also modulate thalamic processing. One remarkable property of hearing is its capacity to follow a signal of interest amongst many others. It seems likely that the descending pathway plays a key role in this type of **signal detection**.

7 Summary

Throughout the ascending auditory pathway, the systematic representation of different frequencies (from low to high tones) set up in the cochlea is maintained as tonotopic maps. Sound signals are delivered via the vestibulocochlear nerve to the cochlear nuclear complex. Here, different features of the sound are extracted and the pathway divides, one tract going to the superior olivary complex where binaural comparisons are made of the intensity and timing of signals to determine where sounds are located in space. The other tract goes to the inferior colliculi that control motor reflexes that help protect the inner ear. Further analysis of what the sound is takes place with other aspects such as intensity being mapped. Integration with vision occurs by means of connections with the superior colliculi which direct the eyes towards a sound source. The auditory pathway then travels on to the medial geniculate nuclei where responses to specific complex sounds are found and further integration with other senses occurs. These are connected to the primary auditory areas and their belt areas in the overlying cerebral cortex. Descending pathways running back down from the cortex to the cochlea are used to select sounds of interest from the surrounding auditory scene.

Imaging central auditory function

Alan Palmer and Debbie Hall

1 Introduction

Over the last decade, advances in a range of non-invasive techniques have allowed the activity in the brains of humans while they are performing a range of tasks to be measured with fine spatial and temporal resolution. In this chapter, we provide an overview of some of the most recent imaging data that highlight the roles of brain areas involved in various aspects of hearing.

As is evident from Chapter 3, *From cochlea to cortex*, the auditory nervous system has many stages of processing before the signals reach the cortex. While it is technically feasible to image activation in these earlier stages, imaging studies of the auditory system have concentrated on the processing at and beyond the primary auditory cortex. The data presented here were acquired using **functional magnetic resonance imaging (fMRI)**, **positron emission tomography (PET)**, **magneto-encephalography (MEG)** and **electrophysiology**. These imaging methods alone or in combination have produced a reasonable consensus as to the brain areas involved in audition. The auditory cortex in the human brain, like that of virtually all other animals, consists of a primary area surrounded by multiple non-primary fields, which are presumed to have specific functions. We first consider the anatomical arrangement of the human auditory cortex. We then discuss imaging studies designed to probe the nature of the processing of *simple* sounds and the function of the non-primary auditory fields. Finally, we consider the way the human brain responds to speech.

2 Anatomy of the human auditory cortex

The **auditory cortex** occupies the **superior temporal gyrus**, lying mostly on its upper surface, known as the **supratemporal plane** (Figure 1 overleaf). This region of cortex is one of the most highly folded in the human brain and the supratemporal plane is located along a deep fold, the **sylvian fissure**, which constitutes the uppermost boundary of the temporal lobe. The **superior temporal sulcus** defines the lower limit of the superior temporal gyrus. Brain areas within the superior temporal sulcus are likely to be involved in higher-level processing such as integrating acoustical information with that from other sensory modalities.

The primary auditory area in both hemispheres occupies the medial portion of **Heschl's gyrus**, which runs transversely across the supratemporal plane. Heschl's gyrus measures approximately 30 mm along its long axis and about 10 mm across. From Heschl's gyrus, a number of non-primary areas extend along the supratemporal plane, anteriorly onto the planum polare and posteriorly onto the planum temporale (Figure 2 overleaf). The degree and pattern of folding of the auditory cortex is highly variable. For example, in some human brains, the normally single Heschl's gyrus is indented by a sulcus along its long axis to create two gyri. In these cases, the primary area lies on the more anterior gyrus.

Multiple auditory fields on the supratemporal plane have been defined based on the distribution and density of neural cells identified by histological methods using stained samples of human brain tissue. These auditory fields are not directly visible from magnetic resonance images and generally their locations do not align precisely with morphological features such as Heschl's gyrus and the **planum temporale**. Thus, it is not possible to define their absolute location from individual structural images.

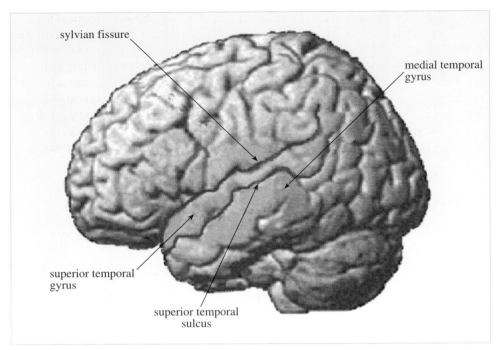

Figure 1 Left side of the human brain showing the lateral view of the auditory cortex on the temporal lobe. The upper surface of the superior temporal gyrus forms the supratemporal plane within the sylvian fissure. The primary auditory cortex is located on Heschl's gyrus, a part of the supratemporal plane. Below this region, the superior temporal gyrus and medial temporal gyrus may play a role in multimodal integration.

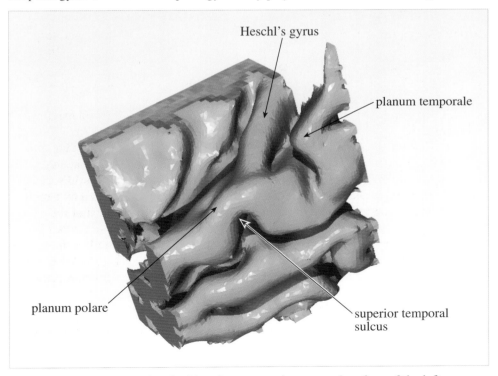

Figure 2 A transverse view looking down upon the exposed surface of the left supratemporal plane and showing the relative locations of Heschl's gyrus, the planum temporale, the planum polare and the superior temporal sulcus.

The histological borders of a number of auditory fields do, however, appear to correspond well with physiological mapping. For example, primary areas exhibit an ordered mapping of neural frequency sensitivity (see Section 3.1). In addition, the greater size of auditory fields occupying the planum temporale on the left than on the right may play a role in the dominance of the left hemisphere for language processing (see Section 4). Thus, the division of the auditory cortex based on histology can provide a more appropriate guide to its functional organization than can that based on gyral patterns. The following section examines the degree of response selectivity in these different auditory areas to certain basic acoustical features.

3 Responses to simple attributes of sounds

The patterns of activity in the peripheral auditory system depend upon a number of features of the sound stimulus. One feature is the distribution of energy across the frequency spectrum, whilst another is the amplitude of the sound component at each frequency. Dynamic variations in the spectrum and the sound level, which are characteristic of all real world sounds, therefore alter the activity patterns within the auditory system. At the cortical level, the spatial position of the sound source, whether it is moving, and if it is moving the direction and speed of movement, also affect the neural representation. Imaging techniques, particularly fMRI and PET, have been used to study the changes in human brain activation that correlate with these sound features. However, the poor temporal resolution of these techniques has resulted in an emphasis on the spatial extent, magnitude and topographical distribution of brain activation, rather than its temporal pattern.

3.1 Sound frequency

Stimulus frequency is the most distinctive organizing principle in the auditory pathway. Each auditory nucleus has a **tonotopic organization**, replicating the progressive change in frequency that occurs along the length of the basilar membrane (Chapter 1, *The mechanics of hearing*). In the cortex of animals and humans, primary, and some non-primary, fields also show such tonotopic organization. In humans, tonotopic organization has been demonstrated using a variety of imaging methods. Electrophysiology provides the most direct demonstration. Using electrodes implanted in epileptic patients to detect the foci of seizures, a lateral progression in frequency sensitivity from high frequency (3360 Hz) to lower frequency (1480 Hz) has been measured along Heschl's gyrus (Figure 3). MEG measures magnetic field changes at the scalp induced by neural activity. Modelling techniques can then be used to estimate the source of the electrical generators giving rise to these surface magnetic fields. Using tones presented at four different frequencies, the source of the response in Heschl's gyrus again moves more laterally as frequency decreases (Figure 4 overleaf). MEG has also revealed a second tonotopic gradient in the planum temporale running from high to low frequency in a posterior direction.

Perhaps surprisingly, there have been few convincing demonstrations of tonotopicity in the human auditory cortex using PET or fMRI, possibly as a result of the limited spatial resolution or the generally low levels of activation induced by pure tones. However, in 2000, Talavage and his co-workers in Boston, USA, have recently combined high-resolution fMRI imaging with narrow-band stimuli that evoke more reliable activation than pure tones. Regions on the supratemporal plane were

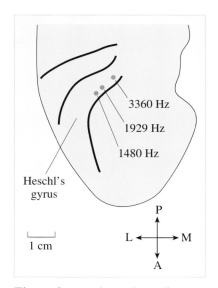

Figure 3   A schematic outline as if looking down on the right supratemporal plane showing electrophysiological measurements of the frequency sensitivity along Heschl's gyrus using three electrodes. The most medially-located electrode was best activated by 3360 Hz tones, while the more laterally-placed electrode was activated by 1480 Hz tones. (M = medial, L = lateral, P = posterior, A = anterior.)

Figure 4 Magnified view of the exposed surface of the left supratemporal plane showing the auditory areas. Superimposed are the electrical sources computed from surface magnetic fields in response to tones of four frequencies (250 Hz: red arrows; 500 Hz: yellow arrows; 1000 Hz: green arrows; 2000 Hz: blue arrows) measured in a single subject.

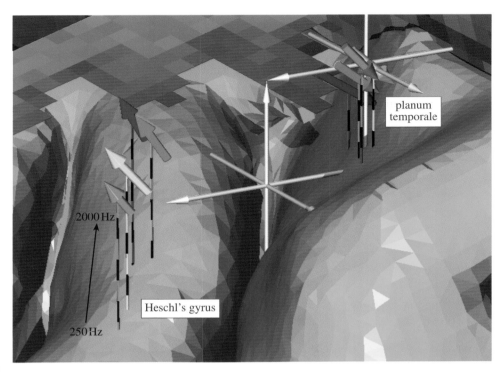

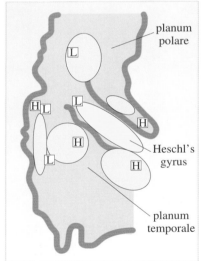

Figure 5 A schematic outline of the left supratemporal plane showing the locations of frequency-dependent regional responses. Foci responding to lower frequencies are denoted by 'L', while those responding to higher frequencies are denoted by 'H'. The frequency-dependent response areas are superimposed on the multiple anatomically-defined areas; the primary area is yellow and the non-primary green.

identified that were more responsive to the high-frequency sounds (above 2490 Hz) than the low-frequency sounds (below 600 Hz) and vice versa. Four response regions were identified that were more strongly activated by the low-frequency sounds and four that were more strongly activated by the high-frequency sounds. These frequency-sensitive regions are widespread across the auditory cortex including Heschl's gyrus, planum polare and the planum temporale, suggesting multiple tonotopic axes. For the purposes of more accurate localization, the locations of the frequency-sensitive regions have been reported relative to anatomically-defined auditory fields (Figure 5). At least some of the frequency-sensitive regions appear to coincide with anatomical divisions of the cortex, such as the region more sensitive to low frequencies at the lateral extreme of the primary area on Heschl's gyrus.

3.2 Sound level

Variations in sound level are important in the perception of a variety of sound features including loudness, spatial position and distance. A major factor in determining the perceived loudness of a sound is its intensity, although other factors, including its spectral content, are also important. Both spectrum and sound level contribute to the observed activation in the brain such that, generally speaking, the higher the sound level or the more extensive the spectral components, the greater the auditory activation. Imaging studies of the cortical response to sound level are therefore important for two reasons: (1) to enhance our understanding of the internal representation of sound level; and (2) to facilitate our interpretation of stimulus-evoked activation, when the auditory response is likely to reflect a combination of several acoustical properties of the stimulus.

Several studies have investigated the changes in auditory activation as a function of sound level. Using MEG, Pantev and his co-workers in Münster, in 1989, showed that the depth of the electrical source generating surface magnetic fields in response to 1000 Hz tones decreased monotonically with level from 30–80 dB above hearing threshold. This result was interpreted as evidence for an **ampliotopic organization**, that is, a systematic gradient of response selectivity to sound level.

Imaging studies have shown that the auditory areas responsive to sound level seem to involve both primary and non-primary areas (Figure 6). Commonly however, imaging techniques reveal an increase in the magnitude of auditory activation and/or in its spatial extent accompanying increases in sound level, rather than ampliotopy *per se* (Figure 7 overleaf). The increase in activation with sound level appears to hold true for both verbal (spoken words or consonant–vowel syllables) and non-verbal (tones) sounds. The exact nature of the relationship between activation and sound level is, however, less clear. For example, in 1999, Lockwood and his co-workers in Buffalo used PET imaging to show a significant linear increase in activation with the level of a 4 kHz tone (30–90 dB SPL) in the medial geniculate nucleus and the primary auditory cortex. Similarly, in 1999, Mohr and co-workers in Gainsville using words with fMRI, found an increase in activation between 60–110 dB SPL, but with evidence for response saturation at 90 to 95 dB SPL. In contrast, in 2001, Hart and her colleagues in Nottingham, also using fMRI, found evidence for a non-linear growth of the auditory response with sound level (42–90 dB SPL) for 300 Hz tones. Most notably for the extent of activation, the nature of the non-linear relationship indicates a relatively flat response to sound level between 42–66 dB SPL, followed by a linear increase, without evidence for response saturation (Figure 7).

Using a rather different approach to measure sound-level effects, Belin and his co-workers in Paris in 1988, used PET to correlate brain activation with the *discriminability* of changes in sound level, rather than with changes in sound level *per se*. The right posterior superior temporal gyrus was activated during the discrimination of sound intensity, independently of performance level, indicating a role for this region of the non-primary auditory cortex in the computation of sound-intensity differences.

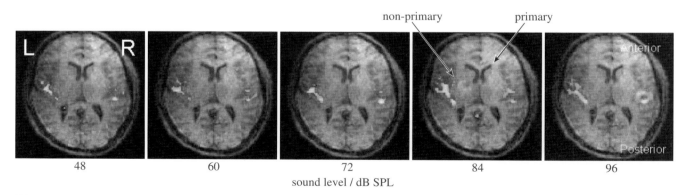

Figure 6   Auditory cortical activation in both hemispheres by a 300 Hz tone presented to the left ear at a range of sound levels (48–96 dB SPL). Activation involves both primary and non-primary auditory areas. Activation for a single subject is overlaid onto a transverse brain image cutting through the superior temporal gyrus from that subject.

Figure 7   The number of voxels (volume elements) activated by a 300 Hz tone as a function of sound level. Data are averaged across 10 subjects.

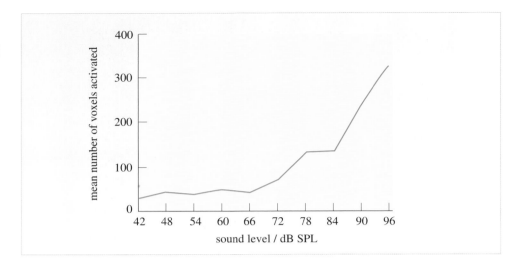

3.3 Spatial attributes of sound: position and motion

Sound source position is computed from three cues: (1) monaural spectral cues generated by the outer ear; (2) differences in the level of the sounds reaching the ears (for high frequencies); and (3) differences in interaural timing (for low frequencies) (see Chapter 5, *Hearing the world*). Moving sound sources generate dynamically varying interaural level and time differences which when slow (2–6 Hz), are perceived by humans as moving.

Several imaging studies have utilized such static and dynamic spatial cues to search for specialized spatial processing within the brain. The inferior parietal lobes (particularly on the right side) are more activated during sound localization tasks than during non-spatial auditory discrimination tasks based on frequency. In 1998, PET and fMRI measurements by Griffiths and his collaborators in Newcastle and London also revealed selective activation of the posterior **parietal cortex**, greater on the right side, in response to moving sounds (Figure 8). These investigators used a 500 Hz tonal stimulus that contained both interaural time and level cues for auditory motion. When the cues were complementary, listeners perceived sound motion. When the cues were opposed they cancelled, resulting in a perception of the sound being stationary. The primary auditory area was activated by both sound conditions relative to silence, but was not differentially activated by perceived motion. In contrast, the right parietal cortex was more active when subjects perceived motion, than when they did not perceive motion, despite the presence of the same dynamic stimulus cues in both conditions. Some of the additional activation in the frontal and left parietal cortices shown by fMRI (Figure 8a), but not by PET (Figure 8b), could perhaps be attributed to the additional demands on auditory selective attention imposed by the scanner noise.

Another fMRI study, in 2000, by Baumgart and his co-workers in Magdeburg, Germany, measured response selectivity to sound motion within the auditory cortex. Part of the auditory cortex on the right supratemporal plane, in an area of the planum temporale lateral to Heschl's gyrus, also appears to be involved in movement processing. Dynamic changes in sound level that were 90° out of phase at the two ears created a moving percept, whereas changes in level that were in phase at the two ears produced only the same variation in loudness at the two ears. Compared to silence, both moving and stationary sounds activated the auditory cortex in both

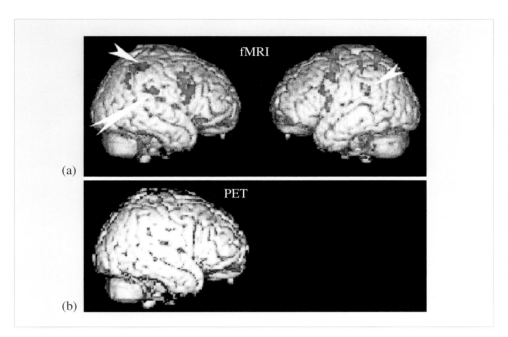

(a)

(b)

Figure 8 (a) Areas more activated by a moving sound than by a stationary sound, measured using fMRI. The data are pooled across three subjects and superimposed onto lateral views of the right and left hemispheres of the brain. Arrows indicate the areas of posterior parietal cortex that show the strongest response to auditory motion. (b) A PET replication of the above study pooled across six subjects. Activation by the moving sounds was observed in an isolated region of the right posterior parietal cortex.

hemispheres (Figure 9a), but only a lateral area on the right planum temporale was more activated by the moving sound than by the stationary sound (Figure 9b).

Activation of the right parietal cortex is consistent with suggestions that processing of the spatial properties of sounds, including their motion, occurs beyond the primary auditory cortex in the right hemisphere and probably involves non-primary auditory regions in the planum temporale as well as higher-level processing in the multimodal parietal cortex. It is unclear why the auditory areas on the right supratemporal plane do not show consistent motion selectivity in all imaging studies.

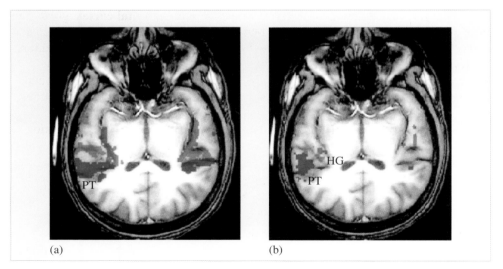

(a)   (b)

Figure 9 (a) A transverse brain image from above showing the auditory regions of the supratemporal plane. Primary and non-primary auditory areas were activated by both moving and stationary sounds, relative to silence. (b) Regions that were more activated by moving than by stationary sounds, pooled across ten subjects. PT: planum temporale; HG: Heschl's gyrus.

4 Responses to speech

Speech is a complex acoustical stimulus that generates widespread activation in the auditory cortex including primary and non-primary areas in both hemispheres. Neuropsychological and psycholinguistic studies, supported by imaging, have also implicated a wider network of brain areas, predominantly in the left hemisphere. The network includes the inferior prefrontal cortex (**Broca's area**), the temporoparietal cortex (**Wernicke's area**) and the middle temporal gyrus. These areas play a specific role in linguistic analysis, particularly in the analysis of lexical, semantic and syntactic information. The exact pattern of activation is highly dependent on the specific requirements of the language task. For example, activation occurs in Broca's area both during auditory word perception and repetition, but is greater during repetition. A comprehensive review of the cortical bases for speech perception extends beyond the scope of this chapter and so we focus on imaging evidence for speech-specific activation *within* and adjacent to the auditory cortex.

Areas of the left auditory cortex are more activated than those of the right by sounds that contain amplitude and spectral changes This differentiation is less pronounced for sounds with a more uniform temporal pattern. Such temporal analysis is a particular requirement in the encoding of acoustic cues for speech perception. **Voice onset time** is a temporal feature that helps us to distinguish between two classes of stop consonants, voiced (e.g. [ba], [da]) and voiceless (e.g. [pa], [a]). Thus, hemispheric differences in the acoustical processing of such stop consonants can indicate selectivity for temporal coding. For example, in 1999, using recordings from electrodes implanted along the supratemporal plane of epilepsy patients, Liégeois-Chauvel and her collaborators in Marseille demonstrated differential responses to voiced and voiceless stop consonants in left, but not right, Heschl's gyrus and planum temporale. Both left and right auditory cortices responded strongly to the syllables, but responses were only time-locked to the different components of the syllable in left auditory areas. Identical time-locked responses were found on the left side for both speech sounds and non-speech analogues, suggesting that the asymmetries in temporal processing in Heschl's gyrus and the planum temporale are unlikely to be speech-specific.

PET and fMRI imaging can distinguish strong from weak brain activation, but because of their relatively poor temporal resolution, they are insensitive to subtle differences in sequential processing in the millisecond time scale. Consequently, for auditory areas such as Heschl's gyrus and the planum temporale, imaging has failed to show asymmetries between speech and non-speech sounds. For example, Binder and his colleagues in Milwaukee, USA, found no difference in the strength of activation in Heschl's gyrus or the planum temporale, in either hemisphere, between listening to sequences of words and sequences of pure tones with different frequency steps. However, activation by words was greater in the superior temporal sulcus on the left side compared to the right, indicating that auditory activation of this area may be more speech specific.

To investigate speech specificity further, in 2000, Binder and his colleagues measured auditory responses to additional sound stimuli, including white noise, reversed speech and pseudowords (e.g. [sked]). Heschl's gyrus responded equally well to all of the stimuli suggesting that it may respond to the basic acoustic elements present in all of the stimuli. In contrast, surrounding non-primary auditory areas, including the planum temporale, responded more strongly to the tones than to the white noise suggesting a preference for the changing frequency over time. An area on the lateral surface of the superior temporal gyrus responded to words more than tones and to tones more than noise, suggesting the emergence of some degree of speech specificity. The areas denoted in red in Figure 10, primarily in the left superior temporal sulcus, were unresponsive to the noise and weakly responsive to the tones, but strongly responsive to the words, pseudowords *and* reversed speech. The speech-like sounds differed from the noise and tones both in terms of their acoustic complexity and their linguistic features. The specific activation in the superior temporal sulcus for 'speech-like' sounds could therefore have arisen from differences in acoustical, phonetic or lexical processing.

To probe the role of the left superior temporal sulcus in the analysis of speech-like sounds further, in 2000, Scott and co-workers in London measured auditory activation differences using a variety of speech and speech-like sounds with equivalent spectral and temporal complexity, but varying intelligibility and phonetic information. While the lateral surface of the superior temporal gyrus and the posterior superior temporal sulcus were activated by all stimuli that contained perceptible phonetic features, regardless of intelligibility, the anterior part of the superior temporal sulcus was specifically activated by only those stimuli that could be understood.

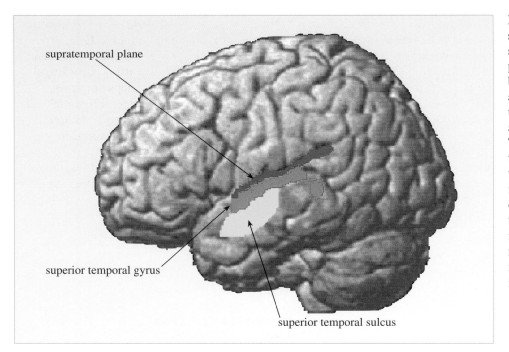

Figure 10   View of the lateral surface of the left hemisphere showing areas involved in speech processing. The region shown in blue includes non-primary auditory areas on the supratemporal plane that appear to be sensitive to the acoustic characteristics of speech. The region coloured in red denotes those auditory areas of the superior temporal gyrus that may be involved in pre-lexical processing of phonetic cues. The region of the superior temporal sulcus shown in yellow shows speech selectivity, responding more strongly to intelligible speech than to non-intelligible speech-like sounds.

5 Summary

On the basis of these imaging results, an anatomical framework for the detection of simple sounds and of speech perception in the auditory cortex can be proposed. Virtually all simple and complex sounds produce activation of the primary auditory cortex which is situated on Heschl's gyrus. This primary area is tonotopically organized and responds to increased sound level, even of single tones, with increased activation up to high sound levels (96 dB SPL). Non-primary auditory areas may also be tonotopically organized.

In general, sounds containing spatial and motion cues activate auditory regions that are posterior to Heschl's gyrus as well as multimodal regions of the posterior parietal cortex. It has been suggested that these brain areas form part of a pathway specialized for the processing of auditory spatial information. In contrast, areas on the anterior part of the supratemporal plane are more activated by complex sounds. Anterior and lateral non-primary auditory areas appear to be critically involved in the processing of auditory patterns, including the acoustical features of speech.

Speech processing seems to involve distinct subsystems in the left temporal lobe that proceed along an anterior pathway. Low-level speech cues are likely to be processed in Heschl's gyrus and surrounding non-primary auditory areas on the supratemporal plane, while pre-lexical processing of phonetic cues and their sequencing probably occurs on the lateral surface of the superior temporal gyrus. At the next stage of analysis, aspects of speech intelligibility are likely to be encoded in the anterior superior temporal sulcus.

Further reading

Binder, J. R. *et al.* (1994) Functional magnetic resonance imaging of the human auditory cortex, *Annals of Neurology*, **35**, pp. 662–672.

Elliott, L. L. (1994) Functional brain imaging and hearing, *Journal of the Acoustical Society of America*, **96**, pp. 1397–1408.

Hickik, G. and Poeppel, D. (2000) Towards a functional neuroanatomy of speech perception, *Trends in Cognitive Sciences*, **4**, No. 4, pp. 131–138.

Hearing the world
Chris Darwin

5

1 Introduction

We hear objects doing: water falling, people talking, glass breaking. Usually there is more than one such auditory source within earshot, so that the ear receives a mixture of their sounds. Yet from this mixture, we can usually recognize the separate auditory sources, each with its own appropriate pitch, timbre and location. We can also tell something about the environment that the sounds are being produced in: are you in a church, a living room or a field?

To understand how the brain solves these difficult problems, you need first to understand what different sounds consist of and what the sensory information about these sounds looks like to the brain.

Although sound enters the ear as a pressure wave, its translation into neural impulses involves a sophisticated frequency analysis on the basilar membrane (see Chapter 1, *The mechanics of hearing*), and a conversion of the movement of each position on the basilar membrane into electrical impulses in different auditory nerve fibres (see Chapter 2, *The transformation of sound stimuli into electrical signals*). You *could* hear sound without the frequency analysis stage, so it is interesting to question why the ear has evolved to carry out frequency analysis.

In this chapter we shall look at the consequences of this frequency analysis for the coding of different properties of complex sounds by the auditory nerve, and how the brain recognizes basic properties of complex sounds such as pitch and timbre from the information in the auditory nerve. We will then look at the different cues that the brain uses to localize sounds in three dimensions, and finally address the intriguing question of how the brain can still perform these operations reliably when, as is usual, it is hearing more than one sound at a time.

2 Structure of complex sounds

A lot of the sound that we listen to is either speech or music. Most of the sounds of speech and almost all musical sounds have a definite pitch to them and are produced by a steadily vibrating sound source (the vocal cords for speech and singing – a string, reed or lips for instrumental music): the faster the vibration the higher the pitch. Such sounds have two very distinctive and related properties: first, their waveforms consist of a repeating pattern, and second, their spectrum consists of discrete harmonic components. The upper panel of Figure 1 (overleaf) shows the first 500 ms of the waveform of an oboe note. The graph shows the change in pressure over time. The oboe is starting to play the F sharp an octave and three tones above middle C. This note has a **fundamental frequency** (or repetition rate) of 740 Hz which corresponds to the rate at which the reed is vibrating. The waveform repeats itself at this rate, with a single cycle taking 1/740 s or 1.35 ms. The lower panel shows a spectrogram of the waveform, which shows how much energy there is at frequencies between 0 and 5000 Hz again with time running along the horizontal axis. The spectrogram shows that there is energy at the **harmonic frequencies** of the 740 Hz fundamental. Each of the horizontal bars in the spectrogram corresponds to a harmonic frequency. The frequencies of these harmonics are all multiples of 740 Hz; the lowest is at 740 Hz itself, the next at 1480 Hz and so on. Notice that for this oboe the second frequency component is stronger, with a darker bar, than the other harmonics.

Figure 1 Waveform and spectrogram of the start of an oboe note. The upper panel shows how the air pressure changes over time, giving a periodic complex waveform with a repetition rate of 740 Hz. The lower panel shows a spectrogram of the same sound. The vertical axis is now frequency, and the horizontal grey bands show that the periodic sound has energy at harmonic frequencies which are multiples of the 740 Hz fundamental.

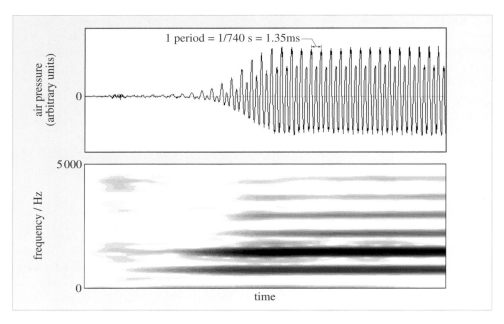

The brain recognizes the **pitch** of this sound (i.e. the F sharp an octave and three tones above middle C) mainly from the frequencies of these first few harmonics. The pitch of speech sounds is also determined by the frequencies of the first few harmonics. In spoken English we use pitch to vary the intonation of the voice ('They won!' versus 'They won?'). Other, so-called tone languages use pitch to distinguish between individual words. The movement of the harmonics that occurs when the pitch of the voice changes is illustrated in the left-hand part of Figure 2.

Figure 2 Waveform and spectrogram of the start of a normally voiced and a whispered vowel [a] – as in British English 'car'. The waveform of the voiced sound (left) is periodic and its spectrogram shows harmonics which fall in frequency over time. The waveform of the whispered sound (right) is noisy rather than periodic and its spectrogram does not have harmonic structure.

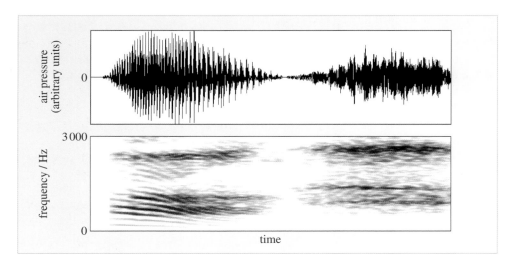

Not all sounds are periodic and have a pitch. For example, whispered speech is generated as a noise when air is blown through the glottis – the gap between the vocal cords. The waveform of such natural noise does not repeat itself, so the spectrum is not harmonic. The waveform and spectrogram of a whispered vowel are shown on the right-hand side of Figure 2.

The **timbre** of the sound (that is whether the sound is like an oboe or some other instrument, or which vowel the sound is) is a more complex percept. Timbre is partly determined by the relative amplitudes of the different harmonics. For the particular note shown in Figure 1, the second harmonic at 1480 Hz is the strongest. In a different instrument, the harmonics will have different relative amplitudes. In speech, different vowels also change the relative amplitudes of the different harmonics. But for musical instruments the onset of a note is also very important in giving the listener clues to what instrument it is. Notice in the spectrogram of Figure 1 that the oboe starts in a complicated way with a burst of noise followed by the different harmonics starting at different times.

3 Auditory excitation patterns

The basilar membrane acts like a bank of band-pass filters, so that each point on the membrane responds to only a narrow band of frequencies. Each auditory neuron therefore hears the world of sound through a filter tuned to a centre frequency and with a particular bandwidth. The bandwidth of the healthy human ear has been measured at different frequencies in masking experiments. These experiments measure how intense a tone must be for listeners to hear it against a background of noise. The noise has a variable-width notch (where there is no sound energy) in a band of frequencies around the frequency of the tone. If the auditory filter in a listener's ear has, say, a bandwidth of 100 Hz, then their ability to hear the tone will not be influenced by noise outside this band. One of the symptoms of sensorineural hearing loss that a hearing aid cannot alleviate is that the auditory filters become substantially broader than in the normal ear (probably as a result of damage to the outer hair cells). Consequently, sounds that someone with a sensorineural hearing impairment wants to listen to are more masked by background sounds than is the case for someone with normal hearing.

We can use the bandwidths measured from these masking experiments to model how the human ear responds to complex sounds. **Auditory excitation patterns** from such a model for a pure tone and for a complex tone (with 25 equal-amplitude harmonics) are shown in Figure 3 (overleaf) together with their line spectra. The left-hand columns show an excitation pattern from an ear with normal bandwidths, and the right-hand columns those from an ear whose bandwidths are twice as broad as normal, as might occur as one of the symptoms of outer hair cell damage in sensorineural hearing loss. The graphs are plotted on a scale that corresponds to distance along the basilar membrane. The excitation pattern shows how much the basilar membrane moves at each position along its length in response to sound. The normal ear is able to resolve out about eight or so harmonics – there are about eight clear peaks in the excitation pattern. But in the ear with the wider bandwidths, only two or three harmonics can be resolved.

The low-frequency part of complex sounds, where the individual harmonics are resolved, is particularly important for pitch perception and for localization of the sound source in the horizontal plane.

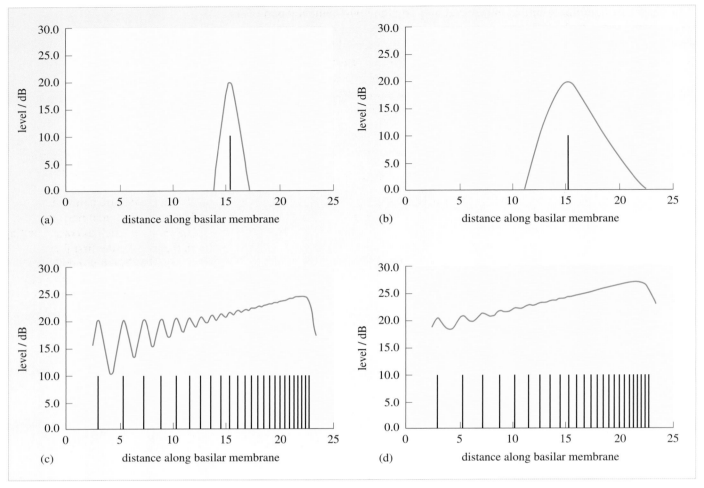

Figure 3 Spectra and auditory excitation patterns. The horizontal axis is a frequency scale representing distance along the basilar membrane. (a) An auditory excitation pattern for a normal human ear in response to a single sine wave (indicated by the vertical line). (b) The broader excitation pattern that occurs as one of the symptoms of sensorineural hearing loss (SNHL) in response to the same single tone. (c) and (d) The normal and SNHL responses to a complex tone consisting of 25 equal-amplitude harmonics. Notice that in the normal ear the first eight or so harmonics are resolved (giving identifiable peaks in the excitation pattern), but in the SNHL ear fewer harmonics are resolved.

4 Recognizing a sound's pitch

Although we hear a periodic complex sound as having a pitch which is the same as its fundamental, it is a surprising fact that it is not necessary to have energy at the fundamental frequency of a complex tone for the pitch to be heard. Hermann von Helmholtz in the mid-nineteenth century put forward the contrary theory of pitch perception, that the presence of the fundamental frequency *was* necessary, and such was his intellectual stature, that it was not until about one hundred years later that his theory was finally discarded. It is now clear that we *can* hear a pitch even in the absence of the fundamental frequency – the so-called 'Case of the Missing Fundamental'. There is now general agreement about the basic experimental facts that a theory of pitch perception has to explain, but it is still not clear whether there is a single mechanism underlying pitch perception, or two separate mechanisms.

The pitch of a complex sound is influenced more by the low-frequency part of its spectrum than by the high-frequency part. The crucial experiment was performed by the Dutch auditory scientist Reiner Plomp in 1967. He created sounds that were composed of two different harmonic series: the first few harmonics were derived from one fundamental, and the remainder from a fundamental that was either 20% higher or lower. Plomp found that the pitch that listeners heard was that of the first few harmonics rather than that of the rest of the sound (Figure 4).

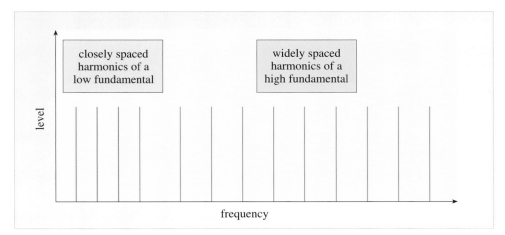

Figure 4 When listeners hear a sound whose first few frequency components are harmonics of a low fundamental frequency and the remainder are harmonics of a higher fundamental frequency, they hear its pitch as corresponding to the pitch of the first few harmonics. The low-numbered harmonics are thus dominant in determining our perception of pitch.

One influential hypothesis about how we recognize pitch is that it is done through a process of pattern recognition. Julius Goldstein, working in the Communications Biophysics Group at the Massachusetts Institute of Technology in the area of biomedical engineering, suggested in the 1970s that the brain identifies the pitch of a complex sound from the frequencies of its resolved harmonics. It finds the harmonic series that best fits the identified frequencies.

But Goldstein's theory is unlikely to be the whole story. We can recognize the pitch of a sound even when there are no resolved harmonics for his theory to work on. The sensation of pitch that we get from the high harmonics of a complex sound was called 'residue' pitch by Jan Schouten working in Holland in the 1940s. He suggested a quite different mechanism of pitch perception for these sounds based on the fact that the basilar membrane responds to the unresolved harmonics by 'beating' at the fundamental frequency. **Beats** are the regular changes in amplitude of a sound that result when two (or more) sine waves are added together. The beats occur at the difference in frequency between the two sine waves (Figure 5 overleaf). Since we know that the temporal pattern of firing in the auditory nerve reflects the rate at which these beats occur, then it is likely that the brain can use this information to measure the pitch of the sound directly, since the beat rate for sounds consisting of mixtures of consecutive harmonics is none other than the fundamental frequency.

One solution to the problem of how we hear the pitch of a complex tone is that we actually have two mechanisms: one like that proposed by Goldstein, which operates on resolved harmonics, and one like that proposed by Schouten which operates on the unresolved harmonics. This proposal is supported by observations that the subjective sensation of pitch from these two types of sound is rather different. Sounds that have resolved harmonics have a more musical quality and we can make rather fine discriminations of their pitches, whereas sounds that only have unresolved harmonics have a less musical quality and we can only make rather coarse discriminations of their pitch.

Figure 5 When a 1000 Hz sine wave (upper panel) is added to a 1100 Hz sine wave (middle panel), the result (lower panel) is a complex wave whose amplitude waxes and wanes or 'beats' at 100 times per second. Two beats appear in the lower figure, which shows 20 ms of the waveform.

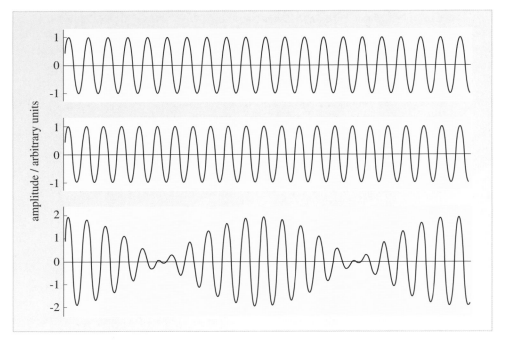

A different solution to the problem dates back to the 1950s when experimental psychologist Joseph Licklider (Figure 6) proposed that a simple neural model based on a delay line could extract the pitch period (the frequency of the perceived harmonic) from a set of resolved harmonics as well as the pitch period of Schouten's unresolved harmonics. **Autocorrelation** compares a waveform with a delayed version of itself. If the waveform is periodic, and the delay is the same as the period, then the original and the delayed versions will look identical. By finding the delay that gives the best correspondence, autocorrelation can give the pitch of a complex tone. Licklider's model, illustrated in Figure 7, performs an 'autocorrelation' on each auditory channel. The comparison of the original and the delayed waveform is carried out by coincidence detectors which will only fire if they get an impulse at the same time from both of their inputs.

Licklider's model has some advantages as an *integrated* theory of pitch perception, since it can handle both resolved and unresolved harmonics, but it has two disadvantages over the two-mechanism approach. First, the Goldstein model uses simpler neural information and provides an impressive quantitative explanation for a large body of experimental data which modern autocorrelation models have not yet matched. Second, there is recent experimental evidence that listeners find it easier to compare two 'Goldstein pitches' or two 'Schouten pitches' than they do to compare one of each. This is a result that is not readily explained by a single-mechanism model such as Licklider's.

Figure 6 Joseph C. R. Licklider (1915–1990). Joseph Licklider was initially an experimental psychologist who subsequently went on to become one of the most influential pioneers of modern computing, yet who today remains virtually unknown. His ideas led to the development of the graphical user interface that is so familiar today, and at the US Department of Defense's Advanced Research Projects Agency (ARPA) he instigated the creation of the ARPAnet, the precursor to the Internet.

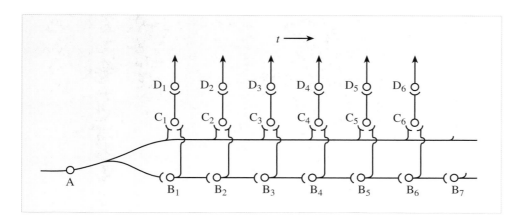

Figure 7 Licklider's neural autocorrelator. The input signal divides in two to provide an undelayed upper version and a lower version that is progressively delayed by the chain of neurons marked B. The neurons marked C fire when both their inputs arrive at the same time. Their firing rate is integrated over a short time period by the neurons marked D.

5 Localizing sounds in space

Many different cues combine to let us localize sound in three-dimensional space. Different types of information are used to localize sound in the horizontal plane, in the vertical plane and in terms of distance.

5.1 Binaural cues to direction in the horizontal plane

Two main cues inform us from what direction in the horizontal plane (left–right) a sound is coming. They both involve comparing the signals at the two ears and this comparison is carried out in parallel (i.e. simultaneously) for each frequency band that the ear analyses.

A sound which comes from the left side will reach the left ear before it reaches the right thus generating an **interaural time difference (ITD)**. The maximum extra distance that a sound travels between the ears is about 23 cm, which takes sound about 690 μs. This is therefore the largest naturally-occurring ITD. We are remarkably sensitive to changes in ITD. Under optimum conditions listeners can distinguish a change of as little as 6 μs in ITD – that is they can distinguish a change of direction of a sound of less than 1°.

The mechanisms underlying this remarkable ability are not fully understood, but it is very likely that we use a delay-line mechanism proposed in 1948 by the American psychologist Lloyd Jeffress. Jeffress's mechanism is similar to Licklider's 'autocorrelation' mechanism except that it performs '**cross-correlation**': it compares two different signals (those from the two ears) rather than two versions of the same signal. In Jeffress's cross-correlator the small delays required to cancel the ITD are produced by neural impulses having to travel different distances down an axon. Figure 8 (overleaf) illustrates this proposed neural mechanism. Neurons that were anatomically and functionally very similar to those proposed by Jeffress were discovered by the American physiologist Tom Yin in the medial superior olive nucleus of the cat brainstem (see Chapter 3, *From cochlea to cortex*).

The second main cue to localization in the horizontal plane is the difference in intensity (or level) of sound at the two ears – the **interaural level difference (ILD)**. There are two reasons why sound might have a higher level at one ear than at the other. The main reason is that the head casts an **acoustic shadow**; this shadow is 'darker' for high-frequency sounds than for low-frequency, since low-frequency sounds diffract around the head. The second reason is that sound will be louder at the ear nearer to a source simply because the energy at a point decreases as the

Figure 8 Jeffress's cross-correlator. Signals from the two ears meet at coincidence detectors after they have travelled different relative distances down their axons. When the difference in conduction times cancels the difference in their starting times (ITD) the appropriate coincidence detector neuron will fire. ITDs are thus converted into a place code according to which of the coincidence detectors fires.

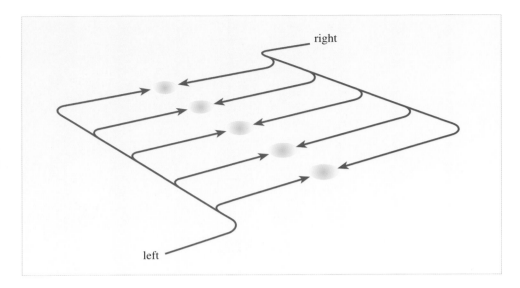

inverse-square of its distance from the source. In practice this second factor is only important for sounds that are within 2 m of the head. For more distant sounds, the head-shadow effect is the only one that can give substantial ILDs; a distant 5 kHz tone coming from a direction opposite one ear will be about 20 dB more intense at the nearer than at the farther ear. It is likely that interaural level differences are initially detected in the lateral superior olive of the cat by so-called excitatory–inhibitory (EI) neurons. These cells show an excitatory response to sound from the ipsilateral ear, and an inhibitory response to sound from the contralateral ear.

The physiological division of function between the medial and the lateral nuclei of the superior olive found in cats sits well with models of human listeners' performance on auditory localization tasks. The human behavioural data are explained well by assuming that ITDs and ILDs are first computed independently and then their separate estimates of the sound's location combined.

For pure tones, the two cues, ITD and ILD are complementary; ILDs are useful for high-frequency sounds, and ITDs are useful for low-frequency sounds. There are two main reasons for this 'duplex' theory (as the famous nineteenth-century physicist Lord Rayleigh called it). First, only high-frequency sounds produce substantial ILDs (since low-frequency sounds diffract round the head). Second, only low-frequency tones give unambiguous ITD information. This second point is not obvious and is due to **phase ambiguity** (Figure 9). For a tone of say 5000 Hz, the individual cycles of the waveform occur five times every millisecond or every 200 μs. This time-interval is shorter than the largest naturally-occurring ITD (about 690 μs). Consequently a 5000 Hz sound that has an ITD of 200 μs will produce signals at the two ears which are identical (apart from their onsets) to those produced by a sound that has an ITD of 0 μs. For both of them, peaks in the waveform will arrive at the two ears at exactly the same time. The brain then has no way of telling whether the sound is coming from straight ahead or from one side. This ambiguity kicks in for pure tones of frequency around 1500 Hz or higher. Human listeners are in fact unable to detect phase differences between the ears for sounds that are higher in frequency than about 1500 Hz.

Most of the behavioural work on humans' ability to localize sound, and also the physiological work on brain mechanisms in animals has used pure tones. However, most of our listening involves complex sounds. The most important cues for

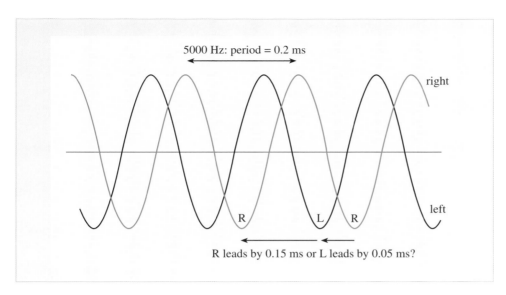

Figure 9 Phase ambiguity. The red waveform is from the right ear and the black from the left. But which ear started first? The right ear could be leading by 0.15 ms, or the left ear could be leading by 0.05 ms. Since both of these values are less than the maximum delay for an adult head (c. 0.7 ms) there is no correct answer and the stimulus is ambiguous. For lower frequencies (< 1500 Hz), with longer periods, the longer of the two possible delays would be greater than 0.7 ms, and so could not have started first. In this case there would be no phase ambiguity.

complex sounds such as speech are the ITDs of the frequency bands in the low-frequency part of the spectrum.

Psychologists Frederic Wightman and Doris Kistler at the University of Wisconsin have shown that if natural localization cues are artificially manipulated so that ITDs indicate that the speech is coming say from the left whereas ILDs indicate that it is coming from the right, then the ITDs win and the speech is heard on the left, provided that it contains low frequencies. If the low frequencies are removed, then ILDs win. (Normally, of course, these two cues will be acting together rather than in opposition.) Notice that the low-frequency region is dominant both in the perception of the pitch of a complex sound and in its location in the horizontal plane.

5.2 Pinna and head movement: cues to direction in the vertical plane

Although the low-frequency part of complex sounds is dominant in localization in the horizontal plane, the very high-frequency part of the spectrum is dominant in localizing sound in the vertical plane (ahead–back–below–above). The main cues to a sound's location in this plane are produced by the interaction of the sound with the external ear or pinna. Since human ears are small, only very high frequency sounds interact with them (for the same reason that only high-frequency sounds give ILDs through the shadowing effect of the head). The physics of how sound interacts with the pinna is complex, but the following may give you a feel for what is happening.

Because the ear is asymmetrical, sounds will be reflected off the pinna into the ear canal in different ways depending on the angle that they come from. A particular direction of sound will give an echo with a particular path length difference compared with the unreflected sound (that goes directly into the ear canal). This applies in particular to sounds that are reflected off the concha (the smooth shell-like surface closest to the ear canal). Depending on the frequency of the sound, a particular path length will give a particular phase difference. If the reflected sound at a particular frequency happens to be 180° out of phase with the unreflected sound and at the same amplitude as they enter the ear, then the two will cancel each other out, producing a notch in the spectrum at that frequency. Conversely, if the reflected sound has the *same* phase as the unreflected sound, the two will add together to produce a peak in the spectrum. The result of this destructive or constructive interference between reflected and unreflected sound is that different directions of sound produce characteristic changes to the spectrum. Perceptual experiments have shown that the frequency of the notches produced by destructive interference are important cues to direction in the median plane. The physiologist Eric Young at Johns Hopkins University in Baltimore has found evidence that a particular cell type in the dorsal cochlear nucleus of cats is specialized for detecting the frequency of these pinna-induced spectral notches.

We are also able to distinguish whether a long or repeating sound is in front of or behind us by moving our heads. When we move our head to the left, a sound that is in front will move (relative to the head) towards the right ear whereas one that is behind will move towards the left ear.

5.3 Cues to distance: how far away is a sound?

Lightning that is close produces a loud crack of thunder; lightning that is distant produces a quieter rumble. So what are the cues to distance? More distant sounds are quieter (as the wavefront spreads out over a greater area), they have relatively less energy at higher frequencies (since air absorbs higher frequencies more than lower) and they have a relatively higher level of echoes than do nearer sounds. To be able to use the first two cues – level and loss of high frequencies – the listener must know something about the intrinsic nature of the sound; the sound might be a quiet muffled one that is close, or a loud, bright one that is distant.

6 Understanding speech and music

Speech is not only the most important type of sound for humans but also the one that we know most about. At a very simple level we can see what properties of sound give the differences in timbre that, for speech, we hear as different vowels.

6.1 Timbre in speech and music

Vowel sounds are produced by a sound source – the vibrating vocal cords – which is filtered by the vocal tract. The regularly vibrating vocal cords produce a harmonic sound with a particular pitch – the faster they vibrate, the higher the pitch – but the distinctive vowel quality comes from the way in which this sound is filtered by the vocal tract, the tube of air between the larynx and the lips. We produce different vowels by changing the shape of this tube through changes to the position of our tongue, jaw and lips; for the vowel [i] 'ee', the tongue is high and forward in the mouth, for [a] 'ah' it is low and back. The different shapes of tube resonate at different frequencies, so that different parts of the spectrum are amplified, with some harmonics becoming louder and others quieter. These **resonant frequencies** are called **formant frequencies** and are different for different vowels. For a man's voice the first formant frequency of [i] is at around 270 Hz and the second at about 2300 Hz, whereas for [a] the values are about 73 Hz and 1100 Hz respectively. Since women on average have smaller heads than men, and children have even smaller heads, their formant frequencies are correspondingly higher. Because of non-linear processes in the ear, the response of the auditory nerve to a vowel-like sound gives increased prominence to the frequencies with higher energy.

Pitch and timbre are therefore cued by different properties of a sound. The frequencies of the low-numbered harmonics are the main determiners of a sound's pitch, but the timbre, or at least vowel quality, is determined by which frequency regions have more energy – the relative intensities of the different harmonics. We can change these two dimensions quite independently – we can sing the same vowel on different pitches, or we can intone on a monotonous pitch and change from one vowel to another. Normally, of course, we change both at the same time.

As we saw at the beginning of this chapter, musical timbre, as in what characterizes the sound of an instrument, is complex, but the concept of a formant is also useful here since instruments can have formant frequencies – the trombone has one around 500 Hz. The presence of formants in a musical instrument's spectrum provides one reason for the unsatisfactory sound of samplers and electronic synthesizers that produce the different pitches of a particular instrument by stretching or compressing in time a template waveform. This process keeps the relative amplitudes of the harmonics constant (so that, say, the second harmonic always has the most energy). But a formant stays constant in frequency, so for a trombone note the harmonic close to 500 Hz should be intense regardless of whether it is the third, the first or the fifth.

The dynamics of a note are particularly important for recognizing a musical instrument – the start of a note is not the same as the middle. The different harmonics of a note start at different times and each harmonic can have complex changes in amplitude before the note settles down. This 'onset transient', which lasts about 50 ms, is particularly important for recognizing the instrument, but we know very little about how rapidly changing complex sounds such as these are coded by the brain.

6.2 Customizing our auditory world

The same sound is heard differently by different people. This customized sound experience is most obvious in the perception of language. Native Japanese speakers find it almost impossible to hear the difference between [r] and [l]. English speakers have similar difficulties distinguishing some Hindi consonants. Why? The intuitive answer is that we learn as a child to hear the difference between the sounds that our particular native language uses. But this intuitive answer is wrong. Surprisingly, infants are born able to hear the difference between sounds that their 'native' language does not contrast, but they lose this ability during the first year of life. By the time they are one year old their perception of the sounds of speech is like that of an adult: they respond to the difference between sounds that their language distinguishes, but not to differences which it does not make. Although it is possible for adults to re-learn these distinctions later, it can be very difficult, as is the case with Japanese adults learning the [r]–[l] distinction. We do, however, now know that substantial reorganization of the way that the brain responds to sound can occur as a result of adult experience.

The importance of early experience in forming the categories of your auditory perception is also found in music. **Perfect** or **absolute pitch** is the ability to recognize the pitch of a note in isolation, without an external reference. Early musical training seems to be a necessary though not a sufficient condition for it. In a recent study, 40% of musicians in conservatories who had begun musical training before they were five reported that they possessed absolute pitch, whereas only 3% of those who had initiated training after they were eight did so. As the music critic Donald Tovey observed, perfect pitch is the pitch of your mother's piano. Perfect pitch might also have a genetic basis since it tends to aggregate in families.

7 Separating mixtures of sounds

Although we now have a fair understanding of what aspects of a sound are important for cueing its pitch, its timbre and its location, our understanding of the mechanisms by which the brain extracts and uses these cues is largely restricted to the unrepresentative situation of a listener hearing a single sound source. Normally, there is more than one sound going on at a time. What problems does this produce?

There are two sorts of problems created by the presence of multiple-sound sources: problems of simultaneous grouping, and problems of sequential grouping.

Consider a snapshot of the sound coming into the ear at any particular time. Now, decide how many different sounds are present, and which parts of the total sound come from each sound source. This illustrates the problem of simultaneous grouping.

The sequential problem can be illustrated as follows: imagine that you have successfully split up the total sound at time t_1 into a number of different sources, and also the total sound at time t_2. Now which (if any) of the sources at t_1 are the same as those at t_2?

Albert Bregman, an experimental psychologist from McGill University, has suggested that there are two different ways that the brain might solve these problems. One is through learned, **schema-based** ('top-down') **mechanisms**, where the listener uses detailed knowledge about what specific sounds are like to select a relevant subset of the total sound. The other is through unlearned, **primitive** ('bottom-up') **grouping mechanisms**, which use generally useful cues to separate sound into different sources. An example of a primitive cue that can be used to help solve the simultaneous grouping problem is onset-time – components of the same sound source (such as a note of a musical instrument or the noise of one object striking another) tend to start at the same time. Another example, that applies to periodic sounds such as music and speech sounds that have a definite pitch, is that the frequency components all form a harmonic series. If two instruments play the same note at exactly the same time, it is difficult to recognize the individual instruments. An example of this is at the beginning of Schubert's *Unfinished Symphony* where the theme is played by two different wind instruments. If the performance is by a good orchestra and the players are well in-tune and perfectly in time then it is very difficult to tell which two wind instruments are playing; but if the players are less accomplished, the task is easier. The fusion of the two well-played instruments' timbres creates a new timbre that is a composite of the two component timbres.

An example of schema-based grouping involves the remarkable ability of listeners to understand **sine-wave speech**. Sine-wave speech is a transformation of natural speech, which consists of just three sine waves on which the speech frequencies are superimposed. These sine waves follow the first three formant frequencies. Although there are few primitive grouping cues to tell listeners that they form a single sound source (the sounds are not harmonically related), nonetheless listeners have little difficulty in interpreting what is being said (albeit by a very peculiar-sounding voice). Here one's knowledge of how formant-frequencies change to produce different speech sounds is probably helping the brain to treat the sound as a single (speech) sound source rather than just as three independent whistles.

An important practical problem linked to sound source separation is the separation of the voice of a single talker from background noise. The problem is important for two reasons: first, individuals with a sensorineural hearing loss have particular difficulty understanding speech against a background of other sounds (such as a TV in the same room). If hearing aids could remove the background noise, they would be much more useful. Second, although computers can recognize speech moderately well when the speech is spoken in quiet conditions (or with a close, directionally sensitive microphone), they are very much worse at recognizing speech when there are background sounds present. It is likely that a solution to this problem will use a combination of both types of mechanism proposed by Bregman.

8 Summary

In this chapter we have seen the effect that cochlear frequency analysis has on the information about complex sounds that is transmitted to the brain. The distinction between low-numbered, resolved harmonics, and higher frequency, unresolved harmonics is an important one when we consider which parts of this information cue the perception of pitch and timbre. The brain uses a variety of different cues to localize sound in three dimensions, with binaural cues being important in the horizontal plane, and spectral changes in the high-frequency spectrum being important in the vertical plane. We also looked at the problem of how the brain can sort out, when it is presented with two simultaneous sounds, which frequency components come from the same sound source.

Further reading

Bregman, A. S. (1990) *Auditory Scene Analysis: The Perceptual Organisation of Sound*, Bradford Books, MIT Press, Cambridge, Mass.

Levin, T. C. and Edgerton, M. E. (1999) The throat singers of Tuva, *Scientific American*, **281**, (9) pp. 80–87.

McAdams, S. and Bigand, E. (eds) (1993) *Cognitive Aspects of Human Audition*, Oxford University Press, Oxford.

Moore, B. C. J. (1997) *An Introduction to the Psychology of Hearing* (4th edn), Academic Press, San Diego and London.

Pierce, J. R. (1983, 1992) *The Science of Musical Sound*, W. H. Freeman, New York.

Hearing impairments: causes, effects and rehabilitation

David Baguley and Don McFerran

6

1 Introduction

> There are two kinds of deafness. One is due to wax and is curable: the other is not due to wax and is not curable.
>
> Sir William Wilde (1815–1876)

It is almost 150 years since Sir William Wilde (Figure 1), one of the first surgeons to call himself an Otologist, and the father of the celebrated writer, Oscar, considered the causes of deafness in this pessimistic way. The present situation is very different, and in this chapter the causes of hearing impairments and the many strategies that can be utilized to rehabilitate hearing-impaired individuals will be considered. Hearing impairments are normally divided into groups based on the anatomical site of the problem. Thus hearing losses can be subdivided into conductive (outer ear or middle ear), cochlear (inner ear), **retrocochlear** (auditory nerve) and central (brain) causes. The standard tests of hearing easily distinguish conductive losses from the other types but are less good at distinguishing cochlear, retrocochlear and central auditory problems from each other. The latter three causes are therefore in practice often amalgamated and the classification is simplified to conductive and sensorineural.

2 Conductive deafness

2.1 Causes

The **conductive pathway** comprises the pinna or external ear, the external auditory meatus or ear canal, the tympanic membrane or eardrum and the middle ear. The middle ear is the small cavity between the eardrum and inner ear, which contains the ossicles. The ossicles are the three tiny bones of hearing, the malleus, incus and stapes or hammer, anvil and stirrup. Disease of any part of this pathway can result in hearing impairment.

Pinna

The pinna can be congenitally deficient or can be damaged by trauma or tumour. Although the pinna has a small effect in funnelling sound and contributing to sound localization it is not of major importance in humans. Some other mammals, such as horses and cats, have more highly developed external ears and have a much enhanced ability to localize sound accurately. Disease of the human pinna can cause marked cosmetic deformity but generally does not cause significant deafness.

External auditory meatus

The external auditory meatus can become blocked due to wax or a foreign body, or it can become swollen due to infection or inflammation. This impedes the passage of sound to the ear drum. It is easy to mimic this hearing impairment by simply putting your fingers in your ears!

Figure 1 Sir William Wilde (1815–1876).

Tympanic membrane

The tympanic membrane can be damaged by trauma, such as a slap to the side of the head, or by fluid resulting from infection in the middle ear (called **acute otitis media**) bursting its way out through the membrane (effusion). These factors can cause holes or perforations of the eardrum, which reduce the amount of sound energy that is captured by the ear thereby causing hearing loss (Figure 2). The eardrum can become scarred as a result of repeated infection. This scarring, referred to as **tympanosclerosis**, increases the stiffness of the membrane, reducing its efficiency as a sound transmitter.

Figure 2   Subtotal perforation of tympanic membrane in left and right ears.

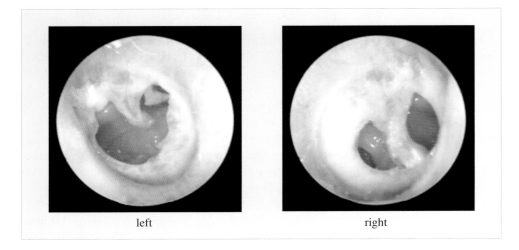

left   right

Middle ear

The middle ear cavity normally contains air which reaches this cavity via a small tube called the Eustachian tube that passes from the back of the nose up to the ear. If this tube malfunctions, air cannot reach the middle ear cavity and the ears feel blocked – most people have experienced a temporary blocked feeling of the ears when they have had a bad head cold. If the tube malfunctions for a longer period, the middle ear cavity gradually fills up with fluid that is produced by the lining of the cavity itself. This fluid may be thin and watery or it may be the thick, viscid (sticky) fluid that gives the condition the colloquial name 'glue ear'. The more correct medical terms are **otitis media with effusion** or **secretory otitis media**. Although otitis media with effusion can occur at any age it is most prevalent in children partly due to immaturity of the Eustachian tube and partly due to the physiological enlargement of adenoid tissue in this age group. The adenoids are swellings of lymphoid tissue at the back of the nose that help the body to respond to infections. Unfortunately the adenoids are very close to the openings of the Eustachian tubes and adenoidal swelling can result in tubal blockage. Otitis media with effusion is by far the most common cause of conductive hearing loss in the UK.

Ossicles

The ossicles can be damaged by infections; acute otitis media is a common condition in childhood that, in addition to causing perforations, can result in scar tissue developing round the ossicles. Persistent negative pressure in the middle ear can suck part of the eardrum inwards. The inside-out portion of the eardrum traps layers of dead skin that can then become infected. This small bag of chronic inflammation is called a **cholesteatoma**, and the infectious material slowly, inexorably, eats away the normal structures in the middle ear. The middle of the three ossicles, the incus or anvil, is especially prone to damage in this process. This uncommon disease tends to occur in later childhood or adulthood. Trauma can also damage the ossicles; a severe head injury can dislocate the delicate joints between the tiny bones. In the condition of **otosclerosis** new bone forms around the footplate of the stapes, fusing the bone rigidly with the bone of the inner ear. This reduces the ear's ability to conduct sound from the ossicular chain to the transduction mechanism of the cochlea.

2.2 Effects

Even with no ear canal, eardrum or ossicles, sound can still reach the inner ear, transmitted through the bones of the skull directly to the cochlea. The maximum effect of a conductive lesion, therefore, is to remove the contribution of the conductive pathway to hearing. An isolated conductive hearing loss has a maximum extent of 40–50 dB.

In addition to measuring the individual's **hearing thresholds** (the quietest sounds they can hear in a sound-proofed environment) it is also necessary to consider **auditory discrimination** while assessing hearing impairment. This is the ability to listen to a sound in a noisy environment and to be able to concentrate on that sound while ignoring the background noise. An individual with reduced hearing thresholds but normal auditory discrimination will be helped simply by making the sound louder. In contrast, an individual with poor auditory discrimination will find that simple amplification will turn a quiet acoustic jumble into a louder acoustic jumble. The clarity may not be improved. Isolated conductive hearing losses generally have normal auditory discrimination.

2.3 Rehabilitation

As they have normal auditory discrimination, individuals with conductive hearing impairments generally do well with hearing aids, but herein lies a great irony, as this is the same group of people that are most likely to benefit from surgery. An offending foreign body or wax can be removed, a perforated tympanic membrane can be repaired with a graft taken from one of the patient's own muscle tendons, and a dislocated ossicular chain can be reset using microsurgical techniques. Cholesteatomas can be excised and the damage they have caused can in many cases be repaired. In cases of otosclerosis the diseased stapes can be replaced with a minute prosthetic ossicle, such stapedectomy surgery often returning hearing sensitivity to normal or near normal levels.

The situation regarding cases of otitis media with effusion has been the cause of much debate and controversy in recent years. The persistence of this condition in a child can undoubtedly impair that child's development, both in educational terms and also in social skills. Surgery has been developed to alleviate the potential handicap. The surgery involves making a tiny incision in the tympanic membrane, removing any fluid in the middle ear and inserting a tiny plastic or metal tube. This ventilation tube or **grommet** (Figure 3) allows air to get from the atmosphere, through a hole in the grommet into the middle ear cavity. This equalizes the pressure on either side of the eardrum, preventing build up of fluid in the middle ear. The tympanic membrane grows throughout life and this normal growth eventually results in the grommet being extruded from the eardrum. This process takes approximately one year and in the majority of cases, by the time extrusion is complete, the patient's Eustachian tube function has returned to normal and the otitis media with effusion does not recur.

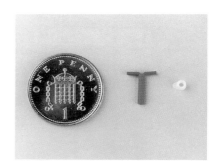

Figure 3   A T tube and Shah grommet.

Initial results were good and the operation became very popular. However, more detailed surveys showed that the otitis media with effusion was short lived in many cases and the insertion of grommets was not without its own problems; scarring of the eardrums often followed grommet insertion and in some cases the degree of hearing improvement was disappointing. In addition, the operation developed a political dimension: grommet insertion became the most frequently performed surgical procedure in the UK with associated financial implications. Healthcare purchasers therefore sought to reduce the number of grommet operations. A sensible middle ground approach has now been adopted whereby most individuals with otitis media with effusion undergo a period of 'watchful waiting' (careful monitoring of a child's hearing over time) prior to consideration of surgery. In some Otology units hearing aids are provided for mild cases, surgery being reserved for the more seriously affected.

3 Cochlear hearing loss

3.1 Causes

The delicate micro-mechanical structures of the cochlea have been described previously (Chapter 2, *The transformation of sound stimuli into electrical signals*) and it will come as no surprise that the cochlea is vulnerable to trauma, infection and degenerative processes, leading to reduction of hearing sensitivity. Noise at excessive levels, even for short periods of time, affects first outer and then inner hair cell function. A decrease in cochlear sensitivity with age is almost universal, the consequent hearing loss being entitled **presbyacusis**. **Menière's disease** is a disorder of the inner ear characterized by episodes of hearing loss, tinnitus and vertigo. The ear often feels blocked prior to these attacks. Between acute episodes the patient may return to normality though as the disease progresses the hearing loss may become permanent. This distressing condition is thought to be due to a build up of endolymph within the inner ear that distorts the delicate membranes of the cochlea and vestibular apparatus, thereby affecting both hearing and balance. In some rare cases the body's immune system may malfunction, attacking normal tissues such as the components of the inner ear causing a sudden or progressive hearing loss. The cochlea is also vulnerable to a number of cochlear-specific viruses. Congenital cochlear impairment will be considered as a separate entity.

3.2 Effects

The extent of cochlear hearing loss can be mild, moderate, severe or profound, and can have almost any conceivable frequency configuration, though most often the extent of loss is greater in the high frequencies. With cochlear deafness due to ageing or noise exposure the loss is usually bilateral and reasonably symmetrical. Some other forms of cochlear loss, including deafness due to Menière's disease or trauma can result in unilateral symptoms. Auditory discrimination tends to be more affected in this type of loss than in conductive losses.

3.3 Rehabilitation

In Menière's disease, specific but controversial treatments are used to prevent or ameliorate attacks. Drugs are used to try and improve cochlear blood flow and also to control the vertigo. Surgery is undertaken in some patients to try and reduce the build up of endolymph. Other patients undergo operations to sever the balance nerves and prevent the disabling vertigo.

However for the majority of patients with cochlear hearing loss there is no operative or drug treatment. The prevalence of cochlear hearing loss in the UK has been investigated, and it appears that about one in ten adults would benefit from hearing aids. Unlike conductive hearing impairment the effect of cochlear damage is not only to reduce hearing sensitivity, but also to reduce the ability to make fine discrimination in frequency and temporal domains. In addition, tolerance to loud sound may be reduced. The consequence for an individual is that sound may be distorted, even when amplified. Thus the benefits of hearing aids in such situations may be limited unless they are carefully prescribed to account for an individual's specific needs in this regard. There are some early indications that hearing aids which utilize digital technology rather than analogue may be better able to meet the requirements of a cochlear hearing-impaired person, though this is as yet unproven. What is generally accepted is the need to match the prescribed hearing aid sound output with the needs of the patient (Figure 4).

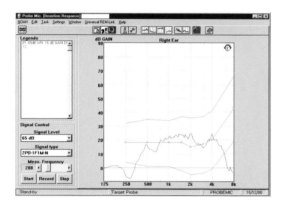

Figure 4   Computerized hearing aid fitting screen, demonstrating hearing aid performance measured in the ear canal of the patient. The blue line represents the hearing aid response, the central red line depicts the ideal response for this patient.

Whilst technological solutions to cochlear hearing impairments are advancing, it should be noted that these do not address the whole problem created by the hearing impairment. Adult individuals who acquire a cochlear hearing loss may experience feelings of isolation and loss of confidence, and a small but significant proportion may go on to experience psychological problems as a result of their hearing impairment. The application of technology to address this in an holistic context appears to be the most effective method of intervention, thus treating people as people rather than dysfunctional hair cells! It is noteworthy however that the opportunity to perform technological and holistic rehabilitative interventions is largely limited to the developed world. The possibilities of cheap and appropriate interventions, such as solar-powered hearing aids and campaigns for the prevention of hearing loss are being investigated for the benefit of the large number of hearing-impaired people in the Third World.

3.4 Congenital cochlear impairment

In the developed world approximately 1 in 1000 live births is a child with a bilateral severe to profound cochlear hearing loss. In approximately two-thirds of these cases the cause of the problem is genetic. In the other third, factors such as intrauterine infection, hypoxia or neonatal jaundice are responsible. Without early identification and treatment such children have almost insurmountable difficulties in the development of speech, and sign language may become vital for communication. Early identification is possible with tests undertaken in the neonatal period, though care has to be taken to allay parental anxiety. Initial treatment of such children is to provide suitable hearing aids, intensive support for both child and parents, and to correct any concomitant conductive hearing loss such as otitis media with effusion. In some cases however, the hearing loss is beyond the reach of even the most powerful and sophisticated hearing aids.

The idea that it is possible to induce sound perception by electrical stimulation dates as far back as Volta who in 1800 undertook electrical stimulation of his own ear after filling the ear canal with saline solution, the electrical charge giving rise to an extremely loud bang – Volta appears not to have repeated the experiment! In the 1970s the possibilities of using electrical stimulation to give the profoundly deaf some experience of sound formed the basis of **cochlear implantation**. Those early devices utilized a single electrode placed in the round window to stimulate the cochlea. Nowadays a multi-channel electrode is usually placed within the cochlea, and complex speech-processing algorithms are used to stimulate the auditory nerve, giving as rich and natural a perception of sound as possible (Figures 5 and 6).

Figure 5   The Clarion® range of external cochlear implant equipment made by the Advanced Bionics Corporation. The sound signal is converted to an electrical signal by a microphone attached to a microprocessor worn either on the belt (top) or behind the ear (bottom, shown with attached headpiece). After processing, the signal is sent to a headpiece, which sends the sound information through the skin to the implant using a radio signal.

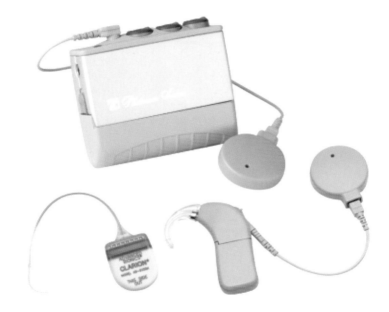

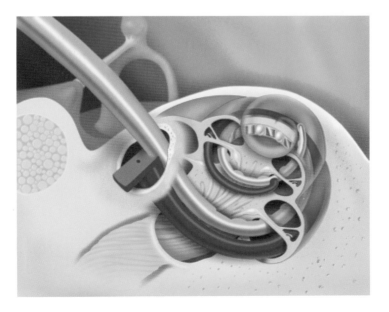

Figure 6   Schematic diagram of the insertion of a cochlear implant electrode into the cochlea.

Initially application of cochlear implants was in deafened adults, many of whom had lost their hearing as the result of meningitis, but cochlear implant surgery is now routinely undertaken in children born with a profound hearing loss.

Patients with a cochlear implant find that at the least the device augments their abilities to lip-read and increases awareness of environmental sound, whilst at best they are able to converse on the telephone and to enjoy music. The reasons for such variability in performance are not fully understood but include the length of time a person has been deaf, the disorder causing that deafness and the number of surviving cells in the auditory nerve. One important factor for congenitally deaf children in the consideration of cochlear implants is the age of the child. It is widely accepted that after the age of approximately eight years the neural plasiticity needed for the auditory system to utilize stimulation from a cochlear implant may not be sufficient to justify this intervention. Cochlear implants do have their opponents; some deaf adults think that cochlear implants are an act of violence upon deaf children, whose natural language is said to be sign language and whose natural home is in the deaf world. Despite this however, developments in the field continue, and it is expected that binaural cochlear implantation may soon become commonplace.

4 Retrocochlear hearing loss

4.1 Causes

The cochlear and vestibular nerves run side by side within the internal auditory meatus (the bony canal that passes through the temporal bone from the inner ear structures towards the brainstem). A region of cellular instability on the vestibular nerve can give rise to a benign tumour, derived from the Schwann cells that surround and insulate nerve fibres. These tumours are correctly known as **vestibular schwannoma** but are more often referred to as **acoustic neuromas**.

4.2 Effects

Vestibular schwannoma usually cause unilateral hearing loss and tinnitus (Section 6). The hearing loss typically results in poor auditory discrimination. Left untreated they can grow to fill the internal auditory meatus, and thence grow out towards the brainstem, where after some years the compressive effects of the tumour compromise the functions vital for life. Vestibular schwannoma are diagnosed in 1 in 50 000 adults per year in the UK, and such diagnosis has been greatly facilitated by magnetic resonance imaging (Figure 7 overleaf).

4.3 Treatment and rehabilitation

At present the usual treatment of this condition is the surgical removal of the tumour, undertaken by a team including both otologists and neurosurgeons, though technologies involving the irradiation of the tumour are being investigated. The surgical procedures commonly employed for this condition cause a unilateral total and permanent hearing loss in the operated ear.

4.4 Other retrocochlear conditions

The move towards neonatal diagnosis of hearing impairment has uncovered another situation of interest. In the 1970s biophysicist David Kemp working in London discovered that normal ears emit a small amount of sound in response to sound

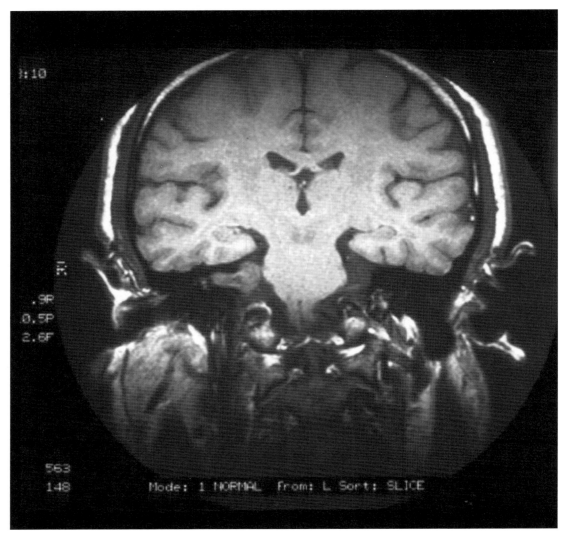

Figure 7   MRI scan demonstrating right vestibular schwannoma.

input. These **otoacoustic emissions** are used as the basis of a hearing test for neonates (newborn infants). A small number of babies have normal otoacoustic emissions suggesting normal cochlear function, but when the activity of the retrocochlear neural pathway is tested using auditory brainstem responses the results are indicative of significant dysfunction. Further investigation has shown that the auditory nerve fibres seem to be unable to respond to sound in a synchronous fashion. This condition has been entitled auditory neuropathy or auditory desynchrony, and is a compelling argument for using a battery of tests for the diagnosis of hearing impairment in young children rather than relying upon one test alone. Similar patterns of auditory nerve dysfunction may be demonstrated in 20% of adult patients with multiple sclerosis, though it is rare for such patients to complain of hearing difficulties.

5 Central auditory processing disorders

5.1 Causes and effects

One interesting group of patients that are referred to audiologists and otologists believe themselves to have a hearing problem although standard hearing tests are normal. More detailed psychoacoustic tests show that their ability to discriminate sound in noise is markedly worse than their peers. In the UK these symptoms were carefully considered in the 1980s and the condition named **Obscure Auditory Dysfunction (OAD)**. In the USA the name **Central Auditory Processing Disorder (CAPD)** has been used, and was coined after the specific investigation of children who had normal hearing acuity on pure tone and otoacoustic emission testing but who had quantifiable and significant difficulties in noisy environments – such as found in classrooms. CAPD is gradually becoming the more accepted terminology. Specific mechanisms involved in this situation have yet to be identified, and indeed there are likely to be a variety of different patho-physiologies involved rather than one alone.

5.2 Rehabilitation

Management of CAPD involves a variety of measures. Increasing the strength of the signal that the individual is striving to hear relative to the competing background noise is the first avenue to investigate. In a classroom this can be accomplished by simple measures such as moving the child closer to the teacher. Careful use of hearing aids or FM radio aids can also help. For adult sufferers it is often more difficult to manipulate the acoustic environment and in these cases counselling and the teaching of specific hearing tactics are the most common treatment options.

6 Tinnitus

Psychologist Dennis McFadden in 1982 defined **tinnitus** as 'the conscious expression of a sound that originates in an involuntary manner in the head of its owner, or may appear to him to do so'. It has been determined that approximately one-third of the UK adult population experience some short-lived (< 5 minutes) spontaneous tinnitus experiences and that in 10% tinnitus experience is persistent. In 1% of the UK population tinnitus has a severe effect upon quality of life, making this an auditory dysfunction worthy of scientific consideration and of effective therapy. Unfortunately, despite considerable scientific endeavour (there being nearly 1700 peer review scientific papers considering tinnitus in the last decade) effective treatments remain elusive. Drug therapy has not been effective, although antidepressant medication can help to alleviate any depression associated with tinnitus. Surgery is not usually recommended, although some conditions that may require surgery (such as vestibular schwannoma and Menière's disease; see above) contain tinnitus within their symptom profile. Treatment strategies rely upon counselling, and the reduction of sympathetic autonomic nervous system (agitation) and limbic system (emotion) responses to tinnitus. A useful model of tinnitus was proposed by neuroscientist Pawel Jastreboff in 1990 (Figure 8 overleaf), pointing out that whilst the generator site of tinnitus may be in the auditory periphery (though not necessarily the cochlea) the mechanisms of persistence and reaction were central and also involve the sympathetic and the limbic system (specifically the amygdalae, structures in the brain that play a critical role in the formation and modulation of emotionally influenced memory).

Figure 8 Jastreboff neurophysiological model of tinnitus. The model postulates that perception of tinnitus becomes associated with negative emotions, thereby involving the limbic system, which in turn activates the autonomic nervous system, resulting in annoyance.

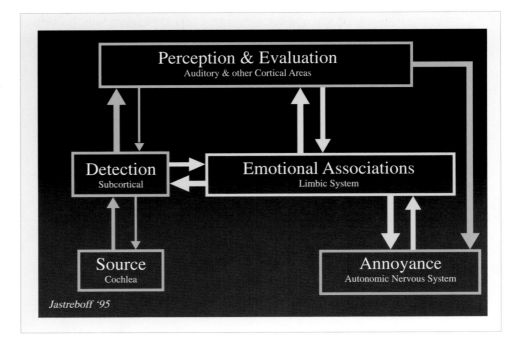

Whilst this model has been criticized for offering little new scientific insight, the clinical impact has been high, with a treatment strategy named 'Tinnitus Retraining Therapy' based upon the model. This approaches the treatment of tinnitus from several different angles; the condition is thoroughly explained, the patient is counselled, relaxation techniques may be taught and sound therapy is used in some cases (Figures 9 and 10).

As yet there are no good properly controlled scientific trials of this therapy but there is considerable ongoing research in the field. There may be some controversy over the methods of tinnitus therapy, but there is a consensus about the objective, that patients should habituate to the signal within their auditory system. One is unlikely

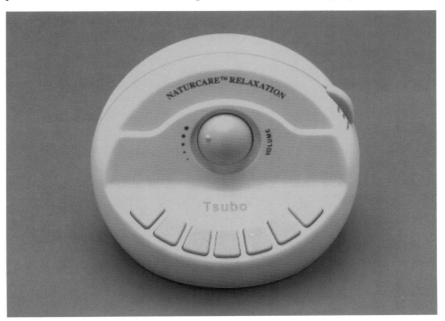

Figure 9 Environmental sound generator used in sound therapy for tinnitus.

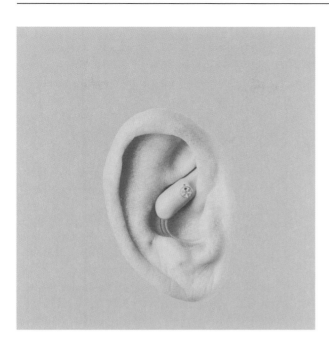

Figure 10   Ear-level wide-band noise generator used in tinnitus therapy.

to do so if anxious or upset by tinnitus, or concerned about the potential seriousness of the sound, and so careful, authoritative reassurance might well be helpful, and indeed has long been utilized by some audiologists and otologists.

Some recent scientific insights into tinnitus may well augur more hope for the future. Whilst tinnitus may well emerge as a consequence of changes in cochlear function, it has been suggested that such changes result in reorganization of the auditory cortex, specifically in regard to the dimensions of the cortex concerned with the perception of particular frequencies close to an area of hearing loss. An analogy is drawn with the situation of losing a finger, wherein the area of the somatosensory cortex concerned with that finger is greatly reduced in activity immediately following that amputation. Some weeks later activity has returned to usual levels, but investigations have shown that this later activity is associated with neighbouring fingers which are thus over-represented in terms of cortical activity. This phenomenon has been associated with the development of phantom pain and the suggestion is that tinnitus represents phantom auditory perception in some cases. Investigation of such hypotheses continues apace, and the hope is that some more effective therapy for people who develop tinnitus may result.

7 Summary

The human auditory system is complex and dysfunction at any level may result in hearing impairment. The simple reduction in sensitivity in conductive hearing loss may be remediated by amplification, but the more complex dysfunction associated with cochlear hearing loss requires careful consideration. Auditory dysfunction beyond the cochlea is also possible, and may result in particular auditory phenomena. Tinnitus is common in the population in general and appears not to bother most of these individuals, but as there is a significant number of people whose lives are significantly affected, this condition therefore warrants careful consideration and the development of effective therapy.

Further reading

Graham, J. and Martin, M. (2001) *Ballantyne's Deafness*, 6th edn, Whurr Publishers, London.

Moore B. C. J. (1998) *Cochlear Hearing Loss*, Whurr Publishers, London.

Tyler R. S. (ed.) (2000) *Tinnitus Handbook*, Singular Press, San Diego, CA.

The vestibular system
David Furness

1 Introduction

The human body is both graceful and highly versatile when in motion, with an economy and accuracy of movement that at times is quite amazing. Consider a tennis player receiving a serve, during which the approaching ball travels at over one hundred miles per hour. The ball is in the air for less than one second before it reaches the position at which the player must return it or lose the point (Figure 1). How does the player manage not only to track the moving ball but also simultaneously, and at high speed, to position the body and arms so as to return it to the opposing end of the court? And having managed to hit the ball, how does the player maintain balance and remain upright ready to play the next ball?

Figure 1   Tim Henman, ready for action on the return of serve.

As described in this chapter the **vestibular apparatus** is vital for such a task; it provides a continuous supply of information about the precise position of the head in three-dimensional space and its direction and speed of motion. In addition, it has direct control over eye and neck muscles via the **vestibulo-ocular** and **vestibulocollic reflex pathways**, through which it stabilizes the gaze by generating compensatory eye and head movements, and it works to maintain posture and balance by controlling body muscles via the spinal cord.

The importance of a functional vestibular system is considerable in everyday life. By the same token, disorders of the vestibular labyrinth can be seriously debilitating, producing effects like vertigo (dizziness and loss of balance) which considerably reduce the quality of life. It is probably true to say that we are actively conscious of the vestibular system only when it is abnormally stimulated or damaged through illness.

2 The organization of the vestibular apparatus

The inner ear consists of a system of tunnels, the bony (osseous) labyrinth in the hardest part (the petrous region) of the temporal bone (Figure 2a). The labyrinth can be divided into three main regions, the cochlea (or hearing organ), vestibule and semicircular canals, the latter two forming the vestibular system. To give some impression of its size, the vestibule in humans is about 3–5 mm across whilst the semicircular canals range from 12 mm up to 22 mm in length. The bony labyrinth is lined by an outer membrane sheath that encloses an inner **membranous labyrinth** (Figure 2b). This arrangement means that the system contains two almost concentric compartments both filled with fluid. The outer compartment contains perilymph, a fluid similar in composition to cerebrospinal fluid and rich in sodium ions, and the inner compartment contains endolymph, a fluid that is rich in potassium ions.

The vestibular system consists of five different sensory organs that can be divided into two types, the two **otolithic organs** which enable us to detect the static position of the head and changes of speed of motion in a straight line (linear acceleration), and the three **semicircular canals** which detect rotation of the head (angular velocity). The otolithic organs are the **utricle** and **saccule**, both located in the **vestibule**, and are often called the organs of *static equilibrium* although they are important in motion too. The three semicircular canals are used for maintaining *dynamic equilibrium*. The canals lie more or less at right angles to each other, so that in each ear one lies parallel to each of the three possible planes of three-dimensional space. At one end of each canal is a swelling of the tube called an **ampulla**. Both ends of each semicircular canal open into the utricle (Figure 2b).

The basic sensory apparatus of all of the inner ear organs is an epithelium containing mechanoreceptive hair cells, the nerve fibres connecting with them, and supporting cells. The detailed structures of an epithelium and the hair cells are shown in Boxes 1 and 2. In the saccule and utricle the sensory epithelium is a flat plaque called a **macula** whilst in the ampullae of the semicircular canals there is a ridge called a **crista** (Figure 5 overleaf). Although basically similar, the sensory epithelia of the semicircular canals and the otolithic organs both show some specific differences in accessory structures which make them especially suited for their particular functions.

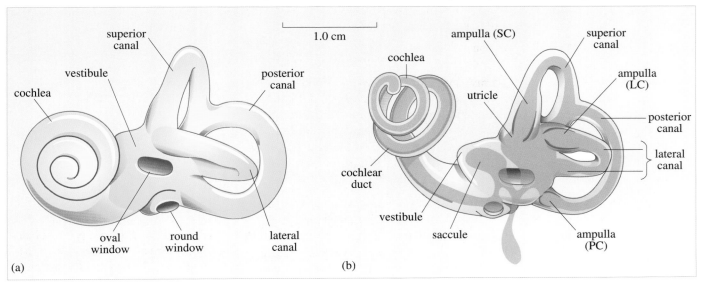

Figure 2   (a) The external appearance of the osseous labyrinth. (b) The organization of the membranous labyrinth (blue) within the osseous labyrinth.

Box 1   The structure of vestibular sensory epithelia

The sensory epithelia contain two types of hair cell (Figure 3a and b). The hair bundles of both project into the otolithic membrane (Figure 3c). Type I hair cells are flask-shaped and are innervated by an afferent nerve calyx around the cell body, sometimes shared with other hair cells. Type II hair cells are cylindrical and have small round afferent endings onto the cell body. At these afferent synaptic contacts, the hair cells contain synaptic bars with neurotransmitter vesicles around them. Efferent nerve fibres end on the afferent calyx rather than on Type I hair cell bodies, but directly onto Type II hair cells. The hair bundle consists of a single kinocilium that contains microtubules and 30–50 stereocilia that contain a stiff core of actin filaments, some of which extend down to anchor the stereocilia into an actin rich fibrous structure, the cuticular plate. The stereocilia and cuticular plate contain complex cytoskeletal networks of actin-associated proteins such as 'unconventional' myosins that influence how the hair bundle moves. The cell body contains the nucleus and cytoplasmic organelles such as mitochondria, Golgi apparatus and endoplasmic reticulum.

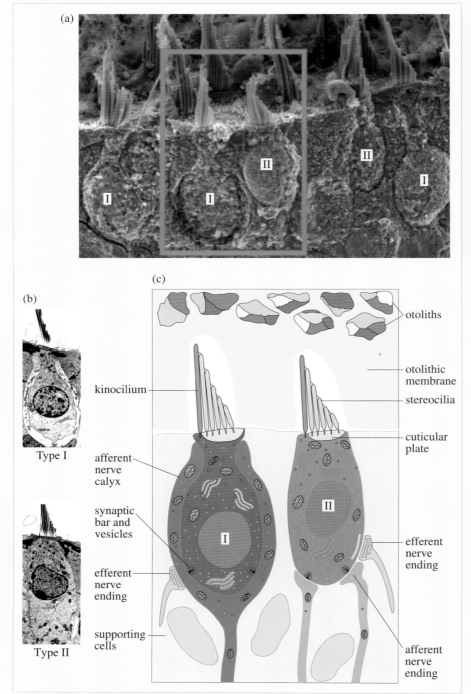

Figure 3 The structure of vestibular sensory epithelia: (a) scanning electron micrograph of a fracture of the utricular macula showing Type I and Type II hair cells; (b) transmission electron micrographs of the two types of hair cell; (c) schematic illustration of the structure of Types I and II hair cells with hair bundles projecting into the otolithic membrane.

Box 2   The morphology and polarity of vestibular hair bundles

In all hair cells the stereocilia form rows increasing in height across the bundle, forming a 'staircase' (see Figure 4). Bundle shapes vary quite considerably (compare these hair bundles with those of cochlear hair cells, Chapter 2) but the functional orientation of the hair cell is always determined by the direction of the staircase. The change in height varies enormously in vestibular hair bundles from ones with virtually no staircase to ones with stereocilia increasing from as little as 0.5 μm to over 9 μm high. The stereocilia are interconnected by fine extracellular filaments called tip links, one of which arises almost directly from each

tip and attaches to the stereocilium immediately behind (Figure 4c). The kinocilium occurs on the side of the hair bundle immediately adjacent to the tallest row. Its position is shown in Figure 4d, which represents a view looking down onto a hair bundle. Deflection of the hair bundle (arrow) towards the kinocilium is excitatory and results in depolarization of the hair cell; deflections in the opposite direction cause the cell to hyperpolarize (see Chapter 2, *The transformation of sound stimuli into electrical signals* for a detailed discussion of this mechano-electrical transduction process).

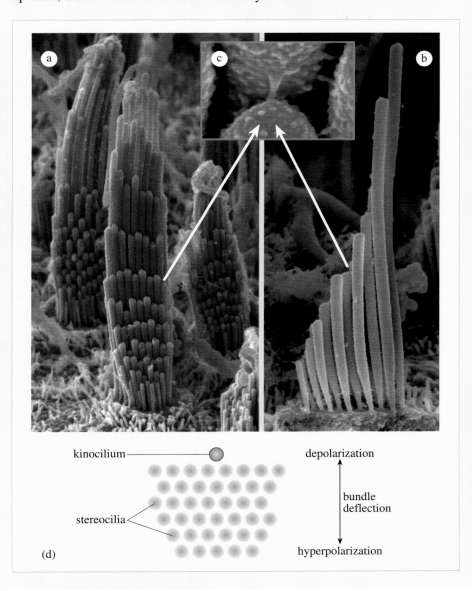

(d)

kinocilium

stereocilia

depolarization

bundle deflection

hyperpolarization

Figure 4   The morphology and polarity of vestibular hair bundles: scanning electron micrographs of (a) a 'front view'; (b) a side view; (c) the tip link between two adjacent stereocilia; (d) schematic diagram of the hair bundle arrangement and position of the kinocilium viewed from above to show how bundle orientation and deflection produce changes in membrane polarization.

2.1 The otolithic organs and the detection of head position

The saccule and utricle are sac-like dilations of the membranous labyrinth filled with endolymph and suspended in the vestibule by straps of connective tissue. With the exception of the macula, the walls of each sac are formed from cuboidal epithelial cells. These, together with the macula lie on a thin connective tissue base. The macula in the utricle is heart-shaped and lies horizontally when the head is upright whilst in the saccule it is comma-shaped and lies more or less vertically. The maculae are covered with a dense population of hair cells (Figure 5), each one characterized by its bundle of tiny hairs or stereocilia which projects into an overlying accessory structure, the jelly-like **otolithic membrane** which also contains crystalline inclusions called **otoliths** (Figure 5, Boxes 1 and 2).

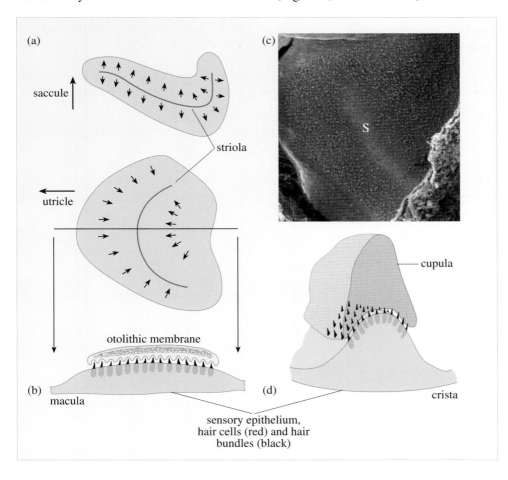

Figure 5   (a) The shape and relative orientation (large arrows) of the maculae of the saccule and utricle, and (b) a cross-section along the line shown. The orientation of the hair bundles is indicated, with the small arrows within each macula showing the excitatory directions. Note that there are two populations of opposing orientation on either side of the striola (red line), but that there is also a systematic change in orientation across each macula. In the scanning electron micrograph (c) of the utricular macula from above, the membrane has been removed so that the hair bundles (white dots) are visible. The striolar region (S) is clearly visible. (d) The structure of an ampulla showing the crista and overlying cupula with hair bundles inserted into it.

The hair bundles in both the utricular and saccular macula form two populations with their functional polarization (Box 2) oriented in opposing directions (see Figure 5). These populations occur on either side of a curved zone, the **striola**, which is distinguishable from the rest of the epithelium by the fact that it contains a larger proportion of small hair bundles. In the utricle, the orientation of the hair bundles reverses along the striola so that the excitatory direction always points towards the striolar axis. In the saccular macula a similar distribution of orientations occurs but they are the opposite of those of the utricle because the excitatory directions in the two populations of hair cells point away from the striola. In both cases, the orientation changes gradually with the curvature of the striola.

Movements in a straight line involving acceleration or deceleration, or a tilt of the head which changes its orientation with respect to gravity, cause the otolithic membrane to move relative to the hair cells and this deflects the hair bundles inserted into the membrane. Provided the axis of hair-bundle orientation lies in the same direction as the motion, the cells on one side of the striola become depolarized and those on the other become hyperpolarized (Box 2). Since the orientations of the hair bundles change progressively along the striolar axis, a different direction of tilt or motion will stimulate a different group of hair cells. As the saccular and utricular maculae also lie at right angles to each other, the otolithic organs are together able to detect and distinguish changes in head orientation and motion in a straight line in both horizontal and vertical directions of any angle.

Depolarization of the hair cell releases a neurotransmitter, probably **glutamate**, at the afferent synapse. This activates receptor molecules on the terminal of the nerve fibre, depolarizing the postsynaptic membrane towards the threshold at which action potentials will be produced in the afferent nerve fibre. In a relatively short time (1–50 ms), the hair cell itself adapts (discussed in Chapter 2) which resets it so that it is able to continue to detect further movements of the otolithic membrane.

The supporting cells provide physical and metabolic support to the hair cells, but may also be directly involved in the transmission process. They contain **glutamate transporter molecules** that rapidly take up extracellular glutamate. These proteins help to terminate glutamate action at the synapses making them ready for further activation. They also provide a vital protective function because glutamate is **excitotoxic**, causing nerve damage if allowed to remain around the nerve endings.

2.2 The semicircular canals and the detection of head rotation

As described above, the three semicircular canals occupy three different planes at right angles to each other (Figure 2). The superior canal (sometimes called the anterior canal) lies vertically, at right angles to the long axis of the petrous bone. The posterior canal is the longest and also lies vertically but parallel to the petrous bone, whilst the lateral (or horizontal) canal which is the shortest slopes downward and backward at an angle of 30° to the horizontal. Each canal forms a spatial pair with one on the opposite side of the head (Figure 6).

The three ampullae all have a similar structure consisting of a spherical cavity containing the crista, which has an epithelium with hair cells and supporting cells in it (Figure 5). The basic structure of the epithelium is similar to that shown in Boxes 1 and 2. However, the cristae differ from the maculae in that they are ridge shaped, the accessory structure into which the hair bundles project (the **cupula**) lacks otoliths, and the orientation of the hair bundles is the same throughout each crista, with the excitatory direction oriented across the crista (Figure 7). In the crista of the lateral ampulla the excitatory direction points *towards* the opening into the utricle but in the other canals it points *away* from it.

The hair cells in the semicircular canals are stimulated by rotations of the head and in consequence the firing rate in their afferent nerve fibres changes (Figure 7). The output in the nerve fibres originating from one canal will be excitatory because the resultant cupular motion will cause hair-cell depolarization, whilst in the complementary canal on the other side of the head the output will be inhibitory. The number of fibres that are active and their rate of firing will depend on how close the rotational motion is to the plane of each pair of canals. The balance of excitation and inhibition of all three pairs of canals can thus represent the *direction* and *speed* of any angular rotation of the head.

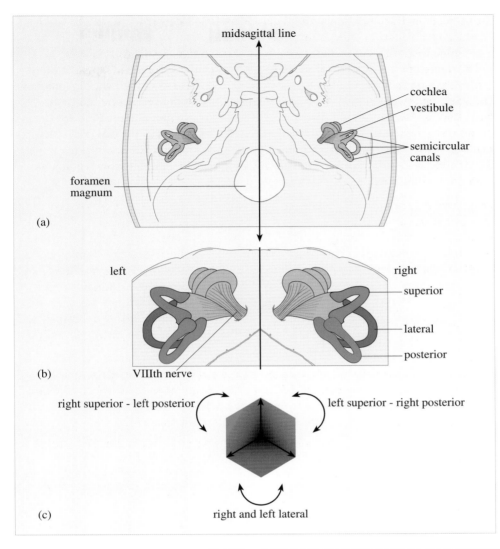

(a)

(b)

(c)

Figure 6   (a) The position of the semicircular canals on the two sides of the head, and (b) their arrangement in spatial pairs. The corresponding canals of each spatial pair are shown in the same colour. The lateral canals on both sides lie in the same plane, whilst the superior canal on one side occupies approximately the same plane as the posterior canal on the other. The different planes of rotation are detected by these pairs, as indicated in (c).

▼ **Figure 7**   Detection of a leftwards head rotation by the lateral semicircular canals. The process is initiated by head rotation (a) which results in fluid motion in the opposite direction in the canals (b) since the endolymph and cupula lag behind because of their inertia. The relative motion of the cupula deflects the stereocilia causing depolarization of the hair cells in the left crista and hyperpolarization in the right (c). The afferent fibres are spontaneously active at rest. During movement, depolarization of the hair cells in the left canal causes an increase in the frequency of action potentials (excitation) whilst hyperpolarization in the right causes a decrease (inhibition) (d).

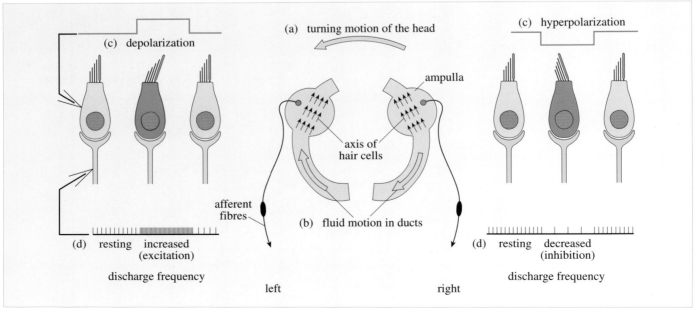

3 The central pathways of the vestibular organs

The nerve fibres that signal the response of vestibular hair cells form one part of the VIIIth cranial nerve (the **vestibulocochlear nerve**), the second part arising from the cochlea. These afferent fibres are peripheral processes arising from **bipolar neurons** (neurons with two processes, one entering each side of the cell body). The cell bodies are located in two subdivisions of **Scarpa's ganglion** (Figure 8). The peripheral process is like a dendrite in that it carries signals to the cell body of the neuron rather than away from it, but is like an axon in that, except where it enters the epithelium, it is myelinated and carries action potentials. The fibre leaving the opposite pole of the cell body is the true axon of the neuron, passing along the **vestibular nerve** to end in the **brainstem vestibular nuclei** (Figure 9). A proportion of these vestibular fibres project directly to or send branches into the cerebellum, which plays a major role in coordination of movements.

The vestibulocochlear nerve on each side enters the brainstem at the junction of the medulla (the lower region of the brainstem) and pons (the upper region of the brainstem) (Figure 9). The majority of vestibular nerve fibres fork into two and branch further to form excitatory primary connections in the different parts of the vestibular nuclear complex. Some enter the cerebellum via the **inferior cerebellar peduncle** also on the same side. (The cerebellar peduncles are large fibre tracts that connect the cerebellum to the brainstem.)

There are four vestibular nuclei (Figure 9) which differ in the pattern of their afferent and efferent fibre connections and in the different populations of cells they possess (their cytoarchitecture). The **superior nucleus**, in the caudal pons, and the **medial** and **inferior nuclei**, in the rostral medulla, contain small to medium-sized neurons. The **lateral nucleus** (also known as Deiters' nucleus) is in the medulla and contains mainly large multipolar neurons. Studies of the physiology of neurons in these nuclei show that some receive inputs from both the utricle and saccule and others from both canals and otolithic organs. Also, many neurons receive inputs

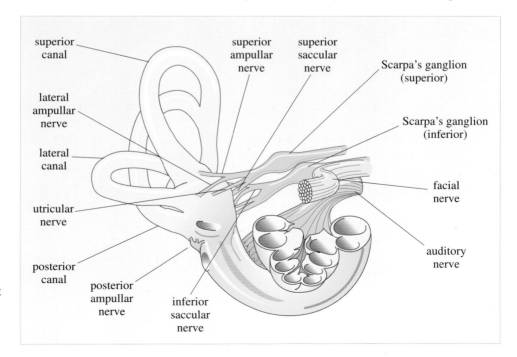

Figure 8　Diagram showing the innervation of the vestibular system. Afferent fibres leave each of the sensory epithelia via distinct nerves and enter the two subdivisions of Scarpa's ganglion before joining the VIIIth nerve.

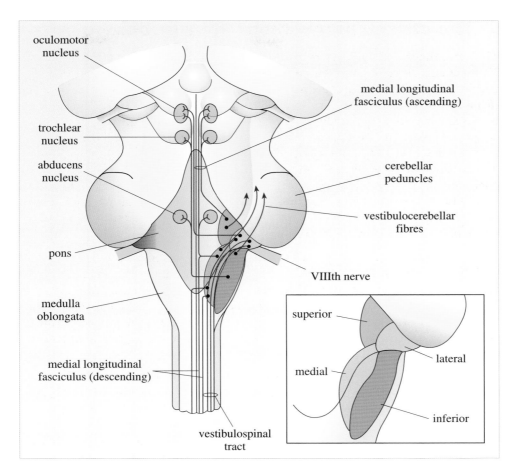

oculomotor nucleus

trochlear nucleus

abducens nucleus

pons

medulla oblongata

medial longitudinal fasciculus (descending)

vestibulospinal tract

medial longitudinal fasciculus (ascending)

cerebellar peduncles

vestibulocerebellar fibres

VIIIth nerve

superior

medial

lateral

inferior

Figure 9 The brainstem nuclei of the vestibular system and their connections to other major pathways and nuclei. The vestibulospinal tract and descending portion of the medial longitudinal fasciculus are involved in the maintenance of posture. Control of eye movements is mediated by the ascending portion of the medial longitudinal fasciculus, and the trochlear, abducens and oculomotor nuclei. The primary vestibular nuclei are coloured to aid identification (see inset) and occur at the junction between the pons and medulla, where the VIIIth nerve enters the brainstem from the inner ear.

from the vestibular systems on both sides. These **convergent inputs** of various kinds mean that information from the different vestibular sensory organs and from both sides of the head is rapidly integrated, increasing the accuracy of the directional information obtained, for example, by reducing the possibility of error from spontaneous or random activity in one organ.

From the vestibular nuclear complex nerve fibres go to various parts of the brainstem, including **oculomotor nuclei** that control eye movements, and also enter two bundles of nerves which pass longitudinally along the spinal cord, the **vestibulospinal tract** and the **medial longitudinal fasciculus** (Figure 9). The vestibular nuclei also send projections to respiratory centres, which alter breathing rate in relation to position. A connection to the visceral centres that influences the digestive system may be the origin of nausea and vomiting in motion sickness, caused by conflicting visual and vestibular signals (see Chapter 28, *Interaction between the senses: vision and the vestibular system*).

As well as the afferent pathways into the brainstem, there are nerve fibres going in the opposite direction from the medulla to the hair cells (see also Box 1). Efferent stimulation has varied effects on hair cells, but the role it plays is not properly understood.

3.1 Maintenance of posture and balance through the vestibulospinal tract

The vestibulospinal tract originates in the lateral vestibular nucleus and the nerve fibres travel down the ventral part of the spinal cord, ending on motor neurons at various points. Especially large numbers end in the regions where motor neurons for limb muscles are concentrated. Signals from the lateral vestibular nucleus derived originally from the vestibular organs affect the tone of the body muscles. This is illustrated by the fact that stimulation of this nucleus results in excitation of extensor muscles and inhibition of flexor muscles in the lower limb, causing the foot to be pressed firmly down to maintain balance. Around 40% of body musculature is involved in maintaining posture and balance against gravity so signals from the otolithic organs are particularly important.

3.2 Maintenance of gaze through brainstem and spinal cord pathways

The maintenance of gaze involves two types of vestibular action, the **vestibulo-ocular reflex** (**VOR**) and the **vestibulocollic reflex** (**VCR**). The VCR maintains the correct positioning of the head via fibres from the medial nucleus which approach the centre of the brainstem and then descend along the medial longitudinal fasciculus. These end on motor neurons in the neck which innervate the muscles that control head and neck position. Other vestibular fibres go to the abducens, trochlear and oculomotor nuclei, and these provide a route for the VOR. The VOR can be subdivided into the *static* VOR which is dependent on information from the otolithic organs and *dynamic* VOR based on semicircular canal activation, but in both cases the pathways lead to and directly control contraction in the eye muscles. This involves two routes, one staying on the same side and one crossing over the midline of the brainstem, both to the abducens and oculomotor nuclei. The crossing over is necessary to enable both eyes to receive appropriate signals from both inner ears. These pathways work together to provide signals directly from the vestibular system to the eye muscles.

Each eye has three pairs of **extraocular muscles** which pull on the eye to rotate it in three planes that match, approximately, the three planes of the semicircular canals. Stimulation signalling, for example, a leftward head movement causes excitation in the left lateral canal and inhibition in the right (Figure 7). These signals go via the vestibular nuclei into the two routes to produce complementary contraction and relaxation of the appropriate muscle pairs on both sides. This produces movement of both eyeballs in synchrony (these are called conjugate eye movements) that compensates for the rotation and keeps the centre of gaze fixed on an object of interest. As well as vestibular input, the VOR is strongly influenced by the visual system, especially information regarding the distance to an object. This is not surprising because an object that is closer would appear to move more than an object that is further away for the same amount of head rotation, which would affect the amount of compensatory movement required to keep the gaze fixed on it.

Other, non-vestibular eye movements are important and can suppress the VOR when the eyes are required to track a moving object whilst the head is moving in a different direction.

4 Summary

The vestibular apparatus is a sensory system that provides precise information about the orientation of the head in three-dimensional space and its rate and direction of motion. It consists of the two otolithic organs that detect position with respect to gravity and the direction of linear accelerations or decelerations, and three semicircular canals that detect head rotations. The basic sensory cells of all of these organs are mechanosensitive hair cells. Motion or changes in orientation cause deflections of the hair bundles on the hair cells and this gives rise to action potentials in the afferent fibres that contact them. The afferent fibres enter the brainstem via the vestibular nerve and terminate in four main vestibular nuclei. Output from these nuclei is used to provide rapid and direct control of the musculature that determines body, head and eye position to maintain posture, balance and gaze. This control gives us the ability to perform rapid and complex three-dimensional actions, such as those that enable the top tennis players to play as well as they do. But it should not be forgotten that the vestibular system is just as vital for everyday activities as basic as walking and running, nodding the head or watching the world go by.

Further reading

Berry, M. M., Bannister, L. H. and Standing, S. M. (1995) Nervous system, in *Gray's Anatomy: The Anatomical Basis of Medicine and Surgery*, 38th edn, Williams, P. L. (ed.), Churchill-Livingstone, Edinburgh, pp. 901–1398.

Goldberg, M. E. and Hudspeth, A. J. (2000) The vestibular system, in *Principles of Neural Science*, 4th edn, Kandel, E. R., Schwartz, J. H. and Jessel, T. M. (eds), McGraw-Hill, New York, pp. 801–815.

Kiernan, J. A. (1998) *Barr's The Human Nervous System: An Anatomical Viewpoint*, 7th edn, Lippincott-Raven, Philadelphia.

PART TWO

VISION

Colour science

Stephen Westland

1 Introduction

Colour vision enriches our view of the world in which we live. We are able to make use of colour in our communication and in our art. Our colour vision derives from the fact that the retina in the eye contains three classes of photoreceptor that have different sensitivities to the wavelength of light. Any colour percept can be described by three terms, such as brightness, colourfulness and hue. A consequence of the fact that our colour vision relies upon just three classes of photoreceptor (see Chapter 10, *The retina*) is that we can provide a match to any colour using mixtures of three primary colours. This remarkable phenomenon has led to the development of colour-reproduction systems such as cameras, cinematography, computer displays and printers that enrich our world today. The measurement and communication of colour is also important to many aspects of our lives. Everything that is manufactured is coloured (even if that colour is white) and systems of colorimetry have been devised to allow colour to be measured, controlled and manipulated. This chapter introduces the basic attributes of colour perception and describes the important principles of additive and subtractive colour mixing. Finally, an international system of colour specification is described which is based upon additive colour mixing and which has widespread use in industry and commerce.

2 Perceptual colour attributes

2.1 The hue circle

When we look at a typical everyday scene there appear to be a great number of different colours in the world. The number of colour names that are used to describe the colours that we see is large enough to fill a small dictionary. Indeed, the *Methuen Handbook of Colour* tells us that there are about 8000 colour names used in the United Kingdom, although many of these (such as *Angel Wing* and *Cinderella*) tell us little about the colours that they represent and are chosen primarily for the commercial promotion of products. In fact we can describe all the colours that we discriminate by using only six terms and their various combinations. These terms are red, yellow, green and blue (the so-called unitary hues) and black and white. If we place all the **hues** in order so that hues that are minimally different from each other are placed next to each other, then we will form a continuous series or closed circle that turns back upon itself.

Inspection of the outer, hue, circle (Figure 1 overleaf) reveals that there are four unique points in the circle. Thus as we move from green to yellow we observe green colours that become increasingly yellow, but eventually yellow becomes the predominant component. If we continue, then the yellow colours become increasingly red, and so on. However, there is a point on the hue circle where the yellow hue is neither red nor green. This is called the unique yellow hue. There are four such unique hues: red, yellow, green and blue. Every other colour that exists can be explained in terms of these four unique hues. Thus orange is a reddish-yellow and aquamarine is a greenish-blue.

The hue circle also makes it clear that there is a relationship between the colours opposite to each other in the circle. Consider the unique hues blue and yellow; these

Figure 1 The colour circle showing the opponent relationships yellow–blue and red–green and the increase in colourfulness from the achromatic grey centre to the yellow hue.

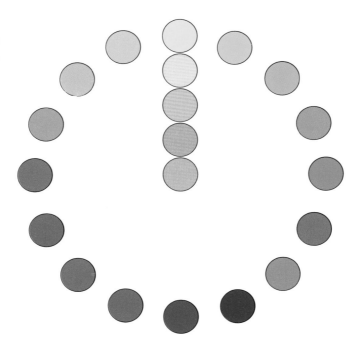

colours are opposite to each other and we therefore describe them as being **complementary**. Note that although there is a gradual transition from red to yellow, there is no such transition from blue to yellow. There are no colours that can be described as yellowish blues nor as reddish greens. The opponency of yellow–blue and red–green that is evident in the hue circle reflects some basic facts about human visual physiology.

2.2 Brightness, colourfulness and hue

The colour circle is useful for describing one attribute of colour perception, namely that of hue. However, hue is only one of three terms that are needed to accurately describe a colour percept. The second term is colourfulness. The concept of colourfulness can be explained if we imagine a grey sample at the centre of the colour circle (Figure 1) and then imagine smooth transitions from the grey centre point outwards in each of the hue directions. The grey centre is referred to as an **achromatic colour** (a colour without hue) whereas the other colours are referred to as **chromatic colours**. As we move outwards from the centre of the colour circle we can imagine samples that differ more and more from the achromatic grey. We say that these samples increase in their **colourfulness**, **saturation** or **chroma**. The third perceptual attribute is **brightness**. This attribute can easily be explained if we realize that there is more than one achromatic colour at the centre of the hue circle. All the different shades of grey, from the extremes of white to black, are achromatic; these samples differ in neither colourfulness nor hue but appear to be of different brightness.

If we consider two different colour stimuli then we require at most three terms to describe the difference in colour appearance between them, reflecting the three dimensions of our perceptual colour experience: brightness, colourfulness and hue (Figure 2). It is important to note, however, that colour is only one aspect of the total appearance of surfaces in the world and many other phenomena, including gloss and texture, contribute to overall appearance.

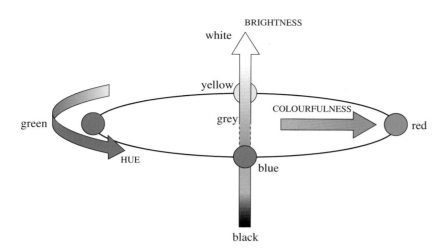

Figure 2   Perceptual colour space. The three-dimensional colour space illustrates a logical arrangement of colour appearance. The vertical axis of the space is brightness. Colours that seem to reflect or emit more light are seen as brighter than those that reflect or emit less light. The limits of the brightness axis result in the perceptions of white and black. Between these limits we have shades of grey. As we move away from the central axis in any direction we increase the colourfulness of the perception. Colours can broadly be categorized as either chromatic or achromatic. Colours that lie along the central brightness axis are achromatic (thus it is not strictly true to say that white and black are colourless; it is better to say that such achromatic colours lack colourfulness). The third perceptual attribute, hue, is arranged in a circle around the brightness axis. The hue of a colour defines whether the colour is red, green, blue, etc. Colours with increasing colourfulness are perceived to possess more of the attribute defined by hue when compared with the achromatic colours.

2.3 Colour-order systems

Material standards have long been used as a basis for colour specification or communication. Colour-order systems typically contain a large number of coloured samples of paint or textile material arranged in a logical order. The purpose of such systems is to enable a particular colour to be identified by its position in the system. The position or notation then provides a specification for that colour and enables the colour to be communicated to other people who have an identical system. There are many ways of constructing a colour-order system based on a number of different basic schemes but the **Munsell colour-order system** is particularly important in the history of colour science and is representative of the many colour-order systems that are still in use today.

Albert H. Munsell was an artist and art teacher with a particular interest in colour, who was born in Boston, Massachusetts in 1858. During the summer of 1898 the thought occurred to him that it might be helpful in teaching students about colour composition to be able to describe colours in definite terms. Eventually, he refined his ideas to generate the *Munsell Color System*, the first edition of which was published in 1905 and entitled *A Color Notation*. The samples are now included in the *Munsell Book of Color*, where they are ordered on the basis of equal hue, value and chroma. In the most recent edition there are 1600 glossy colour paint chips organized in 40 constant-hue charts. On any chart the samples are organized into

10 equally spaced brightness intervals (from top to bottom on the page) but the brightness dimension is given the term **value** by Munsell. From left to right the samples vary in their colourfulness; this dimension of variation is termed chroma by Munsell.

To specify a given colour in Munsell terms, one simply finds the Munsell sample that most closely approximates the colour and quotes the Munsell notation. A typical Munsell notation would be 5Y 4/6. The first term (5Y in this example) specifies the hue chart, the second term (4, not shown in this figure) denotes the Munsell value (brightness) and the third term (6) represents the chroma. The most colourful samples have a chroma of 10 whereas the achromatic samples have a chroma of 0. White has a chroma of 0 and a value of 10 whereas black has a chroma of 0 and a value of 0. Figure 3 shows the arrangement of hues in the Munsell system.

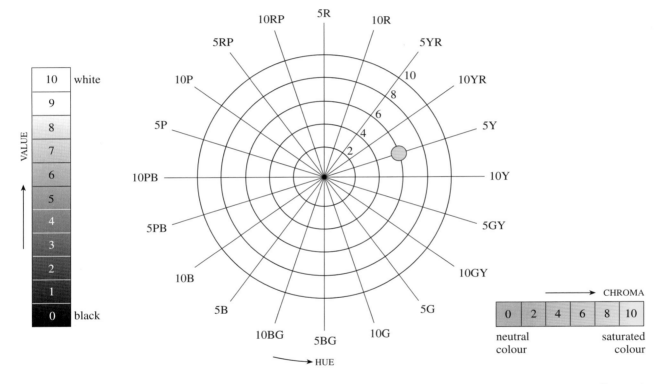

Figure 3   The Munsell system. The colour 5Y 4/6 has the hue yellow, value (brightness) 4 (not shown on diagram) and chroma 6. P = purple; Y = yellow; B = blue; R = red; G = green. The full Munsell chart would include all the values.

Although colour-order systems are still used today for a wide range of practical and educational purposes there are a number of disadvantages of a specification system based upon physical samples. Two of the most critical problems relate to the fact that the colour swatches tend to become dirty or fade over time and the fact that the system contains only a limited number of samples. The consequence of the latter is that it is not always possible to find an exact match to a colour that is to be represented by the system. Fortunately, there is a more exact method of colour specification based upon additive colour mixing.

3 Colour mixing

3.1 Additive colour mixing

The phenomenon of **additive colour mixing** is important because it illustrates some remarkable and surprising attributes of human colour vision and also forms the basis of most colour-reproduction systems in use today. Additive colour mixing can be illustrated by considering the superposition of light from projection lamps. The term light is used to describe electromagnetic energy in the visible spectrum, which is normally considered to be those wavelengths between 380 nm and 780 nm (often generalized to 400–700 nm). Imagine illuminating a white screen with red light from a projection lamp and then illuminating the same part of the screen with green light from a second projection lamp (we can think of each of the lamps as consisting of a standard tungsten-filament bulb and a coloured filter). Where the green light and the red light are superimposed we see a single colour percept of yellow. The process that leads to this single percept (a process that we call additive colour mixing) takes place in the retina of the human eye rather than on the projection screen. If the light from the red projection lamp is monochromatic and at 700 nm, and the light from the green projection lamp is at 560 nm, then assuming that the white screen simply reflects the light back towards the observer, the light reaching the eye still consists of *both* 560 nm and 700 nm contributions. Additive colour mixing occurs because there are three classes of photoreceptor in the human retina each of which produces a single response to these two wavelengths – a response that is identical to the response of the photoreceptors to monochromatic yellow light. Thus, the additive mixture of red and green light produces the perception of yellow light.

Figure 4 illustrates the colour mixing that occurs when lights from red, green and blue projection lamps are mixed together. The effect of mixing red and green to produce yellow is surprising to many who see it for the first time since the effect of mixing red and green paints produces a rather dirty brown. The mixing of paints, however, is a subtractive mixing process (described later). Similarly an additive mixture of red, green and blue of the appropriate intensity can produce a white whereas the subtractive mixture of red, green and blue would produce black.

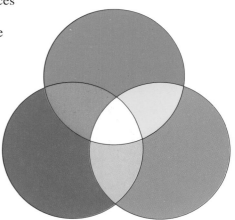

Figure 4   Additive colour mixing.

If a small number of components are used in an additive-mixing process then these components are referred to as **primaries**. Many image-reproduction systems (such as television) are based upon additive colour mixing and use three primaries. The primaries are almost always red, green and blue. Why should the number of primaries be three and why should they be red, green and blue? It has long been known that an additive mixture of three carefully selected primaries can be used to produce a large **gamut** of colours. (The range of colours that can be produced by any colour-reproduction or colour-mixing system is referred to as the gamut.) However, even with the most carefully chosen three primaries, the gamut of colours that can be reproduced is actually only about half of the gamut of physically realizable colours. Nevertheless, for most practical purposes, three primaries are adequate to provide reasonable colour reproduction. The choice of red, green and blue for the additive primaries is similarly pragmatic. This choice of primaries allows the largest gamut of colours to be reproduced. This is not because the spectral sensitivities of the visual photopigments are centred at red (long), green (medium) and blue (short) wavelengths; indeed the peak sensitivities of the long and medium cones turn out to be separated by only about 35 nm. Nevertheless, the choice of red, green and blue primaries is clearly related in some way to the human cone spectral sensitivities.

Additive colour mixing is what is known as a linear process, and as such obeys the important rules of superposition and homogeneity. In other words we can carry out additive operations on the stimuli. The person who first noted this was Grassman, and the linearity of additive colour mixing is usually referred to as **Grassman's additivity law**. Thus if a stimulus I is matched by R units of the red primary [R] and G units of the green primary [G] we can write:

$$I \equiv R[\mathrm{R}] + G[\mathrm{G}] \tag{1}$$

where the symbol $\equiv$ is not a strict equality but means 'is matched by'. This is known as a colour-matching equation. The terms in square brackets refer to the primaries themselves whereas the terms R and G are the amounts or intensities of the primaries that are used to match the test light I. Now if a second stimulus I' is matched by R' and G' units of [R] and [G] respectively, then:

$$I' \equiv R'[\mathrm{R}] + G'[\mathrm{G}] \tag{2}$$

and we could predict the amounts of the primaries [R] and [G] that we would need to use to match the additive mixture of I and I' using Grassman's law thus:

$$I + I' \equiv (R + R')[\mathrm{R}] + (G + G')[\mathrm{G}] \tag{3}$$

3.2 Subtractive colour mixing

Subtractive colour mixing occurs when light is selectively removed from a light path by processes such as absorption and scattering. This most commonly occurs when dyes or pigments selectively absorb light of different wavelengths. The colour of many surfaces, including printed images, is produced by a subtractive colour process. For printing, the paper is normally approximately white, which means that it strongly reflects light at most wavelengths in the visible spectrum. The application of ink to the paper causes light to be selectively absorbed at certain wavelengths depending upon the spectral absorption properties of the pigment in the ink. The subtractive primaries, shown in Figure 5 are usually cyan, magenta and yellow, because this allows the largest gamut of colours to be reproduced.

Subtractive colour mixing is not a linear process and does not obey Grassman's law. Even if we assume that the absorption of light is linearly related to the concentration (more usually film thickness) of the ink applied, there is a non-linear relationship between the amount of light absorbed and the reflectance of the print. Mixtures of cyan and magenta, yellow and cyan, and yellow and magenta can result in blue, green and red respectively. A mixture of cyan, yellow and magenta can produce black. Figure 6 shows how this is achieved.

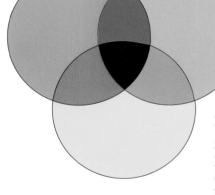

Figure 5   Subtractive primaries.

4 Colour matching functions

4.1 RGB colour matching

The properties of the human visual system can be further understood by considering **colour-matching functions** and the international system for colour specification developed by the International Commission on Illumination (*Commission Internationale de l'Eclairage*) and known as the **CIE system**. The colour-matching

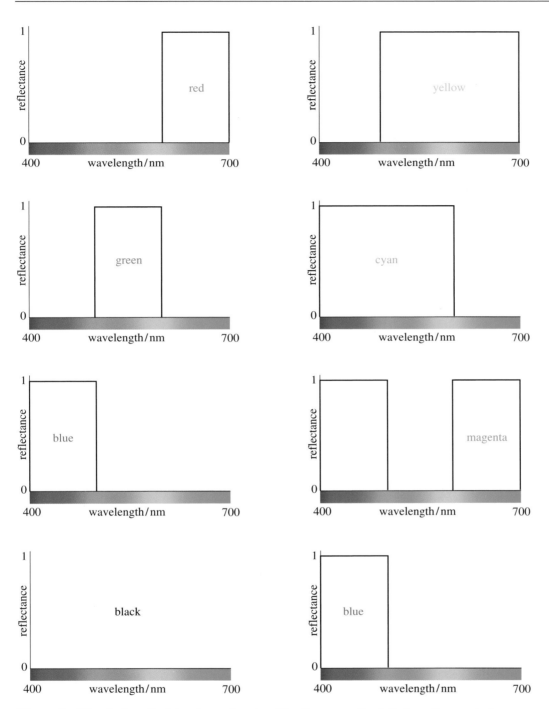

Figure 6 The choice of subtractive primaries. The figures on the left show the spectral reflectances of the ideal red, green and blue subtractive primaries. Each primary absorbs in two-thirds of the spectrum, so that a mixture of any two of the primaries (bottom) will result in black. The figures on the right show the spectral reflectances of the ideal yellow, cyan and magenta primaries. Each primary absorbs in just one-third of the spectrum. A mixture of cyan and magenta for example (bottom) will result in blue.

Figure 7 Measurement of the colour-matching functions.

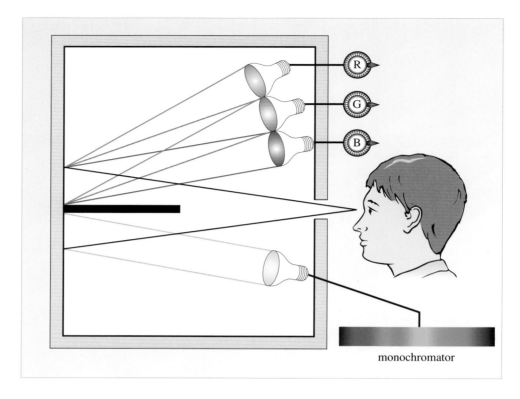

monochromator

functions for an observer describe the amounts of three primaries that provide a match to a unit intensity of light at each wavelength in the visible spectrum. Measurements of the colour-matching functions of an observer can be made using a split-field colorimeter as illustrated in Figure 7.

Figure 7 illustrates an observer viewing a bipartite field. On one half of the field a test light is shown and on the other half of the field an additive mixture of three primary lights is shown. In order to measure the colour-matching functions the test light is set to a monochromatic wavelength of unit intensity and then the relative intensities of the three primaries are adjusted by the observer until the field of view is uniform and the additive mixture is a visual match to the test light. The relative amounts of each of the three primaries that match each wavelength are noted.

The colour-matching functions are therefore three functions (one for each of the primaries) of wavelength and if the primaries are red, green and blue (denoted by [R], [G] and [B] respectively) then for any given monochromatic test light I we can write:

$$I \equiv R[\text{R}] + G[\text{G}] + B[\text{B}] \tag{4}$$

Equation 4 literally means that the stimulus I at a given wavelength is matched by the primaries [R], [G] and [B] at the intensities R, G and B. The values of R, G and B vary with the wavelength of the stimulus, represented by $I(\lambda)$, and therefore the colour-matching functions are given in full by $R(\lambda)$, $G(\lambda)$ and $B(\lambda)$. Figure 8 shows the CIE colour-matching functions that were measured in 1931 for a small group of observers. The physical interpretation of the colour-matching functions is that they define the relative amounts of the three primaries that are required to match one arbitrary unit of radiation at each wavelength.

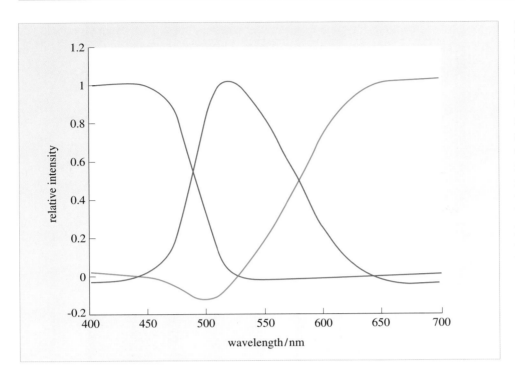

Figure 8   Colour-matching functions for RGB primaries as measured in 1931. At each wavelength, the values of the functions indicate the amounts of the three primaries that formed an additive match to a monochromatic stimulus of that wavelength. For certain wavelengths, one of the functions is negative. This indicates that the stimulus at that wavelength could not be matched by an additive mixture of the three primaries. In such circumstances one of the primaries is added to the stimulus rather than to the other two primaries and this is mathematically equivalent to using a negative amount of that primary.

4.2 The CIE system

Why are the CIE colour-matching functions so important? It had long been known that additive colour mixing could provide a method of colour specification. That is, if an observer were to use three primaries in a split-field colorimeter to match a given stimulus, then the amounts of these primaries that the observer uses would form a specification of the stimulus that takes into account the physical distribution of light I and the response of the observer's visual system. However, such a system would be tedious to implement widely and the specification would be valid for just one observer, since it has been established that there is considerable variation in colour vision between observers. What was needed, therefore, was an objective system of colour specification that would still take into account the visual system and would be easy to implement.

By calibrating the response of the visual system to monochromatic wavelengths, the colour-matching functions can be used to predict the response of the system to *any* colour stimulus without having to resort to actually performing a physical colour match. Equation 5 shows how this is possible.

$$R = \Sigma\, I(\lambda)R(\lambda) \tag{5}$$

$$G = \Sigma\, I(\lambda)G(\lambda)$$

$$B = \Sigma\, I(\lambda)B(\lambda)$$

In equation 5 the colour-matching functions (see Figure 8) are represented by $R(\lambda)$, $G(\lambda)$ and $B(\lambda)$ and the stimulus is represented by $I(\lambda)$. At each wavelength, we multiply the intensity of the stimulus $I(\lambda)$ by the amount of the primary required to match one unit intensity of the stimulus (e.g. $R(\lambda)$). The equation exploits Grassman's law of additivity. Thus, the amounts of the primaries required to match the stimulus at each wavelength are simply added together (implied by the symbol Σ) to provide the amount of the primary required to match the arbitrary stimulus *I*. The amounts of the primaries required to match a stimulus are known as **tristimulus values**. This provides a useful system of equivalence or specification since if two stimuli *I* and *I′* give the same tristimulus values then the two stimuli will be a visual match, even though they may be physically different.

Although the colour-matching functions themselves depend upon the spectral properties of the primaries in whose terms they are represented, it is critical to note that the equivalence of two stimuli is independent of the choice of primaries given the constraint that the primaries must be independent of each other. This constraint simply means that it should not be possible to match any of the primaries using an additive mixture of the other two.

The CIE realized that the colour-matching functions could be used as the basis for a system of colour specification that would take into account the human visual system. In the late 1920s two groups of workers (one group headed by Wright working at Imperial College, London, and another headed by Guild working at the National Physical Laboratory in Teddington) independently measured colour-matching functions each for small groups of observers. These were transformed into a single set of primaries known as [X], [Y] and [Z]. The CIE colour-matching functions $X(\lambda)$, $Y(\lambda)$ and $Z(\lambda)$ define the XYZ tristimulus coordinate system.

The CIE 1931 system allowed the simple computation of the XYZ tristimulus values for any colour stimulus defined by a spectral power distribution *I*. However, the majority of colours in the world around us that we would wish to measure are surfaces rather than emitters of radiation. Fortunately, the amount of light radiating from a surface can be easily computed as the product of the spectral reflectance factor of the surface *S* and the spectral power distribution of the light *E* illuminating the surface, so that $I = SE$. The spectral reflectance of a surface can be readily measured using a reflectance spectrophotometer and the CIE also defined standard illuminants (tables of spectral power distributions) that can be used to compute the colour signal for a surface given only the spectral reflectance factor of the surface. The introduction of standard illuminants allowed the computation of tristimulus values for surface colours as well as for self-luminous colours.

The CIE (1931) colour-matching functions were derived from colour-matching experiments that used a bipartite field that subtended 2° at the retina. A second set of colour-matching functions were measured in 1964 using a larger (10°) field size. The 1931 and 1964 colour-matching functions are based on the same XYZ primaries but exhibit some marked differences. This is because the distribution of photoreceptor classes is not uniform across the retina. For example, it is known that there are no short-wavelength (blue) receptors in the central portion of the retina (the fovea).

The CIE system has important applications in the colour industry (see Box 1).

4.3 Colour spaces

The CIE XYZ tristimulus values specify a colour stimulus in terms of the visual system. It is often useful, however, to compute chromaticity coordinates *x*, *y* from the tristimulus values thus:

$$x = X / (X + Y + Z) \qquad\qquad (6)$$

$$y = Y / (X + Y + Z)$$

Box I Industrial applications of colorimetry

The CIE system allows the specification of colours according to three tristimulus values. This allows colour to be communicated numerically so that, for example, a colour can be designed in one geographical location and communicated, via its tristimulus values, to a separate geographical location for manufacture. The system allows perceptual colour differences to be predicted for a pair of samples. This is important for the manufacturing industries where, typically, a product has been manufactured to match some target colour. The holy grail for colour science has long been the search for a uniform colour space; that is, a space in which the Euclidean distance (i.e. the straight line) between two points would be directly proportional to the perceived colour difference between the colour stimuli represented by the two points. Approximately 70 years after the CIE system was first introduced, there is still no perfectly uniform colour space. However, optimized colour-difference metrics are ubiquitous in the colour industry and are more reliable than the judgements of any individual observer. The importance of colour measurement is increasing with the development of the internet. Colorimetry allows the calibration of VDUs, printers and scanners, and WYSIWYG (what you see is what you get) image processing, and image reproduction allows colour communication throughout the world.

The **chromaticity diagram** is derived by plotting y against x (Figure 9 overleaf) and this provides a useful map of **colour space**. However, it should be noted that stimuli of identical chromaticity but different luminance are collapsed onto the same point in the 2D plane of the chromaticity diagram.

One of the benefits of the chromaticity diagram is that, according to Grassman's law, additive mixtures of two primaries fall on a straight line joining the two points that represent the two primaries in the chromaticity diagram. If three primaries are used then the gamut of the additive system is given by a triangle, with the vertices defined by the three primaries. Figure 9 shows the spectral locus (solid horseshoe-shaped line) and the gamut (edges of the lighter triangle) of a typical computer monitor based upon RGB primaries. The choice of RGB primaries for a typical additive colour-image reproduction system is clearly constrained by the shape of the chromaticity space. Furthermore, the convex shape of the spectral locus illustrates why it is not possible to select any three real primaries whose triangular gamut will enclose the gamut of all realizable colours.

5 Summary

The three basic attributes of human colour perception are brightness, colourfulness and hue. Physical colour-order systems (usually based upon a logical arrangement that is consistent with our perceptual attributes) have been devised and are helpful for the specification and communication of colour. The Munsell system is typical of the many systems that have been developed. However, more useful systems of colour specification are based upon colour mixing. There are two types of colour mixing: additive and subtractive. Additive mixing describes a process that takes place in the human retina and can be used to explain our perception of colour when coloured lights are mixed (on a screen or in a television set for example).

Figure 9 The CIE chromaticity diagram. The *x* and *y* coordinates are calculated from the tristimulus values as explained in the text. The positions of spectral colours are shown by the curved line and are given by the corresponding wavelengths in nm. The points representing non-spectral (pale) colours are inside the curved line, with white in the middle and denoted by W. The straight line at the bottom of the chart connects the red and blue ends of the spectrum so non-spectral red/blue mixtures (e.g. purple) are located along this line. The lighter triangle indicates the typical colour gamut for a VDU (such as a computer screen). The corners of the triangle represent the colours of the three phosphors (or coatings) used on the screen; only colours within the triangle can be reproduced on the screen.

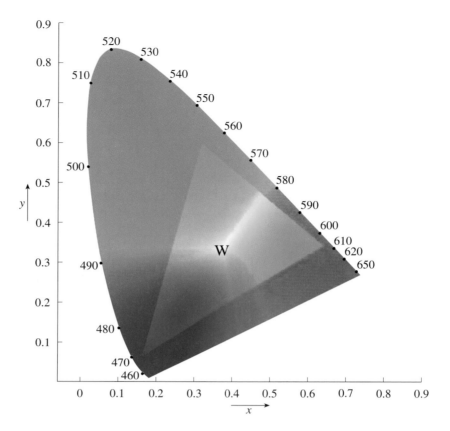

Subtractive colour mixing is caused by absorption and scattering of light by dyes and pigments and occurs when paints, inks and dyestuffs are mixed together. The optimum additive primaries are red, green and blue whereas the subtractive primaries are cyan, magenta and yellow. The phenomenon of additive colour mixing has been exploited in the CIE system of colour specification, which allows colour to be communicated, measured and controlled in many practical and commercial environments.

Further reading

Hurvich, L. M. (1981) *Color Vision*, Sinauer Associates, Sunderland, MA.

Wandell, B. A. (1995) *Foundations of Vision*, Sinauer Associates, Sunderland, MA.

Kaiser, P. K. and Boynton, R. M. (1996) *Human Color Vision*, Optical Society of America, Washington, DC.

McDonald, R. (1997) *Colour Physics for Industry*, Society of Dyers and Colourists, Bradford.

The cornea

Keith Meek

1 Introduction

The **cornea** is the clear part of the eyeball at the front of the eye. If you look at your eye in a mirror, you will see that the white **sclera** (the white of your eye) becomes clear and glassy in the centre, over the coloured **iris** and the **pupil**. This is the cornea. The sclera contains blood vessels (which may be more visible if you get an eye infection or are tired), but the normal cornea does not, and this is a necessary requirement for transparency. This means that nourishment is obtained by diffusion from the aqueous humour bathing the back of the cornea.

The cornea has a number of properties that make it interesting to the physicist, bioengineer, biologist and ophthalmologist. Its principal functions are to be tough enough to protect the eye contents from injury and, as it is the most powerful refracting surface in the eye, to carry out about two-thirds of the focusing of visible light with minimum distortion.[*] The latter requires the cornea to have a very smooth optical surface, a precisely defined curvature, and, most of all, to be very transparent (greater than 95%). Whatever the functional capacity of the ocular system, the cornea is the first part of the eye that light encounters, and without a transparent cornea blindness would ensue.

Visual loss related to corneal dysfunction is a huge problem world-wide, highlighted by the fact that in the United States, corneal diseases and injuries are the primary cause of visits to eye-care clinicians. For this reason, considerable effort is being directed towards furthering our appreciation of how the cornea works. Our current understanding of how the unique properties of the cornea are achieved forms the bulk of this chapter.

2 The cornea as an optical lens

The cornea is more curved than the rest of the eyeball. In fact, the radius of curvature of a typical human eyeball is about 12 mm (the length of a normal eye is thus about 24 mm), whereas the radius of curvature at the centre of the cornea is only 7.8 mm (measured at the front surface) and about 6.3 mm (measured at the back surface) (Figure 1 overleaf). Something that is less obvious is that from the front, the cornea is smaller in the vertical direction (10.6 mm diameter) than in the horizontal direction (11.7 mm diameter).

So how do these dimensions confer the appropriate refracting power to the cornea? To understand this, one has to imagine the cornea as a meniscus lens (i.e. a lens in which both faces curve in the same direction) (Figure 2 overleaf). The front of this lens is in contact with air, and the back is in contact with the aqueous humour.

---

[*] Note that, although the cornea is the main refracting surface in the eye, the term 'lens' is usually used to refer to the crystalline lens situated further back in the eye, which gives the eye the ability to accommodate. Accommodation is the ability of the crystalline lens to change its power by changing its shape: more spherical to increase power to focus on close objects and less spherical to reduce power to focus on distant objects.

Figure 1 A diagrammatic representation of a cross-section of the eye viewed from the side. The cornea (in yellow on the left) has a smaller radius of curvature than the rest of the eye. The front surface of the cornea (blue) forms part of a sphere of diameter about 15.6 mm (its radius of curvature is thus 7.8 mm), whereas the back surface (green) forms part of a sphere of diameter about 12.6 mm. Viewed from the front, the cornea is elliptical (about 10.6 mm high by 11.7 mm wide).

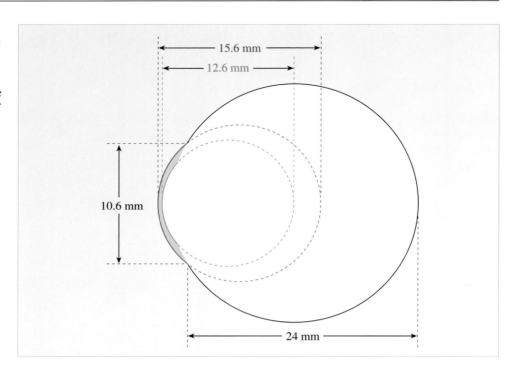

Figure 2 The cornea can be imagined as a thick meniscus lens. Light entering from air is strongly converged. There is a slight divergence as the light leaves the cornea and enters the aqueous humour. In the absence of a crystalline lens, calculations using the appropriate thick lens formula show that light would come to a focus about 32 mm behind the cornea, which is about 8 mm behind the retina.

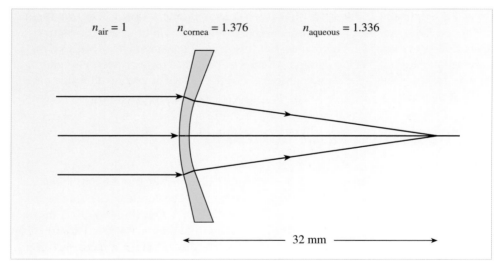

The radii of curvature of the front and back surfaces of the cornea can be used to calculate the **refractive power** P of the surfaces using a well-known relationship in optics:

$$P = (n_2 - n_1) / r \tag{1}$$

where n_2 and n_1 are the **refractive indices** on the refracted and incident side respectively and r is the radius of curvature. We know that $n_{air} = 1$ and $n_{cornea} = 1.376$, so we can calculate the power for light travelling from air into the cornea. We can do the same for light leaving the cornea and entering the aqueous humour, since $n_{cornea} = 1.376$ and $n_{aqueous} = 1.336$. These data give values of 48.2 D (dioptres) for the power of the front face, P_1, and -6.3 D for the back face, P_2. Now we invoke another standard equation in optics that allows us to calculate the equivalent power of the cornea by treating it as a 'thick lens':

$$P = P_1 + P_2 - P_1 P_2 \frac{d}{n} \qquad (2)$$

where, in our case, d is the central corneal thickness (about 0.5 mm) and n is the corneal refractive index. Substituting the above figures in equation 2 we obtain a value of 42 D. Using this value, light from infinity impinging normally near the central cornea, then leaving the cornea and travelling through the aqueous humour would be focused some 32 mm behind the cornea, or about 8 mm behind the retina, resulting in an image which was out of focus. The extra power needed to focus such light on the retina comes from the crystalline lens situated behind the cornea.

While we are considering the cornea as an optical component, it is worth mentioning that any lens-maker wanting to produce an artificial lens that refracts the incoming light with minimum scattering (e.g. for a pair of spectacles) would need to ensure that the surfaces of the lens are machined to a state of optical smoothness. In other words, there cannot be surface irregularities approaching the size of the wavelength of light or else light will be scattered from these in unwanted directions, and the image will be accordingly degraded. The surface of the cornea is coated with a very thin layer of moisture, called the tear film. This film provides lubrication for lid closure and has an antibacterial function, but most importantly, it assists in 'smoothing out' the irregularities on the front surface of the cornea, thus providing a perfect optical surface.

3 The cornea as a tough protective coating

A flexible membrane of high tensile strength inflated by pressure is a very satisfactory way of producing a sphere with a high resistance to external impact. One can liken it to a football, which has to resist severe shock. In such a sphere, the tension resulting from the internal pressure is everywhere equal and is expressed by:

$$T = \frac{pr}{2} \qquad (3)$$

where r is the radius of curvature and p the excess internal pressure over the outside pressure. Since p is constant within the eye, but r is smaller in the human cornea than in the rest of the eye, it follows that the tension in the cornea is less than elsewhere in the globe.

From the discussion in Section 2, you can see that the focusing power of the human cornea, and the quality of the image it produces on the retina, depend on its ability to maintain a particular radius of curvature that is smaller than that of the rest of the eye. It is like a blister on a bubble, and to sustain such a structure is not simple from a mechanical standpoint. In Figure 3 (overleaf), the section along AB is flat or even concave. The tension around the circumference of the cornea (CD) has to contain the internal pressure of the eye (the intra-ocular pressure) by itself, as well as balance any outward force generated by a concavity in the perpendicular direction AB. This tension will be at least twice that in neighbouring regions. To understand how these mechanical constraints are dealt with, we must examine the composition and structure of the cornea.

Figure 3 The curvature of the human cornea is greater than that of the sclera. To maintain this change in curvature along the direction AB requires a greater tension in the tissue around the corneal circumference (direction CD).

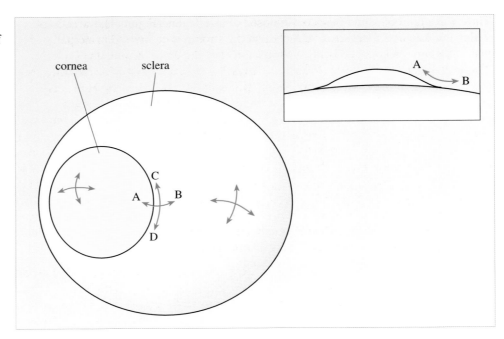

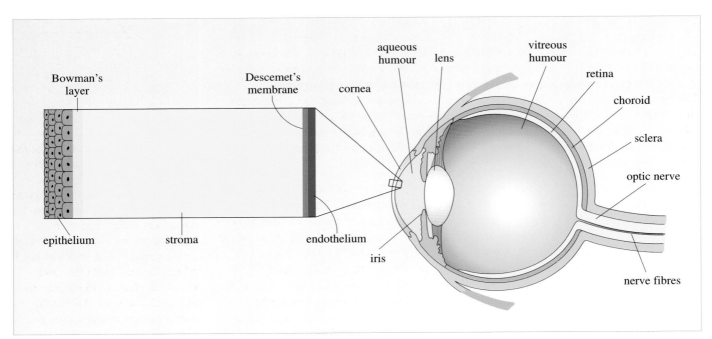

Figure 4 A diagrammatic view of a cross-section through the eye is shown on the right. An expanded view of a cross-section through the cornea is shown on the left. The cornea is composed of five distinct layers. The epithelium at the front surface of the tissue contains about six layers of interconnected cells that protect the surface of the cornea as well as synthesizing numerous proteins vital for corneal function and repair. Bowman's layer is an acellular region containing randomly arranged collagen fibrils. Its exact function is not known. The stroma is a dense connective tissue comprising some 300 or so lamellae, each containing parallel collagen fibrils. Behind the stroma is a thin layer called Descemet's membrane, which acts as the basement membrane of the endothelium. The endothelium itself is a single layer of cells lining the back of the tissue. These cells play an important role in maintaining the correct level of tissue hydration, which is important for the correct packing of the collagen fibrils in the stroma.

The cornea is a connective tissue composed of five layers (Figure 4), the bulk of which is taken up by the **stroma**. Although the stroma is composed principally of water, the protein collagen is the most abundant of the dry constituents (Table 1). This collagen takes the form of fibrils, narrow fibres that consist of approximately parallel collagen triple-helical molecules (Box 1 overleaf). These molecules are connected laterally by strong covalent crosslinks, an arrangement that gives enormous tensile strength along the fibril axis. In fact, collagen fibrils have the tensile strength of steel, and for this reason they are used throughout the body where tissue strength is required. The cornea has to withstand the intra-ocular pressure; in a normal eye this is between 1.4×10^3 Pa and 2.8×10^3 Pa above atmospheric pressure (which is approximately 10^5 Pa). Clearly this pressure will tend to stretch the cornea in all directions in its plane (Figure 5) and to resist this, the collagen has to be disposed in all these directions. There is no tensile stress from the front to the back of the cornea (i.e. through its thickness, AB in Figure 5) because the tissue is under compression in this direction and, as a consequence, no collagen fibrils travel that way.

X-ray scattering (diffraction) techniques allow us to quantify the relative amount of collagen oriented in a given direction at any point in the cornea. The outcome of this kind of analysis is called an orientation distribution plot. Figure 7 shows the results of producing such plots by shining a very intense beam of X-radiation at different points across an imaginary grid extending over the human cornea and into the sclera. This allows us to accurately map the *preferred* orientation within the plane of the cornea (over and above a background that has collagen fibrils in equal numbers in all orientations within this plane). Whereas in most animals the collagen fibrils at any point in the cornea are more or less equally disposed in all radial directions as suggested by Figure 5, the **X-ray diffraction patterns** from human corneas indicate that, over and above this, there are preferred orientations of the collagen. Furthermore, these were identified as the inferior–superior and the nasal–temporal directions (i.e. the vertical and horizontal directions if you look straight at the eye). This vertical/horizontal preferred orientation throughout most of the cornea is obvious from the X-ray results shown in Figure 7. The reasons for this preferential orientation are not yet understood.

The radial strength of the cornea is one engineering problem solved by having collagen disposed in all directions within the plane of the tissue. The second engineering problem is how to progress from a small radius of curvature (the cornea) to a large radius (the eyeball) as illustrated in Figure 1 and Figure 3. Figure 6 clearly indicates that, towards the edge of the cornea where the tissue is flattening or becoming concave, the preferred orientation of the fibrils changes, becoming circumferential, and there is also more collagen here; this is exactly the arrangement of collagen fibrils required to absorb the high circumferential stress (Figure 3).

4 The cornea as a transparent connective tissue

Perhaps the most remarkable property of this unique tissue is its ability to transmit almost 100% of the light in the visible part of the electromagnetic spectrum. You may not think this is such an incredible achievement, but, given that the composition of the cornea is essentially the same as that of the white sclera, and also of skin, tendons and ligaments, which of course are *not* transparent, then how is corneal transparency achieved?

To understand transparency, you need to ask yourself what the requirements are for any substance to be transparent. There are two requirements to consider.

Table 1 Composition of the bovine corneal stroma.

Constituent	%
water	78
collagen	15
other proteins	5
proteoglycans	1
salts	1

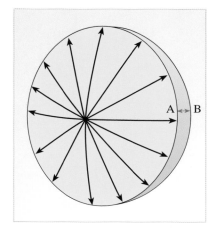

Figure 5 Any small region of the cornea can be approximated to a disc that is under compression through its thickness (AB) because of the pressure from within the eye, and is under tension in all radial directions as indicated. As a consequence, collagen fibrils need to be arranged in all directions within the plane of the cornea to take up this tension. This is the basic structure of the cornea in most animals.

Box I   The structure of collagen fibrils

Collagen is the most abundant protein in the body. There is a family of these molecules, but the most common, and the predominant collagen in the cornea and sclera, is Type 1 collagen. This consists of three **polypeptide** chains, each containing a string of over one thousand amino acids twisted into a helical conformation. The three helices are then coiled into a super-helix, called the collagen triple helix, or simply the collagen molecule. This arrangement makes the molecule very strong, in the same way as coils and super-coils do in the formation of rope. The thin, long collagen molecules then aggregate in a characteristic staggered manner, with a gap between any molecule and the one in front, to form the collagen fibril. The fibril itself is stabilized by a series of covalent cross-links between adjacent molecules.

In Figure 6, the collagen molecules are depicted in two dimensions in their staggered arrangement within the fibril, connected together by cross-links (red lines). The staggered arrangement gives rise to a periodically-repeating axial structure in the collagen fibril (in the figure, the molecular content between the two vertical blue lines is repeated along the length of the fibril). Each repeat is sub-divided into a gap zone (where only four different parts of the molecule contribute) and an overlap zone (where five different parts of the molecule contribute). The molecules are aligned with an electron micrograph of a Type 1 collagen fibril from sclera, such that their length (300 nm) is at the same scale as the micrograph. It is not possible to draw the width of each molecule (1.5 nm) to scale. In fact, there are hundreds of molecules in the cross-section of a corneal collagen fibril. The gaps in the structure allow the penetration of the electron microscope stain and hence appear black when hundreds of molecules are lined up together, such as in the fibril depicted in the electron micrograph.

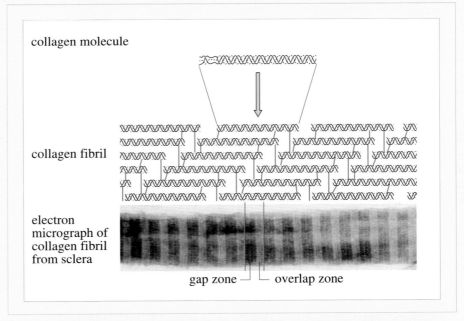

Figure 6 A schematic diagram and an electron micrograph of a collagen fibril.

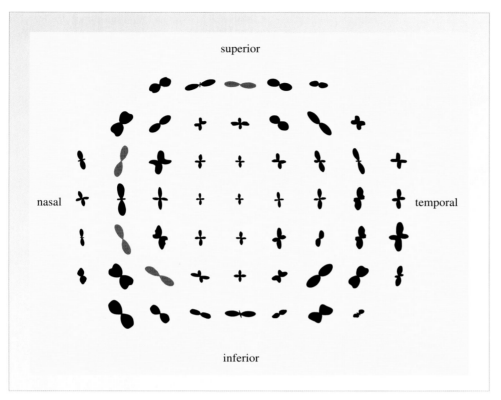

Figure 7   The amount and direction of preferentially-aligned collagen (above a background of collagen aligned equally in all radial directions) in the human corneal stroma. The data were determined from X-ray diffraction patterns (passing a beam of X-rays through the tissue and recording how they are 'bent' away from the incident direction). The tissue was sampled across a grid at 2 mm intervals. The diffraction pattern from each grid point was used to determine the distribution of the preferentially-aligned collagen fibrils averaged throughout the thickness of the tissue at that point. The central propeller-shaped plot in the array comes from the centre of the cornea, whereas plots near the edge come from the region between the cornea and the sclera. Each orientation distribution plot in the array is interpreted as follows: the radial length of the plot in a given direction gives the relative amount of collagen running in that direction (so a large plot indicates a greater amount of collagen at that point in the tissue). Grey plots have been scaled down by a factor of 1.5. You can see that there is generally more collagen at the edge of the cornea than in the centre, which is thinner. The asymmetry in each plot gives the direction of preferentially-aligned collagen at each position. Thus a circular plot would indicate no preferred orientation. You can see that there is a preferred orientation of the collagen in an inferior-superior and a nasal–temporal direction throughout most of the cornea, but there is a circumferential orientation of collagen at the periphery.

1   *For a substance to be transparent it must not absorb light*. It must, therefore not contain pigments or any other absorbing molecules. The space between the collagen fibrils contains various molecules called glycoproteins, some of which absorb in the ultraviolet part of the electromagnetic spectrum below 310 nm. These molecules probably help to cut down the passage of harmful ultraviolet radiation, which could damage the other optical components of the eye. However, the cornea contains nothing that absorbs in the visible region.

2 *For a substance to be transparent it must not scatter light.* You may know that the sky appears blue because particles in the atmosphere scatter light away from its forward path. Blue light is scattered more than red light, so, as we look away from the Sun, the sky takes on a blue coloration. If the spacing between the scattering molecules is *very* much less than the wavelength of light, then the medium has a uniform refractive index different from unity. This has the effect of slowing down the passage of the light, but there is no scattering away from the forward direction.

If you think about it, the components of the eye are the only tissues in the body that need to be, and are, transparent. The aqueous and vitreous humours are transparent for much the same reason as water is – they do not absorb visible wavelengths and they are essentially homogeneous, with a constant refractive index. The crystalline lens and the cornea, on the other hand, are complex structures with densely packed constituents (protein aggregates) that, although smaller than the wavelength of light, have refractive indices different from the refractive indices of the intervening material and would therefore be expected to scatter light significantly. In fact, theoretical calculations for the cornea have shown that, taking into account the size of the collagen fibrils as well as the refractive indices of the fibrils and of the material between them, about two-thirds of the incident light should be scattered at a wavelength of 500 nm (Figure 8). So why does this not happen? The answer to what is essentially a problem of physics, lies in the peculiar structural biology of the cornea.

Figure 8   The dotted line shows the transmission of light through a rabbit cornea as a function of wavelength. The solid line shows the expected transmission through a rabbit cornea on the assumption that each fibril acts as an independent scatterer (i.e. if there are no interference effects).

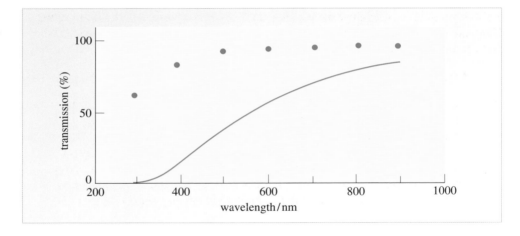

You will remember that to achieve radial strength, the cornea and sclera both need to have collagen fibrils deployed in all directions within the surface of the globe (Figure 5). Indeed, this is what occurs, albeit with certain preferred directions. But whereas the white sclera has fibrils of varying diameters in a kind of meshwork, the cornea has a very distinct layered structure. In fact, through the thickness of the human cornea there are about 300 such *lamellae*, each about 2 μm thick and 9 to 260 μm wide, and each containing *narrow* collagen fibrils with a *constant diameter* (about 30 nm). The fibrils within each lamella are *parallel* to one another and are *evenly spaced*, but fibrils in one lamella make a large angle with those in the adjacent lamella (Figure 9) such that over the 300 lamellae, fibrils are found in all directions parallel to the surface. The space between the fibrils is filled with a number of different molecules, notably a group of molecules called proteoglycans, which are very hydrophilic (i.e. have an affinity for water) and hydrate the tissue in such a way that the collagen fibrils cannot touch each other.

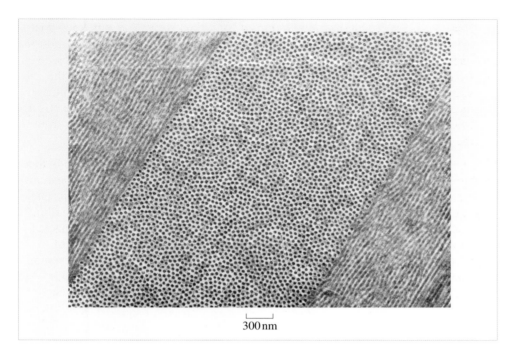

Figure 9   High magnification transmission electron micrograph of the corneal stroma showing three adjacent lamellae. The fibrils in the central lamella are coming directly out of the page; those in the adjacent lamellae make a large angle with those in the central lamella. There is a high uniformity in both the diameters of the fibrils and in their mode of packing.

You may wonder why certain words in the last paragraph are printed in italics. This is because it is these special features of the cornea that account for the passage of light through it. To explain why, we shall start by considering a diffraction grating. The equation that tells us the angles at which we get constructive interference when light impinges perpendicularly on a diffraction grating is:

$$n\lambda = d \sin\theta \qquad (4)$$

where λ is the wavelength of the light, d is the centre-to-centre spacing of the lines on the grating, θ is the angle of **constructive interference** with respect to the incident light and n is an integer 0, 1, 2, etc. Note that the first order of diffraction ($n = 1$) occurs at 90 degrees ($\sin\theta = 1$) when $d = \lambda$. Under these circumstances, only the zeroth order ($n = 0$) occurs (in the forward direction, $\theta = 0$) and there is **destructive interference** in all other directions. This means that all the energy of the incident light goes in the forward direction – the grating appears to be transparent. It follows that:

>   If $d > \lambda$ you will see one or more diffraction orders, if $d < \lambda$ you will see only the zeroth order.

Another property of diffraction gratings is that, if you stack them one behind the other, with the lines at different orientations, they act in such a way that the sentence in italics still holds.

The highly ordered arrangement of the collagen fibrils in the cornea – their parallel arrangement within a given layer and their constant, narrow diameter (compared to the wavelength of light) – led to the proposal that each lamella acts as a multilayered diffraction grating. The parallel collagen fibrils are equivalent to the lines in the diffraction grating. Each collagen fibril scatters a small amount of the incident light, but light scattered from one fibril interferes with light scattered from the others. The centre-to-centre spacing of the fibrils (about 60 nm) is less than the wavelength of visible light, so destructive interference occurs in all directions other than the forward (zeroth order) and the cornea appears transparent. When X-rays are passed through the tissue, however, diffraction orders are seen, because the wavelength of the X-ray is now less than the spacing of the fibrils.

The idea of the cornea acting as a diffraction grating relies on a very high degree of uniformity in the spacing of the collagen fibrils. As you might expect, with the advent of specialist techniques such as electron microscopy and X-ray diffraction, it was found that the uniformity of this spacing only occurs over short distances (Figure 9). More detailed calculations have, however, shown that even with this so called 'short-range' order, there can be sufficient destructive interference of the light scattered from fibrils close to each other to allow the cornea to be transparent.

As with any physiological tissue, the cornea sometimes fails. In some cases this just results in failure of the refractive properties, but at worst it leads to blindness. For example, if the collagen fibrils become disordered, the cornea gets cloudy. This was one of the first pieces of evidence that led to the explanation of transparency in terms of interference effects. Corneal cloudiness can occur following cataract surgery if the endothelial cells (which control the tissue's water content) are damaged, or can result from certain hereditary conditions called endothelial dystrophies. The hydrophilic proteoglycans between the collagen fibrils draw fluid into the tissue from the aqueous humour, with the result that the fibrils move apart somewhat randomly (Figure 10). This spatial disordering leads to the loss of destructive interference of the scattered light waves, resulting in an opaque cornea.

5 Corneal surgery

You may have heard or read about the use of special lasers to correct refractive problems. As mentioned in Section 2, most of the refraction in the eye takes place at the front surface of the cornea. Consequently, a very small change in the curvature of this surface will result in quite a large change in the focusing power. You can see from equation 1 that flattening the surface (increasing r) will reduce the power, whereas increasing the curvature (reducing r) will increase the power. In this way, both **myopia** (short-sightedness) and **hyperopia** (long-sightedness) can be treated. A common method used to change the curvature is to remove a tiny layer from the front of the cornea with a laser; the amount and position of the tissue removed is chosen so as to change the shape of the front of the cornea to compensate for the myopic or hyperopic state of the eye. The technique is called **photorefractive keratectomy (PRK)** (Figure 11). Within the last few years, other refractive surgeries have been introduced. One that is gaining popularity is called **laser in situ keratomileusis (LASIK)**, where, instead of changing the shape of the cornea by removing the surface of the tissue, a thin flap of the cornea is lifted and the laser is then used to remove some of the internal collagen. Other techniques are also being developed to correct refractive problems; the techniques include the use of corneal ring implants, where an artificial ring is introduced into the cornea to change its curvature, and the use of enzyme injections to soften the cornea followed by the application of plastic moulds to reshape it into its new refractive state.

Finally, one important property of the cornea that has not been discussed is its immune privilege. This means that the cornea only produces a low immunological response and so, in the majority of cases, corneas can be transplanted from one person to another without fear of tissue rejection. As a consequence, corneal transplantation has become a common surgical procedure. Nevertheless, in the

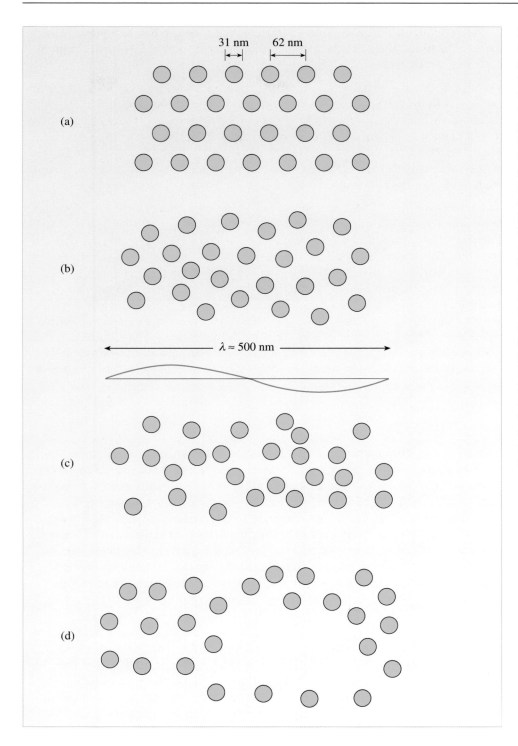

31 nm 62 nm

(a)

(b)

$\lambda \approx 500$ nm

(c)

(d)

Figure 10 Each circle represents a collagen fibril in cross-section. (a) represents fibrils packed on a perfect lattice. (b) is closer to the situation found in the cornea, where there is disorder in the packing, but all fibrils are within a small range of distances from each other. Both (a) and (b) would allow suppression of light scattered away from the forward direction. This occurs by means of destructive interference of the light scattered by each fibril with that scattered by other fibrils nearby. (c) and (d) both show a more disordered arrangement of the fibrils. In (c), many fibrils have moved further apart from each other. In (d) large areas devoid of fibrils have appeared. One of these areas is approaching the wavelength of light in size (a wavelength of about 500 nm is shown to scale in the middle of the figure). (c), and more so (d), would lead to a significant amount of light scattering because of the reduction of the destructive interference.

underdeveloped world there are insufficient surgical facilities, and even in the developed world it is very expensive. This has fuelled the drive to develop an artificial cornea. Several approaches towards a so-called 'keratoprosthesis' are currently under development. One involves the implantation of an artificial lens embedded in a matrix of bone (which is essentially a collagenous tissue like the cornea). Such artificial corneas have restored limited vision in extreme cases where

Figure 11 Photorefractive keratectomy (PRK) is a surgical procedure whereby a laser is used to reshape the surface of the cornea in order to correct refractive errors. To correct for myopia, a flat profile (large radius of curvature) is produced at the centre of the cornea. This lowers the power of the cornea. For hyperopia, a steep curvature is produced at the centre of the cornea in order to increase the power. (The dashed line indicates the shape of the original cornea.) Obviously, both these corrections are less effective if the pupil becomes wider than the central reshaped area. This can lead to deterioration of the image in low light conditions.

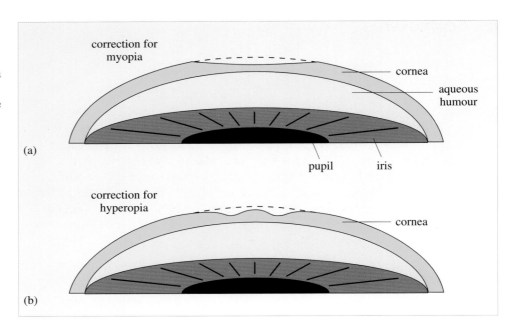

conventional corneal grafting has not been possible. But the ingenious way in which the cornea has developed to simultaneously fulfil its various functions has yet to be replicated by any artificial device.

6 Summary

The purpose of this chapter is to show how the cornea functions as the main refracting component in the eye and to illustrate some of the unusual properties that make it interesting for study in a range of different scientific disciplines. The cornea acts as a powerful lens because of its shape and because there is a large refractive index difference between the cornea and air. Its unique anatomy leads to it being almost totally transparent to visible light yet tough enough to withstand the internal pressure of the eye and to protect the contents of the eye from external knocks. Finally, since it invokes a relatively low immune response it can be transplanted from one person to another, or can be surgically altered to correct for refractive errors such as short-sightedness and long-sightedness.

Further reading

Farrell, R. A. (1994) Corneal transparency, in *Principles and Practice of Ophthalmology*, Albert, D. M. and Jacobiec, S. A. (eds), W. B. Saunders, Philadelphia, PA, pp. 64–81.

Maurice, D. M. (1984) The cornea and sclera, in *The Eye*, Davson, H. (ed.), Academic Press, New York, pp. 1–158.

Meek, K. M. and Newton, R. H. (1999) Organization of collagen fibrils in the corneal stroma in relation to mechanical properties and surgical practice, *J. Refractive Surgery*, **15**, pp. 695–699.

The retina

Jim Bowmaker

1 Introduction

For an animal to see, it must possess an organ that can form an image of the surrounding environment. Such an organ requires several basic components. It must have an optical system to focus an image and a photosensitive surface to detect it. In the vertebrate eye (Figure 1), light passes through the highly refractive and transparent cornea and the aqueous humour of the anterior chamber before being finely focused by the lens. The pupil, the aperture of the lens, is controlled by the smooth muscle of the iris, and ligaments attached to the ciliary body support the lens. The image is focused onto the retina after passing through the jelly-like vitreous humour of the posterior chamber (Figure 1).

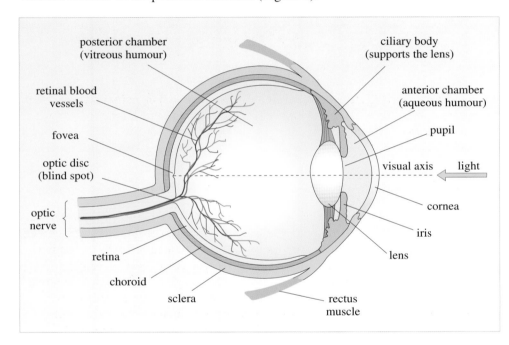

Figure 1 Schematic diagram of the human eye.

The detected image must then be converted from light energy to neural energy and transmitted to the brain for perception. The process of detection and conversion is carried out by the retina. The key components in the system are the **photoreceptors**, which are the transducers of vision. The ultimate constraint on the resolution of the visual system is set by these photoreceptors; no amount of post-receptoral processing, by either the retina or the brain, can reconstruct information that has been lost at the input stage.

2 The retina

The **retina** consists of a complex layer of nerve cells extending across the back of the eye and lying against the **retinal pigment epithelium** (**RPE**) and choroid (Figure 2 overleaf). Its function is to detect and sample the inverted image projected onto it, to carry out initial neural integration and then to transmit the information in a precisely ordered pattern to the higher visual centres in the cortex. The sensitivity

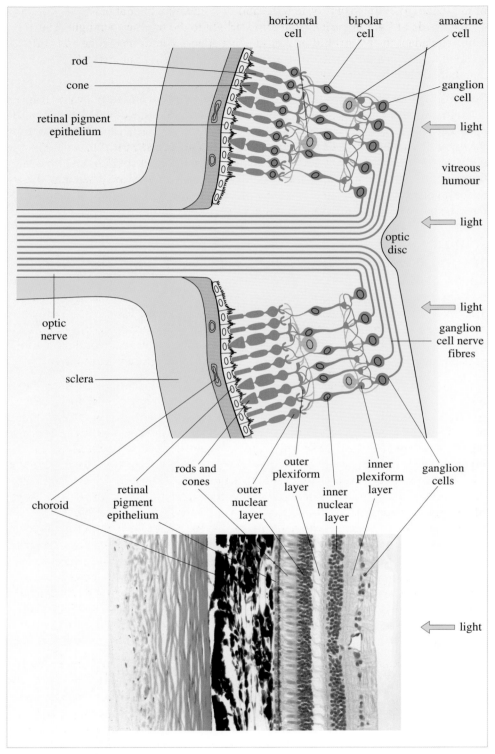

Figure 2   Schematic diagram of the retina and optic nerve, with a photomicrograph of a section through the retina. Note the uniform layers of nerve cells and synaptic plexiform regions.

of the retina gives the visual system the ability to function over about twelve orders of magnitude of light intensity, from dim starlight to the brightest sunlight. The retina can adapt to any level of background brightness within this range and still respond to small changes in intensity, an essential feature if vision is to be maintained across all intensities.

Basically, the retina is composed of a layer of sensory photoreceptors, which connect through a series of **interneurons** to a layer of **ganglion cells**, whose axons form the **optic nerve**. The optic nerve, composed of about 1 000 000 axons, leaves the eye through the **optic disc** or **blind spot** located about 15° from the visual axis of the eye. The eye is richly supplied with blood vessels that enter via the optic disc (Figures 2 and 3a, overleaf). One network radiates throughout the retina, bringing oxygen and nutrients to the inner retina; a second network extends throughout the choroid and supplies the pigment epithelium. Both networks provide a limited supply to the outer retina.

2.1 Retinal organization

The photoreceptor layer, situated at the back of the retina, is composed of two classes of light-sensitive cells, **rods** and **cones**, whose photosensitive outer segments interdigitate with cellular projections of the retinal pigment epithelium (Figure 2). The interneurons connecting through to the ganglion cells include a direct radial link consisting of **bipolar cells**, and two lateral networks composed of **horizontal** and **amacrine cells**. The retina can be considered 'inverted', since incident light has to pass through the retinal neural layers before reaching the rods and cones.

The retina is therefore composed of three layers of nerve cell bodies (the outer and inner nuclear layers and the ganglion cell layer) and two layers of synapses (the plexiform layers) (Figure 2). The **outer nuclear layer** is composed of the cell bodies of the rods and cones; the **inner nuclear layer** comprises the cell bodies of the bipolar, horizontal and amacrine cells. The third nuclear layer, the **ganglion cell layer**, contains the cell bodies of the ganglion cells whose axons form the optic nerve, and 'displaced' amacrine cells similar to those of the inner nuclear layer. Separating these nerve cell layers are the outer plexiform and inner plexiform layers. The **outer plexiform layer** consists of connections between the rods and cones, bipolar and horizontal cells, whereas the **inner plexiform layer** relays information from bipolar cells to ganglion cells as well as integrating signals between amacrine, bipolar and ganglion cells. This organization is not uniform across the retina. The central retina is thicker than the peripheral retina and has a high density of photoreceptors, primarily cones, and their associated interneurons and ganglion cells. In contrast, the peripheral retina is thinner and is dominated by rods with fewer cones (Figure 3b).

2.2 The fovea

In the central retina, close to the visual axis, is a clearly differentiated region about 3–4 mm across, the **macula lutea**, which contains the **fovea**, a region specialized for acute vision (Figure 3a). The macula lutea, or yellow spot, contains screening pigments composed of the **carotenoids** zeaxanthin and lutein located in the cone axons forming the fibre layer of Henle (Figure 3c). Since incident light must pass through the fibres before reaching the cone outer segments, the yellow macular pigment acts as a short-wave filter, screening out blue light. This will improve visual acuity by reducing the amount of chromatic aberration in the image falling on the retina. Carotenoids can also act as antioxidants, scavenging potentially damaging high-energy free radicals that are produced when visual pigments are excited by light. The lens also acts as a major short-wave filter. It is highly transparent throughout the visible spectrum, but effectively limits our vision at short wavelengths by cutting off light below about 390 nm (near ultraviolet). In combination with the macular pigment, this screens the retina from high energy, and potentially damaging, near ultraviolet radiation.

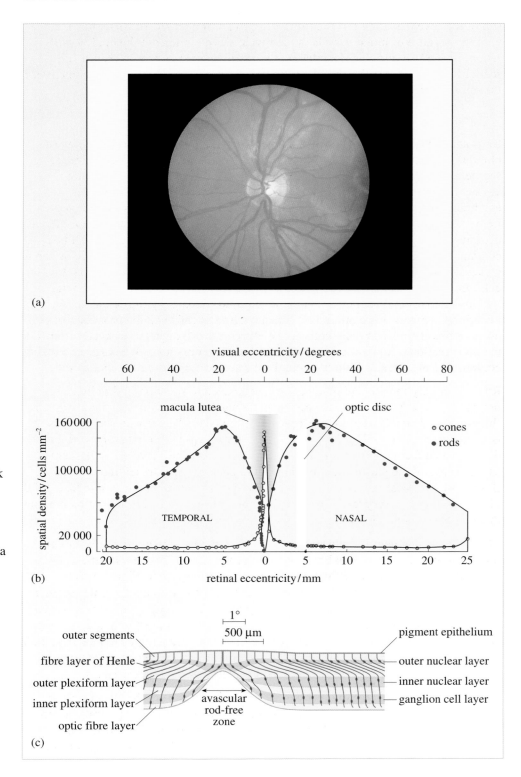

Figure 3 (a) The fundus, or back surface, of the human eye seen through an ophthalmoscope. The blood vessels radiating from the optic disc (blind spot) and the macula lutea surrounding the fovea can be seen. (b) Density of rods and cones across the retina. Note the high density of cones in the central rod-free macular region and the high density of rods away from the fovea. (c) Diagrammatic section of the retina through the foveal region (the thickness of the retina is not to scale). The avascular rod-free foveal pit, and the fibre layer of Henle, which contains the yellow macular pigment are clearly seen.

At the centre of the fovea, the outer nuclear layers of the retina are displaced concentrically forming a foveal pit composed almost entirely of cones. In this rod-free region about 500 µm across (Figure 3c), the cones are elongated and thin, closely packed in an hexagonal mosaic, reaching densities as high as about 175 000 cones per square mm. The displaced interneurons tend to pack together around the rim of the fovea, making this the thickest region of the retina. These features, along with the absence of blood vessels in the fovea, serve to increase the quality of the retinal image by removing the intervening neural layers that would absorb and scatter light. Similarly, the absence of rods and the close packing of cones maximize the retinal sampling of the image (Figure 3b).

2.3 Photoreceptors

Rods and cones (Figure 4 overleaf), whose function is to transduce the energy of photons into a neural signal, are elongated cells consisting of an outer and inner segment joined by a ciliary connection or bridge. Developmentally, the outer segment is a greatly modified **cilium**, with the ciliary fibres or microtubules extending into the length of the outer segment. The microtubules may be involved in the transport of cellular material, most notably the visual pigment proteins, from the inner segment to the outer segment. The inner segment, in effect the cell body, contains the nuclear material and mitochondria, and extends to the synaptic region to make contact via cone pedicles and rod spherules with other photoreceptors, bipolar cells and horizontal cells. **Cone pedicles** (Figure 4) are the specialized synaptic regions of cones that contain a number of **invaginations** or **synaptic clefts**. Each invagination receives the processes of two horizontal cells and the processes of two or more bipolar cells. Bipolar cells also make contact through basal junctions outside the invaginations. **Rod spherules** (Figure 4) contain only a single invagination that contains the processes of two horizontal cells and two or more rod bipolar cells.

Rods are highly sensitive photoreceptors specialized to function in dim light. In mammals, there is only a single spectral class maximally sensitive at about 500 nm (blue-green) which is used for **scotopic** or night vision. This is why scotopic vision is monochromatic or colour blind. Rods have outer segments containing membrane discs isolated from the extracellular domain, whereas cones have discs that remain as infoldings of the plasma membrane and are open to the extracellular domain (Figure 4). A typical rod outer segment in the human retina contains more than 1000 discs, which provide a greatly expanded membrane area. It is this area of membrane that contains a high concentration of photosensitive visual pigment.

The rod outer segment is not a static structure. New discs are continually added by infoldings of the plasma membrane at the ciliary junction and, in rods, these are pinched off to become 'free floating' within the outer segment (Figure 4). The addition of new discs forces the isolated discs to migrate through the outer segment which, if not controlled, would continue to grow in length. However, a major function of the retinal pigment epithelial cells that interdigitate with the photoreceptors is to engulf and pinch off the ends of the outer segments by **phagocytosis**. This process is under circadian control. In mammals some 10% of the outer segment are renewed each day, so that the entire outer segment is replaced about every 10 days.

Cones function at higher light intensities for **photopic** or daylight vision, and are the basis of our trichromatic colour vision. In humans there are three spectral classes maximally sensitive at about 560 nm (long wave), 530 nm (medium wave) and 420 nm (short wave), termed L, M and S cones respectively. The three classes of

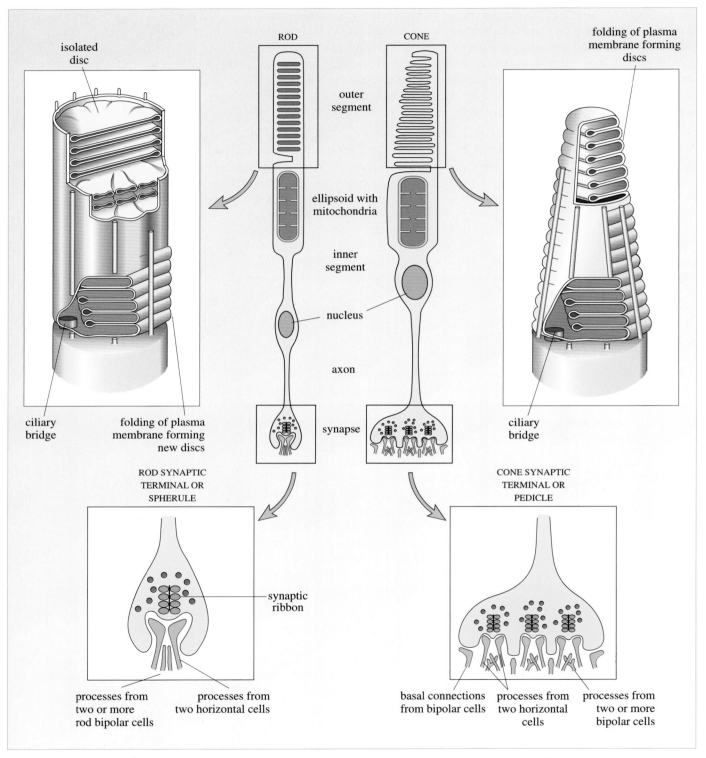

Figure 4   Schematic diagrams of a rod and cone including details of the rod spherule and cone pedicle synaptic terminals. Isolated discs are formed in the rod outer segment, in contrast to the plasma membrane infoldings of the discs in the cone outer segment.

cone are not uniformly distributed across the retina. The central foveal pit is blue-blind (tritanopic) as only L and M cones are present. Within the foveal region the L and M cones appear to be randomly distributed in a ratio of about 2L to 1M, though this varies between individuals from about 1:1 to as high as 5:1. The S cones are rare throughout the retina, but are more concentrated in a ring around the fovea.

2.4 Visual pigments

Visual pigments are partly composed of a protein, **opsin**, which forms a ligand-binding pocket containing **retinal**, the aldehyde of vitamin A (Figure 5). It is the retinal that functions as a **chromophore**, conferring photosensitivity to the visible spectrum on the visual pigment. Opsins belong to a very large family of structurally similar transmembrane proteins that act as receptor molecules in a wide range of different cell types: all function through the activation of a G-protein that binds

Figure 5 (a) The arrangement of a visual pigment molecule within a photoreceptor membrane disc. The schematic representation on the right shows the arrangement of the chain of amino acids in rod opsin. Note that the chromophore retinal is bound within the ring of seven α-helical transmembrane sections. Retinal is attached to opsin via a lysine residue in helix 7.
(b) The structure of retinal. An absorbed photon isomerizes the 11-*cis*-isomer to the all-*trans*-isomer.

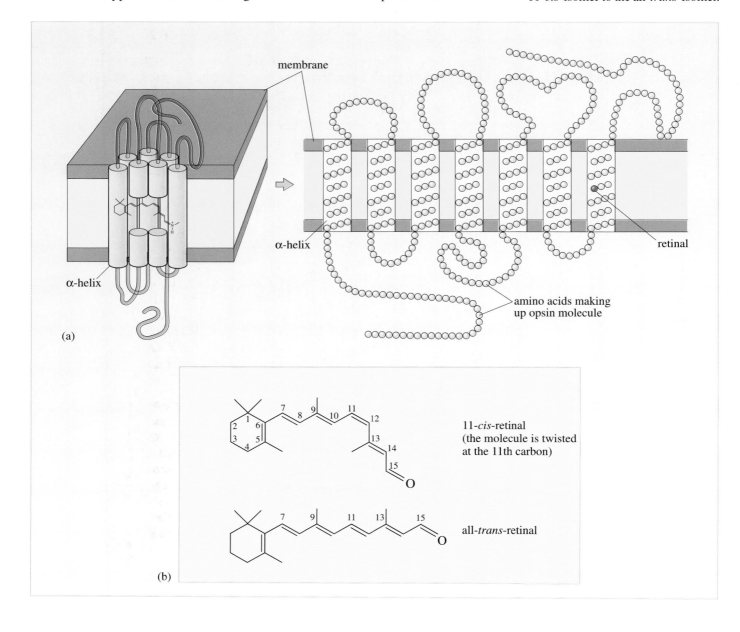

guanosine diphosphate (GDP). They consist of a single polypeptide chain made up of about 350 amino acids that form seven hydrophobic α-helical regions spanning the membrane, linked by extra-membrane straight-chain hydrophilic loops (Figure 5a). The seven helices form a bundle or palisade within the membrane, creating a cavity on the extracellular side that binds retinal. Retinal consists of a ring and conjugated chain of single and double bonds. The **polyene chain** can exist in a number of isomeric forms, but only two isomers are found in photoreceptors, **11-*cis*-retinal**, where the polyene chain is twisted at carbon 11, and **all-*trans*-retinal** which has a straight chain (Figure 5b).

Retinal absorbs maximally at about 380 nm, in the near ultraviolet, whereas opsin, like most proteins, absorbs maximally in the far ultraviolet close to 280 nm. However, when retinal is bound to opsin via a **lysine** in the centre of helix 7 (Figure 5a, position 296 of human rod opsin), the maximum absorbance or sensitivity shifts to longer wavelengths in the visible part of the spectrum. (Helix 7 is referred to in some sources as helix VII or 7th helix.) In the case of most rod pigments, this 'opsin shift' displaces the maximum absorbance into the blue-green at about 500 nm. Such a pigment looks pink or purple in solution and was originally termed 'visual purple'. However, the term **rhodopsin** (from the Greek 'rhodon' for rose) is now applied to the whole family of visual pigments, although it is commonly used for just the rod pigment. In humans, the three classes of cone each contain a distinct opsin that spectrally 'tunes' the visual pigment to its specific spectral location. Each opsin is composed of a different sequence of amino acids and it is the interaction of these different amino acids with retinal, at specific sites within the transmembrane helices, which determines the precise absorbance maximum of the visual pigment.

The energy of a photon absorbed by a visual pigment molecule leads to the photo-isomerization of 11-*cis*-retinal to all-*trans*-retinal (Figure 5b) within picoseconds (10^{-12} seconds). This is followed by a series of rapid thermal conformational changes of opsin through the intermediates bathorhodopsin (pre-lumirhodopsin), lumirhodopsin, and metarhodopsin I, leading to metarhodopsin II within one or two milliseconds. Metarhodopsin II is the active form of rhodopsin (R*), which initiates the enzyme cascade of transduction. An enzyme cascade is an efficient amplification process, since at every stage in the cascade, a single activated molecule can excite hundreds of molecules in the subsequent stage.

3 Transduction

3.1 Activation and the receptor potential

Transduction is the process by which the energy of absorbed photons is converted to a change in the ionic flux across the photoreceptor membrane, the receptor potential, which in turn leads to an alteration of **neurotransmitter** release at the synapse to retinal interneurons. The process must be rapid, amplify the signal, code for the intensity of the signal and adapt to constant illumination so as to respond to small changes in illumination against any intensity of background light.

The enzyme cascade begins with the absorption of a photon and ends with the closure of cation channels in the outer segment plasma membrane. The cascade involves rhodopsin, its G-protein (transducin), a phosphodiesterase (PDE), and a cyclic nucleotide (cGMP) which controls the opening and closing of cation channels. Absorption of a photon by rhodopsin generates activated rhodopsin,

R* (metarhodopsin II) (Figure 6i overleaf). R* binds with its G-protein, **transducin** (T$_{\alpha\beta\gamma}$), a trimer composed of three subunits (Figure 6ii). The action of R* is to catalyse the exchange of **guanosine triphosphate** (**GTP**) for guanosine diphosphate (GDP) on the α-subunit of transducin. Binding of GTP allows the dissociation of the βγ-subunits, leaving the active α-subunit of transducin, T$_\alpha$.GTP. R* then dissociates from the α-subunit and is free to activate further transducin molecules. The **lipid bilayer** of the disc membranes of the outer segments has an oily consistency, so that before it is deactivated, R* is able to diffuse within the disc membrane and catalyse the exchange of GTP on about 500 transducin molecules, producing a significant amplification of the signal.

Activated transducin then binds to and activates a **phosphodiesterase** (**PDE**) that hydrolyses a cyclic nucleotide, **cyclic guanosine monophosphate** (**cGMP**). PDE is a tetramer consisting of an αβ-subunit and two inhibitory γ-subunits (Figure 6iii). Full activation of PDE requires two activated transducins (T$_\alpha$.GTPs) to bind and remove the γ-subunits. The activated PDE$_{\alpha\beta}$ produces a local drop in the cytoplasmic concentration of cGMP, generating a second amplification of the original signal, since each PDE$_{\alpha\beta}$ molecule can catalyse the hydrolysis of about 800–1000 cGMP molecules (Figure 6iv). A drop in the cytoplasmic concentration of cGMP leads to a closure of cation channels in the plasma membrane (Figure 6v), which produces a hyperpolarizing receptor potential. The cation channels are controlled directly by the level of cGMP and are distinct from the voltage-gated Na$^+$ channels of neurons.

In the dark-adapted state, the rod outer segment membrane is permeable to cations, with an inward current carried primarily by Na$^+$ (90%), but also by Ca^{2+} (10%) through non-selective cation channels. In cones, Ca^{2+} accounts for as much as 25% of the inward current. This 'dark' inward current is balanced by an outward K$^+$ current originating from the inner segment, and the cell's ionic balance is maintained by a metabolic Na$^+$/K$^+$ pump. In contrast to a nerve cell, a photoreceptor is relatively depolarized in the dark, with a membrane potential of about −35 mV. Although there is an influx of Ca^{2+} through the cation channels, intracellular Ca^{2+} is maintained at low levels by a Na$^+$/Ca^{2+}:K$^+$ exchanger in the outer segment: four Na$^+$ ions are moved inwards in exchange for a Ca^{2+} and a K$^+$ ion moved out (Figure 6vi).

Light stimulation leads to an increase in membrane resistance due to closure of the cation channels. This inhibits the flow of sodium and calcium ions into the outer segment, causing a reduction in the **dark current**. The inside of the cell thus becomes more negative with respect to the outside creating a hyperpolarizing receptor potential. The degree of **hyperpolarization**, or the magnitude of the receptor potential, is dependent on the intensity of the light stimulus. The receptor potential is therefore graded, or amplitude coded, and over the middle of its operational range the amplitude is linearly related to the logarithm of the stimulus intensity.

Photoreceptors are sensitive to a single absorbed photon, which causes a reduction in the dark current of about 0.5 to 1 pA (from its normal value of 20–30 pA) and which is sufficient to lead to a decrease in transmitter release at the cell synapse. The gain in the system is equivalent to the closing of about 200 to 300 cation channels and a reduction in flow of about 10^6 ions. Rods are very sensitive to low light levels and the absorption of just 200 to 400 photons leads to saturation. However, since a rod contains about 10^{10} molecules of rhodopsin, there will be very little bleaching of the visual pigment. Cones are 30–100 times less sensitive. Rods and cones also differ in their temporal properties. Human cones respond to a brief flash with a

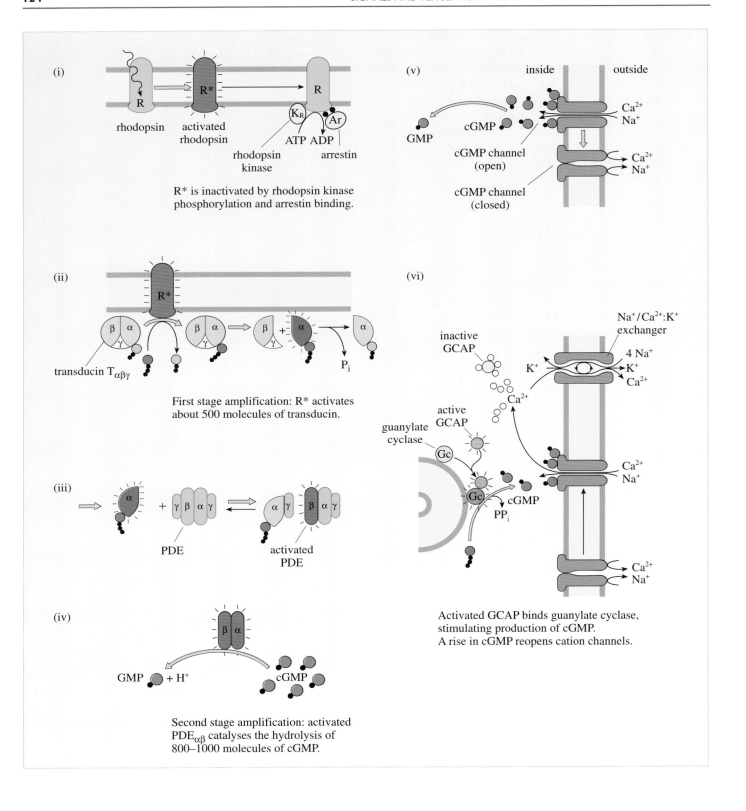

(i) rhodopsin — activated rhodopsin R* — R

R* rhodopsin kinase K_R ATP ADP arrestin Ar

R* is inactivated by rhodopsin kinase phosphorylation and arrestin binding.

(ii) R*

transducin $T_{\alpha\beta\gamma}$ β α γ P_i

First stage amplification: R* activates about 500 molecules of transducin.

(iii) α + PDE γ β α γ → α γ β α γ activated PDE

(iv) β α

GMP + H$^+$ cGMP

Second stage amplification: activated $PDE_{\alpha\beta}$ catalyses the hydrolysis of 800–1000 molecules of cGMP.

(v) inside outside

GMP cGMP Ca^{2+} Na$^+$

cGMP channel (open)

cGMP channel (closed)

Ca^{2+} Na$^+$

(vi) inside

inactive GCAP

active GCAP

guanylate cyclase Gc

Gc PP$_i$ cGMP

Ca^{2+}

Na$^+$/Ca^{2+}:K$^+$ exchanger

4 Na$^+$ K$^+$ Ca^{2+} K$^+$

Ca^{2+} Na$^+$

Ca^{2+} Na$^+$

Activated GCAP binds guanylate cyclase, stimulating production of cGMP.
A rise in cGMP reopens cation channels.

◄ **Figure 6** Schematic diagram of the enzyme cascade involved in transduction, incorporating reactions in both activation, and in recovery and light adaptation. Each of the six sections (i)–(vi) identifies a distinct step in the cascade. Yellow arrows: reactions that lead to the closure of the cGMP-gated cation channels. Black arrows: reactions that lead to recovery from excitation and the reopening of the channels. Activated proteins are darker, with 'rays'. Arched arrows represent catalysed reactions (with the enzyme catalyst above the arch). Straight arrows represent binding reactions. (i) A photon isomerizes a rhodopsin molecule. (ii) R* catalyses the exchange of GTP for GDP on the G-protein, transducin, producing activated transducin, T_α.GTP. (iii) T_α.GTP, in turn, binds to and activates cGMP phosphodiesterase (PDE) by removing 1 inhibitory subunit. (iv) PDE activity produces a local drop in cytoplasmic [cGMP]. (v) Drop in [cGMP] leads to closure of cGMP-gated channel, blocking entry of Na^+ and into the outer segment. (vi) Continued activity of a Na^+/Ca^{2+}:K^+ exchanger causes a local decline in [Ca^{2+}] and removal of Ca^{2+} activates guanylate cyclase activating protein, GCAP. PP_i represents the pyrophosphate ion, $HP_2O_7^{3-}$.

response which lasts about 200 ms and which reaches a maximum in about 50 ms (Figure 7a). In contrast, rods respond considerably more slowly, reaching a maximum response after about 100 ms with the response lasting for seconds (Figure 7b). These differences probably reflect differences in the cascade amplification since rods and cones have separate forms of transducin and PDE.

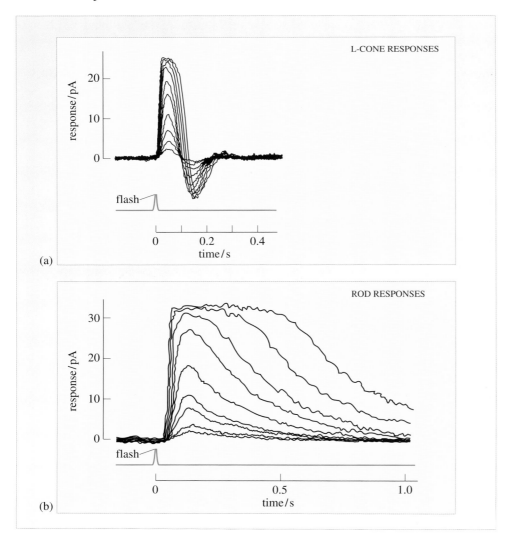

(a)

(b)

Figure 7 Photoreceptor currents produced in response to light. The graphs show families of superimposed responses to brief flashes of increasing strength, with the outer segment current plotted relative to the dark level. Flash strengths were increased by factors of approximately two. (a) L-cone responses; (b) rod responses. Cones are less sensitive than rods and require about 150 times more absorbed photons to reach saturation. Note the much more rapid response characteristics of the cone and the very slow recovery time of the rod response.

3.2 Recovery

A return to the dark condition after a flash requires the 'switching off' of the activated proteins in the enzyme cascade and the resynthesis of cGMP. Transducin is deactivated by an intrinsic GTPase activity that converts T_α.GTP back to T_α.GDP so that it no longer has affinity for PDE_γ. The released inhibitory subunits of PDE_γ reassociate with $PD_{\alpha\beta}$, restoring it to its inactive dark state. R* is inactivated by rhodopsin kinase phosphorylation, in which the enzyme transfers phosphate from ATP to amino acid residues near the C-terminus of rhodopsin (Figure 6i). A protein, arrestin, then binds phosphorylated rhodopsin, which prevents it activating any further transducin molecules.

Synthesis of cGMP is carried out by guanylate cyclase and the activity of the enzyme is determined by the Ca^{2+} concentration. Ca^{2+} inhibition of guanylate cyclase is mediated via a Ca^{2+}-sensitive protein, guanylate cyclase activating protein (GCAP) (Figure 6vi). Following a flash, internal Ca^{2+} levels will fall since cation channels are closed, but the $Na^+/Ca^{2+}:K^+$ exchanger will continue to remove Ca^{2+}. The reduced level of Ca^{2+} will increase the synthesis of cGMP leading to reopening of cation channels (Figure 6vi).

Under continuous light stimulation, equilibrium will be reached between the level of cGMP, the internal calcium concentration and the number of cation channels open. In other words, the cell will adapt to the ambient light level and will then be able to respond to a further change in illumination. The calcium concentration is fundamental to the process of adaptation and affects a number of other stages in the cascade. In addition to its action through GCAP, it also, in combination with **calmodulin**, a small calcium-binding protein similar to GCAP, decreases the affinity of the cation channels for cGMP. It also affects PDE activation and the phosphorylation of activated rhodopsin.

4 Receptive fields

Individual photoreceptors sample light from a specific point in the visual field. Apart from the cones in the central fovea, groups of photoreceptors connect to a single bipolar cell and combine their signals in a process called summation. In turn, a number of bipolar cells may summate onto a single ganglion cell. The ganglion cell therefore receives input from a collection of photoreceptors that together sample an area of thevisual field, termed the ganglion cell's **receptive field**. Since photoreceptors can make many contacts with many bipolar cells, which in turn can make contact with many ganglion cells, the receptive fields of individual bipolar or ganglion cells will overlap.

The receptive fields of ganglion cells can be divided into two types, ON-centre and OFF-centre. In **ON-centre** ganglion cells, light in the central region of the receptive fields excites the ganglion cell whereas light in the peripheral region inhibits the cell. **OFF-centre** ganglion cells respond with opposite polarity.

5 Cone pathway

5.1 Bipolar cells

Cones connect to a variety of different types of bipolar cell (Figure 8). Bipolar cells are distinguished by the spread of their dendritic fields (midget, diffuse and wide-field diffuse) and by their type of synaptic contact with cone pedicles. Each foveal cone connects to one ON-midget bipolar and to one OFF-midget bipolar cell as well as to ON- and OFF-diffuse bipolars. The ON- and OFF-bipolars are differentiated by different classes of glutamate receptor. In ON-bipolars, the receptor is a metabotropic G-protein linked receptor with a cyclic GMP cascade similar to that of the photoreceptors. A decrease in glutamate release from the cone leads to a depolarization of the bipolar cell. These cells make a central ribbon synaptic contact in the three invaginations of the cone pedicle. In contrast, in OFF-bipolars, the glutamate receptor is ionotropic and a decrease in glutamate leads to hyperpolarization. These cells make a basal junction contact with the cone pedicle (Figure 4).

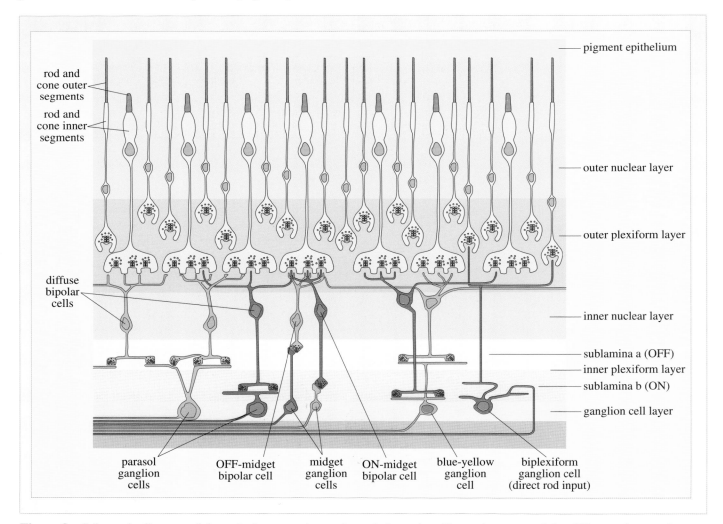

Figure 8 Schematic diagram of the retinal cone pathway through the retina, illustrating some of the different classes of bipolar and ganglion cells.

Each cone **midget bipolar cell** makes direct contact with one midget ganglion cell, with the ON- and OFF-bipolars contacting ganglion cells in different laminae of the inner plexiform layer (Figure 8). The ON-cells make contact in sublamina b of the inner plexiform layer, close to the ganglion cells, whereas OFF-cells make contact in sublamina a, close to the amacrine cells. ON-bipolars activate depolarizing ON-centre ganglion cells and OFF-bipolars activate hyperpolarizing OFF-centre ganglion cells. Away from the fovea, **diffuse bipolars** make contact with from 5–7 cones in the central retina, but up to 12–14 cones in more peripheral retina. The **wide-field bipolars** make contact with even greater numbers of cones. The diffuse bipolars in turn summate onto increasing numbers of ganglion cells so that, with increasing eccentricity, the private 'single cone' pathway of the fovea is lost, with a concomitant reduction in visual acuity.

These two parallel (private) pathways, directly connecting cones with ganglion cells via bipolar cells, are designed to detect contrast. One pathway (OFF-centre) detects darker objects against a lighter background, whereas the other (ON-centre) detects brighter objects against a darker background. Centre-surround organization achieved through lateral inhibition from either horizontal cells at the bipolar level or amacrine cells at the ganglion cell level, leads to simultaneous contrast. This greatly improves image resolution by increasing perceived contrast at edges or borders.

In the fovea, the midget ganglion cells will be concerned primarily with L and M cones, but moving away from the fovea an additional S-cone pathway is incorporated. The S-cone bipolar cells appear to be primarily or possibly solely ON-bipolars, extending down into sublamina b of the inner plexiform layer. The S-cone bipolars normally make contact with several S cones and will have a relatively large receptive field adding to our poor acuity at short wavelengths.

5.2 Ganglion cells

Ganglion cells involved in vision can be classified into three types: midget, blue–yellow and parasol cells (Figure 8). Each of these types probably includes both ON- and OFF-centre varieties. The **midget ganglion cells** are probably involved in high acuity and colour vision. They are referred to as **P cells**, since they project to the **parvocellular (P) layers** of the **lateral geniculate nucleus (LGN)**. The cells, receiving input from a small number of midget bipolar cells, respond in a sustained manner and have axons that are smaller than those of parasol cells. In contrast, the **parasol ganglion cells** are probably involved in achromatic, low spatial vision, and movement and luminance detection. They project to different areas of the LGN, the **magnocellular (M) layers**, and are termed **M cells**. The cells receive input from diffuse bipolar cells, respond in a more transient manner and have larger axons.

The midget ganglion cells have a colour opponent centre-surround organization that can be considered as a red–green opponent mechanism (Figure 9). The ON- or OFF-centres will be derived from a single cone–bipolar pathway and will be chromatically pure, so that there must be four classes, L-ON, M-ON, L-OFF and M-OFF centres. The surrounds will be chromatically opponent, receiving input from other cones via their midget bipolar cells and through neural connections from horizontal cells and amacrine cells. The surround will not necessarily be chromatically pure, since the input will be from a number of cones that may include both L and M cones.

The **blue–yellow ganglion cells** are small bistratified cells with their main dendritic field in the ON-sublamina of the inner plexiform layer (Figure 8). However, they also

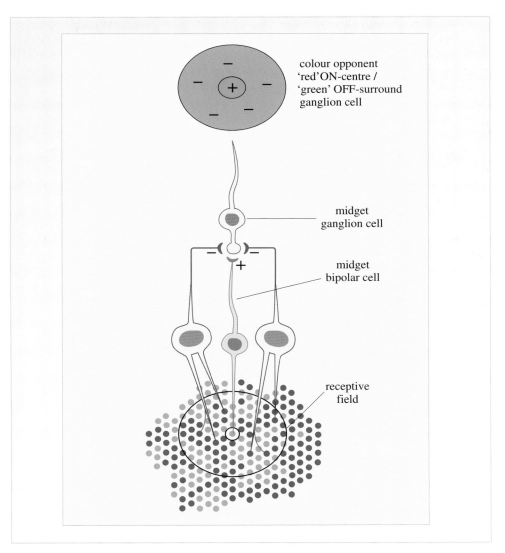

colour opponent
'red' ON-centre /
'green' OFF-surround
ganglion cell

midget
ganglion cell

midget
bipolar cell

receptive
field

Figure 9 Diagrammatic representation of the receptive field of a colour-opponent midget ganglion cell. Note that the input to the 'red' ON-centre is drawn from a single L cone and its single midget bipolar cell, whereas the input to the OFF-surround is drawn from a number of cones, either exclusively from M cones (as shown) or from both L and M cones.

have a somewhat smaller dendritic field in the OFF-layer that connects to OFF-diffuse bipolar cells, which may give a chromatic opponent input from L and M cones.

The division throughout the retina into two colour opponent channels, commonly referred to as red–green and blue–yellow, which continue separately through the LGN to the cortex, reflects the evolution of colour vision in primates and humans. Most mammals are basically 'red–green colour blind' dichromats and generally possess only long-wave- and short-wave-sensitive cones with a 'blue–yellow' opponent mechanism. This is what remains, after a nocturnal mammalian evolutionary phase, of a more complex ancestral vertebrate tetrachromatic system that evolved about 450 million years ago and which is still present in many teleosts (bony fish), reptiles and birds. Primates evolved about 35 million years ago and by duplication of the gene for the single long-wave-sensitive cone, 're-evolved' an additional red–green opponent process to achieve trichromacy. In primates and humans the 'ancient blue–yellow' channel consists of opponency between S and (L+M) cones, whereas the 'modern red–green' channel consists of L and M cone integration.

6 Rod pathway

Rods make specific contact with rod bipolar cells that are depolarizing ON-centre cells (Figure 10). In contrast to the cone pathway, large numbers of rods summate onto a single rod bipolar cell, which results in large visual fields. This greatly increases sensitivity, but results in a severe loss of acuity. Rod bipolars do not make direct contact with ganglion cells, but project to a specific class of small-field amacrine cell, type AII, and to a wide-field amacrine cell, type A17.

The AII amacrine cells project the rod signal onto the cone pathway via two types of connection: chemical synapses to OFF-cone bipolar cells and electrical gap junctions to ON-cone bipolar cells (Figure 10). AII amacrine cells are depolarizing ON-centre cells that feed into the centre of OFF-ganglion cells via a sign-inverting GABAergic connection to cone bipolar cells, but make a sign-conserving depolarization gap junction with cone bipolar cells that connect to ON-centre ganglion cells. This division of signal allows rod depolarizing bipolars to connect to both cone ON-centre and OFF-centre ganglion cells (Figure 10).

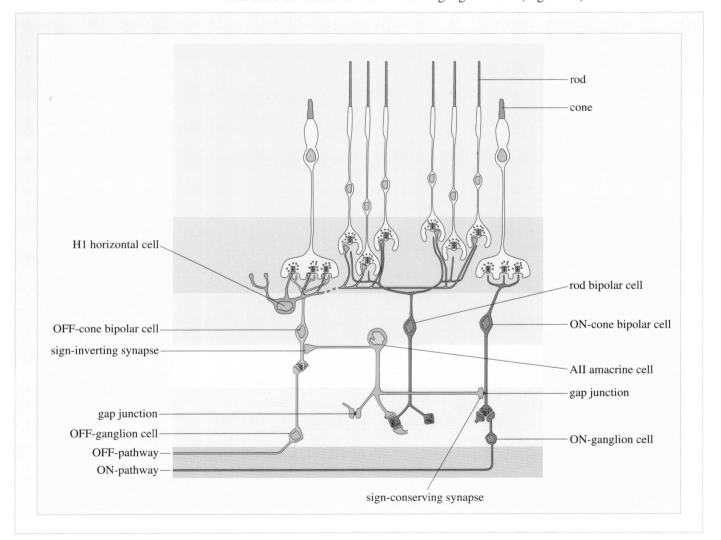

Figure 10   Schematic diagram of the retinal rod pathway, illustrating the connection to the cone pathway through the AII class of amacrine cell.

Rods also make direct contact with a specific class of ganglion cell, the biplexiform cell (Figure 10), thus circumventing bipolar and amacrine cell interactions. These biplexiform cells, which depolarize in response to light, have processes in both the inner and outer plexiform layers. However, their exact visual function is not well understood.

7 Summary

The complex cellular organization of the retina functions to convert a visual image into a series of parallel neural strings of information. Features of the image, such as contrast, colour and movement, are extracted through the interaction of different classes of bipolar, amacrine and ganglion cells and relayed through to the visual cortex. Anatomically these parallel pathways can be clearly identified by neurons which are specific to rod and cone pathways, and which connect at highly organized ON- and OFF-laminae within the plexiform layers. Electrophysiologically, parallel pathways can also be identified by their transient or sustained responses, with transient responses being more closely related to contrast and movement detection, and sustained responses being dominated more by chromatic and high-acuity signals. It is only in the higher visual centres that these parallel pathways are 'reassembled' into a perceptual image.

Functional colour vision

Stephen Westland

1 Introduction

The colour properties of the visual system result from the fact that the cones in the retina contain three different light-sensitive pigments with bell-shaped functions of wavelength and peaks at 420 nm, 530 nm and 560 nm. This chapter describes the operation of the cones and explains how at least two different cone types are necessary for wavelength discrimination. Possible reasons why humans have three cone classes, rather than two or four, are discussed. The existence of three cone types explains the three-dimensional nature of our perceptual colour space; however, the nature of the perceptual dimensions can be explained by a second stage of processing that takes place beyond the retina. Here cone signals are opposed to generate red-green and yellow-blue responses. The nature and basis of opponent processing is described and related to some common perceptual phenomena such as after-images and simultaneous colour contrast.

2 Spectral sensitivity of photopigments

The rods and cones of the retina contain **photopigments** which undergo a chemical transformation when light of an appropriate wavelength is absorbed. In the rods, the photopigment is based upon the compound known as rhodopsin and the events that occur when rhodopsin absorbs light have been studied by psychophysical, biochemical, physiological, and most recently molecular techniques. Rhodopsin consists of a protein called opsin and another component called 11-*cis*-retinal (also known as 11-*cis* vitamin A aldehyde). When rhodopsin absorbs light there is a chemical transformation during which the rhodopsin molecule decomposes into opsin and vitamin A. Once a photon has been absorbed by rhodopsin there is a change from the 11-*cis* isomer to the all-*trans* isomer as the terminal chain connected to opsin rotates (Figure 1 overleaf). The protein then undergoes a series of transformations eventually producing all-*trans*-retinal and opsin. The photopigment loses its colour in a process called bleaching and no longer responds to light. Regeneration of the coloured photopigment is very slow and takes several minutes. The visual pigments are described in more detail in Chapter 10, *The retina*.

The colour properties of the visual system result from the fact that the photopigments in the three types of cone are tuned to different spectral locations. Each has a sensitivity function that is an approximately bell-shaped function of wavelength. The three classes of cone have peak sensitivity at 420 nm, 530 nm and 560 nm and are termed short-, medium- and long-wavelength-sensitive cones respectively. However, when estimated *in vivo*, the peak sensitivities are shifted to longer wavelengths (about 440 nm, 545 nm and 565 nm) (see Figure 2 overleaf) by the transmission properties of the yellowish crystalline lens and the macular pigment of the eye. The abbreviated terms S-, M-, and L-cone classes will be used in this chapter.

It is important to note that when a photopigment molecule absorbs light, the effect upon the photopigment is the same no matter what the wavelength of the absorbed light might be. Thus, even though quanta at 400 nm possess more energy than quanta at 700 nm, the sequence of rhodopsin reactions is identical for each. This important property is known as the **principle of univariance** because a photopigment makes a single-variable response to the incoming light (Box 1).

Figure 1 The chemical transformations involved in the bleaching of rhodopsin.

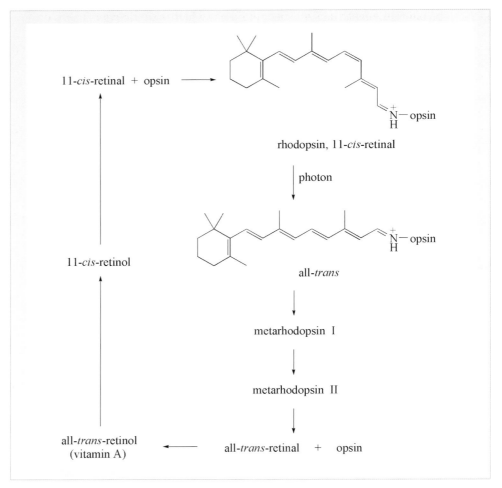

Figure 2 Spectral sensitivities of the three classes of cone in humans.

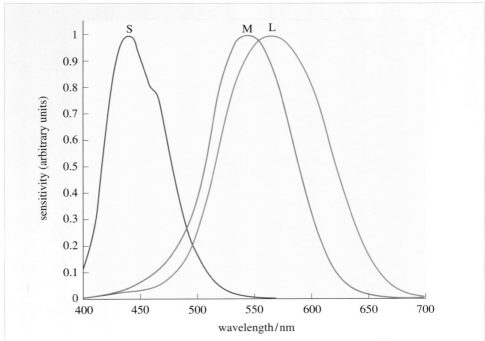

In fact, the photopigment maps all spectral lights (whether single wavelength or broadband) into a single-variable output, the rate of absorption. Thus the response of a single photopigment does not encode any information about the relative spectral composition of the light. Consequently, under scotopic (low light level) viewing conditions, when vision is mediated by a single photopigment in the rods, and the cones do not operate, we cannot discriminate between lights of different spectral compositions. Scotopic vision is achromatic; we simply see shades of grey. Note, however, that even under scotopic conditions the rod photopigment does not respond equally well to all wavelengths. The photopigment is more likely to absorb some wavelengths than others as determined by the spectral sensitivity function.

When the colour signal consists of more than one wavelength, a measure of the response of the photopigment can be estimated by integration over the visible spectrum of the spectral sensitivity of the photopigment and the spectral distribution of the energy in the colour signal.

Box 1 The principle of univariance

Figure 3 shows a sensitivity profile of a visual photopigment, with the sensitivity of the pigment plotted for wavelengths between 400 nm to 700 nm. Technically the vertical axis shows the probability that a given photon of light would be absorbed at each wavelength. The sensitivity is greatest for the middle wavelengths. Thus a certain number of photons of light at 550 nm will cause a stronger response than the same number at 450 nm. However, note that any number of photons at about 505 nm will produce an identical response (about 0.4 in this case) to the same number at about 615 nm. This means that, on the basis of the response of a cone containing this photopigment, it would be impossible to distinguish between light at 505 nm and light at 615 nm. However, although the same number of photons at about 480 nm would give a response of only 0.2, twice that amount of light at this wavelength would also elicit a response of 0.4. This illustrates an important principle that the response of the cones is univariant and consequently the variables of wavelength and intensity are confounded. If monochromatic light is absorbed and the response is 0.4, for example, then no information is retained in the response about the wavelength of the light. A single photopigment is unable to distinguish between wavelengths, and any colour vision system requires at least two such photopigments. This is why scotopic vision, which is mediated by a single photopigment, is totally colour blind.

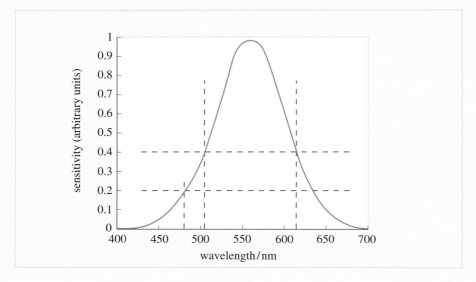

Figure 3 The sensitivity profile of a visual pigment.

3 Trichromacy

In a paper presented to the Manchester Literary and Philosophical Society in 1794, John Dalton systematically described his own colour vision experience which seemed different from that of most others around him. In general, he found that he confused crimsons with blues and scarlets with greens. In order to explain his defect he proposed that his eye must contain a blue filter which selectively absorbs the long wavelengths in the visible spectrum. However, Dalton was mistaken about the cause of his colour deficiency. An alternative explanation was proposed in 1807 by Thomas Young based upon the notion that although the physical variable (wavelength) underlying hue was a continuous one, the visual system imposed a trichromatic limitation on normal colour perception. Young suggested that the eye contained three receptors that are wavelength-selective in their response and that the colours we see are determined by the relative proportions of the responses among the three receptors. We now know that Young's three-receptor hypothesis is an essentially correct account of the first stage of normal colour vision.

Trichromatic vision is achieved by combining the signals from the three cone types: S cones, M cones, and L cones. It is now established that the two main forms of **dichromatic vision**, **protanopia** and **deuteranopia**, are commonly associated with the absence of the L- or M-cone pigment respectively. Individuals with protanopia or deuteranopia are known as protanopes or deuteranopes respectively, and are colloquially referred to as colour-blind or colour-defective observers. It is not accurate to refer to protanopes as being red-blind. Although it is true that protanopes cannot distinguish between many red colours, it is similarly true that they cannot distinguish between greens. Thus protanopes and deuteranopes lack *both* red and green experiences. The only true colour-blind human individuals are **monochromats**; such individuals are extremely rare and have only one cone class. A more common colour defect is shown by **anomalous trichromats**, who possess all three cone classes, but with shifted sensitivities (Figure 4). The protanomalous observer has an L-cone class spectral sensitivity that is shifted to shorter wavelengths, and the deuteranomalous observer has an M-cone class spectral sensitivity that is shifted to longer wavelengths, compared with the normal trichromat. Deuteranomaly is found in about 5% of the male population with protanomaly, protopia and deuteranopia each occurring in about 1% of the male population. Tritanopia, where the S-cone photopigment is absent, is an extremely rare condition. Colour-defective vision may be hereditary or acquired through injury or disease.

Most normal observers enjoy trichromatic vision, and the fact that our colour perception is mediated by three classes of photoreceptor explains why all colour stimuli can be matched by the additive mixture of three primaries. Furthermore, the physiological basis of our trichromatic vision explains why most colour-reproduction systems (printers, cameras, cinematography, cathode-ray tubes, etc.) are based on three additive or subtractive primaries. It is tempting therefore to conclude that trichromacy is caused by the fact that the retina contains L-, M- and S-cone classes, but this provides only a superficial explanation of trichromacy. The question is still open as to *why* we have three cone classes at all, rather than two or four.

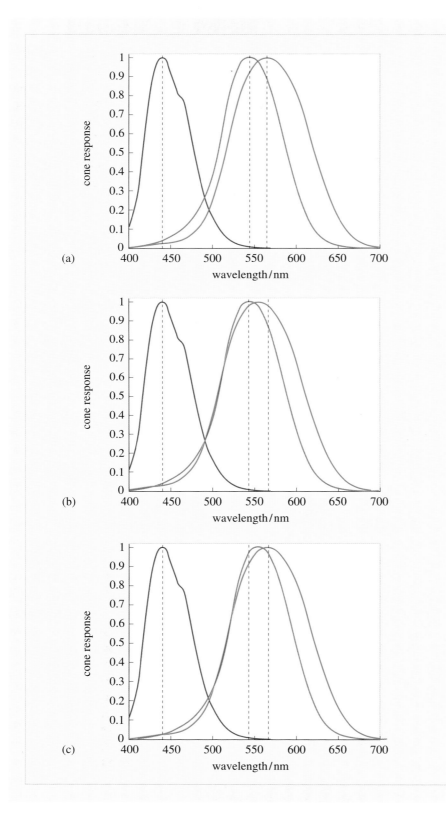

Figure 4 (a) The normal observer has three cone classes with peak sensitivities at 420 nm, 530 nm, and 560 nm, estimated *in vivo* to be 440 nm, 545 nm and 565 nm. Anomalous trichromats also have three cone classes but the peak sensitivities are shifted.

(b) The L-cone sensitivity of the protanomalous observer is shifted to shorter wavelengths. The protanomalous observer is green sensitive compared with the normal observer. Thus, if red and green monochromatic lights are used to match a yellow stimulus, the protanomalous observer will use proportionately less of the green light than the normal observer.

(c) The M-cone sensitivity of the deuteranomalous observer is shifted to longer wavelengths. The deuteranomalous observer is red sensitive compared with the normal observer.

Both types of anomalous trichromats exhibit poorer colour discrimination than normal observers caused by the greater overlap in the spectral sensitivities of their L and M cones.

One possibility is that the visual system has adapted in some way to the colour signals in the world that need to be processed to provide us with useful information. It is interesting to note that trichromacy is not unique to humans and that virtually every animal class has some species with trichromatic vision. Nevertheless, trichromacy is not the norm. Many animals, including squirrels, rabbits, some fishes, and possibly cats and dogs, are dichromats; others, including most birds and goldfish, appear to be **tetrachromats**; with some pigeons and ducks being perhaps **pentachromats**. This implies that two surfaces reflecting light of different spectral compositions could appear to be the same colour to humans (if they excite each of the three cone types equally) but could be discriminated by a bird. Many bird species possess a cone pigment that is sensitive to ultraviolet light and so, like bees and some other insects, are able to discriminate surfaces such as the petals of flowers on the basis of differences in ultraviolet reflectance that are invisible to humans. There is recent evidence that a small proportion of the female human population may be tetrachromats (see Box 2).

Three cone photopigments allow us to benefit from colour vision because, although each on its own is insufficient to allow wavelength discrimination, the ratio of the three responses is different for each monochromatic wavelength. It is the combination of cone signals that provides us with a colour vision system. In fact, it is perhaps surprising that the human visual system has such a remarkable ability to discriminate between different wavelengths. Wavelength discrimination can be measured by presenting an observer with a bipartite field that contains the same wavelength in the two halves and at the same intensity level. The observer is then asked to adjust the wavelength in one half until a just perceptible difference is seen between the two half-fields. The wavelength difference necessary to produce a just noticeable difference varies with wavelength but is about 5 nm at the very short and

Box 2 Do female mutants walk amongst us?

Most of us have colour vision based on three channels, but a tetrachromatic observer would have four classes of cones with the fourth visual pigment having a peak sensitivity between that of the L- and M-cone class pigments. The theoretical possibility of human tetrachromacy was first revealed in 1948, and since about 1993 it has been known that some of the female population (genetics dictates that tetrachromats would all be female) have four different cone photopigments in their retina. Research into female tetrachromacy is currently being carried out by two independent groups: one is headed by Gabriele Jordan at the University of Newcastle and the other is headed by Jay Neitz at the Medical College of Wisconsin in Milwaukee. Experiments carried out by Jordan involved asking observers to perform colour-matching experiments, and revealed two female observers whose responses were consistent with them having a fourth visual pigment. The question still remains, however, whether any of these females possess the neural circuitry that would enable them to enjoy a different (probably richer) visual experience than the normal trichromat. If researchers were to succeed in finding such a practical tetrachromatic observer then this would prove that the human nervous system could adapt to new capabilities. Such flexibility is important, since if someone with four kinds of visual pigment cannot see more colours than others, it would imply that the human nervous system cannot easily take advantage of genetic interventions such as gene therapy for colour blindness.

long wavelengths and less than 1 nm at about 480 nm and 585 nm (see Figure 5). However, wavelength discrimination for dichromats is considerably poorer than it is for normal observers. The dichromat requires a just discriminable wavelength difference that is often ten or more times as great as the corresponding difference for the trichromat. Wavelength discrimination curves for the protanope and the deuteranope have a single minimum of about 2 nm at around 500 nm.

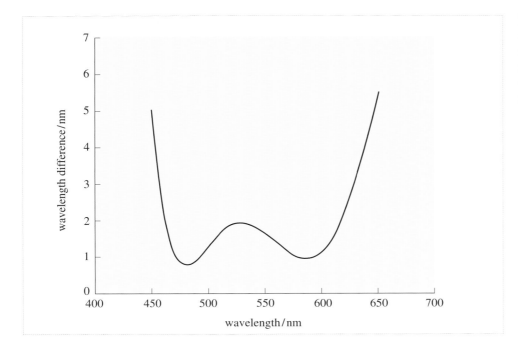

Figure 5 Wavelength discrimination. The wavelength necessary to produce a just noticeable difference between two colour stimuli is shown as a function of wavelength.

4 Colour vision and the natural world

One explanation for the fact that the human visual system possesses three cone types (rather than two or four) is that the number and nature of the cones represent an adaptation to regularities in the natural world. In order to pursue this argument we need to consider the physics of light sources and surfaces. Surfaces in the real world are viewed under a light source that can be defined by a spectral power distribution E as a function of wavelength λ. Although in principle a light source can have any distribution of power, in fact, the various types of daylight are highly constrained to be relatively smooth functions of wavelength (Figure 6 overleaf) and their chromaticities lie upon a locus in the CIE chromaticity diagram (see Chapter 8, *Colour science*). As Figure 6 illustrates, the **spectral power distributions** of many artificial light sources (such as that for tungsten incandescent light) are also smooth functions of wavelength.

It has been shown that the spectral variability of daylight can be represented by a linear model with just three components. These components can be related to three physical constraints on the variation of natural daylight.

1   The first dimension of variation is *light–dark*; this is the dimension in overall intensity that can occur without much change in chromatic composition. This kind of chromatically non-selective filtering can occur whenever light reaches a scene after being scattered to it from chromatically neutral surfaces such as white clouds, grey cliffs or the moon.

Figure 6 Relative spectral power distributions for natural daylight (orange line) and tungsten light (green line).

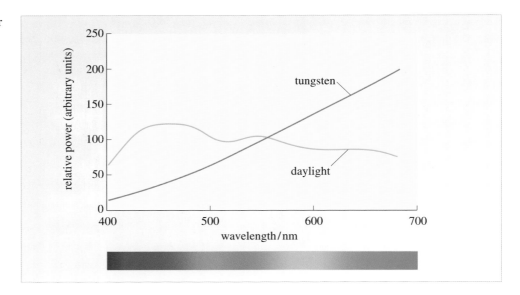

2   The second dimension of variation in the spectral composition of daylight is *yellow–blue* and this arises primarily because of **Rayleigh scattering**. The shortest (blue and violet) wavelengths of light are scattered by small particles in the atmosphere to a far greater extent than the longer wavelengths. A blue extreme in natural lighting therefore occurs when no direct sunlight falls on an object but the illumination is provided by an otherwise clear (blue) sky. The contrasting yellow extreme occurs when an object is illuminated by direct sunlight.

3   The third dimension of variation is *red–green* and this depends upon the elevation of the sun and on the atmospheric burden of water vapour. The longest (red) wavelengths of light are absorbed most by any water that they encounter. When the atmosphere carries a high burden of water vapour the penetrating light will contain a reduced component of long-wavelength light. The angle of elevation of the sun will also affect the amount of light absorbed by water vapour as the path length through the atmosphere varies.

A typical linear model that accounts for the spectral variations of daylight assumes that the energy distribution $E(\lambda)$ for a given light source can be represented by the linear sum of three so-called basis functions $E_i(\lambda)$ of wavelength, thus:

$$E(\lambda) \approx a_1 E_1(\lambda) + a_2 E_2(\lambda) + a_3 E_3(\lambda) \tag{1}$$

where the values of a_i are constants for a particular light source.

If we were to represent the various types of daylight by such a linear model the basis functions $E_i(\lambda)$ would be common for all of the types whereas the coefficients a_i would be specific for each type. The main point is that only three numbers, a_1, a_2 and a_3 are necessary to define (almost) completely the variation in spectral power distributions.

Similarly, the **spectral reflectance** $S(\lambda)$ properties of many natural surfaces are smooth functions of wavelength. The colour signal that reaches the eye when we view a surface S under a light source E is given by the product $E(\lambda)S(\lambda)$ at each wavelength (Figure 7). Recent analyses of reflectance spectra for some sets of surfaces suggest that they can also be represented by a linear model with just three

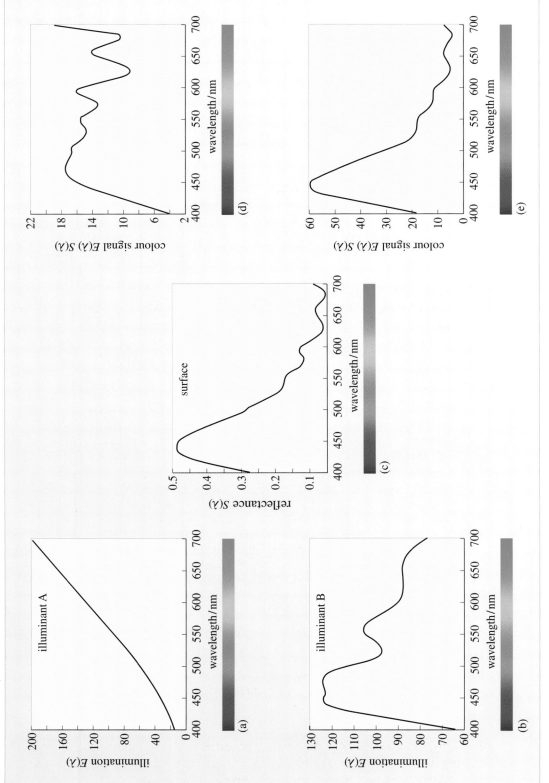

Figure 7 The colour signal depends as much on the illumination *E* as it does on the reflectance spectrum *S*.
(a) Energy distribution for illuminant A;
(b) energy distribution for illuminant B;
(c) reflectance spectrum for a typical surface;
(d) colour signal for the surface under illuminant A;
(e) colour signal for the surface under illuminant B.

parameters. If this finding were to be confirmed then the trichromatic nature of the visual system might be explained in terms of the constraints on the spectral variation of natural light sources and natural surfaces. However, the explanation would not be complete unless we could show how the visual system might recover the reflectance spectrum for a surface S from the cone responses to a colour signal ES. The problem lies in the fact that the colour signal ES depends as much on the illumination E as on the reflectance S, and yet our perception of surface colours appears to be relatively independent of the colour of the illumination. This phenomenon is known as colour constancy and is described in much more detail in Chapter 15, *Colour in context: contrast and constancy*.

Could perceptual colour constancy be explained by the fact that the visual system can recover the reflectance spectrum S from the cone excitations that result from a colour signal ES? In fact, it has been shown that the visual system can discount the illumination in this way and can recover the reflectance spectrum S but that a system with n receptors can only recover the reflectance to the accuracy of an $(n-1)$-basis function linear model; one degree of freedom is used up to discount the illuminant. Since humans possess only three cone classes, this means that we could only recover estimates of the reflectance spectra of surfaces to the accuracy of a linear model with just two parameters. Furthermore, it now seems that the original estimates of the smoothness of reflectance spectra were optimistic for reflectance spectra generally and it is now considered that between six and nine basis functions are required for a reasonable approximation of many reflectance spectra. It therefore seems unlikely that trichromacy can be explained by the global statistics of reflectance spectra of surfaces in the world. However, it is still suggested by some researchers that the roots of trichromacy may be explained by the fact that natural illumination can be represented by a linear model with just three parameters, if it is considered that the main computational task of the visual system is to discount the illumination, so that surfaces retain their approximate daylight appearance no matter which natural illumination they are viewed in.

In summary, it seems unlikely that trichromacy can be explained by the global statistics of reflectance spectra of surfaces in the world although trichromacy may result from an adaptation to the regularities in terrestrial illumination. However, a complete characterization of the challenges faced by colour perception must include changes in surface surround and illuminant changes due to inter-reflections between surfaces in cluttered scenes. The majority of contemporary vision scientists regard the three-dimensionality of human colour representation as a more pragmatic (somewhat arbitrary) compromise between competing pressures towards the one-dimensional simplicity of achromatic vision on the one hand, and the high-dimensional complexity of the truly full-colour vision that would wholly capture the intrinsic spectral reflectance distribution of each and every external surface on the other. The *fewer* types of cone class we possess the better our spatial resolution but the worse our colour resolution; the *more* types of cone class we possess the better our colour resolution but the worse our spatial resolution. Thus, trichromacy may simply be a trade-off between colour and spatial resolution.

If the trade-off theory is correct then it is likely that we will need to look to genetic science and evolutionary pressures to fully understand the reasons for trichromacy in humans. Textbooks often represent the three types of human cone as equal elements in a trichromatic scheme. However, the evidence strongly suggests that they evolved at different times and for different purposes. Our own colour vision seems to depend upon two, relatively independent, subsystems: a recent subsystem (red-green) overlaid on a much more ancient dichromatic (blue-yellow) subsystem. If our distant ancestors had only two classes of cone they might have been at a slight (but in the long run significant) disadvantage in identifying food compared with ancestors that through spontaneous mutation developed trichromatic vision. Our trichromatic system may therefore have evolved to allow the detection of brownish-reddish edibles against greenish backgrounds.

5 Opponent-colours theory

Trichromacy provides us with the ability to discriminate wavelengths independently of their relative intensities but the notion of **colour contrast** is essential to a modern understanding of colour perception. Colours are always seen in some visual context; for example, a colour patch is always seen in relation to some background colour. A yellow patch on a green background appears more reddish than it does on a red background (Figure 8).

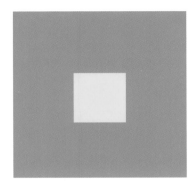 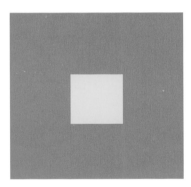

Figure 8 A yellow patch on a green background appears more reddish than it does on a red background.

The *simultaneous* colour contrast illustrated in Figure 8 can also be demonstrated temporally as *successive* colour contrast or afterimages (Figure 9 overleaf). We usually notice these kinds of phenomena only when we are presented with artificial displays but both kinds of contrast are continually operative in our visual field. Indeed, we know that triplets of cone excitations do not uniquely or efficiently specify the colours that we see. Simultaneous colour contrast indicates that the colours we see in a complex scene depend on the cone responses caused by those colours and also on the cone responses caused by surrounding colours.

Physiological data have been used to show that postreceptoral processing of cone excitations is antagonistic or opponent in nature; for example, cone excitations from different spatial locations in the retina are combined, but with, in effect, opposite sign. **Spatial antagonism** is fundamental in the operation of the visual system and implies that the visual system responds primarily to contrasts rather than to absolute magnitudes. If cone excitations are combined from different cone types then **spectral antagonism** can also take place. **Opponent processing** allows the cone excitations to be recombined to generate three new channels that code luminance, redness–greenness, and yellowness–blueness (Figure 10 overleaf).

Two properties distinguish a cell as an opponent response cell. First, an opponent cell has a spontaneous rate of firing and, second, the cell shows an increased rate of firing in the presence of lights whose dominant wavelengths are from certain regions of the spectrum, while lights from the complementary spectral regions will decrease the rate of firing below its normal rate. Such cells have been found in the lateral

Figure 9 Temporal colour contrast. Stare at the central cross in the top figure for about 30 seconds and then transfer your attention to the cross in the bottom figure.

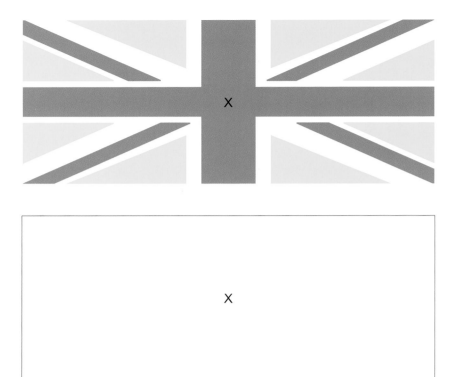

Figure 10 Schematic diagram to show opponent processing of cone responses. The top square boxes represent the firing rates, or responses, of the L, M and S cones to any arbitrary stimulus. The lines below the boxes show how these are combined to produce opponent responses. The luminance channel receives a combined response from the L and M cones; the red–green channel receives antagonistic signals from the L and M cones; the yellow–blue channel receives signals from the S cones opposed by a combined response from the L and M cones.

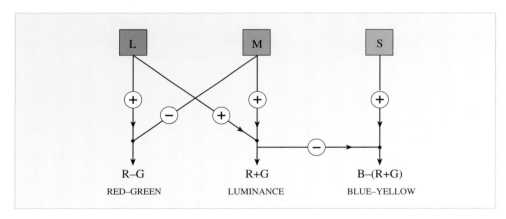

geniculate nucleus (a central area of the brain) of macaque monkeys whose visual system is known be similar to that of humans. Thus, whilst colour is coded for at the retinal level by the relative responses from the three types of cone, this representation is transformed beyond the retina into three different signals; a luminance signal and two opponent-colour signals (red–green and yellow–blue). It is the relative strengths of the opponent signals that directly determine perceived hue.

Whereas the fact that there are three cone types explains the three-dimensional nature of our perceptual colour space, the opponent channels can be related to the nature of the perceptual dimensions (see the earlier discussion in Chapter 8, *Colour science*). The brightness dimension is clearly related to the presence of a luminance channel whereas the hue and colourfulness dimensions can be alternatively coded as redness–greenness and yellowness–blueness.

Opponent processing also provides an explanation for observations by psychologists such as Ewald Hering in the early twentieth century. Hering argued that any colour appears subjectively either as one of four pure hues (red, green, yellow or blue) or as a mixture of these unique hues. In fact, Hering claimed that all colours other than the unique hues could be seen to consist of the simultaneous perception of two of the primaries. Thus, orange could be considered to be a simultaneous perception of red and yellow whereas purple could be considered to be a simultaneous perception of red and blue. Hering also observed that red and green could not be simultaneously observed and neither could yellow and blue. Hering's observations were striking given that in his time there was no knowledge of the antagonistic neural processes that we now know take place in the human brain. We are now able to measure the response functions for spectrally opponent cells in, for example, the lateral geniculate nucleus. It is interesting to note that crosspoints of such response functions occur at approximately the same wavelengths as the two minima in the wavelength discrimination function (Figure 5). Thus, the spectral sensitivity of opponent cells that take their input as L−M, crosses with the spectral sensitivity of opponent cells that take their input as M−L at about 590 nm whereas the (L+M)−S and S−(L+M) spectral sensitivities cross at about 480 nm.

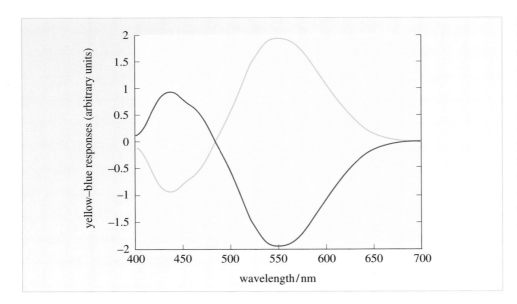

Figure 11 The yellow–blue and blue–yellow opponent channels crossover close to 480 nm which is a minimum in the wavelength discrimination function (Figure 5). The yellow–blue and blue–yellow responses are symmetrical around the null response and can be either positive or negative since they result from opponent processes (e.g. yellow minus blue). When a channel is negative then that channel is considered to be sending an inhibitory response.

If fine wavelength discriminations are based on the activity of the cell type which is most sensitive then one would predict a double minimum in the wavelength discrimination function based upon the spectral properties of the two opponent channels. Thus at about 480 nm the yellow–blue channel would be most sensitive because a small shift in wavelength might be expected to cause the (L+M)−S response to switch from excitation to inhibition.

Opponent processing may also be responsible for the circularity of the perceived hue dimension (the CIE diagram). A transformation by the visual system from the outputs of three classes of cones to an opponent representation has the effect of bending the continuum of wavelength into a closed cycle of spectral hues.

6 Summary

Three cone photopigments allow us to benefit from colour vision because, although each on its own is insufficient to allow wavelength discrimination, the ratio of the three responses is different for each monochromatic wavelength. Furthermore, the fact that our colour perception is mediated by three classes of photoreceptors explains why all colour stimuli can be matched by the additive mixture of three primaries. Possible explanations for trichromacy have been discussed and it seems likely that the reason that we have three cone types may be the result of a trade-off between colour and spatial resolution. Evolutionary evidence suggests that at some time in our distant past we were all dichromats and some scientists suggest that we evolved a third cone pigment in order to improve our ability to discriminate between fruit and foliage or between ripe and unripe fruit. Wavelength discrimination for normal trichromats is surprisingly good – differences of less than 1 nm can be discriminated at certain wavelengths. Explanations for the shape of the wavelength discrimination curve and for the existence of four unique hues can be found in the opponent-colours theory. It is now established that the cone signals are transformed beyond the retina into a luminance signal and two chromatic opponent signals, red–green and yellow–blue. The excitation of the three cone classes is not sufficient to explain the complex nature of our colour perception. In addition to colour-opponent processing, it is necessary to understand spatial and temporal contrast in order to explain many perceptual phenomena such as afterimages and simultaneous contrast. These phenomena, and the biological processes that underlie them, are described in more detail in Chapter 15, *Colour in context: contrast and constancy*.

Further reading

Hurlbert, A. (1991) Deciphering the colour code, *Nature*, **349**, pp. 191–193.

Hurvich, L. M. (1981) *Color Vision*, Sinauer Associates.

Marrimont, D. A. and Wandell, B. A. (1992) Linear models of surface and illuminant spectra, *Journal of the Optical Society of America A*, **9** (11), pp. 1905–1913.

Maloney, L. T. (1986) Evaluation of linear models of surface spectral reflectance with small numbers of parameters, *Journal of the Optical Society of America A*, **3**, pp. 1673–1683.

Wandell, B. A. (1995) *Foundations of Vision*, Sinauer Associates.

Byrne, A. and Hilbert, D. A. (1997) *The Science of Colour*, MIT Press.

From retina to cortex

Andrew Derrington

1 Introduction

A great deal can be learned about the processing of information in sensory pathways by studying maps that show how the sensory world is projected onto the brain structures that process it, and by studying receptive fields, which show what information is represented by the electrical signals of individual neurons. Maps and receptive field properties are important in understanding all sensory pathways, but they are particularly useful in understanding visual processing.

Most sensory pathways contain maps of the stimulus space. Neurons are positioned in the map according to their responses to some stimulus parameter, so that those that have similar responses are close together. The maps contain two different kinds of clue to the way in which information is processed. First, they show which parameters of the stimulus are being analysed by showing which parameters are mapped in an orderly way. They also show what kinds of information are segregated so that they can be processed independently, and what kinds of information are combined. Second, the relative amounts of the map devoted to different parts of the stimulus space show the relative importance of each. The first part of this chapter deals with the maps that exist in the visual pathway and shows us that maps tell us a great deal about the function of the lateral geniculate nucleus (LGN).

The receptive field properties of a neuron tell us what makes the neuron fire, which in turn tells us the meaning of the signals carried by that neuron – what information it encodes and how. At each level, neurons encode particular attributes or features of the stimulus by responding selectively to those features. All the visible information in the stimulus must somehow be encoded by the responses of the whole ensemble of neurons, but some information about the stimulus is represented explicitly in the responses of individual neurons whereas other information can only be derived by analysing the responses of many neurons.

At each stage of processing, the signals of different sets of neurons can be combined so that attributes of the stimulus that are represented by combinations of neurons at one stage of the pathway become explicitly represented in the responses of individual neurons at the next. The second part of this chapter deals with receptive field properties and explains that they tell us little about the function of the LGN but a great deal about the function of the primary visual cortex.

2 Maps and pathways

2.1 Visual maps and visual fields

In humans and other animals with forward facing eyes, a substantial part of the visual field is **binocular**: it is seen by both eyes. One of the distinctive features of the organization of the visual pathway (which is shown in Figure 1 overleaf) is that signals from the two eyes are sorted and combined so that those relating to stimuli in the same part of the visual field end up in the same part of the brain even if they arise in different eyes. In order for this to happen, the projection from each eye into the brain is divided at the **optic chiasm**. Fibres originating in the **nasal** half of each retina cross the midline to join those from the **temporal** half of the other retina. This

Figure 1   The visual pathway.

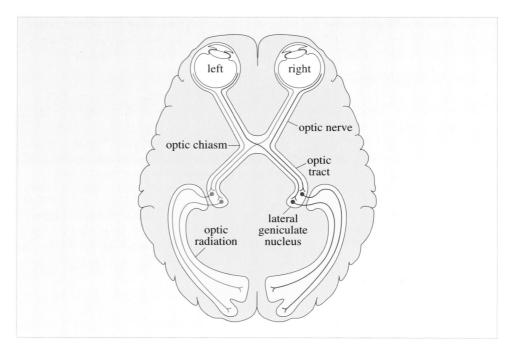

mixture of fibres from both optic nerves forms the **optic tract**, which carries all the output from both retinae relating to the contralateral visual field.

There is no synapse in the optic chiasm. Axons of retinal ganglion cells run the length of the optic nerve and optic tract and synapse with relay cells in the LGN. Axons of relay cells in the LGN form the **optic radiation,** which projects to the **primary visual cortex** (also called the **striate cortex**). Figure 2 illustrates how the visual field is mapped onto the human primary visual cortex. The fovea is mapped onto the most dorsal part of the medial surface of the occipital lobe, and the map is inverted so that the upper visual field is mapped onto the lower part of the cortex, and vice versa. The map is hugely distorted by a variation in scale between the

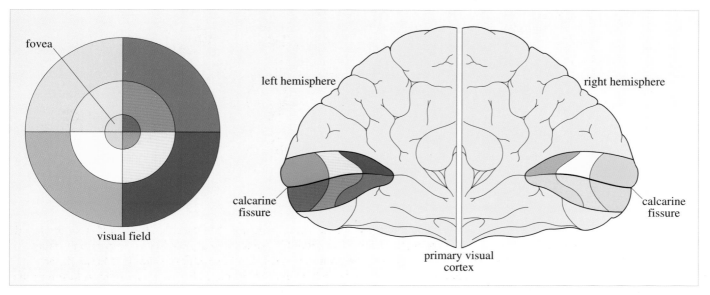

Figure 2   The map of the visual field on the human primary visual cortex. (Note that the brain is shown as having been sliced sagitally and opened out.)

fovea, where a tiny area of the visual field is mapped onto a huge expanse of cortex, and the periphery of the visual field, where a large area of visual field is mapped onto a small area of cortex. Most of the cortex is occupied by the central few degrees of the visual field.

The distortion in the map of the visual field on the striate cortex makes sense of the everyday fact that visual acuity falls rapidly with distance from the fovea. The fall in acuity reflects the fact that, in the peripheral visual field, less cortex is available to process image detail. It also explains the fact that the pattern of visual field loss following a lesion to the striate cortex very often spares the fovea; the foveal representation in the cortex is so large that it is rare for it to be completely destroyed by a lesion.

The organization of the visual pathway means that lesions at different levels produce distinctively different patterns of visual field defect. These are illustrated in Figure 3. The patterns of field loss can be useful in diagnosis: a tumour of the pituitary gland, which is located just behind the optic chiasm, may selectively damage the fibres that project across the midline, producing a pattern of laterally symmetrical monocular defects like that in position 2 in Figure 3b.

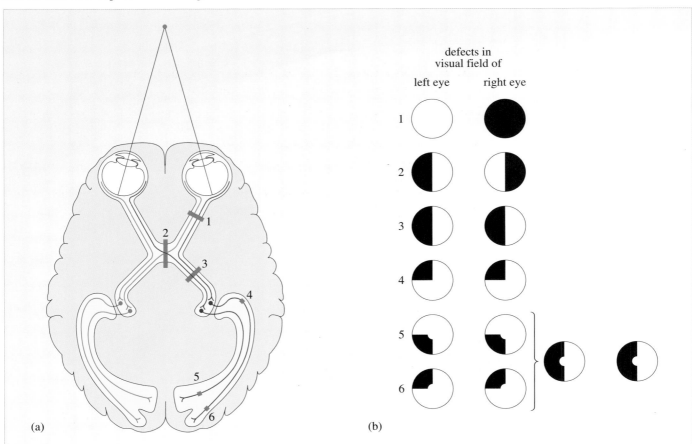

Figure 3 (a) Map of the positions of lesions at different points in the visual pathway. (b) Defects in the visual field produced by lesions at the different levels shown in (a). Cutting the right optic nerve (1) produces complete loss of vision in the right eye. Cutting the optic chiasm (2) produces a complete loss of the temporal visual field in each eye. The field losses do not overlap. Cutting the optic tract (3) causes a complete loss of vision in both eyes in the contralateral visual field. A lesion of the optic radiation fibres that pass through the temporal lobe (Meyer's loop) (4) produces a loss in both eyes of the upper visual field on the opposite side. A lesion of the upper bank of the calcarine sulcus (5) causes a loss of the lower visual field on the opposite side. A lesion of the lower bank (6) causes a loss of the upper visual field.

2.2 Segregation of information in the pathways from retina to visual cortex

The lateral geniculate nucleus is a multi-layered structure and contains several superimposed maps of the contralateral half of the visual field. The fact that within each layer there is an orderly map of the visual field indicates that signals from neighbouring parts of the visual field are being kept together for processing. Conversely, the fact that there are multiple layers, each with a separate map of the same region of visual space, indicates that information in different layers is being segregated so that it can be processed independently.

The logic by which signals are segregated between the layers of the LGN and even the anatomical details of the layering are not universally agreed among scientists. However there is agreement on a number of main points shown in Figure 4. Each layer is monocular and has a companion layer driven by the other eye. Four prominent dorsal layers contain small cells, known as parvocellular or P layers from the Latin *parvus* meaning small. The P layers relay signals that originate in midget ganglion cells. Two prominent ventral layers, known as magnocellular or M layers because they contain large cells, relay signals from parasol ganglion cells. The magnocellular and parvocellular layers of the LGN project to different sub-layers of the visual cortex. These details of the geniculo-cortical projection are shown in Figure 4.

Between the layers of the LGN illustrated in Figure 4 is another set of layers, known as the **intercalated (I)** or **koniocellular (K) layers**, which are much harder to identify. The I layers project patchily to layer 2 of the cortex. The patches coincide with the areas that are known as **blobs**, because they stain densely for the enzyme cytochrome oxidase.

Each layer of the LGN contains a map of the relevant part of the visual field. This means that there are up to 12 separate quasi-independent pathways through the nuclei, 6 for each eye. As the following paragraphs show, although a good deal is known about differences between the signals relayed through the three groups of layers (P, M and I), it is not yet clear whether the finer subdivisions of the P and I layers have any functional significance.

The general properties of the signals carried by magnocellular and parvocellular neurons are well established. Both types of neuron have receptive fields that are driven by antagonistic excitatory and inhibitory mechanisms. Stimuli make the neurons respond if they cause a temporary imbalance in which the excitatory mechanism dominates over the inhibitory mechanism.

Magnocellular neurons have centre-surround antagonism in their receptive fields. The receptive field consists of a small central region, the centre, within which light has an excitatory or inhibitory effect, depending on whether the cell is ON-centre or OFF-centre respectively (see Chapter 10, *The retina*), and a surrounding region in which the effect of light is opposite to its effect in the centre. When the receptive field is uniformly illuminated, the antagonistic effects of light on the centre and surround balance out. When there is an imbalance between the light levels in the centre and surround, as when the image of a bright object on a dark background fills the centre of an ON-centre receptive field or a high spatial-frequency grating moves across the receptive field, alternately increasing and decreasing its level of illumination, the cell generates a response.

Magnocellular receptive fields are generally not colour coded. Centre and surround are driven by the same classes of cone so changing the colour of the light has no effect on responses.

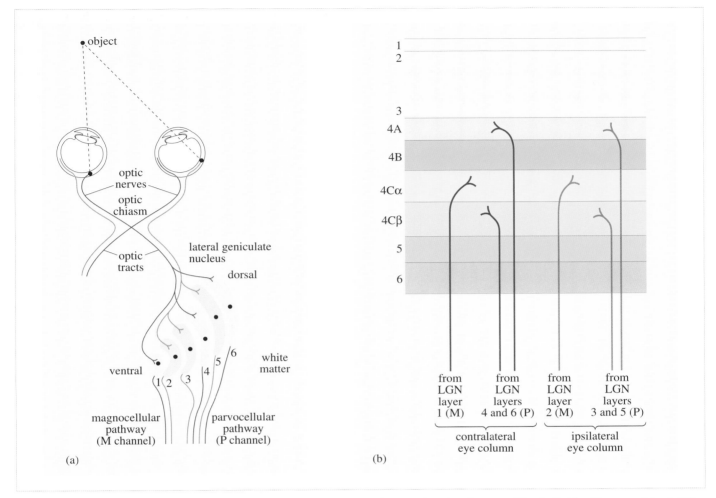

Figure 4   (a) M and P pathways through the lateral geniculate nucleus to the visual cortex. The individual layers of the LGN are coloured to indicate whether their input is from the contralateral (blue) or ipsilateral (green) eye. (b) LGN axons from different eyes and from different layers arrive in different sub-layers or in different zones of the cortex.

The properties of parvocellular neurons, illustrated in Figure 5 overleaf, are different from magnocellular neurons in that their receptive fields combine centre-surround antagonism with red–green opponent colour coding. The signals for the centre and the surround originate in different cone types (L and M). The fact that centre and surround of P cells are driven by different cone types has no effect on the responses of the cell to small stimuli or to high spatial-frequency gratings. These make the cell respond by causing different intensities of light to fall on centre and surround. However large stimuli reveal the cell's colour-coding properties: variations in colour between red and green make the cell respond because these colour changes produce a differential effect on the L and M cones.

Two of the I layers (those associated with the more ventral pair of P layers) relay signals from blue–yellow colour-opponent ganglion cells. These have receptive fields with no centre-surround antagonism. Cells respond as if they had received signals of one sign from S cones and of the opposite sign from a mix of L and M cones from throughout the receptive field. The cells respond to colour variations between blue and yellow because these cause maximal changes in the relative activities of S cones against L and M cones.

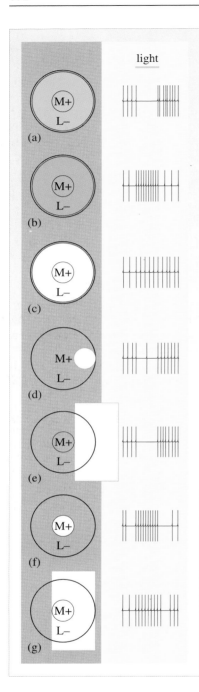

◄ **Figure 5** The properties of parvocellular neurons. (a) A large red stimulus causes a response in the L cones driving the inhibitory surround, resulting in a reduction in response. (b) A large green stimulus causes a response in the M cones driving the excitatory centre, resulting in an increase in response. (c) A large white stimulus excites both the L and M cones so that excitatory and inhibitory influences balance each other, resulting in no change in response. (d) A small white stimulus in the inhibitory surround causes a decrease in response. (e) A larger white stimulus in the inhibitory surround causes a greater decrease in response. (f) A small white stimulus in the excitatory centre causes an increase in response. (g) A large white stimulus covering the whole excitatory centre and part of the inhibitory surround causes a moderate increase in response; all the excitatory influence but only part of the inhibitory influence is recruited. A magnocellular neuron would show the same responses to stimuli (c) to (g) but, because both sub-regions of the receptive field are driven by the same class of cones, it would show no change in response to stimulus (a) or (b).

3 Signals in the lateral geniculate nucleus

3.1 What processing occurs in the lateral geniculate nucleus?

Analysis of the relationship between responses of LGN cells and those of their retinal inputs suggests that the processing that occurs in the nucleus does not involve any wholesale reorganization of retinal signals. In qualitative terms the receptive fields of LGN cells are the same as those of their retinal inputs. No new receptive field properties emerge. Simultaneous recordings from LGN neurons and their retinal inputs show that, in the cat at least, individual LGN cells are driven directly by one or a small number of retinal ganglion cells. What then is the point of having a synapse at this point in the pathway?

The projections to the LGN and its circuitry suggest that its function may be to allow signals from other structures to influence those from the retina, rather than to allow retinal signals to influence each other. Although individual geniculate neurons receive dominant input from a very small number of retinal ganglion cells (see Figure 6) the retinal inputs to the nucleus account for only a small proportion of the synapses on relay neurons – possibly as little as 10%. The most important input in terms of the numbers of synapses is probably from the visual cortex, which provides more than half the synapses in the nucleus. Other important sources of LGN synapses include midbrain visual structures such as the superior colliculus, and non-visual structures such as the **reticular formation**.

3.2 Modulatory influences in the lateral geniculate nucleus

Although retinal synapses are in the minority, Figure 6 shows that they are extremely effective in driving the responses of relay cells; three of the five retinal ganglion-cell action potentials cause an action potential in the LGN cell. Thus retinal ganglion cells drive LGN relay cells approximately one-to-one. Non-retinal inputs to the nucleus modulate the effectiveness with which the retina drives the output. Figure 7 shows a schematic diagram of the microcircuit by which retinal and non-retinal inputs are combined to determine the responses of the LGN cell. The input from the retina arrives at a synapse close to the cell body and is thus in an excellent position to drive the output of the cell. The inputs from the cortex and other structures act to change the effectiveness with which the retinal input drives the relay rather than to drive it directly.

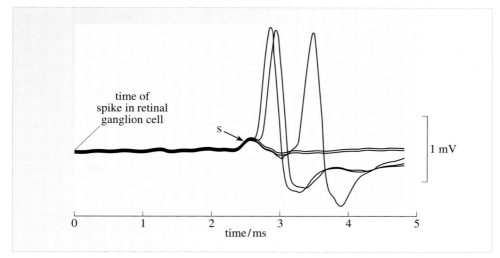

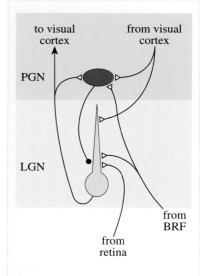

Figure 6 Results from an experiment in which recordings were made simultaneously from a retinal ganglion cell and a geniculate relay cell to which it was connected. The trace shows the signal recorded from the micro-electrode in the LGN, synchronized to the occurrence of a spike in the retinal ganglion cell. Every LGN trace shows a small upward deflection that is tightly time-locked to the retinal spike and occurs about 2.5 ms after it. This is the 's' potential, which is believed to be the excitatory post-synaptic potential triggered by the retinal ganglion cell's synapse on the LGN cell. Of the five LGN traces, three also show action potentials.

One of the challenges of visual neuroscience is to understand how and why the cortical feedback modulates the responsiveness of the LGN. Under some circumstances cortical feedback suppresses LGN responsiveness and under others it appears to enhance it. Understanding the rules that determine whether the feedback is excitatory or inhibitory would, in principle, enable us to understand the function of the nucleus.

Figure 7 Diagram of the microcircuit by which cortical and other inputs to the LGN affect the transmission of signals from retinal ganglion cells to LGN cells. Inputs from the retina synapse on the relay cell close to the cell body. Inputs from the cortex and the brainstem reticular formation (BRF) modulate the cell either directly through more distal synapses, or indirectly through interneurons in the LGN or in the perigeniculate nucleus (PGN).

4 Receptive fields of striate cortical neurons

Unlike the LGN, the cortex radically transforms the signals it receives. The transformation is such that cortical cells explicitly represent several stimulus parameters that are not represented by individual LGN cells. These include the orientation, the breadth and the length of contrast features, and their direction of motion.

4.1 Circuitry in the striate cortex

Figure 8 (overleaf) shows the morphology of the main types of neuron in the striate cortex, and a schematic diagram of the cortical circuit. There are rich interconnections between different inputs to the cortex that make it possible for the cortex not only to generate new forms of selectivity, such as orientation selectivity, but also for neurons to generalize across some stimulus parameters while responding selectively to others. The clearest example of this comes from a comparison of the two most commonly encountered receptive field types: **simple cells** and **complex cells**.

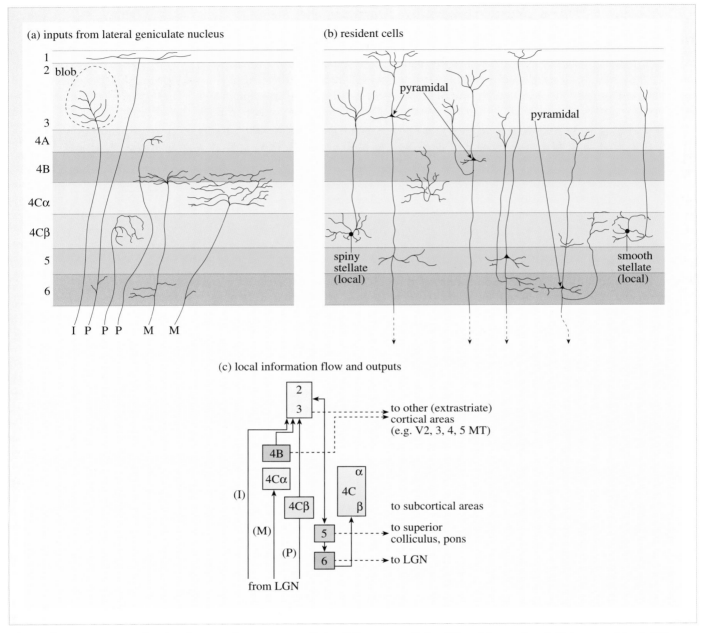

Figure 8 (a) Inputs to the visual cortex from magnocellular (M), parvocellular (P) and intercalated (I) layers of the LGN terminate in different cortical regions. (b) Resident interneurons and output neurons. Spiny stellate cells and pyramidal cells are excitatory; smooth stellate cells are inhibitory. Pyramidal cells project out of the cortex: those in layers 2, 3 and 4B project to higher cortical areas, those in layer 5 project to the midbrain, those in layer 6 project to the LGN. (c) Diagram of the information flow through the visual cortex.

4.2 Receptive fields in the cortex: orientation selectivity

Simple cells

Like most cells in the lateral geniculate nucleus and the retina, the receptive fields of simple cells consist of separate sub-regions within which light has opposite effects on the activity of the cell – excitatory or inhibitory. Figure 9 shows some examples. It immediately reveals an obvious difference between cortex and earlier stages of the visual pathway. The excitatory and inhibitory zones of the cortical receptive field are elongated instead of being circular. They are arranged either as a central zone of one type flanked by two zones of the opposite type (Figure 9a, b and c), or as two abutting zones of opposite type (Figure 9d).

The receptive field map of a simple cell allows us to predict the optimal stimulus, one that would illuminate the parts of the receptive field where the effect of light is excitatory and leave in darkness the parts where it is inhibitory. For the receptive field illustrated in Figure 9d the predicted optimal stimulus would be an elongated edge; for the receptive fields illustrated in Figure 9a, b and c it would be a dark or bright line of appropriate width. The defining property of the simple cell is that this prediction works; the receptive field map allows an accurate prediction of the shape and location of the optimal stimulus.

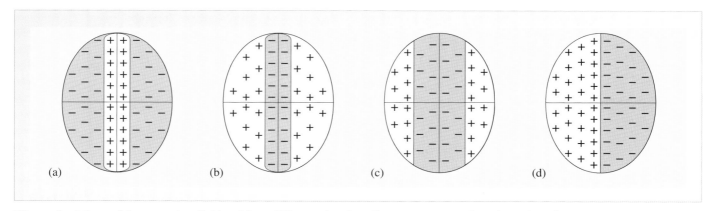

Figure 9 Maps of the receptive fields of four different simple cells: + represents a location where light has an excitatory effect; – represents a location where it is inhibitory.

For all the cells shown in Figure 9, the long axis of the optimal stimulus is vertical. As Figure 10 (overleaf) shows, cells tend to be very selective for their optimal orientation; changing the orientation of the stimulus, even by only a few degrees, reduces its effectiveness in driving the cell. This means that in order to signal edges and lines of all possible orientations the cortex must contain a range of cells selective for all orientations. This is in fact the case; a microelectrode moved through the cortex encounters cells tuned to different orientations, although cells tuned to the same orientation tend to be grouped together. Thus orientation preference is a property that is mapped onto the cortex in an orderly way.

Figure 11 (overleaf) shows a hypothetical wiring scheme for connecting geniculate inputs to a cortical cell in a configuration that makes the cortical cell selective for a bar of vertical orientation. Clearly the same geniculate cells must be connected in different configurations to cortical cells selective for other stimulus patterns, sizes and orientations in the same region of the retina.

Figure 10   Responses of a simple cell to (a) a bar of different orientations, and (b) a small spot in different positions and a large spot. The response is shown as a train of action potentials to the right of each stimulus. The best response to the bar is obtained when it is vertical (av). A small spot elicits a response at stimulus onset when it is presented in the excitatory zone or ON area and at stimulus offset when it is presented in the inhibitory zone or OFF area. The large spot elicits no response (biii).

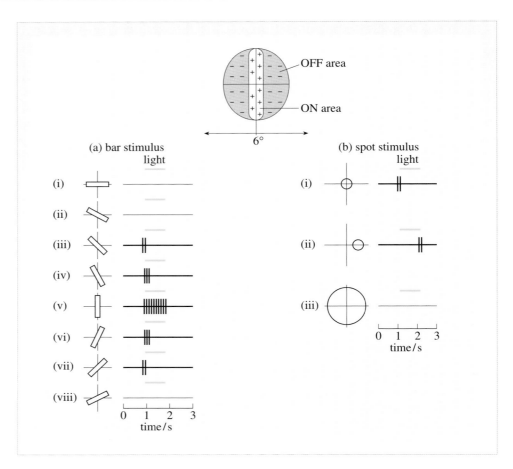

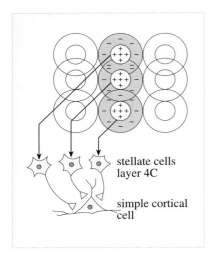

Figure 11   Hypothetical connection scheme from LGN cells through stellate cells to a cortical pyramidal cell that has a bright vertical bar as its optimal stimulus.

Complex cells

Complex cells respond well to the same types of stimuli that are optimal for simple cells although they tend to have much larger receptive fields. However the most striking difference between the two cell types is that in general it is not possible to map the receptive field of a complex cell with simple stimuli in a way that makes it possible to predict the optimal stimulus. Either a map cannot be obtained because the cell does not respond, or it gives the same pattern of responses throughout the receptive field, making the map uninformative.

Like simple cells, the orientation, polarity and type of stimulus are crucial in determining whether a complex cell responds; a given complex cell, for example, might respond only to vertical edges that are light on the left and dark on the right. However, unlike simple cells, the position of the stimulus within the receptive field is much less crucial: the cell responds well to an appropriate stimulus in a range of positions within the receptive field. It shares the simple-cell's selectivity for the kind of stimulus, but it generalizes its response across a range of positions. Hubel and Wiesel, in their seminal work which began in the 1960s, hypothesized that the complex cell might be driven by a group of simple cells all of which are tuned to the same optimal stimulus in slightly different positions. Each simple cell signals the presence of the stimulus and its precise position. The complex cell signals the presence of the stimulus but not its precise position. Figure 12 illustrates how connections between simple and complex cells could implement Hubel and Wiesel's proposed model.

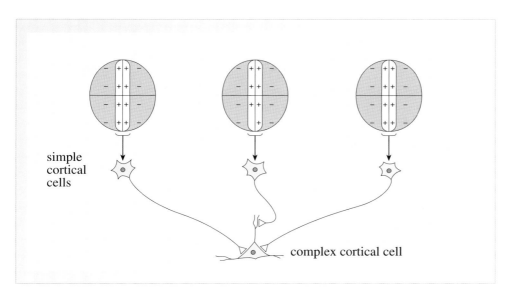

Figure 12 The hypothetical connection scheme from simple cells to complex cells. The receptive fields of the three cells in the lateral geniculate nucleus respond preferentially to a vertical bar in their receptive field, but the complex cell will respond if any one of the three LGN cells is active.

Many cortical cells are also selective for the length of a visual stimulus, for its direction of motion, its colour and for its relative position in the two eyes, although these selectivities are more variable than selectivity for orientation.

Selectivity for length and curvature

Early descriptions of the visual cortex identified a distinct class of cell called the **hypercomplex cell**, which has the additional requirement to those of a simple or complex cell that the stimulus not be longer than a certain length. Figure 13 shows an example of a paired recording in which one of the cells is a hypercomplex cell. The hypercomplex cell completely fails to respond to a long stimulus that extends into inhibitory regions at each end of its receptive field although it responds vigorously to a short one.

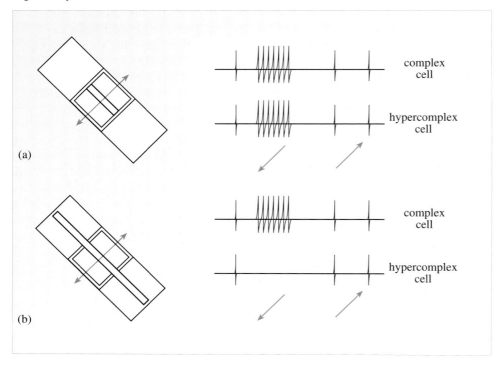

Figure 13 Responses of a hypercomplex cell and a complex cell recorded simultaneously with superimposed receptive fields. The hypercomplex cell only responds to the short bar (a), not to the long bar (b). Both cells also exhibit direction selectivity (see overleaf).

Although the simplest description of the hypercomplex cell is that it is selective for stimulus length, a different view is possible. The inhibitory end zones of its receptive field are selective for orientation. This means that a long curved stimulus might not elicit the inhibition that a long straight stimulus does, and so might drive the cell as effectively as a stimulus of optimal length.

In early descriptions of the striate cortex, which relied extensively on subjective evaluations of responses to hand-held stimuli, hypercomplex cells were described as a rare and distinct class of cell. However more recently, quantitative measurements have revealed that a substantial proportion of cortical cells are length-tuned to some degree. However it should be pointed out that weak length tuning is a property that cortical cells might well inherit from their geniculate inputs.

Direction selectivity

Both the cells shown in Figure 13 respond only to one direction of stimulus motion. Direction selectivity is another type of stimulus selectivity generated by cortical processing. About 20% of cells in monkey striate cortex are direction-selective. Chapter 16, *Motion perception*, discusses some possible mechanisms for producing direction selectivity.

Spatial frequency selectivity

Although receptive field maps can give an indication of the nature of the optimal stimulus of a simple cell, they do not allow us to quantify the selectivity in any direct way and in the case of complex cells they give no useful information. However, if sinusoidal gratings are used as stimuli, selectivity can be measured directly as the range of spatial frequencies and orientations to which the cell responds. This gives a very clear picture of what has been achieved by cortical processing. Parvocellular neurons in the LGN constitute a single channel for the whole range of spatial information. Individual neurons respond to the whole range of spatial frequencies and orientations. Each cortical cell on the other hand responds to a narrow range of orientations and spatial frequencies. The optimal stimuli of cortical cells – oriented edges and lines of particular sizes – are elements from which one could construct a recognizable picture of a visual scene. Thus if we take the activity of a cortical cell as a signal that its optimal stimulus is present we could reconstruct a recognizable representation of a visual scene from the signals carried by the very small percentage of active cells in primary visual cortex.

4.3 The fine grain of the cortical map: organization of selectivities into hypercolumns and pinwheels

In examining the cortical map of the visual field at fine scale, it becomes clear that, at this scale, the representation of the visual field gives way to a representation of stimulus preferences such as orientation, and eye of origin. The full range of stimulus preferences is represented within a unit of cortical surface about 1 mm across. Each sub-unit, often known as a **hypercolumn**, contains a more-or-less orderly grouping of neurons according to selectivity for eye of input and orientation. Hubel and Wiesel deduced this basic principle of cortical organization from micro-electrode and anatomical tracer studies. Subsequent work using functional imaging and refined anatomical techniques has added the suggestion that within the hypercolumn there is also a grouping of neurons by spatial frequency preference and colour preference.

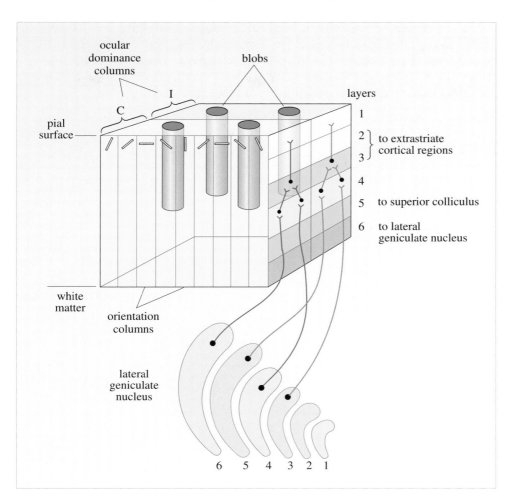

Figure 14 Distribution of orientation selectivity and eye dominance within a block of cortex about 1 mm square. (Contralateral (C) input to LGN is coloured blue, ipsilateral (I) green. The pial surface is the surface of the brain, pia mater.)

5 Modulation of signals in the visual cortex

Primary visual cortex contains extensive lateral connections and receives substantial feedback from the higher cortical areas to which it projects. Like the cortical feedback projections to the LGN, the functions of the feedback projections are not known. However it is known that activity in the visual cortex can be influenced by visual imagery, by memory tasks and by attention. This suggests that the signals about different features of the image that are provided by simple, complex and hypercomplex cortical neurons are also influenced by these higher cognitive processes. Although speculative, it is clearly tempting to suppose that such feedback might provide one neural link between bottom-up and top-down processes.

6 Summary

The retina projects via the LGN to the visual cortex. Both the LGN and visual cortex are organized into multiple retinotopic maps in which cells with similar properties are grouped together into distinct anatomical structures. LGN cells have similar properties to retinal cells; they are monocularly driven and have circular receptive fields. Cells in the visual cortex have different properties; they typically have elongated receptive fields, may be binocularly driven, and may respond better to a particular direction of stimulus motion. Individual cortical cells are consequently more selective than retinal or LGN cells. Whereas an individual retinal cell might respond to a wide range of edges, an individual cortical cell might respond only if the edge has the right orientation, size, and motion direction.

Functional imaging of the human visual system

Krish Singh

13

1 Introduction

The visual world is the richest and most complex of all our sensory environments. In our normal everyday lives we process a huge amount of visual information, every fraction of a second. We are exquisitely sensitive to brightness, contrast, colour, form, depth and visual motion, and we are able to use of all these **low-level visual attributes** in order to perform extremely complicated tasks such as face and object recognition. It is therefore not surprising that a large proportion of the brain (approximately 20% in humans) is devoted to the processing of visual information, and since the 1970s, scientists have used increasingly sophisticated tools to study the working of human visual cortex.

Initially, scientists used indirect methods, such as post-mortem studies of the structure of the brain, invasive animal experiments, experiments during neurosurgery and studies of what happens to perception and cognition when people suffer brain damage from tumours, strokes and other trauma. Since the 1970s, researchers have been able to use **structural** and **functional imaging techniques** in order to see what the living human brain looks like, and what functions are carried out in specific parts of the brain; these tools have in some ways contributed to the great success in studying the visual cortex.

This chapter looks at the development of different methods of imaging the human visual system.

2 Anatomical studies

It has been known since the time of the Ancient Greeks that the brain is divided into several anatomical regions, with the most obvious division being the separation of the brain into two hemispheres. Less obviously, the brain can also be divided into sub-regions or lobes: the temporal lobe, the frontal lobe, the parietal lobe and the occipital lobe. Each lobe is generally thought of as carrying out a specific class of function. For example, the **frontal lobe** is considered to be the seat of **higher-level cognitive functions** such as language and reasoning. These divisions are ill defined and controversial, however, except in the case of the **occipital lobe** which is clearly specialized for visual function.

At the end of the nineteenth century, scientists performed detailed anatomical studies of post-mortem brains. Using microscopy, and the application of dyes that selectively stain different types of neurons, one of these scientists, Brodmann, was able to show that the brain was divided into many different areas (**Brodmann's areas**, Figure 1 overleaf). For example, in a region of the brain in the occipital lobe (Brodmann's area 17), the cells are oriented in stripes and columns, leading to this area being termed the striate cortex. At a certain point in the brain, this striped organization ends abruptly, and this change defines a boundary between one area and the next. This type of study of the distribution of cell types and organization is know as the study of **cytoarchitectonics**, and Brodmann and later workers identified over 200 different cortical areas, many of which are in the occipital, or visual, cortex.

Figure 1 Diagram showing the Brodmann areas of the brain. Areas 17, 18 and 19 are within the occipital lobe.

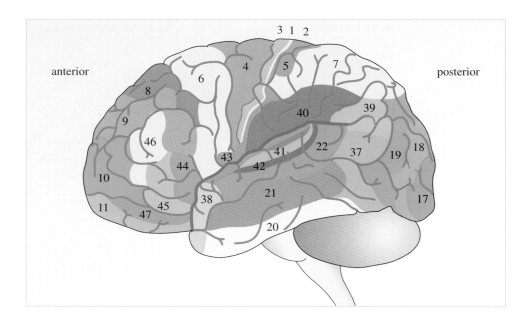

Note that Brodmann himself only identified three different areas within the occipital lobe: 17, 18 and 19. We now know this to be much too simplistic a picture of the complexity of the visual cortex.

3 Retinotopic organization

In humans, stroke or injury to the back of the head can often result in partial blindness or other visual problems. This is indirect evidence that the rear part of the brain, the occipital lobe, is specialized for the processing of visual information. After the end of the First World War, Holmes and others studied visual processing in patients who had suffered gunshot and other traumas to the occipital lobe of the brain. The range of defects observed clearly indicated that certain regions of visual cortex represented certain portions of the visual field. This is known as a **visuotopic** or **retinotopic representation**.

In the 1950s, Penfield carried out a series of groundbreaking experiments during neurosurgery to treat intractable epilepsy. Penfield woke his patients during the surgery (the brain itself feels no pain as it has no pain receptors, and the scalp was anaesthetized using a local anaesthetic) and stimulated the exposed surface of the brain using small electrodes. Penfield found that stimulating a specific part of the brain generated a very specific response by the patient. For example, stimulating one part of the brain might elicit speech or interfere with the patient's ability to comprehend language. Stimulating another part of the brain's surface might produce movement of the fingers. Penfield and co-workers also electrically stimulated various portions of the occipital lobe, and noted that patients reported the perception of flashing points of light (known as phosphenes). They also noted that stimulating a particular portion of cortex always generated a phosphene in the same visual field location. This again indicated that the brain contained a retinotopic map of the visual field.

Invasive studies in animals also confirmed that the mammalian visual system is **retinotopically organized**. This means that a specific point in the external visual world is mapped directly to a specific group of neurons in the brain, and that an adjacent point in visual space is mapped to an adjacent group of neurons. This remarkable fact tells us that there is a complete neuronal map of the external visual field within the visual cortex.

4 The visual areas of the brain

When scientists study animals with brains similar to ours, such as cats or macaque monkeys, the functional specialization of the visual system can be revealed in fine detail. Hubel and Wiesel, who were awarded the Nobel Prize in 1981 for their work, pioneered this type of study. Using recording electrodes implanted in the brains of monkeys, scientists have discovered that groups of neurons within the occipital lobe respond directly to visual stimulation within a specific part of the visual field – known as the receptive field of the neuron.

It was also found that certain types of neuron were preferentially sensitive to specific types of visual stimulus. For example, some neurons only fire if a bar of a particular orientation is placed within its receptive field. Other neurons only fire if a visual stimulus is moving in a particular direction, with a particular speed. The spatial distribution of these different types of neuron is not uniform, and this led to the discovery that the visual system is modular in nature, with different regions of the occipital lobe performing different visual functions, such as the analysis of visual motion or the processing of colour information. In monkeys, such as the owl and macaque, approximately 30 different visual regions have been discovered within a complex system with many interconnections.

The 'modules' within the visual system are known as visual areas and are named V1, V2, V3, etc. V1 is the first visual area in the brain, as it receives its neural input directly from the retina, via the optic chiasm and the lateral geniculate nucleus. Figure 2 (overleaf), constructed from data collected by Felleman and Van Essen in 1991, shows our current understanding of the visual areas, and their various interconnections, in the macaque monkey.

Animal studies also confirmed the presence of a retinotopic organization within the visual cortex. In fact multiple retinotopic maps were found, as some of the visual areas (such as V1, V2, etc.) have their own copy of the map.

In the owl monkey, a region of the brain in the middle temporal (MT) area was shown to contain neurons that only responded to moving visual stimuli. The implication was that the MT is functionally specialized for motion processing, and once it had been identified in several different monkeys, including the macaque, by workers such as Zeki and others in 1980, the question was: does a version of MT exist in humans?

In 1983, Zihl and his co-workers reported on a study carried out on a patient known as LM. LM had suffered a stroke that selectively damaged an area of the brain close to where the temporal, occipital and parietal lobes meet. Unusually, this damage occurred on both sides of the brain. Remarkably, although the patient had essentially normal cognitive function and most of her visual perception was normal, she had great difficulty perceiving moving objects. This motion-blindness or **akinetopsia** in a patient with localized damage was deeply suggestive of a localized motion perception region in humans. In neuroscience terminology this was the human homologue of the monkey area MT. In fact this motion area is in the middle temporal region of the brain in the owl monkey but not in humans. This has led many authors, including Zeki, to name the motion sensitive area V5. From here on it will be called V5/MT.

Figure 2 This figure shows all the currently known areas within the macaque monkey visual pathway. The boxes represent the areas, and the lines represent the known neural connections between all the visual areas. Note that boxes within the lower part of the diagram are true visual areas within the monkey retina, lateral geniculate nucleus and occipital lobe. Cortical regions at the top of the diagram are in other parts of the brain such as the temporal and parietal lobes. (The labels in the boxes refer to specific areas in the brain, which are not described here.)

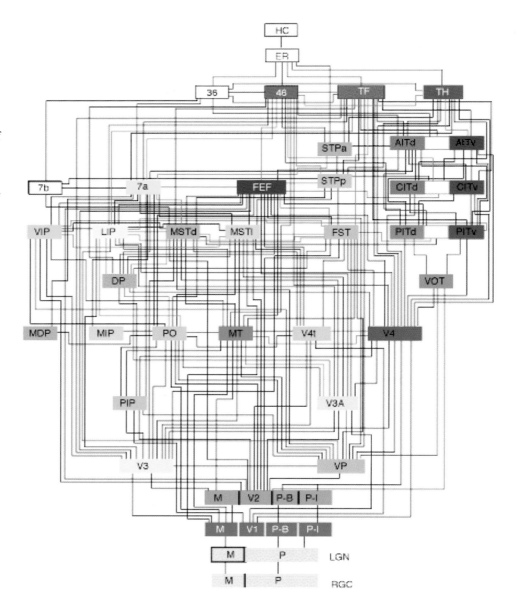

5 The need for a new tool

The above story of the discovery of a possible human V5/MT is a good example of how decades of work in several areas of neuroscience can lead us to a theory of how at least one part of the human brain might work. It also gives us an inkling of the complexity of the problem. To get to this point, we had to bring together evidence from the microscopic properties of individual neurons, i.e. the fact that certain neurons in a specific part of monkey cortex fired when a moving object was seen, and the reported behaviour of an entire human being (the patient LM).

In the case of the visual system, we know about the neuronal properties of cells in great detail (albeit in monkeys). We also know a lot about the ability of humans to detect different types of visual stimulus, the study of which is known as **visual psychophysics**. What visual neuroscience researchers needed was a tool that enabled them to identify the visual areas, non-invasively, in humans and then to investigate what function each of these visual areas was carrying out. Such a tool would bridge the gap between the microscopic level of neuronal function, and the amazing visual performance of humans. Such tools now exist, and are known as functional imaging techniques. In the study of human visual function, the two predominant techniques are positron emission tomography (PET) and functional magnetic resonance imaging (fMRI).

6 Positron emission tomography (PET)

In PET, a radioactive isotope of, for example, oxygen is inhaled or injected. Regions of the brain that are working hard will need more oxygen, and so will receive more of the radioactive tracer. A ring of detectors outside the head can be used to assess the amount of radioactive emission in each part of the brain. PET was the first true functional imaging technique, and has been used in several studies of the visual system. In 1985, Fox and co-workers used a flashing visual stimulus, and showed that the optimum frequency of stimulation in V1 appeared to be at approximately 8–10 Hz. This is one of the first examples of a *parametric* study of brain function, in which, rather than simply localizing brain function, researchers looked at how the amplitude of the activation varied as a function of the stimulus parameters.

Some seminal PET papers have described the first identification of the human visual areas in normal subjects. In 1989, Lueck and co-workers used PET to show that there was an area of the brain which was stimulated by visual stimuli containing colour. This appeared to be the human homologue of area V4 found by Zeki and others in monkeys. In 1991, Watson and co-workers (including Zeki) used PET to show the position of a visual area sensitive to visual motion. This area was close to the junction of the parietal, occipital and temporal lobes, and was consistent with the area of damage in Zihl's patient, LM, described above. The authors were therefore able to claim that they had identified the human homologue of V5/MT. The role of V4 in colour processing is still controversial, but the identification of the motion centre, V5/MT, has been replicated in many studies using both PET and fMRI.

There are several problems with PET that mean that it is not the best choice for imaging the visual cortex. However, the main problem is that the signal-to-noise ratio is rather low, which means that the experiments have to be performed on several different people (the same person cannot be scanned more than once because of radiation dosage regulations) and the results averaged to form a 'group' functional image. This is problematical for studies of visual function because we know that there is a large amount of variability in the size and position of the visual areas between people. For example, post-mortem anatomical studies by Andrews and co-workers have shown that the size of V1 can vary by a factor of 2 between individuals. This means that when we average our functional images, we may be 'mixing' the contribution from different visual areas. Ideally, we would like a functional imaging technique that has a better spatial resolution than PET and is sensitive enough to be able to measure brain function in a single subject. Such a technique is functional magnetic resonance imaging (fMRI).

7 Functional magnetic resonance imaging (fMRI) of the human visual cortex

Magnetic resonance imaging technology utilizes strong magnetic fields in order to give an image of the distribution of hydrogen nuclei within the body. As well as giving an image of tissue density, the MR image also contains information about the type of material in which the hydrogen nuclei are embedded, and can therefore be used to differentiate between different types of tissue, such as the grey and white matter of the brain.

Although the technique was initially developed to give anatomical images of the brain, it was soon realized that the magnetic properties of **deoxygenated haemoglobin** could be used to generate an MR image that was sensitive to local cortical metabolism and hence cortical function. In 1989, Kwong and co-workers were the first to show a measurable fMRI response in human visual cortex. By 2001, a computerized literature search would show at least 1500 papers reporting fMRI studies of vision. These papers report studies of many aspects of vision, including the low-level processing of simple visual stimuli, and the representation of complex visual objects such as faces.

Many of the initial studies were carried out by researchers repeating the experiments using PET to confirm the location of visual areas such as V5/MT. In 1995, Tootell and co-workers localized V5/MT and investigated many of its properties using fMRI. They were able to demonstrate that if one varied the contrast of a moving visual pattern, the magnitude of the fMRI response varied in a characteristic way. Specifically, the response saturated at a very low contrast, i.e. V5/MT appears to 'switch on' to its maximum value at a low contrast. This fits well with what is known about the properties of neurons in macaque V5. There is now much evidence to show that the fMRI signal, at least in the visual system, is quite tightly linked to the underlying neural activity. In a recent study (2000), Rees and co-workers showed that as the amount of coherent motion in a visual stimulus changes, the fMRI response in V5 increases in the precise way that one would predict from the behaviour of neurons, as described in the literature on monkey studies.

fMRI has been most successful in its ability to identify the boundaries between the retinotopic visual areas V1, V2, V3, V3A, etc. The experimental design and computer software techniques needed for this were developed in the early and mid-1990s by Engel, Wandell, Teo, Fischl, Sereno, Dale, Tootell and other researchers, and have provided vision scientists with a remarkably powerful tool. Collectively these techniques are known as retinotopic mapping.

8 Retinotopic mapping: determining the boundaries of the visual areas

Retinotopic mapping involves sequentially stimulating parts of the visual field. Consider the visual stimulus shown in Figure 3, which is a wedge with a checkerboard pattern. The checkerboard is made to reverse (black to white, white to black) at a frequency of 8 Hz, which is known to be a strong stimulator of the visual cortex. At all times the subject concentrates his or her gaze on the central fixation dot. All the neurons in the brain that are linked retinotopically to the position of the flickering wedge stimulus will be activated by the stimulus. Those cells that represent other parts of the visual field will not be stimulated. After three seconds,

Figure 3 A checkerboard 'wedge' used as a stimulus in retinotopic mapping experiments.

the wedge rotates to a new position and a new group of cells is stimulated. Throughout the whole fMRI experiment the wedge stimulus rotates slowly round the visual field at approximately 1 revolution per minute (rpm). Groups of cells are switched on and then off in a cyclical fashion. At each point in the visual cortex, the fMRI response will increase and decrease with a frequency of about 1 rpm, but different parts of the brain will reach maximum intensity at different parts of the cycle. This *phase* information tells us which part of the external visual world is connected to each part of the brain, and we can then colour-code the occipital lobe of the brain accordingly. Figure 4 shows an example. Areas of the brain that are coloured blue are activated when the wedge stimulus is flickering in the upper midline, i.e. directly above the fixation spot. Those parts of the brain that are coloured green are stimulated when the wedge is on the lower midline i.e. when the wedge is flickering directly below the fixation spot. Red and orange represent parts of the brain that are stimulated when the visual stimulus is on the horizontal line.

It was soon realized that these retinotopic maps were extremely difficult to interpret when viewed on a 3D image of the brain. The brain is made up of white matter (which can be thought of as the 'wiring' of the brain) covered with a thin layer of grey matter, known as the cortex. In the visual system it is the grey matter cortex that processes the visual information. The grey matter is essentially a large two-dimensional structure that is folded in a highly convoluted way so that it fits inside the skull. Using computer software techniques, the grey matter can be detached from the white matter and flattened out – as if it were gently squashed. When retinotopic mapping data are superimposed on a flattened representation of the occipital lobe, it becomes much easier to interpret. Figure 5 shows such a **retinotopic flatmap** of a subject's left occipital lobe. Stripes of colour are clearly visible, which show where particular parts of the visual field are represented on the brain. The stripes also represent the boundaries between the visual areas. For example, the blue stripe towards the bottom right of the flatmap delineates the border between V1 and V2.

Once the boundaries have been identified on the flatmap, they can be visualized in three dimensions on the original MR image. An example of this for a single subject is shown in Figure 6.

Retinotopic mapping and flatmap techniques are extremely important for the functional imaging of vision in that they allow most of the visual areas in any one individual to be identified using fMRI. This only has to be done once, and neuroscientists then have a functional map of that subject's visual system. The subject can then be studied in many different experiments at later dates, and for

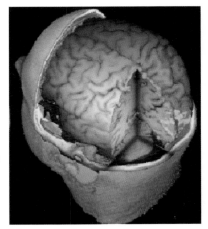

Figure 4 Retinotopic data superimposed on a 3D MR image. Those areas of the brain that respond to stimuli on the upper vertical midline, i.e. directly above the fixation spot, are colour-coded blue (see for example the small patch in the middle of the larger red area); those which respond to the lower vertical midline are coloured green. Red and orange represent parts of the brain that are stimulated when the visual stimulus is on the horizontal line.

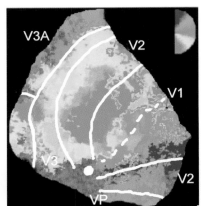

Figure 5 Retinotopic mapping data shown superimposed on a flattened representation of the subject's left visual cortex. The key at the top right shows how the colours represent different parts of the visual field.

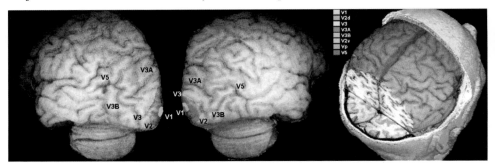

Figure 6 The boundaries between some of the visual areas, identified using retinotopic mapping techniques, in a single human subject. The left and middle panels depict the boundaries of the visual areas on the external or lateral aspect of the brain. The panel on the right shows the boundaries revealed by cutting into the occipital lobe.

each experiment, the researcher will be able to say how much activity is present in each of the different visual areas. This allows a direct comparison with animal studies that detail the response properties of neurons in many different visual areas.

It is these *parametric studies* of visual function that are the most exciting applications of fMRI. Rather than just using functional imaging to try to identify the position of a cortical area, neuroscientists are now investigating the precise properties of these areas. The results of these investigations can then be compared with both studies of the properties of neurons, and the visual performance of human subjects.

9 fMRI of complex visual perception and interactions

More recently, scientists have begun to use functional imaging techniques to investigate more complex visual functions, and to investigate how the visual cortex interacts with other areas of the brain such as the sensory-motor and auditory cortex.

One important research area is that of attention. Functional imaging researchers have found that the amount of activity in a specific part of the visual cortex, say in V1, depends on whether the person is attending to the part of the visual field that is retinotopically mapped to that part of the cortex. This is a surprising finding, as V1 is conventionally thought of as a low-level visual area that receives direct input from the retina, via the lateral geniculate nucleus. These findings suggest that there are feedback connections from other parts of the brain (in this case the visual attention system) that are used to directly modulate the activity in V1. The same is true of other visual areas. The motion area V5/MT was originally considered to be a low-level motion perception area, but there are many studies showing that the activity in V5/MT is affected by higher-level functions. For example, the perception of complex moving objects, such as walking human figures, increases the amount of activity in certain regions of V5/MT. Recent (2000) fMRI studies by Senior and colleagues have shown that if subjects are shown photographs that imply motion – such as a photograph of a falling cup – then V5/MT is strongly activated. This is a surprising finding as there is no visual motion present in these stimuli and so one would not expect the motion-sensitive neurons in V5/MT to be activated. The fact that they are is a strong indication that there are feedback connections to V5/MT from higher, more cognitive, areas of the brain.

10 Summary

The brain is a highly complex system and understanding how it performs even the simplest of visual tasks is highly challenging. In order to make significant progress, visual neuroscience researchers must utilize a wide range of techniques. At the microscopic level, these include single-cell studies of how individual neurons respond when a specific visual stimulus is placed in the visual field of an animal. At the other end of the scale, visual psychophysicists measure in exquisite detail our ability to detect and interact with our visual environment. Since the 1970s, functional imaging studies have allowed researchers to measure activation within the modular visual areas non-invasively, and thus bridge the gap between single cell studies and psychophysical performance. Using retinotopic mapping techniques, researchers can 'label' the visual areas in each subject. Once this map has been generated, experiments can be performed to determine how the activity in each visual area varies when that subject views a particular stimulus or performs a specific task. As well as studies of low-level visual function, such as simple motion and colour perception, functional imaging studies have revealed areas of visual cortex that perform more complex tasks such as object and face recognition. Finally, functional imaging techniques are starting to reveal how visual cortex interacts with other cortical systems such as the auditory, sensory-motor and attention mechanisms.

Spatial vision

Tim Meese

14

1 Introduction

To the layperson, vision is all about 'seeing' – we open our eyes and, effortlessly, we see the world 'out there'. We can recognize objects and people, we can interact with them in sensible and useful ways and we can successfully navigate our way about the environment. Of course, the only information that we are really able to act upon is that which is encoded as neural activity by our nervous system. These visual codes, the essence of all of our perceptions, are constructed from information arriving from each of two directions. Image data arrive **bottom-up** from our sensory apparatus and knowledge-based rules and inferences arrive **top-down** from memory. This chapter focuses primarily on one aspect of the bottom-up process, sometimes called early vision: the processing and encoding of spatial information in the two-dimensional retinal image.

2 From retinal image to neural image

The job of early vision is to encode the retinal image ready for subsequent processing stages where more complex tasks such as object recognition are performed. Clearly, to be able to recognize an object it is important to be able to segment it from its background. As objects usually reflect different amounts of light from their background the identification of luminance boundaries in the retinal image might be a useful starting point. The initial stage of this process is performed very early in the visual pathway, by retinal ganglion cells (see Chapter 10, *The retina*).

Central to understanding this aspect of retinal processing is the concept of a cell's receptive field. This is the region on the retina that, when stimulated, can produce a change in the retinal cell's response. Not surprisingly, neighbouring retinal ganglion cells have neighbouring, though slightly overlapping, receptive fields. Importantly, the receptive fields of retinal ganglion cells have distinct ON and OFF regions like those shown in Figure 1. When light falls onto an ON region the response of the cell increases and when it falls onto an OFF region it decreases. This means that a cell with an ON-centre receptive field would respond most strongly to a bright spot on a dark background and a cell with an OFF-centre receptive field would respond most strongly to a dark spot on a bright background.

However, the construction of these receptive fields means that they respond to other stimuli, particularly luminance boundaries, in interesting and useful ways. Figure 2a (overleaf) is an image of a white square on a black background, and Figure 2b illustrates the set of responses of many ON-centre retinal ganglion cells whose receptive fields cover the image. In this figure, white represents a strong response, black represents no response and other grey levels represent intermediate responses. This representation of neural responses provides a convenient way of thinking about the two-dimensional distribution of responses of visual neurons and it is easy to see why it is sometimes called a neural image.

An interesting feature of the neural image in Figure 2b is that most regions of the image are mid-grey. This response level is the same as each cell's spontaneous discharge (i.e. that produced in the absence of any stimulation), implying that the

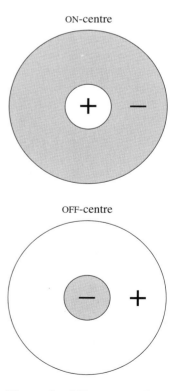

Figure 1 ON-centre and OFF-centre receptive fields of retinal ganglion cells.

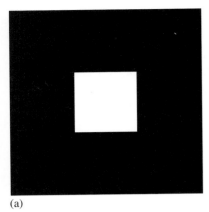

(a)

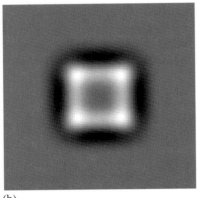

(b)

Figure 2 A stimulus and a neural image. (a) An image of a white square on a black background. (b) The response to the retinal image is sometimes called a neural image and is shown for ON-centre retinal ganglion cells. Mid-grey represents a response level equal to the dark current, and response levels greater than or less than this are represented by lighter and darker shades respectively.

image contains nothing of interest in these regions. The only responses that deviate from these are those close to the boundaries. On the (dark) outside of the square, the responses are very low and on the (light) inside they are high, giving the object boundaries a characteristic signature. Exactly why boundaries produce this signature is described in Box 1.

The neural image for OFF-centre retinal ganglion cells would look very much like that in Figure 2b, but the dark regions would be light and vice versa. In other words, the neural images for the two classes of cell would be of opposite polarity. Conceptually, these two images can be thought of as superimposed on top of one another. This is a clever feature of the retina because it means that image features are encoded by both increases and decreases in neural response effectively doubling the number of distinct response levels that can be usefully employed in the visual code.

3 Spatial frequency selectivity

Most images are much more complex than that in Figure 2 and consequently, the visual system employs an extra level of complexity to deal with it. The problem is illustrated by the cartoon of the cat in Figure 3. At one level of analysis we might conclude that the contour orientation midway along the cat's back is approximately horizontal and that this indicates the boundary of the cat's body. On the other hand, around the same general region, the orientations of the raised hairs are close to vertical. In other words, different visual information is being conveyed at different spatial scales: a coarse scale for information about general shape and a fine scale for details about the hairs. To solve this problem, vision operates at several different spatial scales using receptive fields of different sizes. In Figure 5 (overleaf), three different sized ON-centre receptive fields are shown superimposed on images containing luminance changes at three different spatial frequencies. As the spatial frequency of these images increases, the receptive fields that provide the best match to the images become smaller. The better the match between the receptive field structure and the image, the greater the response. For this reason, vision contains superimposed receptive fields of several different sizes (which are said to be 'tuned' to different spatial frequencies) to analyse the different image information that is conveyed at different spatial scales. This also means that we should think of vision as containing neural images at multiple spatial scales (or multiple resolutions) as well as ON- and OFF-centre images.

In fact, this introduces a completely different way of thinking about vision. An astonishing fact is that all images can be constructed by adding together a sufficiently large number of **sine-wave gratings** such as those in Figure 5, at different spatial frequencies and different orientations. For example, an image containing vertical black and white stripes with sharp boundaries can be produced by summing together a series of vertical sine waves with fuzzy boundaries (see Box 2). Because all images are made from sine waves, it is useful to know how the visual system processes sine-wave stimuli. Indeed, by characterizing vision in terms of its response to different sine-wave stimuli, it is possible to make reasonable predictions as to how vision processes any one of an infinite number of natural images constructed from those sine waves.

Figure 3 A cat. The orientation of the hairs on the cat's back are vertical, but the orientation of the back itself is approximately horizontal.

Box 1   Responses of retinal ganglion cells to luminance borders

Figure 4 shows a horizontal cross section of the light level of the image in Figure 2a, the receptive field locations of a selection of retinal ganglion cells and the pattern of responses of these cells. Receptive fields are also shown in cross section. For each cell, the contribution from its excitatory centre is matched to that from its inhibitory surround, meaning that when stimulation is the same in both regions the effects cancel out.

For cells 1 and 2 there is no stimulation in any part of their receptive fields and so these cells respond with spontaneous discharge. For cell 3, however, some light from the central square falls into its inhibitory surround. This means that the cell's spontaneous discharge is slightly inhibited and so its response is less

than for the previous two cells. For cell 4, even more light falls into the inhibitory surround and so its response drops even further. For cell 5, although more light falls into the inhibitory surround, which would have the effect of reducing the response still further, light is also falling into half of the excitatory centre. Because the same proportion of both centre and surround are stimulated, the two effects cancel out and the result is spontaneous discharge. For cell 6, much of the inhibitory surround is stimulated but all of the excitatory centre is stimulated so the net contribution is one of excitation and the response is greater than spontaneous discharge. For cell 7, the level of excitation is the same as that for cell 6, but the level of inhibition is greater and so the response decreases. Finally, for cells 8 and 9, light fills the entire receptive field and so the contributions from the two regions are equal and the response is the same as spontaneous discharge.

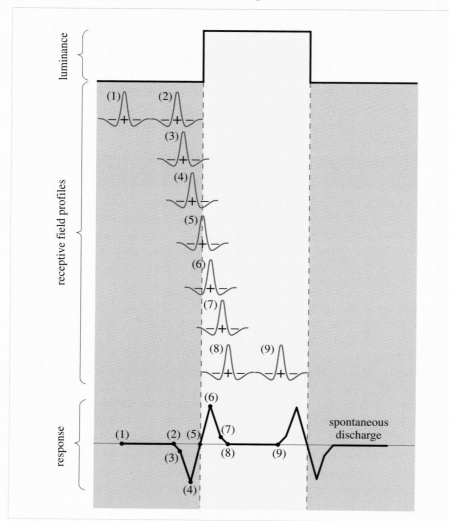

Figure 4   A cross section of the luminance profile of the image in Figure 2a is shown at the top of the figure. The locations and receptive field profiles of nine different retinal ganglion cells (1–9) are shown in the centre, and the responses of these cells are shown at the bottom. Note that the response profile at the bottom of the figure is a horizontal cross section through the response profile in Figure 2b.

Figure 5　Three vertical sine-wave gratings whose spatial frequency increases from left to right. Superimposed on each are the receptive fields of three ON-centre retinal ganglion cells.

Box 2 Synthesizing a square wave from a series of sine waves

The left-hand side of Figure 6 shows an image of a square wave and, below it, the first few in the series of sine waves from which it can be constructed.

At first glance it is not at all clear how this is going to work. For example, the square wave has sharp edges, the sine waves do not, and the square wave has flat plateaus, whereas the sine waves have ripples. The construction process is illustrated in the remaining two columns of Figure 6. The centre column shows a set of sine-wave gratings, with decreasing amplitude and increasing spatial frequency from top to bottom. In the right hand column is shown a square-wave grating, with the sine waves progressively superimposed upon

it. As the sine waves of increasingly higher spatial frequency are included in the summing process, the result is an image profile with increasingly sharp edges and increasingly flat plateaus, which looks more and more like the square wave. If the process is continued indefinitely, adding higher and higher spatial frequencies, then a perfect square wave is obtained. Of course, a square wave can be generated only with the correct combinations of sine waves at the correct spatial frequencies and amplitudes; different combinations of different sine waves will produce different images.

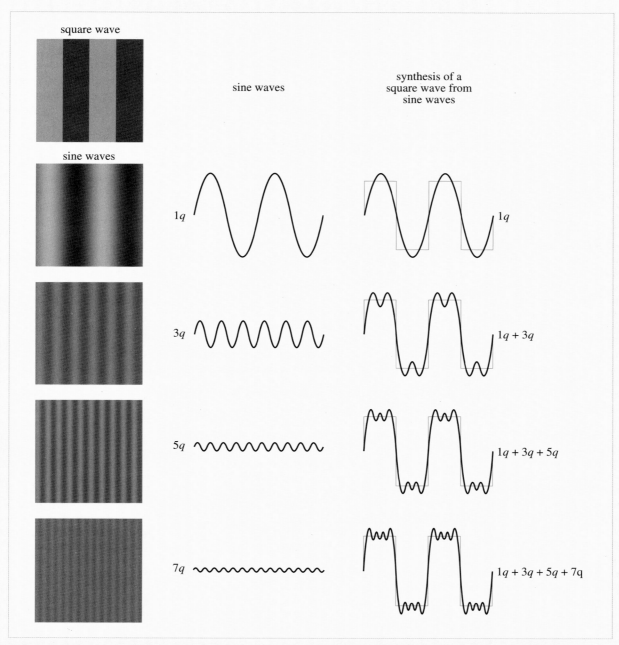

Figure 6 The construction of a square wave (top) from sine waves of different frequencies. The symbol *q* represents spatial frequency, thus a sine wave of 3*q* has a spatial frequency three times that of a sine wave of 1*q*.

4 The contrast sensitivity function

The visual system's sensitivity to (vertical) sine waves is illustrated psychophysically by the **contrast sensitivity function** (**CSF**) shown in Figure 7. The CSF is generated by measuring the lowest contrasts at which sine-wave gratings of different spatial frequencies can be just detected. A popular way of doing this is to use the **two-interval forced choice technique** (**2IFC**) described in Box 3. The CSF illustrates the range of spatial frequencies to which the human visual system responds and has a characteristic inverted-U shape. In other words, vision attenuates high and low spatial frequencies in the image. The CSF is sometimes referred to as the window of visibility because for an image to be visible it must contain sine-wave components that fall within the bounds of the CSF. In principle it would be possible to construct images from sine waves that fall entirely outside the CSF. For human observers, these images would be invisible.

Figure 7 Typical contrast sensitivity function (CSF). Note the inverted U-shape of the CSF.

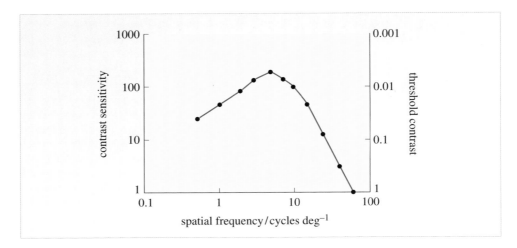

So, the CSF characterizes human spatial vision and tells us what can and cannot be seen by the visual system, but why does it have the shape that it does? The low spatial frequency attenuation is readily explained by the inhibitory surrounds of retinal ganglion cells that we have met already. For example, in Figure 5, the cell with the medium-sized receptive field would not respond very well to the low-frequency grating (the one on the left) because both its excitatory centre and its inhibitory surround are stimulated by the light bar of the sine-wave grating. Of course, in Figure 5 this is not a problem because there is a cell with a larger receptive field that *will* respond to this spatial frequency. However, there will clearly be a lower spatial frequency to which this cell would not respond and this will always be true, no matter how large the receptive field.

To understand the high spatial frequency attenuation we must turn our attention to the very earliest stages of vision. In order for the retinal image to be converted to a neural image it must be sampled by light receptors in the retina. To be able to represent a high spatial frequency grating correctly these receptors must be packed very closely together so as to convey the rapidly changing light levels across the retina. The physical size of light receptors imposes a limit on their packing density and so this imposes a limit on the highest spatial frequency that can be correctly encoded.

Box 3 Two-interval forced choice (2IFC)

This psychophysical technique is widely used in vision science in a variety of experimental contexts. Its use is illustrated here by considering how to measure the contrast detection threshold of a sine-wave grating. A single experimental trial consists of two temporal intervals (two brief presentations of a stimulus separated in time) each signalled by an auditory beep. One of the intervals, chosen at random, contains a sine wave and the other contains no stimulus, just a blank display with the same mean luminance as that in the test interval. The observer has to decide in which interval the test stimulus was contained and indicates his or her response by pressing one of two buttons. If the observer could see the stimulus then the response would be correct, whereas if they could not, they would have to guess. If the observer guesses, then the probability of pressing the correct button would be 0.5 (i.e. 50% correct). By performing many trials at a range of contrasts it is possible to generate a **psychometric function** such as that shown in Figure 8. Contrast detection threshold is then taken as being the contrast level associated with some criterion level of performance, such as 75% correct. In the figure this gives a detection threshold of 1%, or 0.01, and the reciprocal of this number gives sensitivity, in this case 100.

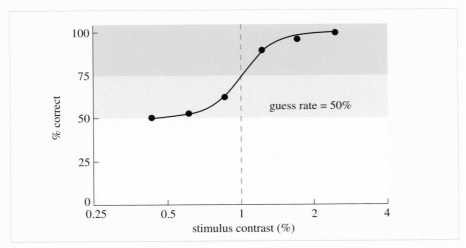

Figure 8 Psychometric function generated in a two-interval forced choice (2IFC) experiment.

However, there is a problem, because as explained in Box 4 (overleaf), spatial frequencies that are higher than the limit imposed by the sampling density result in the encoding of spurious low spatial frequency components known as **aliases**. In other words, we might expect that very high spatial frequencies can in fact be detected by vision (i.e. they can be discriminated from mean luminance; see Box 3), but that they would look like low spatial frequencies. This state of affairs is clearly unfortunate because not only would vision be removing some information from the image (the high spatial frequencies), but by misrepresenting it as low spatial frequencies it would introduce distortions: sine-wave components that are seen but are not present in the original image.

Box 4 Sampling and aliasing

Figure 9 shows the pattern of responses of retinal receptors for sine-wave gratings of different spatial frequencies. For the lower spatial frequencies, the pattern of responses captures the luminance changes contained in the image. However, for spatial frequencies that are so high that they are sampled less than twice per stimulus cycle, the pattern of responses does not correctly convey the original image information. This spurious pattern of responses is similar to that which would occur for a stimulus containing lower spatial frequencies. These spurious components are called *aliases*.

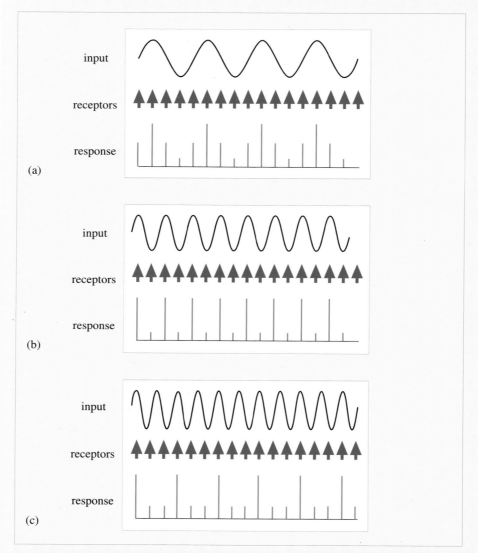

Figure 9   Aliasing due to under-sampling. Each panel shows the pattern of receptor responses to a different sine-wave grating stimulus. The sampling frequency of the receptors in the retina is fixed. (a) The sampling frequency is more than twice the spatial frequency of the input. (b) The sampling frequency is exactly twice the spatial frequency of the input. (c) The sampling frequency is less than twice the spatial frequency of the input. Only in (c) does the pattern of responses incorrectly convey the spatial frequency of the input. This spurious response pattern of responses is known as an alias.

Fortunately, the visual system has evolved a neat trick for rectifying this problem. The optics of the eye are not perfect but blur the image. As shown in Figure 6, sharp image structure is conveyed by high spatial frequencies and so blurring the image actually removes the very high spatial frequency content. In other words, a substantial part of the high spatial frequency attenuation of the CSF is due to optical deficiencies but this provides the benefit of removing the high spatial frequency components that would have resulted in aliasing. For this reason, the eye's optics can be thought of as acting as an anti-aliasing filter.

5 Primary visual cortex

So far, we have seen that spatial vision responds to a broad range of spatial frequencies (the CSF) and that retinal processing operates at different spatial scales. As we move up the primary visual pathway from the retina to the lateral geniculate nucleus and then the primary visual cortex, this operation becomes increasingly refined. For example, although retinal ganglion cells are tuned to spatial frequency, each cell does in fact respond to a rather broad range of spatial frequencies. Cells in the lateral geniculate nucleus are very similar to those in the retina but each one responds to a narrower range of spatial frequencies and cortical cells respond to a narrower range still. In fact, cortical cells are so selective that if the spatial frequency of a sine-wave grating at a cortical cell's preferred spatial frequency is increased by a factor of three, then the cell would respond weakly or not at all. This means that the CSF can be thought of as the envelope of the sensitivities of a collection of cells each tuned to a different spatial frequency as illustrated in Figure 10.

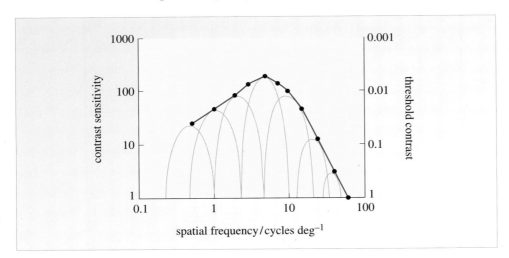

Figure 10 Underlying the CSF is a set of cortical cells tuned for different spatial frequencies (here the selectivities of seven cells are shown by the seven arches), each of which responds to a much narrower range of spatial frequencies than the overall CSF.

There is good supporting evidence for this from experiments using a psychophysical paradigm known as adaptation. In this paradigm, an observer first inspects a high contrast sine-wave grating at a particular spatial frequency (known as an **adapting grating**) for a couple of minutes. This prolonged stimulation fatigues the cortical cells that respond to the adapting grating, and when the CSF is subsequently measured, this shows up as a reduction in sensitivity. Most importantly, however, sensitivity is not reduced for all spatial frequencies, just those around the spatial frequency of the adapting grating. This implies that the unaffected spatial frequencies are detected by cells that do not respond to the adapting grating, meaning that there must be cells that are tuned for several different spatial frequencies.

All this leads to the surprising conclusion that different spatial frequency components of the square wave in Figure 6 are processed by different cells in the primary visual cortex. Again, there is good psychophysical evidence for this. A low contrast square-wave grating is detected only when its lowest spatial frequency component (the one with the greatest amplitude in Figure 6) reaches its own detection threshold. Furthermore, the square wave is only discriminable from a sine-wave grating when its sine-wave component with the next highest amplitude (the $3q$ component in Figure 6) reaches *its* own detection threshold.

As we have learned already, one reason that vision operates at multiple spatial scales is so that it can read the different image information that the different scales convey. However, in the case of the square wave, for example, there seems to be little benefit in this. Although the details are still far from clear, it seems that where appropriate, subsequent visual processes are involved in recombining spatial frequency information across spatial scale.

One particularly important feature of cortical cells is that, in marked contrast to those encountered earlier in the primary visual pathway, they are selective for orientation (Chapter 12, *From retina to cortex*). Receptive fields of a class of cortical cells known as simple cells are similar to those shown in Figure 11a and can be generated by wiring together an array of LGN cells in the way shown in Figure 11b. Their elongated structure means that, unlike retinal ganglion cells, a stimulus such as a sine-wave grating would have to be at a particular orientation for the cell to respond. This makes these cells ideally suited to coding the orientation of image structure. For example, retinal ganglion cells highlight both the vertical and horizontal borders in Figure 2, whereas the neural images for vertical and horizontal simple cells only pick out their preferred orientations, as shown in Figure 12. Thus,

Figure 11   Receptive fields of cortical simple cells. (a) Simple cells have oriented receptive fields of various sizes, orientations and polarity, a small selection of which are shown. Some simple cells have more or less than the number of sub-regions shown. (b) The receptive field of a simple cell is approximately equivalent to summing together the receptive fields of an array of ON- or OFF-centre cells. This is achieved by making neural connections from an array of cells in the LGN onto a single simple cell in the cortex.

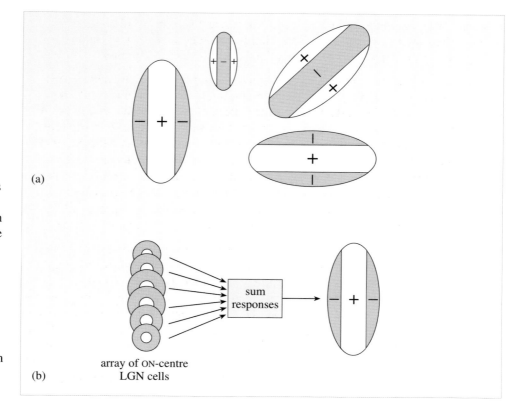

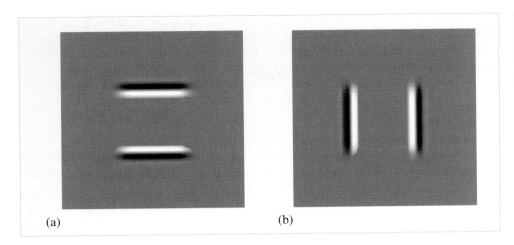

(a)   (b)

Figure 12 Neural images for simple cells with (a) horizontal, and (b) vertical receptive fields. The stimulus was the same as in Figure 2.

orientation adds yet another dimension to the neural image representations in vision. How this rather fragmented view of the world is useful to spatial vision is illustrated in the next section by considering the details of orientation coding in the cortex.

6 Population coding

The first thing to realize is that the response of a single simple cell cannot provide unambiguous information about the stimulus that stimulated it. To see this, consider the simple cell whose receptive field is shown in Figure 11b. It would respond strongly to a high contrast vertical grating. Importantly, however, the response of the cell could be reduced in at least two very different ways: first, by reducing stimulus contrast, and second by changing stimulus orientation. Thus, by inspecting the response rate of a single cell, later stages of the visual system could not know whether the stimulus was at the cell's preferred orientation but of low contrast, or of high contrast but oriented away from the cell's preferred orientation.

The solution to the problem is to consider the *distribution* of activity across cells that look at the same region of the image but through receptive fields at different orientations. Figure 13 (overleaf) shows the pattern of responses that would occur for a vertical grating at two different contrasts. Although the response of each cell changes with stimulus contrast, the shape of the distribution across the population of cells does not and in both cases the peak of the distribution indicates the orientation of the stimulus. This is known as a **population code** because a population of cells are required to encode the stimulus attribute, in this case, orientation. A psychophysical phenomenon known as the **tilt after-effect (TAE)** suggests that this is in fact the way that orientation is encoded in human vision.

The TAE is another important psychophysical phenomenon that has been revealed using the adaptation paradigm that we met earlier. If an observer adapts to a slightly tilted grating (oriented at say 15° from vertical), a subsequently presented vertical test grating appears tilted in a direction opposite from that of the adapter. As the perceived orientation of the grating is different from the physical orientation of the test image on the retina, the visual system must have made an orientation coding error, but how does this relate to the earlier idea about a population code? Figure 14b shows the response distribution (population code) for a vertical grating. The peak of the distribution is for a cell with a vertical receptive field and so this is the orientation that is seen. Now suppose that the observer adapts to a grating oriented at 15°.

Figure 13 Population coding. Response distributions are shown for a population of simple cells for vertical gratings with high and low contrast.

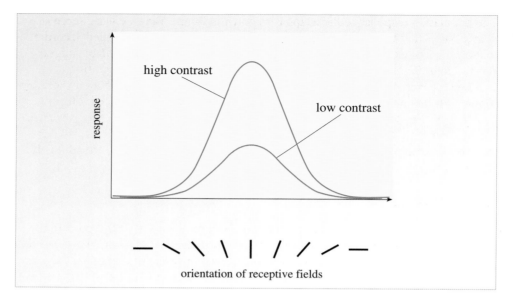

Figure 14 The tilt after-effect. (a) An adapting grating oriented at 15° and the population response. (b) A vertical test grating, distribution of fatigue and unadapted population response for the vertical test grating. (c) Perceived orientation of a vertical test grating after adapting to the grating in (a). The distorted population code is shown after taking into consideration the effect of fatigue.

You might be able to demonstrate the TAE for yourself. Look at the grating stimulus in (a) for about 30 seconds and then transfer your gaze to the vertical grating below it. You should notice that the grating now appears tilted in the same direction as the grating in (c), although the magnitude of the after-effect might not be as large as that illustrated.

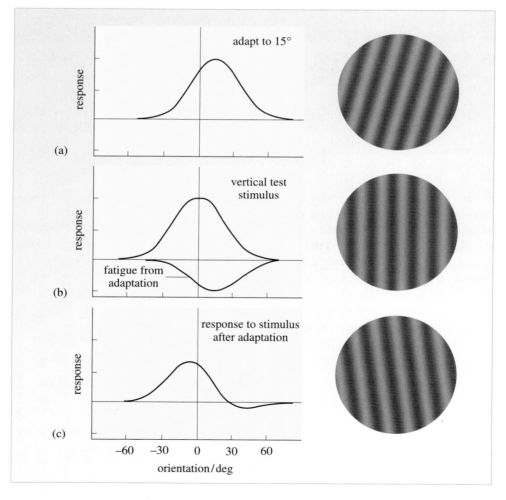

The population response to the adapter is shown in Figure 14a. A consequence of adaptation is that the cells that responded to the adapter become fatigued according to their level of excitation by the adapter. This leads to the distribution of fatigue illustrated in Figure 14b. The adapter is now removed and a vertical grating is presented. Normally this stimulus would produce the response distribution shown in Figure 14b, but because of fatigue, the response distribution is distorted. This is shown in Figure 14c and was calculated simply by summing the expected response distribution with the fatigue distribution (the two distributions in Figure 14b). Because the peak of this distribution is oriented anticlockwise from vertical this is the way that the stimulus is seen.

7 Summary

Our visual perception of the world is the end result of extensive neural processing that starts in the retina by decomposing the retinal image into a collection of parallel neural images of different polarity and multiple spatial scales (different spatial frequency bands). A crucial feature at the very front end of the visual system is that an imperfect optical system blurs the image, removing very high spatial frequency components that would otherwise cause visual distortions due to under-sampling by retinal receptors. The overall effect of this blurring and the properties of spatial processing by retinal ganglion cells are characterized by the contrast sensitivity function: the window through which we view the world. At the level of the primary visual cortex, spatial frequency tuning is tighter than at earlier stages and the representation of visual information has further branched into neural images for multiple orientations. The spatial decomposition of the image in the visual cortex achieves at least two things. First, images convey different information at different spatial scales and so a useful starting point for spatial analysis is the independent representation of different spatial frequency bands in the image. Second, it provides a direct means by which individual stimulus features such as orientation (as illustrated here) and size can be measured. This is done using population codes in which image features are represented by the distribution of activity across a set of cells whose receptive fields look at the same location in the image but with selectivity for different stimulus attributes such as orientation. The end result of all this early visual processing is the transformation of a two-dimensional array of light (the retinal image) into multiple neural representations that encode useful image features for subsequent stages such as object recognition.

Colour in context: contrast and constancy

15

Anya Hurlbert

1 Introduction

Mention to a casual acquaintance that you are studying colour vision, and almost invariably you will be asked: 'So, are the colours I see the same as the colours you see?' This question has been a philosopher's favourite for centuries. The answer has not changed; it is still impossible to verify that the colours you see are the same as the colours he or she sees. But with the advent of ever more quantitative and functional methods of exploring brain function, we can now say much more about *why* you see the colours you do see. Since then, our knowledge of the perceptual subtleties of colour vision – from adaptation and afterimages, to colour contrast and colour constancy – has vastly increased, as has our understanding of the neurophysiological mechanisms that mediate colour vision. Yet there is still an immense gap between the two.

Colour is a perception. The starting-point in the study of colour perception is to understand that the term 'perceived colour' is redundant. Colour is itself a perception, not a fixed, physical attribute of an object. Colour is constructed by mechanisms in the brain, starting from the light signal that objects send to the eye. And as we shall see below, the spectrum of light reflected from an object is not all that determines its colour.

2 How colour is encoded by neurons

The light signal is captured by the three distinct types of cone photoreceptor in our retinae: the long- (L), medium- (M), and short- (S) wavelength-selective cones. Because at the most fundamental level, we have only these three cone types, each responsive to a broad segment of the spectrum, we cannot resolve the individual wavelengths of light (see Figure 2 in Chapter 11, *Functional colour vision*). In this sense, colour vision is inferior to hearing. We can detect individual frequencies of sound – aurally decompose a C major triad into its distinct constituents of C, E and G – but we cannot see the separate wavelengths of light that yellow rose petals reflect. None the less, we can discriminate many millions of colours, corresponding to millions of distinct cone-response triplets.

Thus, at the first stage of retinal processing, colour is encoded by triplets of cone responses. Immediately afterwards, still in the retina, this triplet code is thought to be transformed into a new code formed by two types of colour-opponent neurons that combine the cone responses: (L−M) and (S−(L+M)); and a luminance neuron: (L+M). The colour-opponent neurons may mediate our perception of certain colours as opponent pairs: red–green and blue–yellow.

In the visual cortex, the colour selectivities of neurons are scattered throughout colour space, not clustered on the colour-opponent dimensions (see Figure 9 in Chapter 8, *Colour science*). So, in the third stage of processing, colours are encoded not just by two types of opponent neuron, but by many distinct neural types representing many discriminable colours. In the primary visual cortex and at higher levels, the responses of neurons are also influenced by the cone excitations from stimuli outside their classical receptive fields, as recent studies show. Such interactions between cone responses across the visual field may help to explain the phenomena of colour constancy and colour contrast.

3 Colour contrast, adaptation and assimilation

Two lights in a black void that evoke the same triplet of cone responses will appear the same – these are known as metamers. But two lights that evoke the same triplet of cone responses will not appear the same if they are lights reflected from surfaces, and the surfaces are *embedded in different contexts*. In other words, the colours of surfaces are not governed solely by the cone responses they elicit at one time in one place. The colour of an object depends on the colours of other objects in the scene, and on the colours of objects seen just before.

In the late nineteenth century, Chevreul, Director of Dyeing at the Gobelin factory in Paris, found that the appearance of one colour could be dramatically influenced by nearby colours. Dyeing was therefore an unpredictable art, not unlike that practised by the great painters who deliberately applied contrasting colours to convey distance or mood. Chevreul formulated the law of simultaneous contrast, based on his meticulous observations of colour combinations, which stated, amongst other things, that red would be enhanced if surrounded by green.

One simple rule that predicts the effects of colour contrast remarkably well is illustrated in Figure 1, a version of a demonstration by the British psychologist Paul Whittle. The inks used to print the four squares in the top row have each been chosen so that they elicit a particular set of cone responses relative to the grey background. For example, light from the pink square evokes a greater response from the L cones than does the background grey.

Figure 1   The pink squares in the top and bottom rows appear the same colour, yet are printed with different inks. You can verify the difference by viewing the squares through small cut-outs in a card that covers the background.

The inks used to print the four squares in the bottom row are different from those in the top row. And yet, the two rows look very similar. Why? Because the squares in the bottom row elicit approximately the same *relative* cone responses with respect to their *green* background as the top squares do with respect to their grey background.

This simple principle explains the effect: colour appearance is determined by the ratio between the cone excitations from a surface and its background. (Note that the effect is not perfect because the printing is not perfectly calibrated for our cone sensitivities.)

Other experiments show that for more complex images, colour contrast is even more complex. Distant regions of a scene may influence the colour of a central surface, in a way that cannot be explained simply by the cone contrast between the surface and its immediate background. These global contrast effects are often small, but nonetheless real.

In 1905, the German scientist von Kries proposed that the responses of the different colour receptors in the eye (at that time still unidentified) must be scaled by a measure of their average stimulation over the scene. We now know that **chromatic adaptation** occurs in the cones and that it reinforces colour contrast. For example, when the eye is exposed to a large red background, the L cones decrease in sensitivity. A small grey patch seen subsequently will evoke a larger response from the M cones than from the desensitized L cones, and will therefore appear greenish.

Simultaneous colour contrast is perhaps the best known illustration of how the colour of a surface depends on its surround. But it is only one of many such effects. In contrast effects, the surrounding colour induces its opponent colour in the central surface. In **assimilation**, the surrounding colour induces the *same* colour as itself in the central surface. Why does assimilation occur in some images, and contrast in others? As the American neuroscientists Russell and Karen DeValois argue, the surround effect may depend on the particular spatial scale and configuration of the image. Figure 2 (overleaf) illustrates this dependence. The assimilation in Figure 2a (also called the Bezold effect) may occur because we are more sensitive to colour changes on a coarse spatial scale than on a fine spatial scale.

These effects and others show that predicting colour appearance is not just a fine art, but an exceedingly complex, multi-parameter scientific problem. In the following sections, we will explore one of the reasons why such effects may have evolved.

4 Colour constancy

A red apple is red, whether seen under a yellow tungsten light bulb in the kitchen, or beneath a cloudless blue sky at the picnic table. The fact that it appears red even under large changes in the spectrum of the illuminating light is due to **colour constancy**, a fundamental property of the way our brains construct colour.

Colour constancy is traditionally defined as the stability of an object's colour under changes in the spectrum of the light illuminating the object. Its purpose is presumably to enable us (and other primates and animals such as goldfish and honeybees who also possess the ability) to use colour as a reliable cue for object recognition. Why is colour constancy such a remarkable achievement? Consider what determines the spectrum of light that an object reflects to our eyes.

(a)

(b)

Figure 2   (a) View the checkerboard from a distance of about 2 feet. The two oblong patterns are made up of the same grey squares, but on the left they appear pinkish, and on the right, greenish. The explanation is that we are more sensitive to the difference in average colour between the two oblongs, rather than to the differences between the squares making up each oblong. (b) In a different configuration, with the same colours, contrast effects occur. Now the left grey square appears greenish and the right grey square pinkish.

The **surface spectral reflectance function** describes the fraction of incident light at each wavelength that an object reflects and is an invariant property of the material from which it is made. But the total amount of light reflected at any wavelength depends, of course, on the total amount of incident light at that wavelength. The following equation sums up the relationship, and is key to understanding what the brain must do to achieve colour constancy:

$$I(\lambda) = S(\lambda) \times E(\lambda) \tag{1}$$

where $S(\lambda)$ is the spectral reflectance at a particular wavelength λ (i.e. a number between 0 and 1), $E(\lambda)$ is the energy at wavelength λ of the incident light, and $I(\lambda)$ is the energy of the reflected light, again at wavelength λ. Clearly, the spectrum of the reflected light will change when the incident light spectrum changes. Yet, our brains must extract a measure of the invariant reflectance $S(\lambda)$ from this changing signal.

Photographic film captures these changes in the light spectra because it does not have the inbuilt compensatory mechanisms that our brains do. Witness the change in the banana's colour recorded by the film from greenish-yellow when the fruit are illuminated by fluorescent light (Figure 3a) to yellow when they are illuminated by tungsten light (Figure 3b). You would not see the same dramatic change in colour if you viewed the actual fruit first under one light source and then under the other. You see the change in colour now because the two pictures have become objects in their own right, with different spectral reflectance properties, illuminated by yet another light source, the lamp (or daylight) illuminating the page.

(a)

(b)

Figure 3   The same fruit are illuminated by fluorescent light (a), and by tungsten light (b). Notice that the photographic film does not have colour constancy.

Some artists exaggerate these differences, perhaps to emphasize the ambience of illumination rather than the material object; in effect, they disable colour constancy in order to capture the colour differences (see Box 1).

When the light illuminating a scene changes, the effects are not confined to changes in the spectrum of the reflected light. The overall intensity may change; parts of the scene may become darker or brighter as they fall in and out of shadow; or the whole scene may be dimmed. Conversely, it is not only changes in the colour of the primary light source that may affect the colour of light reflected by objects. Objects that face each other can reflect light onto each other, creating secondary light sources (mutual illumination) that add to the primary light source. Pigments may fade or age: as a red apple ripens, its red pigment becomes more concentrated, and the depth of its colour increases. Colour constancy compensates for some of these changes, and confers stability on our perception of objects.

4.1 Experimental demonstrations of colour constancy

Colour constancy has fascinated scientists for centuries, but it has proved an elusive phenomenon to quantify or explain. In 1789, the French scientist Monge demonstrated to members of the Royal Academy in Paris that white objects continued to appear white even when viewed through a piece of red glass, i.e. under red illumination. But this was only true when the white objects were seen against a richly coloured background. When viewed through the red filter placed at the end of a long tube, so that the background was eliminated from view, the white object now looked red. Thus, he also demonstrated a key feature of colour constancy: it depends on the presence of other objects in the scene. Solitary surfaces seen in a black void do not display constant colours under changing illumination.

In 1860, in his great *Treatise on Physiological Optics*, Hermann von Helmholtz attributed the phenomenon of colour constancy to acts of learning and judgement, rather than 'pure' sensation. He wrote that: '… by seeing objects of the same colour under … various illuminations … we learn to form a correct idea of the colours of bodies, that is, to judge how such a body would look in white light … .'

In 1971, the American inventor Edwin Land revived interest in experimental demonstrations of colour constancy. To prove that colour constancy was not just an illusion foisted on our brains by the forces of memory or learning, he showed that it did not occur just for familiar objects whose colours we had memorized over repeated exposure. Land constructed large vibrant collages of coloured paper, cut into various rectangular flat shapes, which he called 'Mondrians' after the twentieth-century Dutch painter Piet Mondrian (Figure 4 overleaf).

In one demonstration, Land illuminated a Mondrian with three different light beams (red, green and blue), created by putting a different narrow-band filter on each of three projector bulbs. He measured the light intensity reflected from, say, the pink paper under each of the three lights separately. He then adjusted the relative strengths of the three lights so that now the blue paper reflected exactly the same three intensities as the pink paper formerly had reflected. Yet the pink paper looked pink, and the blue paper looked blue.

Land concluded that each paper remained roughly constant in colour even under the change in illumination because the red, green and blue light reflected by each paper *relative to the other papers in the Mondrian* remained constant. In other words, the blue paper always reflected more blue light than the other papers, even when the

Box 1 Monet and colour constancy

La Cathédrale de Rouen

Cathédrale de Rouen, symphonie en gris et rose

The colours of objects in paintings may appear unusual when viewed out of the context of the light source in which they were painted. In his series of paintings of Rouen Cathedral, Monet exaggerated the changes in colour caused by changes in sunlight as the day progressed. In a late afternoon view (5–5.30 pm) from the Louvet apartment, (*La Cathédrale de Rouen*), he portrayed its western façade with brilliant yellow and gold; in the evening view (6.30 pm) from the same location (*Cathédrale de Rouen, symphonie en gris et rose*), he used swirling blues and purples. Monet's skills were not just in putting paint on canvas, but also in knowing how to counteract the hard-wired effects of colour constancy. Like other artists, he might have used reduction viewing to isolate the colour of one small element of the scene – say, an arch or portal – from the influence of surrounding colours. Since colour constancy is known to be achieved in part by

comparisons between the light reflected from different surfaces across the scene, he would not only eliminate colour contrast in this way but also reduce colour constancy. But the artist views small portions of the scene in isolation in order to choose the paint that matches them perfectly. And by using paints that mimic the reflection of the surface under the natural illumination that existed when the artist viewed it, he reproduces the effect of the illumination as well. The whole painting will therefore carry the tinge of the light source colour if it is viewed in a different context, say, under a spotlight in a museum. If he did not disable his colour constancy in this way, Monet might have painted each view of the Cathedral as if it were illuminated by the same neutral daylight. But it seems that he also exaggerated the contribution of the light source colour to the spectrum of light reflected from individual surfaces.

Figure 4 Edwin Land demonstrated that the colour of a surface is not solely determined by the spectrum of its reflected light. By adjusting the intensities of the three lamps to produce greenish light on the left, and reddish light on the right, he caused two different papers (whose reflectances are shown) to produce the same reflected light. The same reflected light looks pink in the Mondrian under greenish light and blue in the Mondrian under reddish light.

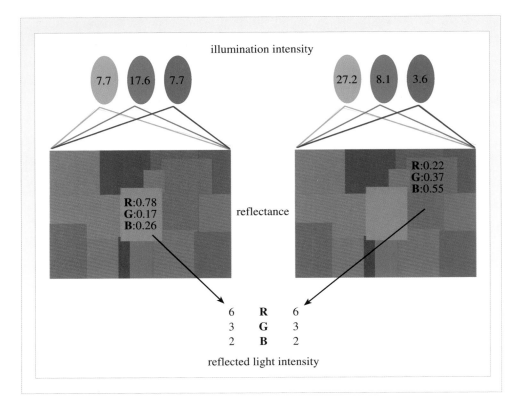

amount of blue light shining on it was reduced. He argued that the colour of each paper was determined by its 'lightness' (or relative reflectance) in each of the three colour channels specified by the three lamps: red, green and blue. Land emphasized not the fact that the colours remained perfectly constant, but that their colours could be predicted from their three lightness values. Since the time of Land's demonstrations, much effort has gone into obtaining accurate assessments of just how good colour constancy is.

'Mondrian' images have remained the stimuli of choice for colour constancy experiments, but are now usually generated by computer and displayed on cathode-ray tube screens (VDUs). In a typical **asymmetric matching experiment**, the observer views two computer-simulated Mondrians side by side, or in rapid succession, each under a different light source. The task is to adjust the colour of a patch in one Mondrian to match its colour in the other. Perfect colour constancy would mean that the same pale green paper would appear exactly the same colour under bluish daylight as under yellowish daylight, despite the difference in its reflected light (Figure 5). The observer must therefore match relative reflectances, not absolute reflected light spectra.

American experimental psychologists Larry Arend and Adam Reeves reported in 1986 that the observer's performance depended on the exact phrasing of the task. When asked to match the colour that the patch would be if it were *cut from the same piece of paper* as in the other Mondrian, observers show much better colour constancy than when asked simply to match its colour. Colour constancy is also better when the two Mondrians are viewed **haploscopically**, so that each eye sees only one Mondrian, and is therefore differentially adapted.

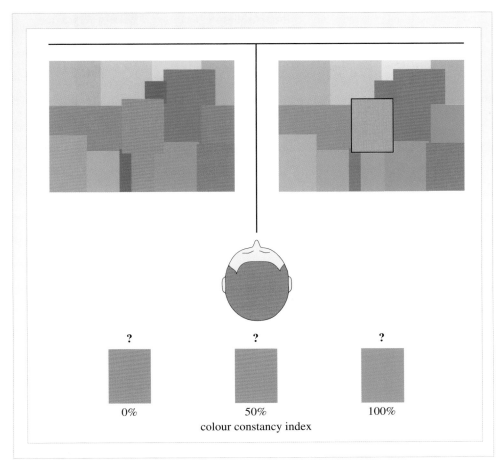

Figure 5 In a typical colour constancy experiment, the observer views the same Mondrian simulated under two different light sources (bluish daylight on the right; yellowish daylight on the left). The task is to adjust the colour of the central patch on the right to match its colour on the left. For 100% colour constancy, the observer would adjust it to have the same relative reflectance as its matching paper, but with a different spectrum of reflected light due to it being under a different light source. For 0% colour constancy, the observer would match the spectrum of reflected light, not the relative reflectance.

From such experiments using artificial Mondrians, reports vary as to the extent to which we possess colour constancy, ranging from 20% to 120% (overcompensation for the illumination difference). Perhaps the best recent estimate of colour constancy comes from an experiment using real papers under real light sources in a viewing box. In 1999, American scientists Jamie Kraft and David Brainard used special techniques to allow observers to adjust the colour of a grey paper in the box, and found the best constancy to be approximately 80–90%. The consensus now is that colour constancy is not perfect, and that it varies between observers and depends on the task. But it is always better than a camera's.

4.2 Computational explanations of colour constancy

The phenomenon of colour constancy presents an enticing theoretical problem summarized in equation 1: the light that an object reflects to the eye is the product of the object's inherent reflectance properties – which are constant – and the spectrum of the light source – which is variable. A robot that tried to sort fruit by measuring their reflected light spectra might confuse apples and oranges under changing daylight in an outdoor market. How would it extract the apple's surface reflectance from the changing signal it measured? In the computational approach to colour constancy, scientists try to find solutions that could be implemented by robots, as well as elucidate mechanisms possibly used by the human visual system.

Land proposed his 'Retinex' algorithm to compute lightness values of Mondrian papers in each of the three colour channels. To obtain lightness in, say, the 'red' channel, the Retinex divided the 'red' intensity of a particular paper by the average 'red' intensity of the whole scene. The clever trick was the way it computed the average 'red' intensity: the Retinex tracked changes in measured intensity across the Mondrian along random paths, and discarded small changes due to minor fluctuations in the illumination. It ensured that the 'red' lightness of the paper was a fairly accurate measure of its 'red' *reflectance* relative to the other papers, irrespective of changes in the amount of incident long-wavelength light that might be caused by shading or shadows.

The Retinex is a prototypical example of the computational approach to colour constancy. We can evaluate it and other computational solutions on three criteria:

1   How good is the method, in an absolute sense, in achieving colour constancy? That is, do the computed lightness values stay constant under changing illumination?

2   How good is the method at predicting human performance? Do the lightness values predict the colours that human observers see?

3   Does it tell us how the human visual system achieves colour constancy?

Taking the last criterion first, in one sense the Retinex algorithm tells us nothing new about the human visual system; we already know from the phenomena of chromatic adaptation and simultaneous contrast that, in seeing colours, the human visual system compares the light reflected from a surface with that from its surround.

What Land's Retinex algorithm and others of its type tell us is that contrast and adaptation might have evolved to help achieve colour constancy. Looking at the other two criteria shows us why. First, the Retinex method does not yield perfect colour constancy. But, second, under certain conditions, lightness values predict the colour matches that human observers make.

Cone contrasts (the human visual system's version of lightness values) are even better predictors of colour matches. And changes in daylight illumination tend to preserve the cone contrasts between surfaces in a scene (Figure 6). For example, as

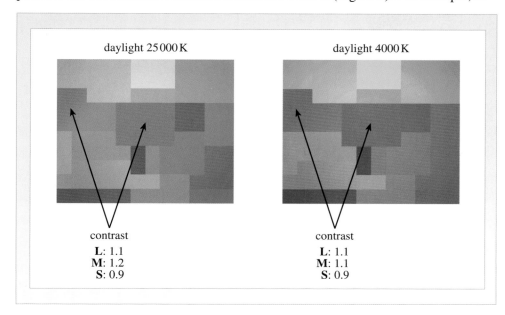

Figure 6   The ratios between the cone excitations elicited from the green and purple papers stay roughly constant under the change in illumination from daylight, with a colour temperature of 25 000 K, to daylight with a colour temperature of 4000 K.

the sun sets, the reflected long-wavelength light increases over the whole scene, so the local relative excitations of the L cones stay the same. So it would make sense for the human visual system to encode colours as cone contrasts, because these will tend to stay constant under changing illumination.

Recently, the British vision scientist Foster and his colleagues showed that to an astonishing extent the human visual system does interpret colour changes that preserve cone contrasts as true changes in the illumination, even when the colour change could not actually be achieved by an illumination shift. Thus the human visual system seems to have adopted the rule that constancy of cone contrasts means constancy of objects, even if the rule sometimes fails.

But simple cone contrasts cannot be the whole story underlying colour constancy; if it were, objects would noticeably change in colour when placed against different coloured backgrounds, even under the same light source. There must be other information from across the scene that helps to balance any skew in the background colour particular to an object. One such piece of information may be the range of colours in the scene, not just their average.

Figure 7 illustrates one influence of the range of colours. Against the grey background in Figure 7a, the pastel coloured patches appear vividly coloured. Against the multi-coloured background in Figure 7b, which has the same average colour as the grey, the pastel patches now appear dull and insipid. Brown and MacLeod, in 1997, called this enhancement of colourfulness 'gamut expansion'. Its purpose may be to achieve colour constancy under illumination changes caused by interactions that the light undergoes with particles in its path, such as fog, mist, or smoke. These changes tend to dilute all colours with white, reducing the gamut of colours in a scene to a pale version of its former self. Hence, in order to recognize that the scene has not changed, the visual system must take account of the full range of colours, not just their average.

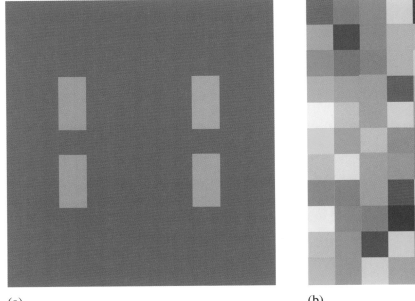

(a)   (b)

Figure 7 The same four pastel rectangles appear more saturated in colour against the grey background (a) than against the multi-coloured background (b), which elicits approximately the same space-averaged cone responses.

Other computational solutions propose that colour constancy may be achieved by using the information contained in highlights produced by **specular reflection** from glossy surfaces, such as vegetable skin, paints, eggshells and plastics. The highlights from these inhomogeneous materials are almost perfect mirror reflections of the light source, and therefore their colour provides a clue to the colour of the light source. Similarly, mutual reflections, the light that surfaces reflect onto each other, contain information about the reflectance properties of the surfaces involved.

In some cases, these other computational solutions yield better colour constancy than the Retinex or cone-contrast algorithms, but they have not been thoroughly tested on the last two criteria. Whereas cone-contrast algorithms could readily be implemented by the retina, at the purely sensory level, the other solutions may be classified as on a perceptual level, because they require the visual system to segregate surfaces and recognize features such as specular highlights. On a yet higher level, there are cognitive solutions which propose that we recognize and memorize the colour of familiar objects such as bananas, and use their colour under changing light sources to calibrate the colours of other objects in the scene.

4.3 The neurophysiological substrate of colour constancy

Where and how are the long-range interactions necessary for colour constancy carried out in the human visual system? The British neuroscientist Semir Zeki has argued that neurons in monkey V4, a visual area relatively high in the presumed hierarchy of processing from retinal signal to perception, possess the appropriate properties to mediate colour constancy:

1   They have large receptive fields capable of summing information from a large region of the image.

2   Many neurons in V4 have spectrally opponent responses: if excited by a particular wavelength inside its receptive field, the neuron is inhibited by the same wavelength outside. Such neurons compute spectral contrast, and American neurophysiologists Stan Schein and Robert Desimone therefore christened them 'lightness' neurons.

3   Most importantly, some V4 neurons display unchanging responses to surfaces that appear unchanged in colour to a human observer, irrespective of changes in the wavelength composition of the light. In support of the argument for V4 as the site of colour constancy, British neuroscientist Alan Cowey and his colleagues showed that monkeys experimentally deprived of V4 perform badly on colour constancy tasks, while performing normally on hue discrimination tasks.

Whether or not a discrete cortical locus of colour constancy exists in humans is still an open question. People with the rare condition of cerebral achromatopsia see no colour at all, typically as a consequence of an illness-induced brain lesion in a relatively circumscribed region of the visual cortex (the temporo-occipital cortex). But this region, the putative colour centre in humans, is unlikely to be the homologue of monkey V4, since unlike V4-deprived monkeys, people with cerebral achromatopsia are unimpaired in pattern discrimination but severely impaired on hue discrimination tasks. On the other hand, there are patients with lesions in other higher visual areas who display normal colour discrimination abilities, yet fail on tests of colour constancy. And one patient with cerebral achromatopsia, although unable to recognize colours *per se*, can detect differences between a simple patch and its surround, resulting from changes in local cone contrast. The evidence suggests, therefore, that local contrast and adaptation mechanisms occur early in the visual cortex (between the retina and the primary visual cortex), whereas more global mechanisms that contribute to colour constancy occur at higher levels.

5 Summary

The colours of solitary lights (in a black void) are determined by the responses they elicit from the three cone types. Surface colours (in the context of other surfaces) depend not only on the cone responses they evoke, but also on the cone responses from surrounding lights and lights recently seen. The phenomena of colour contrast and colour assimilation illustrate how colours depend on their context. In simple images, the colour appearance of a surface is determined by its cone contrast with the background. Colour constancy is the tendency for object colours to remain constant under changes in the illumination spectrum, and it is a fundamental property of the way our brains construct colour. Cone contrasts between surfaces tend to be preserved under natural changes in daylight illumination. Thus, by encoding surface colours as cone contrasts our brains keep colours constant as the illumination changes. Chromatic adaptation of the cones also aids colour constancy. Other mechanisms contribute to colour constancy, including global contrast, the use of chromatic information from specular highlights and mutual reflections, and colour memory. Local cone contrast mechanisms and chromatic adaptation probably occur in early stages of the visual pathway, but other mechanisms occur at higher levels in the visual cortex.

Motion vision

Mike Harris

16

1 Introduction

We consciously perceive a stable visual world in which movement is rare and therefore significant. But although the visual world *is* stable, the retinal image is not; it jumps and flows as we move our eyes or move around the world. From a moving car, for example, the image of a distant object slowly expands as we approach, until it rushes past and disappears behind us. We perceive this, correctly, as our own movement through a stationary world, rather than as an image that stretches, expands and rushes about. Because we are more aware of the stable result than the changing input on which it is based, it is easy to overlook the importance of visual motion. But, in fact, it is useful in a wide variety of tasks, from maintaining balance to recognizing familiar objects. This chapter sets out to illustrate this usefulness by considering an everyday task – deciding when and how hard to brake when driving. To understand how this is done, we need to think about three stages in the processing of retinal motion:

- encoding the speed and direction of individual moving points;
- placing these individual motions into the general context of retinal motion;
- deriving measures that are useful in controlling behaviour.

2 Signalling the direction and speed of individual moving points

2.1 Two motion systems

We have two separate systems for encoding the speed and direction of retinal motion. The first is indirect, *inferring* motion from a sequence of static frames. This is the kind of motion we experience at the cinema and, of course, it is totally compelling. However, we also have a second system that can *directly* record retinal speed and direction, rather than simply inferring them. This chapter is concerned with this second, direct, system.

2.2 Simple motion detectors

One simple way to detect motion directly is illustrated in Figure 1. Two receptor cells, R_1 and R_2, at slightly different retinal positions, are connected to the motion-detecting cell, M. R_1 directly excites M almost as soon as it responds. R_2 inhibits M but the effect is delayed so that it lags slightly behind the initial response. When a stimulus moves over the receptors from left to right, R_1 responds first and causes M to respond. A moment later R_2 responds and, after a short delay, inhibits M. The motion detector thus responds to leftward movement. But, when the stimulus moves from right to left, R_2 responds first and its inhibitory signal starts on its way to M. R_1 then responds and immediately sends an excitatory signal to M. If things are set up correctly, the immediate excitation from R_1 and the delayed inhibition from R_2 arrive simultaneously, cancelling each other out so that M does not respond to rightward movement. M is thus a simple motion detector that responds better to one direction than the other and can thus signal the direction of the stimulus.

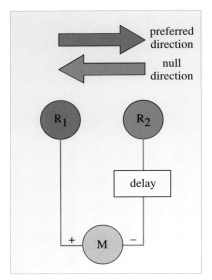

Figure 1 Schematic diagram of a simple motion detector based on delayed, lateral inhibition. The motion detector (M) responds to motion in one direction but not the other.

Mechanisms like this, based on delayed, lateral inhibition, are found in the retinas of simple mammals like rabbits. Similar principles are also involved in motion detection in primates, but here the situation is more complex. Animals such as rabbits have relatively small brains so their sensory systems must place minimal demands on central processes. They therefore filter out most of the input data at a very early stage of processing, passing on only essential 'trigger features', such as movement. Primates have relatively larger brains and can afford to pass on more of the input data for later processing. Initial sensory processes produce a more complete description of the stimulus, rather than preserving only a few essential trigger features. Thus, rather than simple motion detectors, the primate retina has mechanisms that record general information about the spatial and temporal characteristics of the image. Motion detection, *per se*, does not emerge until later, when cortical processing occurs.

2.3 Separate mechanisms for encoding spatial and temporal detail

The white background of this page looks constant and uniform but the amount of light it reflects actually varies widely from one position to the next and from one instant to the next. This continual, random variation in both space and time is an inherent property of light and is called visual 'noise'. To get rid of the noise and so gain the 'correct' impression of constancy and uniformity, we must collect together and average several measures. Whether we collect these measures over different positions or different times depends crucially upon what we are trying to do, and is one key to understanding the early stages of motion processing.

If we want to preserve the spatial detail in the image, we can't collect and average measures from many different positions because that would blur out the very detail that we are trying to preserve. To reduce noise while preserving spatial detail, we can collect samples over time but not across positions. Conversely, if we want to preserve temporal detail, about the way the stimulus varies over time, we can collect and average measures across different positions, but not over time. Instead of a single general mechanism that collects light over both space and time, we have evolved two separate mechanisms, with different spatial and temporal properties, for picking up spatial and temporal detail.

Retinal mechanisms for picking up spatial detail are well known (see Chapter 14, *Spatial vision*). Retinal ganglion cells pick out spatial details, such as edges, using a simple system of **lateral inhibition**. The receptive fields of these cells are relatively small so that they collect light from a small range of retinal positions and thus preserve spatial detail. On the other hand, these cells continue to respond for as long as a suitable stimulus is present within the receptive field – they collect light over an extended period of time. There is a separate population of retinal ganglion cells for picking up temporal detail. The receptive fields of these cells are larger, indicating that they collect light over a larger range of positions. On the other hand, they only respond briefly to the onset or offset of a suitable stimulus – they collect light only over a short time period and so preserve temporal detail about the way the stimulus changes from instant to instant.

2.4 Combining spatial and temporal information to encode direction and speed of motion

Motion involves both a change in position and a change in time so, while the first stages of motion processing deal separately with spatial and temporal information, these two aspects must subsequently be combined in order to extract both the direction and speed of the stimulus. Temporal information alone, for example, is not enough to distinguish the direction of the stimulus. As an edge moves over a given position on the retina, a cell concerned with temporal detail might signal the direction in which the light changes, say from dark to light. But, as shown in Figure 2a, this direction could be produced either by a light/dark edge moving to the right, or by a dark/light edge moving to the left. To distinguish motion direction, we need to know not only the direction of *temporal* change (i.e. dark to light or light to dark) but also the direction of *spatial* change; in other words, information from the spatial and temporal systems must be combined. Similarly, recording the *rate* of temporal change is not enough, by itself, to signal the speed of the stimulus. Figure 2b shows that the same rate of temporal change could be produced either by a sharp edge moving slowly or by a broad edge moving quickly. To distinguish the speed of the stimulus, we need to know not only the rate of temporal change but also the rate of spatial change; again, information from the spatial and temporal systems must be combined.

Spatial and temporal information are combined within the primate motion system by a slightly fancier version of the simple scheme shown in Figure 1. The motion detector shown there combines lateral and delayed inhibition in a single stage.

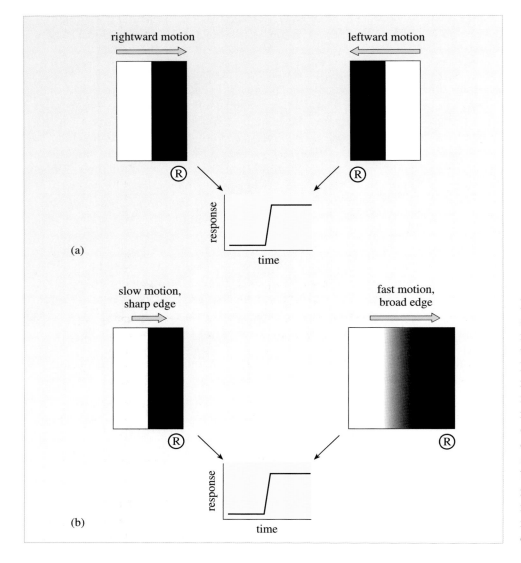

Figure 2   To recover the direction and speed of retinal motion, we need to know both the spatial and temporal properties of the image. Both panels show the response of a receptor (R) as an edge drifts over its receptive field. (a) The same response is produced by a light/dark edge drifting rightwards and a dark/light edge drifting leftwards, so R alone cannot distinguish between them. (b) The same response is produced by a slowly-moving sharp edge, and a rapidly-moving broad edge, so R alone cannot distinguish between them.

In the primate system these two types of inhibition are performed separately in the retina and then combined in the cortex. In general, inhibition provides a convenient neural mechanism for subtracting one input from another, and so calculating the difference between them. It can therefore be used to work out the *rate* at which the stimulus is changing, either across position or over time. The spatial system uses lateral inhibition to compare the response at neighbouring points and thus to signal both the direction and rate of change of light across *position*. The temporal system uses **delayed inhibition** to compare the response at a single position from one instant to the next, and thus to signal both the direction and rate of change in light over *time*. As shown, in Figure 2, both these different types of information are needed to signal the direction and speed of a moving stimulus.

2.5 Putting local motion into a more general context

When we move about, the image flows and transforms as we change our position relative to visual targets and we make compensatory eye movements to keep interesting targets stable on the retina. Consequently, it is impossible to make sense of the motion of an *individual* retinal point, as signalled by the sort of mechanisms that we have considered so far, without putting it into the context of this overall complex pattern of retinal motion. Only then can we decide whether it is caused by our own movements about the world, by eye movements, by the movement of other objects about the world, or by some combination of all these things.

Part of the solution to this problem is to make use of our own expectations. Since our brain controls our movements it might be able to predict what sort of retinal motion will be produced. Certainly the apparent stability of our visual world during eye movements does depend upon this kind of prediction. You can easily demonstrate this by closing one eye and very carefully and very gently touching your finger to the side of the other eye so that you move it very slightly in its socket. Under these circumstances, the visual world seems to jerk about alarmingly, because the retinal motion produced by the eye movement is not 'cancelled' by normal expectations and associated eye movement commands. However, expectations only partly solve the problem of making sense of retinal motion. They rely on the brain being able to translate general movement commands into the precise pattern of retinal motion that the movements will produce. While this is plausible for eye movements, it is much more difficult for our movements about the world. Nonetheless, different types of movement do produce different characteristic patterns of retinal motion, and it turns out that only two types of movement matter. We can move in a straight line from one position to another, which is called a translation. Or we can remain at the same position but change our angle of view, which is called a rotation. Eye movements are a simple example of a rotation. Moving in a straight line is an obvious example of a translation. Moving in a curve is just a combination of translation and rotation.

Figure 3 shows a convenient way to think about the visual motion produced by rotation. Figure 3a shows a simple case in which we are looking down from directly above the observer's viewpoint during a rotation about a vertical axis (e.g. a horizontal eye movement). Only a few visual targets are shown, all in the same horizontal plane as the viewpoint, and all stationary in the world. Note that, as the observer rotates, the images of all targets move through the *same angle* in the opposite direction to the rotation. This angle depends only upon the amount of rotation and not upon the distance of the targets (compare, for example, the motion of points P_1 and P_2). Figure 3b extends the same idea to all possible visible

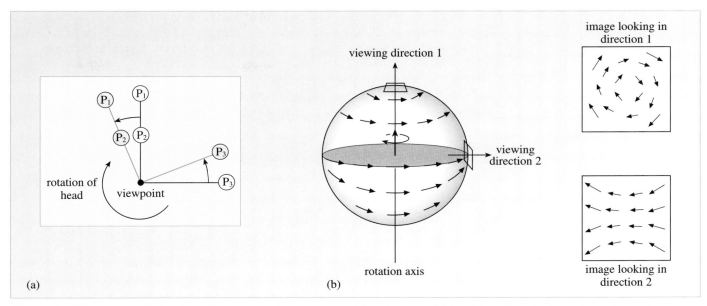

Figure 3 The pattern of visual motion produced by rotation of the observer. (a) Looking directly down from above the observer's viewpoint as he or she makes a horizontal eye movement (a rotation about the vertical axis) in a stationary world. The images of all points move through the same angle, irrespective of their distance (compare P_1 and P_2). (b) Imagine the observer at the centre of a transparent sphere. Each arrow shows the visual motion, on the surface of the sphere, of a target in that visual direction, during a rotation about the vertical axis. The insets show the image motion experienced by the observer looking in a given direction.

directions by placing the observer at the centre of an imaginary sphere; the arrows depict the visual motion of stationary targets during a horizontal eye movement. Notice that the pattern of motion depends on the direction of the target relative to the axis of rotation. The images of targets at right angles to the axis move fastest, those in the same direction as the axis do not move at all. The small insets in Figure 3b show examples of the retinal motion experienced when we look in particular directions relative to the rotation axis. The retinal motion produced by rotation is actually rather simple; we can exactly reproduce the whole pattern if we know only the axis and speed of rotation. This simplicity is what allows the use of predictions to maintain the stability of the visual world during eye movements.

Figure 4 (overleaf) shows the equivalent pattern of motions produced by linear translations. Figure 4a shows the same view from above as in Figure 3a. This situation is more complicated because the retinal motion depends not only upon how fast we are translating, and the direction of the target relative to the direction of translation, but also, importantly, upon the *distance* of the target (compare, for example, the motion of points P_1 and P_2). Figure 4b shows the extension to all possible directions, and the equivalent insets for retinal motion for particular viewing directions. The images of stationary targets at right angles to the direction of translation tend to move fastest, while those in the same direction as the translation do not move at all. For translations, however, although the overall pattern of motion *directions* can be simply worked out from the direction of motion, the pattern of retinal *speeds* can only be predicted if we know the distances of all the targets. In general near targets produce faster motion than distant targets. This dependence on distance makes it very difficult to predict the exact pattern of retinal motion that will result from a given translation.

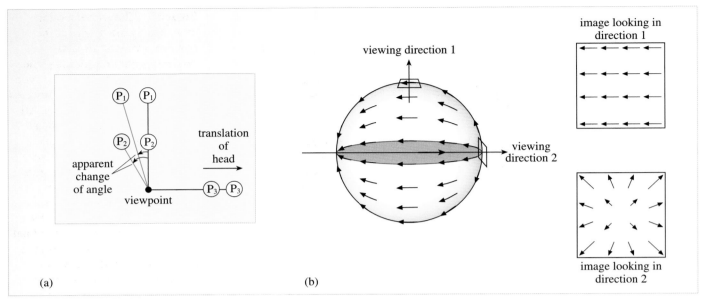

Figure 4 The pattern of visual motion produced by translation of the observer. (a) Looking directly down from above the observer's viewpoint as he or she translates in the direction of P_3. Note that movement of the observer to the right is the same as moving all targets by the same distance to the left. The images of distant points move less than those of nearby points (compare P_1 and P_2). The image of a target in the direction of translation does not move at all (P_3). (b) Imagine the observer at the centre of a transparent sphere. Each arrow shows the visual motion, on the surface of the sphere, of a target in that visual direction, during a rightward translation. The insets show the image motion experienced by the observer looking in a given direction.

Figure 5 shows a specific example of the retinal motion actually experienced when looking ahead while moving relative to a stationary, randomly textured ground plane. Each line represents the retinal motion of one point, with the length of the line representing the speed. Figure 5a shows the effect of a forward translation towards a target in the direction of the red point. Notice in particular that all the motion expands smoothly away from a single point, and that this point coincides exactly with the direction in which we are translating. (Remember from Figure 4 that the images of objects in the direction of translation *do not move at all*.) Figure 5b shows the combined motion produced by a forward translation in the same direction as in Figure 5a, accompanied by a compensatory eye movement (i.e. a rotation) to keep the red point stable upon the retina. Notice that the motion still emanates from a single point, but that this point now coincides with the direction of the target we are fixating rather than the direction in which we are moving. This is the kind of complex retinal motion that we most commonly experience and it clearly illustrates why the motion of any individual point can only be understood in the context of the overall pattern of retinal motion.

We do not yet know exactly how the visual system makes sense of the complicated moving patterns to which it is exposed, but one suggestion is that we actually decompose the type of complex motion shown in Figure 5b back into the simpler patterns shown in the insets to Figure 3b and Figure 4b. Although this is not the only possible approach, it is certainly simple to understand and, perhaps, to carry out. It is indirectly supported by the types of motion-sensitive mechanism found in the visual cortex. In the later stages of cortical motion processing, for example, there are cells with very large receptive fields capable of 'looking at' large areas of the

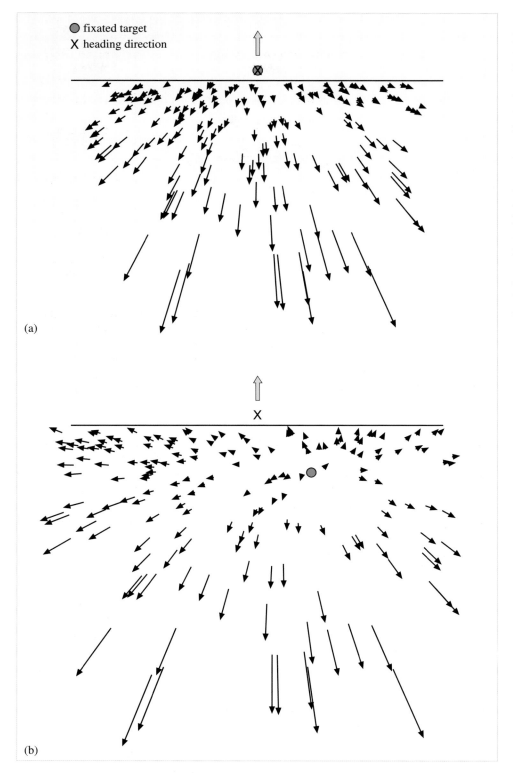

○ fixated target
X heading direction

(a)

(b)

Figure 5 The retinal motion produced by movement of the observer over a stationary, randomly-textured ground plane. (a) Translation only: the observer translates in the direction indicated without moving his/her eyes. All retinal motion expands from a single point, which coincides with the direction of translation. (b) Translation and rotation: the observer moves in the same direction as in (a) but rotates his/her eyes to keep the red dot stationary on the retina. All retinal motion expands in curves from a single point, but the point now coincides with the direction of the fixated target rather than the direction of translation.

retinal pattern. Some of these cells respond only to the particular patterns of retinal motion associated with either translation or rotation (the types of pattern shown in the insets to Figure 3b and Figure 4b). Perhaps they act as 'templates', somehow picking out and signalling only the appropriate components of complex retinal motion. Whatever the details of this process, it is at least clear, as we shall see in the next section, that human beings are extremely good at using complex retinal motion to guide and time their actions.

2.6 Using retinal motion to time actions

There is no doubt that human beings can use complex retinal motion in a variety of ways. For example, when shown patterns of motion like the one depicted in Figure 5b, they can accurately judge the direction in which they are currently heading. This suggests that the visual system can decompose complex motion into its component parts, as described in the previous section, because only when this has been done are heading judgements easy to explain. As shown in Figure 5a, the component of motion due to translation contains a point from which everything expands smoothly. This point is called the Focus of Expansion (FOE) and, as explained in the previous section, it coincides exactly with the direction in which we are currently heading. To know where we are going, then, we only need to locate the FOE – although this is obviously tricky when faced with patterns like Figure 5b.

But, in addition to guiding basic movements, complex retinal motion can also be used to control more subtle behaviour, such as knowing when and how hard to brake while driving a car. At first glance, knowing when to brake in order to stop at a particular goal seems complex, requiring knowledge about both our current speed and our current distance from the goal. But these two factors can be combined to generate a much more useful measure, called **time-to-contact** (**TTC**). Just as it sounds, TTC is the time needed to reach a particular goal. It can easily be worked out by dividing *current distance* from the goal by *current speed* – just as, when trapped 10 miles from our destination in a traffic jam moving at 2 mph, we can easily work out that we will need another 5 hours to get there. The remarkable thing is that TTC is *directly* available from retinal motion, without any knowledge about current speed and distance.

The logic behind this surprising property is illustrated in Figure 6. Because of simple geometry, the ratio of retinal distance to retinal speed (d_r/s_r) is exactly equal to the ratio of current distance to current speed in the world (d_w/s_w). Since TTC is equal to d_w/s_w, we can measure TTC directly from the retinal information. Specifically, for any retinal point, we just divide its retinal distance from the FOE (d_r) by its retinal speed away from the FOE (s_r). Notice that this tells us nothing about current distance and speed – retinal distance does *not* correspond to real distance, and retinal speed does *not* correspond to real speed – but the ratio of these two things *does* correspond to TTC. This means that we cannot distinguish a distant object approaching rapidly from a nearby object approaching slowly, because both will have the same TTC. But TTC is otherwise ideal for timing our behaviour. When driving, for example, we want to know *when* to do things, not how far we are from a target and how fast we are moving. Indeed, this remarkable property of retinal motion may well account for our surprising ability to cope with driving at all. How else could we cope with speeds of 70 mph and more, using a visual system that evolved to cope with a maximum natural speed of 20 mph or less?

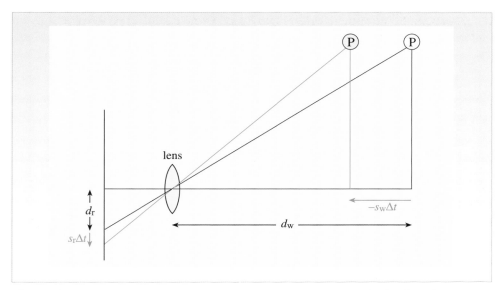

Figure 6 The geometry of time-to-contact (TTC). The observer looks directly where he or she is going, so that the direction of translation coincides with the centre of the image. A point (P) at distance d_w in the world produces an image at distance d_r from the centre of the retinal image. The observer translates to the right at speed s_w. This is the same as moving P to the left at speed s_w. In a small time Δt the object has moved a distance $-s_w \Delta t$ as shown. The image of P on the retina moves away from the centre of the image at speed s_r so, in the same small time interval, the image moves on the retina by a distance $s_r \Delta t$. A geometrical argument (using similar triangles) can be used to show that $d_w/s_w = d_r/s_r$. The time-to-contact with the plane containing P is d_w/s_w. This can be measured directly from the image by calculating d_r/s_r.

When people are shown complex retinal motion like that in Figure 5a or b, they can make accurate judgements about how long it will take them to reach a specified target. This suggests that they can make use of the kind of information described above. But they can go beyond this and make even more subtle judgements about whether or not they will stop in time when shown complex motion depicting braking. Again, at first glance, this seems very sophisticated behaviour, involving complex calculations with speeds, distances and accelerations. But, again, it turns out that the required information is available directly from complex retinal motion.

When we move at a constant speed, TTC declines predictably over time, as shown by the solid line in Figure 7 (overleaf). A target with an initial TTC of 3 seconds, for example, will have a TTC of 2 seconds after 1 second, 1 second after 2 seconds, and so on. When we brake, our speed declines and TTC declines more slowly than normal.

It is easy to show from the basic equations of motion, that to stop exactly at a target with an initial TTC of T seconds, takes exactly $2T$ seconds (see Box 1). Thus, if we are braking correctly, the TTC will decline to zero with a slope of exactly -0.5 (as represented by the dotted line in Figure 7). The visual system does not need to know anything about our acceleration and speed, or our instantaneous distance from the target, but can simply monitor the rate at which the instantaneous time-to-contact changes over time. And, of course, TTC can be obtained directly from the instantaneous rate of expansion of the image. So long as we can brake hard enough to reduce TTC by half the rate before braking, we can stop in time.

Figure 7   Using TTC to control braking. The solid line, labelled 'constant speed', shows that TTC with a given target declines with a slope of −1 as we translate towards the target at constant speed. Speed decreases during braking, so that TTC declines at a slower rate. The dashed line, with slope −0.5, shows how TTC must decline if we are to brake to a stop exactly at the target. Braking harder than this means that TTC declines at a slower rate and we will stop before the target (green area). Braking more gently than this means that TTC declines at a faster rate and we will not stop before the target (red area).

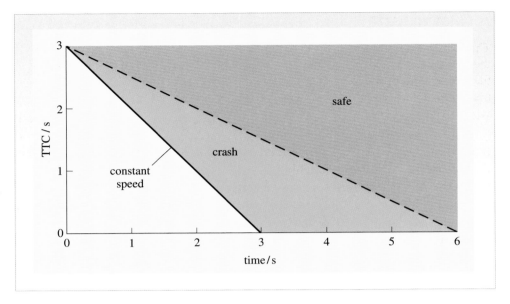

In real driving, of course, we generally brake as hard as possible when faced with an emergency and can very quickly tell whether this is hard enough. We may well reach this quick decision by looking at the rate of change of TTC. If we are braking as hard as possible but TTC is still declining faster than half the rate before braking, we know that we need to take some other emergency action, such as swerving.

As these few examples illustrate, the analysis of retinal motion is complex but worthwhile. It is certainly worthwhile for the perceiver. And, though it is complex for vision scientists trying to understand it, for them too, it is certainly worthwhile.

Box 1   Time to stop

If you are mathematically inclined, you may wish to see the proof of the statement that the time taken to stop exactly at a target with an initial time-to-contact of T seconds is $2T$.

If the distance to collision is S, and the instantaneous speed is V, then the initial TTC (T) is S/V.

The acceleration required to stop before reaching the target can be calculated from the standard constant acceleration equation:

$$v^2 - u^2 = 2as$$

where u = initial speed, v = final speed, a = acceleration and s = distance.

Putting $v = 0$, and $u = V$ gives $a = -V^2/2S = -V/2T$ (the negative sign indicating deceleration).

Substituting (from above) $T = S/V$ gives $a = -V/2T$.

The standard equation:

$$v = u + at$$

where t = time, can then be used to show that the time taken to reach zero speed is $2T$.

3 Summary

The motion of individual retinal points can be recovered by combining measures of the rate at which the light in the image changes from one position to the next, and of the rate at which the light at one image position changes over time. These measures are based on lateral and delayed inhibition, respectively.

The retinal motion of individual points can only be understood in the context of the overall pattern of retinal motion. All movements of the observer can be broken down into a translation and a rotation. So, if retinal motion is produced by movements of the observer, it can be understood in terms of the distinctive patterns produced by these two types of movement.

Once the overall pattern of retinal motion has been understood, it can provide direct measures, such as time-to-contact (TTC), that are extremely useful for controlling apparently complex behaviour, such as braking in a car.

17

The perception of words

Peter Naish

1 Introduction

When evolution first gave animals the ability to detect changes in their environments, the facility was used directly to control behaviour. For example, this kind of perceiving can cause an animal to move to a more benign location, or to capture food, but it is not the conscious perception of the sort that we can employ. In fact we too have those kinds of primitive perceptual mechanism; if our temperature sensors detect a fall in body temperature, then shivering is initiated, and if we touch something painfully hot our hand is snatched away before we become consciously aware of what happened. Processes such as these are of interest, but the level of explanation involved in describing them need not go beyond the physiological. The kind of perception to be discussed in this chapter is that which, in humans, leads to experiences such as knowing and understanding, and this is the province of psychology.

The behaviour which is often cited as setting humans apart from the rest of the animal kingdom is the use of language. Some animals do appear to use communication systems that might qualify for the label 'language', but none approaches the rich complexity of human communication. The impressive thing about spoken language is that words are symbols: they represent thoughts and things, and the objects represented need not even be present when referred to. Through the medium of language, our brains are able to manipulate ideas, and to plan for events that are yet to happen, or to describe those that are long past. It is perhaps no accident that young children really start to master their language at the same age as they begin, in play, to use objects to represent other things, i.e. like words, the objects are used as symbols.

If language is impressive, then the ability to read and write must be still more so. The printed word is merely a pattern of lines, but it represents a spoken word from the language. Hence, text is also symbolic, but it is a symbol of a symbol, and this is a remarkable level of abstraction. For example, the pattern 'DOG' is a symbol that represents a spoken word, which is itself a symbol used by English speakers to represent a certain kind of animal. To understand how reading takes place is really to understand what conscious perception means for a human being. It addresses the question of how a pattern of stimulation (in this case visual) is able to give rise to meaningfulness.

2 From text to language

Somehow, printed words have to generate appropriate activity in our language systems, and there appear to be two ways by which text might achieve this. The possible entry points are easily explained by considering the options available to a child learning to read. A beginning reader can already do two very relevant things: he or she can recognize many different objects and name them, and also can understand speech. If a child can recognize and name objects, then in principle he or she could learn to distinguish the patterns of different printed words, and put appropriate names to each. If this were mastered, then a sentence could be read by stringing together the sequence of word names. In the past this mechanism has been assumed to exist, at least tacitly, when children have been taught to read by the 'look and say' technique. Typically, classroom walls would be festooned with printed words, so that their shapes would gradually become familiar; the words were in lower case letters, since these are more distinctive than capitals.

As pointed out above, children can understand speech, and this provides an alternative potential route from text to language. Our printed words are not arbitrary collections of letters; they are, by and large, representations of the spoken sounds. If a child can master the correspondence between letters and pronunciation, then it becomes possible to convert each word into the appropriate sound pattern, and the child need only listen to him- or herself to 'hear' the text as if it were speech. This mechanism is also represented in teaching, when children are taught by the 'phonic' (sometimes called 'phonetic') method.

Neither of the word recognition routes is without problems. The chief difficulty with the so-called **visual route** (recognizing whole words) is that there are so many words to learn. We can gain some measure of the magnitude of the task by considering the situation for Chinese children. Chinese characters are **ideograms**; they have names and represent whole words, but their pronunciation cannot be deduced from the pattern. Indeed, different regions of China speak different dialects (e.g. Mandarin or Cantonese), so put entirely different words to the ideograms. However, ideograms retain the same meaning, so people who cannot speak to one another can write to each other. We too use ideograms; for example two parallel, horizontal lines (i.e. =) cannot be pronounced, but we know they represent 'equals'. So, how do Chinese children get on with their ideogram learning? It turns out that they have to work at acquiring a written vocabulary, right up into teenage years. Since Western children would hope to have mastered reading by that age, it is tempting to assume that they do not use the visual route to read. However, we must reserve judgement.

English has a notoriously difficult system of spelling. What are called **spelling-to-sound correspondence rules** do apply to most of our words, but there is a large proportion of irregular words, some which are downright bizarre! Infamous examples are: cough, plough, rough, through and dough. Even if we discount the more extreme vagaries of the language, a child attempting to read by what is termed the **phonological route** still has a difficult task in trying to make the letters map onto sounds. For a start, some letters, in some situations, are silent, but serve to change the pronunciations of other letters (e.g. putting an 'e' on the end of 'hat'). Consonants can be a source of difficulty, because it is difficult to speak their sounds without also introducing some vowel sound. Thus, children are often asked to 'sound out' the letters, as in c - a - t, but the result becomes rendered as something like 'ker-atter', a sound very far removed from 'cat'. Looking to other languages again, for comparison, it turns out that children learning to read a very regularly spelled language, such as Finnish, do acquire the skill faster than English speakers. The relative slowness with English may indicate that the phonological route is used, although with difficulty, or it might mean that some children are trying to employ the visual route, at least some of the time. More often than not, the children who find reading particularly difficult are boys. Men tend to be slightly better than women at visuo-spatial tasks, such as map reading; women are considered better at linguistic skills. It has been suggested that some boys try to capitalize on their relative visuo-spatial strength, and attempt to use the visual route. This gives them a task as hard as for the Chinese. The girls, in contrast, discover the imperfect, but altogether easier phonological approach.

Before we consider the various pieces of evidence that point to how adults process text, try to read the following, imagining that it was written by a terrible speller:

> Althoe theeze wurds ar orl kompleetly rong, yoo shood kope kwite eezilly.

If indeed you did cope quite easily, it looks as if you have a very effective phonological route. Even primary school teachers are unlikely to have encountered quite such a disastrous collection of misspellings, so it is safe to assume that no reader will have seen many of them before. That means that reading by visual recognition was impossible, so presumably you used spelling-to-sound rules. However, before concluding that all your reading is done like that, have a look at the following example of bad spelling:

> Hear eye no ewe ah shore two fined it hard, four these ah knot awl the write spellings.

All of those words have genuine (if inappropriate) spellings, but most of them are **homophones**, i.e. words that, although differently spelled, have the same pronunciation. If you found it difficult to get the sense of the sentence you might complain that it was because it was too ambiguous: so many homophones made it confusing. This explanation would claim, for example, that when you reached the word 'two' you were unable to tell whether it stood for to, two, or too. However, English has many homophones, and we seem to deal with them very well. Try reading the offending sentence to someone who is not looking at it. It will be found that, in spite of the many ambiguous words, they will understand it without difficulty. Since all the words above have the correct sounds to fit the sentence, the only possible explanation for the reading difficulty is that you were recognizing their shapes, and so finding the inappropriate (for the sentence) meanings. It looks as if you are a bit of a visual route user too! Those were rather informal tests of your approach to reading; we will now look at the results of properly conducted research, to see whether it confirms the implication that we read by both routes.

3 Letters and words

Words are, of course, composed of letters, so it seems reasonable to assume that word perception proceeds via letter perception. That would certainly be expected if letters were used to derive the pronunciation of the word (i.e. if the phonological route were used), but purely visual analysis (the visual route) should proceed from the entire pattern, rather than on a letter-by-letter basis. There have been many experiments which can throw light upon the extent to which individual letters are important. Many of these experiments have used a piece of apparatus called a **tachistoscope**. 'Tachi' means fast, as in the medical condition tachycardia – a racing heart. The 'scope' part of the word implies that this is something for seeing. In fact the apparatus is designed to give a visual display for a very brief, but accurately measured length of time. Early examples of the tachistoscope used shutters, like a camera, but the modern version simply displays material on a computer screen for a short time, short meaning a duration of the order of 50 milliseconds, or one twentieth of a second.

When a person is flashed a group of, say, ten random letters for a fraction of a second, it turns out that they will probably be able to identify only three of them. However, if they are shown two five-letter words for the same duration they will probably be able to say what both the words were; that is, they have somehow managed to report ten, rather than three letters. In itself, this may tell us little more than something of how the memory works. Thus, it certainly takes longer than 50 ms to remember a set of ten letters; on the other hand, one can read and remember just two words very quickly. The fact that two items are easier to remember than ten does not say much about the route used to recognize the words.

The memory issue raised above has been addressed by getting people to remember just one letter – either on its own, or in a word. In one phase of the study, people are flashed a single letter, for a very brief period, and asked what it was. Thus, a 'd' might appear, and the viewer has to try to say what was displayed. In the next phase, a complete word is flashed for the same time; it might be 'hand'. The viewer is then asked what the last letter was, and it turns out that they actually do better at spotting 'd' in a word than on its own. This is remarkable, because it means that we can see a letter better when there are three others to analyse too. The phenomenon has been named the **word superiority effect**.

You might spot a flaw in the above description. It could be argued that the 'd' was not really seen any better in the word, but if one or two of the other letters were glimpsed, then the last letter could probably be guessed. Someone would guess correctly a sufficient number of times to make the averages suggest that looking for letters in words was easier. Later studies found a way of controlling for guessing. The word 'han-' could potentially end with 'd' or 'g', so instead of asking people what was the last letter, they were asked simply whether it was a 'd' or 'g'. Of course, many other similar examples were used, such as showing 'bell' and asking whether the last letter was 'l' or 't'. If people were really guessing, then they should have averaged 50% correct; in fact they did rather better, at around 60%. This is not a high score (the reading conditions were very difficult), but the results did show that putting a letter in a word makes it easier to identify.

Clearly all the words we know are stored in some form in our memories, like the entries in a dictionary. Our word storage system is referred to as a **lexicon**, and each item (word) is said to have a **lexical entry**. The word superiority effect can be explained by assuming that enough of a word is seen in the time available, for the appropriate lexical entry to be activated. If someone asks you the last letter of the stimulated entry, the task is not much different from being asked 'How do you spell 'hand'?' This is a reasonable explanation, but unfortunately it does not tell us what we want to know: whether the lexical entry is activated simply by the visual appearance of the word, or whether it is first translated into 'sound'. We can begin to address this issue by using nonwords, instead of words. People shown the unpronounceable 'agbd' and asked 'Was the last letter 'd' or 'g'?' are hopeless! This is not surprising, because we do not have 'agbd' in our lexicons, but what if we flash the letters 'kand' and ask the same question? This time people do rather better. That cannot be because we have a lexical entry for 'kand' or 'kang', but must have something to do with the fact that these nonwords are pronounceable. If pronunciation is a factor, then the phonological route is implicated.

Researchers felt uneasy about drawing strong conclusions about the reading of words, upon the basis of our behaviour with nonwords. They looked for another kind of test material, and decided upon homophones (like sent and cent), stimuli to which researchers in this field often seem to return. Suppose you had just seen 'sent' flashed for a moment and were asked whether the first letter was a 'c' or 's'. How would you expect to do? If all you had registered was the *sound* of the word, you would have no idea what initial letter had been used. That is exactly what was found; people could do no better than the chance hit rate of 50%, suggesting strongly that a phonological route was employed to register the words.

There is one last twist to this part of the story. When people were given plenty of practice with homophones the sent/cent problem went away, and the word superiority effect returned. This can be explained by assuming that people have some control over the route they use; if they find the phonological approach unhelpful they can switch to the visual route and escape the confusion. Clearly the mechanisms of word perception are difficult to pin down, so a variety of test procedures is needed to try to determine exactly what is going on. As well as looking at the analysis of letters within words, it has proved useful to investigate the perception of the word itself.

4 The lexical decision task

Varieties of the **lexical decision task** are probably the most widely used investigative tools in the field of reading research. The task merely requires a person to decide whether or not a group of letters is represented in their lexicon; put simply, they are asked whether the letters spell a word, and they have to decide as quickly as possible. Typically the letters are shown on a computer screen, and the viewer has to press one of two keys on the keyboard, representing 'yes' and 'no', for word or nonword. The computer measures how long this takes, from the moment the letters appear, to the point when the key is pressed. Response times are of the order of half to three quarters of a second, with 'no' decisions taking longer than 'yes', and common words like 'the' producing faster responses than rare words such as 'thy'.

Early researchers assumed that lexical entries were located by their sounds; in other words, a phonological route was used. Once a word entry was accessed, information such as its meaning would become available. Importantly, there would also be information on how to spell the word, so this could be checked with the letters presented, to ensure that this was indeed a word. In support of this position, it was found that people took longer to say 'no' to a nonword like 'brane', than to one such as 'brame'. The most obvious difference between these is that 'brane' sounds like 'brain'; it is a kind of homophone. Since it is a nonword, it is called a **pseudohomophone**. The explanation given for the additional slowness is that the pronunciation of 'brame' does not find a lexical entry, whereas 'brane' does. Having found the entry for 'brain' a spelling check is performed, and of course it fails, so 'no' is pressed. However, all this checking will have taken extra time, hence the slower response to pseudohomophones.

The above results sound like good evidence for phonological analysis, but as stated earlier, people are reluctant to base too many conclusions upon responses to *non*words, when the goal is to discover how we process words. Once again, researchers turned to homophones to settle the matter. Consider the words 'week' and 'weak'. The former is encountered far more frequently than the latter; it is said to be a higher frequency word. As explained above, high-frequency words elicit 'yes' responses more quickly than do low-frequency words; the lexical entries of common words are presumably located more easily. What should we expect if the low frequency word 'weak' is presented in the lexical decision task? If its location were found by visual recognition, then it would eventually be located, a little slowly, as for any low-frequency word, but with nothing out of the ordinary. However, the 'phonological story' would be rather more complicated. Having derived the pronunciation for 'weak', the lexicon would be searched, finding the high-frequency entry first. On doing a spelling check it would be found that this entry represented the sound by the letters 'week'; this is a mismatch, so searching must continue, eventually to find the matching entry for 'weak'. The 'false alarm' would have taken extra time, so the 'yes' should come even more slowly than for other low frequency words. The crucial test, to distinguish between the visual and phonological routes, is whether responses to the lower frequency members of homophone pairs (not 'pears' or 'pares'!) are merely slow, or whether they are extra slow. Unfortunately, the results are far from clear; some researchers report the additional slowing, but others have failed to find it. There is some indication that the slowing is present, unless the stimulus list used for the lexical decisions contains a lot of homophones and pseudohomophones. This implies, once again, that people move from phonological to visual analysis, when they find that the pronunciations are unhelpful, or confusing.

5 Deliberate confusion

Discovering how people respond in a confusing situation can sometimes be very revealing. One of the most confusing phenomena, devised by psychologists, is the **Stroop effect**, named after the researcher who first described it. To experience the effect for yourself you have a very simple task to perform, and you do not even have to know how to read to carry it out. In the table below there are columns of words, printed in coloured inks. Go down each column, as quickly as possible, calling out the ink colours of each word, but not bothering to read the words. See how quickly you can go, using a stopwatch if you want to be precise.

round	big	fine
great	long	thin
square	round	great
big	fine	round
fine	great	long
round	square	big
long	long	square

That no doubt seemed a reasonably straightforward task, and if you followed the instructions about not reading you will probably be unable to remember many of the words used. Now try to repeat your performance on the next set of words. Remember not to read them; just name the inks as fast as possible.

green	blue	red
blue	black	black
black	red	green
red	blue	blue
green	black	green
blue	green	red
yellow	blue	yellow

If that seemed very difficult it must be that, in spite of the instructions, you did read the words, and of course found them confusing. Although reading the words was detrimental to the task, you were unable to prevent yourself processing them. It seems that, once we have learned to read, it is a very difficult skill to 'turn off'. In the preceding sections it has been suggested that readers can change the reading route used, if the current one is leading to confusion. However, in the case of the Stroop effect, a situation of great confusion, it is clear that there is a limit to how much a reader can abandon the word processing routes. Perhaps one can be dropped, but not both, or maybe the route usually used has to be retained. These are speculations; what we need is a means of testing the routes individually.

Some years ago this was attempted, by using what is known as **articulatory suppression**. It is known that the muscles of the vocal apparatus can be active when people read, as if they are speaking under their breath. Even if the reader is unaware of doing this, small electrical signals can be picked up from the articulatory muscles, so it has been claimed that speech movements are an integral part of reading by the phonological route. If that were true, then suppressing the movement ought to make phonological reading impossible. The best way of stopping the muscles from following the print is to give them something else to say; this cannot be anything too complicated, because that would distract from the reading, when all we wish to do is keep the muscles busy. A favourite approach is to ask people to keep repeating 'Double, double, double …'. You might try it now; read a few lines of this text, while saying double over and over again. If you were able to make sense of what you were reading, in spite of the articulatory suppression, then perhaps you were using the visual route; on the other hand, it may just be that 'doubling' does not actually interfere with finding the pronunciation of words. There is controversy about this issue, but nevertheless, articulatory suppression, or **concurrent vocalization**, as it is also called, has been attempted with the Stroop test.

If you have followed the story so far, you may be wondering how one can call out ink colours and say double, double at the same time. The trick is to change the nature of the Stroop task. Each word is written on a separate card, then the pack is shuffled. The task is then to sort the cards as quickly as possible into piles of the same ink colour (ignoring the word). The same confusion arises as before when the words are colour names, and by timing how long it takes to sort the pack, a measure of the confusion can be gained. With the sorting being done by hand, the mouth is free to say double. What does 'doubling' do to card sorting times? Well, when this idea was first explored, the concurrent vocalization seemed to enable the colour-name cards to be sorted as quickly as cards bearing neutral words. It looked very much as if the people tested would usually read phonologically (and get confused by the words as a result), but the suppression stopped the phonological processing, and so removed the confusion. Unfortunately for this neat account, other researchers have failed to get similar results. This, together with the fact that a question mark hangs over the action of articulatory suppression, suggests that it would be dangerous to conclude too much from suppression experiments. A different approach to the Stroop effect is required if we are to gain a clearer view of the relative importance of reading 'by shape' and 'by sound'.

I tested the phonological route by means of pseudohomophones, nonwords that would be pronounced like colour names. They were 'BLOO', 'WYTE', 'YELLOE', 'GREAN' and 'PERPLE', written in upper case, with coloured inks, one to a card. A complete pack comprised 25 cards, each 'word' repeated five times. To get a measure of how confusing (or not) these stimuli might be, I needed two 'anchor points'. I used the real versions of the colour names (BLUE, WHITE, YELLOW, GREEN and PURPLE), which would certainly be very confusing, and another set of nonwords, as unlike colour names as possible, except that they had the same numbers of letters and syllables. They were 'FRON', 'MOBE', 'DEVORT', 'BLATE' and 'STEGIN'. Presumably these would cause little confusion. These two sets of stimuli were also printed on two further packs of 25 cards. With these three packs almost everything was in place to test whether people doing the Stroop test, and trying not to read, found themselves doing so by the phonological route. However, there was one problem. It is true that GREAN, say, sounds just like GREEN, and so should confuse a phonological reader, but it also *looks* a lot like the real word, with 80% of the letters in common. Thus, a person who read by visual appearance might also be confused by my nonwords, because they look so similar to the real thing. If I found that people were slowed by my pseudohomophones I would not know whether it was the shape, the pronunciation, or both that were being analysed. To get round this difficulty I produced one last pack of cards. These were to have nonwords that had just as many letters in common with the proper spellings as before, but they would not be pronounced like colour names. I used 'BLOD', 'WOTE', 'YELLOT', 'GRELN' and 'PARPLE'. If people found these confusing, it could only be that they tended to read by the visual route. I gave my four packs to 24 men and 24 women to sort, measuring how long each pack took. The results have been averaged and summarized in Figure 1.

Figure 1 Times taken to sort packs of colour cards.

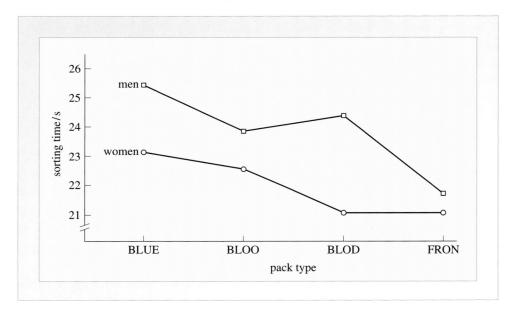

As can be seen, women tended to be about two seconds quicker than men, and the pattern of the results also differed between the sexes. Consider how the women behaved first. Not surprisingly, they were slowest with the real word pack, and quickest with nonwords like FRON. With pseudohomophones (e.g. BLOO) they were almost as slow as for the real words, so they must have processed these stimuli almost as if they *were* real words. The question is, were they confused by the similarity of shape or of pronunciation? The answer lies with the remaining pack, the shape-like nonwords, such as BLOD. Women could deal with this pack as quickly as the FRON pack, so presumably they were quite immune to shape. If BLOO caused confusion, it must have been produced by its pronunciation. The women were phonological readers.

The men I tested behaved rather differently. They did not find BLOO and the rest of the pseudohomophones nearly as confusing as the real words, although they were processed more slowly than the FRON set, so there must have been some confusion. Since the pseudohomophones sounded *exactly* like the real words, one might have expected complete confusion, but only if the nonwords were processed phonologically. It is tempting to suggest that the *partial* confusion results from BLOO looking just somewhat like BLUE. This seems to be confirmed by the fact that men found the similar shape nonwords (e.g. BLOD), almost as confusing as the real thing. It seems that the men were using a visual route.

It would be unwise to read into this single study the conclusion that all men, in all reading situations, process text by its shape, whereas women always derive its pronunciation. However, the results do fit in with the idea mentioned earlier, that men tend to have a facility for spatial processing, while women are stronger in language-based tasks. A far more recent study than mine seems to show phonological processing in everyone. The method was ingenious; it used people bilingual in Hebrew and English, and gave them a Stroop test using rather special pseudohomophones. The study got round the problem of separating 'sound alike' from 'look alike' by using the letters of one language to spell (phonetically) the *sound* of a colour word in the other language. With the two scripts being so very different (see Figure 2) these mixed language pseudohomophones *looked* absolutely nothing like the colour names in either language. Nevertheless, they generated the usual slowing associated with the Stroop effect.

| real colour word | red | צדם |
| pronunciation in other script | רצד | edam |

Figure 2 Hebrew and English representations of the colour red. (Note: Hebrew is read from right to left)

Interestingly, brain-mapping studies are beginning to throw some light on the issue of sex differences in reading. People were given a task requiring rhyming judgements to be made about printed words, an activity assumed to involve phonological processes. Using fMRI, it was found that a region of the brain involved in speech (called Broca's area) was active during the task; in men the activity tended to be concentrated in the left hemisphere, whereas for women it was more bilateral. What is more, it was later shown that people with stronger bilateral activity are also more likely to be slowed down by homophones, during lexical decision tasks.

6 Japanese Stroop

The Japanese use a form of writing inherited from the Chinese; it is called Kanji. As it comprises ideographs, it can only be read by visual recognition, just as with Chinese writing. However, in Japan the problem of getting children to learn all the characters, before they can advance in their reading, is avoided by using another writing system in parallel. This one is called Kana, and like the Western system of writing, it is designed to convey the sounds of words. However, whereas most languages use alphabets, Kana employs a syllabary; instead of characters representing small sound elements (as in English), they correspond to complete syllables. Here is an Anglicized example. Suppose we used the symbol ϑ to represent the sound 'cat'; we would then put ϑ when we wanted to write about a cat. In the same way we could use ζ to represent 'pill', and perhaps $\wedge$ to indicate the sound 'er'. What do you suppose $\vartheta \wedge \zeta \wedge$ would spell? You should have read 'caterpillar'. That, apart from the fact that Japanese is written vertically, is how Kana works, and even if one cannot read Japanese, it is at least possible to see how many syllables there are in a word! Because Kana is so straightforward and completely regular (no equivalents to 'sleigh', for example), the children learn to read very quickly, then acquire the Kanji in 'slow time'. You might wonder why they bother at all, but it is considered that Kanji characters (whole words, remember) convey a richness that is lost in a rigid spelling system. As pointed out earlier, Kanji (like Chinese) must be read visually; Kana could be processed by a visual route too, but being so easy to pronounce it seems likely that the processing is largely phonological.

Figure 3 Colour words in two Japanese orthographies.

English name	Japanese pronunciation	Kana	Kanji
red	**aka**	あか	赤
green	**midori**	みどり	緑

As in any language, it is possible to devise Stroop stimuli in Japanese, and there is the added interest of being able to see whether the sound-based or visually-based script produces more confusion. Moreover, this offers the opportunity of seeing just what it is that concurrent vocalization does. If it really impacts just upon the phonological route, then it ought to reduce the Stroop effect for Kana words, but not those written in the 'visual' Kanji. I was able to put these ideas to the test when a Japanese colleague took some packs of Stroop cards back to Japan, to test on her friends. Three packs were prepared, one each for Kana and Kanji (Figure 3), and one where the cards contained just XXX, written in coloured ink. XXX does not look like a Japanese word, so that pack served as a baseline, against which to judge the extent of the slowing. The volunteers sorted all three packs, twice over, once in silence and once with concurrent vocalization. My colleague was able to find sixteen people willing to participate; ideally one would use more, to get dependable averages, but the results obtained were informative. They are summarized in Table 1.

Table 1   Number of seconds taken to sort Japanese colour-word packs.

	pack type		
	XXX	Kana	Kanji
silent	14.9	21.6	19.1
vocalizing	15.6	19.9	19.0

As can be seen, both Kana and Kanji words produced confusion; these packs were sorted five or six seconds more slowly than the XXX pack. When the task was carried out in silence, Kana words seemed slightly more troublesome than the Kanji equivalents, but that difference was eliminated by concurrent articulation; i.e. talking made the sound-based Kana less confusing. In contrast, the articulation had little impact upon the sorting times for the Kanji pack. Importantly, articulatory suppression did not stop the Kana confusion altogether; it remained as bad as the Kanji. One interpretation of these results is as follows. Concurrent vocalization does indeed disrupt phonological processing, and prevents characters from being read by that route. Since Kanji is read only by shape, vocalization has no impact upon it. Colour names are quite high-frequency words (i.e. they are commonly encountered in print), so Japanese readers become familiar with the *visual* appearance of colour names written in Kana, as well as knowing how to derive their sounds. Consequently, Kana words are, if anything, more confusing in the Stroop test, because their disrupting information gets in by two routes. However, during concurrent vocalization the phonological route is cut, so only the visual interference remains.

More research would be required to confirm the various components of the above story, but it at least reminds us that colour words are common. Consequently, it is likely that English readers, like their Japanese counterparts, are good at recognizing a word such as RED, both from its visual appearance and from its pronunciation. This ability to use both routes might account for why conflicting results have been obtained from different articulatory suppression experiments. The more practised the reader, and the higher the frequency of the words used, the more likely it is that the words will be recognized visually. Many psychological studies use university undergraduate volunteers, a population which can be assumed to do a great deal of reading. The first Stroop/suppression study that I described earlier used members of the general public, many of whom may have been relatively infrequent readers who relied upon a phonological approach.

7 Confusing sentences

There are two difficulties associated with using the Stroop effect to examine how reading takes place. First, discovering how people read when they are trying not to do so, may not be a very good way of determining what processes are used when they do wish to read. Second, like so many studies, the reading tested is for individual words. Reading usually takes place with sentences, and studies have shown the context of a sentence to influence the processing of individual words within it. Nevertheless, seeing how people cope with confusion can be illuminating, and for a confusing sentence one could do worse than use the sort mentioned in Section 2 (*Hear eye no ewe ah shore two fined it hard, four these ah knot awl the write spellings*).

My examples, which almost certainly will have worked appropriately for you, were not a formal test of reading by sight or by sound. I mentioned that one of the potential difficulties with the homophonic sentence was that most of the words had at least two meanings; that level of ambiguity might slow the reader, irrespective of the spelling. I dismissed this idea at the time, pointing out that people can understand the sentences if they hear them, rather than see them printed, but for a formal experiment we really need to compare correctly spelled sentences, homophonic sentences, and pseudohomophonic sentences. For a proper comparison, these should all be versions of the same sentence, just in case some sentences are inherently harder to read than others. A typical sentence, in its three forms, would be:

Lady Godiva rode a horse bare through Coventry.   (correct)

Lady Godiva road a hoarse bear threw Coventry.   (homophonic)

Lady Godiva roed a horss bair thrue Coventry.   (pseudohomophonic)

We need to know how long it takes people to understand such sentences, and an easy way is to make them part of a true-or-false task. The reader has to indicate, as quickly as possible, whether the sense of the sentence (not its spelling) is true or not. Since Lady Godiva allegedly rode naked through Coventry the above sentences should all have elicited 'true' responses. Examples of a false sentence would be:

The knight is a piece in draughts.   (correct)

The night is a peace in drafts.   (homophonic)

The nite is a peess in drarphts.   (pseudohomophonic)

I produced 24 sets of sentences, each in three versions, and presented them, one at a time, on a computer screen. As soon as the readers had decided whether the sentence was correct they typed a 'yes' or 'no' key, and the computer recorded how long it had taken, from when the sentence was first displayed. People saw only one version of each sentence, eight correct, eight homophonic and eight pseudohomophonic. Different people saw different sets of eight. The average timings are shown in Table 2.

Table 2 Mean times taken (seconds) to understand different sentence types.

sentence type		
Lady Godiva rode...	Lady Godiva road...	Lady Godive roed...
1.86	2.90	2.54

As expected, the correct sentences were processed the fastest, taking, on average, 1.9 seconds. Again as you might expect from your own experience, the homophonic sentences were the slowest at 2.9 seconds, but this was only marginally slower than the pseudohomophones, which averaged 2.5 seconds. Statistical analysis showed this small difference to be insignificant; in other words, it was probably just chance that made the 'hoarse bear' type of sentence a little slower than 'horss bair'. You may well feel that this is at variance with your own experience, where complete misspelling seemed so much easier to read than the correctly spelled, but inappropriate homophones. There appear to be two factors at work. First, in order to generate pronunciations which sounded like words, but which were not spelled like a word (i.e. pseudohomophones), it was necessary to resort to some very odd letter combinations. Remember that I was trying to generate nonword equivalents for sounds that already had two proper spellings associated with them. That did not leave many conventional letter groupings, and resulted in examples such as 'kawd' (chord/cord), 'knun' (none/nun) and 'klyme' (clime/climb). Although these nonwords were sufficiently unlike the real equivalents that confusion by shape was unlikely, it is probable that readers' unfamiliarity with deriving pronunciations from such combinations would make them rather slow. Thus, anything gained by the absence of visual confusion was lost in the time taken to work out the sounds.

In addition to the influence of the bizarre spellings, there seemed to be a practice factor at work. For the first few presentations of sentences of the 'hoarse bear' type, people did indeed seem extra slow, but they quickly improved, so that the average time was very similar to the 'horss bair' sentences. Presumably this was another example of readers selecting the route they would use, on the basis of whether it produced confusion. Previous cases mentioned have suggested that the phonological route can be abandoned; here it may be that it is the visual route which loses favour.

8 Evidence from damaged brains

Thus far, the evidence seems to be not only that we have the *theoretical* possibility of reading by one of two routes, but also that we actually *do* use both of them. Here and there in the descriptions I have injected a note of caution, but I have tried to show how a wide range of techniques all tend to point to broadly similar conclusions, so supporting the same story. The beauty of the experimental approach to answering questions is that all the various potential influences upon human behaviour can be controlled rigorously, the minutiae of an issue can be addressed, and there can be no doubt about the final results of the study. Unfortunately, and as you may have noticed from what I have presented so far, although the results might be sound, they are often found to be open to more than one interpretation. Many an experimental psychologist makes a good living from finding alternative explanations for others' results, then devising experiments of his or her own to test the alternative story! In this section we shall be considering a different approach to the reading question; we shall be trying to deduce how the system works by observing the errors that occur when it is not working. Such a failure can occur when people suffer strokes or head injuries.

At the heart of this approach to reading research lies the assumption that different processes take place in different regions of the brain; i.e. the brain is modular. That has long been known to be the case in broad terms: visual analysis at the back, speech on the left (for most right-handed people), and so on, but here we are also assuming that reading is further subdivided into visual and phonological regions, if indeed those two routes exist. In fact there are even more facets to reading than that, because in addition to basic analysis of a word, for reading to be useful the word's meaning has to be found. Also, if one is reading aloud, and has processed the text visually (as must be the case with mathematical symbols, even if not all words), then the pronunciation has to be found, together with the 'instructions' that are sent to the vocal apparatus to generate speech. Not surprisingly, damage in many areas of the brain can result in an impairment in one or another aspect of reading; here we shall concentrate principally upon evidence that might show whether there are separate visual and phonological pathways. It should be noted that all reading, whether visual or phonological, would have to commence with an initial visual analysis of the patterns on the paper.

Many patients have been kind enough to allow their impairments to be investigated and published. To preserve their anonymity, it has become traditional to refer to them by their initials. One, JC, was reported as being able to read (which in this context means speak aloud) about half the regular words he was shown, but less than a third of the irregular. Thus, he might manage to pronounce a word like 'gland', but make 'glove' rhyme with 'cove'. A more extreme example was MP, who could get over 90% of regular words correct, even if they were low-frequency words. However, with low-frequency irregular words he managed only 40% correct. This condition, which has become known as **surface dyslexia**, implies that the sufferer can successfully use spelling-to-sound rules to convert letters to sounds, as long as a word is regular; if it disobeys the rules the wrong pronunciation results. It would seem that the patient has lost the visual route, which would lead him directly to word recognition, and would presumably allow him to retrieve the pronunciation of the word, just as he would if using it in conversation. A further test of this explanation can be made by asking a patient to read pronounceable nonwords, such as 'brame'. As there is no lexical entry for 'brame', the letters cannot be recognized via a visual route; success at pronunciation can come only through phonological analysis. KT could do all that; he read nonwords as well as an unimpaired person, but misread over half the irregular words that he was shown. With regular words of similar frequency he achieved a perfect score.

The cases cited all support the idea that visual analysis can become impaired, while leaving a phonological route relatively intact. That sounds very much as if there are two routes, one of which can be damaged while sparing the other, but the account would be strengthened if the reverse pattern of results could be found, with sound derivation damaged, but visual recognition intact. Such cases have indeed been reported; the condition is known as **phonological dyslexia**, because there seems to be an inability to use the phonological route. RG was tested with 40 words and 40 nonwords. He could read all the words, but only managed to pronounce 4 of the nonwords. WB could read most words he was shown, including quite low-frequency, polysyllabic words, such as 'satirical'. In contrast, he was unable to read even the simplest nonword, such as 'nust', a failure that implied he had lost the ability to convert from letters to sounds. All the words he read must have been recognized from their patterns, rather than their pronunciations.

It has been a tenet of **neuropsychology** (the discipline that links behaviour to neural structures in the brain) that when complementary patterns of deficit can be found, then it is virtual proof for the existence of two structures. Thus, the descriptions above of people who have lost the ability to read either irregular words, or simple nonwords, have generally been taken as very strong support for what is known as the **dual route theory of reading**. In fact the behaviour of some brain damaged patients suggests that a third route may be available, at least for generating speech from text. I pointed out at the beginning of this section that patients were generally tested by getting them to read aloud the printed words placed in front of them. Strictly, being able to speak a printed word does not guarantee that the reader has understood it, and after all, understanding is what reading should be all about. Is one being pedantic to make this distinction? Well, we should consider the issue a little further.

It seems entirely possible that a person confined to the phonological route might produce an appropriate pronunciation, without having any idea of what the word meant. For example, you are likely to be able to pronounce 'gunter' correctly, but unless you have boating interests and know that it is a type of sailing rig, the word will have no meaning for you: it might as well have been a nonword. We know that surface dyslexics can read nonwords, so perhaps real words are just as nonsensical to them. That probably is not the case, because to take part in the tests these patients can obviously understand the spoken requests of the experimenter. For them, words that they hear spoken are intelligible, and that must include the words they speak themselves.

The case of phonological dyslexics appears at first to be even more cut and dried. Since these patients are unable to deduce a word sound, they recognize words visually, and then find a pronunciation (if required to read aloud). It has often been assumed that the visual recognition stage takes the reader direct to the word's meaning (and pronunciation details), so the idea of phonological dyslexics reading aloud without understanding seems implausible. However, the patient WB calls this simple reasoning into question. To remind you, he could read a word like 'brush', but not a nonword such as 'grush'. His investigator tested his understanding by showing him a pair of pictures, and asking which matched the word. So, to go with 'brush' he might be shown a picture of a brush, and one of a cup. He could select the right picture: so far so good. The test was repeated with pictures of a brush and a comb. This time he picked the comb. It seems that for WB the letters b-r-u-s-h triggered some concept of a 'hair tidier', which was clear enough to distinguish it from a cup, but was too fuzzy to avoid confusion with a comb. Presumably there was damage to his meaning storage area too. That is not unique; there have been cases of patients who shown the word 'lightning' might say aloud 'thunder'. However, this does not happen with WB; if he used his faulty understanding to discover a word's pronunciation he should have read 'brush' as 'comb'. He did not make that kind of error, so must have had another way of getting from the visual pattern of the word to its pronunciation.

Once again, a field of research has provided puzzles as well as answers. The difficulty for investigators in this area is that they cannot set up experiments to order. They have to wait for patients to appear with just the right set of symptoms; many patients may have lost the ability to read altogether, or be more or less equally impaired on all kinds of words and nonwords. Clearly, such cases cannot contribute useful data to this particular debate. Nevertheless, enough information has been gleaned from neuropsychological data, and from conventional laboratory experiments, that psychologists are willing to suggest likely pathways by which words can be understood, or spoken. One possibility is shown in Figure 4 (overleaf).

Figure 4   Routes by which speech and the printed word might be understood.

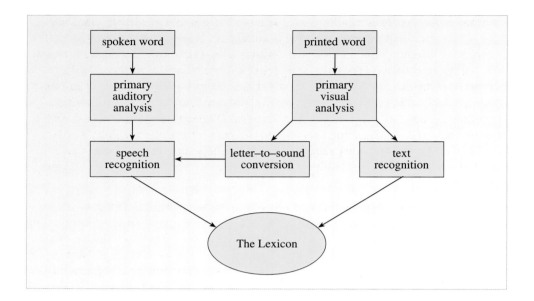

9 Connectionism and computer modelling

In recent years computers have become sufficiently powerful for them to implement models of human mental processes; i.e. the computers are set up to simulate human behaviour. In fact, modelling of a sort has been used for several decades, but early attempts were merely implementations of the program-writer's idea of how humans behaved. If the program worked, that proved that the writer's ideas were not impossible, but of course this was not proof that the ideas were actually correct. To make this point more concrete, suppose that someone devised a program that could read text, and that part of the system was written to recognize the word shapes, while another part was programmed to deduce pronunciations for regular letter combinations. That would make a very nice model of the dual route theory, but just because the programmer put two routes in the program does not mean that there are two in our heads. Recently a very different approach has developed, based upon the ideas of **connectionism**.

The connectionist approach recognizes that the brain is modular at a coarse level, i.e. with major functions carried out in different regions, but below this level there is presumed to be no specialization. Microscopic study of brain material seems to confirm that there are large, amorphous areas of neurons, which are not divided into sub-groups as might be expected from a 'box-and-arrow' picture such as illustrated in Figure 4. The neurons are extensively interconnected, with some receiving as many as one thousand links from others. The connections, or synapses, are of course the means by which one neuron influences the activity of another and, with so many connections involved, an exceedingly large number of different activity patterns can be achieved. Different patterns could (in the appropriate region of the brain) represent different words, and the activity might be triggered if one heard or read a word. Learning (such as when learning to read) takes place by changing the strengths of synapses. In other words, some are made to exert more influence upon the receiving neuron, while others become weaker. These adjustments lead to very specific activity patterns being associated with specific triggering signals. (Presumably, WB, with his brush and comb confusion, had lost some of this specificity.)

From the above brief description, which it should be emphasized hardly does the topic justice, you will see why the field is known as connectionism. Central to connectionist thinking is the belief that neurons do not have to be 'pre-wired' in any way. All that is required is to have a large number of brain cells, with a very large number of connections between them, and through experience the connections will adjust until the whole group has achieved its own wiring. Intuitively this position is appealing, because to be born with special neural connections in place would require an enormous amount of genetic encoding to define all the necessary links. In the case of reading, it is only very recently, in evolutionary terms, that humans have invented writing, so it is impossible that we have had time to evolve special reading connections.

Computers are now fast enough, and have sufficient memory, that they can be programmed to mimic some of the processes described above. They certainly cannot emulate the brain in terms of numbers of neurons; the brain has many billions, whereas programmers cannot currently do better than a few hundred equivalent units. Nevertheless, this can be sufficient to start to find answers to important questions. In the current context, the crux of the matter is whether the visual/phonological distinction exists at the level where the brain is accepted as modular, or whether all reading is mediated by the same set of brain cells which just behave as if there are two routes. The remainder of this section will look very briefly at a few attempts to model reading in this way.

An early model did not attempt to mimic reading for understanding; it was far closer to reading aloud, as it was taught to give pronunciations when presented with words or nonwords. The program did not literally pronounce (although that would have been possible); for ease, it produced the kind of representations used in dictionaries to indicate pronunciations. To teach these kinds of model, the computer repeatedly works through a list of all the items it is supposed to learn, while simultaneously checking against a matching list of correct responses, which in this case were the pronunciations. The computer monitors its own output, which will be wrong at first, and then makes small adjustments to its simulated synapses, in order to do a little better. It then moves on to the next item it has to learn, and so on, round and round the list. Eventually, probably after thousands of attempts, the model neurons should learn, and produce the correct responses for each input. You may wonder why the program does not simply make one large adjustment to the synapses, and get things right straight away. The problem is, a set of connections that work well for one item will probably be completely inappropriate for another. With large numbers of neurons and connections there are many possible combinations that could link one set of letters to their correct pronunciation, but not very many combinations that can get it right for all the letter sets. An individual neuron does not 'know' anything; all that can be done is for the group as a whole to inch its way, by trial and error, to a successful pattern of connections.

The model described here did manage to learn to pronounce its word list, and interestingly the list contained a mix of regular and irregular words. It is generally assumed that irregular words like 'yacht' or 'pint' must be read visually, since spelling-to-sound rules would produce a completely wrong pronunciation. On this basis, it would seem that the model had learned to mimic the visual route of human reading. However, the list did contain regular words, like 'patch' or 'mint', and these can be processed phonologically. The fact that a phonological pathway *can* be used does not mean that it is, so perhaps all the words, irrespective of regularity, were being recognized 'by sight'. The test for this was to give the program a nonword to read. A phonological system should be able to find a pronunciation for a pronounceable nonword; that is what surface dyslexics can do. On the other hand, if this system was, as suggested, reading all the words visually, then it would be like a phonological dyslexic, and be unable to read nonwords. Well, this early model was able to provide reasonable pronunciations for some nonwords. It was not too good at it, but it did seem that the single set of undifferentiated 'neurons' had gone some way to producing behaviour that mimicked both visual and phonological processing.

A more advanced **neural network**, as these models are called, used a similar pronunciation system, but also added simulated neurons that were to deal with meanings. For training this network, it had to be told not only how to pronounce each set of letters, but also some elementary detail about what the word meant. This was just a simple set of category representations, such as 'animal'. Once this network had learned, the researchers were able to do something denied to those working with humans: they could damage it to order. It is possible with a computer model to eliminate some of the simulated neurons or synapses, as if it had a stroke. Having done this to their model, it was unable to produce pronunciations, but curiously, it was still able to give some indication of meaning. It was behaving like a person who could not read a word, but knew what it meant. Such cases have been reported; people are sometimes able to say to what category a word belongs, even when they cannot say the word aloud. One person looked at the word 'nice' for a long time, and finally said, 'I can't read it, but I think it's a place in France'. He must have been thinking of Nice.

The model I have just described had meaning elements, but they were not linked to the pronunciation system. As discussed in Section 8, although WB seemed not to use a meaning-pronunciation route, unimpaired readers would be expected to have such a pathway. A very recent neural network did model the meaning-phonology link, and its performance was probably the most human-like yet, although it was still not perfect. There was one very interesting finding. You will recall that the first network I described had only one section, and it seemed, rather imperfectly, to process both regular and irregular words through it. This latest improved model was found, after it had been well trained, to be using the original section to derive just the regular pronunciations, but was obtaining the pronunciations of irregular words via the meaning-phonology pathway. It is important to note that the programmers had not designed the model to do this; the particular pattern of behaviour developed spontaneously, given the basic links. This sounds suspiciously like the development of visual and phonological pathways!

Connectionist modelling is still a relatively new approach to reading research, but the results do seem to confirm that reading can take place through different routes, even when the starting 'material' (the neural circuitry) is relatively amorphous. However, the kinds of 'route' that may develop are probably not the distinct pathways that early reading researchers had in mind.

10 Some concluding thoughts

Just how powerful written words are is underlined by the Stroop effect. It is remarkable that, having once learned to read, we are quite unable to prevent ourselves from being aware of the distracting word meanings. This happens soon after learning to read; thus children as young as six or seven can display a very convincing Stroop effect. Although colour words are found to be distracting in the task, other meanings can also degrade performance. This observation has given rise to the **emotional Stroop test**. You will recall that the demonstration in Section 5 compared colour names with non-colour words, such as 'round' and 'big'. In this context, they are described as neutral words, and are assumed to form a good baseline against which to measure the slowness of colour words. In fact those innocent words may not feel quite so neutral to someone who was trying to lose weight. For someone with a real eating disorder, such as anorexia, words like those, together with 'fat', 'chocolate', 'food', 'weight' and the like might generate detectable sensations of anxiety. For them, truly neutral words might be 'garden', or 'traffic'. It turns out that if two Stroop lists are prepared, one with 'fat' words, and the other with 'garden' words, then anorexics name the colours more slowly on the first list. Of course for most people there would be no difference in the naming times, so finding a slowing effect can be a useful diagnostic tool. My example happens to be related to eating, but the same technique can be employed with any potentially emotive vocabulary. Even if people do not believe that they have a problem, their perception of the coloured words is sufficiently influenced to produce measurable timing differences. As a note of caution, it should be pointed out that there are many reasons why some words may produce more slowing than others, including factors such as part of speech (e.g. noun or verb) or word frequency. It would be unwise to put a quick couple of lists together, and from trying them on oneself or friends start to believe that many were suffering from all manner of fears!

To have our perceptions affected, as a result of knowledge or beliefs that we already hold, is an example of top-down analysis. The early stages of analysis of a printed word, from the initial detection of the various line segments onwards, can be described as bottom-up, with the outcome of the analysis determined more or less entirely (not necessarily completely; recall the word superiority effect in Section 3) by the information derived from the retina. The further the analysis proceeds, the more it is influenced by prior knowledge and expectancy. The effect is not restricted to words that have high emotional saliency; it is a process that goes on all the time, especially when we are reading sentences.

Most reading, of course, deals with sentences, and as the meaning is extracted it is used to influence the meanings we give to later words. Take the following sentences, for example:

> Many Americans defend their right to bear arms vociferously, a reasonable
> position for members of rifle clubs, but potentially an invitation to tragedy.
> The shooting of the President came as a great shock to the First Lady; she had
> always believed him to be an excellent marksman!

Almost certainly you had to do something of a 'double take' as you read that. The problem is at the beginning of the second sentence, with the ambiguous word 'shooting'. The ambiguity is not finally resolved until the last word of the sentence, but you are unlikely to have noticed the ambiguity before then, since the earlier reference to tragedy inevitably biased your interpretation. Examples like this are often called 'garden path' sentences, because that is where they lead you! Apparatus exists which can detect precisely where a reader is looking; it can show whether he or she spends longer on some words than others. It turns out that ambiguity invites longer inspection times, but that where a meaning has been well signalled by the preceding text there is no unusual delay; that is an example of top-down processing working as it should. Unless deliberately trying to achieve some 'jolting' effect, good writers avoid leading their readers astray, as it slows the reading and makes it feel more arduous.

Well, I trust that I have not led you astray too often. As the Stroop effect shows, after learning to read one never sees things in quite the same way again. I hope that after reading this chapter you will never think of reading in quite the same way. As the Inca king Atahualpa observes, in Shaffer's play *The Royal Hunt of the Sun*: 'There is great power in these marks.'

11 Summary

This chapter has been concerned with how printed words are perceived. It assumed that basic visual processing had taken place, and then addressed the question of how the results of that early analysis could eventually give rise to a sense of meaning. It is its ability to convey meaning which makes the written word arguably the greatest invention of humankind.

Two mechanisms for the recognition of words have been identified: the visual route and the phonological route. The two common methods for teaching children to read, namely 'look and say' and 'phonic' techniques, assume that these two routes are operative. Evidence for the operation of one or both of these mechanisms comes from the application of the Stroop effect and from the variety of impairments in word recognition found for individuals with damaged brains. Investigations using the Stroop effect rely on different degrees of confusion, manifest by an increase in the time taken to undertake various tasks involving words. These studies variously involve the use of concurrent vocalization, homophones, pseudohomophones, nonwords and alternative language alphabets. The different approach of connectionism and computer modelling provides supporting evidence for the modular nature of the brain and the existence of the two word recognition routes. However, much about the way in which we recognize and interpret words still remains to be established.

PART THREE

TOUCH AND PAIN

18

Somatosensory Coding
Stanley Bolanowski

1 Introduction

Somatosensation is unique among the sensory systems. It is a multifaceted, multimodal sensory experience. It is multifaceted in that it is composed of sensations imposed on the body not only from the outside environment but also from the internal environment of the body as well as **proprioceptor** information about body movement. It is multimodal in that somatic perceptions arise as a result of the activation of tactile (mechanical stimulation), thermal (warmth and cold) and the receptors of noxious stimuli (or **nociceptors**). It is responsible for our feelings of well-being, hunger, thirst and even romantic love, to mention only a few primal, and not so primal, aspects of life. Pain and thermal perception, and the physiological mechanisms and anatomical organization mediating them, will be discussed in later chapters of this text. Here, we focus on the mechanical aspects of somatosensation, called **taction**.

2 Overview of somatosensation

The peripheral basis of tactile sensations arises by the activation of sensory receptors, located in the skin, that are responsive to mechanical stimuli. These sensory receptors are typically complex in structure (see below), but the basic organization is that of a neuron that has an unmyelinated terminal ending responsible for mechano-electric conversion. The remainder of the neuron is typically myelinated and conveys action potentials to the central nervous system. These neurons, called **mechanoreceptors**, do not have a synapse between the site of mechanoelectric conversion and action potential generation, unlike the mechanosensitive hair cells located in the cochlea of the auditory system (see Chapter 2, *Auditory signal transduction*). The tactile mechanoreceptors have their cell bodies located in structures called dorsal root ganglia. These ganglia are arranged along both sides of the dorsal aspect of the spinal column. Each vertebra of the spinal column has two (left and right) dorsal root ganglia associated with them, and they form the basis of the spinal nerves, which innervate regions of body surface called **dermatomes**. Nature has developed a separate, but parallel system for sensing the mechanical and other somatosensory experiences on the face. This system is called the **trigeminal system** and it operates in a manner quite similar to that of the spinal nerves and will only be briefly discussed here.

Neural activity arising in the spinal nerves as a result of mechanical stimulation of the mechanoreceptors is passed across the dorsal root ganglion and enters the spinal column, where it takes one of three routes. Following the first pathway, the activity is directly passed upward in the spinal column via tracts called the dorsal columns (Figure 1). These bilateral dorsal columns are myelinated fibre tracts in the posterior region of the spinal cord. It is a direct pathway of activity to brain structures called the **dorsal column nuclei** (**DCN**), located in the brain stem. Since it is a direct pathway, no synapse is present between the site of mechano-electric conversion and the dorsal column nuclei. Consequently, these neurons are quite long, some being more than a metre in length. The synapses are located within the dorsal column nuclei and the projection neurons from the dorsal column nuclei are considered the second-order neurons of the somatosensory system.

These secondary neurons form a pathway called the medial-lemniscal system, which projects directly to the **thalamus** (Figure 1).

The second avenue of travel for the activity arising in the mechanoreceptor is a pathway that originates in the synaptic regions within the spinal cord, the central grey matter. Via a single synapse, the neural activity is relayed towards the brain by a pathway called the spino-cervical-thalamic tract. As the name implies, the pathway originates in the spinal column, projects to the cervical nucleus at the level of the neck and, after synapsing there, the projection neurons merge with the dorsal-column/medial lemniscal system, subsequently synapsing in the thalamus (Figure 1).

The third avenue of information does not go to higher, central nervous system regions like the thalamus, but operates at the spinal-cord level to control responses of motor neurons. These neurons are involved in controlling muscles that are responsible for the movements of the body.

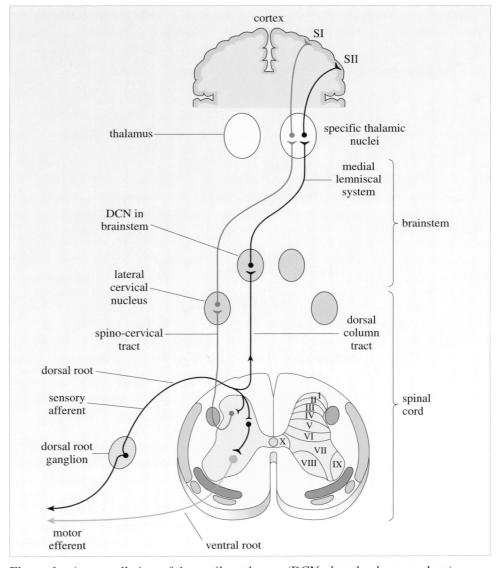

Figure 1   An overall view of the tactile pathways (DCN=dorsal column nucleus).

Information arising from the mechanoreceptors of the body and face goes to specific regions within the thalamus, specifically the posterior and ventral-medial aspects. Processing of information occurs at the level of the thalamus, and its output goes to primary and secondary somatosensory cortex. **Primary somatosensory cortex** is located in the post-central gyrus of the cerebral cortex, a region known as the parietal lobe. Secondary somatosensory cortex is located just lateral to this region (Figure 2).

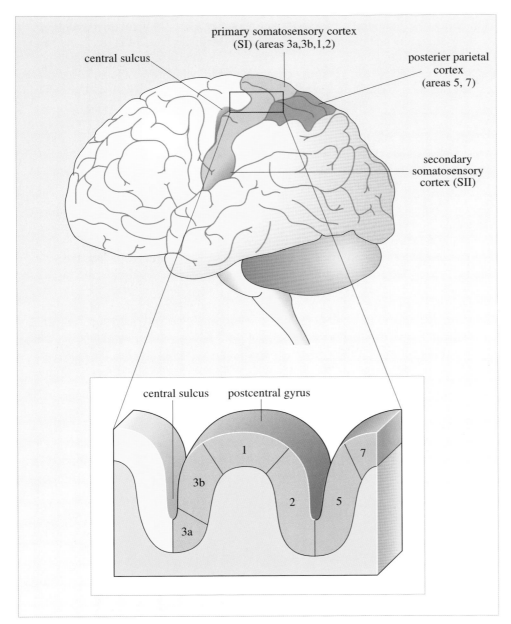

Figure 2   Somatic sensory areas of the cortex. All of the illustrated areas lie in the parietal lobe. The lower drawing shows that the postcentral gyrus contains SI, which consists of four different cortical areas that retain the numbering assigned by Brodmann.

3 Anatomy of skin and mechanoreceptors

The sensory receptors responsible for tactile sensations reside in the body organ which we call skin, a multilayered coating covering the entire body, inside and out. In fact, it is the largest organ of the human body. This organ is a highly complex living structure that incorporates not only the tactile mechanoreceptors and nerve fibres innervating them, but also blood vessels, sweat glands, and other specialized structures.

Skin is classified into three specific types, each having its own complement of mechanoreceptors and internal structure: (1) **glabrous** or hairless skin typified by the skin of the palm and the soles of the feet; (2) **hairy skin**, so called because of the presence of body hair; (3) **mucocutaneous skin**, which lines the entrances to the inside of the body. The different organization of these three types of skin imparts differences to their sensory capabilities because the sensory receptors and the mechanical properties of the three types are different. Furthermore, the mechanical properties of skin and the types and density of mechanoreceptors within it vary across body site and with the age of the individual. For example, the lips and the fingertips are highly sensitive when compared with the thigh or the back. With age, as with all sensory systems, the sensitivity of the tactile system declines.

Glabrous and hairy skin are both composed of an outside layer called the **epidermis** and an inside layer called the **dermis**. Figure 3 shows schematic cross-sections through glabrous and hairy skin. Also shown in the figure are some of the mechanoreceptors found in these two types of skin. The dermis separates the epidermis from the underlying muscle, ligaments and bone. The border between the epidermis and dermis is specialized in that somatic or epithelial cells are generated in this region and these cells migrate over time to the surface of the skin. As they migrate they begin to die, and eventually they form a relatively hard surface called the **stratum corneum**. It is the dead cells of the stratum corneum which are brushed away during everyday activities such as washing and grooming. For the most part few, if any, tactile receptors are located within the epidermis.

The dermis is quite different from the epidermis. It is not formed by epithelial cells, but is composed of connective tissue and elastic fibres floating in a semi-fluid mixture called the ground substance. Also embedded in the dermis are fat cells, blood vessels, smooth muscle, sweat glands, the lymphatic supply and, most importantly, the tactile receptors and the nerve fibres innervating these. Another major distinction between the epidermis and dermis is that epidermis does not receive a major blood supply.

The mechanoreceptors in the dermis that are innervated by the peripheral nerve fibres originating in the spinal cord come in a variety of shapes and forms. The four main types of mechanoreceptor are called **Pacinian corpuscles**, **Meissner's corpuscles**, **Merkel's discs** and **Ruffini endings**, after the nineteenth-century biologists who discovered them. A fifth group of endings innervate the hairs found in hairy skin. Some of these tactile receptors have non-neural elements attached or adjacent to them. The non-neural elements, referred to as accessory structures, are thought to participate in imparting particular response properties and perhaps even regulating the metabolic capabilities of the mechanoreceptors. One major class of tactile receptor has accessory structures called capsules, in which the tip of the neuron is embedded. The capsules of these receptors are organized in specific ways, depending upon receptor type. The capsule surrounding the Pacinian corpuscle

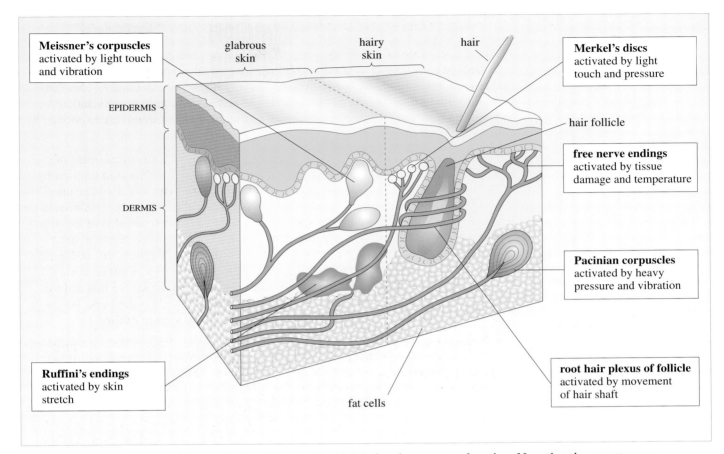

Figure 3 The anatomy of glabrous (left) and hairy skin (right) showing receptor location. Note that the receptors are diagrammatic and not drawn to scale.

mechanoreceptor, for example, has an onion-like, layered arrangement (see Figure 4). The Ruffini receptor capsule resembles a small muscle spindle, while the Meissner receptor has a capsule that looks like a woven basket. A second class of endings has accessory structures to which the sensory receptors are merely attached; these are called the Merkel-cell **neurite** complex, the Iggo corpuscle or touch pad, and the circumferential and pallisade nerve fibres on the shafts of hairs within the hair follicle. The last major class of endings in the skin are the free nerve endings, which are not attached to any accessory structure. This class of receptor is not involved in mechanotransduction but in signalling thermal and/or noxious (i.e. painful) stimuli, and is discussed in detail in Chapter 21, *The neurophysiological basis of pain*.

4 The physics of cutaneous stimulation and stimulus control

From a physical standpoint, the skin can be thought of as an incompressible, viscoelastic medium possessing the mechanical properties of viscous resistance (friction), stiffness (elastic restoring capabilities) and mass. Mechanical stimuli applied to the skin surface produce stresses and strains within the skin itself. Stresses are the forces that are applied to objects within the skin, such as the mechanoreceptors, while strains correspond to deformation or stretches of such objects. In a medium such as skin there are three kinds of mechanical disturbance that are possible as a result of the application of mechanical stimuli to the skin surface. The first is called the incompressible shear wave. These waves travel obliquely with respect to the stimulus presented to the surface of the skin. The second is the irrotational (linear) compression wave. These waves travel normally (i.e. at right angles to) with respect to the stimulus applied to the skin surface. It is these stresses and strains that are transmitted to the mechanoreceptors located in the dermis. The third type of wave is a travelling wave that propagates along the body surface from the point of stimulus excitation. This wave of excitation activates mechanoreceptors located away from the point of skin stimulation. As can be appreciated from the above discussion, the skin has complex mechanical properties. Because of this the skin responds differently to different kinds of mechanical stimuli, and its reaction to them is also a function of skin type (i.e. glabrous, hairy or mucocutaneous). Furthermore, the skin at different body sites responds differently to mechanical stimulation and, as with the tactile sense in general, the mechanical properties of the skin vary with gender and age.

Because of all of the above mentioned factors, many types of mechanical stimulus have been used to understand how the tactile system works. For example, mechanical stimuli produced by pins or probes applied perpendicularly or tangentially to the skin have been used to determine the basic properties of transduction and the transmission of the induced electrochemical signals to the central nervous system. These stimuli indent the skin and can be of a 'vibratory' nature or of the 'ramp-and-hold' variety. The vibratory stimuli that are typically used range in frequency from 0.4 to1000 Hz and in amplitude up to 3–4 mm. Ramp-and-hold stimuli consist of a variable indentation of the skin by the probe, followed by a period when the probe is held at a constant static indentation until such time as the stimulus is withdrawn. The rate and depth of the initial ramp indentation and the duration of the hold state can be varied widely, as can the rate of withdrawal. Other types of stimulus that have been used to understand taction include periodic and aperiodic gratings moved across the skin surface, air puffs, embossed letters, and even everyday items such as sandpaper, cloth and steel wool. Each of these stimuli has provided knowledge about tactile mechanisms, although the precise relationship between stimuli applied to the skin surface and the actual stimulus impinging on the tactile end organs is still an area requiring much more research. More details of the perceptual aspects of taction are given in Chapter 19, *The perception of touch*.

5 Mechano-electric transduction

The manner in which mechanical stimuli applied to the skin are transduced by the various tactile mechanoreceptors into the electrochemical energy used by the nervous system has only partially been determined. One reason for the lack of knowledge regarding the transduction mechanisms is that the receptors are embedded in the highly vascularized skin, making it difficult, if not impossible, to obtain receptor-potential activity via electrophysiological techniques. What is known regarding the transduction mechanisms of these mechanoreceptors has been learned mostly by performing experiments on Pacinian corpuscles isolated from the mesentery (the membrane enclosing the intestines) of the cat, these corpuscles being anatomically and physiologically similar to those located within human skin. Figure 4 shows a light micrograph of a single Pacinian corpuscle (a) and a schematic diagram defining the various components forming the Pacinian corpuscle (b).

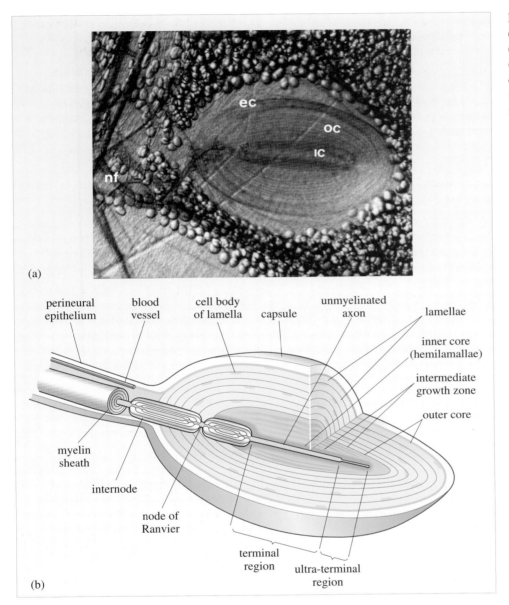

It is generally accepted that the mechanisms of transduction found for the Pacinian corpuscle are common to the other tactile receptors.

It is commonly thought that the normal strains set up within the skin by mechanical stimulation is the adequate stimulus for transduction in tactile mechanoreceptors. This is to be contrasted with the shear strain which apparently is ineffective in inducing transduction. The idea that normal strain is the adequate stimulus has been confirmed in work on isolated Pacinian corpuscles.

Mechanotransduction mechanisms in tactile receptors work in the following way. When a mechanical stimulus is applied to the receptor, for example a Pacinian corpuscle, either via the skin or directly, the accessory structure acts as a mechanical filter, transmitting the applied strain to the unmyelinated transductive membrane. The strain at the level of the mechanosensitive membrane induces hypothesized strain (stretch)-sensitive channels to respond by increasing their conductance to certain ions, Na$^+$ ions in particular, although a contribution from K$^+$ ions may also occur. The electrochemical forces on Na$^+$ are such that if Na$^+$ channels increase their conductance then Na$^+$ ions will rush into the neuron, causing depolarization. The increase in conductance as a result of activating strain-sensitive channels is evidenced by the transmembrane electrical event known as the receptor potential. It has been determined that the receptor potential is probably not mediated by transmitters or other neuroactive substances being released by the surrounding accessory structure. If the receptor potential is of sufficient amplitude an action potential will be generated and propagated along the peripheral nerve to locations within the central nervous system.

The action potential set up on the more proximal portion of the tactile receptor operates as typically described in most textbooks. Voltage-sensitive Na$^+$ ion channels are opened once a threshold has been reached. They are subsequently closed and the receptor returns to its resting potential via activation of K$^+$ channels. It is believed that the site of receptor-potential generation and action-potential initiation are different. Specifically, the receptor potential arises in the unmyelinated portion of the neurite and the action potential probably originates near the unmyelinated/myelinated juncture, perhaps at the most distal node of Ranvier. The specific location of the mechanoreceptive channels responsible for the receptor potential is speculated to be in elements called filopodia that project from the unmyelinated nerve terminal, although other theories regarding the locus of transduction as it relates to the shape of the terminal neurite have also been proposed. An electron micrograph of a filopodium and associated structures is shown in Figure 5.

The relationship between the amplitude of a stimulus and the magnitude of the receptor potential is linear at low stimulus amplitudes and saturated at higher intensities (Figure 6). As the size of the receptor potential increases, the greater the number of action potentials produced on the myelinated fibre innervating the receptor. This means that as stimulus amplitude increases, there is an increase in the firing rate as measured in action potentials per second. It has been proposed that the mechanism that produces increased amplitude of the receptor potential for increases in stimulus amplitude is a result of a spatial summation of activity from discrete transduction sites. It has been speculated that these transduction sites are the filopodia and the suspected stretch-sensitive channels that are probably located on them.

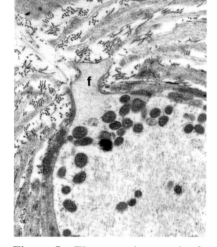

Figure 5 Electron micrograph of a filopodium (f = filopodium).

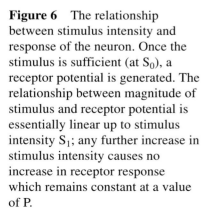

Figure 6 The relationship between stimulus intensity and response of the neuron. Once the stimulus is sufficient (at S_0), a receptor potential is generated. The relationship between magnitude of stimulus and receptor potential is essentially linear up to stimulus intensity S_1; any further increase in stimulus intensity causes no increase in receptor response which remains constant at a value of P.

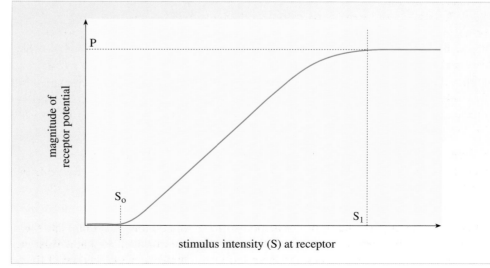

In response to stimuli that rapidly indent and remain in contact with the mechanoreceptors, (i.e. a **ramp-and-hold stimulus**) the receptor potential, especially as measured in Pacinian corpuscles, first rises rapidly and is then seen to decay. This phenomenon, commonly called adaptation, is the basis for the fast-adapting properties in the action potential responses seen in activity recorded from certain tactile receptors (see below).

6 Physiological classification of mechanoreceptors

The physiological scheme for the classification of mechanoreceptors, both in the periphery and more centrally in the nervous system, follows a two-class designation based on the receptor's responses to ramp-and-hold-like stimuli, although response properties to other forms of stimulation add to the taxonomy. The two general classes are fast adapting (FA, also called quickly adapting and rapidly adapting) and slowly adapting (SA). Here, adaptation refers to the rate of decline in action-potential firing rate in response to ramp-and-hold-like stimuli. This can be seen in the central portion of Figure 7. There are two subclasses of FA and SA mechanoreceptors: FAI and FAII and SAI and SAII. The differences in response properties for these four mechanoreceptor types can be seen in the figure. For example, FAI mechanoreceptors respond mostly to the ramp portion of the stimulus while FAIIs only respond to the corners of the ramp-and-hold stimulus. SAIs, on the other hand, respond not only to the ramp portion of the stimulus but also to the hold portion with an irregular firing pattern. Finally, SAIIs display a more regular firing rate and also have spontaneous activity, this activity occurring in the absence of controlled stimulation.

This classification scheme, while descriptive of the mechanoreceptor response properties, does not take into account receptor anatomy. However, it has been fairly well established that the FAIs are the Meissner corpuscles, the FAIIs are the Pacinian corpuscles, the SAIs are the Merkel cell–neurite complexes and the SAIIs are the Ruffini endings (see Section 3). For hairy skin, the FAIs are the hair-follicle endings, as Meissner corpuscles are not found in hairy skin.

Another characteristic that helps define the various response properties of the tactile receptors is their receptive-field organization. The receptive field is that region which, when stimulated with a given stimulus, activates the mechanoreceptor. Stimuli outside the receptive field will fail to activate the mechanoreceptor. As can be seen in Figure 7 (overleaf), FAIs and SAIs have small, well-defined receptive fields while FAIIs and SAIIs have fairly large receptive fields. It is also noteworthy that while the FA and SA type responses are found all along the pathways even within the **somatosensory cortex**, the receptive fields increase in size dramatically from the periphery to the cortex. This indicates that activity from many adjacent mechanoreceptors is converging on cortical neurons, thus increasing the receptive field size.

Figure 7 also shows the different densities of the various receptor types. For example, the FAIs and SAIs have a fairly high density in the fingertips, the density decreasing from the fingertips to the palm. In fact, this is one reason why the fingertip is more sensitive than the palm or the arm.

There are at least two other types of response characteristic that help delineate the mechanoreceptor types: rate–intensity characteristics and frequency characteristics. Rate–intensity characteristics define the relationship between action-potential firing

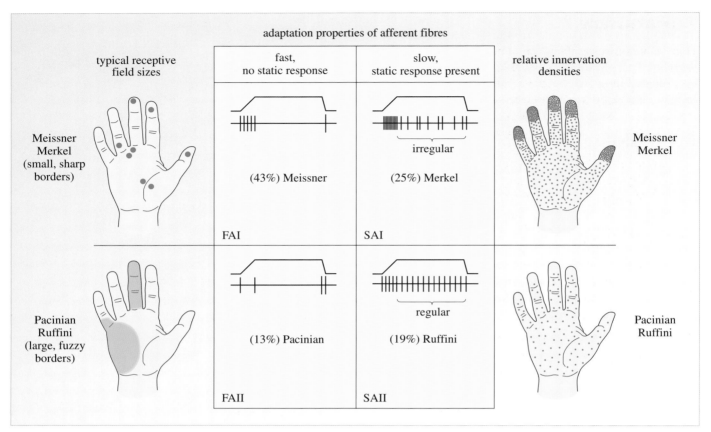

Figure 7   Physiological classification of the mechanoreceptive afferent fibres found in the skin of human hands. The different patterning of action potential discharge in response to a 'ramp and hold' stimulation is shown in the four central pale yellow boxes. These boxes also show the relative numbers of each afferent type and their presumed receptor anatomy. The hands to the left of the central panel show that type I afferents have small discrete receptive fields whilst type II afferents have large receptive fields with fuzzy borders. The hands on the right show that type I afferents innervate the fingertips more densely than they do the palm of the hand.

rate and stimulus intensity. Generally speaking, the firing rates of mechanoreceptors increase with increasing stimulus intensity. This suggests that one of the codes for stimulus intensity is increased activity on the various mechanoreceptors. Frequency characteristics are unique in that they can only be determined using vibratory stimuli. The frequency characteristics relate the intensity of the stimulus to stimulus frequency for a given firing rate criterion. All of the tactile receptors have this type of response property but the range in stimulus frequency over which the various mechanoreceptors operate is different. FAIIs, for example, are very sensitive in the high-frequency range, around 20–600 Hz. FAIs, by contrast, are more sensitive in the 3–40 Hz range. The significance of these response properties will be discussed further in Chapter 19, *The perception of touch*.

7 Summary

This chapter presents information on the organization of the somatosensory system at both the peripheral and central nervous system levels. Furthermore, the issue of the effective stimuli that are needed to activate the mechanoreceptors within the skin and the manner by which these stimuli, presented to the skin surface, are transduced at the level of the sensory endings within the skin is detailed, as are the mechanisms by which this information is passed to higher brain centres. In particular, it is noted that there are multiple receptor types responsible for mediating neural activity from their origin in skin receptors all the way to the brain. The activity carried over the various receptors and the relay neurons to which they are attached all ultimately combine to produce somatosensory perceptions.

Further reading

Bolanowski, S. J. (1996) Information processing channels in the sense of touch, in Franzén, O., Johansson, R. and Tarenius, L. (eds) *Wenner-Gren International Series: Somesthesis and the Neurobiology of the Somatosensory Cortex*, pp. 49–58, Birkhäuser Verlag AB, Basel.

Greenspan, J. D. and Bolanowski, S. J. (1996) The psychophysics of tactile perception and its peripheral physiological basis, in Kruger, L. (ed.) *Handbook of Perception and Cognition, 7: Pain and Touch*, pp. 25–103, Academic Press, San Diego.

Iggo, A. (ed.) (1973) *Handbook of Sensory Physiology, II Somatosensory System*, Springer-Verlag, Berlin.

Bell, J., Bolanowski, S. J. and Holmes, M. H. (1993) The structure and function of Pacinian corpuscles: a review, *Prog. Neurobiol.*, Vol. 42, pp. 79–128.

Halata, Z. (1990) Sensory innervation of the hairless and hairy skin in mammals including humans, in Zenker, W. and Neuhuber, W. L. (eds) *The Primary Afferent Neuron*, pp. 19–34, Plenum, New York.

The perception of touch

Peter Cahusac

19

1 Introduction

Touch is generally regarded as the experience of physically encountering objects in our environment. But touch is much more than this, so the title of this chapter is slightly misleading. This chapter will cover our somatosensory experience associated with touching objects, such as their weight, stiffness, temperature and thermal conductivity, even pain – properties that quickly tell us what the felt object is and what it is made from. By necessity, the active searching out of information involves the motor and proprioceptive systems. In contrast, when we are passively touched by an object, much less information is obtained (although our experience of tickle and pain is actually enhanced). This chapter will also review a few recent neuropsychological studies into disorders of touch produced by nerve and brain damage, and lead us to the distinct concepts of body image and body schema.

2 The exploratory sense

The bright red mango at the supermarket's fruit counter catches your eye and you pick it up to give it a gentle squeeze. This one's too soft – it's overripe. Another one you test is too hard, but the next one yields ever so slightly to gentle pressure from the thumb – it's perfect. This fruit testing procedure can be performed successfully through what is called **active touch** (also known as **haptics**). What we have done is to test the softness (or hardness) of the mango. Hardness is a property of an object that can best be determined by active touch; if instead the mango was pushed passively against your immobile hands you would not get the same experience of hardness, and your judgement would be poor. Our hands are most suitably adapted to perform active touch as they work together to grasp, palpate, prod, press, rub and heft the tested object. The pulp of the fingertips is equipped with a dense array of highly sensitive tactile receptors that map to a large somatosensory cortical representation in the brain. The tactile acuity of the fingertips is only surpassed by the tip of the tongue (though curiously the tongue is unable to feel a pulse at the wrist).

The fact that the tip of the tongue has the highest acuity results in the common experience of the magnified perception of small objects in the mouth, for example, food stuck in the teeth, (known as Weber's illusion because Ernst Heinrich Weber (1795–1878), Professor of Physiology at Leipzig University, was the first person to study the acuity of different regions of the body).

Testing for ripeness of fruit is just one situation where touch perception provides more reliable information about the world than vision. Others might be judging the sharpness of a knife (without the aid of a microscope) and assessing the finish of a sanded wood surface during DIY. Active touch contrasts with **passive touch**, where the object is merely pushed against the immobile hand. You can experience both active and passive touch if you examine one immobile arm using the hand of your other arm. Your own tests (say with a mango) will confirm, as experiments have, that active rather than passive touch is the superior method of obtaining information about objects through our somatosensory system.

In fact active touch is used more in our daily lives than we are normally aware of – reaching into a pocket to retrieve a handkerchief, keys or coins; getting dressed;

doing buttons up; peeling an orange; and so on – although usually these operations are accompanied by other sensory input from vision and hearing. All these manoeuvres require the remarkable exploratory, manipulative and sensory capacities of our hands – capacities that we very much take for granted. The motor and sensory computing required to perform these 'simple' tasks is comparable to that for tasks performed by the visual system. The neural representations devoted to sensory and motor processing in the cortex are strongly correlated for the different parts of the body, as shown by the two homunculi in Figure 1. Some nocturnal animals use their mobile facial whiskers to scan their immediate environment instead of using vision. In these animals tactile sensitivity and acuity is equal or superior to that of our fingertips. This enhanced tactual perception is provided by a proportionately larger somatosensory cortical representation.

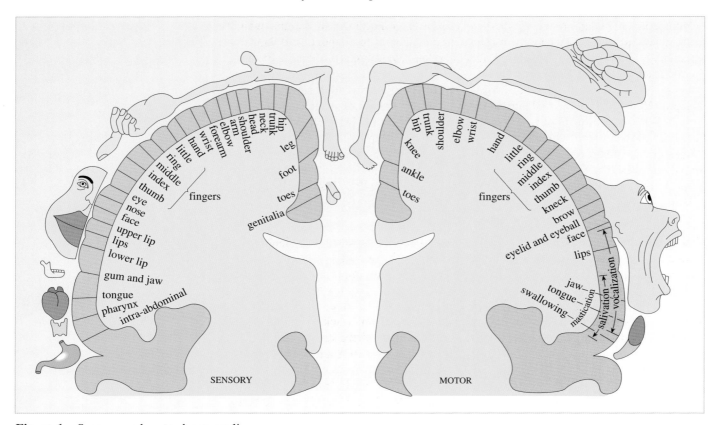

Figure 1   Sensory and motor homunculi.

It is interesting that when a congenitally blind person produces a plastic model of a person the same areas of increased acuity (the hands and mouth) are exaggerated relative to other parts.

In picking up an object to feel its weight, movement is essential for accurate performance. Weber was perhaps the first to emphasize the importance of movement in touch:

> 'Surprisingly, however, man is in some way helped by the knowledge of his own bodily movement when he examines objects by touch. When we move our arms in a particular direction intentionally and deliberately, we achieve the best

perception of the direction of the object under examination. In this way we gain information about the shape of objects that we handle and touch all over. We also perceive weights more clearly when we feel by kinaesthesis the muscular or nervous force necessary to lift the objects.'

(From E. H. Weber, *The Sense of Touch*, Academic Press. Translated by Helen Ross, 1978, with the author's permission.)

This seems somewhat counterintuitive because you might think that weight would be better determined by controlled activation of the relevant cutaneous receptors produced by placing the object onto the palm of a stationary hand resting on a table top (as in accurately weighing out flour on a kitchen scale). In fact, if you watch someone judging the weight of an object you will find them hefting the object up and down and even tossing it from hand to hand. These movements take time, and what appears to be happening is that the particular information being sought (weight) is being isolated as an *invariant* from the changing flux of movements and their correlated tactile sensations. This is how American psychologist James J. Gibson, in his influential book *The Senses Considered as Perceptual Systems*, described the process, adding that it is a kind of filtering out of proprioceptive information (see Chapter 20, *Proprioception*), leaving the 'pure' information about the manipulated object. What is striking about our experience of feeling an object with our hands is the unity of the object despite the multiple tactile sensations from up to ten moving fingertips. This is directly comparable to the stability of the visual world when we move our eyes. The tactual sense of object unity can be upset when the positions of fingers are forced out of their usual order, as with the so-called Aristotle illusion, where the index and middle fingers are crossed and their tips moved laterally over the nose to give the impression of two noses.

During hand movements, tactile detection thresholds are increased for areas of skin that are not in contact with the target of exploration (object), while they are decreased for the involved skin areas. This 'sensory gating' improves the signal-to-noise ratio, allowing manipulated objects to become the focus of attention. Somewhat surprisingly, Weiskrantz and Zhang at Oxford described a related effect that was apparent in a patient suffering from hemianaesthesia (lack of touch sensation on one side of the body) following a right hemisphere stroke. The patient (who was examined when blindfolded) could accurately localize a touch on her left insensate hand only when she used her good (right) hand to do this. Another person's touch to the insensate hand was not perceived or localizable. Thus, active touch by the patient's good hand reduced the tactile threshold in the insensate hand.

Electrical recordings of single brain cells in the somatosensory cortex of the monkey reveal that responses occur to the manipulation of complex tactile objects rather than to discrete tactile stimuli. Iwamura and colleagues from Tokyo found that at the level of the primary somatosensory cortex features of objects, such as edges, were being coded for by cell firing. The cells had very large receptive fields on the contralateral hand, comprising a whole finger or more. There were also cells that coded the joint positions of individual fingers. What is more, cells in Brodmann's area 2 were especially sensitive to the active manipulation of particular object shapes (either a sphere or a rectangular block shape). Indeed, many cells *only* fired during active grasping of an object, since passive probing or movement of fingers gave no response. Johnson and colleagues from Johns Hopkins University in Baltimore recently found that in the monkey the responses of neurons in Brodmann's area 3b to dot patterns presented to the finger pads were independent of the application velocity of the pattern. We have here, therefore, the complex integration of **kinesthetic** and tactile information to extract shape and roughness information about objects; as Gibson said 'The covariance of cutaneous and articular motion …'. The responses of these cells appear to represent a low-level analysis necessary for object recognition by active touch. The cortical area that fully integrates the necessary sensory and motor information may be an area within the parietal cortex, such as area 5.

Another good example of active touch is of blind or visually impaired subjects using active movement of their fingertips over raised dot patterns representing letter symbols (Braille). The spacing of the dots within Braille patterns are just within the two-point discriminative power of the fingertips. Slowly adapting receptors, associated with **Merkel cells**, in the superficial skin of the fingertips are responsible for the acuity demanded by Braille reading and other fine discriminative abilities of our hands. (However, the tongue, which has the greatest tactile acuity, lacks Merkel cells.) Experienced braillists can read up to 100 words per minute, a third of the rate for silent visual reading by sighted subjects. Better braillists tend to use a 'reading' finger from each hand, for example the index fingers side by side. There is evidence that areas of cortex used in sighted people (occipital cortex) are recruited during Braille reading in people blind from an early age. Experiments by Cohen and colleagues, from the National Institute of Neurological Disorders and Stroke, Bethesda, USA and elsewhere, used brief periods of transcranial magnetic stimulation (TMS) to transiently disrupt the occipital cortex during tactual reading tasks. Braille reading was disrupted by this stimulation in early blind subjects, who reported 'missing dots', 'phantom dots' or that the 'dots don't make sense'. It is worth noting that speech, and language in general, was not affected by the stimulation. The same stimulation in sighted subjects had little effect on the tactile reading of embossed roman letters, and in these subjects the stimulation only interfered with visual discriminations. It seems then that some of the special tactile discriminative abilities underlying Braille reading can be explained by redeployment of the 'visual' cortex for tactile reading skills. Other studies using TMS in sighted people have shown that the visual cortex is important for tactile discrimination of orientation, indicating that cross-modal processing of information in sensory cortical areas may be more widespread than was previously thought.

Touch is also used by the deaf-blind in the Tadoma method of 'listening' to speech. The 'listener' places their hand lightly across one side of the speaker's face such that the thumb is placed over the lips and the fingers splayed out across the cheek and neck. In this way, vibrations and movements of the jaw and lips are used to perceive speech. One device intended to help the blind to detect remote objects uses a large array of tactile stimulators placed on the blind person's back. The brightness output of a video camera is then converted into a vibrating 'image' on the tactile array. What interested Paul Bach-y-Rita, the first investigator to do this, was that blind people began to experience objects (such as a cup on a table) as being 'out there' rather than as a felt image on their backs. This 'seeing' experience depended upon the subject being able to manipulate the camera to scan the scene – again illustrating the importance of active self-initiated movement. To what extent blind people using this method are able to see, in the same way as sighted people do, is debatable. However it was intriguing that when the zoom was inadvertently operated, an experienced user raised his arms in front of his face to avoid collision with the 'looming' object. Given the involvement of the redundant visual cortex to perform Braille, it is interesting to speculate whether the same area is also deployed for this substituted vision in the blind. Despite the initial successes of these laboratory studies over 30 years ago it has proved technically difficult to implement such tactile-visual substitution systems for practical use by the blind. Bach-y-Rita is currently developing a miniaturized video system with a 49-point electro-tactile array on a dental retainer accessed by the tongue.

The so-called 'facial vision' where blind people are aware of objects and can navigate around them is reported to be a 'tactile' experience involving the face, but experiments show that it is in fact due to the auditory pickup of changes in the nature of reflected sounds while moving the head around. It is thought that the 'tactile' perception results from synaesthesia between the auditory, vestibular and kinaesthetic senses.

In animals, active touch often involves various appendages, such as hair, nails, claws, beak, etc. These extensions are used to probe and explore the environment. Using one of your fingernails, try probing into the wood grain of a table and consider where you are actually experiencing the scraping sensation. It is perhaps surprising to realize that the sensation is localized to the tips of the fingernails themselves, yet the mechanoreceptors responsible are located at the root of the nail. There seems no limit to how far we can extend our perception in this way, and we shall examine this later. The blind or sighted person with a stick feels the explored ground and experiences the gravel, tarmac or carpet at the end of the stick. Similarly, grasping a bolt in pair of pliers results in feeling the contact at the jaws of the pliers, yet all the receptors are in the hands, arm muscles and tendons. Cutting paper with scissors gives us a sensation at the very cutting edge of the scissors (Figure 2).

Active touch is also used to explore objects and to determine their hazardous nature. This involves the transient activation of nociceptors in the skin, free nerve endings, which signal potential or actual tissue damage. Hence we might warily check the sharpness of the edges of a flint stone before grasping and throwing it.

Figure 2   Cutting paper with a pair of scissors. We feel the cutting action at the blades of the scissors even though our sensory receptors are in the skin, joints and muscles associated with the hand. It is interesting that the control and sensation are attributed to the wrong blade because of their crossed construction (i.e. we experience the top blade as being controlled by our thumb, whereas it is in fact controlled by our finger/s).

Self-application affects pain and pleasure sensations: it is the very predictability of movements made during active touch that explain why it is difficult to tickle oneself (see Figure 3); and one is less sensitive to a noxious stimulus that is self-applied. Active touch is routinely used in many professions: the surgeon's palpation and percussion of an afflicted body region, and a wool grader's judgement of the wool quality as determined from the softness and fineness of the fleece, to give just two examples. The perceived temperature of an actively manipulated object is important in assessing its material nature. Objects that feel cold at room temperature, such as those made from metal, have a high thermal conductivity. Skin surface temperature (the face is especially sensitive) is closely monitored to provide information about the ambient temperature as part of the body's thermoregulatory system. Rapid adaptation to skin temperature occurs so that within a certain range of temperatures we experience *relative* temperature. That is, if one of your hands is cool adapted by placing it in a 20 °C water bath for a couple of minutes, and then you move it to a 30 °C water bath, you will feel the latter to be warm. If on the other hand (literally) you adapt at 40 °C and then place it in the 30 °C water bath, it feels cool. In a demonstration attributed to Locke (1690) the cool and warm adaptations for both hands are done at the same time. The hands are then transferred to the same 30 °C water bath and the contrasting warm and cool sensations experienced simultaneously. Probably because cold is more of a threat to survival than heat, there are more cool than warm sensitive spots on the skin's surface: most people do not feel the warmth of a full coffee (china) mug (not too hot!) pressed against the end of their nose, but do feel the temperature of a cold (empty) mug.

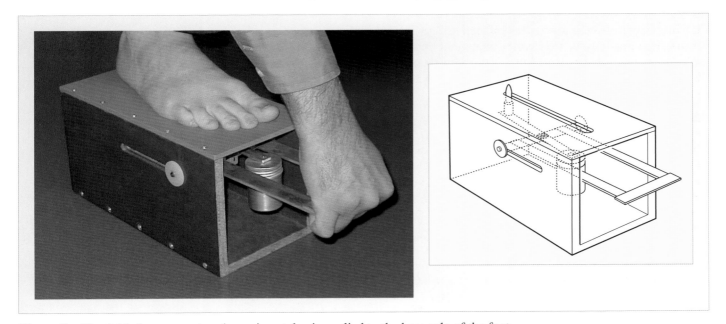

Figure 3 The tickle box apparatus. A moving stylus is applied to the bare sole of the foot.

3 The salience of touch

In evolutionary terms, touch is the oldest and most fundamental sense of all. Primitive unicellular organisms can feel but not see or hear. Serious disorders, or congenital defects, of the sense of touch are extremely rare, more so than for other senses (which traditional medical texts refer to as the 'special senses' of sight and hearing). This may explain the common notion of the salience of touch: when we think we might be dreaming we pinch ourselves, and when we are suspicious about the authenticity of coins or a bunch of flowers, we subject them to various mechanical tactile tests. It has been said that touch educates the other senses. There are revealing figurative uses of the words derived from touch perception. So, for example, when we say that a person is 'in touch' we mean that the person is in direct communication. Other phrases tap common experience and emotions: deeply touching, a gripping experience, get a grip, be tactful or tactless, to be touchy, rub someone the wrong way, tickles my fancy, a ticklish problem, a soft touch, a palpable lie, grasp an idea, a slap in the face or just a slap on the wrist. The importance of touching for social communication is well known, but it is an area neglected by perceptual psychologists. We shake hands, pat each other on the back, stroke and kiss. Touch plays a crucial role in a wide range of human experience, from infant bonding, through aggression, to courting and sexual relationships.

Perhaps the most sensitive somatosensory sense is that used to detect vibration, and this is nicely exploited by mobile phone technology which provides the option of discrete vibratory rather than obtrusive auditory signals to alert the owner to incoming calls. At the receptor level it is estimated that Pacinian corpuscles can detect 300 Hz tissue oscillations as small as half a micrometre. These large (at 2 mm long they are the body's largest sensory receptors) distinctive corpuscles consist of concentric layers of membrane, resembling an onion, which encapsulate a central rod-like neuronal terminal – a physical arrangement that acts as a high-pass filter to the mechanically sensitive neurite terminal. The corpuscles occur deep in both hairy and glabrous skin, the soles of our feet, and in other more unusual places such as in the diaphragm and the peritoneal connective tissues (see Chapter 18, *Somatosensory coding*). In this respect it is interesting that the profoundly deaf musician, Evelyn Glennie, reports that she can hear (feel) low frequency sounds with her feet, and higher frequency sounds with her face, neck and chest. This also explains how deaf-mute people can learn to dance to music.

Having stated how salient touch is, it is clear that, like other senses, the somatosensory system is subject to illusions and can be fooled. In fact, some of these illusions are direct analogues of common ones found in vision – the Müller-Lyer, the vertical-horizontal, and the Bourdon illusion (see Figure 4 overleaf) – and indeed these illusions cross-adapt when subjects are pre-exposed to the illusion in the other sense. An illusion that depends on a curious interaction between mechanical and thermal stimulation is the silver Thaler illusion. Weber described this illusion in 1846 using large (heavier than 50 g) coins (silver Thalers) at different temperatures, placed upon the forehead. One freezing cold coin felt as heavy as two body temperature warm coins stacked on top of each other. You can readily demonstrate this for yourself using three modern £2 coins at different temperatures. The basis of this illusion appears to depend on the fact that some slowly adapting mechanoreceptors in the skin also respond to cooling, although Ainsley Iggo, of the University of Edinburgh, who studied these responses in primate skin, thought it unlikely that such 'spurious' responses could affect perception.

You will come across another illusion in Chapter 20, *Proprioception*, involving the artificial stimulation of muscle stretch receptors by the application of a vibratory stimulus to a large muscle, such as the forearm. Activation of the muscle spindles results in the perception that the arm has moved to a new position in space, despite remaining stationary. An interesting change to the body image can be produced by this illusion. The subject touches the end of his nose with an index finger. While the

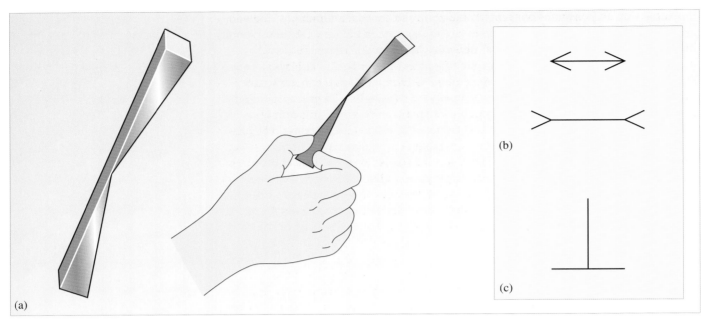

Figure 4   (a) The Bourdon illusion. This image is a visual analogue of the tactile Bourdon illusion. The top (straight) surface feels curved. (b) The Muller-Lyer illusion, both lines are the same length but the top one looks shorter. (c) Again both lines are the same length but the vertical one looks longer.

Figure 5   The size–weight illusion using objects of different sizes but the same weight. When compared with each other they are perceived to be of different weight

biceps muscle is vibrated the subject feels the arm extending and his finger and nose feel longer too. However, perhaps the most impressive and important of all somatosensory illusions is the size-weight illusion (see Figure 5). Two objects of exactly the same mass but of different size (volume) are perceived to be of different weight, such that the larger object feels lighter than the smaller object. The illusion also occurs in blindfolded subjects, as long as they are allowed to feel the size of the two objects before lifting them. To control for an effect that might be due to differences in pressure on the skin that the different-sized objects cause, the objects can be fitted with identical lifting rings, but the illusion remains unchanged and is extremely robust. Augustin Charpentier, who first described this illusion in 1891, used two spheres, one 40 mm in diameter and the other 100 mm in diameter, of identical mass (266 g). Subjects perceived the larger sphere to be lighter than the smaller sphere, an effect that could be nullified by increasing the weight of the larger sphere by 66 g (nearly 25% of the total weight: this is a large effect). What's more, the illusion is present from an early age, from three years of age, and even occurs under microgravity (i.e. in space). It is of interest that the size–weight illusion can also be produced by placing the lifted objects in the context of the railroad track illusion: greater lift force is applied to the apparently larger object further up the track. The size-weight illusion is of some significance because it shows us how important expectations are (this is why the unexpectedly empty suitcase feels so light), and challenges the simple notion that the neural outputs of sensory receptors in the skin, muscles and tendons can directly code the perceived properties (in this case heaviness) of an object.

If you are sitting comfortably, then close your eyes and touch your nose with your index finger. Easy? You have just passed one item from a battery of clinical tests for somatosensory function. Unless you are suffering from a rare disorder, this manoeuvre should be accomplished easily and fairly accurately (say, with an error of a centimetre). The tip of your finger is separated from your nose by nine joints, so this little trick demonstrates our remarkable ability to coordinate limb position and movement information (proprioception and kinaesthesis) with touch. A few individuals suffering from **peripheral neuropathy**, a condition that destroys proprioceptive neuronal fibres, are unable to do this. Oliver Sacks, in his well-known book *The Man Who Mistook his Wife for a Hat*, includes a chapter entitled *The Disembodied Lady*, which described a woman who suffered a precipitous and permanent loss of her sense of proprioception. That is, she was unable to feel the position or posture of her trunk and head, or the disposition of her limbs. Other cases have arisen among health faddists who over-indulge in vitamin B_6, though in these cases the symptoms are reversible when a normal diet is resumed. Two more cases of peripheral neuropathy were described in great detail by Cole and Paillard in 1995. In one of these the proprioceptive loss was from the neck down, and in the other, from the mouth down. Both individuals also had a loss in the sense of touch but not temperature and pain. One of them was said to no longer experience tickle, but did feel itch. In Sacks' case the deficit was more purely proprioceptive as all the other senses of touch, temperature and pain were only marginally affected. All of the cases had normal vestibular function, so that they could position, move and orient their heads normally according to gravity. What seems to have been lost in these and other cases is what the physiologist Sir Henry Head in 1911 described as the '**body schema**'. The concept, of some importance, is clearly explained by him in the following:

> 'For this combined standard, against which all subsequent changes of posture are measured before they enter consciousness, we propose the word 'schema'. By means of perpetual alterations in position we are always building up a postural model of ourselves which constantly changes.'

The idea, then, is that all parts our body (including the hierarchy of joints, e.g. from trunk to fingertip) are continuously mapped and updated by information from receptors in our muscles, joints and skin. Although peripheral neuropathy sufferers have no body schema, they do have some experience of a **body image** – and this largely depends on visual feedback. Hence one of the cases (as described in Chapter 20, *Proprioception*) was tested for the ability to localize a thermal stimulus presented to a small patch of skin on one arm. If her entire body from neck down was covered with a sheet so that it was unavailable to visual inspection then she was unable to point using her other arm to where the stimulus was presented. However she could describe where the stimulus was given and mark on a schematic body diagram the precise position.

In discussing neurological syndromes, Paillard suggested a distinction between awareness of the 'what' and the 'where' of the stimulus, corresponding to the terms suggested by Larry Weiskrantz: awareness *that* and awareness *of*, in talking about conscious experience. It seems that individuals lacking a body schema due to proprioceptive nerve damage can both locate *where* the tactile stimulus was presented on their own body (when allowed visual feedback) and know *what* the stimulus was: their perception of the stimulus is accurate in relation to their body image. However, access to somatosensory information about limb position and body posture is completely lost in these cases: their defective body schema denies them access to sensorimotor space. A further interesting finding from these cases is that they show normal performance in what we will call the waiter's tray effect. That is, they are able to lift off an object (say a filled wine glass) with one hand from a tray held in the other hand, without the tray rising up due to the sudden decreased load.

This is performed by an appropriate postural reduction in the upward force applied to the tray in synchrony with the lifting of the glass. The timing is crucial. The appropriate adjustment fails to occur when another person lifts the glass, and is the reason why you shouldn't remove items from a tray carried by a waiter! The normal response in neuropathy sufferers suggests that the neural mechanisms for this form of postural adjustment are centrally programmed through the motor system, and are not dependent on proprioceptive feedback.

The existence of a body schema allows elaboration of that schema in surprising ways. Sir Henry Head noted in this respect that objects that become part of conscious body movements become incorporated into the schema, even '…a woman's power of localization may extend to the feather in her hat'. The blind man's stick was mentioned earlier as an extension to our perception. Another example is the use of sticks, cues, clubs, bats and rackets to hit balls in sport. These become part of the person's schema. Proficient racket sport players are able to switch quickly between sports, even though the so-called 'sweet spot' moves by as much as 30 cm from the grip when changing from a table tennis bat to a badminton racket. Some gifted sports players are said to have 'touch', reflecting their uncanny ability to gently 'feel' or 'stroke' the ball (or shuttlecock), rather than just hit it. More bizarrely, perhaps, is our ability to incorporate a motor vehicle into our body schema as we drive it along. The experienced driver has a reasonably accurate idea of the width and length of a gap necessary to traverse through or to park the vehicle. The expanded body image might partly explain how 'touchy' we get about driving behaviour, for example when we get 'cut up' by another driver. When hit by another vehicle we feel it as a direct assault on the person. Even a minor bump not involving anyone else can cause considerable shock. It is tempting to speculate that short-term alterations are made to the cortical representation shown in Figure 1 to accommodate an expanded body schema.

4 Summary

In this chapter we have considered the importance of active touch for normal interactions with the world. We have discussed how significant the somatosensory system is and how, in some respects, it maintains primacy over other senses. Much of its information is not directly accessible to conscious awareness, and therefore taken for granted. This is particularly well illustrated by what happens when proprioception and touch are lost in the tragic cases of peripheral neuropathy. Like other senses we have seen that various somatosensory illusions can occur. The study of these illusions often reveals how the somatosensory system normally functions. The size-weight illusion, for example, shows us how important expectation is – we lift an object using a force, learned from experience, to be appropriate for the size of the grasped object.

Finally, we have considered the crucially important concept of the body schema. The body schema is a system for representing and coordinating our body posture, movement and feeling. It operates largely hidden from conscious scrutiny, but encompasses all of a person's self-identified body and its varied extensions.

20

Proprioception

Ian Lyon

1 Introduction

This chapter is an introduction to **proprioception**, the sense we have of our own position and movement. It reviews some of the underlying neurophysiology and discusses some of the experimental approaches that have been used. It then looks at the central importance of proprioception in our balance control, and our perception of our orientation. This leads into a discussion of the part that proprioception plays in our overall experience of ourselves. Studies of people who have lost their proprioception are discussed in relation to all of the above. Finally, the important role of proprioception in our perception of the three-dimensional world in which we live is considered.

2 Proprioception

2.1 What is proprioception?

Around the beginning of the last century, the English neurophysiologist Sir Charles Sherrington coined the term 'proprioception', deriving it from the Latin *proprius*, meaning 'own'. Sherrington defined proprioceptors as receptors sensitive to stimuli that '… are traceable to the actions of the organism itself'. In one sense then, all of our receptors can be seen as proprioceptors. If for example you move your arm, you may see or even hear it move. You may feel the movement of the skin over the joints and muscles. If you move your head you will stimulate the vestibular apparatus of the inner ear, and probably the visual system too. Generally, however, the term proprioception is used more narrowly than this. It is reserved for a series of receptors in our joints, muscles and tendons that can provide the central nervous system (CNS) with information about the position (or angle) and movement of our joints. One exception is the touch receptors in the skin – although these clearly have an **exteroceptive** function, it appears that they can also contribute to our sense of joint position.

It isn't immediately obvious what a sense of joint position and movement might be for. It is not something of which we are ordinarily very aware. We can perhaps see how it might be important for the maintenance of posture and the control of movement. If the CNS needs to maintain a joint at a particular position, information that the joint is drifting away from this position is clearly useful. If it needs to move an arm in order that you can pick up a mug of tea, it needs to know where the arm is at the outset in order to work out what movement is required. However, it turns out that this sense of the position and movement of our own bodies has a deeper significance than this. It has become apparent that it is fundamental to the way we experience not only ourselves, but also the outside world. This is far from intuitively apparent and it seems that one reason for this is that you cannot turn your proprioceptors off, in the same way that you can close your eyes, block up your ears or anaesthetize your skin. This sense is always with us and so integral to our experience that we cannot really imagine what it would be like to be without it.

2.2 Which receptors tell us about the position and movement of our joints?

We have receptors in our joints, muscles, tendons and skin, all of which might theoretically provide the CNS with information about joint position. Joint receptors, for example, have been shown to change their firing rate with changes in joint position and velocity. **Muscle receptors** (or **muscle spindles**) are sensitive to stretch of the muscle, and movement of joints generally results in muscles being stretched. Sherrington suggested that it was likely that all of the receptor types contributed: 'whenever we've got sensory receptors we expect them to be used'. But by the 1960s it was thought that only joint receptors were behind position sense. One reason for this was that a decade earlier it had been discovered that muscle spindles have a motor as well as sensory nerve supply, suggesting that they were 'driven' by the CNS as well as by stretch of the muscle (more about this later). How then could they provide an unambiguous signal of joint angle? It also seemed that, since it is joint position rather than muscle stretch that we sense, joint receptors were the obvious choice.

However, the advent of joint replacement surgery posed a problem for this idea. Patients with artificial hips in which the joint capsule (and therefore receptors) had been entirely removed were still able accurately to detect position and movement of the joint.

Then, in the 1970s, it was discovered that vibrating a muscle (or its tendon), a stimulus known to cause muscle spindles to fire rapidly, could produce illusions of joint movement. It was also suggested that the CNS could subtract the level of 'drive' it was sending to the muscle spindles from the signal it was receiving back from them, and thus derive an unambiguous signal of muscle stretch.

The sceptics, however, were not convinced and in the early 1980s the Australian physiologist Ian McCloskey felt it necessary to go to the heroic lengths of having the tendon of his extensor hallucis longus muscle surgically exposed and cut in order that the effect of stretching the muscle could be investigated. This muscle is in the front compartment of the lower leg. Its tendon runs down over the top of the foot and inserts into the top of the terminal joint of the big toe. Contraction of the muscle results in extension (i.e. lifting) of the big toe. Under local anaesthetic an incision was made on the foot and the tendon exposed and cut (Figure 1). The foot and joints of the toes were carefully immobilized in a cast. McCloskey could readily detect pulls of less than 1mm imposed on the muscle and reported that it felt like flexion of

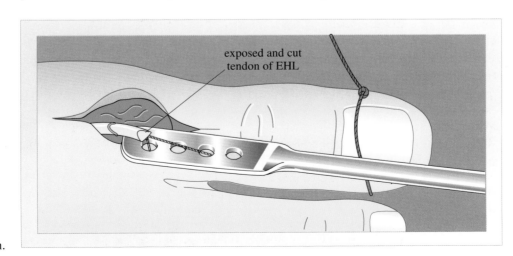

Figure 1 The exposed and cut tendon of Ian McCloskey's extensor hallucis longus (EHL) muscle attached to a manipulandum with which it was pulled. The foot was embedded in a cast before the experiment began.

the terminal joint of the big toe (the movement that would normally stretch this muscle). This work was reported in the neurological journal *Brain* in 1983. It seems, however, that no degree of self-sacrifice is enough! For in the very same issue, the Swedish surgeon and physiologist Erik Moberg reported similar experiments, this time in the hand, and a different conclusion. Moberg reported that pulling on tendons in the hand produced little or no sensation of joint movement, and suggested that any such sensation that was produced could be due to movement of the skin over the muscle as it moved when its tendon was pulled.

The present view is that all receptor types contribute to our joint position and movement sense, some perhaps having a more prominent role at certain joints than at others, a position reminiscent of that proposed by Sherrington almost 100 years ago. In fact, recent anatomical studies on proprioceptive pathways in the CNS reveal that, at higher processing levels, there is much convergence between the signals from skin, joint and muscle receptors. However, the controversy over the relative importance of the various receptors has led to a great deal of research into them, and some of the fruits of this research are described in the next section.

2.3 Adjustment of receptor sensitivity according to task: 'tuning in' the muscle spindles

The proprioceptors in muscles, muscle spindles, are specialized muscle fibres connected in parallel to the ordinary fibres which produce the contractile force. They are sensitive to being stretched and provide the CNS with signals of muscle length, and rate of change of length. As already noted, they have a motor as well as a sensory nerve supply. We now have evidence that the motor supply is used to set the sensitivity of the spindles according to the prevailing circumstances.

Let's start our discussion with some terminology. The motor neurons that project from the CNS to the spindles are called gamma (γ) motor neurons, whereas those projecting to the ordinary contractile fibres are alpha (α) motor neurons. The motor system of the spindles is often referred to in its entirety as the **fusimotor system**. The sensory neurons projecting from the muscle spindles to the CNS are referred to as spindle afferents, afferent meaning a fibre transmitting impulses from the periphery to the CNS.

When a muscle contracts (due to firing of its α motor neurons), the resultant shortening of the muscle would cause the spindles to become slack and unresponsive were it not for the fact that the γ motor neurons also fire. This activity, which tracks that in the main muscle, stretches the central sensory parts of the spindles, effectively taking up the slack and keeping them in the operating range (Figure 2 overleaf). This pattern of activity is described as **alpha-gamma co-activation (α-γ co-activation)**.

The very presence of a separate motor system for the spindles suggests that it must in some way function independently. There must be more to it than just α-γ co-activation. In practice, however, evidence for such independent function has proved difficult to find, not least because the γ fibres are of such small diameter that it is very difficult to record from them. The first demonstration of independent control of the γ fibres was made in the mid-1980s by the physiologists Arthur Prochazka and Manuel Hulliger in a series of ingenious and technically demanding experiments. Prochazka and Hulliger worked with cats which were instrumented but free to move, the various electrodes being connected to a small transmitter worn by the cats. Because, under these conditions, it isn't possible to measure activity in

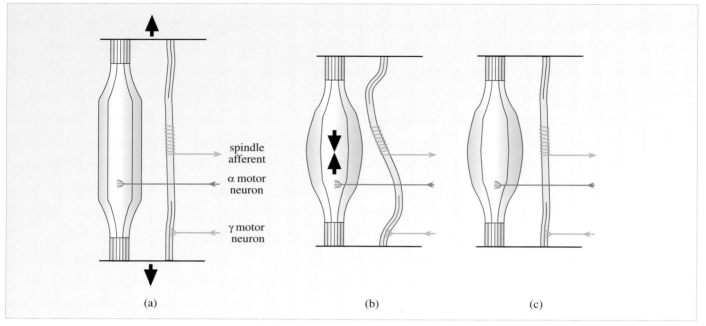

Figure 2   Diagrammatic representation of the basic action of the fusimotor system. (a) The muscle at rest and under normal physiological stretch. The alpha (α) motor neuron projects to the main muscle, the gamma (γ) motor neuron projects to the spindle. Note that the contractile elements of the spindle are at the two ends, and the sensory part is in the middle. (b) When the muscle contracts, the spindle would become slack and unresponsive were it not for the simultaneous contraction of its end portions due to activity in the γ motor neuron (c).

γ fibres directly, their activity had to be inferred from other measurements. The output of muscle spindles, that is the activity in the spindle afferents, depends on three things: (1) the contractile activity in the muscle; (2) the degree of stretch of the muscle; (3) the activity in the fusimotor system. If you measure (1) and (2), together with spindle afferent activity, you can estimate the level of γ activity.

Prochazka and Hulliger found that the background level of fusimotor activity was set at different levels according to the circumstances, or to what the cat was doing. These results are summarized in Figure 3. As can be seen from the figure, two types of fusimotor fibre have been distinguished. Firing in dynamic γ fibres increases the sensitivity of the spindles to the rate of muscle stretch, whereas firing in static fibres increases sensitivity to absolute muscle length. Recruitment of these two types of γ fibre can be predicted from the type of activity in which the animal is engaged. During activities in which muscle length changes slowly and in a predictable fashion, only the static γ neurons are active. However, under conditions in which muscle length may change rapidly and unpredictably, dynamic γ neurons are activated.

This, then, is an example of the CNS adjusting an incoming signal at source. It is effectively 'tuning in' the receptor based on the prevailing conditions. It also appears to be a fine tuning, with independent control of dynamic and static fibres. It is worth noting that this behaviour is often predictive in nature. The animal is preparing itself for what is likely to happen. It will now be apparent why, despite the technical difficulties involved, it was necessary for the animals to be free to move. Results such as these could only have been found in animals free to engage in a range of natural activities. Similar results have also been found in monkeys, but it has not yet

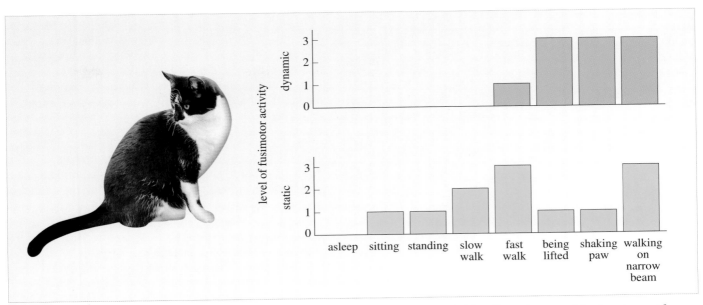

Figure 3 Activity in two types of cat fusimotor fibre measured for a range of activities. Recruitment of the two types of γ fibre can be predicted from the nature of the activity. Static fibres are active where muscle length changes slowly and predictably; dynamic fibres are active where muscle length may change rapidly and unpredictably.

proved possible to demonstrate independent fusimotor control in humans. It seems likely, however, that the human CNS uses similar strategies to provide itself with information about the state of the body of the highest possible fidelity.

2.4 Role of proprioceptors in balance control and perception of whole-body orientation

Proprioceptors play an important role in human balance control. Our balance when standing is a rather precarious state of affairs. Our centre of mass is high (about the level of the top of the hips) compared to the size of our base of support (the area bounded by the outer edges of the feet). A relatively slight tilt in any direction is therefore enough to cause us to lose our balance. For this reason, life-size statues of human figures have to be made with large and heavy bases.

The CNS must, then, maintain the orientation of our body with respect to gravity within very tight limits. We have what are effectively 'gravity receptors' in the vestibular system of the inner ear. But these alone can only tell the CNS about the orientation, with respect to gravity, of the head. In order for the CNS to know about the orientation of the trunk it needs to know the position of the head relative to the trunk. This information is best provided by proprioceptors in the neck, and it is interesting to note that the neck musculature is unusually richly endowed with muscle spindles.

There is considerable evidence that proprioceptors are involved not only in the control of our orientation but also in our perception of it. Part of this body of evidence has come from muscle vibration studies. Vibration of a muscle or its tendon stimulates the spindles and the CNS appears to interpret this as stretch of the muscle. For example, if the flexor muscles of the wrist are vibrated, an illusion of extension of the wrist is produced. Conversely, vibration of the extensor muscles produces an illusion of wrist flexion. Figure 4 shows an interesting further finding.

If a subject leans against a wall with his or her hand and the flexor muscles or tendons of the wrist are vibrated, the illusion produced is now of whole-body movement. Furthermore, the direction of the whole-body movement is reversed simply by changing the orientation of the hand (and still vibrating the flexor muscles). With the fingers pointing forward the illusion is of the body swaying forward, and vice versa. In both cases this is how the body would move were the wrist really extending.

Results such as these demonstrate that proprioceptive signals from the whole body are integrated by the CNS in arriving at an estimate of body orientation and movement. In this case the signals from the wrist flexor muscles in the arm are interpreted according to the posture of the arm and wrist, and indeed of the whole of the rest of the body.

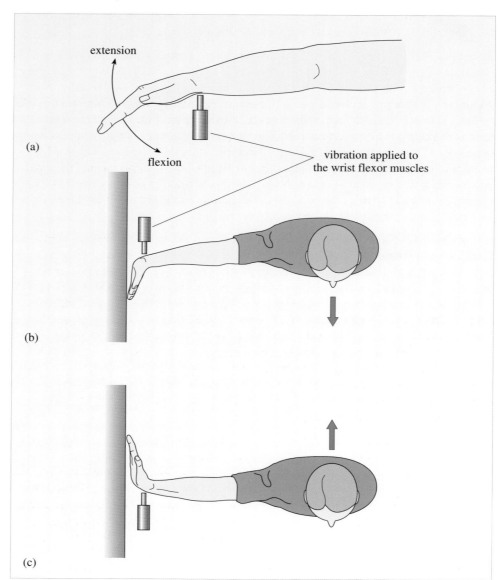

Figure 4 Vibration applied to the muscles of the wrist flexors produces an illusion of wrist extension when the hand is free (a), but an illusion of whole-body motion when the body is partly supported by the hand (b, c). The whole-body illusion is always consistent with the illusion of wrist extension. Thus in (b) this is forwards; in (c) it is backwards.

3 The consequences of proprioception loss

3.1 Pathology

A number of cases of subjects suffering a large fibre sensory **neuropathy** have been reported. This is a condition in which the afferent nerve fibres are selectively destroyed, leading to a loss of proprioception. Only the large (myelinated) fibres are affected. These convey impulses from proprioceptors and touch receptors in the skin. The small fibres, which convey heat and pain, are spared. In some cases this condition has arisen following a viral infection. From a scientific point of view these cases are extremely interesting in that the loss is so specific. The motor fibres are apparently entirely unaffected so that motor function, or muscle strength, is normal. This of course is not the case when spinal injury leads to complete severance of the spinal cord. Here, the motor as well as sensory signals are interrupted, resulting in total inability to contract the muscles below the level of the injury.

Subjects suffering a large fibre sensory neuropathy find that, although their motor function is intact, they are initially unable to move purposefully. To begin with they are typically unable even to support themselves in a sitting position. In order to regain any purposeful motor function they have painstakingly to relearn how to hold and move themselves. However, they never regain anything like normal motor function. Their posture and movements are impoverished and critically dependent on vision. Furthermore, they require considerable attention. Sitting in a chair, for example, requires constant vigilance to avoid falling out of it, and closing the eyes is likely to lead to such a fall regardless of the concentration given to avoiding it. Observations such as these give us some indication of the central importance of proprioception to the control of our everyday movements.

But of more direct interest here is the perceptual loss experienced by these subjects. Lacking proprioception, they have no idea where the various parts of themselves are unless they can see them. If you ask them to close their eyes and you move their arm, they have almost no idea where you have moved it to and cannot reach out and touch it with the other hand. It is of course simple to demonstrate that normal subjects have no difficulty with this. However, the sparing of the small sensory fibres means that such subjects do have some bodily sensibility, for example to heat. One such subject, GL, can tell you to which part of her arm a thermal stimulus has been applied. She might say for example, 'It's over my left wrist'. But, without being able to see her arm, she does not know where her left wrist is. This is demonstrated by the fact that she cannot (without vision) point to the stimulus position with her right index finger.

This situation can be contrasted with another pathological condition that apparently results in a loss of proprioception, this time within the central nervous system. The French neuroscientist Jacques Paillard describes the interesting case of a subject who experienced damage to the left parietal area of the cerebral cortex. Parts of the parietal cortex are thought to be involved in the representation of three-dimensional space within the brain. Among other deficits, this subject lost the sense of touch in her right arm. She was completely unaware of pressure applied to her right arm, even when the pressure was very strong. However, Paillard now tried a very interesting thing. He asked the subject to put on a blindfold and then with his finger applied pressure to a point on her insentient right hand. After one second's pressure he removed his finger and said 'here'. This was a cue for the subject to reach across with her left hand and touch the spot where pressure had been applied.

Now of course this subject was not conscious of any pressure having been applied but nonetheless, cued by the word 'here', obediently reached across and touched a location on her right hand. Remarkably, she was able to touch the correct location, albeit with some degree of error. The test was repeated for a total of 18 stimulus sites on the right hand. This task must have felt to this subject like pure guesswork, and Paillard reports that she made comments such as, 'But I don't understand that … I don't feel anything and yet I go there with my finger. How does that happen ?'. As an extra control, Paillard interspersed at random ten 'false' trials in which he said 'here' without having applied any pressure to the right hand. Although the subject was not conscious of these trials being any different from the legitimate ones, she did not respond (by reaching with her left arm) in any of them.

Thus this subject's loss is apparently only of the *consciousness* of her proprioception. Below the level of her consciousness the system is working relatively well, and this is reflected in the fact that her movement control is much better than that of deafferented subjects such as GL. On the other hand, because GL's small afferents are intact, she can detect some peripheral stimuli and can tell which part of her is being stimulated, something that Paillard's subject cannot do. Thus GL must have some sort of internal 'mapping' or 'image' of her body. It is just that this image has become detached from any positional information, a state of affairs which it is impossible for us to imagine.

3.2 Wider issues

Most people report that, under normal circumstances, they are not particularly aware of the position and movement of their own bodies. Interestingly, the very wording of the previous sentence hides an assumption or preconception, namely that our bodies are separate in some way from 'us' – my body is something that the real me 'owns', or, when some part of it hurts, just puts up with. This conception of ourselves is particularly marked in Western culture.

In his book *A leg to stand on*, the celebrated American neurologist Oliver Sacks describes his experience of a temporary loss of proprioception and sensation in a leg following an accident. Sacks was shocked and dismayed to discover that, rather than feeling like himself minus a leg, he now felt almost like someone else. A part of *him* had been taken away. The presence of his leg had been an integral part of his everyday experience of himself, but, because it had always been there, he wasn't aware of this. Sacks found that experiences similar to his own were common in others who had suffered one or another form of 'de-afferentation'. These reports suggest that our conception that our bodies are somehow not the real us, but just a convenient bit of machinery 'bolted on', may be seriously misleading.

4 The role of proprioception and our perception of the external world

We are able to reach out and touch things in the space around us without having to watch what we're doing. This is easy to demonstrate. Just select an object, close your eyes and reach out and touch it, then open your eyes and see how you've done (a patterned tablecloth can be used to help you gauge your error). This apparently simple feat is cleverer than it first seems. When you look at something, the eye is rotated to bring the image of the thing onto the most sensitive part of the retina, the fovea. Then, in order to relate the position of the object being looked at to 'your' position (say the position of the shoulder of the reaching arm) the CNS needs to make some computation based on the position of the eye in the head and the position of the head with respect to the torso.

A deafferented subject lacking proprioception from the neck down (such as GL) cannot perform this task, partly because they cannot determine the position in space of a visual target relative to their shoulder. In order to reach for things, they have to watch closely what they're doing. This is in stark contrast to our everyday behaviour, where the most cursory glance at, say, a mug of tea is all that is needed for us to reach out and pick it up successfully.

This, then, is an illustration of the role of proprioception in the control of movement. But this same proprioceptive information (and possibly some similar type of computation) also shapes our perception of the space around us. A group headed by the French neuroscientist Marc Jeannerod investigated this using the technique of muscle vibration. In Jeannerod's experiment, subjects sat in darkness looking at a small illuminated target in front of them. When vibration was applied to their neck muscles on one side, subjects reported that they saw the target move to the other side (no head movement had occured). When asked to point to the target they in fact pointed to the side of it, consistent with the illusion of target movement.

The explanation for this is that the CNS interprets the vibration, let's say of the left side of the neck, as a stretching of the muscles on this side, something that would normally occur when the head turns to the right. If the head were to turn to the right (and the eyes remained in the same position in the head), the target would appear to move to the left. Since in this case the target does not move to the left (because the head hasn't actually moved – it's an illusion) the CNS interprets this as a movement of the target to the right (Figure 5).

This experiment demonstrates that our perception of the position (with respect to ourselves) of objects that we see is dependent on proprioception. Interestingly, it also suggests that what we think of as 'ourselves' in this context is the torso, rather than the head. This in turn suggests that our spatial perception arises out of a movement (in this case reaching) control system. For it seems that the harder you look, the deeper the influence of proprioception goes. It may the basis of our understanding of the three-dimensional world in which we live. This can be more easily appreciated by comparing the abilities of jointed animals like ourselves with soft-bodied creatures such as the octopus. It is because we bend in relatively few and well-defined places (i.e. our joints) that we are able reasonably easily to compute the position of our body parts. This is not so for an octopus, where the position of each part depends upon the degree of contraction of muscles all over the rest of the body. As a result, the jointless animal appears to lack the equivalent of our proprioceptive position sense.

We can pick up and examine an object, say a cube, with our hands. Without needing to see it we can build up a mental picture of its shape by turning it in our hands and moving our fingers over it. We can do this because we know throughout where our fingers are relative to each another. We could easily distinguish between, say, a cube and a pyramid in this fashion. An octopus, however, appears unable to do this. It cannot (for a food reward) learn to distinguish by touch a cube from a sphere. In contrast, it is very much able to distinguish between different textures.

Similarly, creatures like the octopus appear limited in their ability to understand the three-dimensional space in which they move. They are for example unable to learn

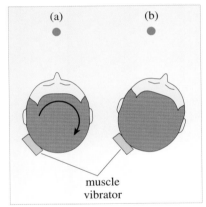

Figure 5 Vibration of the left neck muscles (a) produces the illusion of rotation of the head to the right. (b) If the head were really to move to the right a stationary target would move to the left of the visual field. Since the head does not actually move and neither does the target, the subject interprets this as a movement of the target to the right.

to negotiate all but the simplest mazes. Jointed creatures, on the other hand, can monitor the number of steps they have taken and the angle of any turns that they have made. They can readily learn to run even quite complex mazes without the need for exteroceptive cues. They can build structures, such as honeycombs and spiders' webs, which necessitate accurate measurement of lengths and angles. It seems likely that our very ability to understand the three-dimensional space we live in, which appears as two-dimensional representations on the retinae, is based on proprioception. In fact, philosophers have suggested that cognition in general might be based on our early experience of moving in our environment since this is how we first learn to distinguish between ourselves and the rest of the world.

5 Parting thoughts

The most startling thing about proprioception is how enormously important it is to us and yet how totally unaware we seem to be of it. It appears to be at the basis of both our control of posture and movement, and our perception of ourselves and the external world. In fact, our exploration of proprioception seems to have suggested a close connection between the way we move and the way we think.

6 Summary

Proprioceptors provide the CNS with information about the state of the muscles and joints, and provide us with a sense of our own position and movement. This information appears to be an essential part of our balance and movement mechanisms, and is also fundamental to our experience of both ourselves and the external world.

Experiments to find out which receptors provide the CNS with proprioceptive information have proved technically difficult, but a consensus has begun to emerge that various receptor types can contribute, the relative importance of each depending on the joint in question. It has also been demonstrated that the CNS does not merely passively receive this information, but 'tunes in' the receptors according to context.

We cannot 'turn off' proprioception in the way that we can other senses, and so people who lose their proprioception, through disease or accident, provide a unique insight into the role and importance of this sense. Not only are balance and movement control impoverished, but the very sense of 'self' may be profoundly changed.

Experiments also show that our perception of the three-dimensional world in which we live is dependent on proprioception. For example, we use our sense of the position of our various parts in the process of judging where things in the external world are.

Further reading

Cole, J. (1995) *Pride and a Daily Marathon*, MIT Press, Cambridge, MA.

Sacks, O. (1991) *A Leg to Stand On*, Picador, London.

Paillard, J. (ed.) (1991) *Brain and Space*, Oxford University Press, Oxford.

21

The neurophysiological basis of pain

Julian Millar

1 Introduction

Pain is a conscious sensation, normally, but not always, correlated with tissue damage. This chapter discusses the sensory apparatus for the detection of tissue damage (nociceptors) and how information about this damage is conveyed to the central nervous system. It then explains how the information is transformed and modulated at the level of the spinal cord and higher levels of the central nervous system to create the sensation of pain. Mechanisms by which the brain can reduce the effect of nociceptor input in activating pain sensations are discussed in detail. Finally, the modes of action of several analgesic drugs are discussed in terms of their interactions with the nervous system.

2 The purpose of pain

Why do we feel pain? One key concept is that pain protects us from further injury. We pull away our hand if it accidentally touches a flame. We try to minimize the pain by cooling the burn with ice water. By reducing the pain in this way we also reduce the tissue injury. This may seem a trivial point but its importance is dramatically illustrated by the experiences of the few unfortunate individuals who are born without the capacity to feel pain. They are usually admitted to hospital in the first few months of life with severe body injuries, and most do not survive to adulthood. If a baby with this condition gets something too hot in his mouth he does not spit it out, and therefore is likely to burn his tongue and palate. If he rests too long in one position he does not feel cramped, does not move to restore the blood flow to the compressed joint, and therefore damages the joint. Such babies get bedsores normally associated with the old and infirm. Perhaps worse, because a wound does not hurt, the child will not reflexly protect and immobilize the injured limb. The wounds are constantly challenged by movement and are thus unable to heal, leading to permanent damage or atrophy. Such individuals are rare but there are more common conditions where the ability to detect pain is lost later in life and similar problems arise. Sufferers from leprosy lose the ability to feel pain and the sad consequences of this loss can be seen in their mutilated limbs. Pain is without doubt our great protector and arguably our most important sensation.

2.1 Pain is not an ordinary sensation

The sensation of pain is something that can only be experienced by a conscious individual. If someone is unconscious we do not regard him or her as being able to feel pain, even though he or she may show reflex responses to painful stimuli. In this respect pain is a sense like that of vision, hearing, or touch. However, in one very important way it is completely different from these other senses.

If we flash a spot of light into someone's eye, we know that there will be activation of neurons in the retina, the lateral geniculate nucleus and the visual cortex. We can record a brief cortical evoked potential (indicative of the activation of cortical neurons) from the scalp over the visual cortex a few tens of milliseconds after the flash. Now suppose we repeat the flash a second or so later; we expect to record an evoked potential identical or very similar to the first. After the first stimulus the visual system returns quickly to its prestimulus state and so, when stimulated by the second flash, responds in the same way as it did to the first. The same of course would be true in the auditory cortex after a brief click or in the somatosensory cortex after a light touch. In each case the system returns quickly to the prestimulus state at the end of the stimulus. But suppose you accidentally cut yourself with a knife. The skin and other tissue damaged by the knife clearly do not return to normal in a few milliseconds. Instead, this single stimulus initiates a whole series of irreversible biochemical and physiological processes. Blood clotting cascades are activated to stem the bleeding; the immune system is alerted and sends white cells into the damaged area; the sympathetic nervous system is activated. These changes are progressive, and they will persist not for milliseconds but for days, weeks or longer until the wound is finally healed. In other words, unlike other senses, receptors for tissue damage do not return to their prestimulus state after activation but remain 'switched on' for an indefinite period.

In the last two decades neuroscientists have shown that not only is the sensitivity of damage-detecting sensory nerve endings altered following injury, but also that their synaptic connections inside the central nervous system may be significantly modified and reorganized. The connectivity and sensitivity only return to normal when the wound is completely healed, and even then there can be permanent changes in central connections, just like there can be permanent scar tissue after serious injuries. In other words, pain is not like the sensations of vision, touch, etc; the pain felt in response to a repeated injuring stimulus is not constant (but often augments). Pain is part of an integrated response to injury, and is part of a mechanism triggered by injury to prevent further injury and promote healing.

There is one more important consideration. Pain is not linked in a hard and fast way to tissue damage. Our own experience tells us that mild or moderate tissue injury normally causes pain. However, this correlation does not hold in all circumstances. Pain can be reduced or even obliterated in conditions of great excitement or arousal. For example, a soldier in battle may completely deny feeling pain even after suffering severe injuries.

On the other hand, some unfortunate individuals may suffer severe pain without having any detectable tissue damage. Patients complaining of severe pain without overt tissue damage were once considered to have psychiatric disturbances, but now it is recognized that such pain is very real. It is a form of **neuropathic pain**. Thus there can be a '**double dissociation**' between the physical condition of tissue damage and the psychological state of pain.

2 Nociceptors

In order to understand the mechanisms of pain caused by tissue injury we need to understand some of the anatomy of peripheral nerves. Peripheral nerve fibres can be grouped into two main types: myelinated or 'A' type and unmyelinated or 'C' type. The myelinated fibres are further divided into several subgroups with Greek suffixes: $A\alpha$, $A\beta$, $A\gamma$ and so on. Different types with different conduction velocities mediate different sensations, as shown in Table 1.

A variety of receptors connected to $A\beta$ fibres detect light touch, pressure, vibration and other innocuous cutaneous sensations. However, two types of fibre are only sensitive to stimuli that cause tissue damage. We call these fibres and their sensory endings nociceptors. The majority are unmyelinated axons (C fibres). These nerve fibres are always less than 1 μm in diameter and thus conduct action potentials

Table 1   Classification of human peripheral nerves.

Type	Special name	Diameter (µm)	Function	Velocity (m s⁻¹)
Aα	alpha-motor neuron '1a' or muscle spindle afferent '1b' or golgi tendon afferent	10+	motor to skeletal muscle sensory from muscle spindle sensory from Golgi tendon organ	60+
Aβ	general sensory afferents	6–10	sensory from skin, viscera, etc. sensory from secondary endings in muscle spindles	36–60
Aγ	gamma-motor neuron	5–8	motor to muscle spindles	30–48
Aδ	nociceptor or thermoreceptor	1–6	'fast' pain from skin, muscle, joints; thermoreceptors	6–36
C	nociceptor or thermoreceptor	< 1	'slow' pain from skin, muscle, viscera; thermoreceptors	< 1

relatively slowly. The other type is small myelinated Aδ fibres. (Note: this classification is not strictly true as some C and Aδ fibres are thermoreceptors, and respond to warm or cold, not noxious, stimulation; see Table 1.)

If you stub your toe or tread on a sharp object, you will often be aware of two components of the pain sensation. There is an initial sharp or 'pricking' pain followed perhaps half a second later by a dull aching or burning pain. These two components of pain are called 'fast pain' and 'slow pain'. The fast pain appears to be carried by the Aδ fibres and the slow pain by the C fibres.

Both types of fibre terminate in the skin and other body tissues as extensively branching networks of very fine (< 0.5 µm) nerve terminals (Figure 1). Because they have no specialized connective tissue capsule around them, these terminals are called free nerve endings.

Free nerve endings are found in all parts of the body except inside bones and in the interior of the brain. In the cornea of the eye, free nerve endings make up the vast majority of nerve endings, and it is known that abrasions of the cornea (sometimes caused by badly fitting contact lenses) can be intensely painful.

The free nerve endings are polymodal receptors. Unlike Aβ afferents, which have mechanoreceptive nerve endings 'tuned' by their connective tissue capsule to a particular kind of movement stimulus, free nerve endings have a variety of receptors on their surface which can respond to mechanical or chemical stimulation.

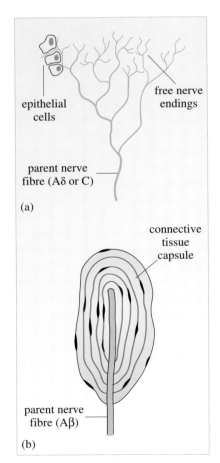

Figure 1   The structure of free and encapsulated nerve endings. (a) Receptors for noxious stimuli are formed from axons with bare ('free') nerve endings. These fine axons branch profusely in the tissue and form a fine matrix in all organs of the body. (b) Receptors for touch, vibration and other non-noxious stimuli have specialized connective tissue 'capsules' around the end of the axons. These capsules form mechanical filters so that the endings only respond to certain specific forms of mechanical distortion of the tissue.

Physical distortion of the terminal axon membrane, changes in the concentration of various ions in the extracellular fluid, or changes in pH, can trigger inward sodium currents which generate potential and, when this is sufficiently large, a train of action potentials. Unlike the mechanoreceptors at the ends of Aβ fibres, whose discharge adapts more or less rapidly to a sustained stimulus, C fibre activity can be non-adapting. In other words, after a single noxious stimulus, they may continue firing action potentials for some time. Just as a wound does not disappear when the injuring stimulus is removed, so the activated C fibres do not stop firing and similarly the pain may continue.

How do nociceptors work? When tissue is damaged, cell walls are ruptured and intracellular materials spill out into the extracellular space. A number of the chemicals released into the extracellular space in injured tissue can activate free nerve endings or potentiate their response to other physical or chemical stimulation.

Potassium ions are normally at a low concentration in the extracellular space, but leakage from damaged cells will increase this. Some free nerve endings are activated directly by this rise in extracellular potassium concentration. Tissue damage often leads to an increase in extracellular acidity, which can activate free nerve endings. Damaged tissue causes mast cells (a part of the immune system) to release a number of chemical factors including histamine, ATP, serotonin and cytokines such as nerve growth factor (NGF). All these compounds produce pain or itch if injected into the skin. Factors released by tissue injury can activate enzyme cascades. For example, the enzyme phospholipase catalyses the conversion of arachidonic acid in cell membranes to arachidonate, which in turn is converted to prostaglandins by the action of the enzyme cyclo-oxygenase (COX). Prostaglandins powerfully sensitize the free nerve endings. Aspirin (acetylsalicylic acid) is a good analgesic for minor injuries because it blocks the enzyme COX and stops the synthesis of prostaglandins at the injury site. NSAIDs (non-steroidal anti-inflammatory drugs) also inhibit prostaglandin formation. Finally, free nerve endings are also activated by peptides, especially bradykinin. This peptide is produced at the site of tissue injury or anoxia by the action of enzymes on a precursor protein called a kininogen. Bradykinin can activate nitric oxide synthase in endothelial cells in blood vessels at the site of injury, and thus generate nitric oxide which, together with other factors, triggers a complex series of reactions in the tissue, leading to inflammation.

We can see from this complicated set of changes that the responsiveness of nociceptors may be increased by a variety of chemical changes in injured or inflamed tissue. This is the basis of inflammatory pain. This increase in response is reflected in **hyperalgesia**, that is when more extreme pain is felt in response to a given stimulus in the inflamed tissue, and **allodynia** when a normally non-painful stimulus elicits pain when applied to inflamed tissue (for example the pain felt when warm water touches sunburnt skin).

2.1 Spinal modulation of nociceptive transmission

Sensory nerve fibres enter the spinal cord in the dorsal roots. A cross-section of the spinal cord is shown diagrammatically in Figure 2.

 The grey matter contains the cell bodies and dendrites of cells; the white matter contains only nerve fibres (axons). Grey matter consists of the motor or ventral horn and the sensory or dorsal horn, which is divided into six approximately horizontal layers known as Rexed's laminae. Aδ and C fibres enter the spinal cord laterally and terminate mainly in lamina I, the marginal layer, and lamina II, the **substantia**

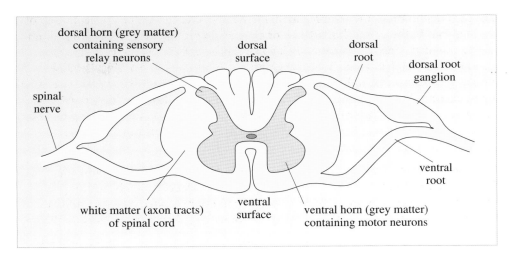

Figure 2 Cross-section of spinal cord.

gelatinosa (SG), which is very important in pain transmission. Researchers now recognize a difference between the inner and outer layers of the SG, known as II_i and II_o. Below the SG are laminae III, IV, V and VI (Figure 3).

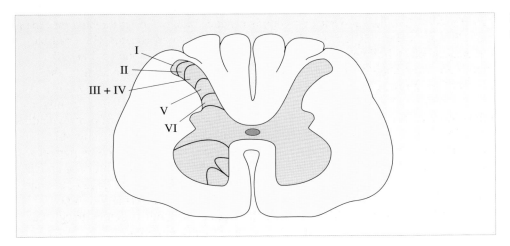

Figure 3 Rexed's laminae of the dorsal horn.

Aδ and C fibres branch when they enter the spinal cord. Some branches terminate in lamina I on large cells (lamina I neurons) that send axons down through the other laminae and then ventrally across the spinal cord to form part of the **spinothalamic tract (STT)**, ascending to the brain on the *opposite* side of the spinal cord to the afferent input (Figure 4 overleaf).

Some Aδ fibres may project down to the base of the dorsal horn (lamina VI) to connect to interneurons controlling flexion reflexes. The function of 'fast pain' may thus be to activate flexion reflexes so that a limb is quickly withdrawn from a damaging stimulus. (Slow pain, in contrast, may be a means of forcing an individual to keep an injured limb immobile so that healing may occur.)

The majority of lamina I cells, like the Aδ and C fibres, respond only to tissue damaging stimuli. (A few respond to innocuous heating or cooling of the skin). They can thus be thought of as the 'second-order neurons' of the pain pathway. The spinothalamic tract has been recognized for over a century as the main 'pain pathway' in the spinal cord. A famous medical condition first recognized in the nineteenth-century is the Brown-Sequard syndrome (Figure 5 overleaf).

Figure 4   The spinothalamic tract.

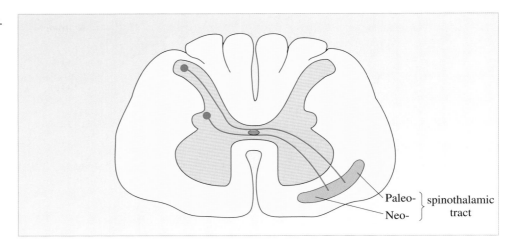

Figure 5   The Brown-Sequard syndrome. The patient has loss of pain and temperature on the right side of the body below the lesion, and loss of proprioception on the left side of the body below the lesion.

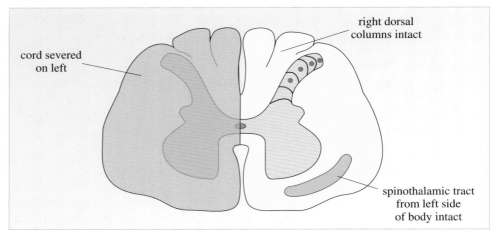

In this condition the patient has damage to one complete half of the spinal cord. Because the spinothalamic tract ascends the cord on the opposite side to the afferent input, the patient loses pain (and temperature) sense on the opposite side to the lesion. Cutting the spinothalamic tract surgically on one side of the cord similarly abolishes pain and temperature sense on the opposite side of the body below the cut. So are all the axons in the spinothalamic tract nociceptive-specific? No! One of the great surprises in pain research was the discovery that most of the fibres in the spinothalamic tract could be excited by brushing or touching the skin. They respond to either low threshold (touch) or high threshold (noxious) cutaneous stimulation. This is because the lamina I axons only make up a small fraction of the spinothalamic tract. Most of the axons arise from other neurons, which also have their cell bodies in the dorsal horn on the opposite side of the cord but in deeper laminae (usually lamina IV, V or VI). These other cells receive input synapses from both noxious ($A\delta$ and C) and non-noxious ($A\beta$) afferents, and have dendrites that project up through the dorsal horn into lamina I, where they can make contact with the terminals of the $A\delta$ and C fibres. $A\beta$ sensory fibres make synaptic contacts lower down the dendrites of these deep cells, as shown in Figure 6.

Cells that receive inputs from both high and low threshold afferents are called wide dynamic range cells.

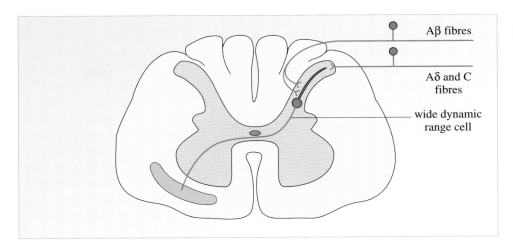

Figure 6 Input to wide dynamic range cells. Aβ fibres synapse on middle and lower parts of lamina V neuron dendrites; Aδ and C fibres synapse on the extreme tip.

Thus the spinothalamic tract has two kinds of neuron: those that are nociceptor-specific (cell bodies in lamina I) and those that have both nociceptive and non-nociceptive inputs (cell bodies in deeper laminae). The deep cells make up the majority of the spinothalamic tract and have small receptive fields, small enough to signal the precise location of a stimulus on the skin. The lamina I cells are very much fewer in number and do not have small enough receptive fields to indicate the precise location of a painful stimulus. The receptive field of a lamina I cell might, for example, cover the whole of one finger, whereas we can localize pain specifically to an injured fingernail.

The fact that most of the cells in the spinothalamic tract are wide dynamic range presents a fundamental problem. Suppose there is activity in these wide dynamic range axons. The forebrain can only know the number of action potentials arriving in the thalamus, not what stimuli caused them. How is the forebrain to know which type of input is activating the cells, the nociceptors or the low threshold afferents?

Suppose the lamina I cells send an 'alerting' signal to the brain to signify that injury has occurred, but only specify in a general way where on the body surface. The brain then sends signals down descending axons in the spinal cord, which modulate the output of the deep cells so that low threshold inputs to these cells are suppressed. Then only those wide dynamic range cells with inputs from nociceptors will be active, and the brain will be able to localize the injury.

This idea, that the brain does not simply passively receive input from the spinal cord but that instead it actively modulates the spinal relay cells to filter and control the signals they send up to the forebrain has been of major importance in pain research. It was put forward by Patrick Wall at University College London in the 1960s and was a major step in the development of the famous gate-control theory of pain.

3 The Gate-Control Theory of Pain

The gate-control theory of pain, put forward by Patrick Wall and Ronald Melzack, was published in 1965. It was enormously influential in the development of ideas of how the whole brain, not just the pain system, worked. Research in the last two decades has shown that the original model has several significant errors of detail; nevertheless, the model has led to many new strategies and drugs for pain relief. The original theory is represented diagrammatically in Figure 7 (overleaf).

Figure 7 The original Gate-Control Theory of Pain.

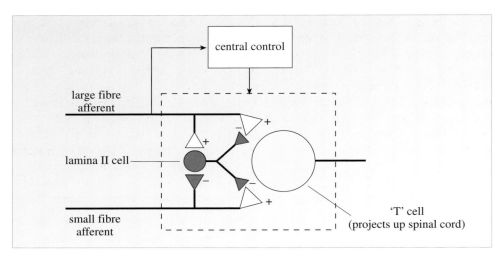

In the gate-control theory large diameter sensory nerve fibres (which we can identify as Aβ fibres) excite a relay cell or T cell which projects up the spinal cord. The T cell activity is felt as pain. They also activate lamina II cells, which have short axons that synapse locally. The lamina II cells inhibit the T cells, either presynaptically or postsynaptically or both. Small diameter fibres (Aδ and C) excite the T cell but they inhibit the lamina II cell. There is also a 'central control' activated from the large fibre.

Crucial to the gate theory is the operation of the lamina II cells. These constitute the actual 'gate' mechanism in the system. In its simplest form, the theory says that when these cells are active, the input to the T cell is shut off, the gate is closed, and pain information does not reach the forebrain. Action potentials arriving in large fibre afferents have a dual role on the T system. They initially excite the T cells but then, via 'feedforward' inhibition through the lamina II cells, inhibit them. Thus the effect of large fibre inputs can only cause transient pain. Activity in small diameter afferents will also directly excite the T cells but will block any lamina II inhibition of the cells. Thus the small diameter afferents will produce powerful and non-adapting excitation of T cells, and thus severe pain.

In support of the theory we can identify the T cell as a deep dorsal horn cell projecting to the spinothalamic tract, with excitatory input from both large and small (i.e. wide dynamic range) fibres. But the theory does not predict or explain the presence of two types of spinothalamic tract cell, wide dynamic range and nociceptor specific. It is now known that lamina II cells may contain the inhibitory transmitter GABA (gamma-amino-butyric acid). These GABA-ergic interneurons could produce presynaptic or postsynaptic inhibition on relay cells. This also would fit with the gate theory. The theory suggests that lamina II cells should have low threshold receptive fields, as they are activated by large diameter sensory fibres. This has been confirmed for some cells in lamina II. However, the theory predicts that lamina II cells with low threshold receptive fields (from large diameter afferents) should also have an *inhibitory* input from high threshold (small diameter) afferents. Such cells have not been found. Furthermore, it is clear that there are at least two anatomically different types of cell in lamina II with different physiological properties: 'stalked cells' and 'islet cells'. Stalked cells are found in the outer part of lamina II (next to lamina I). Their axons project into lamina I and their dendrites arborize in laminae II and III. Stalked cells have nociceptor-specific or wide dynamic range receptive fields. Islet cells have axons and dendrites wholly within lamina II and most have only low-threshold receptive fields or wide-dynamic range receptive fields. Many contain GABA, which is not found in stalked cells. So islet cells could fit the role of inhibitory interneurons postulated in the gate theory, except that they do not have the type of receptive fields necessary for an exact fit to the model. However, stalked cells could be excitatory. Finally, interneurons have been found in lamina I, which may be inhibitory or excitatory for the larger relay cells of lamina I. Perhaps the most powerful criticism of the gate theory has focused on its prediction that the small fibre input could have two types of synaptic contact: excitatory (on to T cells) and inhibitory (on to lamina II cells). It is now accepted that all synapses from primary afferent sensory nerve fibres are excitatory, regardless of what type of cell they contact, so this aspect of the model is clearly incorrect.

In summary, it is clear that anatomically and physiologically the gate theory is a considerable oversimplification of the actual situation in the spinal cord. But is it *functionally* correct? Is there a gating mechanism at this level of the neuraxis to block or attenuate pain transmission?

Since in the model the large fibres excite the lamina II cells and therefore produce feedforward inhibition of the T cells, one prediction of the theory is that input in large fibres can shut the gate and therefore reduce pain. This has been proved to be at least partially true, and has led to the development of **TENS (transcutaneous electrical nerve stimulation)** as a means of reducing pain. It can be very effective in certain conditions, such as pain during childbirth, when drug intervention is undesirable. TENS machines, now widely available in pharmacies and health stores, excite peripheral sensory nerve fibres by electrical shocks applied through the skin. Electrical stimuli preferentially excite myelinated fibres, so TENS machines are thought to work by activating Aβ fibres and thus block pain by activating inhibitory neurons, as in the gate theory. However, even with TENS the situation is complex, as the most effective treatment appears to be when the electrical stimulation itself is just short of painful. It may be that weak stimulation of Aδ and Aβ fibres releases **endorphins**, pain-suppressing chemicals within the brain.

3.1 Arousal analgesia

Can the gate theory explain the analgesia seen during intense excitement or arousal? Yes it can, because the theory includes another input to the spinal cord gate from the 'central control' box. This was envisaged as a descending control system from the brain to the spinal cord. This prediction was verified by the discovery of neurons in the brainstem reticular formation that send axons down the spinal cord to synapse in the dorsal and ventral horns. Two groups of reticular cells in particular appear to be significant in pain control: noradrenaline-containing cells in the locus coeruleus and adjacent structures in the pons, and serotonin- (5-HT) containing cells from the raphe nuclei in the medulla. Some of these descending axons appear to synapse on primary afferents, others on cells in laminae I and II.

During stressful 'fight or flight' situations, the locus coeruleus neurons are active and release noradrenaline from axon terminals in the substantia gelatinosa. This noradrenaline release has a powerful pain blocking effect. Drugs which enhance noradrenergic transmission in the spinal cord are powerful analgesics. Thus descending noradrenergic neurons somehow close the gate in a very effective way. Several mechanisms have been postulated for this, but so far none has been proved. Three mechanisms are shown in Figure 8 (overleaf).

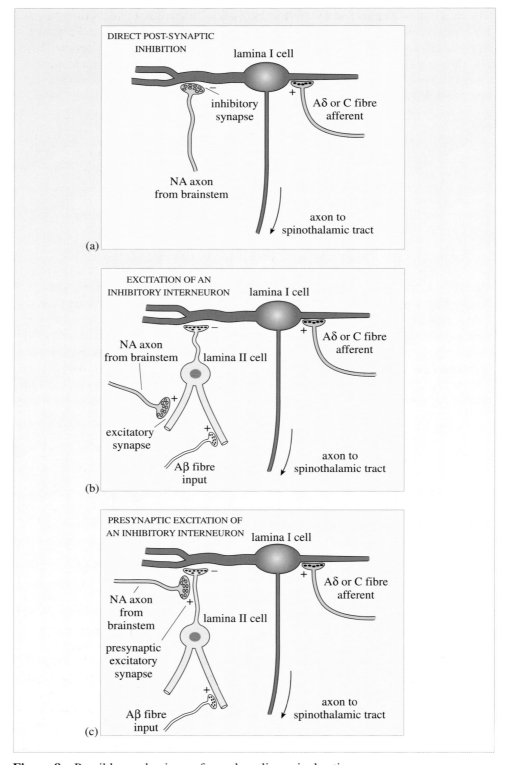

Figure 8 Possible mechanisms of noradrenaline spinal action.

The simplest mechanism would be that the noradrenaline has a direct post-synaptic inhibitory synapse on lamina 1 cells (Figure 8a). An alternative more in keeping with the known anatomy is that the noradrenaline has an excitatory effect on inhibitory interneurons such as islet cells (Figure 8b). A third possibility for which there is some evidence is that noradrenaline has a presynaptic excitatory effect on inhibitory interneurons (Figure 8c).

It has often been pointed out that some forms of arousal, such as anxiety about an anticipated injury (e.g. a hypodermic needle injection), may appear to *increase,* not decrease, the painfulness of the stimulus. However, in such circumstances, it has been observed that the actual pain is often much less than the anticipated pain. This may be a situation where the spinal cord has been primed by descending activity to expect a much larger noxious input than it actually receives.

In contrast to the situation with noradrenaline, the function of the serotoninergic descending system is more difficult to analyse. These neurons also synapse on cells in laminae I and II, and electrical stimulation of the raphe nuclei produces a powerful analgesia in experimental animals, but drugs which excite serotonin receptors do not have specific analgesic effects. It has been suggested that the descending serotonin neurons may have a more general inhibitory effect, possibly helping the brain to filter somatosensory input so that it can concentrate on what is important to it at that particular moment. Serotonin certainly seems to be involved in the initiation of sleep, possibly by lowering somatosensory input to the reticular formation and thus reducing arousal. A complicating factor is that serotonin receptors are found in many places in the dorsal horn, including presynaptically on primary afferents from C fibres.

One further possibility is that serotonin is involved in the changes in synaptic connectivity known to occur in the spinal cord after injury (synaptic plasticity), and their restoration to normal after wound healing. This is an area where much research can be anticipated in the next few years.

3.2 Opiate analgesia

Both stalked and islet cells of lamina II may contain peptides called **enkephalins**, which bind to the same receptors as the classic analgesic drug opium and its derivatives morphine, heroin, codeine, etc. (opiate drugs). It is now accepted that morphine and other opiate drugs are analgesic because they mimic the effect of enkephalins released by lamina II cells.

It has not yet been established fully how the enkephalins operate to block pain transmission. They are released together with amino-acid transmitters such as GABA, glutamate or glycine when the lamina II cells are activated. Peptide receptors can be found both on the dendrites of spinothalamic relay cells and also on the terminals of primary afferent (C and Aδ) fibres. When the enkephalin binds to them these receptors do not open ion channels and initiate post-synaptic potential changes in their membranes. Instead they undergo a shape change, which activates an intracellular protein (one of the G-protein family) which then acts on various metabolic processes in the cell, for example the sodium pumps that control the resting potential. Because their receptors do not open ion channels, enkephalins and other peptides are often referred to as neuromodulators rather than neurotransmitters. The G-protein mechanism of action is called the 'second messenger' system. They do not by themselves initiate action potentials in the cells but modulate the effect of the primary transmitter in some way, perhaps by amplifying or prolonging its effect. They may also modulate the effect of other transmitters on the cell. For example, they could enhance the effect of noradrenaline on the cell by increasing the number or sensitivity of active noradrenaline receptors.

Several other peptides, including substance P, galanin, dynorphin, neurotensin and cholecystokinin, are found in the dorsal horn. Their function is still somewhat obscure. Because some C fibres release substance P together with an amino acid transmitter (glutamate or aspartate), it was initially thought that substance P was the 'pain transmitter'. However, more recent work suggests that all of these peptides work in the same way as the enkephalins, that is they act as neuromodulators. In several cases it has been shown that more than one peptide is co-released with the main transmitter. Indeed, it has been suggested that there is co-release of one or more peptides at every synapse in the nervous system.

3.3 Neuropathic pain

It is clear from the studies with opiates and adrenergic agonist drugs that powerful mechanisms exist in the spinal cord to modulate the patterns of spinothalamic activity that are interpreted by the forebrain as pain. It is also clear that just as peripheral nociceptors can change their responsiveness, so too can the synapses between nociceptors and relay cells in the spinal cord change their connectivity after injury. After injury, new genes are expressed in the afferents and spinal cells, and synapses may sprout or be withdrawn. This reorganization may be temporary, and the connectivity returns to normal if the tissue heals completely. But there are situations where a return to normal is impossible, for example when a limb is amputated. In such cases many cells in the spinal cord die and the changes in connectivity may become permanent. This change in connectivity can produce deranged or abnormal patterns of spinothalamic activity, which is felt as pain in the non-existent limb. Such **phantom limb pain** is an example of neuropathic pain, that is, pain caused by abnormal patterns of activity in neurons rather than by actual tissue damage. Neuropathic pain is often intense and difficult to treat with normal analgesic drugs. Clearly, aspirin or other peripherally acting analgesics are of little use, as there is no peripheral limb injury, but opiates also may be relatively ineffective, owing to changes in the connectivity in lamina II. Some relief has been obtained by the use of TENS-type electrical stimulation of the spinal cord or thalamus. The rationale behind such treatment is that there may be neuronal gates in the thalamus that can be closed by activity in appropriate neurons. This kind of therapy is still in its infancy, but we may expect to see it applied much more in future years.

3.4 Brainstem mechanisms of pain modulation

Many spinothalamic tract fibres have branches that project to the reticular formation in the medulla and brainstem (Figure 9). These branches stimulate the cells in the reticular formation and underlie the arousal effects of painful stimuli (chronic pain is a common cause of insomnia).

Adjacent to the reticular formation in the midbrain is the **periaqueductal gray (PAG)**. This area is an important centre in the descending control of pain. It receives an input from the limbic system, in particular the hypothalamus. Electrical stimulation (via implanted microelectrodes) of the PAG can produce powerful analgesia, more powerful than stimulation of either the raphe nuclei or the locus coeruleus. It is thought that PAG neurons project to the raphe and/or locus coeruleus

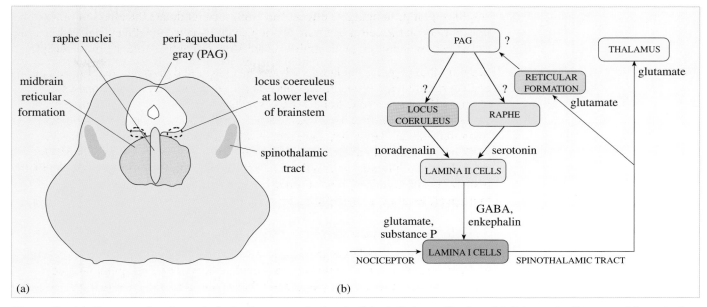

Figure 9 (a) Cross-section through the brainstem at the level of the inferior colliculus. (b) Schematic diagram of the spinal cord and brainstem pathways.

and activate the amine-containing cells that in turn project down the spinal cord to block pain transmission. Enkephalin-containing neurons are found in the PAG and in other parts of the reticular formation, and in the hypothalamus. The euphoric (and addictive) qualities of opiates appear to be due to their effects at the midbrain and hypothalamic opiate receptors.

It can be seen that pain-stimulated arousal could be part of a negative feedback pain control system (Figure 9b). Activity in the spinothalamic tract generates activity in the PAG, which in turn activates the locus coeruleus and raphe nuclei, which generates descending inhibition of the spinothalamic tract.

3.5 Forebrain mechanisms

Spinothalamic tract fibres innervate several thalamic nuclei, including the specific somatosensory relay nuclei (the ventrobasal group), the posterior thalamic nucleus, and the nonspecific 'reticular' nuclei of the thalamus. The question of whether there are nociceptor-specific cells in the thalamus is controversial. There is a powerful corticofugal control system from the somatosensory cortex to the thalamus, and this projection may control and modulate the receptive fields of thalamic cells much in the same way that descending control from the reticular formation modulates the receptive fields of spinothalamic relay cells.

Damage to the thalamus caused by a stroke can lead to the so-called thalamic syndrome. Sufferers feel intense, usually burning or crushing pain from any sort of skin contact with the affected limb. This is a severe form of allodynia which is neuropathic in origin. As might have been expected, since the origin of the pain is above the brainstem, this form of pain often cannot be controlled by opiate analgesics. Some recent studies have suggested that local electrical stimulation by electrodes implanted into the thalamus may provide some relief.

The cells in the 'classic' somatosensory cortices (Brodmann's areas 3, 1 and 2) do not normally respond to stimulation of nociceptors. However, recently PET (positron emission tomography) scans have shown that these areas may be needed for the localization of pain and judgement of its intensity. Nociceptor-specific responses are, however, found in cells in the anterior cingulate gyrus of the cerebral cortex (Figure 10).

Cells in the anterior insula (a fold of cortex between the temporal and frontal lobes) are also activated by noxious stimulation. These two cortical areas (insula and cingulate gyrus) both receive input from the posterior thalamus and both have projections to structures in the limbic system. They may mediate the 'unpleasant' or 'affective' aspect of pain.

Overall, our knowledge of the forebrain mechanisms mediating pain perception is much less than our knowledge of the peripheral nociceptors and spinal cord mechanisms. Different aspects of pain may be processed in several cortical and subcortical areas at the same time.

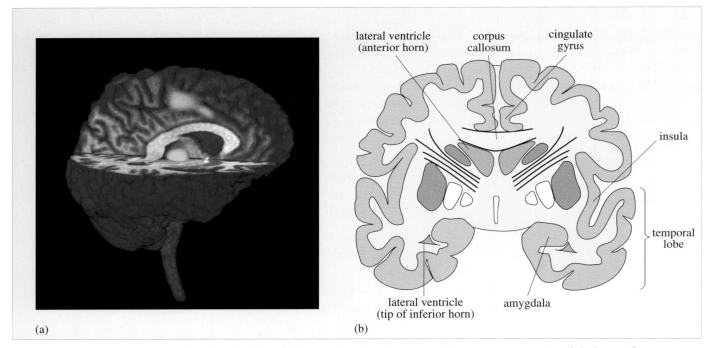

(a)   (b)

Figure 10   (a) Pain intensity-related activation of the anterior cingulate cortex (upper orange area) and thalamus (lower orange area) superimposed upon a blue MRI image. Positron emission tomography of cerebral blood flow in normal healthy volunteers reveals that painful heat stimuli produce activation of a number of brain regions. The regions were activated in direct proportion to the intensity of pain that subjects perceived, indicating that sensory dimensions of the pain experience are processed in a highly distributed fashion. (b) Vertical cross-section (coronal section) through the brain at level of anterior commissure.

4 Summary

Pain is vital; without it we quickly become seriously injured. It is not like other sensations; it does not stop when the stimulus is discontinued. It is part of an integrated response to injury and may last until the related wound is healed.

Tissue damage does not always result in pain, and pain can be felt without tissue damage. Pain is a psychological response that is usually but not always coupled to tissue damage.

Pain is transmitted by nociceptors, specialized peripheral nerve fibres with bare endings that specifically detect tissue damage. These endings are sensitized by many chemicals released from injured tissue.

Nociceptor afferents synapse in the dorsal horn of the spinal cord. Pain signals pass up the spinothalamic tract on the opposite side of the spinal cord to the afferent input. Spinothalamic tract activity may be modulated by descending control from the forebrain.

The gate theory of pain postulated that lamina II cells of the dorsal horn form a 'gate' that can close and block pain transmission at the spinal cord. The theory led to much research and the introduction of TENS for pain relief, but has been shown to be an oversimplification, in particular in its explanation of the function of lamina II cells. There are now known to be several different types of lamina II cells and more than one type of spinothalamic relay cell.

Arousal analgesia is mediated by noradrenaline- (and possibly serotonin-) containing nerve fibres that descend from the brainstem and inhibit lamina I cells, thus closing the gate and blocking pain. Their exact mode of action is still not clear.

Opiate drugs block pain by mimicking the actions of enkephalins. Enkephalins are found in lamina II cells, and enkephalin receptors on relay and other cells. Enkephalins are often referred to as 'neuromodulators' as they act by modulating metabolic processes in cells, not by directly initiating or inhibiting action potentials.

Neuropathic pain is due to abnormal patterns of activity in nociceptor relay cells. It is a considerable clinical problem as it is often unresponsive to treatment with analgesic drugs.

The reticular formation plays a crucial role in the transmission of nociceptive information to the forebrain. Descending messages to close the pain gate in the spinal cord may originate from here.

Pain is processed in several parts of the forebrain, but not predominantly in the classic somatosensory cortex. In particular, the emotional and affective qualities of pain may be processed in the limbic system.

Further reading

Wall, P. D. and Melzack, R. (1976) *The Challenge of Pain*, Penguin Books, London.

Wall, P. D. (2000) *Pain: The Science of Suffering*, Phoenix, London.

The function and control of pain

Robin Orchardson

22

1 Introduction

Pain is a complex and highly variable phenomenon. Minor injuries can cause a lot of pain, yet some severe injuries may not be very painful. It has been reported that nearly 40% of people who attended a hospital accident and emergency department as a result of an injury did not feel any pain until some time after the injury occurred (the other 60% presumably did complain of pain). In contrast, around 70% of patients with chronic back pain have no obvious physical injury. These variations can pose considerable problems for the treatment of pain, which in the past has focused on removing the physical causes or dealing with their effects.

It has long been known that sports and battle injuries may not be painful at the time. This is well illustrated by an account in Homer's *Iliad*, the epic poem about the Trojan War, written over 2500 years ago. Here, Homer describes how Agamemnon (commander of the Greek armies in the war) continues to fight even after being wounded:

> 'As long as the blood was still running warm from his wound, Agamemnon continued to harry the enemy ranks with spear and sword and boulder. But when the blood staunched and the wound began to dry, he felt a stabbing pain, sharp as the pangs which seize a woman in childbirth.'

> Homer, Iliad, Book XI, translated by E. V. Rieu, Penguin Classics, 1950.

This description is typical of stress analgesia, which is probably mediated by release of opioid peptides and other chemicals in the brain and spinal cord. Stress analgesia is apparently not confined to humans. The racehorse Henbit won the 1981 Derby despite fracturing a bone in its leg a short distance from the finishing post.

2 Factors affecting pain

Pain is extremely variable; the perceptions evoked by apparently similar injuries can vary in different people at different times, and the amount of pain can even vary in one person at different times. A person's pain reaction can be influenced by many factors operating at different levels (Figure 1). Psychological factors in particular are well known to affect pain perception and behaviour; these include individual characteristics such as age, gender and personality as well as elements such as the

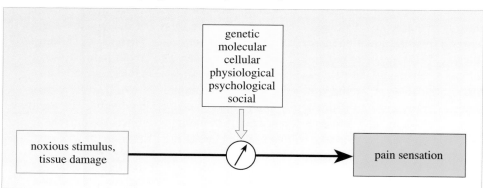

Figure 1 Factors influencing the amount of pain experienced in response to a noxious stimulus or injury. These factors are depicted as acting through a neural 'gate' mechanism located somewhere in the nociceptive pathway.

pain context and emotional factors (Figure 2). These various factors are depicted as operating through a 'volume control' or 'gate' mechanism located somewhere in the nociceptive pathway (see Chapter 21, *The neurophysiological basis of pain*, for more details).

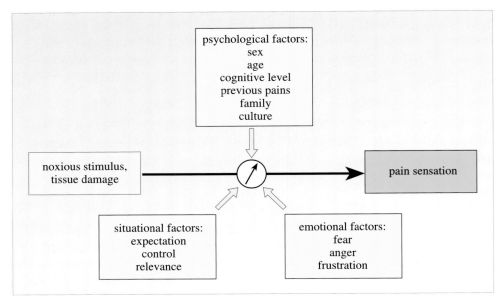

Figure 2   The role of psychological factors in modifying pain perception.

2.1 Psychological factors

Pain-related perceptions and expressions vary with the sufferer's age (for example a child is liable to cry over a minor graze that would not bother an adult), gender and previous pain experience. As we grow up, our behaviour is shaped by the family and cultural attitudes to pain; in some societies, people are expected to be stoical, while other cultures may encourage or tolerate more open expression of feelings. An individual's personality may influence how they behave when in pain; extroverts may make a big fuss about a minor injury, while introverts tend to suffer in silence. Many clinical pain states are generally more prevalent in females, who do not seem to be more 'sensitive' to pain than males but may be less reluctant than males to admit to feeling pain and to seek treatment for it.

2.2 Situational factors

Situational factors refer to the interactions between psychological and contextual factors in a given pain situation. Understanding the source of the pain and degree of control over the situation can affect how much pain is felt. The pain of childbirth is intense, but it has meaning, unlike the pain of cancer. The labour pain has an obvious cause, and the pain eases with the delivery of the baby. Context is also important; soldiers wounded in battle generally complain less of pain from their injuries than a civilian with comparable injuries sustained in a road-traffic accident. These variations may reflect differences in how the injury affects the current lifestyle of the individual (the soldier is taken out of the firing line, but the civilian has to worry about loss of earnings, etc.).

2.3 Emotional factors

Pain provokes a range of emotional responses, which again vary depending on the individual and circumstances. Pain can cause anxiety, especially if the cause is not known. Is a chest pain due to indigestion or a heart attack? People debilitated with chronic pain can become frustrated, angry, depressed. Once again, these reactions tend to vary from person to person.

3 Functions of pain

3.1 Pain as a warning

The physiologist Sir Charles Sherrington described pain as the 'psychical adjunct of a protective reflex'. (This is a useful statement as it distinguishes between the physical response to the injury and the separate perceptual experience usually evoked by it.) This description applies mainly to nociceptive pains. In this respect, acute (nociceptive) pain is useful in that it serves as a warning sign of tissue injury. Such pain is a component of acute inflammation.

Pain prompts the sufferer to rest the injured part so as to avoid further damage and promote healing. Although pain can be regarded as a nuisance, this 'alarm-bell' function is extremely important. This is evident especially in people who are unable to feel pain, as described in Chapter 21, *The neurophysiological basis of pain*. Such individuals experience numerous injuries, and develop arthritis due to excessive joint loading. They do not feel the abdominal pain associated with appendicitis, and so may die from peritonitis.

Not all pain is so useful or beneficial. Chronic pains may persist long after the injury or disease has apparently healed, and the terminal stages of cancer are often associated with severe pain that serves no obvious purpose. The word pain derives from the Latin *poena* (meaning penalty) and was once regarded as a form of punishment for past sins. Pain used to be seen as 'character-building'; strong analgesics were often withheld and the patient's pain was not effectively relieved. These attitudes stemmed from misplaced anxiety about the possible side-effects of strong analgesics (e.g. addiction). Until relatively recently, it was widely believed that the foetus (and even the newborn child) could not feel pain because their nervous systems were not sufficiently developed. Fortunately, understanding has improved and pain is are now managed more effectively.

3.2 Pain in diagnosis

Pain has an important diagnostic function. A patient's description of their pain can often be sufficiently informative to lead to a diagnosis. The relevant features can include the severity of the pain (what limitations does it impose on daily life?), its timing (constant, intermittent, occurs on walking?), its nature (throbbing, burning?), and its location (see Figure 3 overleaf). Is the pain relieved by lying still, or does it drive the patient 'up the wall'? Sometimes the location of the felt pain is not the site of the actual injury or pathology; such pains are said to be **referred**. The pain itself does not actually shift, but the inputs to the CNS cause the brain to interpret the pain as arising from a different structure. Pain usually refers between structures that have similar embryological origins and thus have a common nerve supply.

For example, in the embryo, the heart develops under the chin. As the embryo grows, the heart migrates to the chest, taking its nerve supply with it. Pains from the heart are referred to structures with the same segmental nerve supply – neck, shoulder, arm (Figure 4).

Figure 3 A schematic representation of the relative time course and intensity of different types of pain. The three upper lines depict 'somatic' pains. The two lower examples illustrate 'visceral' pains, which typically have a longer, slower time course. (Note that sensations from the face and mouth are relayed by the trigeminal nerve, the fifth cranial nerve. **Trigeminal neuralgia** represents episodes of intense facial pain caused by a disorder of this nerve.)

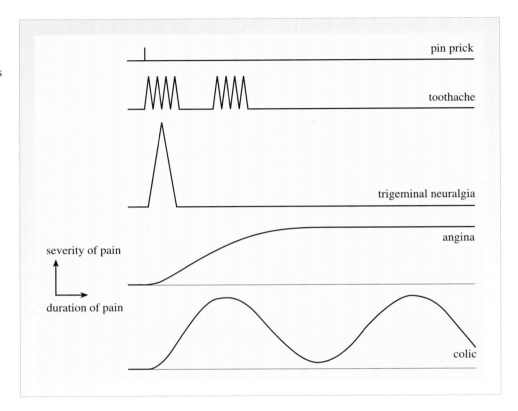

Figure 4 Common patterns of pain referral. Kidney pains can refer to the groin; cardiac pain to the neck, shoulder and arm; pain from the spleen can refer to the left shoulder.

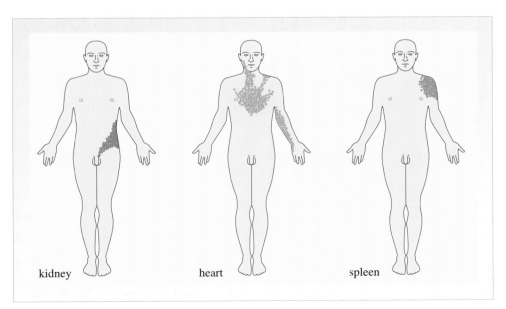

3.3 Pain as a determinant of behaviour

Pain also influences learning and shapes behaviour. The consequences of an action can either promote or suppress that behaviour (e.g. **operant conditioning**) – noxious stimuli provoke an avoidance reaction, and such stimuli are avoided in the future. Melzack and Scott in 1958 showed that a dog's ability to learn to avoid noxious stimuli was impaired if it was not exposed to these stimuli during puppyhood.

These naturally aversive reactions can be modified by appropriate **conditioning**. Amongst his many experiments, Ivan Pavlov conditioned dogs to salivate in response to a noxious stimulus applied to a paw. Such a stimulus normally evokes a violent reaction. The conditioning was very selective and if the stimulus was applied to a different paw (not one used in the conditioning process) the dog reacted violently.

4 Pain control

Pain may be controlled in various ways and by intervention at different levels in the nervous system. The treatment is usually chosen according to the type or severity of pain. Acute (nociceptive) pains tend to be managed with drugs that target specific sites in the nociceptive pathway – the receptors, nerves, spinal cord or higher centres (Figure 5). Chronic pain is now recognized as a distinct entity, rather than merely being an acute pain that has lasted a long time; it is not merely a symptom of disease, but is a problem (syndrome) in its own right. It is associated with depression, helplessness, etc. Treatments that are effective for acute pains may not be effective for chronic pains. Indeed, evidence is accumulating to support the view that in many chronic pains, the 'injury' involves the nervous system itself (see below). These types of pain that involve changes to the nervous system are said to be neuropathic.

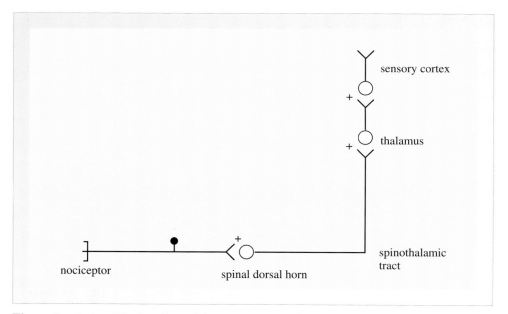

Figure 5   A simplified outline of the components of the nociceptive pathway. The anatomical details are described in Chapter 21, *The neurophysiological basis of pain*. (Note: sensations from the face and mouth are relayed by the trigeminal nerve, the fifth cranial nerve. Here, the first synapse in the nociceptive pathway is in the trigeminal spinal nucleus, located in the medulla oblongata of the brainstem.)

A range of approaches may be used to treat pain. These include pharmacological methods, various forms of stimulation, surgery, behavioural therapy, pain clinics, and pain management programmes, as well as various forms of alternative and complementary medicine (Table 1).

Table 1   A summary of the various methods that can be used for pain control.

Method	Description
pharmacological	use of drugs to block or modify cell signalling or impulse transmission in the nociceptive pathway
stimulation	procedures such as TENS, acupuncture and other forms of counter-irritation
surgical	cutting or lesioning of the presumed nociceptive pathway
pain clinics	multidisciplinary centres that specialize in treating chronic pains by a combination of various methods
behavioural therapy	designed to eliminate specific and 'negative' pain-related behaviours
pain management programme	a form of behavioural therapy using a multidisciplinary approach to help patients cope with their pain
complementary and alternative medicine	use of a wide range of techniques that are not part of 'mainstream' medicine

4.1 Pain control by drugs

Drugs may act at various points in the nociceptive pathway from receptor to the brain (Figure 5).

4.1.1 Drugs acting on nociceptors

Tissue injury provokes a complex response mediated by an inflammatory 'soup' of many chemical mediators that cause nociceptor sensitization. A number of analgesic drugs act to prevent this (see Figure 6). The most widely used are the non-steroidal anti-inflammatory drugs (NSAIDs), many of which are available without prescription. NSAIDS act to block the enzyme cyclo-oxygenase (COX), which acts on arachidonic acid to synthesize the prostaglandins that sensitize nociceptors. Most 'everyday' analgesics (e.g. aspirin, ibuprofen) are in this category. Notable exceptions are paracetamol, which has little or no anti-inflammatory effects and codeine, which acts in the CNS. While NSAIDs are effective analgesics, they can have a number of side effects (e.g. gastric bleeding and ulceration). There are two forms of cyclo-oxygenase. COX-1 is active all the time and mediates the production of prostaglandins, that have a physiological role in protecting gastric mucosa, maintaining renal blood flow and promoting haemostasis. The COX-2 form is induced mainly during inflammation, and is responsible for nociceptor sensitization,

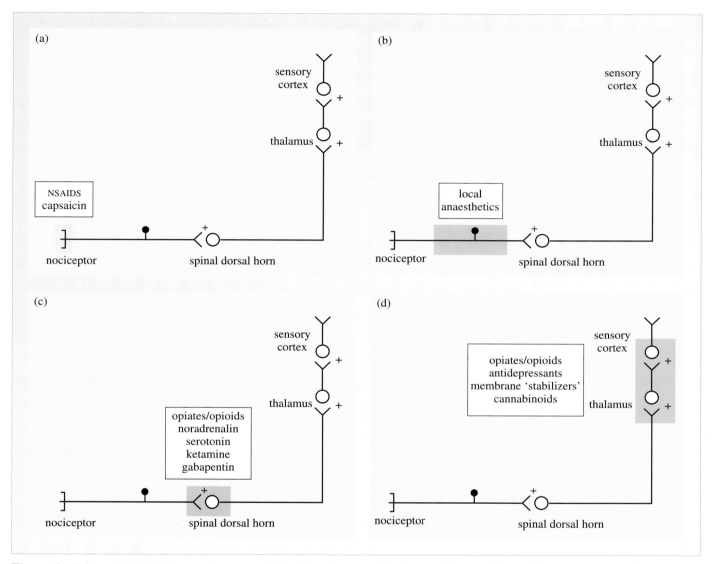

Figure 6   Pain control: (a) drugs acting on peripheral nociceptors; (b) drugs acting on afferent fibres (axons); (c) drugs acting on synapses in the spinal cord dorsal horn (and also the spinal nucleus of the trigeminal nerve, which is the sensory nerve supply to the face and mouth); (d) drugs acting on higher centres in the CNS (forebrain and brainstem reticular formation).

although it too has some protective function. COX-2 generates essentially the same range of prostaglandins, but in much greater amounts. The latter are responsible for essentially pathological effects (Figure 7 overleaf). Specific COX-2 inhibitors are now becoming available (celecoxib, rofecoxib). These seem to be as effective as the original NSAIDs, but are reported to produce fewer adverse side effects.

Capsaicin, the active ingredient in chilli peppers, can be used to treat the pain of arthritis. It is available in an ointment that is applied to the skin over the inflamed joint. Capsaicin causes release of substance P from nociceptors, and repeated exposure results in depletion of substance P levels and so less pain.

Figure 7 Two forms of the cyclo-oxygenase enzyme and their effects.

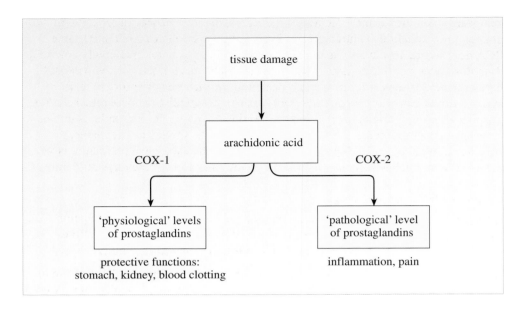

4.1.2 Drugs acting on the primary afferent axon

Local anaesthetics such as lignocaine (lidocaine) act by blocking voltage-gated Na^+ channels in axon membranes, so preventing action potential regeneration and propagation (Figure 6b). Small diameter axons ($A\delta$ and C fibres) are the most susceptible to local anaesthetic block; this is convenient, as nociceptor nerves have small diameter axons. Local anaesthesia is suitable for preventing pain during minor surgery, for example tooth extraction or the removal of an ingrowing toenail, and can also be used during limb surgery and childbirth (spinal and epidural anaesthetics), either alone or as a supplement to a general anaesthetic.

4.1.3 Drugs acting in the central nervous system

The first synapse in the CNS (spinal cord dorsal horn or trigeminal spinal nucleus) is a major site of analgesic drug action (Figure 6c).

Opiates

The opiates include a range of drugs of varying analgesic 'potency' and include codeine, dihydrocodeine, morphine and diamorphine (heroin). These act on various opiate receptors in the CNS and act principally to inhibit transmission in the nociceptive pathways. The actions are quite complex, as they can act both on interneurons and on the main projection neurons. Tramadol is a new analgesic that acts on opiate receptors and also via the **monoaminergic pathways** (serotonin and noradrenaline). In addition to actions in the spinal cord, opiates also act in the forebrain to alter mood and to produce euphoria (the patient may still feel the pain, but it does not bother them; see Figure 6d).

Patient controlled analgesia

A recent development that has improved the delivery of effective analgesia in hospitals is Patient Controlled Analgesia (PCA). Here, the patient takes charge of their analgesic needs, rather than having to call for a nurse or wait for the routine ward round. The drug is contained in a reservoir, which is linked to the patient via an intravenous line. The patient can press a button to receive a small dose of analgesic when they want it. To avoid overdoses, the PCA device is set so that it will not deliver another dose until a pre-set interval has passed ('lock-out'). Portable PCA devices are now available in the form of 'syringe-drivers' that slowly deliver a drug dose over a period of time. Such devices can be used in patients who cannot take oral medications and for whom repeated injections are not appropriate. A syringe-driver can allow a patient to receive analgesia whilst at home rather than in hospital – an important consideration for terminally-ill people. For patients unable to cope with attached devices, implantable drug delivery systems are available. Another way of administering strong analgesics, such as the opiate fentanyl, is via adhesive skin patches, which contain enough drug for about three days of therapy.

Other centrally-acting drugs

Gabapentin is a new drug reported to be effective in treating neuropathic pains such as post-herpetic neuralgia and diabetic neuropathy. It mimics the action of the inhibitory transmitter GABA but may have additional analgesic actions.

Ketamine has been used as a veterinary anaesthetic for several decades, but can be used to relieve pain through its effect in blocking the NMDA (*N*-methyl D-aspartate) receptors in dorsal horn neurons that are now recognized as playing a major role in the development of chronic pain.

Anticonvulsant ('membrane stabilizing') drugs (such as carbamazepine, lamotrigine, phenytoin) can be effective for treating neuropathic pains such as trigeminal neuralgia. They have various actions, such as blocking Na^+ channels in neuronal membranes and acting as GABA **agonists**.

Cannabinoids (cannabis and derivatives) are reported to have analgesic effects, but the evidence in humans is mainly anecdotal and their use is controversial. Cannabinoids are mild hallucinogens and exert their effects by acting on specific receptors in the CNS. At the time of writing (December 2001), cannabis is a Class B controlled drug in the UK (although the government proposes to 'downgrade' it to Class C). A recent review of a number of clinical trials concluded that cannabinoids give about the same level of pain relief as codeine for acute post-operative pain. Another study reported that the cannabis derivative dronabinol and the synthetic cannabinoid nabilone are useful antiemetics in patients receiving chemotherapy.

Higher centres

Tricyclic antidepressants such as amitriptyline and dothiepin are used in treating neuropathic pains. In addition to their effects on mood, they seem to have some analgesic action that may be due to increased availability of the amines serotonin and noradrenaline, both of which are implicated in descending 'anti-nociceptive' pathways originating in the brainstem (see Chapter 21, *The neurophysiological basis of pain*). Similar effects are obtained with the selective serotonin reuptake inhibitors (SSRIs), which increase brain levels of serotonin.

4.1.4 Adjuvants

Glucocorticoids such as dexamethasone and prednisolone can be used along with analgesics as part of a pain control regimen. They are not analgesics, but as corticosteroids they have powerful anti-inflammatory effects and reduce the tissue swelling (oedema) that often contributes to the pain.

4.2 Stimulation methods

Stimulation techniques may be applied either to peripheral nerves, where they operate as segmental inhibitory controls (e.g. TENS, acupuncture), or to parts of the CNS via implanted electrodes (descending controls) (Figure 8).

Stimulation of spinal cord pathways can be achieved by means of an electrode placed over the spinal cord within the vertebral canal. It is an invasive procedure, but is reported to be effective in relieving visceral pains, especially angina. The electrode may be inserted through the skin into the epidural space or can be permanently placed by a spinal operation.

Figure 8 Pain control by stimulation methods (green) and neurosurgery (blue). (A) TENS; (B) spinal cord stimulation; (C) peripheral nerve lesioning; (D) lesioning spinal cord pathways (e.g. cordotomy).

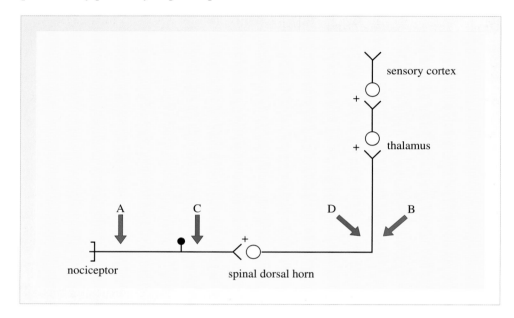

4.3 Surgery

Many neurosurgical procedures have been described for interrupting the presumed 'pain pathway' at some point in the peripheral or central nervous system (Figure 8). 'Open' surgical approaches, such as cordotomy, are less common nowadays. Neurolytic techniques may be used to block peripheral nerve pathways with phenol or alcohol injection. Alternatively, the neural pathway can be lesioned with a thermal probe (either heating – thermocoagulation, or cooling – cryotherapy). These procedures are often used in treating cases of trigeminal neuralgia that fail to respond to drug therapy.

4.4 Pain clinics

When pain is a symptom of a condition, it usually disappears once the condition has been treated. However, some pains persist and become chronic. In the past, chronic pains were dealt with according to which body system was involved. In the 1950s, the anaesthetist John Bonica of the University of Washington Medical School advocated a more integrated approach to pain management by suggesting that chronic pains should be tackled as a medical problem in their own right. Pain clinics provide a multidisciplinary approach to pain management. They allow all aspects of the patient's pain (physical, emotional, behavioural, social) to be treated at the same time. They are staffed by a team of pain specialists from various healthcare backgrounds, and the combined expertise allows a more coordinated approach, taking account of emotional, psychological, family and social aspects of a patient's pain.

According to Dolin and coworkers the aim of pain clinics is to:

- decrease the subjective level of pain;
- enable the patient to be more active;
- reduce drug intake;
- improve quality of life, and enable a return to work;
- reduce the load on health care resources.

4.5 Behavioural therapy

An individual's behaviour tends to be influenced by experience. If a particular action has a favourable outcome (e.g. a reward), the action is likely to be repeated. Similarly, if an action results in something unpleasant (e.g. punishment), it is less likely to be repeated. This is the principle of the learning technique known as operant conditioning. As already mentioned, acute pain causes an individual to rest the injured part. If the pain persists, the sufferer may receive more attention from the family and be allowed to rest; in addition, they can avoid work and anything else they don't want to do. These actions are negative coping strategies. In time these can become linked with feelings of helplessness, dependency, isolation and depression. Positive coping strategies include activities such as exercise, increased mobility, and social encounters. The aims of behavioural therapy are much the same as for the pain clinics, except that the former deals with patients who may not have had success with the pain clinic. The approaches are designed more specifically to alter the sufferer's attitude, to be more positive and to raise their self-esteem. They involve more specific behavioural strategies, such as cognitive therapy to encourage more positive thinking, coping skills such as relaxation techniques, and hypnosis (see Chapter 29, *Perceiving, misperceiving and hypnotic hallucinations*).

4.6 Pain management programmes

Despite the success of pain clinics, chronic pain is still very common. Pain management programmes use a multidisciplinary approach to help sufferers cope with their pain. The main aim is to improve the quality of life, rather than trying to reduce the level of pain. (Pain relief is not neglected, but it is often not the primary focus.) The basic approach is to educate patients so that they are better informed about the causes of their pain and to reduce their consumption of analgesics. Participants are treated in groups, comprising several patients at different stages in the programme. Thus, people starting the programme can learn from fellow-sufferers how it works and can see the benefits. The patients are active in developing a programme that suits their own needs. The expert team includes pain specialists, psychologists, pain nurses, physiotherapists and occupational therapists. Alternative and complementary therapists can also contribute.

4.7 Complementary and alternative medicine

Complementary and alternative medicine (CAM) includes acupuncture, aromatherapy, chiropractic, homeopathy, massage and reflexology. Over the course of a year, such CAMs are used by around 20% of the UK population. The popularity of CAM is even greater in France and Germany, where 50% and 60% of the population respectively have used it. People use CAM for 'positive reasons', for example the 'high touch, low tech' approach is perceived as 'holistic' or 'natural'; or 'negative reasons', such as dissatisfaction with conventional healthcare methods. CAM techniques are very popular, but there is little hard evidence that they work.

Often, reports of efficacy are anecdotal or opinions, rather than being based on rigorous **double-blind clinical trials**. Although some individual studies may suggest a beneficial effect, the evidence is less impressive when it is put under the scrutiny of a systematic review. In other words, the methods are not consistently effective. While there is evidence for positive effects of some herbal remedies (e.g. St John's wort as treatment for depression) there is little convincing evidence for efficacy of CAM in pain relief.

4.8 Placebo effects

No account of pain management is complete without some consideration of the placebo effect. This has gained a bad reputation over the years, mainly because it is often associated with quackery. However, it can be a very powerful adjunct to pain therapy. The placebo effect is influenced by the mode of delivery: an injected placebo is more effective than a pill; large pills are more effective than small ones. Melzack and Wall established that it seems to rely on the patient's expectation; if they believe the treatment is going to work, it probably will.

Double-blind clinical trials

Patients are randomly assigned to one of two groups: an active drug group or an inactive control or placebo group. At the end of the trial, both groups tend to show some reduction in symptoms. In order to demonstrate the efficacy of the active agent or drug, it must perform significantly better than the placebo.

Experimental placebo

Voudouris and coworkers have studied the mechanism of the placebo effect. They tested the ability of an 'analgesic cream' to reduce experimentally induced pain. Their subjects were initially tested with and without the cream to assess placebo responses. (There is evidence that the placebo effect is stronger in some people than in others.) Some subjects received painful (electrical) stimuli to their arm (the first test). The cream was applied and the stimuli repeated. Unknown to the subjects, the stimulus intensity was reduced, so they now felt only a tingle. Then the cream was reapplied, but this time the stimulus intensity was increased to the original level. Remarkably, the subjects reported a lower level of pain than in the first test. Other work showed that this placebo analgesia did not work if the subjects were made aware that the stimulus levels had been manipulated during the experiment. This evidence suggests that the placebo response relies on the subject's expectation. (A placebo does not work if the patient does not know it has been given or it is given under general anaesthesia.)

5 Conclusion

Pain is a necessary evil. It has survival value by assisting recovery from injury and can help to shape behaviour. It is a prominent symptom of many diseases and is an important diagnostic feature. Although most pains arise from an obvious injury or disease, the amount of pain felt often bears no relation to the (apparent) extent of the injury. Pain is a complex emotional experience and can be affected by a wide range of factors. The nociceptive pathway is not a passive conduit like an electric cable; the various components of the pathway can be modified either to suppress or to enhance pain. In addition, there has been a radical change in pain management strategies in recent years. Treatments have switched from 'doctor-centred' to being more 'patient-centred'. Analgesics are given when the patient needs them, rather than when someone else thinks they should be given. Pain treatment is also geared towards helping sufferers to live with their pain, rather than allowing it to dominate their lives. As we learn more about the molecular and genetic mechanisms of nociception and nociceptive systems, it will become possible to develop new treatments. Many of these will continue to use drugs. For example, there is potential to develop drugs that block components of both the peripheral and central sensitization processes.

6 Summary

Pain is more than a sensation. It is a complex and variable emotional experience. The amount of pain felt can be influenced by genetic, cellular, physiological, psychological and social factors. Pain serves primarily as a warning of injury or disease. It can modify behaviour (e.g. once bitten, twice shy). In this context, pain has survival value. However, chronic pains and the pain of terminal cancer serve no obvious purpose. Pain is an important clinical symptom, and often the character and location of the pain can aid diagnosis. In the past, pain was treated medically (with drugs) or surgically (removing the cause of the pain). Drug therapy remains the mainstay of pain management and drugs can target all parts of the nociceptive pathway from peripheral nociceptor to the brain. As more is learned about neural mechanisms, it is becoming possible to develop new drugs designed to block transmission of impulses involved in the generation of pain. Surgery is now less commonly used for pain management and has been replaced by other approaches, including stimulation methods such as TENS (transcutaneous electrical nerve stimulation). Chronic pain is now regarded as a syndrome in its own right, and is treated in specialist pain clinics. Conventional approaches using analgesic drugs are augmented by a range of behavioural methods that are designed to help the patient cope with their pain.

Further reading

McGrath, P. A. (1994) Psychological aspects of pain perception, *Archives of Oral Biology*, **39**, Suppl. pp. 55S–62S.

Melzack, R. and Wall, P. D. (1996) *The challenge of Pain,* 2nd edn, Penguin Books, London.

Melzack, R, and Wall, P. D. (eds) (1999) *The Textbook of Pain*, 4th edn, Churchill Livingstone.

Nurmikko, T., Nash, T. P., Wiles, J. R. (1998) Recent advances: control of chronic pain, *British Medical Journal*, **317**, pp. 1438–1441.

Voudouris, N. J., Peck, C. L., Coleman, G. (1989) Conditioned response models of placebo phenomena: further support, *Pain*, **38**, pp. 109–116.

Wall, P. D. (1999) *Pain: the science of suffering*, Weidenfeld and Nicolson, London.

PART FOUR

SMELL AND TASTE

23

The olfactory sensory system
Tim Jacob

1 Introduction

Smell and taste, sometimes referred to as the 'chemical senses', provide us with information about our environment, each other, and warn us about potential hazards. We can detect in excess of 4000 different smells and the recent discovery of the large gene family that codes for the olfactory receptors goes a long way to explaining how we are able to do this. Smell plays a far greater role in our everyday life than most of us realize. No two humans have the same smell (except identical twins) and our smell may contain information about us, for example, our mood, gender, immunotype and age. While recent research has confirmed the existence of human pheromones – chemicals that transmit information from one individual to another of the same species – the existence of a functional vomeronasal organ to detect them is highly controversial.

When it comes to our sense of smell, our conscious mind doesn't always know what is going on. Oliver Sacks drew attention to this point in his book *The man who mistook his wife for a hat*. In it he describes what happens to a medical student who is suddenly exposed to the full blast of his olfactory sense, no longer attenuated by the inhibition imposed by higher centres in the brain. As we will see later on in the section on the olfactory pathway (Section 5), olfactory information enters more primitive areas of the brain (the limbic system) before being passed to the neocortex for perception, although in some cases such information may not be relayed there at all and the effects are entirely subconscious. The areas of the brain that process olfactory information and how they interconnect functionally are being studied using the latest brain imaging technology (e.g. fMRI) but we are still a long way from understanding how it all works.

2 Odours and olfactory receptors

To possess smell a molecule must be small. Most odour molecules (odorants) have a relative molecular mass less than 300–400. This means that they have a relatively high vapour pressure, and can get airborne and enter the nose (Figure 1a). Here they must dissolve in the **olfactory mucus**. This is an aqueous solution containing mucopolysaccharides, immunoglobulins and detoxifying enzymes secreted by Bowman's glands in the olfactory epithelium. Many odorants are hydrophobic, posing the problem of how they reach the receptors embedded in the nasal mucus. Two factors assist in this process, firstly the presence of lipids in the mucus secreted by the Bowman's glands (located in the connective tissue between the cribriform plate and the olfactory epithelium) and, secondly, odorant binding proteins.

Odorant binding proteins (OBPs) are members of a superfamily that transport small hydrophobic molecules. Retinol binding protein, which binds the hydrophobic retinol (vitamin A) in the photoreceptors of the retina, is another member of this family. OBPs bind odour molecules and assist in their diffusion through the olfactory mucus to the receptors, which are located on the cilia of the olfactory neurons (Figure 1b). OBPs are also responsible for odorant removal and clearance. It is important that odorants, once they have generated a signal, are removed and degraded to allow new odorants to stimulate the receptors and to prevent build up in the mucosal layer. The detoxification enzymes secreted by Bowman's glands then break down the odorants.

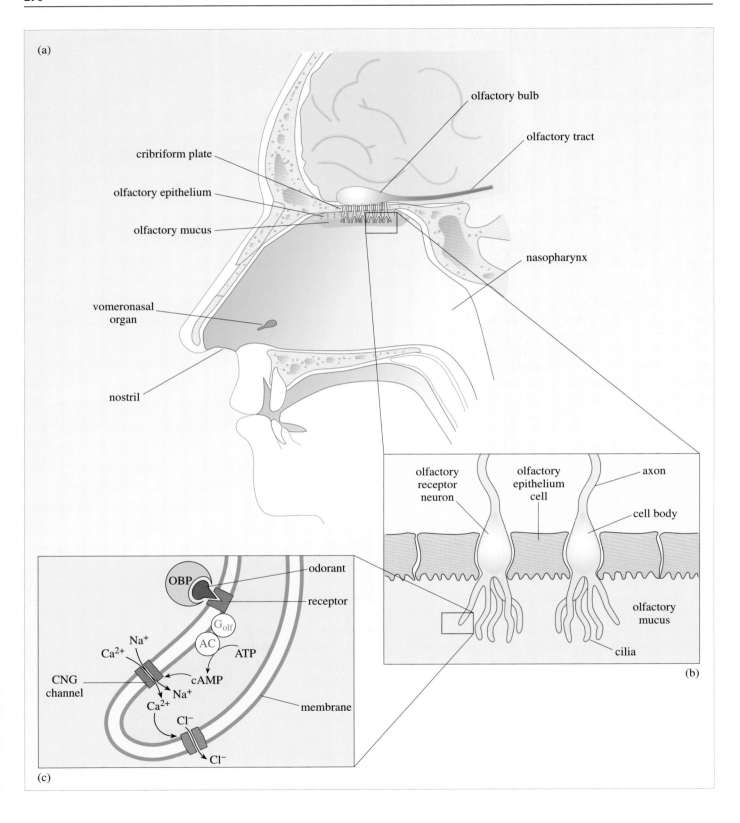

◀ **Figure 1**   The front end of the olfactory system. (a) The olfactory epithelium is located in the roof of the nasal cavity. The receptor cells (olfactory neurons) send axons through the bone (cribriform plate) to the olfactory bulb. At the other end of the receptor cells, cilia containing the receptor proteins project into the olfactory mucus. The vomeronasal organ is a pit located about 1–1.5 cm into the nostril at the base of the nasal septum (the tissue dividing the nostrils) and may be responsible for detecting human pheromones (but see Section 7 below). (b) The olfactory epithelium contains specialized receptor cells, the olfactory neurons, that project cilia into the nasal mucus. (c) The olfactory neurons contain the olfactory receptor proteins and the machinery for olfactory transduction. The smell (odorant) binds to an odorant binding protein (OBP) and is ferried to the receptor – a G-protein-coupled 7-transmembrane receptor – in the membrane. Adenylate cyclase (AC) is activated by a G-protein (G_{olf}) which causes an increase in cyclic AMP. This rise in cAMP opens cyclic nucleotide-gated (CNG) cation channels resulting in an influx of Na^+ and Ca^{2+}. The rise in intracellular Ca^{2+} increases the probability of Ca-activated chloride channels being open. The increased activity of both these channel types causes a depolarization of the olfactory receptor neuron – the receptor potential.

To be detected the odorant must bind to an olfactory receptor. These are situated on the cilia of the olfactory neurons, which are neuroepithelial cells that derive from basal cells within the olfactory epithelium. Estimates of the area of this epithelium are of the order of 2–4 cm^2 in a human, while the dog has 18 cm^2 and the cat 21 cm^2. Dotted about this epithelium humans have about 6×10^6 or six million olfactory neurons in each nostril which compares with 50 million in the rat and between 125–220 million in dogs depending upon the variety. This huge number of olfactory receptor cells in dogs endows them with a very sensitive sense of smell. For example, their detection limit for acetic acid is 5×10^5 molecules per cm^3 of air (2 molecules in 10^{14} molecules of air, or 20 parts per quadrillion) compared with 5×10^{13} molecules per cm^3 of air (2 molecules in 10^6 molecules of air, or 2 parts per million) for a human. Because of their superior sense of smell, dogs can be trained to detect low levels of specific odours and are used to detect explosives and drugs. A bloodhound can identify a person in a line-up after sniffing a 24-hour-old trail, and in a truly extraordinary feat of physiological detective work, can intersect a 20 minute-old trail at right angles and determine its direction after following it for only 2–5 steps.

The olfactory neurons are unusual in a number of ways: first, they are exposed to the external environment, making them particularly vulnerable to damage by toxins, bacteria and viruses; and second, they possess the remarkable ability of regeneration, unlike any other neuron. It is not known for how long an adult human olfactory receptor neuron lives, but the presence of mitotic cells, young receptor cells, mature receptor cells and dying cells coexisting within the olfactory epithelium suggests a process of continual renewal.

Each olfactory neuron possesses between 8–20 non-motile cilia that project from a 'knob' into the olfactory mucus (see Figure 1b). It is on these cilia that the olfactory receptors are located. These cilia sample the air entering the nostrils and thus the olfactory system monitors the external environment. At the other end of the olfactory neuron is an unmyelinated axon. Between ten and one hundred such axons form into a bundle, each bundle becoming a primary olfactory nerve fibre that passes through little perforations in the cribriform plate on its way to the olfactory bulb (see Figure 1a). When these olfactory neurons develop from precursor epithelial cells, this axon grows and must find its way, through the cribriform plate, to a particular glomerulus within the olfactory bulb where it forms a synapse with a mitral cell. This is the first synapse in the olfactory system (Figure 2).

Each olfactory neuron expresses one, or at most a few olfactory receptors, and olfactory neurons expressing the same type of receptor synapse on the same glomeruli within the olfactory bulb.

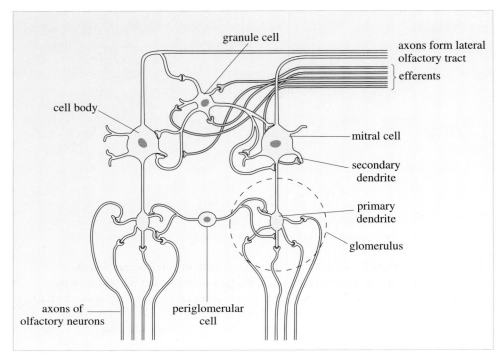

Figure 2   Olfactory bulb connections. The axons from the olfactory neurons synapse onto the primary dendrites of the mitral cells in the bulb. Many axons synapse onto one dendrite and dendrites from several mitral cells contribute to a tangle of axons and dendrites called a 'glomerulus'. The axons of the mitral cells form the olfactory tracts which project to the primary olfactory cortex (septal area, pyriform cortex). Two types of interneuron, granule cells and periglomerular cells, mediate lateral inhibition between mitral cells and possibly other types of modulation. Efferent neurons project from the brain to mitral cells and serve to alter the activity of the mitral cells, for example, to reduce inhibition when a person is hungry.

3 Olfactory transduction

The **olfactory receptor gene** was cloned recently and forms the largest gene family so far discovered, with around 1000 members. It is a 7-transmembrane G-protein-coupled receptor (Figure 3) made up of about 310–340 amino acid residues. Our olfactory system can discriminate between more than 4000 different odorants so this discovery goes part of the way to explaining how this large sensitivity repertoire is achieved.

Each olfactory receptor binds (recognizes) a number of odorants, thus a particular odorant will bind to a number of different olfactory receptors. This binding occurs according to specific molecular features of the odorant, such as its shape, the functional groups it contains, and the distribution of charge within the odorant. Binding of a single odorant molecule may be enough to activate the olfactory neuron.

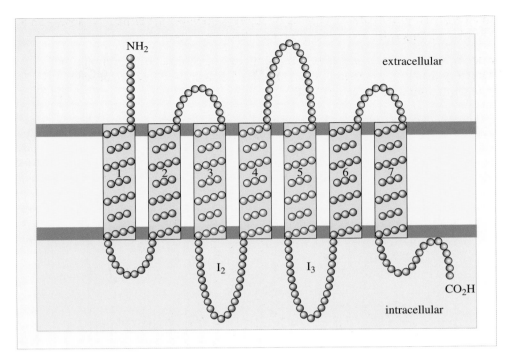

Figure 3   The olfactory receptor protein. A G-protein-coupled receptor with 7 transmembrane domains. Domains 3–5 are highly variable and are probably the odorant binding site. The C-terminus, and the intracellular loops I_2 and I_3 function as the G-protein binding domains.

Odour discrimination is achieved according to a **combinatorial odour code** – each different odour will activate a different pattern of olfactory neurons across the olfactory epithelium. There are 350–400 functional human olfactory receptors (the remainder are pseudogenes), thus one odour (odour 1) might stimulate receptors 1, 3, 5, 6, 17 and 18, while another odour (odour 2) might activate a different selection of receptors, 1, 6, 9, 10 and 19 as shown in Figure 4.

	olfactory receptor																		
	1	2	3	4	5	6	7	8	9	10	11	12	13	14	15	16	17	18	19
odour 1	●		●		●	●											●	●	
odour 2	●					●			●	●									●

Figure 4   The combinatorial odour code. The dots indicate which receptors are bound to and activated by two imaginary odours.

This 'odour code' will in turn be represented by a distinctive pattern of activation in the olfactory bulb. This pattern of activation has been studied by Walter Freeman in the rabbit olfactory bulb. Freeman found that the pattern of activity was encoded by oscillatory activity, called gamma waves (40–80 Hz). This oscillatory activity can be recorded simultaneously in the bulb and the olfactory cortex. He was able to produce 'odour maps' based on the gamma wave activity (Figure 5) and demonstrated that these maps were reproducible following repetitive stimulation

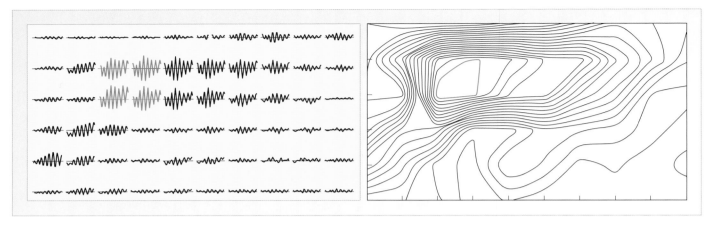

Figure 5   Gamma oscillations (40–80 Hz) recorded from an array of 60 EEG electrodes illustrates the spatial pattern of amplitude from the olfactory cortex of a rabbit as it recognised a scent (left). The wave is nearly the same in each recording, except that the amplitude varies. The shape of the carrier wave does not indicate the identity of the scent. That information is contained in the spatial pattern of amplitude across the cortex, which can be displayed as a contour plot (right), much like the plots of elevations in topographic maps. The coloured contours represent the highest amplitude; successive contours represent the lower amplitudes.

with the same odour. However, if a new odour stimulus was introduced the map changed slightly. The response to the original odour was modified in a way that incorporated the experience of the new odour. The system is therefore 'plastic' and capable of learning.

The binding of an odour to the olfactory receptor activates a G-protein, G_{olf} (Figure 1c), via a mechanism that is not yet understood. There has been a variety of theories attempting to explain the process of olfactory transduction over the years, from those involving molecular shape to those involving a piezo-electric semiconductor current (caused by a voltage brought about by deformation of molecular structure). In 1996 Luca Turin proposed that the nose acted as a spectroscope tuned to the molecular vibrational frequency of the odorant occupying the binding site of the olfactory receptor molecule. While his theory is plausible and attractive there is as yet no evidence that it is correct, and the problem remains unsolved.

Following activation of G_{olf}, adenylyl cyclase is activated, generating increased levels of cAMP which in turn opens a particular class of ion channel, the cyclic nucleotide-gated non-selective cation channel or CNG channel. The resultant influx of cations (mainly sodium and calcium) depolarizes the olfactory neuron. The rise in intracellular calcium activates a calcium-sensitive chloride channel, further depolarizing the cell. This depolarization, if it is large enough (≈ 20 mV), causes the cell to fire an action potential.

The flow diagram in Figure 6 illustrates the sequence of events following the entry of an odour molecule into the nose. The binding of an odorant molecule to receptors situated on the cilia of the olfactory neuron causes a depolarization which is integrated at the cell body. This determines the rate of action potential generation of the olfactory neuron in a manner proportional to the strength of the stimulus – the stronger the stimulus the faster the rate of firing of action potentials. The subsequent change is relayed along the axon to the first synapse in the olfactory bulb.

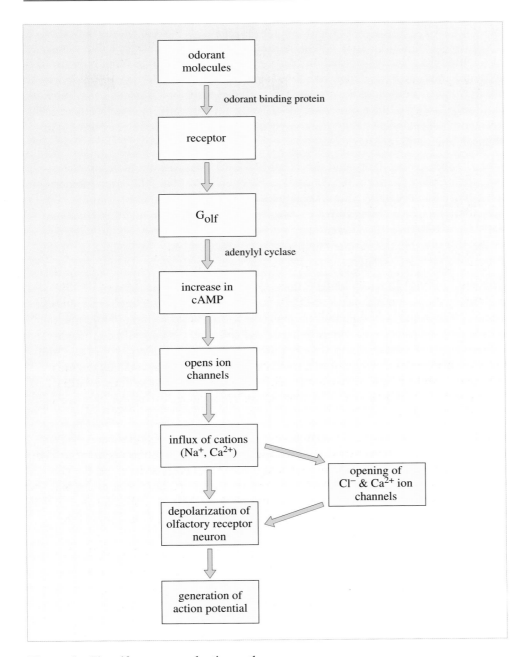

Figure 6   The olfactory transduction pathway.

4 The olfactory bulb

We have two olfactory bulbs situated inside the skull at about the level of the bridge
of the nose. The bulbs are the first relay station in the olfactory pathway and it is to
here that the olfactory neurons send their output. Incoming axons synapse onto the
primary dendrites of the mitral cells. The mitral cells, so called because they
resemble a bishop's mitre in outline, are the main processing cell in the bulb
(Figure 2). There are about 45 000 mitral cells in each bulb of the rat and about
50 000 in the human. They have a large and distinctive primary dendrite onto which
many incoming axons synapse to form a tangled mass of neural tissue called a

'glomerulus' (Figure 2). One extraordinary fact that has recently been discovered about these structures is that, although olfactory neurons are distributed randomly throughout the olfactory epithelium, a single glomerulus receives input only from those olfactory neurons expressing the same type of olfactory receptor. This raises the intriguing question of how, when regenerating, the axon of the olfactory receptor cell finds its way to the appropriate glomerulus. Functionally, this means that each glomerulus 'specializes' in just one molecular feature of an odour, for example its shape, side groups, charge, etc.

One glomerulus may consist of the axons of 17–25 000 olfactory neurons synapsing onto the primary dendrites of 25 mitral cells. There are about 2000 such glomeruli in the rabbit olfactory bulb. This arrangement means that the output of a lot of olfactory receptor neurons converges on a single mitral cell, in fact there is about 1:1000 convergence. This makes the system exquisitely sensitive but at the expense of the ability to localize a smell in the external environment – we cannot tell if the source is to our left or right.

The wiring of the olfactory bulbs is complex (see Figure 2) with many interconnections and interneurons. The function of most of these interconnections is unclear. The periglomerular cells are interneurons that mediate lateral inhibition at the level of the primary dendrites of the mitral cell. The granule cell, on the other hand, mediates inhibition at the level of the cell body of the mitral cell. In addition there are efferent fibres that project from the brain to the olfactory bulb and are thought to have a 'wipe clean' role preparing the olfactory system for the next smell as well as a dis-inhibitory function that increases smell sensitivity, for instance, when we are hungry.

Glutamate is thought to be the olfactory cell neurotransmitter mediating transmission at the first synapse in the pathway (between the olfactory neuron and the mitral cell in the bulb) and there is evidence that noradrenaline is a neurotransmitter in the olfactory bulb. Dopamine receptors have been found to modulate input to the olfactory bulb from the olfactory receptor neurons in rats. Other inhibitory transmitters are also involved (e.g. GABA and glycine) but their contribution has yet to be elucidated.

5 The olfactory pathway

The neuroanatomy of olfaction is unusual (Figure 7). The olfactory tracts project directly to primitive regions of the brain, achieving effects before we are aware of any smell stimulus. All other sensory systems pass first through the thalamus and then on to the neocortex. This gives smell its unique quality – the ability to influence emotion, memory and behaviour.

The axons of the mitral cells join up to form the olfactory tracts, one for each bulb. This divides into the lateral and medial olfactory tracts (or stria). Some neurons of the medial olfactory tract cross over via the anterior commissure to terminate in the contralateral septal area, the rest terminate in the ipsilateral septal area and anterior perforated area. The lateral olfactory tracts project to the primary olfactory cortex which includes such structures as the uncus, amygdala, hippocampus, prepyriform and pyriform areas. These areas are collectively referred to as the limbic system. The term 'limbic system' was first coined by Broca in 1878, the system being distinguished on anatomical grounds. Later Papez, in 1937, suggested its role in emotional behaviour.

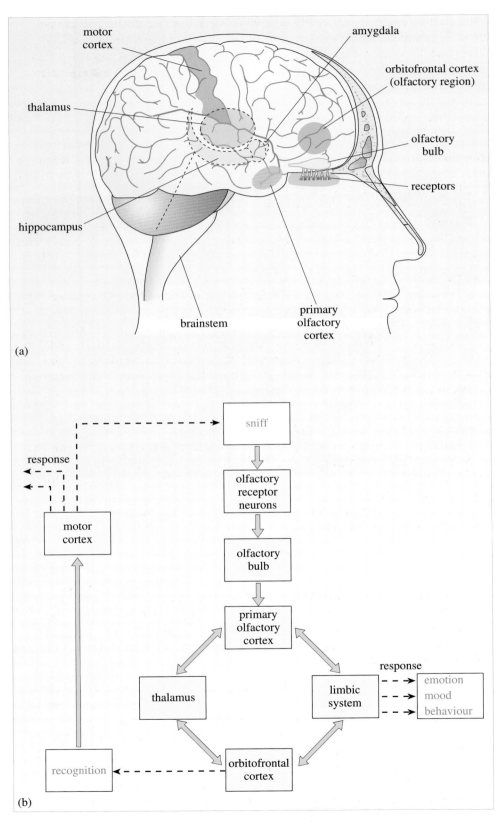

Figure 7 Olfactory pathways in the brain. (a) The diagram illustrates the relative positions in the brain of the structures in the olfactory pathway. (b) The processing of information is indicated in the flow diagram. From the receptors the information flows to the olfactory bulbs and then to the primary olfactory cortex. From here it has two major routes: one to the limbic system (including the amygdala and hippocampus), and the other to the neocortex (orbitofrontal olfactory region) via the thalamus. It is the limbic system that is responsible for the 'affective' component of smell (memory, physiological, endocrine and emotional responses). Recognition is thought to occur in the right orbitofrontal region of the brain.

The olfactory system is intimately involved with the limbic system, indeed is listed as part of the limbic system in *Gray's Anatomy* thus emphasizing the importance of smell to our psychological state. It is via the limbic system that smell influences emotion and achieves subliminal effects such as memory recall and a sense of déjà vu.

The conscious perception of smell is mediated by a pathway which runs from the primary olfactory cortex to the orbitofrontal cortex, via the thalamus. Functional magnetic resonance imaging techniques have demonstrated that it is primarily the right orbitofrontal cortex that is activated following an olfactory stimulus (Figure 8).

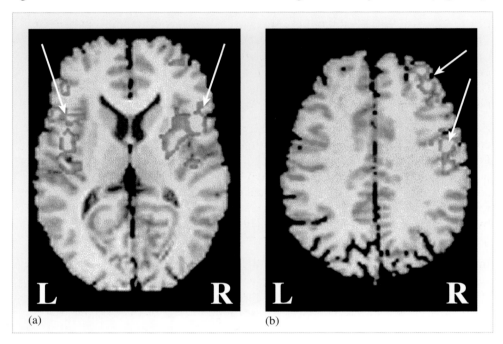

Figure 8   Functional magnetic imaging of the brain. Horizontal sections through the brain showing activation in: (a) the peri-insular region (including the pyriform cortex), and (b) the right orbitofrontal cortex.

6 Olfactory conditioning

One consequence of the interconnections between the olfactory system and regions involved with memory, such as the hippocampus and the temporal lobe, is that smell sometimes becomes associated with a particular memory of a place or experience. To be exposed to the smell again is to relive the experience. This has been termed the 'Proust effect' after a passage in Marcel Proust's book *Swann's Way* in which he describes how the smell of madeleines (a kind of small French cake) dipped in tea brought back long forgotten memories of his childhood.

This phenomenon can be taken advantage of, for example during exam revision. It has been shown that students learning in the presence of a particular smell (conditioning stimulus) obtained better results when recalling the information in the presence of the conditioning odour than a control group. Odour cues were better than colour cues in this context-dependent memory task.

Responses can be conditioned in a classical, Pavlovian maner. For example, human eyeblink can be conditioned to a smell stimulus if an air-puff stimulus to the eye (to cause a blink) is paired with an olfactory stimulus. It may be possible to take advantage of this phenomenon therapeutically by conditioning an immune or endocrine response to an odour stimulus.

7 Human pheromones

Pheromones are chemical signals that induce behavioural changes in another member of the same species. This is a contentious area of science. Nevertheless, there is research demonstrating the influence of such chemical factors in humans. The pioneering work of Martha McClintock, on menstrual synchrony in women, has demonstrated that there are factors, secreted in human sweat, that can act as pheromones. Mothers can recognize their own babies by smell alone and vice versa. Our first responses to the world we inhabit are probably dictated by smell and we respond to smell in ways that we cannot voluntarily control.

It has been shown that there is a relationship between the major histocompatibility complex (MHC), which determines our immunity, and body odour in humans. People with strong aversions to the smell of another individual have been shown to possess similar immunotypes (similar MHCs) to those individuals and there is a stronger brain response in men to the smell of other men with similar MHCs. Other research has demonstrated that mood can be relayed from one individual to another by chemical signals and that the assessment of attractiveness can be altered by human body odour.

In lower mammals it is the vomeronasal organ (VNO; see Figure 1a) that mediates such pheromonal signalling, but to date there is no concrete evidence of a functional VNO in adult humans. That the VNO exists in adults is beyond doubt but there is argument as to whether it is connected to the brain. Thus, the pheromonal effects reported above may well be mediated by the olfactory system.

8 Summary

We now know that the nasal epithelium contains olfactory neurons that house the olfactory receptor proteins. When odorant molecules bind to these proteins they bring about a depolarization of the olfactory neuron that can cause it to fire an action potential. This signal is transmitted to glomeruli in the olfactory bulb from where it is forwarded to the primary olfactory cortex thence to the orbitofrontal cortex via the thalamus where the smell is consciously perceived and to the limbic system which links smell to memory and emotion. Smell appears to be encoded by the pattern of olfactory neurons that are activated when an odorant binds to one or more of the 350 or so different types of known olfactory receptor.

Our understanding of the sense of smell has come a long way in the last ten years. Having said that, we still do not fully understand how the brain discriminates between different odours. Cracking this 'odour code' is the next big research goal. The code will consist of a series of numbers corresponding to which of the 350 or so receptors are activated by each odorant. It will not be an easy task since there are hundreds of receptors and tens of thousands of different odours, but similar reservations were raised before the mapping of the human genome.

Further reading

Bozza, T. C. and Mombaerts P. (2001) Olfactory coding: revealing intrinsic representations of odor, *Current Biology*, **11**, pp. R687–R690.

Doty, R. L. (1994) *Handbook of Olfaction and Gustation*, Marcel Dekker, New York.

Finger, T. E., Silver, W. L. and Restrepo, D. (2000) *The Neurobiology of Taste and Smell* (2nd edn), Wiley-Liss, New York.

Firestein, S. (2001) How the olfactory system makes sense of scents, *Nature*, **413**, pp. 211–218.

Freeman, W. J. (1991) The physiology of perception, *Scientific American*, Feb, pp. 34–41.

Meredith, M. (2001) Human vomeronasal organ function: a critical review of best and worst cases, *Chemical Senses*, **26**, pp. 433–445.

Sacks, O. (1985) The dog beneath the skin, in *The man who mistook his wife for a hat*, Gerald Duckworth and Co. Ltd., pp. 149–153.

The perception of smell

Tyler Lorig

1 Introduction

Brodal, in his excellent and now famous text on neuroanatomy, states that:

> From a clinical point of view the importance of the olfactory system is slight, just as the sense of smell is of relatively minor importance in the normal life of civilized man.

Ironically, that statement begins the chapter on the limbic system, the longest chapter in the book. Brodal's statement is representative of the way that many scientists and lay people view the sense of smell. Most people believe that smell is a vestigial remnant of our four-legged ancestors. Certainly our own experience leads us to that conclusion. When we watch our pets enter a new environment they enter with nostrils flared to find the faintest of odours on the surface of their new surroundings. Our experience is remarkably different. We do not purposely sniff strangers on the street as we pass. We do not begin sniffing the surface of the chair where we've been invited to sit. But we do still use olfactory information in far more ways than most people imagine.

For instance, we take great care to scent and soap our bodies so that we are attractive, or at least inoffensive, to others. Leffingwell & Associates (2001) report industry estimates that the worldwide market for fragranced products reached $12 billion (USD) in year 2000. Just consider the diversity of products where odour is added to enhance the product. Perfume is the most popular example, but fragranced products are everywhere. Tissues, detergents, shampoo, deodorant, paper, leather, cleaning products and many others contain fragrance. In addition to its use in product enhancement, fragrance is added to many products to mask offensive odours that arise in the manufacturing process. If olfaction has become vestigial and unimportant, it is curious that humans spend so much money on it. To better understand this paradox, we will examine the anatomical basis and psychological phenomena associated with the sense of smell.

2 The olfactory system

2.1 The nose

Certainly one of the most often joked about portions of the body, the nose, serves as our chemosensory air scoop. The two nostrils, or more properly, **nares**, are divided by a septum and lead to a large cavity known collectively as the nasal passage. The medial wall of this cavity (Figure 1) is formed by three protuberances. The protuberances are the **inferior**, **medial** and **superior turbinates** and, as can be gathered from their name, they produce turbulent airflow in the cavity. This increased turbulent flow probably leads to a broader distribution of molecules across the portions of the nasal cavity and increases sensitivity to odours.

The nasal cavity is served by two, or possibly three, nerves sensitive to chemosensory stimuli. While the olfactory nerve (cranial nerve I) is the most often discussed, the trigeminal nerve (cranial nerve V) is also critically important to odour perception. Both the ophthalmic and maxillary branches of the trigeminal nerve serve the nasal cavity. The endings from this nerve are more widely distributed than

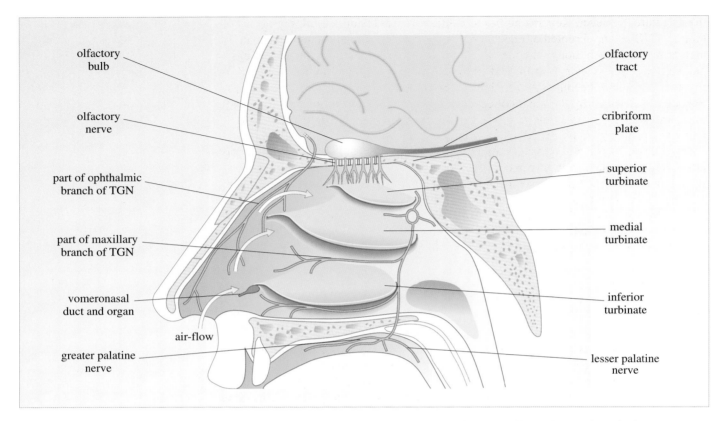

Figure 1   Midsaggital section of the human face showing the nasal cavity and olfactory bulbs (TGN = trigeminal nerve).

the olfactory receptors (Figure 1) and can be found in many portions of the nasal cavity. Activity in this nerve is produced by chemicals such as CO_2, menthol, and camphor and is associated with perceptions of burning, stinging, and pungency. Most of the odours we smell in our daily lives are complex mixtures of chemicals that stimulate both nerves. As you might expect, activity from the two nerves works in a synergistic way to produce perception. For example, a pure odorant (one that doesn't activate the trigeminal nerve) might be rated as a 3 on a 10-point intensity scale. Carbon dioxide, a chemical that is odorless but stimulates the trigeminal nerve, might also be rated as a 3. When the two chemosensory agents are combined, however, subjects would rate them as 8 or 9 on the same intensity scale. This is one of the reasons why carbonated beverages seem so different when the carbonation has dissipated.

The other, and more speculative, nerve that is purported to serve the nasal cavity of humans is associated with the **vomeronasal organ** (**VNO**) (see Figure 1). This organ is found in most mammals where it is associated with the response to pheromones. Pheromones are chemical signals such as those produced during oestrus or scent marking of territory that lead to social communication. In most mammals, activity in the VNO is associated with activity in the vomeronasal nerve. While some humans have an indentation in their nasal cavity that is identifiable as the home of the vomeronasal organ, its association with a nerve is far less clear. Monti-Bloch and coworkers have reported electrophysiological responses in the VNO after stimulation with a purported human pheromone. They conclude that responses do occur under the proper stimulation conditions. In a recent review of

the literature, however, Keverne comes to a different conclusion, describing the human VNO as unafferented or unattached to a nerve. This remains a controversial area of research even though the idea that humans may respond to social odours has gained recent acceptance. Martha McClintock demonstrated that females living together eventually become synchronized in the periodicity of their menstrual cycles. Subsequent research by Preti and colleages in 1986 identified chemicals in urine and underarm secretions that could also produce this response. While controversial for many years, recent studies by McClintock and her colleagues
have addressed some of the earlier methodological criticisms and found chemosensory effects on menstrual synchrony and mood. This is strong evidence for the presence of human pheromones. While some investigators seem to equate the evidence for human pheromones as evidence of a functional VNO, this is not necessarily true. Social chemosensory communication is not defined by the action of any particular nerve and may be the result of activity in the olfactory bulb or trigeminal nerve. VNO activity is not the *sine qua non* of pheromones.

2.2 The olfactory bulb and epithelium

At the topmost extension of the nasal cavity, one finds the olfactory epithelium. This is an area dense with olfactory neurons, cilia, and support cells. The area is bathed in mucus secretions and the cilia 'beat' to move the secretions away from the epithelium and down the back of the throat. When an odour plume enters the nose it is forced up to the epithelium where the odorant molecules embed in the mucus. Once in the mucus, the odorants can stimulate the receptor cells. One of the greatest mysteries in the study of olfaction is why odours don't continue to produce sensations whilst in the mucus adjacent to receptors. Consider that a 'volley' of odorous molecules from the sniff of a rose is estimated to be in the area of the olfactory epithelium for 4 to 6 minutes even though the sensation lasts only a second or so.

Olfactory neurons send their axons into the olfactory bulb. These axons form small groups as they pass through the cribriform plate, the bone that separates the cranial cavity from the nasal cavity (see Figure 1). The axons from the receptor cells enter the superficial regions of the olfactory bulb where they form discrete clusters in an area called the periglomerular layer. Here, many of these axons synapse on mitral cells (see Figure 2). Axons from mitral cells form the pathways that leave the bulb and form the olfactory tracts. This is not the whole story, however. Activity in the mitral cells is affected by a number of other cell types. For instance, tufted cells present in the bulb also synapse with olfactory neurons. These tufted cells significantly influence activity in mitral cells as do granule cells located deep within the olfactory bulb.

One of the most interesting aspects of the olfactory bulb is the large number of neurons that return to the bulb. Most people think of the sensory channels as one-way corridors through which information travels to some central processor. In fact, all sensory systems are two-way streets conveying information to the central processor but also accepting information from it. The olfactory system is somewhat unusual in that so much information is sent back to it. Fibres providing this re-entrant input are called centrifugal fibres. In the olfactory bulb, most of the centrifugal fibres arise in a small nucleus deep in the forebrain called the **anterior olfactory nucleus (AON)**. Other olfactory centrifugal fibres come from the amygdala, pyriform cortex, and locus coeruleus. Interestingly, all of these fibres project ipsilaterally, just as do the tracts of mitral cells that project deep into the brain forming the olfactory tracts.

Figure 2 Schematic diagram of the olfactory bulb showing the information pathway from the odorant molecules to the olfactory tract.

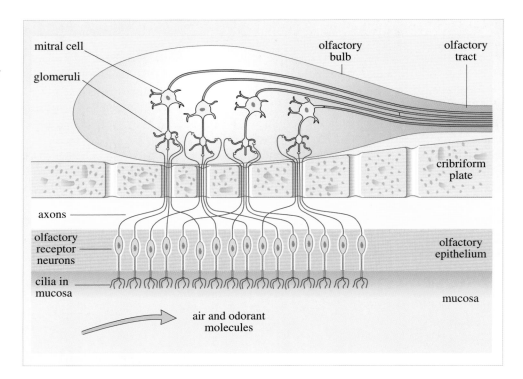

The primary tract in the olfactory system is known as the **lateral olfactory tract** (**LOT**). This tract leaves the olfactory bulb and projects back through the middle of the brain. As mentioned previously, projections from each bulb are ipsilateral. Some of the fibres synapse on the AON. The fibres from this nucleus project back to the bulb ipsilaterally although some cross through the anterior commissure and project to the contralateral bulb.

Olfactory nerve fibres that bypass the AON go to a variety of areas along the anterior to posterior axis of the medial temporal lobe. Most fibres reach the **pyriform** and **prepyriform cortices** and large numbers also reach the **olfactory tubercule**, **amygdala** and **entorhinal cortex**. Second order fibres leaving the amygdala, prepyriform cortex and olfactory tubercule reach the hypothalamus but also cross the midline through the anterior commissure and project to homologous cortical regions in the opposite hemisphere. Second order fibres from the entorhinal cortex project primarily to the hippocampus.

2.3 The olfactory cortex

The pyriform cortex has been identified as the primary cortical projection for the olfactory system. This area would be considered analogous to the occipital lobe for vision or Heschel's gyrus for audition. The pyriform cortex is located on the medial aspect of the temporal lobe. Because this area is on the midline side of the temporal lobe, it can't be seen from the typical lateral views of the cortex so often depicted in texts. It can be seen when the brain is viewed from beneath (see Figure 3).

Anatomical evidence, based on fibre tracing, for the inclusion of this area as the cortical receiving area of olfaction is strong. Electrophysiological recordings have recently demonstrated the presence of fast gamma band activity (30 Hz) in the pyriform cortex of rats during olfactory stimulation presented during an air flow.

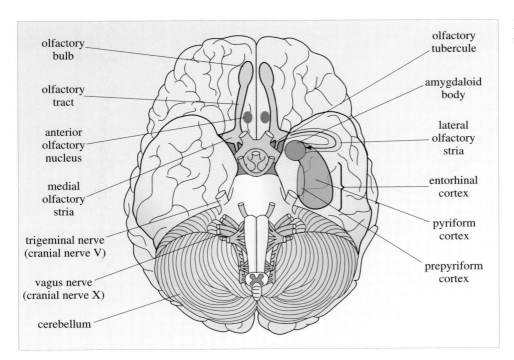

Figure 3 Schematic diagram of the lateral olfactory tract.

Gamma activity is a relatively recently discovered type of EEG rhythm and appears to be very important in communicating sensory information between diverse cortical regions. Thus when odorized air was available to rats, the ipsilateral pyriform cortex showed evidence of gamma activity. It was concluded that the presence of the odour rather than the air flow contributed to the occurrence of gamma. Interestingly, this issue will resurface when we consider human fMRI responses to olfactory stimulation.

Neuroimaging data have been somewhat less convincing about the role of the pyriform cortex. In 1992 Zatorre demonstrated bilateral activation of the pyriform cortex following monorhinic (one nostril) olfactory stimulation, although other investigations have shown much less consistency. However, when pyriform activity is present, it appears to occur bilaterally even though stimulation occurs in a single nostril. Indeed, Kobal and Kettenmann have also found that monorhinic stimulation leads to bilateral activity that is independent of the stimulated nostril. These are very important findings since many investigators have attempted to make statements about the lateralization of olfactory processes based on monorhinic presentation using paradigms analogous to divided visual fields.

In the visual system, the left and right visual fields project contralaterally to the primary visual cortex. Brief activation of one visual field leads to activation of the contralateral visual cortex. In olfaction one would expect the same to be true except that, since the olfactory pathways are uncrossed, activation should occur on the ipsilateral side of stimulation. Unfortunately for many researchers interested in laterality questions, this doesn't hold true. Activation occurs bilaterally following single nostril olfactory stimulation, probably due to close interconnectivity of the two pyriform cortices through the anterior commissure. This leads to great difficulty in interpreting studies about the lateralization of olfaction that use single-nostril presentation of odours. Interestingly, no one has found evidence for the ability of people to identify which nostril is being stimulated during monorhinic presentation of a nontrigeminal odorant. In fact, the absence of this ability is so well known that it is used to test odour mixtures for trigeminally active compounds. Pure olfactory stimuli (e.g. vanilla, low concentrations of phenethyl alcohol or butanol) can't be localized to the stimulated nostril but stimuli containing substances that activate the trigeminal nerve can be. This may be because of the bilateral activation of the pyriform and other cortices during single-nostril odour stimulation.

While on the topic of the pyriform cortex and its activation during olfaction, it is also important to discuss breathing. This seems an unlikely topic and to many investigators it is an annoyance and source of artefacts during recording. Breathing may, however, be much more important to the process of olfaction.

Sniffing appears to be the most effective way to smell and researchers using human brain electrophysiology and fMRI have found that the pattern of brain activity is quite different for odours processed passively versus those actively inhaled through the nose (see Figure 4). This difference is identified as one source of inconsistency in studies of the pyriform cortex, since pyriform activity tends to be present during sniffing. It is possible that the pyriform cortex activity is due to mechanical stimulation of the nostrils as air passes through the nasal cavity. It is also possible that the 'unodorized' air actually contains olfactory stimuli that are below detection levels. There is now clear evidence from several different laboratories using EEG, fMRI and PET that odour chemicals below detection level produce alterations in brain activity (see Figure 5).

The most provocative and plausible explanation for the occurrence of pyriform activity during sniffing is '**priming**'. Since olfactory stimulation tends to occur during the first stages of inhalation, it is possible that activation of brain regions used to process olfactory stimuli are 'primed' by the breathing cycle. Work in 1982

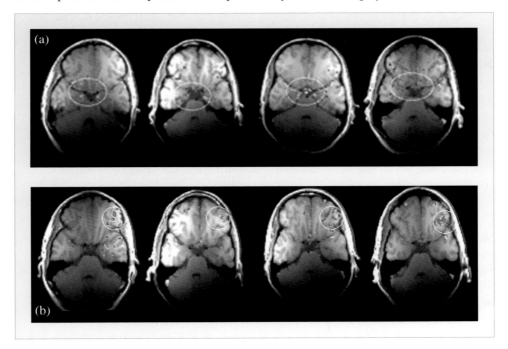

Figure 4   fMRI findings from Sobel *et al.* (1998) illustrating the areas of high response following sniffing. (a) Shows four subjects sniffing in the absence of any odour and (b) shows the same four people sniffing an odour.

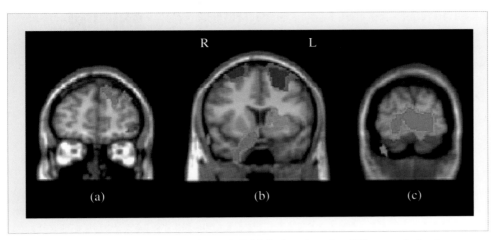

Figure 5 PET findings from Jacob *et al.* (2001) showing the difference in brain activity between subjects experiencing first a mixture of androstadienone + clove and second clove alone. Red areas indicate a significant increase in metabolism when androstadienone is present and blue areas indicate a decrease. The presence of the androstadienone, a purported pheromone, was not perceptible to subjects (i.e. subjects had the same experience despite very different brain responses). Note that activity is occurring in many areas including cortical areas typically associated with vision and language. (a = prefrontal cortex, b = amygdala, basal ganglia, and premotor cortex, and c = primary visual cortex, L = left side, R = right side.)

by Freeman and Schneider in rabbits has shown that the pattern of electrical activity on the surface of the olfactory bulb changes as a function of breathing and the consistency of the stimuli. Their work suggests that an odour, after multiple presentations, achieves a relatively stable pattern of activity (although different between subjects), a template of sorts, and that this pattern is produced in synchrony with the inhalation cycle. Since the pyriform cortex contains efferent nerve fibres that return to the bulb this may be a likely source for the coordination of olfactory activity with breathing.

The implications of respiratory priming of the olfactory system may be very important for understanding many olfactory phenomena. In fact, neuroimaging studies that normally seek to reduce breathing effects by subtraction or random administration of odours during the respiratory cycle will need to be re-evaluated. If they are not, we are likely to treat areas of the brain essential to the olfactory process as artefacts.

2.4 Other cortical projections

Until recently, few investigators believed that olfactory tracts led to cortical regions other than the pyriform cortex. Neuroimaging data from PET, fMRI, magnetoencephalography (MEG), and modelling of sources of evoked potentials all point to projections in surprising areas of the cortex. For example, in a study combining MEG and fMRI, Kobel and Kettenmann found that the orbitofrontal cortex, lateral and medial frontal cortex, and portions of the temporal lobe (insula and superior temporal sulcus) showed activity in response to a pure odorant. In fact, the most consistent component of brain activity in the MEG study was found to occur 518–730 milliseconds after olfactory stimulation. This component was most consistent in the left superior temporal sulcus, an area most often associated with language processing. Based on these data and findings on language processing and odour interference, Lorig has proposed that processing of complex odour stimuli is similar to the processing of words. This rather odd comparison is due to the fact that both odour mixtures and words are temporal streams of information that contain highly overlapping components with very similar temporal features. Different chemicals that comprise an odour mixture may have very different rates for activating olfactory receptors. Some may act quickly and others quite slowly. Thus, in a single mixture, some chemical components will begin producing responses first followed by others. In this way, odour mixtures have a time course like the sounds that make up words. Because the left superior temporal gyrus is an area important to both the interpretation of speech sounds and odour perception, the overlap in processing can lead to interference when one is simultaneously required to process both types of stimuli. This is, of course, a controversial hypothesis but it raises a more general question regarding the hemispheric processing of olfactory information.

The literature on the hemispheric processing of odours contains an amazing array of studies. Some, as mentioned earlier, concentrate on monorhinic stimulus presentations and others use comparisons between brain-injured subjects and normal controls. Still others compare physiological responses between odour conditions and a no-odour control. Used appropriately, valid information may be obtained from these experimental approaches. Unfortunately, it is quite difficult to use these three approaches in a valid way and many of these studies have serious flaws of methodology or logic. This complexity is compounded by the fact that no two laboratories have the same questions in mind when designing experiments. Even so, hemispheric differences do arise. There are clear differences in the effects of lesions of the left and right hemisphere when it comes to detecting odours with the right hemisphere dominant in that ability. The rest of the olfactory world – **hedonics**, memory, semantics, associations, intensity, and the other phenomena collectively known as 'higher' functions – seem to be a complex property of the interaction among hemispheres.

While we have touched upon only a few olfactory phenomena, one in particular, deserves mention here. That is the association of odour memory with the hippocampus. Most people have had the unusual experience of having an odour evoke an important memory from long ago. The phenomenon is known as the '**Proust effect**' owing to Marcel Proust's multi-volume reflections after smelling small pastries. Despite the ubiquitous nature of this phenomenon, it has proven especially difficult to study in the laboratory. This has made the question of why odours evoke memories quite difficult to answer. Perhaps because of the information void and our desire to explain these dramatic memories, a logically flawed answer has emerged. This *incorrect* answer is that the Proust effect is a result of the direct connections between the olfactory bulb and limbic system. Since the limbic system contains the hippocampus, the purported 'centre' for memory, and other areas associated with emotion, odours are believed to have a 'more direct' connection to memory and emotion than any other sense.

This statement seems innocent enough but it contains several errors. For instance, the presumption that the hippocampus is the centre for memory is not entirely accurate. At best, the hippocampus seems necessary to encode new memories, not to recall them. Odours should therefore be more helpful in the encoding process than the retrieval process. Such a statement might really be true if odours produced some sort of non-specific activation of the limbic system that made the system somehow more efficient. If odours and other types of activity in the limbic system produced activation then we might reasonably expect psychological phenomena associated with limbic activity to be more prevalent. If that were true, anger, fear or happiness should lead to enhanced memory. Unfortunately, the data suggest otherwise. Odours may produce fearful emotions, but the converse, fear producing phantom smells, is decidedly unusual. Neural pathways tend to be quite precise and adjacent areas of the brain, especially below the level of the cortex, may be essentially autonomous. It is unreasonable to assume that the proximity of the olfactory system to the hippocampus or even the direct connections between olfactory bulb and amygdala are the reason for some psychological phenomena. Phrenology was unsuccessful in its first incarnation. To say that amygdala activation is the same as fear is just as absurd as saying that the orbitofrontal cortex is the seat of loyalty.

Research by R. S. Herz does support the idea that olfaction is slightly better at evoking emotional memories than other stimuli. However, while it is appealing to try and provide a neurological explanation of these findings, a functional explanation may be just as good. Odours can be very salient cues for emotions because of their association, not necessarily because of the proximity of their neural pathways.

3 Conclusions

While it is tempting to try to understand odour processing by exclusively examining the neurophysiological underpinnings of the pathways and nuclei, much is lost by this 'bottom up' approach. The same is true when one considers only the phenomenology of olfaction (top down). The best approach is to ask 'how some cognitive or behavioural response works' then constrain one's answer by the possibilities provided for by the neurophysiological and anatomical substrate.

Real progress has been made in our understanding of olfaction. We now understand that odours have important but remarkably subtle influence on behavior and we have come to that understanding by a combination of both behavioral and neurophysiological techniques.

4 Summary

Olfactory information is used for product enhancement and to influence social interaction, in particular for the promotion of desirable smells and the masking of unwanted ones.

The olfactory system comprises the nose, our chemosensory air scoop which effects a broad distribution of molecules across the receptive neural surface; the olfactory epithelium and bulb where the olfactory neurons are located and the neuronal stimuli are generated; and the olfactory cortex in the brain where stimuli are processed. In particular, the overlap between regions that process olfactory information and those that process language might well suggest that the two are processed similarly.

Experimental techniques used to establish olfactory mechanisms have been difficult to validate but modern imaging techniques in combination with behavioural studies have recently provided new insights into central processing of olfactory stimulation.

Further reading

Brand, G. (1999) Olfactory lateralization in humans: a review of the literature, *Neurophysiologie Clinique/Clinical Neurophysiology*, **29**, pp. 495–506.

Keverne, E. B. (1999) The vomeronasal organ, *Science*, **286**, pp. 716–720.

Lanza, D. C. and Clerico, D. M. (1995) Anatomy of the human nasal passages, in Doty, R. L. (ed.) *Handbook of olfaction and gustation*, pp. 53–74, Marcel Dekker, New York.

Lorig, T. S. (1999) On the similarity of odor and language perception. *Neuroscience and Biobehavioral Reviews*, **23**, pp. 391–398.

Monti-Bloch, L., Jennings-White, C., and Berliner, D. L. (1998) The human vomeronasal system – a review, *Annals of the New York Academy of Sciences*, **855**, pp. 373–389.

Price, J. L. (1990) The olfactory system, in Paxinos, G. (ed.), *The human nervous system*, pp. 979–998, Academic Press, New York.

Royet, J. P., Koenig, O., Gregoire, M. C., Cinotti, L., Lavenne, F., Le Bars, D., Costes, N., Vigouroux, M., Farget, V,. Sicard, G., Holley, A., Mauguiere, F., Comar, D. and Froment, J. C. (1999) Functional anatomy of perceptual and semantic processing for odors, *Journal of Cognitive Neuroscience*, **11**, pp. 94–109.

Shepherd, M. (1990) *The synaptic organization of the brain*, 4th edn, Oxford University Press.

Silver, W. L. and Finger, T. E. (1991) The trigeminal system, in Getchell, T. V., Doty, R. L., Bartoshuk, L. M., and Snow, J. B. Jr. (eds), *Smell and taste in health and disease*, pp. 97–108, Raven Press, New York.

The gustatory sensory system

Tim Jacob

25

1 Introduction

Taste, more formally referred to as gustation, is one of the two chemical senses. Smell, the other chemical sense, is dealt with in Chapter 23, *The olfactory sensory system*, and Chapter 24, *The perception of smell*. But what most people think of as taste is in fact 'flavour'. Flavour is the result of the combination of information from a number of different senses, in particular taste and smell. Should we eat or drink without our sense of smell we have lost a very important sensory dimension and we have to rely more heavily on our sense of taste. It then becomes very difficult to distinguish tastes that we would normally have no difficulty in identifying. Try drinking coffee while holding your nose. Anosmics (those individuals who have lost their sense of smell) generally lose the pleasure in eating and, disturbingly, have even been reported to forget to eat when living alone. For them eating is merely a refuelling operation and easily overlooked. All the finer qualities of food and drink appreciation are the result of the brain receiving pooled information from taste *and* smell neurons. It is the information from our olfactory receptors that is primarily responsible for flavour. Taste has more basic functions – to provide information about the essential components of our diet and as a last line of defence against poisons.

The taste system is stimulated by a wide range of chemicals that are usually grouped into four basic tastes: salty, sweet, sour and bitter. This grouping is probably too restrictive and other tastes that are difficult to describe such as 'metallic', 'astringent', and 'umami' should also be considered. **Umami** (pronounced 'oo-MOM-ee') is a taste that has been described recently. The word is Japanese and means 'delicious savoury taste'. This taste, common in oriental foods, is the taste of amino acids, in particular glutamate and aspartate.

2 The anatomy and physiology of taste

Why do things have taste? Things only have taste if we put them into our mouths and they come into contact with taste cells on the tongue. Generally, we only do this with food and drink. We have an absolute requirement for certain foods in our diet such as carbohydrates, salt and protein (amino acids) and we have specific detectors for these tastes. Thus, an appetite (desire) for these tastes in food will ensure that we get the essential components of our diet. Taste therefore drives appetite and eating behaviour and protects us against poisons and bad food.

Soluble components of our diet find their way to taste detectors. The latter are membrane proteins in taste cells. Taste cells are found in taste buds – collections of cells in a densely packed spherical arrangement – and these taste buds are located in taste papillae on the tongue, which are often mistakenly referred to as taste buds.

2.1 Papillae

The papillae are specific structures on the tongue. There are four classes of papillae: filiform, fungiform, foliate and circumvallate (or vallate). Each class of papilla, with the exception of filiform, contains taste buds.

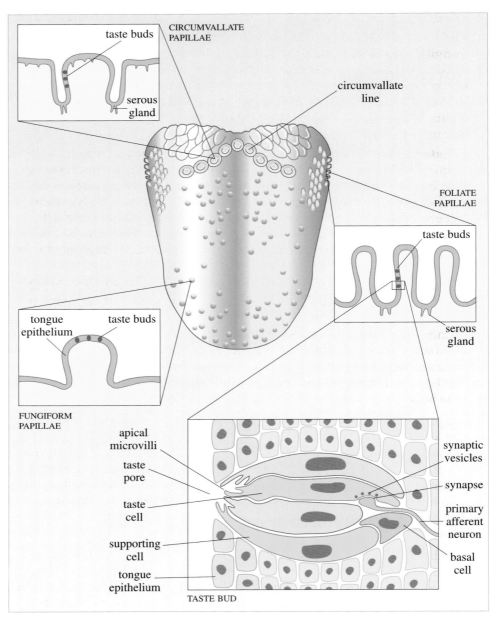

Figure 1   The tongue with its regional distribution of taste papillae. Circumvallate papillae are found along a line at the back of the tongue, foliate papillae are situated at the back edge of the tongue on either side and fungiform papillae are distributed over the front of the tongue, particularly at the tip and the sides. There is an area in the middle of the tongue that is devoid of taste papillae. The small inset diagrams illustrate the basic structure of the papillae; fungiform papillae are raised structures, while foliate and circumvallate papillae are both sunken structures containing serous glands to clean them. The enlargement shows the segmented structure of a taste bud closely packed with taste cells, supporting cells and basal cells. A primary afferent neuron enters the base of the taste bud and synapses onto the taste cell. See text for more detailed information.

- **Filiform papillae** are thread-like in structure and non-gustatory (not involved in taste). They probably have mechanical and somatosensory functions.

- **Fungiform papillae** are raised structures on the surface of the tongue that look a little like miniature mushrooms (Figure 1). There are about 320 in total on the human tongue with an average of 3.5 taste buds per fungiform papilla, giving a total of 1120 fungiform taste buds (about 24 per cent of the total number of lingual taste buds). They are visible as small red dots on your tongue – red because they are richly supplied with blood vessels.

- **Foliate papillae** are situated on either side of the tongue towards the back (Figure 1). They are folds and ridges in the posterior margins of the tongue. The taste buds are situated on the sides of the folds. There are about 5–6 folds on each side with 118 taste buds per fold (total = 1280 foliate taste buds or about 28 per cent of total lingual taste buds). At intervals in the base of the trough between folds there is a serous gland that secretes a clear fluid. This fluid is responsible for removing taste particles and clearing the taste buds ready for the next stimulus.

- **Circumvallate papillae** are found at the back of the tongue along a V-shaped line, the circumvallate line, that runs across the upper surface of the tongue at the level of the foliate papillae (Figure 1). They are sunken, roughly circular cylinders surrounded by a trough. Most of the taste buds are situated on the walls of the central portion of the papillae. There are only about 9 or 10 of these large structures each containing around 240 taste buds, giving a total of about 2200 circumvallate taste buds per tongue (48 per cent of total number of lingual taste buds).

Taste papillae can contain varying numbers of taste buds, for example, fungiform papillae have been found to contain anything from zero to 15 taste buds. Studies have shown that those papillae with no taste buds are not sensitive to any tastes and those with increasing numbers of taste buds are sensitive to a greater variety of tastes. But, even with one taste bud some papillae possess sensitivity to salt, sweet, sour and bitter tastes. Thus a single taste bud can be sensitive to multiple tastes.

2.2 Taste buds

Taste buds, which consist of tightly packed clusters of cells (around 50) embedded in the surface epithelium (Figure 1), are mainly found in the taste papillae. However, there are a few additional taste buds situated on the palate, pharynx and larynx. The cells in taste buds are arranged rather like the segments of an orange; most of the segments are columnar epithelial cells and some are sensory cells. Like all epithelial cells these cells are polarized, possessing apical and basolateral membrane domains. At their apical end, they have microvilli which project into the taste pore. It is here that the food is 'tasted'. Neighbouring epithelial cells perform a supporting function for the sensory cells, and apical tight junctions between the top edges of the cells in the taste bud prevent the passage of food or fluid past the taste pore and into the taste bud. At the base of the taste bud are basal cells that grow and divide giving rise to new taste sensory cells.

Taste buds can be responsive to a range of different tastes. Exactly which tastes they are responsive to depends upon the number and variety of different taste cells they possess. Each individual taste cell is thought to respond preferentially to one stimulus class according to which taste receptor mechanisms it expresses.

2.3 Taste cells

Taste cells are specialized epithelial cells. They tend to be long and thin with microvilli at the apical end that project into the taste pore (see Figure 1). The apical domain contains the taste receptors and ion channels involved with taste transduction while the basolateral domain contains, among other things, the voltage-dependent Na^+, Ca^{2+} and K^+ ion channels (Figure 2). These ion channels give the taste cell the ability to fire action potentials. At the basal end of the cell there is a concentration of vesicles containing neurotransmitter in the region where the cell makes synaptic contact with the primary gustatory nerve.

Taste cells appear to be tuned to respond to one particular taste; this is achieved by their expressing one taste receptor more than others.

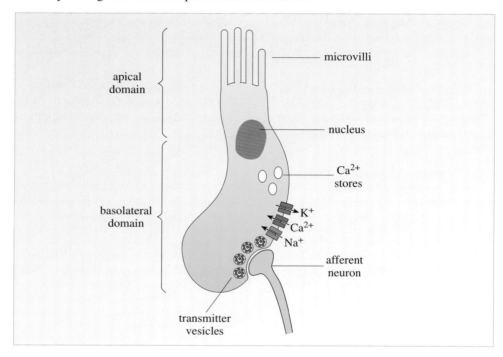

Figure 2   The structure of a taste cell. The sensory cell has two membrane domains: the apical domain and basolateral domain. The apical domain possesses microvilli that project into the taste pore and detect the taste of food. The taste receptors are situated on these microvilli. The basolateral domain contains the ion channels involved in intracellular signalling.

2.4 Regional localization of taste on the tongue

There has been some controversy as to whether the familiar taste maps of the human tongue, which appear in every textbook, are correct. Taste sensation can be localized on the tongue but does the tongue have regions that are more sensitive to one taste modality than another? In humans, the fungiform papillae are concentrated on the anterior tip and lateral margins of the tongue. It has been demonstrated that sensitivity to salt (NaCl) is directly related to the number of fungiform papillae present: the more papillae, the greater the sensitivity to NaCl and the lower the NaCl threshold. However, it has been shown that in addition to responding to NaCl, some taste buds of human fungiform papillae can also respond to sucrose. The response to NaCl and sucrose occurs in different cells within the taste bud.

Therefore, although fungiform papillae are primarily salt sensitive, they are not insensitive to other tastes.

Bitter receptors are not uniformly distributed over the tongue. In rats the bitter receptors are expressed in a subset of taste cells in all papillae but they are more concentrated in foliate and circumvallate papillae situated at the sides and the back of the tongue. Furthermore, α-gustducin, which is the G-protein coupled to the T2R bitter receptors (see below), is expressed more in circumvallate than fungiform papillae in the rat.

One rather more empirical approach to resolving the question of whether the 'classic' map is correct is to stimulate the different areas of the tongue directly. Thermal stimulation of the anterior sides of the tongue in humans (fungiform papillae and the chorda tympani nerve) evokes sweet and salt/sour taste while thermal stimulation of the rear of the tongue (foliate/circumvallate papillae and glossopharyngeal nerve) reveals a different relationship between temperature and taste to that of the anterior stimulation.

One can conclude that the classical 'taste map' is an over-simplification. Sensitivity to all tastes is distributed across the whole tongue and indeed to other regions of the mouth where there are taste buds (epiglottis, soft palate), but some areas are indeed more responsive to certain tastes than others.

3 Taste detection

The molecules that effect each different taste have different chemical properties, for example, shape, acidity, size, electric charge, etc., and there are receptor mechanisms responsive to these characteristics. Some chemicals will activate more than one such mechanism. The mechanisms of some of the more basic tastes have been characterized in some detail and are outlined below.

3.1 Salt taste

Salt taste is conveyed by chlorides, in particular sodium ions and chloride ions (Na^+Cl^-); potassium chloride (K^+Cl^-) has a similar taste. Sodium ions enter the taste cells through sodium channels that can be blocked by the diuretic drug amiloride. However, amiloride, a blocker of epithelial Na^+ channels, does not entirely prevent the detection of salty tastes in humans and thus there must be other mechanisms whereby Na^+ enters the sensory cell. Being positively charged, Na^+ ions depolarize the cell causing activation of voltage-dependent Ca^{2+} channels (Figure 3). The increase in intracellular Ca^{2+} ion concentration causes the migration of the transmitter vesicles to the presynaptic membrane, fusion with the membrane and release of the vesicle contents into the synaptic cleft. This opens channels on the post-synaptic membrane, activating the afferent neuron that fires action potentials.

3.2 Sour taste

Sour tastes are generally effected by acids and acids contain hydrogen ions (H^+ or protons). There are two mechanisms for transducing sour taste. The first involves the inhibition of voltage-sensitive potassium channels. These channels are pH-sensitive and are inhibited by a fall in pH (increase in H^+ ion concentration). The inhibition of these potassium channels removes a hyperpolarizing influence and causes the taste cells to depolarize. The receptor potential then causes stimulation of the afferent nerve by the same mechanisms as above (see Figure 3). The second mechanism for

Figure 3 Taste receptors and the transduction pathways. Salt taste is mediated by Na$^+$ channels and sour taste by H$^+$ inhibition of K$^+$ channels. Sweet, bitter and umami tastes have specific G-protein coupled membrane receptors. The basolateral membrane contains the ion channels (voltage-sensitive Ca^{2+}, Na$^+$ and K$^+$ channels) and pumps (Na$^+$/K$^+$-ATPase) associated with the generation of the receptor potential and maintenance of the resting membrane potential. Salt, sour, and sweet tastes cause a depolarization – the receptor potential – by the mechanisms indicated. Bitter tastes cause an elevation of intracellular calcium by release from internal stores (see Figure 2) as well as a reduction in cAMP. The consequences of this are at present unclear. Umami taste may activate the receptor cell by two mechanisms; first by activation of glutamate receptors and the entry of Na$^+$ and Ca^{2+}, and secondly via activation of phosphodiesterase and a reduction in cAMP. See text for further and more detailed explanation.

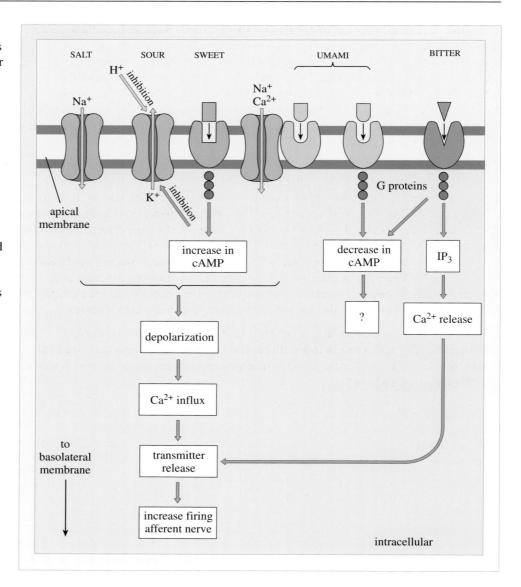

transducing sour tastes is by H$^+$ entry through Na$^+$ channels. Protons (H$^+$) are positively charged and when they enter the cell cause depolarization. Clearly other mechanisms must be involved or it would not be possible to distinguish sour from salt tastes. Following depolarization, the sequence of events leading to increased firing of the afferent nerve is the same as for salt taste (see above).

3.3 Sweet taste

Sweet tasting compounds generally have a structure that is similar to glucose (although artificial sweeteners present some notable exceptions; see Figure 4). Homogenized membranes of taste cells were shown to contain a fraction that binds sucrose (fructose-glucose joined end-to-end) leading to the idea of specific receptors having a binding site that recognizes a glucose-shaped molecule. The recent discovery of T1R1 receptors, which are G-protein-coupled 7-transmembrane proteins found predominantly in the taste buds of fungiform papillae, has suggested a possible mechanism for the transduction of sweet taste. Sucrose binding leads to a GTP-dependent increase in cAMP which depolarizes the cell via closure of K^+ channels (Figure 3). The depolarization then activates voltage-dependent Ca^{2+} channels leading to an influx of Ca^{2+}, transmitter release and activation of the afferent nerve. However, T1R1 receptors are found in cells that do not express α-gustducin and since sweet-responsive cells express gustducin this has been taken to imply that the receptors may not mediate sweet tastes. Confirmation of the exact identities of the sweet receptors therefore awaits further investigation.

Artificial sweeteners have a very different structure to sucrose (see Figure 4). Most artificial sweeteners have been discovered by 'accident' – actually by poor laboratory practice. Three have been discovered on separate occasions by laboratory workers licking their fingers in order to pick up a piece of paper (saccharin, aspartame and acesulfame), a fourth was discovered by a smoker putting his cigarette down on the edge of the bench and tasting something sweet when he next put it into his mouth (cyclamate). Sucralose was discovered when a foreign graduate student misheard 'testing' for 'tasting'. Some plant proteins are sweet, for example monellin and thaumatin (10 000 times as sweet as sucrose), and some simple salts, for example those of lead and beryllium also taste sweet (although they are highly toxic).

Certain artificial sweeteners (e.g. saccharin) lead to the generation of inositol triphosphate (IP_3) and a rise in intracellular Ca^{2+} ions due to release from internal stores; this suggests a different receptor mechanism to sweet receptors which elevate Ca^{2+} by influx (see above).

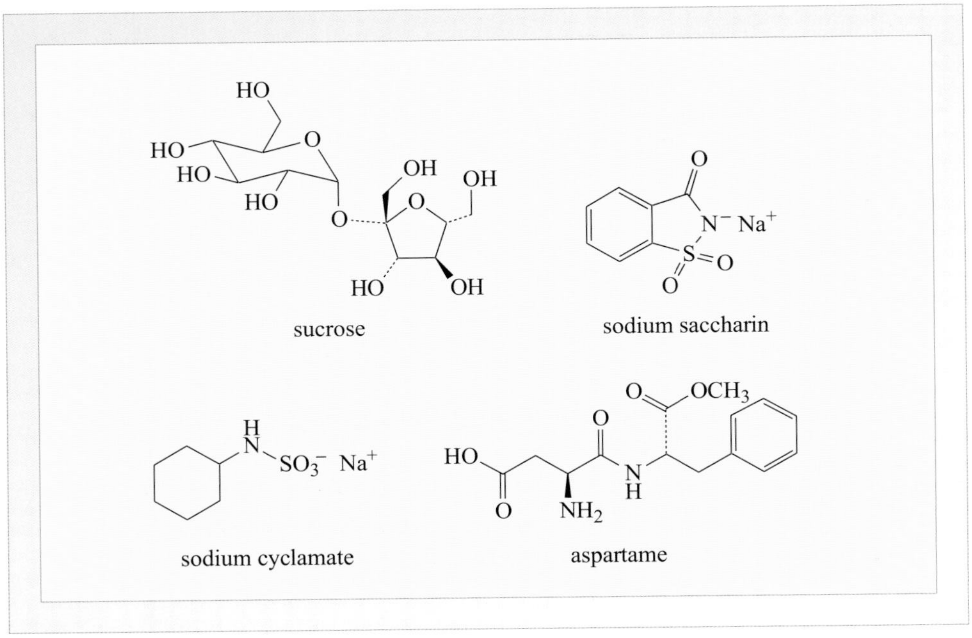

Figure 4   The chemical structures of sucrose and some artificial sweeteners.

3.4 Bitter taste

Many structurally unrelated substances taste bitter – for example quinine and caffeine. We cannot distinguish different qualities of bitterness – bitter is bitter. Bitter taste usually means that the substance is poisonous and warns us not to swallow – this is why most medicines taste bitter. Medicines are of course poisonous in high doses. Recently a family of genes was cloned that code for bitter receptors and these are known as the T2R receptors. This is a large gene family with about

100 members, many of which involve the G-protein, α-gustducin. These receptors are expressed in a small subset of taste receptor cells in all papillae but their predominant expression is in circumvallate and foliate papillae at the back of the tongue. Blocking these receptors inhibits gustatory responses to bitter compounds in mice. Binding of a bitter substance to a T2R receptor results in a receptor potential via an as yet undetermined mechanism, possibly involving the entry of Na^+ and Ca^{2+} through cation channels.

Another recently cloned taste receptor, called T1R2, is also expressed in circumvallate and foliate papillae, but in those that do not express α-gustducin. The T1R2 receptor acts via an IP_3 pathway and may also detect bitter substances.

This variety of receptors coupled with a diversity of second messenger systems enables the detection of a great number of different potentially hazardous compounds.

3.5 Umami taste

Umami is a Japanese word meaning 'delicious savoury flavour' and has been applied to the taste of amino acids, particularly glutamate and aspartate. It came to prominence as a 'new' taste modality with the cloning of a glutamate receptor (mGluR4) from taste buds. This receptor is predominantly expressed in foliate and vallate taste cells in rats and stimulation with glutamate results in a sustained response mediated by the closure of nonselective cation channels. The mGluR4 receptor is linked to a G-protein coupled to phosphodiesterase, and activation therefore leads to a fall in cAMP which would in turn close a class of cation channels called CNG channels (for cyclic nucleotide gated), hyperpolarizing the cell. The consequences of this are at present unclear. It is likely that there are other receptors for amino acids, for example the NMDA (N-methyl-D-aspartate) receptor. Binding to this receptor activates a non-selective cation channel. Binding of glutamate (umami) to this receptor would allow entry of Na^+ and Ca^{2+} ions to depolarize the cell. In electrophysiological studies, rat taste cells produce two different responses to glutamate stimulation: one a sustained hyperpolarization, the other a transient depolarization, both of which are thought to be mediated by cation channels.

Monosodium glutamate, the principle component of soy sauce, may activate the mGluR4 umami receptor (as do some 5'-ribonucleotides, e.g. IMP and GMP) as well as activating the NMDA-receptor.

3.6 Fat taste

Fat is an important part of our diet and a high-energy food. There is some suggestion that there is a taste component to fat perception raising the possibility of a 'fat' receptor. Fatty acids have been shown to control ion channels, for example inhibiting K^+ channels and causing a prolonged depolarization in taste receptor cells. This may lead to heightened intensity of other tastes as well as signalling the presence of fat and could explain why fat-free foods are generally not as appealing as their full-fat counterparts.

3.7 Adaptation and suppression

When the palate is continuously exposed to a stimulus, the taste perception fades to almost nothing in seconds. Taste exhibits almost complete adaptation. Cross adaptation can occur between tastes of the same modality. For example citric acid reduces the sourness of other acids and NaCl reduces the saltiness of other chlorides. Sweet and bitter tastes do not cross-adapt to the same extent because there is more than one receptor for these tastes. Adaptation of a small area of the tongue affects non-stimulated areas suggesting that adaptation is not just a peripheral phenomenon but also has a central neural component.

Certain tastes can be suppressed by topical application of drugs and naturally occurring compounds. For example, local anaesthetics applied to the tongue will temporarily abolish sensitivity to all tastes. Amiloride, a blocker of epithelial Na^+ channels, reduces salt taste in humans and adenosine monophosphate (AMP) may block the bitterness of several bitter tasting agents. Naturally occurring compounds include gymnemic acid, an extract from the Indian tree *Gymnema sylvestre*, which decreases sweet perception by competitive inhibition of the sweet receptor. Artichokes have the opposite effect – enhancing sweet taste. Chlorogenic acid and cynarin, both isolated from artichokes, when applied to the tongue cause water to taste sweet by a mechanism that may involve suppression of sour and bitter taste receptors. Miracle fruit (*Synsepalum dulcificum*) turns sour tastes sweet such that lemons can be eaten like oranges. The fruit contains a glycoprotein, miraculin, which binds near to the sweet receptor site. When subsequently exposed to acid, the sensory cell membrane alters conformation in such a way that the glycoprotein is brought into contact with the sweet receptor.

4 Connections to the brain

4.1 The neuronal pathway of taste

During development, taste buds only form once the nerve fibres extend to the papillae. Once formed, taste cells degenerate without the presence of their nerves and will reappear if the nerve regenerates. Taste cells appear to be replaced every ten days so how a constancy of sensory information is maintained while the receptor cell population is changing is a mystery.

The anterior tongue is innervated by the **chorda tympani**, a branch of the **facial nerve (VIIth cranial nerve)**. This is the region of the tongue containing fungiform papillae, thus the chorda tympani relays information from the taste receptor cells of the fungiform papillae. The posterior region of the tongue, the region of the circumvallate and foliate papillae, is innervated by the **glossopharyngeal nerve (IXth cranial nerve)**.

The **vagus (Xth cranial nerve)** innervates taste buds on the epiglottis, larynx and the soft palate. The tongue (and taste papillae) is also innervated by the trigeminal (Vth cranial nerve) that provides somatosensory information.

Taste information is relayed to the medulla (nucleus of the solitary tract) by first order gustatory neurons of the cranial nerves VII (chorda tympani nerve), IX (glossopharyngeal nerve) and X (vagus nerve) (see Figure 5). From here neurons project to the ventroposteromedial (VPM) nucleus of the thalamus as well as to the amygdala and the hypothalamus. These latter two regions link the gustatory system to the limbic system (affecting emotion, memory, behaviour) and control salivation and feeding behaviour. From the thalamus there are projections to the **primary gustatory cortex** (Brodmann's area 43). It is this area that is responsible for conscious perception of taste.

Figure 5 Schematic diagram showing the neural pathway for taste. Nerves from the tongue (cranial nerves VII, IX) and from inside the mouth (cranial nerve X) relay information from taste buds to the nucleus of the solitary tract that runs through the medulla. From here neurons project to the limbic system (amygdala, hypothalamus) and via the thalamus to the primary gustatory cortex (see text for further detail).

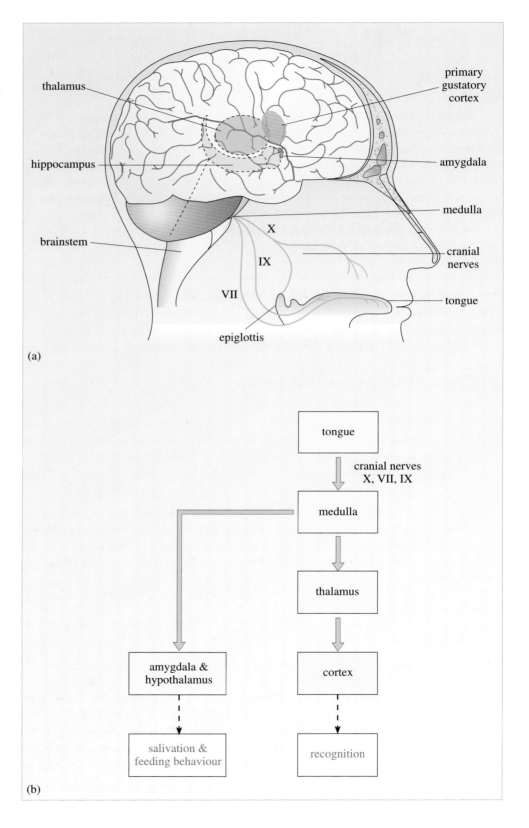

4.2 Neural taste coding

Gustatory neurons often innervate more than one taste bud and will therefore relay information about more than one taste. Analysis of the taste responsiveness of the chorda tympani in primates has demonstrated that there are four clusters of nerves, those primarily responding to sweet, acid, quinine (bitter) and salt (NaCl). The biggest clusters were the salt and sweet responsive nerves. Thus, although the chorda tympani is sensitive to sour and bitter tastes, it is predominantly responsive to salt and sweet tastes. On the other hand, in the glossopharyngeal nerve there are only three response clusters. The bitter response cluster was the largest, followed by the sweet cluster and a third group sensitive to monosodium glutamate, salt and acids. Neurons in the gustatory pathway become increasingly selective the higher up they are in the pathway. Primary afferents are broadly tuned and respond to many tastes, often responding best to one particular taste, while cells of the gustatory cortex are very finely tuned and respond to very few tastes.

4.3 How is taste discrimination achieved?

There are two main theories: (1) '**labelled-line**' and (2) '**pattern**' **theory**. The labelled-line theory proposes independent taste channels extending from receptor to cortex whereas the pattern theory suggests that neurons do not carry exclusive information but cooperate with other neurons in the pathway to provide a pattern of activity. Each taste creates a different pattern that can be recognized in the primary gustatory cortex. Current evidence supports the pattern theory but the two theories need not be mutually exclusive and it is possible that both processes are used, either in series or in parallel.

There is evidence that at least some of this ability to discriminate tastes is inborn. For example, babies a few hours old are capable of distinguishing tastes labelled by adults as 'sweet', 'sour', 'bitter' and 'umami'. The response to 'salty' is more difficult to interpret but ranges from indifference to aversion. While not impossible, it is difficult to imagine how a taste pattern code could be innate and for this innate component of taste the labelled-line theory is the more plausible. There is great redundancy in taste receptors and any changes in perception are likely to depend on central rather than peripheral processing changes during development. The development of the taste pattern code could therefore be a feature of the gustatory system that develops later in life. In support of this theory, children develop a preference for salty tasting foodstuffs and this is maintained during childhood and adolescence.

4.4 Taste and smell

Taste and smell are very closely linked. Mice that are made anosmic (lacking the ability to smell) are no longer able to differentiate tastes. In humans, anosmia leads to a loss in apparent taste sensitivity, although what is actually lost is flavour, a combination of olfactory, gustatory and somatosensory information. The cortical areas of the brain concerned with processing tastes and smells are next to one another in the neocortex and there are cells in the brain that receive input from both taste and smell neurons that will only respond if they receive both stimuli.

Astronauts lose their sense of taste in space because they cannot smell. This is thought to result from the reduced blood flow in the nose under zero gravity conditions.

5 Summary

There are four basic tastes, salt, sweet, sour and bitter, to which a fifth category has recently been added, that of 'umami', which represents savoury taste. Recent advances have seen the cloning of the receptors for bitter and sweet tastes and the identification of possible receptor mechanisms for umami tastes. How we achieve taste discrimination is still the subject of debate and is not as simple as was initially thought. Taste bud stimulation results in the complex activation of many nerves and the brain has to interpret the pattern that it receives from them. To complicate matters further, without smell, taste loses its impact. This is because of the interactions between the smell and taste nerve pathways occurring at higher centres in the brain. So, what we often attribute to taste, is in fact a mixture of information coming from a variety of different sensory systems including smell and taste.

Further reading

Arvidson, K. and Friberg, U. (1980) Human taste: response and taste bud number in fungiform papillae, *Science*, **209**, pp. 807–808.

Breslin, P. A. S. (2000) Human gustation, in T. E. Finger, W. L. Silver, D. Restrepo (eds) *The Neurobiology of Taste and Smell*, 2nd edn, Wiley-Liss, New York, pp. 423–462.

Glendinning, J. I., Chaudhari, N., and Kinnamon, S. C. (2000) Taste transduction and molecular biology, in T. E. Finger, W. L. Silver and D. Restrepo (eds) *The Neurobiology of Taste and Smell*, 2nd edn, Wiley-Liss, New York, pp. 315–352.

Miller, I. J. (1995) Anatomy of the peripheral taste system, in R. L. Doty (ed.) *Handbook of Olfaction and Gustation*, Marcel Dekker, New York, pp. 521–547.

Smith, D. V. and Margolskee, R. F. (2001) Making sense of taste, *Scientific American*, **284**, (3) pp. 32–39.

Taste perception

Steve Van Toller

26

1 Introduction

Like the sense of smell, the sense of taste is strategically placed for the detection of ingested materials. Social and cultural factors apart, the sensation of eating or more accurately, flavour, is a perception comprising the sensory interaction of texture, mouth-feel, temperature, acidity and alkalinity, as well as smell and taste. Eating may also involve the sensation of pain induced by chemical factors such as hot peppers and spices. People describe eating in terms of 'pleasant', or talk of food as tasting 'nice' and rarely attempt to identify the components of the food.

Box 1 Historical points

The Greek philosopher Alcmaeon believed that the tongue had tiny holes that allowed tastes to reach a sensorium in the brain. Democritus explained taste qualities by stating that sourness was related to angular shapes, sweetness to round shapes and bitterness to round shapes with small hooks. These molecule theories were superseded by Aristotle's identification of the four basic tastes that we speak of today plus astringent, pungent and harsh. Modern theories can basically be classified into two groups consisting of direct-line labelling theories and pattern theories.

2 Taste

Examination of the number of taste cells in the mouth reveals that they are relatively few in number and generally it is accepted that there are four basic types of taste quality: salty, sweet, bitter and sour. Some workers have argued for other types of taste quality but often these authors are referring to taste-active components in food rather than basic tastes. Japanese workers have argued powerfully for an additional taste quality that they call umami; and this will be discussed separately. Eating involves the interaction of a number of sensory processes in addition to that of basic taste qualities, that is, touch and the sense of smell. Rarely do we hear people attempting to break down and analyse the fine details related to eating. For example, 'this celery is tasty but the crunchy noise is not quite right', would produce laughter yet it might be an accurate observation.

Flavour consists of smell, taste, texture (this may relate to sound), temperature (chemical and thermal), touch, acidity and alkalinity balance (pH) and the stimulation of pain receptors. In 1990, Ney's flavourgram, shown in Figure 1, provided a heuristic overview of the components of flavour. Ney proposed combinations of three basic categories; smell, taste and consistency.

Examples of the last category would be the presence of fat, which gives a creamy feel in the mouth to ingested butter and ice cream; or the presence of alcohol in food producing dilation of blood vessels. Overall, flavour is an agglomeration of many sensations. However, if you recall the last time that you had a heavy cold which blocked or restricted your nasal passages, you will appreciate the overwhelming importance of the sense of smell in the eating process.

Figure 1 Ney's flavourgram. The top layer of the vertical boxes in the diagram relates to the different classes of smells associated with foods. The top layer of horizontal boxes includes the taste umami, and incorporates the important contribution of the trigeminal nerve that mediates astringency, pungency, as well as chemical coolness. The bottom layer of the two taste layers refers to the four basic taste qualities. The bottom two layers labelled consistency are important factors in experiencing the flavour of food.

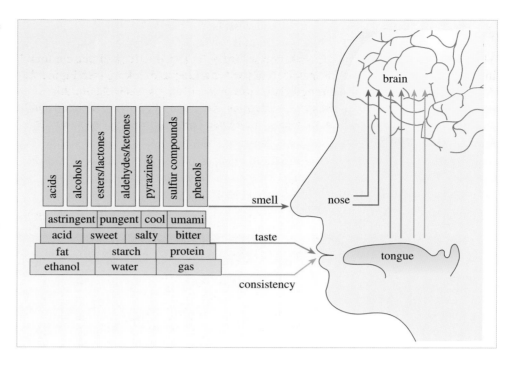

Not being able to smell renders food bland and tasteless. In 1987, Cain suggested that smell contributes over ninety per cent of the sensory input to the perception of eating. Receptors mediating the sense of smell are capable of detecting tens of thousands of different odours and these, together with all their possible combinations, make for a very wide variety of odour perceptions. By comparison, the sense of taste is restricted to a very limited number of different tastes.

Box 2 The effect of anosmia on taste

Loss of the sense of smell, anosmia, sometimes described as smell blindness, means that sufferers may have permanently lost their ability to smell. Anosmics often state that as well as not being able to smell they have also lost their ability to taste. This is rarely true because the neural routes related to the sense of smell are quite different from the nervous pathways of the sense of taste. There is no anatomical reason why loss of the sense of smell should alter the threshold of taste, but we usually find that anosmics have diminished taste thresholds. This finding highlights the limited understanding and research into the interactions between different sensory inputs into the brain. A major problem for these sufferers is that they all report lack of sympathy for their condition by the medical profession. If doctors are using common beliefs and attitudes about food tastes then they will not be aware of the massive contribution that smell makes to the perception of food. Therefore, doctors presumably reason that an anosmic patient can still 'taste' food. This assumption is naïve and incorrect.

The clinical condition of patients who have lost their sense of taste is called ageusia. Taste distortion, often found in the elderly or patients undergoing certain drug treatments, is called dysgeusia.

3 The tongue

The tongue is a versatile, strong and, unless bitten, largely overlooked muscle found inside the mouth. It is used for masticating food, sucking and licking (see Figure 2). Another important role of the tongue is its use in modifying speech. Again this points to the importance of sensory interactions. The ear is a decoder of sounds and, as mentioned above in relation to celery, sound may be an important aspect to the enjoyment of some foods.

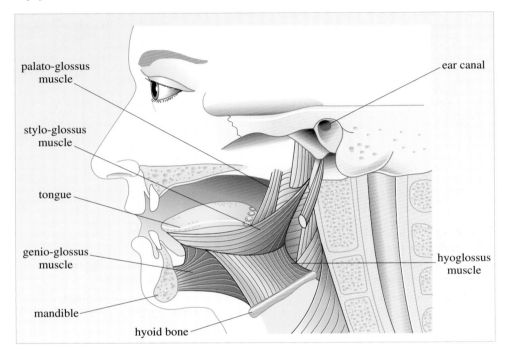

Figure 2   The tongue is a strong muscle found in the mouth or buccal cavity. As well as being the site of many of the basic taste receptors in its upper epithelial surface it also has an important role in helping to masticate food. Its role in modulating speech should not be overlooked.

The taste receptors in mammals are found on the tongue plus the pharyngeal and laryngeal areas of the mouth or buccal cavity (see Chapter 25). Humans have approximately 10 000 taste cells, a very small number compared to the visual and smell senses which each have about 50 000 000 receptor cells. The visual and hearing senses transduce electromagnetic or sound waves to produce perception but the chemoreceptive sensory systems require a finite amount of a substance to reach the receptor cells. A taste cell needs to be stimulated by the appropriate salt, sweet, bitter or sour chemical compounds. Taste receptor information is carried into the brain by three main cranial nerves, the facial (VII), the glossopharyngeal (IX) and the vagus (X).

The tongue is characterized by clefts over its surface. Unlike the sense of smell, which is noted for rapid habituation rates, overall taste shows little or no habituation. The last crisp in a packet will taste as salty as the first one. Taste cells show habituation rates that are equivalent to other sensory cells but taste cells are located in the folds found over the surface of the tongue (see Figure 3). The tongue's movements during eating will result in the constant exposure of unstimulated receptors. Unlike smell receptors, it is not possible for the majority of taste receptors to become saturated simultaneously. The opening and closing of the folds allows recovery time for the receptors.

4 Taste perception

As pointed out in the previous chapter, taste cells or buds are located in papillae (Figure 3). Histologically, four types of taste papillae have been described, filiform, foliate, **vallate** and fungiform. It is generally accepted that taste cells respond to sweet, salt, sour and bitter (metallic has also been proposed as a taste quality). The four types of taste cell have maximal effect in different parts of the tongue but specific tastes can be found over all parts of the tongue and marked individual variations are found. Sour taste cells are said to be located mainly on the side edges of the tongue. Sweet and salty taste cells are located at the front of the tongue. Bitter taste cells are located in the epithelial cells of the soft palate at the back of the tongue and buccal cavity.

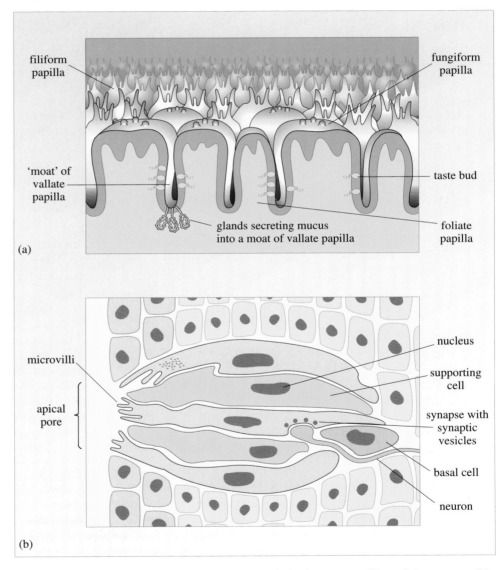

Figure 3   (a) Taste cells are housed in taste buds in the taste papillae of the tongue. (b) The components of a taste bud.

Taste buds are embedded in the epithelial cells of the tongue and mouth and have a protruding apical surface that permits stimulation by **sapid** substances carrying the taste. During the last decade, using biological clamp-cell techniques which allow for individual cells to be stimulated over long time periods, it has become possible to study taste reactions to different stimulations. Within a papilla, taste cells are closely packed together to protect them from injurious foreign substances. They have a life cycle of 10 to 14 days and new taste cells are constantly being generated. It has been suggested that as a result of ageing the life cycle of the taste cells might be extended. This would result in increased degradation of an individual cell due to its longer life cycle. Such a longer life cycle might account for lower taste sensitivity found in older people.

Box 3 Loss of taste sensitivity through ageing

An age effect is shown in the dislike by young children of the bitter thiocyanate taste in vegetables such as cabbage, sprouts and turnips. The bitter taste is not detected by the children's parents who, because of reduced sensitivity due to ageing, are less sensitive to this compound and this may lead them, erroneously, to deny any undue bitter taste. It also explains how children may come to like these vegetables when age has produced the inevitable increase in their taste thresholds.

5 The physiology of taste

Although current research is now questioning the older view that each taste sensation is related to a particular type of receptor, the precise mechanisms have still to be agreed. Saltiness is best exemplified by sodium and lithium chloride. The salty taste appears to be transduced by an ion channel located on the tip of a salt taste bud. It has been found that a compound called amiloride is able to inhibit salt taste transduction. When the salt threshold in the mouth exceeds threshold levels, sodium ions pass into receptor cells causing depolarization. An interesting observation is that salt detection utilizes an epithelial sodium ion channel. Although the precise mechanism of the transduction of sourness is still not clear it is known to be related to the presence of hydrogen ions in solution. Two proposed biophysical mechanisms for sourness have been discovered for the lower order animals but remain to be tested for humans. There is a very wide variety of compounds that give rise to the perception of sweetness. Many do not fit the classical chemical sweetness structure, for example, chloroform and lead acetate. Because of the 'empty' calories associated with sweet foods, attempts have been made to develop sweeteners that have low calorific values. Examples of these are saccharin, developed at the beginning of the last century and, more recently, the dipeptide, aspartame. Most scientific explanations offered at the present time to explain sweet taste involve a second chemical messenger in the receptor cells. The taste of bitterness is also found in a wide variety of compounds and it is thought that more than one mechanism is involved. Cell cloning techniques used by molecular biologists give hope for the future identification of the various taste cells. The fact that there are relatively small numbers of taste cells should help the chances of resolving this problem.

6 Umami taste receptors

The word umami roughly translates as 'savoury and delicious' and the possibility of an umami taste receptor is largely supported by Japanese taste research. The prototypical umami tastant is monosodium L-glutamate. To a Westerner the taste is yeast extract or soy sauce-like and they are unable to make the distinctions that the Japanese make. This raises the possibility that the umami taste is a learned taste, with the Japanese being educated to make fine judgements about it. Critically, learning about the taste requires access to a vocabulary through which this particular taste sensation can be examined and discussed. In 1986, O'Mahony and Ishii carried out an experiment which supported the idea that Asians were better able to describe the umami taste than were Western people. The problem of lack of lexical information to describe foods and liquids is highlighted in Box 4.

Bearing in mind problems that may be related to experimental bias, it should be pointed out that Japanese researchers have reported a large amount of data from different animal species that is believed to demonstrate the existence of umami receptors.

Box 4 The role of language

The ability of people to describe smells is usually extremely poor. However, certain groups of professional people like perfumers, wine tasters and sensory evaluators show that it is possible to learn a vocabulary that allows meaningful discussion about smells. For example, wine tasters use labels like balance, corky, dumb, finish, foxy, grip, hard, long, oaky, spicy, stalky, fruity, green, harsh, mellow/rounded, robust, cloying and crisp.

7 Taste pathways in the brain

The nervous input to the brain related to taste is shown schematically in Figure 4. Nerves from the tongue, the mouth and part of the throat gather into three nerve bundles (the VIIth, IXth and Xth cranial nerves) that travel to the thalamic and hypothalamic areas of the brain. These pathways also connect to the areas of the limbic system that are involved with motivation and emotional states. A collateral pathway has been traced to the amygdala. The amygdala might be responsible for emotional reactions to food which could result in its rejection prior to cortical evaluation. The pathways mediating taste then travel on to an area on the cortical surface called the gustatory neocortex. This is a somatosensory part of the cortex related to touch. Although, as pointed out earlier, taste is a sensory system with few primary receptor cells, interestingly it has, unlike the sense of smell, direct representation on the neocortical surface of the brain. Primarily the taste system extracts three types of information from chemical stimuli: quality, intensity and hedonic value. Clearly these are not independent of each other because, as discussed below, hedonic or emotional feelings depend on many factors. It has been shown that various sub-populations of taste cells respond differentially to taste quality. For example, facial nerve fibres (VIIth cranial nerve) are more responsive to sweet and salt tastes, whereas glossopharyngeal nerve fibres (IXth cranial nerve) are more responsive to unpleasant stimuli such as acids and bitter tasting quinine. The vagal nerve fibres (Xth cranial nerve) are responsive to stimuli that lie outside the normal physiological range of acidity and alkalinity (see Figure 4).

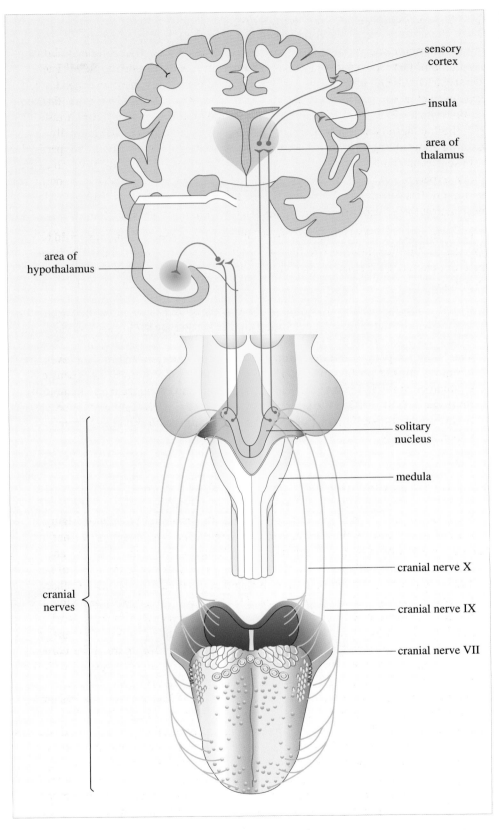

sensory cortex

insula

area of thalamus

area of hypothalamus

solitary nucleus

medula

cranial nerve X

cranial nerve IX

cranial nerve VII

cranial nerves

Figure 4   A diagram showing the pathways linking the sense of taste with the brain. Three main central nervous system nerves (VIIth, IXth and Xth) are involved. The interconnections involve the hypothalamus, limbic system and thalamus, as well as areas of the sensory cortex.

Theories of taste coding have been vigorously debated over many years. In the early 1940s, Pfaffmann, one of the founders of taste research, proposed an across-fibre pattern theory that argued that taste quality was coded by relative activity across a population of fibres. This theory accommodated the multiple sensitivities of taste fibres and had the advantage that it did not require specificity of fibre or receptor types. However, the persistent view that there are only a few different primary taste qualities has led to a revision of the across-fibre pattern theory to a 'best stimulus' rather than a basic taste quality. Other workers have argued for amplitude coding of the fibre information.

8 Psychophysics and sensory analysis

Sensory analysis is concerned with scientific measurement of how humans respond to sensory input. Psychophysics refers to various measuring techniques that allow meaningful quantification of the characteristics of sensory stimuli and human responses. This research area is important both for academic and industrial research. Detection and recognition thresholds may be several hundred dilution steps apart. The detection threshold is where a person reliably can say that they detect the presence of something. The recognition threshold is where they reliably can name the stimulating material. As indicated above, many studies have shown that the ability to evaluate and describe a taste sensation can be dramatically improved by providing an appropriate vocabulary or lexical information. Improvements to sensory research are constantly being made. For example, genetic effects of bitter taste were intially examined by using the chemical PTC (phenylthiocarbamide) and more recently by using PROP (6-propylthiouracil). PROP is used because, importantly, it is odourless and the testee will be using taste rather than a possible combination of taste and smell.

9 Individual taste variations

Detection threshold differences between individuals with normal taste and those who have come to be called supertasters will typically be about 300-fold. Recently psychophysics has switched from merely establishing threshold levels to testing subjects at suprathreshold levels. Suprathreshold levels have relevance to taste levels experienced by people in their daily lives.

Box 5 Psychometric testing

Testing of sensory materials often involves the use of psychometric tests using monopolar and bipolar rating scales that have food or mood descriptors at the end anchor points.

'Please mark the point on the scale that corresponds to your sensation of the taste'

Strong——————————————————————————————Weak

This is an example of a unipolar scale that ranges from weak to strong.

'Please mark the point on the scale that corresponds to your feeling about the taste'

Happy——————————————————————————————Sad

This is an example of a bipolar scale where the '0' point is in the middle of the scale.

Individual taste sensation is a function of genetic make-up plus experiential and learnt factors. Using an analogy with computers these two aspects are often spoken of as the 'hardware' and 'software'. For example, the earlier psychophysical studies asked subjects whether or not a particular substance tasted sweet, bitter, sour or salty, but more recent studies ask subjects about the quality of the taste. This type of questioning has given rise to studies of supertasters mentioned in this section.

10 Is the sense of taste analytic or synthetic?

Whether or not the perception of taste is analytic or synthetic has long been a basic research question. In an analytic sense, any two stimuli presented together maintain their individual sensory qualities; in a synthetic sense, two stimuli presented together give rise to a completely new sensation. In a similar manner to the sense of sound, taste can give rise to three different types of sensation. The first is a binary mixture where it is possible for the two elements to be identified separately. Secondly, it is possible for a binary mixture to give rise to a completely new sensation. Finally, certain mixtures allow for both of the above conditions, with the two stimuli being identified separately whilst at the same time giving rise to a totally new perception. This would be similar to a visual figure ground perception. Thus, taste may be considered to be both an analytic and a synthetic sense. We should note that taste perceptions can be fooled. To take a classic example, when asking for tea but given coffee it can take a surprisingly long time for a person to realize that they have been given the wrong drink. An interesting example of altering a taste perception is to rub the tip of the tongue with salt and then taste a lemon – the lemon will taste sweet. The sweetness perceived does seem slightly strange but it will definitely be a sweet taste that is experienced. Another example is that of gymnemic acid, obtained from the tree *Gymnema sylvestre* – ingestion of this abolishes the sweet taste of both natural and artificial sweetners. The 'miracle fruit' of West Africa is also capable of producing a change of taste from sour to sweet.

11 Food preferences and individual differences

Food likes and dislikes are largely culturally driven and overall it is learning that plays the most important role in personal food preferences, with colour and texture being vital components.

Box 6 The learned nature of food preferences

During a teaching year in Bucknell University, Pennsylvania, periodically I would crave the particular taste of English fish and chips. The first time this happened I went to a well-known American food outlet which had a sign outside boasting that it sold 'English' fish and chips, only to come away bitterly disappointed. The taste did not match my food/taste memory. At other times I found that I craved the taste of European cheeses rather than the bland pasteurised American cheeses or the imported European cheeses that had been subjected to pasteurisation that, for me, destroyed the taste I was craving. These specific taste cravings or deprivations were the result of learned experiences.

Box 7 Social conditioning of food likes

Social conditioning, plus toys and novelties, lies behind the clever marketing by the leading fast food outlets, who, together with parents, condition children to look upon the salty, but otherwise bland, food they serve up as a great gastronomic treat. The children in turn will come to condition their own children about the food outlet experience, setting up a perpetuating commercial cycle. Some nationalities place a different emphasis on the gastronomic influence that children experience. For example, French children are more likely to be taught to appreciate fine foods. Eating with French people can be educational in terms of the amount they know about the food and preparations they are eating. A lack of basic food education could explain a great deal about the general absence of food awareness shown by the English. Interestingly, over the last few years there has been a debate in France about the role that the leading fast food outlets play in the gastronomic lives of the French.

It might be commonly felt that an important aspect of a chef's occupation would be a refined taste ability. However, a study examining the sensory taste and smelling ability of ten chefs who worked in the most highly rated restaurants in Chicago revealed that the top chefs tended to be younger men. The same report found that about 20 per cent of the diners in the restaurants would have scored better on the smell test than the average score achieved by the chefs. Three of the chefs' scores met the criterion for hyposmia, indicating a poor sense of smell ability. Overall, the taste thresholds of the chefs were low but two individuals showed difficulty in detecting salt and seven out of the ten were shown to have difficulty in distinguishing between sour and bitter tastes. The chefs scored high on smell and taste adaptation tests and were able to reliably reproduce taste sensations such as sweet and salty. These would be important in a cooking environment where there would be a need to maintain consistency between dishes on a day-to-day basis.

12 Taste modifiers and enhancers

The idea behind taste enhancers is to provide increased sensation without actually increasing the amount of the compound itself. Such methods are widespread in the food industry where taste and economic factors are important. The two-taste sensations that have attracted most attention are saltiness and sweetness and attempts to increase sales of a food product usually involves additional salt and sugar. Both sweet and salty substances have produced problems in Western societies. Intake of sweet foods has led to obesity. Consequently, since early in the last century attempts have been made to produce a sweet taste with low calories. Also, there is a known causal relationship between salt consumption and increased blood pressure. This problem can occur as a result of oriental restaurant cooking where high levels of monosodium glutamate (MSG), a common taste modifier used to intensify tastes, are sometimes used. Intake of high levels of MSG can lead to 'Chinese restaurant syndrome' where the increased sodium content of the diet leads to increased blood pressure.

Summary

Taste perception begins with the stimulation of taste cells in taste buds in the mouth by ingested materials. There are at least five taste qualities: sweet, salt, bitter, sour and umami. Cultural differences in the perception of the latter may suggest that recognition of some taste categories is the result of having a suitable vocabulary available to describe them. These categories, together with smell, texture, temperature, pH and pain stimuli, contribute to the perception of flavour.

Taste information is carried from the tongue and mouth by the cranial nerves, VII, IX, and X, to the thalamus, hypothalamus and amygdala, and from these regions to the gustatory cortex. Individual detection and recognition thresholds of various taste qualities can vary by about 300-fold, the more sensitive individuals being classified as supertasters. Such differences are the result of both genetics and of learning. Food preferences seem to be culturally driven.

Further reading

Bartoshuk, L. M. (1978) History of taste research, in Carterette, E. C. and Friedman, M. P. (eds) *Handbook of perception*, Volume VIA, Academic Press, New York.

Beauchamp, G. K. (ed.) (1994) International symposium on bitter taste, *Physiology and Behaviour*, **56**, pp. 1121–1266.

Beauchamp, G. K. and Bartoshuk, L. (eds) (1997) *Tasting and smelling*, Academic Press, New York.

Evans, D. (2001) *Emotion, the science of sentiment*, Oxford University Press, Oxford.

Logue, A. W. (1991) *The psychology of eating and drinking*, 2nd edition, Freeman, New York.

LeDoux, J. (1994) Emotion, memory and the brain, *Scientific American*, **270**, (6), pp. 50–57.

Van Toller, S. (1993) The psychology and neuropsychology of flavor, in Ho, C-T., and Manley, C. H. (eds) *Flavor measurement*, Marcel Dekker, New York.

PART FIVE

INTEGRATING THE SENSES

Multisensory integration, attention and perception

27

Charles Spence

1 Introduction

> To attend to an event means to seek and accept every sort of information about it, regardless of its modality, and to integrate all the information as it becomes available.
>
> Ulric Neisser, 1976, Cognition and reality, p. 29.

Most textbooks on perception consider each sense (vision, audition, touch, gustation, olfaction) in isolation. This modality-independent approach is consistent with the fact that, at the very earliest stages of information processing, stimuli for each sensory system are transduced by spatially-distinct sensory epithelia (e.g. the retina for vision, the cochlea for audition, and the skin for touch). However, the majority of objects and events in our environment are *multisensory*, providing correlated and partially redundant information to several senses simultaneously. For example, our perception of the food we eat comes not only from its taste and smell (gustatory and olfactory cues respectively), but also from what it looks, feels and sounds like. As pointed out by Ulric Neisser more than 25 years ago, we continuously bind together, or integrate, all of these various sensory cues to form the multisensory objects and events of everyday life. It is surprising then that the majority of empirical research on human sensation and perception has focused on understanding how each sensory system operates in isolation, especially given that all creatures possessing more than one sensory system have been shown to integrate that information to facilitate the coherent control of action.

When perception is considered within a more 'ecologically-valid' multisensory framework, two key research questions emerge. First, how do we select just that subset of information that is relevant to our current goals and actions from amongst the abundance of information impinging on the various sensory receptors at any one time? And second, what rules govern the integration of that multisensory information once it has been selected? A number of the most important recent studies to have investigated multisensory attentional selection and multisensory integration are reviewed below.

2 Multisensory selective attention

For many years, cognitive psychologists have argued that we need mechanisms of auditory selective attention to be able to pick out just one voice from the many competing voices at a noisy cocktail party (the so-called cocktail party problem; see Figure 1). The efficacy of auditory selective attention has been demonstrated primarily in **dichotic listening** studies, where participants are presented with a different stream of speech to each ear over headphones, and are required to shadow (i.e. repeat) one 'relevant' message, while ignoring the other 'irrelevant' message. It has been shown that people can selectively direct their auditory attention to a particular location in space (to one ear, in these investigations) to selectively enhance the processing of stimuli coming from the attended location, while

Figure 1   How is it that we can selectively listen to what a particular person is saying at a noisy social gathering (the so-called 'cocktail party' problem)? Although it has often been considered to be simply a problem of unimodal auditory selection, closer inspection reveals it to be a multisensory selection problem. In order to understand what someone is saying at such a noisy social gathering, one needs not only to select one particular voice from amongst many others, but also to extract relevant visual information from lip movements, facial expressions, and even gestures. One may also need to ignore irrelevant competing stimuli impinging on the other senses – such as, for example, the feel of the clothes on one's body (tactile), the smell of someone's perfume (olfactory), and perhaps even the taste of one's drink (gustatory).

simultaneously inhibiting, or filtering out, irrelevant sounds (voices) from other locations. In fact, people appear to have very little memory for, or awareness of, messages presented from 'unattended' locations.

It is important to note, however, that the cocktail party problem does not just involve *auditory* selective attention, as the person we are trying to listen to typically generates visual cues concerning what they are saying through their lip movements, facial expressions, and gestures. The provision of relevant visual lip-reading cues can improve comprehension by an amount equivalent to increasing the auditory signal-to-noise ratio by 15–20 decibels in noisy conditions. Therefore, in order to facilitate the processing of just the relevant audiovisual speech signal at a cocktail party, we need to be able to direct both our auditory and visual selective attention to the speaker simultaneously. Given that the multisensory cues associated with particular environmental stimuli typically emanate from the same location (i.e. from the mouth of the speaker in the present example), it would make sense for mechanisms of auditory and visual spatial attention to be coordinated, such that they too are directed to a single location.

My colleague, Jon Driver, and I investigated the nature of any multisensory, or **crossmodal**, links in audiovisual attention by creating a simplified cocktail party in the laboratory. Participants were presented with two audiovisual speech streams, and had to shadow one 'relevant' stream. The relevant auditory and visual information were either presented from the same external position – as in a real cocktail party – or from different positions (the relevant auditory stream from one side and the matching visual lip-reading information from the other side of fixation; see Figure 2). We believed that the existence of any crossmodal links in spatial attention should result in participants finding it easier to shadow when the relevant auditory and visual information were presented from the *same*, rather than *different*, positions. By contrast, if the modality-specific view of attention were correct, participants should find it just as easy to direct their auditory and visual attention to different positions as to the same positions, because the attentional systems in the two modalities would be independent.

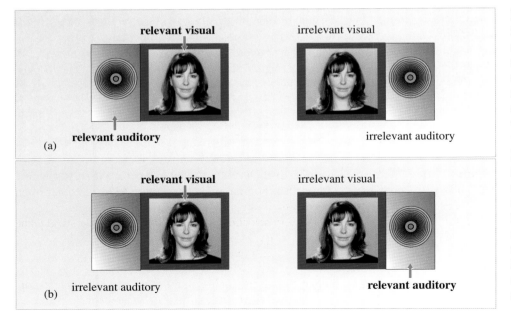

(a)

relevant visual / irrelevant visual

relevant auditory / irrelevant auditory

(b)

relevant visual / irrelevant visual

irrelevant auditory / **relevant auditory**

Figure 2 An experiment was modelled on the cocktail party situation, to investigate the nature of any crossmodal links in spatial attention. Participants were required to shadow one 'relevant' stream of audiovisual speech, while trying to ignore an 'irrelevant' distractor message. In different blocks of trials, the auditory and visual information could either be presented from (a) the same or (b) different locations. Participants found it significantly easier to shadow the relevant message in the same location blocks, demonstrating the existence of crossmodal links in spatial attention.

It turned out that participants found it significantly easier to shadow the target message when the relevant auditory and visual stimuli were presented from the same position, supporting the existence of crossmodal links in spatial attention. Subsequent research has revealed that similar crossmodal links also constrain performance when people are required to perform different tasks in the two modalities, such as, for example, shadowing auditory speech while simultaneously monitoring a rapidly presented stream of visual stimuli for occasional targets.

Researchers studying spatial attention have made a distinction between two forms of attentional selection: **endogenous** and **exogenous** attention. Endogenous attention is typically involved in the voluntary orienting of attention to a particular event or spatial location, such as when we choose to attend to a particular person at the cocktail party. By contrast, exogenous (or involuntary) orienting occurs when attention is reflexively shifted to the sudden and unexpected (or uninformative) onset of a peripheral event, such as someone calling your name at a cocktail party, or a fly suddenly landing on your arm. Orthogonal to this distinction between endogenous and exogenous attention, is another important distinction between overt and covert attentional orienting. **Overt orienting** refers to shifts of receptors (as in eye, head, or hand movements), whereas **covert orienting** (which is of most interest to cognitive psychologists) refers to purely internal shifts of attention (e.g. as when we observe someone out of the corner of our eye).

My colleagues and I investigated the nature of any crossmodal links in specifically exogenous covert orienting. Participants were presented with spatially-nonpredictive tactile cues (brief, pulsed, vibrotactile stimuli) touching either the left or right hand. In other words, a tactile stimulus was presented to indicate that a target would appear, but the hand that was stimulated did not give an indication of whether the target would be presented on the left or the right. People were instructed to ignore which hand was touched, since that was irrelevant to the task. An auditory or visual target was then presented shortly after the cue, on either the same or opposite side (note that the target was just as likely to be presented on the same side as on the opposite side, thus making the cue spatially uninformative). Responses to the auditory and visual targets were more rapid when the target was presented on the same, rather than the opposite, side as the cue, showing that the tactile cues elicited a rapid crossmodal shift of exogenous attention toward the cued hand. Moreover, subsequent research has shown that crossmodal links in exogenous attention are sensitive to posture, such as when the hands are crossed over the midline (see Figure 3), or the eyes are deviated with respect to the head, thus ensuring that attention is always directed to the correct external location.

Taken together, the results of studies of both endogenous and exogenous multisensory spatial attention demonstrate that there are extensive crossmodal links in attention between vision, audition, and touch. Not only are these findings inconsistent with the modality-specific account of attention, they are also hard to reconcile with another idea, the supramodal theory. This is set out in Figure 4.

It is important to note that a better understanding of the nature of these crossmodal links in spatial attention may also help to provide future constraints on the effective design of multimodal interfaces. For example, there is now a growing body of empirical research showing that people find it particularly difficult to hold a conversation on a mobile phone, while simultaneously driving a car. One of the major problems in this multisensory dual-task situation may be that people find it difficult to attend visually out of the windscreen to watch the road ahead, while

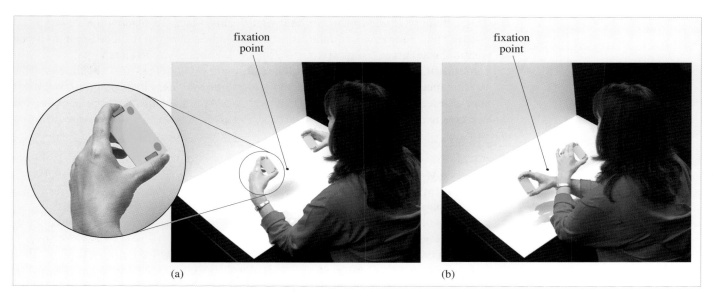

fixation point

fixation point

(a)　　　　　　　　　　　　　　　　　(b)

Figure 3 Researchers interested in the effects of posture change on crossmodal links in spatial attention have compared the behaviour of participants when they adopt (a) uncrossed or (b) crossed hands postures. In the uncrossed posture, the presentation of a spatially-nonpredictive tactile cue to the left hand leads to the facilitation of elevation discrimination responses (made using two foot pedals under the right foot) for lights presented on the left. When the hands are crossed over the midline, the same tactile cue presented to the left hand will now lead to a shift of visual attention to the right lights instead, thus demonstrating that crossmodal links in exogenous spatial attention are updated following changes in posture.

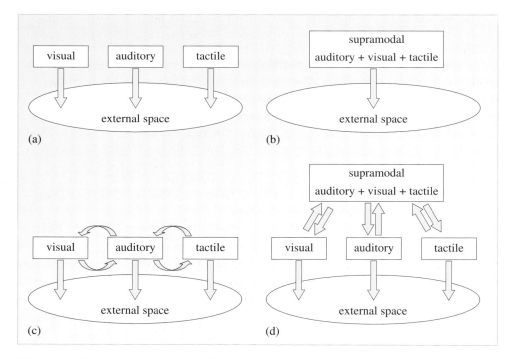

Figure 4 Schematic illustration of the ways in which researchers have conceptualized how the attentional systems might be coordinated across the different sensory modalities. (a) Independent modality-specific attentional resources; (b) single supramodal attention system; (c) separable-but-linked attentional systems; and (d) hierarchical supramodal plus modality-specific attentional systems.

simultaneously trying to listen to the voice coming from the phone by their ear. It is possible that performance in this situation could be improved if the speaker's voice were to be presented from directly in front of the driver (i.e. via a 'talking windscreen'), to take advantage of the underlying crossmodal links in endogenous spatial attention. A better understanding of crossmodal links in *exogenous* orienting may also lead to the design of more effective multimodal warning signals, where for example an alarm could be arranged to sound from the direction which required attention (e.g. alarm and early-warning signals in airplanes and/or cars).

3 Multisensory integration

Having selected certain 'relevant' multisensory stimuli for further processing, the next question is to try to understand the rules that determine how this information is integrated in the brain. For example, is the sensory information presented to each modality weighted equally, or does one sense tend to dominate perception? Normally, the multisensory cues regarding a particular object or event provide convergent and partially-redundant information, making it difficult to assess the relative contribution of each of the senses to our multisensorily-determined percepts. Psychologists have therefore used conflict situations, in which different (i.e. non-convergent or discrepant) cues are provided to each sensory modality, to examine how the senses are integrated.

McGurk and MacDonald in 1976 used the conflict methodology to study the relative contributions of audition and vision to speech perception. Participants in their study were presented with a voice repeatedly uttering a particular syllable (e.g. 'ba'), while they simultaneously saw synchronized lip movements associated with another syllable (e.g. 'ga'). Surprisingly, the majority of participants reported hearing a different syllable in this situation (e.g. 'da'), demonstrating that the **phoneme** which people *hear* can be modulated by *seen* lip-movements. One of the most remarkable aspects of the **McGurk effect**, as it is called, is that it occurs even when people know that what they are hearing and seeing are incongruent, suggesting that the audiovisual integration leading to speech perception may occur automatically. Since the mid-1970s, when the effect was first reported, similar multisensory effects have been shown to occur in a number of other domains. For example, people's judgement of the emotional tone in which a sentence is spoken (happy versus fearful) can be modulated by the simultaneous visual presentation of a face displaying either extreme happiness or fear (i.e. showing that *vocal* emotion can be modified by **affective visual information**).

Visual dominance over audition has also been shown to occur when people resolve situations of spatial conflict or discrepancy. For example, whenever we go to the cinema, the spoken soundtrack of the film is perceived as emanating from the lips of the actors seen on the screen, despite the fact that the sounds are actually presented from loudspeakers situated elsewhere. This multisensory illusion, known as the 'ventriloquism effect', shows that we mislocalize sounds toward their apparent visual source. Although ventriloquism effects are particularly strong in the case of audiovisual speech, similar intersensory biasing effects have also been reported when people try to localize other types of spatially discrepant audiovisual stimuli, such as whistling kettles, bongo drums and even pure tone bursts, when presented with spatially separated flashing lights. Taken together, these studies show that auditory localization is biased more by spatially-discrepant visual cues than vice versa, demonstrating that vision tends to dominate our perception when the senses provide conflicting spatial information.

Vision can also dominate over touch and proprioception. Participants in one study placed their left arm behind an occluding screen on a table in front of them. A life-sized model of a left hand and arm was also placed on a table in full view of the participant, somewhat misaligned with their real hand. The experimenter then started to stroke both arms in temporal synchrony, while participants fixated the artificial limb. After a few minutes of feeling their own hand being stroked, while simultaneously seeing the rubber arm being stroked in a different (or conflicting) location, participants reported experiencing the artificial arm as part of their own body. That is, they were more likely to rate it as appearing to be their own following stroking than before stroking, agreeing strongly with statements such as: 'It seemed as if I were feeling the touch of the paintbrush in the location where I saw the rubber hand touched'. The participants' proprioceptive sense of hand position drifted toward the rubber hand, as revealed when they pointed with their right hand under the table to the unseen location of their left hand. These results demonstrate that visual information regarding apparent hand position can also 'capture' or dominate spatially-discrepant proprioceptive information. Once again, just as for the McGurk illusion discussed earlier, the rubber arm illusion cannot be overcome by will, though it does break down if the rubber arm is placed in an anatomically implausible posture, or the two arms are stroked out of synchrony. (You should be able to experience this illusion at home using a rubber arm such as those sold in joke shops.)

As a last example, it has been shown that vision can dominate over taste (gustation) and smell (olfaction). Participants in one study were presented with three fruit-flavoured soft drinks (cherry, orange, and lime) and one flavourless drink, all of which were independently coloured either orange, cherry-red, lime-green, or else remained colourless. Participants tried to identify the flavour of these beverages by tasting them: their judgements were shown to be strongly affected by the colour of the drinks. For example, when tasting the cherry-flavoured beverage, participants frequently reported it as having an orange flavour when coloured orange, and lime flavour when coloured lime-green. Researchers have also shown that the apparent intensity and hedonic quality of both food and drink can be modulated by changing the visual cues associated with them – a finding whose importance has not been lost on the food industry!

4 Visual dominance versus modality-appropriateness

All of the multisensory illusions discussed so far show that when the senses are put into conflict, the brain resolves the discrepancy by weighting visual information more heavily than information presented to the other modalities. For example, in the case of the ventriloquism illusion, we hear the sound as coming from the position in which we see the lips moving, rather than seeing the lips moving in the position where the sound comes from. It has been suggested that visual dominance effects might be caused by people attending preferentially to vision, rather than dividing their attention equally between the sensory modalities. Any such bias toward attending visually should enhance the relative saliency of visual stimuli over those presented to other modalities, and so might lead to the visual dominance effects seen in conflict situations.

However, recent evidence has shown that audition can also dominate over vision under certain conditions. For example, participants were presented with repetitive visual and auditory stimuli at rates of 4, 6, 8, or 10 Hz. The stimuli were either presented in isolation or else were presented simultaneously. Participants were required to judge the temporal rate at which the light flickered or the sound fluttered using a direct magnitude estimation procedure. When stimuli with conflicting rates of repetition were presented simultaneously, peoples' judgments of the rate at which the light 'flickered' were more affected by the auditory 'flutter' than vice versa. In fact, the auditory bias of vision was nearly five times greater than the visual bias of audition. This result, and others like it, show that auditory dominance occurs under situations where temporal judgments are required.

The existence of both visual and auditory dominance effects have been explained in terms of their **modality-appropriateness**. It is argued that the sense that provides the most accurate sensory information will dominate perceptual judgements. For spatial judgements, vision has the best spatial resolution and so dominates the other senses; by contrast, audition has much better temporal resolution than the other modalities and so it dominates over vision when people make temporal judgments. It should be noted, though, that there may still be a role for the attentional account here, if it is assumed that people do not always bias their attention toward vision, but instead bias it toward whichever modality provides the most accurate sensory information. An important goal for future research is to determine precisely what role attentional biases play in sensory dominance effects, and whether, in fact, it might be possible to reduce, eliminate, or even reverse a particular pattern of sensory dominance simply by experimentally manipulating which modality participants attend to. Moreover, it will also be important to determine under what conditions information from other sensory modalities, such as touch and olfaction, may be weighted more heavily, and so dominate perception and/or behaviour.

5 Neural substrates for multisensory integration and attention

Researchers have known for many years that the superficial layers of the cerebral cortex are separated into numerous different areas, some of which, the primary sensory cortices, are specialized for the processing of sensory information specific to a particular sensory modality. Meanwhile, several other areas have been shown to be specialized for the integration of information from different sensory modalities, such as the association areas, the **parietal lobe** and superior colliculus. For example, over the last 30 years, Barry Stein, Alex Meredith and colleagues have demonstrated the existence of a wide variety of multisensory interaction effects in single cells in the superior colliculus – a sub-cortical neural structure involved in controlling attentive orienting responses, such as reflexive eye and head movements. They have shown that the firing rates of many of the neurons in this structure increase dramatically when multisensory stimuli are presented in spatiotemporal correspondence (i.e. from the same spatial location and at about the same time). Typically, multisensory stimuli presented from the same location at approximately the same time lead to multisensory enhancement

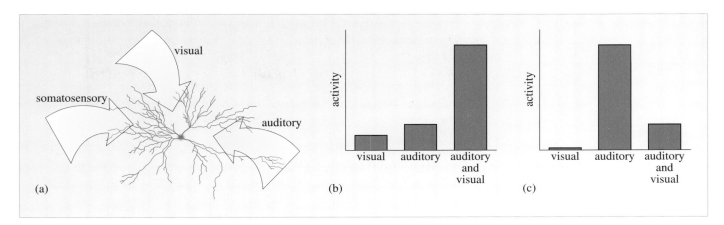

Figure 5 Neurophysiologists have demonstrated multisensory integration effects within single cells in a number of multisensory brain structures, such as the superior colliculus (a). Two types of effect have been observed: multisensory response enhancement effects, whereby a given neuron responds weakly to auditory and visual stimuli presented in isolation, but fires very vigorously when both stimuli are presented simultaneously (b); and also multisensory response suppression effects when a neuron's activity is actually suppressed by the simultaneous presentation of multisensory stimuli (c).

effects, while multisensory suppression effects (or else no interaction) are often reported when multisensory stimuli are presented from different locations and/or at different times (see Figure 5). The most dramatic multisensory interactions have been reported for stimuli that are presented at near-threshold (i.e. barely perceptible) levels, when the enhancement in neuronal activity elicited by spatially congruent multisensory cues can be supra-additive (i.e. greater than the sum of the individual sensory responses), thus making these cells ideal for responding to stimuli in noisy environments.

The multisensory interactions seen at the level of the single neuron can also be seen in the performance of behaving animals. For example, a cat's ability to detect and orient toward a visual target is significantly enhanced when it happens to be paired with an irrelevant sound from the same spatial location. However, just as seen in the single cell, orienting responses are suppressed if the auditory event happens to be presented from a different spatial location. (It is interesting to note here the similarity between these multisensory integration effects, and the exogenous multisensory attention effects described earlier.)

Multisensory integration effects do not, however, occur solely within multimodal brain structures. Recent neuroimaging studies, using techniques such as positron emission tomography (PET) and functional magnetic resonance imaging (fMRI) have shown that multimodal brain structures also feed back information to influence 'earlier' cortical areas, traditionally thought of as being purely **unimodal** (see Figure 6). For example, using fMRI, Gemma Calvert and colleagues have shown that the *sight* of lip movements directly activates the primary auditory cortex in the absence of any auditory speech sounds, presumably via back-projections. Meanwhile, other researchers have shown that neural responses to visual stimuli within unimodal visual cortex in the **lingual gyrus**, can also be enhanced by the simultaneous presentation of a tactile cue from the same spatial location.

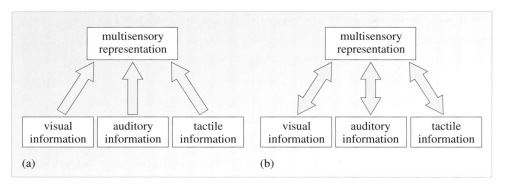

Figure 6   (a) Schematic illustration of the conventional view of multisensory interactions taking place via feedforward convergence of information from different sensory modalities, which are combined in multisensory structures, such as the superior colliculus, to generate multisensory stimulus representations. (b) Schematic illustration of the more recent view that multisensory structures may also feed back to influence earlier brain structures traditionally thought of as being 'unimodal'. The existence of feedback pathways could help to explain why multisensorily determined percepts, such as audiovisual speech perception, are still experienced unimodally (as when *seen* lip movements influence the sound that is *heard* in the McGurk illusion).

6 Summary

Multisensory integration effects play a central role in determining how we perceive the objects and events in the world around us. Extensive crossmodal links in spatial attention ensure that when we selectively attend to a particular stimulus, we are able to enhance the processing of all the sensory attributes associated with that stimulus, regardless of their modality. Having selected the relevant sensory information available to each sensory system, we integrate that information, weighting information from the most accurate sensory modality more highly (typically vision in the majority of laboratory studies). Neurophysiologists have demonstrated the existence of a number of multisensory convergence sites in the brain, such as the superior colliculus and parietal lobe; recent neuroimaging studies have shown how back projections from these multimodal convergence sites can feed back to influence activity within 'unimodal' brain structures. One of the most important tasks for future research is to try and elucidate how mechanisms of multisensory selective attention interact with the processes of multisensory integration to derive the multisensorily-determined percepts of everyday life.

Further reading

Driver, J. and Spence, C. (1998) Attention and the crossmodal construction of space, *Trends in Cognitive Sciences*, **2**, pp. 254–262.

Driver, J. and Spence, C. (2000) Multisensory perception: beyond modularity and convergence, *Current Biology*, **10**, pp. R731–R735.

28

Interaction between the senses: vision and the vestibular system

Rollin Stott

1 Introduction

For any free-living organism a sense of orientation, an ability to sense a spatial relationship to its immediate environment, is a fundamental requirement. Even quite primitive organisms such as some jellyfish, members of the phylum Coelenterata, possess specialized sense organs that detect the direction of gravity and enable them to distinguish up from down. The evolutionary analogue of this structure is present in fishes, where it has acquired a degree of complexity that makes it recognizably similar to the balance organ of land-dwelling vertebrates, including humans.

The human inner ear is a complicated looking structure (Figure 1). With its interconnecting series of canals and chambers it is not surprising that it is also known as the labyrinth. It lies at the base of the skull, embedded in the most dense piece of bone in the body, the petrous temporal bone. It is therefore well protected and firmly coupled to the skull. The inner ear has two functional parts, the cochlea, which contains the organ of hearing, and the **vestibular labyrinth**, the organ of balance. The vestibular labyrinth together with its neural connections within the central nervous system constitutes the vestibular system. The following section will give an overview of the principal vestibular structures; for more detail see Chapter 7, *The vestibular system*.

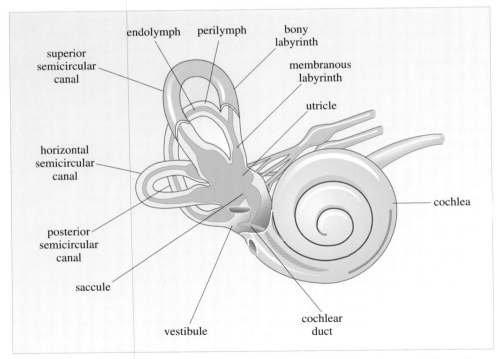

Figure 1 The human inner ear. The three semicircular canals in planes at right angles to each other communicate with the utricular cavity. Below the utricle is the saccule. These two chambers contain the otolithic organs. The canals and otolithic organs constitute the vestibular component of the inner ear. The coiled snail-like cochlea is the auditory component.

2 The vestibular system: a detector of force and movement

The vestibular system is a transducer of the forces we experience in our environment, and sends neural signals relating to the direction and intensity of the linear and angular forces (i.e. turning) that act upon it to the brain. Both linear and angular forces occur as a result of locomotor activities such as walking, running or jumping, or from head rotations associated with visual scanning. However, for a terrestrial animal the most important linear force acting on the body is that due to gravity. Whereas all other forces are transient and variable in intensity, that due to gravity is dependably constant in both direction and intensity. Despite its familiarity, gravity is a force that is potentially injurious and continuous muscle activity is required during waking life in order to avoid its unopposed action.

The vestibular system contains two distinct mechanisms for the transduction of angular and linear forces. At the heart of the process of transduction are hair cells, goblet-shaped cells (Type I) or cylindrical (Type II) which convert a mechanical distortion of the hairs on one end of the cell to a change in the rate of firing in the nerve fibre attached to the opposite end (Figure 2). These cells have a directional orientation determined by the arrangement of hairs in a cluster of diminishing height. Deflection of the hairs in the direction of the tallest will increase the rate of neural impulses in the nerve fibre and when deflected in the opposite direction will decrease it.

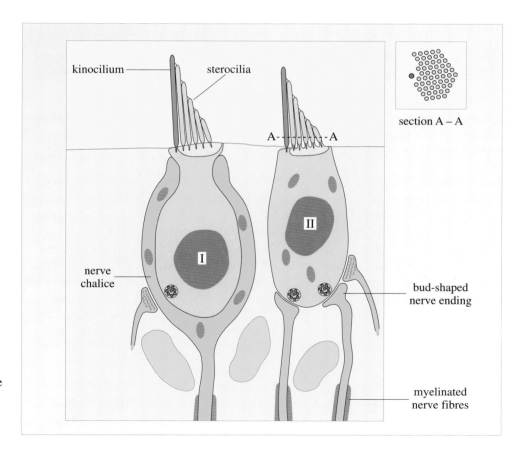

Figure 2   Type I and II hair cells of the inner ear. The rate of depolarization of the underlying cell is changed by deflection of the hairs, the arrangement of which gives the cell a directional sensitivity.

The three semicircular canals in each ear are detectors of **angular acceleration** whereas the otolithic organs are responsive to **linear accelerations** including that of gravity. As a result of the orientation of the semicircular canals in planes at right angles to each other, each canal will detect a component of any imposed rotational acceleration whatever its plane of action. Each semicircular canal communicates with a central chamber, the **utricular cavity**, and can therefore be thought of as enclosing a continuous ring of fluid (Figure 3). The only break in the continuity of the fluid ring is formed by the cupula, a gelatinous curtain-like structure that extends across a dilated portion of the canal near its junction with the utricular cavity. Movement of the fluid within the canal results in distortion of the cupula and this is detected by hair cells at its base, the hairs of which extend into the cupula.

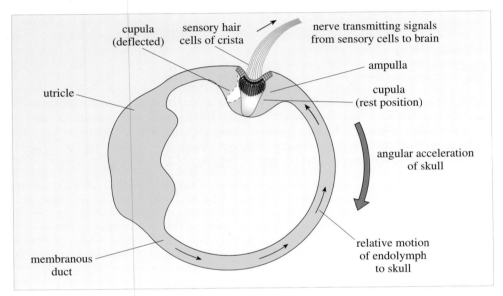

Figure 3   Diagram of a semicircular canal. Rotation in the plane of the canal results in fluid movement within the canal which distorts the cupula and changes the rate of depolarization of hair cells embedded in its base.

The otolithic organs, of which there are two in each inner ear, lie in two fluid-filled cavities immediately below the semicircular canals (Figure 4 overleaf). They consist of a carpet of hair cells overlain by a gelatinous membrane, which contains crystals of calcium carbonate in its outer layers. These give the membrane a stony appearance, and led to the term otolith, meaning 'ear stone'. The otoliths have the effect of increasing the density of the membrane so that it is greater than that of the surrounding fluid. In consequence, if an initially horizontal hair cell surface is tilted, the membrane will, under the influence of gravity, tend to slide downwards and in so doing bend the hairs of the underlying cells and change their rate of firing. The otolithic organs are therefore principally tilt sensors with respect to gravity, though they are also responsive to any accelerative force acting in the plane of the hair cell surface.

One function of the neural output from the vestibular system is to contribute to postural stability. A patient with malfunction of this sense organ, which might occur as a result of acute labyrinthitis or during an attack of Menière's disease, may be unable to stand unaided and may be reduced to crawling in order to move about. By contrast, an individual with total absence of vestibular function may, under most

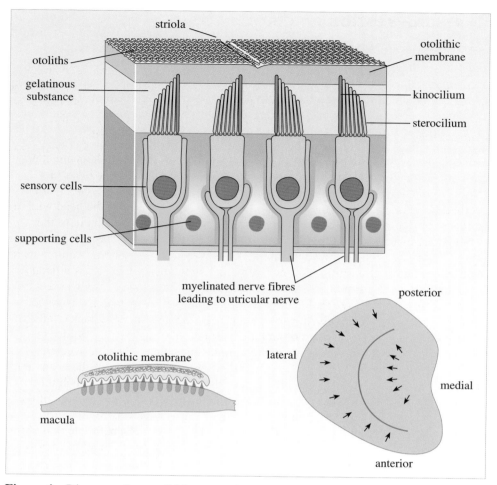

Figure 4 Diagram of an otolithic organ. A carpet of hair cells is overlain by the otolithic membrane, rendered more dense than the surrounding fluid by calcium carbonate crystals within it. Accelerations, including that of gravity, cause movement of the membrane relative to the hair cells and change their rate of depolarization. The diagram bottom right shows the pattern of directional sensitivity of the hair cells.

circumstances, be able to walk and run normally. Such a condition could be the result of toxicity from a group of antibiotics, the amino-glycosides, that are important in the treatment of severe infections but which in excess dose can permanently damage the hair cells of both the auditory and vestibular components of the inner ear. Other sensory mechanisms contribute to postural stability, in particular, pressure receptors in the skin of the soles of the feet, stretch receptors in muscle and tendon, and most importantly, vision. One problem that a vestibular-deficient individual will, however, experience is that, during activities that produce jolting movement of the head such as when walking, running, or travelling in a vehicle over rough terrain, the visual world does not appear static but itself appears to be jolted about. In consequence, the visual detail of the scene is lost.

3 Visual–vestibular cooperation: the vestibulo-ocular reflex

In normal individuals the visual and vestibular mechanisms are interdependent. Head movement is sensed by the vestibular system and this information is used to stabilize the eyes with respect to the visual world. In turn, visual information is relayed to the vestibular nuclei in the brainstem and contributes to postural stability and the perception of orientation and motion with respect to the outside world.

Here is a simple experiment you might like to try. With the palm of the hand at a typical reading distance from the eyes, look at the fine detail of the skin surface. Observe how the ability to discriminate this detail is altered by either side to side oscillation of the hand with the head still, or side to side rotation of the head with the hand stationary. Increase the frequency of oscillation in each condition until the detail is no longer visible. Provided vestibular function is normal, it should be observed that vision is degraded at a much lower frequency of hand movement than head movement. The ability to follow a moving target when the head is stationary involves the **visual pursuit reflex**, an ability to sense the velocity of movement of a visual image across the retina and to generate eye movement to match this velocity. This reflex involves relatively slow cortical processing and in consequence fails to operate at the higher frequencies of target movement. By contrast, the ability to maintain visual acuity for a stationary target in the presence of head movement involves the vestibulo-ocular reflex. This reflex senses the rotation of the head and stimulates an equal and opposite deflection of the eyes, as a result of which the image of a stationary visual scene remains in the same position on the retina of the eye. The reflex operates through a series of three neurons that link the sensory elements of the vestibular system to the eye muscles. The neural path length is short and the synaptic junctions between the neurons add only a short synaptic delay, so that this reflex continues to operate at much higher frequencies.

The vestibulo-ocular reflex can be elicited in the absence of vision. One clinical test of vestibular function is to seat a subject on a turntable in the dark and to measure the eye movements that occur in response to sinusoidal oscillation of the chair. If the amplitude of chair oscillation is less than $\pm 5°$, the eye movement response is also sinusoidal and of similar though not necessarily exactly the same amplitude and in opposite phase, so that when the chair moves to the left the eyes move right and vice versa (Figure 5a). If the amplitude of chair oscillation is increased, the eye movement amplitude is also increased but is interrupted by **saccades**, rapid jumps in eye position to bring the eye back to a more central position (Figure 5b). When measured in the dark, the amplitude of eye movement response in relation to the amplitude of chair movement depends on the frequency of oscillation of the chair. At a frequency of 0.1 Hz the amplitude of eye movement may be only 0.6 of the amplitude of chair movement whereas at 1 Hz the amplitudes may be more nearly the same. If the test were to be repeated in the light with normal visual surroundings the amplitude of the eye movement response would at all frequencies be exactly equal to that of the chair and in opposite phase, implying perfect compensation. In everyday life the pursuit response and the vestibulo-ocular response work together to promote stability of the retinal image. At lower frequencies of head movement the vestibulo-ocular response is augmented by the pursuit response. At higher frequencies where the pursuit response becomes ineffective the vestibulo-ocular response is dominant.

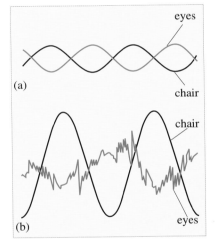

Figure 5 (a) A recording of eye movements generated by a subject undergoing sinusoidal angular oscillation at 0.5 Hz on a turntable in the dark. For small angular displacements of the turntable sinusoidal eye movements are generated which are in opposite phase to the chair movement. (b) With larger amplitudes of angular motion the underlying sinusoidal eye movement response is broken up by rapid eye movements, called saccades, that return the eye to a more central position.

4 The visual component of movement detection and balance

Like the vestibular system, vision has also evolved to be a sensitive detector of motion. To an animal in quest of its next meal, or seeking to avoid becoming someone else's, this ability has obvious survival value. Where visual image movement is of the whole visual scene rather than of objects within it, the resulting perception is of self-motion with respect to a stable outside world. The individual pictured in Figure 6 has advanced towards an umbrella-sized rotating hemisphere of black dots on a white background mounted at eye level. Once he is close enough for the umbrella to encompass the whole of his visual field he will tend to lose balance sideways in the direction of its rotation particularly if his feet are kept close together, or one behind the other. Anti-clockwise rotation of the visual scene, even if only dots on a white background, implies clockwise self-motion, to which the subject responds with an anti-clockwise body tilt. However, only a small rim of peripheral vision of the stable surroundings is sufficient to prevent this inappropriate postural response. Similarly, with feet apart the difference in pressure sensed on the soles of the feet as a result of body tilt countermands further postural change.

Figure 6   The spotty umbrella. The umbrella, rotating anti-clockwise, tends to cause the subject to fall in the same direction when he can no longer see the static visual world in his peripheral vision.

A similar laboratory visual motion stimulus that has been extensively studied is that generated by the optokinetic drum (Figure 7). This consists of a vertically mounted hollow cylinder, large enough for a subject to sit within it, whose inside walls are painted with alternating black and white stripes. When the drum is rotated around a stationary subject there is an initial awareness of rotation of the drum which, after a variable latency of 5 to 30 seconds, is gradually replaced by a perception of self-rotation against a static visual background. This illusion of self-motion is very dependent on the visual motion stimulus falling on the peripheral rather than central visual fields.

There is a multiplicity of sensory information reaching the brain that contributes to a perception of spatial orientation and movement with respect to the outside world. This information arises from the two components of the vestibular system, the semicircular canals and the otoliths, from the visual and auditory systems, and from pressure receptors in skin and stretch receptors in muscle. Other sensory mechanisms such as electric or magnetic fields or chemical stimuli may be particularly important for orientation in some organisms. There are potential problems in having too many sources of information particularly if they send conflicting messages. The brain seems to possess a mechanism for detecting inconsistencies between the signals indicative of motion arising from vision and from the vestibular system. Furthermore, the detection of persistent inconsistencies provokes a pattern of symptoms that include lethargy, light-headedness, sweating, nausea and ultimately vomiting, a phenomenon we know as **motion sickness**.

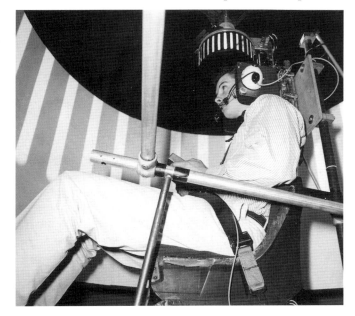

Figure 7   An optokinetic drum. In this arrangement the alternating dark and light stripes are projected from a rotating drum above the subject's head on to a static screen that surrounds the subject. Continuous motion of the striped pattern in one direction tends to provoke a sense of self-rotation in the opposite direction relative to a stationary visual background.

5 Visual and vestibular functions in conflict

Motion sickness has for long puzzled both sufferers and scientists, perhaps for different reasons. What is the nature of the stimulus that provokes it, what is its purpose and how can it be prevented? An observation made in 1882, at a time when the function of the vestibular system was being elucidated, was that individuals who could not be made dizzy on a turntable, and therefore, it was inferred, lacked vestibular function, did not suffer from seasickness, however rough the sea. Since that era, a time when sea travel was becoming increasingly popular, the same pattern of symptoms has been recognized in car and coach sickness, airsickness and most recently, space sickness. Furthermore, sickness can be provoked from travel by camel (Lawrence of Arabia was a sufferer) and elephant, although not on horseback. The enjoyment of fairground rides can also be marred by nausea and sickness. Of particular relevance is the finding that these symptoms can appear in individuals watching a cinema screen in which motion of themselves is implied by what they see on the screen.

The theory that best explains these diverse observations is that motion sickness is provoked by conditions that lead to sensory conflict either within the vestibular system itself or between visual and vestibular evidence of motion. Sensory conflict is best understood in terms of what would constitute sensory accord. All pedestrian motion takes place against a background of a fixed visual environment and a gravitational force that is constant in direction and magnitude. In consequence of this it is possible to formulate three simple rules that determine the interaction between visual and vestibular sensors of motion.

Rule I

The rule that links the visual with the vestibular systems is that when rotational motion is sensed by the semicircular canals there should be an equivalent rotation of the visual scene in the opposite direction. Provided this rule pertains we see the external world as remaining stationary, principally as a consequence of the vestibulo-ocular reflex whose response is linked to this expectation. Viewing the visual scene through magnifying or minifying lenses produces a world that appears to move with every turn of the head.

An even more striking response occurs when an individual is asked to try to walk down a corridor wearing spectacles that invert right and left (Figure 8). In these circumstances a leftward head movement produces a movement of the visual scene in the same direction as the head movement and at twice the angular velocity. When attempting to walk down the corridor in a straight line, subjects, depending on their temperament, either take shuffling wide-based steps with frequent pauses to re-orient themselves or else set off confidently, and rapidly walk into the wall. With persistence, the ability to move about improves, though this may require several days. The attempt to adapt to the wearing of image-reversing spectacles is often accompanied by motion sickness, which may be evident after just 10–15 minutes of spectacle use. Sequential measurements of the vestibulo-ocular response in the dark during the period of adaptation have shown a gradual diminution of the amplitude of the expected eye movement response and the establishment of some degree of reflex eye movement in the opposite direction. Such eye movements would thus be compensatory for the image-reversed movement of the visual world produced by the spectacles. Also with adaptation, the tendency to become motion sick diminishes.

Figure 8   The subject is wearing spectacles that invert his view of the visual scene from left to right. Orientation is easily lost and attempts to move about are difficult and tentative. Repeated efforts tend to provoke nausea, a form of motion sickness.

The individual who becomes sick when watching a wide-screen film taken from a moving vehicle may receive visual evidence of turning without experiencing any corresponding signal from the semicircular canals, or visual evidence of acceleration and deceleration without any corresponding signal from the otoliths. Nausea may also complicate the use of **virtual reality headsets**. In more sophisticated systems movement of the wearer's head is sensed and the view of the visual scene appropriate to the new direction of gaze is generated by computer. However, depending on the rapidity of head movement and the complexity of the visual scene that is portrayed, the time delay in computing the visual image may give the wearer a sense of instability of the visual world. Time delays of the order of 50 ms are perceptible and exposure of subjects to random angular motion on a turntable while viewing a time-delayed visual image is associated with a greater degree of nausea as the time delay is increased.

The remaining two rules of sensory accord apply to the vestibular system itself and the expected interaction of its component parts.

Rule 2

If the head is rotated either forwards or backwards or to left or right there is an expectation that the degree of rotation sensed by the semicircular canals is matched by an equivalent change in the direction of gravity as sensed by the otoliths. Transgression of this rule is readily achieved in aircraft and in vehicles cornering at speed (Figure 9). Dynamic forces are generated whenever a moving body changes direction and are determined by the radius of the turn and the forward velocity of the vehicle. These forces add to the force of gravity and create a resultant force that no longer indicates the true vertical. In a car that is cornering on a flat road there is an apparent change in the direction of gravity without a corresponding rotation. In a turning aircraft there is a sensation of roll as the aircraft assumes a banked attitude but no perceived change in the direction of gravity.

Figure 9 Vehicles that change direction generate radial forces (F) that are proportional to the rate of turning multiplied by the forward velocity. When added to the force of gravity (G), the resultant (R) may feel indistinguishable from gravity alone but no longer indicates the true vertical.

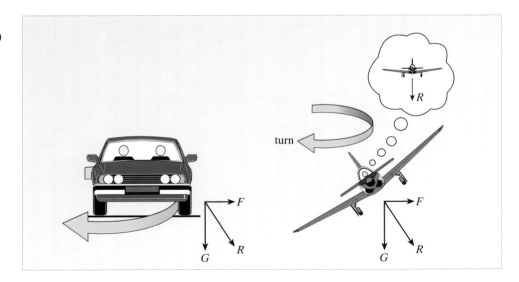

Rule 3

The final rule relates to the constancy of the intensity of gravity. Normal locomotor activities such as walking or running generate alternating vertical forces corresponding to the up and down movement involved. These forces are sensed by the otolithic receptors as transient oscillations in the intensity of gravity. The brain seems to recognize as illegitimate frequencies of oscillation that are significantly below those found in everyday activities and exposure to vertical oscillation at frequencies below 0.5 Hz will give rise to nausea and vomiting. This type of motion stimulus predominates in rough conditions at sea and its measured intensity aboard ships correlates well with the incidence of seasickness. Similarly, motion sickness can also result from low-frequency horizontal oscillation, equivalent to alternate acceleration and deceleration in a road vehicle.

6 Why motion sickness?

While the notion of sensory conflict offers an explanation of the characteristics of motion that result in sickness it has little to say about the relevance of the symptoms of nausea and vomiting to these types of motion. It is perhaps even more puzzling to find that many animals exposed to similar types of motion will also vomit. Even fish have been observed to vomit in response to motion. Neither these creatures, nor indeed humans can have evolved this emetic mechanism as a purposeful response to types of motion that they could never have encountered in their evolutionary past. On the other hand, vomiting *per se* has a more obvious evolutionary benefit if it results in the removal from the stomach of potentially toxic substances. The most convincing explanation for the emetic response we call motion sickness is that the brain has evolved to use the constancy of the gravitational and visual environment as a form of self-calibration. If the expected integration between vestibular and visual sensory information is not found, this is interpreted as a malfunction of the brain itself. If such malfunction were the result of some ingested neurotoxin then vomiting might be an appropriate response to eliminate any that still remained in the gut.

Next time the reader is feeling none too good on some rough sea crossing, it might be of some comfort to reflect that the seemingly useless emetic mechanism that we call motion sickness has only persisted because it conferred some survival benefit on our evolutionary ancestors, and that without it, we just might not be here at all.

7 Summary

In order to orient ourselves in the world we need the ability to sense a spatial relationship to our environment. This we achieve not only through visual awareness of our surroundings but also through the ability to sense the force environment, the transient forces associated with locomotion and, most importantly, the continuous force of gravity.

The vestibular system has evolved as a specialized sensor of forces acting on the head, both linear forces sensed through the otolithic organs and angular forces through the semicircular canals. These two components of the vestibular system, together with the visual system, act as an integrated motion and orientation sensory mechanism. Because the visual environment remains stable and gravity remains constant in direction and intensity, there are functional links between these separate components and only certain patterns of sensory information can occur.

Many forms of transport generate sensory patterns that do not conform to the normal expectations and it has become evident that exposure to these unfamiliar patterns is the common theme, termed sensory conflict, that underlies what is known as motion or travel sickness.

As a response to certain types of motion, the nausea and vomiting of motion sickness appear to serve no useful purpose. Rather, the phenomenon of motion sickness has revealed an emetic mechanism that evolution has designed as a protective response to the detection of an apparent malfunction in the way in which the sensory information relating to motion and orientation is integrated within the brain.

Perceiving, misperceiving, and hypnotic hallucinations

29

Peter Naish

1 Introduction

For completeness, a book dealing with perception should have something to say about misperception. Misperceiving, of course, is something we do often; we 'hear' what we expect someone to say, rather than what they did say, we misread a word, and so on. However, although those sorts of errors can be quite informative about how our perceptual systems work, they are rather unsurprising mistakes. In this chapter we will be consideing quite major misperceptions, where, for example, a person might believe that they can see a cat sitting in their lap when none is in fact present, or where they are apparently oblivious to what for most people would be a painful medical procedure.

Those two examples could be drug-induced; a chemical that gives rise to excess transmitter substance can cause neural activity leading to hallucinations, and one that blocks transmitter action can behave as an analgesic. Again, the perceptual errors associated with chemicals are not surprising. The truly puzzling effects that we will address are those which can often be brought about through hypnosis. In discussing these misperceptions it will be necessary to consider how hypnosis itself occurs. In fact, not only does an understanding of hypnotic effects help to explain hallucinations, but they in turn are a phenomenon which can inform theories of hypnosis. This chapter will attempt to integrate the two topics. Since many readers will be unfamiliar with the nature of hypnosis, the scene will be set by describing something of what it is like, and how it might be explained.

Most people's experience of hypnosis, if they have had any at all, will be as spectators of stage hypnosis. If they have had personal experience it might be through hypnotherapy for giving up smoking, weight loss, or the like. Anyone who has had both those experiences, as spectator and participant, is likely to be struck by the apparent difference: the stage version looks dramatic, while the therapeutic feels rather mundane. The difference sometimes leads people to ask whether hypnosis shows are merely fraudulent stage tricks. Alternatively, after experiencing a seemingly uneventful session themselves, they may observe, 'Oh dear, I don't think I was hypnotized.'

The first issue that we shall need to consider is how to detect when a person *is* hypnotized, and how to distinguish him or her from one who is just acting, or for whom it is not working. A related issue is whether people can be 'slightly hypnotized', or whether it is an all-or-nothing kind of process. If it can range from 'not at all' to 'very deep', then a researcher would want to be able to measure whereabouts between those extremes a particular person came.

2 Hypnotic behaviour and hypnotic susceptibility

To answer the all-or-nothing question straight away, it is the case that people cover the whole spectrum of responsiveness to hypnosis. Some seem quite unaffected, a few are very responsive, and most of us fall between the extremes. To explain exactly what it means to be affected by hypnosis is more difficult than might be expected; that will become clearer as we go on.

There is a limit to what a person can achieve through being hypnotized. If you ever attend a show where people are made to float in mid-air, then that *is* a stage trick! However, you may see someone told that they are like a plank of wood, straight and unbending. They are then placed horizontally between two chairs, one supporting the head and the other the heels, with nothing in between. That is not a trick, it looks very impressive, and the audience is suitably awed by the power of hypnosis. The stage hypnotist wants us to be impressed, but as scientific enquirers should we be? Well, not really, because hypnosis is largely irrelevant to the exercise. This is easily demonstrated: it needs three people, two reasonably strong and one who is not too heavy, and who does not have any back problems. The exercise should be carried out over a soft surface. The light person stretches out, face up, on the floor, and tries to hold him- or herself as rigid as possible. One of the others holds the human plank's ankles (the easy job) and the last links fingers together under the plank's neck (the heavier job). They then lift carefully, and the horizontal volunteer discovers that it is not a very difficult position to hold for a while; certainly not as tiring as for the person lifting the head end. Notice that the use of hypnosis is completely unnecessary to make this work. What is more, it turns out to be nigh impossible to find *anything* that can be done only as a result of hypnosis. This presents quite a problem to anyone hoping to distinguish between success and failure at inducing hypnosis, or between fraud and reality on the stage.

The problem of detecting 'real' hypnosis was demonstrated very dramatically by an eminent American researcher in the field, called Martin Orne. He had an assistant attempt hypnosis with a large number of volunteers, some of whom were responsive, others not. The assistant then said to the participants, 'You are all going to be hypnotized by Dr Orne, and those of you who are unresponsive should try to *act* as if you are hypnotized. Make it convincing, because as soon as he detects that you are a fraud he will stop!' Meanwhile, Orne, who had considerable experience of working with hypnosis, expected that he would quickly spot the impostors from among the genuinely hypnotized people. To his surprise, he could not!

The important point in the above story is that the 'cheats' had not been given any special coaching on how they should respond. They simply took their cue from what the hypnotist seemed to expect, and used their own assumptions as to what being hypnotized should be like; there was no additional hypnotic 'magic' that they were unable to simulate. It is an easy step from this observation to claim that the so-called genuine cases were also acting: they just didn't let on! Why should anyone behave like that? Well, it is the case that, as social animals, humans tend to feel that they should conform. We do not like to 'hurt someone's feelings'; we feel embarrassed about being 'difficult', or standing out as 'odd'. These sorts of effects are particularly evident when there is a status difference between a person expecting particular behaviour and the one who might comply. A researcher with the title Doctor, and an official university post, might well seem, in the eyes of a nervous volunteer, to be of a status that demands appropriate responses. Of course, not everyone would be so awed by a hypnotist that they felt that they simply had to put on a show, but then not everyone *does* 'put on a show'; some respond to hypnosis, others do not.

The 'anxious-to-please actor' story may seem terribly far-fetched, but by the last decade of the twentieth century the majority of scientific researchers concerned with hypnosis were of the opinion that something of the sort was taking place, when people responded to hypnotic suggestions. They did not believe that hypnosis was an 'altered state of consciousness', as some people had claimed it to be. Even seemingly impressive effects, such as pain control, were seen as rather mundane. It was explained that, when someone is very relaxed, as they usually are when taken through a standard **hypnotic induction**, painful stimuli become far less distressing. Any residual discomfort is denied, as part of the hypnosis 'act'. I may as well make my own position clear at this point. For reasons that will emerge as we go on, I do think that at least some people genuinely experience the effects that they claim to have as a result of hypnosis. I can give an example from the field of pain control. I once saw a lady who had required the partial amputation of one foot. This had left her with intractable pain, very much like an amputee's phantom limb pain, except that it was not a whole limb. This patient had been attending a hospital pain clinic, where they tried everything, but without success, so as something of a last resort they referred her for hypnosis. She happened to be hypnotically responsive, and by the end of the session claimed to be pain-free. A month or so later she was still saying that she was without pain, and she wrote to thank me and stopped attending the pain clinic. It does seem implausible that this lady was going round in a relaxed daze, so that she could cope, and denying that there was anything wrong, in case she should cause offence!

Section 1 ended by mentioning that researchers need to know whereabouts a person comes on the hypnotic continuum. There are not any very effective tests that can be carried out in advance of hypnosis, to see if it is worth trying; the usual approach is to hypnotize a volunteer and see how they respond. For scientific rigour this cannot be a subjective assessment, so standardized **hypnotic susceptibility scales** have been devised. Typically, they contain a series of suggestions for effects that might occur such as an arm getting lighter, and floating up, or seeing something that is not there. Some effects are rather easy, and most people respond, while others are hard to achieve, and only the most susceptible succeed. Paradoxically, the researchers who have claimed that hypnosis is a matter of **compliance** are scrupulous in employing susceptibility scales in their work. One wonders why an embarrassed volunteer feels duty bound to perform some tests, but not others. If they really were acting, why not act the lot? After all, as pointed out earlier, hypnosis does not make the impossible possible, so *all* the tests could be performed by a person wishing to deceive. The situation seems more like a tacit agreement between researcher and volunteer, where the latter is in effect saying 'I know I *could* do any of these things you are asking for, but I promise only to let them happen if they happen by themselves.' Certainly, people whose arms start to lift up will claim that the limbs seem to be moving by themselves. I once gave some demonstrations with a group of students, and one young man could achieve a variety of effects, such as feeling a (non-existent) fly walking on his face, but his arm refused to budge, and he was very disappointed. The sceptic would have to produce an elaborate story to explain this, because the student must have decided to fake some effects, but then decided not to do so for the arm levitation, and instead feign disappointment that it had not worked. It all sounds very implausible to me! It seems all together more likely that this individual was only moderately susceptible, with the result that he experienced a certain number of effects, but that the more difficult ones were beyond him. Note that the effects were beyond the volunteer, not the hypnotist. The hypnotist has no power, merely acting in the role of a guide, who helps a person to achieve as much as they can. It has rightly been said that all hypnosis is self-hypnosis, although it is the case that many people do find it easier to obtain the effects if there is someone else present to lead them through the process.

3 How does it work?

There have been many theories to account for hypnotic behaviour, the sceptical account outlined above being just one. Since this is not a course on hypnosis we will not look at a large number but instead set the scene for a physiological explanation. As yet, this is not an explanation that is complete, but a number of recent studies appear to be producing convergent evidence that implicates attentional areas of the brain.

Although mentioning the wish to account for hypnotic *behaviour*, it is not really the behaviour which needs explanation, although it can sometimes appear to be odd. It can look strange, for example, to see a hypnotized person stroking the air above their lap, but that is no longer surprising if one knows that they can 'see' a cat sitting there. It is the *perception* that is surprising and which needs to be explained. There is a ready-made theory in Psychology, which can account for people experiencing things that are not there, or missing ones that are: it is called **signal detection theory**. This theory, abbreviated to **SDT**, was developed originally to explain the behaviour of people such as radar operators, who sometimes missed signals, or occasionally thought they had seen something when there was nothing. Central to the account is the recognition that our neural system is 'noisy'. By this is meant that neurons can have a resting level of activity, in the absence of any real stimulus. Moreover, the level of this activity is not constant; it rises and falls, quite randomly. Any real neural signal, resulting from an actual stimulus, has to be superimposed upon the inconstant background activity. A useful analogy is the behaviour of a hi-fi system. Good ones have a very quiet background, but if one turns up the volume when there is nothing playing a hiss will become discernible. It is still there when there is music, but in a reasonably high quality system what is known as the signal-to-noise ratio is so high that the music 'drowns out' the background noise, although it could become noticeable if there were a very quiet passage of music. We too suffer from 'noise', which is similarly still present while there is a wanted signal. Fortunately, we do not experience a radio-like hiss during periods of quietness (unless one has tinnitus), because the noise is filtered out before it reaches a conscious level. Nevertheless, it still has an effect and, as with the hi-fi analogy, it is noticeable when the desired signal is of low intensity, such as a tiny flash of light on a radar screen, or a very quiet sound. To explain, sound will be used as an example, but do not assume from this that the term **neural noise** applies only to hearing; 'noise' in this context refers to any random neural activity.

Spectators at a firework display can be in no doubt about when there are explosions; neural noise is drowned out by the bangs, as with the hiss of the hi-fi by loud music. The situation is different when 'it is so quiet you could hear a pin drop'. What would happen if a pin did drop? Well, that really is a very quiet sound, so some people might hear it, others not. If we repeated the experiment no doubt there would again be some who heard and others who missed the event, although they would not necessarily be the same people as last time. Suppose we change the test slightly. I hold my hand out of sight and say 'I may or may not drop a pin this time. There! Did you hear one?' In such circumstances some people say 'No', when there had been a pin, but others say 'Yes', even when there was no sound. This is all explained by the degree of randomness in neural behaviour. The level of activity varies, both when there is no true stimulus, and also when there is an event, such as a pin dropping. Of course, if there has been a sound, the associated neurons will *on average* respond more vigorously, but because of the randomness there may be little or none of the expected increase. The level of activity that occurs at any time can be expressed graphically, as in Figure 1.

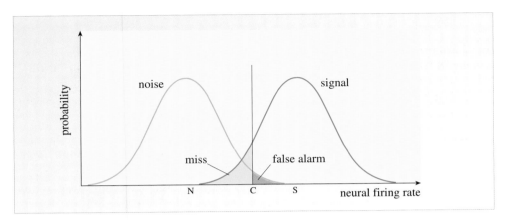

Figure 1   A graphical representation of the signal detection theory.

The horizontal axis represents neural activity, and it can be seen that the curve labelled 'signal' lies further to the right, reflecting the fact that a true signal will make a neuron respond more actively. The curve labelled 'noise' shows the background activity. The vertical axis represents probability: the higher the point on a curve, the more likely it is that the activity level will occur. The highest points of the two curves (marked S and N) indicate where the average levels of activity are to be found, respectively when there is a signal, and when there is only background noise. Because of the random element, the activity can sometimes be either less than, or more than the average, but the more extreme the value, the less likely it is to occur, reflected by the fact that the curves get lower (less probable), away from points S and N. Curves of this shape (mathematically known as *normal* curves) spread a long way from side to side (theoretically to infinity), so inevitably the signal and noise curves will have areas of overlap. An overlap is a problem area for our perceptual system, because it implies that a given level of activity might have come about either as a result of a real event, or simply because of some rather more intense noise than usual. How are we to know the difference? We cannot; there is no way to identify the *cause* of a neuron firing, only the fact that it fired. It seems that our compromise is to set a criterion point (marked C in the figure), and this is the cut off level, which determines whether neural activity is to be recognized as an event or not. Any activity level that falls below C is treated as if it was noise (even if it was from a real event), and it fails to reach conscious awareness. In contrast, activity that exceeds C will lead to a conscious perception of an event *even if it was not a real event*. It can be seen that this leads to two possible errors: if random noise happens to produce high activity an event will be perceived, and if the randomness leads to a real signal producing less activity than normal, then the signal will not reach awareness. These two mistakes are referred to as **false alarms** and **misses** respectively; they are the errors that people tend to make when trying to decide whether they heard a pin drop.

There are times when an error of one sort or the other can have serious consequences, and we appear able to get around that problem by shifting our criterion point. Suppose, for example, that there is an anxious parent, whose baby has not been well. It is supposed to be asleep upstairs, but should it awake and cry the parent does not want to miss it. Consequently, the criterion level of activity for that particular sound is moved very low, as shown in Figure 2. It will be seen that, by adopting such a low position, the proportion of events leading to misses has become very small: the baby is very unlikely to cry without being noticed. However,

Figure 2 The shift of the criterion position when it is important not to miss a signal.

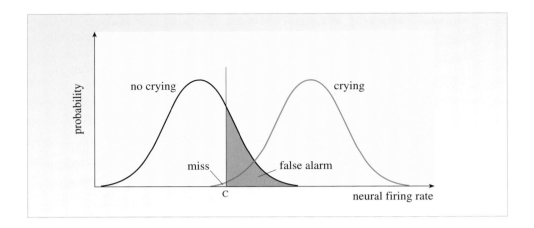

the low criterion position has resulted in the number of false alarms increasing dramatically: there is a much higher chance that the parent will *think* he or she heard the baby crying and hurry upstairs, only to find that all is well. It is not possible to avoid one type of error, without at the same time increasing the chances of experiencing the other type. An example of reducing false alarms at the expense of experiencing misses is to be found when we are 'lost in thought'. We raise our criteria, so as not to be interrupted as we walk down the road thinking great thoughts, and may look a friend in the face, yet not notice (nor acknowledge) their presence. Later they ask what they had done to offend!

If the needs of the moment can cause us to shift our perceptual criteria, it is not difficult to see how hypnosis might do the same. In this way, by making the 'cat' criterion very low, a person might register the noise in their cat-related neurons as representing a real cat, sitting in their lap. Conversely, if the criterion associated with sensation in the teeth were raised sufficiently, the pain signals of toothache might be treated as noise, and fail to reach consciousness (see Figure 3). I have carried out experiments that have lent some support to this picture of hypnosis, but it must be appreciated that the account is very far from being complete. It does not explain *how* hypnosis might achieve this result, and it certainly fails to account for the enduring quality of hypnotic misperceptions: the person who mistakenly goes to check the baby soon realizes that it was not crying, but a hypnotized person can persist in erroneous perceptions for a long period. The explanation does show, at a descriptive level, how misperceptions could occur, but we will return later to a consideration of the processes that might be involved.

4 Hypnotic hallucinations

Although some more hypnotizable people appear able to hallucinate all manner of experiences 'to order', research into the area has tended to focus upon more mundane misperceptions. These are easier to apply in a controlled way, and are more likely to be achievable by people with a wider range of hypnotic abilities. Before the availability of methods for recording brain activity, it was difficult to carry out convincing research on hypnotic hallucinations. If the volunteer claimed an experience, the sceptic would inevitably ask how we knew that they were telling the truth. Researchers in the USA have reported controversial results, using EEG techniques. Volunteers sat watching (hypnotized people can open their eyes) a computer monitor displaying a checkerboard pattern, in which the squares repeatedly switched between black and white. The flashing produced a detectable EEG response – a so-called **event-related potential** (**ERP**). The viewers were then told to 'see' a cardboard box being placed between themselves and the screen, so obstructing their view. In reality there was no box, but for participants who were hypnotically highly susceptible the EEG activity was reduced, as if the monitor had really been concealed. Not all researchers have been able to obtain comparable results, and it has been suggested that the viewers may have achieved the effect by letting their eyes go out of focus, so blurring the image of the black and white pattern. If the effect *is* what it seems, it is impressive, because the neural response picked up by the EEG electrodes might be thought to be automatic, and beyond the control of hypnosis or anything else. However, it is known that different attention strategies can have an impact upon the size of ERPs, so it is possible that the volunteers changed the way in which they attended to the stimulus.

Attention has been cited as the modulating influence in pain control. Pain has often been used in this kind of research, because it is intuitively not the kind of thing a person is going to pretend about: if they say they can stand more pain, then presumably it is genuinely not hurting as much. In fact one of the earliest uses of hypnosis was as an analgesic, in the days before chemical anaesthesia. Figure 3 shows a dental extraction taking place under hypnosis, in 1836. To carry out research on pain requires a pain-inducer which can give quantifiable levels of painful stimulus, without causing any actual harm. A recent technique involves the delivery of potassium ions to receptors in the skin. A person places the palm of his or her hand on a metal plate, which is connected to the negative side of an adjustable electrical supply. On the back of the hand is placed a cotton wool pad, soaked with potassium chloride solution, and this pad is connected to electrical positive. The potassium ions in the solution are themselves positively charged, so tend to diffuse away from the positive pad (same-polarity charges repel) and into the negative-connected hand. There, the change in potassium ion concentration causes action potentials in sensory neurons, and the signal is interpreted as heat. The number of ions migrating, and hence the strength of the stimulation, is precisely determined by the amount of electric current flowing, so the experimenter knows exactly how strong the stimulus is. At higher levels it is experienced as a strong burning sensation, although no physical damage is done. Hypnotized individuals are sometimes able to withstand stronger stimuli of this sort, an achievement which more sceptical researchers have ascribed to 'attending away'; in other words, the person tolerates the pain by trying to think about something else. However, one extensive study, which required the volunteers to try a number of different strategies, found that the highly hypnotizable actually achieved the best pain reduction by focusing their attention on the painful stimulus.

An interesting suggestion has been that hypnosis might cause the release of endorphins in the brain. These are naturally occurring substances that are chemically related to the analgesic morphine. They are probably released in situations such as the heat of battle, when soldiers have been reported to have received wounds to which they were oblivious until after the excitement had died down. If hypnosis produced endorphins, it would certainly explain any elevation in pain threshold, and undermine the signal detection account. The endorphin hypothesis was tested by giving participants naloxone, while evaluating the impact of hypnosis upon their pain tolerance. Naloxone is a morphine antagonist; it blocks the analgesic properties of morphine, and does the same to endorphins. If hypnotic

Figure 3   An early example of hypnotic analgesia during dental extraction.

pain tolerance is due to the brain's analogues of morphine, then naloxone should return people to their normal, sensitive state. It turns out that it does not; the volunteers were still able to stand raised levels of pain, so perhaps were changing their perceptions in some way.

PET and fMRI techniques are now beginning to give a rather better picture of what is taking place when hypnotized people tolerate pain. A number of studies have shown that an important region of activity lies at the centre front of the brain, where the cortex of each hemisphere curves inwards (Figure 4). This is the **cingulate cortex**, an area known to be involved in attentive mechanisms. It would seem that attention is indeed involved in pain reduction, but probably in more complex ways than the simple self-distraction idea would suggest. The possible role of the cingulate region is considered in more detail below.

Figure 4 Location of the cingulate region of the cortex. It is shown in light pink, and the anterior section (to the right in the picture) appears to be active in hypnosis.

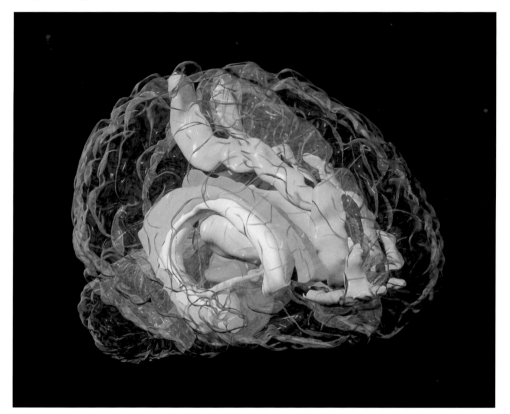

5 Mimicking illness

One of the most distressing types of hallucination suffered is the hearing of voices, in schizophrenia. Patients often experience the voice (or voices) as giving a critical running commentary upon their every action. Sometimes the voice intrudes to tell the patient what he or she should do. Brain-mapping studies of schizophrenics are difficult to conduct, because the hallucinations cannot be relied upon to appear 'to order'. Also there is a problem in researching patients who require brain-affecting medication, since it is not always easy to separate the effects of the condition from the drugs. An ingenious study has circumvented these difficulties by using very highly hypnotizable participants to mimic the effects of schizophrenia.

During hypnosis, and while being PET scanned, the volunteers were either played a tape of someone speaking, or they were asked to *imagine* that they could hear the tape (when it was not in fact turned on). Finally, they were told to listen to the speech again and they heard the cassette player being switched on. What they were not told was that it now contained a blank tape. These highly responsive people actually believed that they could hear the voice, and some took a great deal of convincing, at the end of the experiment, when told that there had in fact been nothing playing. In this hallucinating phase the participants' brains showed a different pattern of activity from that of the imagination, or real listening sections of the experiment. The region of brain that distinguished the phases was the cingulate cortex which showed increased activity during hypnosis.

This experiment appears to weaken a simplistic attention-based account of hypnotic misperception. Certainly, a person listening to a tape is paying attention to it, but it seems implausible that the style of attending is of the same sort as in pain control, where sceptics claimed that the participant was *dis*attending. Simple attention strategies seem even less likely to have played a part in recent studies, involving the universities of Cardiff and Oxford, and University College, London. The research began with the investigation of a case of **hysterical paralysis**. Sufferers become unable to move some part (in this case a leg), in spite of there being absolutely no identifiable physical problem. The patient was PET scanned, in an attempt to discover why a healthy limb was not being moved. The next stage of the study was to find a hypnotizable man, who was particularly responsive to suggestions of paralysis. (It had to be a man, since, unless there are good medical reasons, there is a reluctance to employ the mildly radioactive PET technique with women of child-bearing age.) He was given suggestions that he could not move one leg, and then he was scanned, while trying to move either the good or the 'paralysed' leg. The pattern of results was very much as had been obtained with the genuine patient: the motor cortex in the hemisphere driving the good side showed activity, but the other hemisphere did not. What was evident, in patient and volunteer alike, was that, during unsuccessful attempts to move the bad leg, the cingulate cortex became active. The close parallels between patient and mimic suggest that hysterical paralysis is the result of something akin to self-hypnosis.

6 Putting it all together: experience and agency

The cingulate cortex seems to be implicated in any study of hypnosis in which brain-mapping has been used. The region is probably involved in a number of neural circuits and functions; attention, emotion, motivation and motor control have all been identified as being modulated in the cingulate area. Any or all of these might be involved in hypnotic effects, but one function stands out as being a particularly good candidate. It has been reported that injury to the anterior cingulate results in dramatic **reality monitoring** failures. As a result, a patient can experience imagined events as being real.

One of humanity's most powerful abilities is that of imagining; it enables us to plan, remember, answer 'what if?' questions, and engage in a multitude of inner experiences, without ever having to enact them in reality. Although these imaginative activities must use many of the same brain regions as the corresponding real events, we are usually (and fortunately) able to distinguish what we have imagined from what has taken place. Hypnosis is known sometimes to break down that distinction, resulting in what are known as **source attribution errors**. In other words, when the source of an experience was a session of hypnosis, it may later be wrongly attributed to a real event. This process has occasionally taken place during misguided therapy, giving rise to false memories – recollections of events that never took place.

Many of the effects of hypnosis can be explained as examples of wrongly attributing experiences to an external agency. Thus, people whose arms obediently float up, in response to suggestions that the arm is getting lighter, are clearly using their own muscles to do the lifting, but their experience is that the arm is moving by itself. Returning to our example of a parent thinking that the baby was crying (Section 3), the normal response is something like 'Oh, I must have imagined it.' The hypnotized person seems not to know that he or she is 'imagining it'; they do not engage in proper reality monitoring, instead they accept their experiences as being real.

7 Summary

In summary, many of the neural processes involved in perception can be activated both by external stimulation and by internal processes, such as criterion shifting or imagination. Normally, we have the essential ability to distinguish between external and internal sources, using a reality testing process that probably involves the cingulate cortex. The misperceptions that can be produced in hypnosis, and also some types of hallucination, may well arise as a result of unusual activity in that region of the brain.

Acknowledgements

Grateful acknowledgement is made to the following sources for permission to reproduce material in this book:

Cover

Luciferase activity in stained cortical slice neurons. Reprinted from *Neuron*, Vol. 20, (4), 1998, with permission from Elsevier Science.

Chapter 1

Figure 2: Geisler, C. D. (1988) *From Sound to Synapse: Physiology of the Mammalian Ear*, copyright © 1988 by C. Daniel Geisler. Used by permission of Oxford University Press; *Figure 4*: Science Museum/Science & Society Picture Library; *Figures 5, 6*: Rosowski, J. J. (1996) 'Chapter 2: Models of External and Middle ear Function', Hawkins, H. L. *et al.* (eds), *Auditory Computation*, Springer-Verlag; *Figure 9a*: courtesy of Professor Andy Forge, UCL Centre for Auditory Research, University College London; *Figure 11*: The Nobel Foundation.

Chapter 2

Figure 5a: Furness, D. N. *et al.* (1997) *Proceedings of the Royal Society of London*, Vol. 264, 1997, The Royal Society of London; *Figure 7*: Reprinted from *Hearing Research*, Vol. 24, Palmer, A. R. and Russell, I. J., Copyright (1986), with permission of Elsevier Science; *Figure 8*: Rose, J. E. Galambos, R. and Hughes, J. R. (1959) *Bulletin of the Johns Hopkins Hospital*, Vol. 104, 1959, © Johns Hopkins Hospital. Reprinted by permission of The Johns Hopkins University Press; *Figure 9*: Reprinted from *Hearing Research*, **22**, Kiang, N. Y. S. *et al.*, Copyright (1986), with permission from Elsevier Science; *Figure 10*: Reprinted from *Current Opinion in Neurobiology*, Vol. 4, Ashmore, J. F. and Kolston, P. J., Copyright (1994), with permission from Elsevier Science.

Chapter 3

Figures 1, 11: Bear, M. F., Connors, B. W. and Paradiso, M. A. (1996) *Neuroscience: Exploring the Brain*, Williams & Wilkins. Copyright © 1996 Williams & Wilkins; *Figures 3a, 3b, 6b, 6c, 6d (right)*: Hackney, C. M., Osen, K. K. and Kolston, J. (1990) *Anatomy and Embryology*, **182**, 1990, Springer-Verlag; *Figure 4*: Pickles, J. O. (1988) *An Introduction to the Physiology of Hearing*, Academic Press; *Figure 5*: Lorente de Nó, R. (1981) *The Primary Acoustic Nuclei*, Raven Press; *Figures 6a, 7a, 7b (left)*: Ehret, G. and Romand, R. (1997) *The Central Auditory System*, copyright © 1997 by Oxford University Press. Used by permission of Oxford University Press; *Figures 7a (right), 7b (right)*: Thompson, R. F. (1993) *The Brain: A Neuroscience Primer*, W. H. Freeman and Company; *Figure 8*: England, M. J. and Wakely, J. (1991) *A Colour Atlas of the Brain and Spinal Cord*, W. B. Saunders & Co. Inc.; *Figure 9a*: Servière, J., Webster, W. R. and Calford, M. B. (1984), *The Journal of Comparative Neurology*, **228**, 1984. Reprinted by permission of Wiley-Liss, Inc., a subsidiary of John Wiley & Sons, Inc.; *Figure 9b*: Reprinted from *Neuroscience Letters*, Vol. 65, Stieber, I. Copyright (1986), with permission from Elsevier Science.

Chapter 4

Figures 1, 10: England, M. J. and Wakely, J. (1991) *A Colour Atlas of the Brain and Spinal Cord*, W. B. Saunders & Co. Inc.; *Figures 2, 4*: Steinstrater, O. and Lutkenhomer, B. (1998) *Audiology & Neuro-Otology*, Vol. 3, 1998, S. Karger, AG; *Figure 3*: Reprinted from *Brain Research*, **724**, Howard III, M. A. *et al*. Copyright (1994) with permission from Elsevier Science; *Figures 6, 7*: Courtesy of Heledd Hart (2002) PhD dissertation, MRC Institute of Hearing Research, Nottingham; *Figure 8*: Griffiths, T. D. *et al*. (1998) *Nature Neuroscience*, **1**, No. 1, 1998, Nature Publishing Co.; *Figure 9*: Baumgart, F. *et al*. (1999) *Nature*, **400**, 1999, Nature Publishing Co.

Chapter 5

Figure 6: Courtesy of Research Laboratory of Electronic, MIT.

Chapter 6

Figure 2: Courtesy of Roy F Sullivan, PhD, www.rcsullivan.com; *Figures 5, 6*: Reproduced with permission of Advanced Bionics; *Figure 8*: Tyler, R. *Tinnitus Handbook*, © 2000. Reproduced with permission of Delmar, a division of Thompson Learning.

Chapter 7

Figure 1: Dave Caulkin/AP; *Figures 3a, 3b*: Reprinted from *Hearing Research*, Vol. 118, Quint, E., Furness, D. N. and Hackney, C. M., Copyright (1998), with permission from Elsevier Science; *Figures 3c, 6a, 6b, 7a*: Kandel, E. R., Schwartz, J. H. and Jessell, T. M. (1991) *Principles of Neural Science*, Reproduced with permission of The McGraw-Hill Companies, Inc.

Chapter 9

Figures

Figure 3: Davson, H. (ed.), (1969) Chapter 7 The Cornea and Sclera, *The Eye*, Vol. 1, 2nd edn, Academic Press (London) Limited; *Figure 7*: Forrester, D. *et al*. (2002) *The Eye: Basic Sciences in Practice*, 2nd edn, Harcourt Health Sciences; *Figure 8*: Hart, R. W. and Farrell, R. A. (1969) *Journal of the Optical of America*, **59**, (6), 1969, Optical Society of America; *Figure 9*: Giraud, J. P. *et al*. (1975), *Experimental Eye Research*, **21**, 1975, Academic Press (London) Limited.

Tables

Table 1: Davson, H. (ed.), (1969) Chapter 7 The Cornea and Sclera, *The Eye*, Vol. 1, 2nd edn, Academic Press (London) Limited.

Chapter 10

Figure 2a: Tortora, G. J. and Anagnostakos, N. P. (1987) *Principles of Anatomy and Physiology*, 5th edn, Harper & Row, Publishers, New York, Professor Michael H. Ross; *Figure 2b*: Biophotos Associates/Science Photo Library; *Figure 3a*: Rory McClenaghan/Science Photo Library; *Figure 3c*: Rodieck, R. W. (1998) *The First Steps in Seeing*, Sinauer Associates, Inc.; *Figure 6*: Reprinted from *Vision Research*, **30**, Pugh, E. N. and Lamb, T. D., copyright (1990), with permission from Elsevier Science; *Figure 7a*: Baylor, D. A., Nunn, B. J. and Schnapf, J. L. (1987) *Journal of*

Physiology, **390**, 1987, The Physiological Society, Cambridge University Press; *Figure 7b*: Baylor, D. A., Nunn, B. J. and Schnapf, J. L. (1984) *Journal of Physiology*, **357**, 1984, The Physiological Society, Cambridge University Press.

Chapter 12

Figures 2, 3, 4a, 8: Kandel, E. R., Schwartz, J. H. and Jessell, T. M. (2000) *Principles of Neural Science*. Reproduced with permission of The McGraw-Hill Companies, Inc.; *Figure 6*: Cleland, B. G., Dubin, M. W. and Levick, W. R. (1971) *Journal of Physiology*, **217**, 1971, The Physiological Society, Cambridge University Press; *Figure 10*: Hubel, D. H. and Wiesel, T. N. (1959), *Journal of Physiology*, **148**, 1959, The Physiological Society, Cambridge University Press; *Figure 14*: Kandel, E. R., Schwartz, J. H. and Jessell, T. M. (1995) *Essentials of Neural Science and Behavior*, Copyright © 1995 by Appleton & Lange.

Chapter 13

Figure 2: Felleman, D. J. and Van Essen, D. C. 'Distributed hierarchical processing in the primate cerebral cortex', *Cerebal Cortex*, (1991) Vol. 1. Reproduced by permission of Oxford University Press.

Chapter 15

Box 1 (left): Scala Picture Library;

Box 1 (right): National Museums and Galleries of Wales.

Chapter 17

p. 222: Cartoon drawn by Alastair Parvin.

Chapter 18

Figure 7: Courtsey of Göran K Westling (1986), *Sensori-Motor Mechanisms during Precision Grip in Man*, Umeå University Dissertation No 171, ISSN 0346-6612.

Chapter 22

Figure 10a: Courtesy of Dr Robert C. Coghill, School of Medicine, Wake Forest University.

Chapter 23

Figure 5: Freeman, W. J. (1991) 'The physiology of perception', *Scientific American*, 264 (2), February 1991; *Figure 8*: Yousem, D. M. *et al.* (1999) 'Gender effects on odor-stimulated functional magnetic resonance imaging', *Brain Research*, **818**. Copyright © 1999 Elsevier Science Publishers Ltd. Reproduced with permission from Elsevier Science.

Chapter 24

Figure 4: Sobel, N. *et al.* (1998) 'Sniffing and smelling: separate subsystems in the human olfactory cortex', *Nature*, **392**, 19 March 1998. Reproduced by permission from *Nature*. Copyright © 1998 Macmillan Magazines Limited; *Figure 5*: Jacob, S. *et al.* (2001) 'Sustained human chemosignal unconsciously alters brain function', *NeuroReport*, Vol. 12, Lippincott Williams & Wilkins.

Chapter 27

Figure 1: Cover Design by Nigel Hynes, *Trends in Cognitive Sciences*, July 1998, **2**, No.7, (16) Elsevier Science Ltd.

Chapter 29

Figure 3: Mary Evans Picture Library; *Figure 4*: Science Photo Library.

Every effort has been made to trace all the copyright owners, but if any has been inadvertently overlooked, the publishers will be pleased to make the necessary arrangements at the first opportunity.

Glossary

absolute pitch *See* perfect pitch.

achromatic colour An achromatic colour is one that is without hue. Black, white and all the grey colours are examples of achromatic colours.

acoustic impedance A measure of how readily the particles of the conducting medium can be displaced by sound waves. It is measured as the ratio of the sound pressure to the flow velocity of the particles of the transmitting medium.

acoustic neuroma *See* vestibular schwannoma.

acoustic shadow A region in a field in which the sound is reduced owing to an object which blocks, obscures, absorbs or reflects the physical energy. The sound shadow produced by one's head serves as a cue in the location of sounds of relatively high frequencies.

acoustic threshold The amplitude of a sound pressure wave that can just be heard when presented to a listener.

activation curve The relationship between the number of mechanosensitive channels open and hair bundle displacement.

active touch The type of intentional touch used to assess the properties of objects.

acute otitis media Acute inflammation of the middle ear.

adaptation Change in sensitivity in response to continued stimulation. For hair cells, the shifting of the activation curve to a new working point as a result of maintained deflection of the hair bundle. This ensures that the sensitivity of hair cells is always at a maximum close to the resting position.

adapting grating A grating used to fatigue the cells that it activates by the process of adaptation, employed in psychophysical studies of spatial vision.

additive colour mixing Additive colour mixing describes the process by which light from different primaries is superimposed to generate a particular colour. Additive colour mixing is used to produce images in television and on computer screens.

affective visual information Visual stimulus or situation which produces an emotional response.

afferent nerve fibre A nerve fibre that carries neural information from the periphery to the brain.

agonist A chemical substance capable of mimicking the physiological effect of a neurotransmitter by specifically interacting with its natural receptors.

akinetopsia The inability to detect or interpret visual motion.

aliases Spurious low spatial frequency components that arise from spatial frequencies in a stimulus that are too high for the sampling rate used.

allodynia Pain experienced when the subject is stimulated by a previously innocuous stimulus.

all-*trans*-retinal The substance formed during the visual process by the action of light on 11-*cis*-retinal.

alpha-gamma co-activation (α-γ co-activation) The pattern of neuronal activity in muscles when both α and γ motor neurons fire causing simultaneous extrafusal muscle contraction (α motor neurons) and a stretching of the central portion of the spindle as a consequence of the contraction of their end portions (γ motor neurons).

amacrine cells A type of nerve cell without axons whose cell bodies lie in the inner nuclear layer of the retina. They connect laterally in the inner plexiform layer with bipolar and ganglion cells.

ampliotopic organization The systematic gradient of response selectivity to sound level.

ampulla The bulge at one end of each semicircular canal which contains the hair cells that are stimulated by rotation of the head.

amygdala An almond-shaped body located at the tip of the inferior horn of the lateral ventricle of the brain between the hypothalamus and the cerebral cortex. In general, the amygdala can be viewed as an area that is involved in regulation of awareness of behaviour.

angular acceleration Acceleration leading to a change in the rate of rotation, e.g. in shaking or nodding the head.

anomalous trichromats Individuals with three types of cone pigment but with one or more of the pigments having a slightly different spectral sensitivity to that found in a normal human observer. Anomalous trichromats have good colour vision but are unable to discriminate all the colours that a normal observer can.

anterior olfactory nucleus (AON)   A sheet of cells just posterior to the olfactory bulb from which centrifugal fibres project to the olfactory bulb.

anteroventral cochlear nucleus   The anteroventral division of the cochlear nucleus.

articulatory suppression   The use of continuous speech to make it impossible to 'sound out' words while reading. Also called concurrent vocalization.

assimilation   The reduction of colour (or brightness) differences, or enhancement of colour similarity, between adjacent surfaces, caused when the surfaces are of particular sizes and arranged in a particular spatial configuration.

asymmetric matching experiment   A technique used in psychophysical experiments in which the observer must compare and judge the perceptual equality of two stimuli that are presented against different backgrounds or in different contexts.

audiogram   An auditory threshold curve. A plot of the minimum stimulus that evokes a response for a range of frequencies.

auditory cortex   The part of the brain that is involved with processing auditory information. Located in the temporal lobe adjacent to a deep groove or convolution in the brain called the lateral (sylvian) fissure.

auditory discrimination   The ability to pick out a sound in a noisy environment and concentrate on that sound while ignoring the background noise. Can also be used to refer to the ability to discern a difference between two sounds.

auditory excitation pattern   The pattern of basilar membrane movement in response to complex sounds; usually plotted as a graph on a frequency scale represented as distance along the basilar membrane against response level in dB.

auditory nerve (cochlear nerve)   The part of the VIIIth cranial nerve that carries information from the auditory system to the brain (via afferent neurons) and from the brain to the auditory system (via efferent neurons).

autocorrelation   The technique used to compare a waveform with a delayed version of itself.

basilar membrane   A membrane that runs the length of the cochlear canal. It separates the scala media from the scala tympani and supports the organ of Corti.

beats   The regular changes in amplitude of a sound that results when two (or more) sine waves of similar frequency are added together.

binocular   Used to describe either a visual structure that processes information from both eyes or a part of the visual field that can be seen through both eyes.

bipolar cell   A nerve cell with two axons extending from opposite sides of the cell body. In the retina these interneurons connect photoreceptors with ganglion cells.

bipolar neurons   Neurons with just two processes.

blind spot   *See* optic disc.

blobs   Areas of striate cortex with high levels of the enzyme cytochrome oxidase, which appear dark when stained for microscopic examination with a substance specific for the enzyme.

blue–yellow ganglion cell   A retinal ganglion cell with a receptive field that responds as if it had received signals of one sign for blue light and the opposite sign for yellow light.

body image   A perception of body shape, position and appearance, largely effected by visual feedback.

body schema   An awareness of where all the body parts are at any one moment; the continuous, subconscious update of our postural model.

bone conduction   The conduction of sound to the inner ear through the temporal bone.

bottom-up   A form of information processing in which the results are determined solely by the nature of the incoming stimulus. Synonymous with data driven, this is the converse of top-down or concept driven.

brainstem vestibular nuclei   Nuclei in the brainstem that receive input from the vestibular labyrinth of the inner ear. Also called simply vestibular nuclei.

brightness   The perceptual correlate of illumination.

Broca's area   The inferior prefrontal cortex of the brain, an area involved in linguistic analysis, specifically auditory word perception and repetition.

Brodmann's areas   The 47 separate zones of the cerebral cortex differentiated by the German neuroscientist Korbinian Brodmann on the basis of their visually distinct appearance.

calcium-activated potassium channels   Special potassium channels in the hair cell which open in response to calcium ion influx thereby allowing potassium ions to leave the cell.

calmodulin   A small regulatory calcium-binding protein found in almost all tissues.

carotenoids   A family of yellow, orange or red pigments manufactured by bacteria, fungi and plants. It contains two sub-groups: carotenes and xanthophylls.

Central Auditory Processing Disorder (CAPD)
The condition in which individuals perform standard hearing tests normally but have difficulty in discriminating sound in noisy environments, such as found in classrooms.

characteristic frequency (CF)   The sound frequency to which a neuron in the auditory system gives the greatest response.

cholesteatoma   A small bag of chronic inflammation that may progressively infect and damage the structures of the middle ear; caused when persistent negative pressure in the middle ear sucks part of the eardrum inwards and the inside-out portion of eardrum traps layers of dead skin which then become infected.

chorda tympani   A branch of the facial nerve (VIIth cranial nerve).

chroma   The degree to which a colour contains hue; equivalent terms are saturation and colourfulness. Vividness and purity are also sometimes used to describe the degree to which a colour differs from being achromatic. It is one of the three attributes used to specify a colour in the Munsell system, the others being hue and value.

chromatic adaptation   The adjustment of visual sensitivity caused by selective exposure to particular wavelengths or bands of wavelengths of light.

chromatic colours   All colours are either chromatic or achromatic. Chromatic colours are those that possess hue.

chromaticity diagram   The CIE chromaticity diagram is a two-dimensional map of colour space where colours of equal luminance are plotted. The chromaticity coordinates are derived from normalized tristimulus values.

chromophore   A group of atoms in a molecule that gives colour to that substance. In the rod and cone visual pigments, 11-*cis*-retinal, which is bound to the protein opsin, is the chromophore and gives the pigment its colour.

CIE system   The CIE system refers to a method of colour specification that was introduced in 1931 by the Commission Internationale de l'Eclairage. It includes the colour-matching functions of the standard observer and definitions of standard illuminants and viewing geometries.

cilium   A cell organelle consisting of a characteristic organization of internal fibres or tubules. In rods and cones the outer and inner segments are connected by a ciliary bridge in which the characteristic organization has lost the central two tubules.

cingulate cortex   A region of cortex on the inward-facing surfaces of the frontal lobes.

circumvallate papillae   Cylindrical structures surrounded by a trough that form a V-shaped line across the back of the tongue. The nine or ten circumvallate papillae together house almost half of the lingual taste buds, and the taste cells are innervated by the glossopharyngeal nerve.

cochlea   A spirally-coiled, tapered bony tube of about two and three-quarter turns located within the inner ear. It contains the receptors essential for hearing.

cochlear amplifier   Outer hair cells, including the motor protein in the outer hair cell membrane, responsible for amplifying the displacements of the basilar membrane in the cochlea.

cochlear implantation   The insertion of a device into the cochlea to induce sound perception. The device is a multi-channel electrode and complex speech-processing algorithms are used to stimulate the auditory nerve directly.

cochlear nerve   *See* auditory nerve.

cochlear nuclear complex   The first stage of the central auditory pathway, located in the brainstem, and which consists of the dorsal cochlear nucleus and the two divisions of the ventral cochlear nucleus.

colour constancy   The phenomenon whereby the apparent colour of an object does not change even though the spectral distribution of the illuminating light, and hence of the reflected light, has changed.

colour contrast   The enhancement of colour differences between adjacent surfaces; typically, the effect caused when one surface induces its opponent colour in an adjacent surface, e.g. when a green background induces a reddish tint in a figure that it encloses.

colourfulness *See* chroma.

colour-matching functions The colour-matching functions result from experiments to determine the amounts of each of three primaries that in an additive mixture produce a match to a monochromatic stimulus, determined experimentally over the range of the visible spectrum. The XYZ colour-matching functions of the CIE system form the basis of modern colorimetry.

colour space A colour space is a two- or three-dimensional map used to plot colour stimuli. The CIE system is a very well known colour space that has many applications in applied colour science.

combinatorial odour code The way in which an odour is coded by a particular pattern, or combination, of olfactory neurons being activated.

complementary (hue) Each hue has a complementary hue, that when the two are mixed additively, results in white or grey. Examples of complementary pairs are blue/yellow and red/cyan.

complex cells A type of cell in the primary visual cortex that responds to an appropriately oriented stimulus anywhere within its receptive field.

compliance Action made in accordance with a request.

concha The deep central portion of the pinna. It has a diameter of 1 to 2 cm.

concurrent vocalization *See* articulatory suppression.

conditioning A procedure for producing behavioural modification.

conductive pathway The pathway that comprises the pinna, the external auditory meatus, the tympanic membrane and the middle ear.

cone pedicles Specialized synaptic terminals of cones consisting of many 'triads'. Each triad is composed of an invagination or infolding of the membrane that is occupied by two horizontal cell processes associated with a synaptic ribbon. Bipolar cells contact the pedicle through invaginating processes below the synaptic ribbon and also at the base of the pedicle.

cones Visual photoreceptors in the retina that respond to normal light levels. In humans there are three spectral classes, with peak sensitivities to short-, medium-, and long-wavelength light conferring trichromatic colour vision.

connectionism A school of thought which proposes that mental processes are implemented in large networks of interconnected neurons (neural nets), where the strengths of the interconnections (synapses) determine the behaviour of the network.

constructive interference Occurs when two waves superpose such that their combined displacements add together in phase. This results in a wave with a larger amplitude than either of the contributing waves.

contrast sensitivity function (CSF) The contrast sensitivity of the eye expressed as a function of spatial frequency.

convergent inputs Inputs received by neurons which have come from various sources (e.g. from both utricle and saccule, or from both canals and otolithic organs). Information from convergent inputs can be rapidly integrated, with a reduced possibility of error from spontaneous or random activity in the organs.

cornea A transparent layer of tissue that forms the front part of the eye, over the iris and lens. The cornea carries out most of the refraction of the light entering the eye, enabling it to be focused on the retina.

covert orienting Internal shift of attention (e.g. as when observing something out of the corner of the eye). *See also* overt orienting.

crista The sensory structure within the ampulla of the semicircular canals. The cristae respond to changes in the rate of movement of the head.

cross-correlation The comparison of two waveforms where one is delayed relative to the other by finding the compensatory delay time necessary to cancel out the original delay. The mechanism proposed to explain our remarkable sensitivity to changes in interaural time difference. The delays required to cancel the ITD are produced by electrical impulses having to travel different distances down an axon. The subsequent firing pattern of coincidence detector neurons provides a place code.

crossmodal Linking across more than one 'modality' (i.e. sensory system), such as vision and hearing.

cupula A gelatinous body in the ampulla of the semicircular canals in which the hair cells of the crista are embedded.

cyclic guanosine monophosphate (cGMP) A cyclic nucleotide that in rods and cones controls the opening of cation channels in the outer segment. A drop in concentration leads to the closure of the channels.

cytoarchitectonics The microscopic study of the distribution of neural cell types and organization within the brain.

dark current The flow of sodium ions into the outer segment that occurs in photoreceptors in the dark. The sodium movement is balanced by an active sodium pump on the inner segment. Light stimulation causes a reduction in the dark current.

delayed inhibition The inhibition of a retinal cell by a receptor cell only after a delay following the initial response to a stimulus. The phenomenon of delayed inhibition is the key to the function of a cell acting as a motion detector.

deoxygenated haemoglobin Haemoglobin is the oxygen-carrying molecule within red blood cells. It is able to transport oxygen around the body because it can exist in two forms, oxygenated and deoxygenated. It is in the latter form when it has 'delivered' its oxygen load to, for example, a region of the brain. Of the two, only deoxygenated haemoglobin has suitable magnetic properties to give a magnetic resonance image.

dermatomes The area of skin whose sensory receptors are modified sensory neurons that lie in one single dorsal root ganglion.

dermis The inside layer of skin separating the epidermis from the underlying muscle, ligaments and bone; composed of connective tissue and elastic fibres floating in a semi-fluid called the ground substance, and containing many different cell types including tactile receptors and a rich blood vascular supply.

descending auditory pathway Descending projections from the auditory cortex to the medial geniculate nucleus, the inferior colliculi and the brainstem auditory nuclei.

destructive interference Occurs when two waves superpose such that their combined displacements add together out of phase. This results in a wave with a smaller amplitude than either of the contributing waves; when they are exactly out of phase, the resultant displacement is zero.

deuteranopia Deuteranopia refers to a form of dichromatic vision where the normal M-cone pigment is absent.

dichotic listening Listening simultaneously to two different messages, delivered by headphones, one message to each ear.

dichromatic vision The colour vision that is experienced by humans with only two classes of cones rather than the usual three. Dichromats are therefore colour-defective observers.

diffuse bipolar (cell) A bipolar cell located away from the fovea whose broad (diffuse) dendritic tree makes contact with from 5 to 14 cones.

dorsal cochlear nucleus The dorsal division of the cochlear nucleus.

dorsal column nuclei The nuclei in the dorsal part of the medulla where the axons of the dorsal columns terminate. The neurons of the dorsal column nuclei relay touch information to the ventrobasal nucleus of the thalamus on the opposite side of the brain.

double-blind clinical trials A protocol whereby neither the subjects nor the practitioners administering the treatment and the scientist analysing the results know which group received which treatment.

double dissociation The situation where two events that are usually causally linked become separate from one another. So event A is usually a necessary precursor of event B but if event A can occur without triggering event B and event B is manifest without event A having occurred, there is a double dissociation.

dual route theory of reading A theory about the process of reading which claims that printed words are analysed by two routes: visual and phonological.

efferent nerve fibre A nerve fibre that carries neural information from the brain to the periphery.

electrophysiology The various techniques used to measure the electrical changes caused by the activity of neurons in the central and peripheral nervous system. An example is electroencephalography, which involves measurement of the currents in the brain using electrodes attached to the scalp.

emotional Stroop test The use of the Stroop effect as a diagnostic test to detect words that have particular emotional significance to the reader.

end-bulb of Held The final terminal made by each Type I cochlear afferent neuron in the anteroventral cochlear nucleus. They ensure rapid and precise transmission of every incoming action potential to the spherical bushy cells.

endocochlear potential The potential of about 80 mV that exists between the endolymph surrounding the stereocilia and the perilymph bathing the basal region of the hair cell.

endogenous A process arising from within, generally implying that it is carried out with conscious intent. *See also* exogenous.

endolymph A watery fluid contained within the membranous labyrinth. It is thought to be secreted by the stria vascularis.

endorphins Naturally secreted substances, chemically like morphine, which produce analgesic effects.

enkephalins Peptides produced in the brain which bind to opiate receptors to block pain transmission; often referred to as neuromodulators.

entorhinal cortex A caudally placed region of the layered cortex also found medial to the rhinal sulcus. This cortical area receives information from association cortical areas of all sensory systems and transmits information to the hippocampal formation.

epidermis The outer layer of skin; formed from epithelial cells and containing few, if any, tactile receptors.

Eustachian tube The small tube that connects the middle ear to the back of the throat (the pharynx). It equalizes the pressure on each side of the tympanic membrane.

event-related potential (ERP) A small voltage change, detected at the scalp, as a result of an event to which neurons have reacted.

excitotoxic The toxicity that excessive amounts of a substance presents to cells. Excessive amounts of glutamate are highly toxic to neurons, known as glutamate excitotoxicity.

exogenous A process triggered from the outside, generally involuntary. *See also* endogenous.

external auditory canal (meatus) The canal that conducts sound vibrations from the pinna to the tympanic membrane.

external ear An alternative name for the outer ear.

exteroceptive Responding to stimuli that are external to the animal.

extraocular muscles Three pairs of muscles attached to the eye which control the rotation of the eye in three planes.

facial nerve (VIIth cranial nerve) Also known as cranial nerve VII, the chorda tympani branch of this nerve innervates the taste buds in the anterior two-thirds of the tongue.

false alarm The detection of an apparent stimulation, which was in fact merely neural noise. *See also* miss.

filiform papillae Thread-like structures that cover the dorsal surface of the tongue; they have no gustatory function.

foliate papillae Flat-topped structures that have deep clefts between them, these papillae are found on the edge of the posterior one-third of the tongue at about the same level as the circumvallate papillae. Their appearance makes them look like leaves of a book (the word 'foliate' means 'leaflike'). Foliate papillae house approximately one-quarter of the lingual taste buds.

formant frequencies In humans, the vocal tract (between the larynx and the lips) resonates at different frequencies so that different parts of the frequency spectrum are amplified. These amplified frequencies are known as formant frequencies. Musical instruments also have formant frequencies, which stay constant regardless of the note being played.

fovea A depression or pit in the centre of the retina containing densely packed cones and no overlying interneurons, which is specialized for high visual resolution.

frequency The number of cycles of a periodic process occurring per unit time. The SI unit of frequency is the hertz (Hz), where $1\,\text{Hz} = 1\,\text{s}^{-1}$.

frontal lobe One of the four lobes of the cerebral cortex situated at the front of the brain. It is associated with motor control and higher mental processes.

functional imaging techniques The use of imaging techniques such as MEG, EEG, PET and fMRI to locate distinct anatomical regions of the brain that perform particular sensory, motor or cognitive functions in response to a carefully controlled stimulus.

functional magnetic resonance imaging (fMRI) This is an indirect functional imaging technique which, in one version, is able to detect local increases in blood flow in activated areas of the brain and display these on a conventional MRI scan.

fundamental frequency The lowest frequency component in a harmonic series.

fungiform papillae   Raised structures on the surface and tip of the tongue that resemble miniature mushrooms. There are about 320 fungiform papillae on a human tongue and they house about a quarter of the lingual taste buds. Taste cells in fungiform papillae are innervated by the chorda tympani branch of the facial nerve.

fusimotor system   The motor system of the muscle spindles.

gamut   The gamut of a colour-reproduction device is the range of colours that can be physically reproduced by that device. Most colour-reproduction devices have a gamut that is no more than 50 per cent of all the possible colours that could be reproduced.

ganglion cell   Nerve cells located in the retina whose axons form the optic nerve, which connects to the lateral geniculate nucleus in the middle of the brain. They receive their inputs from the photoreceptors (rods and cones) via intermediate horizontal, amacrine and bipolar cells.

ganglion cell layer   The layer in the retina where the retinal ganglion cells are located. It is the first layer that incident light meets and is next to the inner plexiform layer.

glabrous (skin)   Hairless skin; one of three skin types, typified by skin on the palms and soles.

glossopharyngeal nerve (IXth cranial nerve)   Otherwise known as cranial nerve IX, this nerve innervates the taste buds in the posterior one-third of the tongue.

glutamate   An amino acid that acts as a neurotransmitter. In the ear, glutamate is released by hair cells at the afferent synapse as a result of depolarization of the hair cell, thereby initiating an action potential in the associated neuron.

glutamate transporter molecules   Proteins which take up extracellular glutamate, terminating its action and making it ready for further activation. The take-up of glutamate prevents it becoming excitotoxic (toxic to neurons).

Grassman's additivity law   Grassman's law states that stimuli of the same colour produce identical effects in mixtures regardless of their spectral composition.

grommet   A tiny plastic or metal ventilation tube inserted into the tympanic membrane to allow air to get from the atmosphere into the middle ear cavity.

guanosine diphosphate (GDP)   A nucleotide that when further phosphorylated becomes a high energy molecule, guanosine triphosphate (similar to ATP). It is involved in the energy-requiring activation of transducin.

guanosine triphosphate (GTP)   A high energy molecule (similar to ATP) that is involved in energy-requiring processes such as the activation of transducin in the visual system.

hair bundles   *See* stereocilia.

hair cells   Sensory receptor cells for hearing and balance. Ciliated epithelial cells located within the organ of Corti (hearing) and the vestibular system (balance). In the organ of Corti there are two types: inner and outer hair cells. The bases of the hair cells are in contact with the dendritic processes of the neurons of the spiral ganglion of the cochlea.

hairy skin   One of three skin types characterized by the presence of hair.

haploscopically   Term used to describe the presentation of two images side-by-side to an observer so that each eye views just one of the images, a technique used in colour matching experiments.

haptics   Active touch.

harmonic frequencies   Frequencies that are whole number multiples of the fundamental frequency.

hearing threshold   The quietest sound that an individual can hear in a soundproofed environment.

hedonics   The branch of psychology that deals with pleasurable and unpleasurable states of consciousness.

helicotrema   A narrow aperture within the apex of the cochlea that allows communication between the scala vestibuli and the scala tympani.

Heschl's gyrus   An area of the auditory cortex running transversely across the supratemporal plane; the primary auditory cortex is located here and virtually all simple and complex sounds produce activation of this area.

higher-level cognitive functions   The more complex 'thinking' processes of the brain.

homophone   A word with the same pronunciation as another, but with different spelling.

horizontal cell   A nerve cell whose fibres extend laterally (horizontally), located in the outer plexiform layer. They are involved in lateral inhibition.

hue　The quality of a colour that determines whether it is red, green, blue, etc. It is one of the three attributes used to specify a colour in the Munsell system, the others being chroma and value.

hyperalgesia　An increase in sensitivity to pain experienced in response to a given stimulus.

hypercolumn　The set of cells in the primary visual cortex that processes one small region of the retinal image.

hypercomplex cells　A type of cell in the primary visual cortex with a receptive field similar to a complex cell, but that responds only if an appropriately oriented stimulus ends somewhere within the receptive field.

hyperopia　A defect of vision commonly known as long-sightedness in which the near point of the eye is considerably further away than normal. The eyeball is too short, or the refracting power of the eye is too weak to focus on near objects, and light from an object located at the normal near point would be focused behind the retina. Long-sightedness is also known as hypermetropia.

hyperpolarization　An increase in the potential difference (voltage) across the cell membrane making the interior of the cell more negative than at rest. Rods and cones hyperpolarize on activation.

hypnotic induction　The process of inducing hypnosis.

hypnotic susceptibility scale　A series of tests, graded in difficulty, administered to a hypnotized individual, to determine the level of hypnosis that has been achieved.

hysterical paralysis　A condition in which sufferers are unable to move a body part in spite of there being no identifiable physical problem.

ideogram　A symbol (as opposed to a printed word) that represents an object or concept.

incus　The central member of the three auditory ossicles which are located in the middle ear. The body of the incus is attached to the head of the malleus and the rounded projection at the lower end of the incus is attached to the head of the stapes.

inferior cerebellar peduncle　A large fibre tract connecting the cerebellum to the brainstem.

inferior colliculi　Nuclei in the midbrain from which all ascending auditory signals project to the medial geniculate nucleus. The inferior colliculi are involved with hearing and pair up with the superior colliculi, which are involved with vision.

inferior nucleus　One of the four vestibular nuclei, it is located in the rostral medulla and contains small to medium-sized neurons.

inferior turbinate　One of the three structures that arise from the wall of the nasal cavity, the function of which is to create turbulent air flow and to clean, moisten and warm the inhaled air. The inferior turbinate is the lowest and largest of the three turbinates.

inner ear　Part of the ear that consists of the cochlea and vestibular system.

inner hair cells　*See* hair cells.

inner nuclear layer　A layer in the retina consisting of the cell bodies of bipolar, horizontal and amacrine cells.

inner plexiform layer　A layer in the retina composed of the synaptic connections of bipolar, ganglion and amacrine cells.

intensity　The sound power transmitted through a given area in a sound field. It is expressed in watts per square metre. The term is also used as a generic name for any quantity relating to the amount of sound, such as power or energy, although this is not technically correct.

interaural intensity difference　*See* interaural level difference.

interaural level difference (ILD)　The difference in intensity of sound at the two ears.

interaural time delay　*See* interaural time difference.

interaural time difference (ITD)　The time difference between a sound reaching one ear and then the other ear.

intercalated (I) layer　One of the set of layers lying between the P and M layers of the LGN, also called koniocellular (K) layers. They contain a morphologically and physiologically distinct class of neurons.

interneuron　Nerve cell connecting two or more other neurons. In the retina these link photoreceptors with ganglion cells.

invagination　The pocket or pockets at the base of rods and cones (synaptic region) that partially enclose the processes of horizontal and bipolar cells.

iris　The adjustable diaphragm in the human eye, located just in front of the crystalline lens, which gives the eye its characteristic colour. The hole at the centre of the iris, through which light enters the eye, is the pupil.

isofrequency layers Layers in the central nucleus of the inferior colliculus, made up of bands of cells with flattened dendrite fields in which the neurons are tuned to the same frequency. High-frequency layers are found towards the mid-line, low-frequency layers towards the outside.

kinesthetic The type of information provided about the movement of body parts.

koniocellular (K) layer *See* intercalated (I) layer.

labelled-line theory The theory that independent taste channels extend from receptor to cortex.

laser in-situ keratomileusis (LASIK) A surgical technique used to effect a refractive correction to the eye. A thin flap of cornea is lifted and some of the central stroma is removed with a laser such that when the flap is replaced, the corneal shape is changed.

lateral fissure The pronounced groove on the surface of the brain that separates the frontal lobe from the temporal lobe. Also called the sylvian fissure.

lateral geniculate nucleus (LGN) One of a pair of nuclei in the thalamus to which retinal ganglion cells project and which relays visual information to the primary visual cortex.

lateral inhibition The output neurons of the retina (ganglion cells) are connected to the photoreceptors (rods and cones) by interneurons (horizontal, bipolar and amacrine cells). The connections are such that each ganglion cell receives two types of information: excitatory from a particular photoreceptor and inhibitory from adjacent receptors. This latter effect is lateral inhibition.

lateral lemniscus A prominent neural tract that carries axons (a lemniscus is a collection of axons) of the superior olivary nucleus to the inferior colliculus of the midbrain.

lateral nucleus One of the four vestibular nuclei, it is located in the medulla and contains mainly large multipolar neurons.

lateral olfactory tract The nerve formed by the bundle of axons projecting from the mitral cells. The tract projects primarily to the pyriform cortex and also to the anterior olfactory nuclei, the olfactory tubercule, the entorhinal cortex and the amygdala.

lexical decision task The task of deciding whether a string of letters is a correctly spelled word or not.

lexical entry An entry (i.e. a word) in the lexicon.

lexicon The mental store of words known to the user, presumed to contain meanings, pronunciations and spellings.

LGN *See* lateral geniculate nucleus.

linear acceleration A change in speed along a straight line; e.g. the rise and fall (i.e. a vertical straight line) of the head, when a person is running.

lingual gyrus Region of cortex on the ventral surface of the brain, hidden by the cerebellum; part of the primary visual cortex.

lipid bilayer Lipids (e.g. phosphoglycerides) have a polar head and a hydrophobic tail. In an aqueous medium they form a bilayer with their hydrophobic tails inside and their hydrophilic polar heads pointing outwards. A lipid bilayer constitutes the basic structure of biological cell membranes.

low-level visual attributes Simple visual features that can be processed in early visual areas. One example is the detection of edges in a visual scene.

lysine A naturally occurring amino acid with a side chain containing an amino group ($-NH_2$). 11-*cis*-retinal attaches to opsin in rhodopsin and iodopsin by linking with the side chain amino group of a lysine residue.

M cell *See* parasol ganglion cell.

McGurk effect The misperception of a spoken sound, resulting from listening to one speech sound while watching a speaker's lips forming a different sound.

macula A sensory epithelium found in the otolithic organs (saccule and utricle) of the inner ear.

macula lutea A 3–4 mm diameter central region of the retina, including the fovea and often referred to as the yellow spot, which contains a yellow screening pigment consisting of a mixture of carotenoids.

magnetoencephalography (MEG) This is a direct functional imaging technique that is able to detect, and locate, the very weak magnetic fields associated with the electrical currents caused by neuronal activity.

magnocellular (M) layers The two lower or ventral layers of the six main layers of the LGN, composed of neurons with larger cell bodies than those in the four dorsal layers. This region receives input from the retina primarily from parasol ganglion cells (M cells). The term is also used to describe the retinal ganglion cells that project to the magnocellular layers of the LGN.

malleus   The outermost of the three auditory ossicles that are located in the middle ear. The handle of the malleus is attached to the tympanic membrane and the head is attached to the body of the incus.

meatus   *See* external auditory canal.

mechanical spectrum analyser   The function of the basilar membrane. The mechanics of the basilar membrane are such that different frequencies excite hair cells in different areas of the membrane, with high frequencies at the base and low frequencies at the apex.

mechano-electrical transduction   The conversion of a mechanical stimulus (movement of the stereocilia) into an electrical signal (the receptor potential).

mechanoreceptor   A sensory receptor cell activated by mechanical forces such as pressure. They are involved in hearing, balance and touch sensations.

mechanosensitive ion channels   Channels in the hair cells which are activated by movement of the stereocilia, allowing entry of positively-charged ions which depolarize the cells.

medial geniculate nucleus   A relay nucleus in the thalamus through which all auditory information passes on its way from the inferior colliculus to the auditory cortex.

medial longitudinal fasciculus   A complex of connections among the nuclei of the cranial nerves that control movement of the eyes (the oculomotor, trochlear and abducens nerves).

medial nucleus   One of the four vestibular nuclei, it is located in the rostral medulla and contains small to medium-sized neurons.

medial turbinate   One of the three structures that arise from the nasal wall, the function of which is to create turbulent air flow and to clean, moisten and warm the inhaled air. The medial turbinate is a bony projection of the ethmoid bone, is the second largest of the three turbinates and lies between the inferior and superior turbinates.

Meissner's corpuscle   A type of cutaneous sensory receptor cell (found in glabrous skin) that responds to light touch and vibration.

membranous labyrinth   A membranous compartment inside the bony labyrinth of the inner ear, surrounded by an outer membrane sheath.

Menières disease   A disorder of the inner ear characterized by episodes of hearing loss, tinnitus and vertigo.

Merkel cells   *See* Merkel's disc.

Merkel's disc   A type of cutaneous sensory receptor cell that responds to light touch and pressure.

middle ear   The air-filled chamber within the mastoid portion of the temporal bone, which contains the three auditory ossicles.

middle ear reflex   The spontaneous contraction of the muscles in the middle ear in response to the sudden onset of a loud sound.

midget bipolar cell   A bipolar cell in the central retina (fovea) that receives input from one cone (or occasionally two) and connects with a single midget ganglion cell.

midget ganglion cell   Ganglion cell (P cell) identified in the foveal part of the retina. It receives input from one cone photoreceptor (or occasionally two) through a single midget bipolar cell. Their axons connect to the parvocellular layers of the LGN.

miss   Failure consciously to detect a stimulus, when the resultant level of neural activity is insufficient to exceed an internally-set criterion. *See also* false alarm.

modality-appropriateness   The tendency of one modality (sense) to exert more influence than other modalities, in situations where the favoured sense is likely to convey more accurate information.

modiolus   The conically-shaped central core of the cochlea. It contains the spiral ganglion of the cochlea and forms the inner wall of the scala vestibuli and scala tympani.

monoaminergic pathways   Neuronal pathways that use monoamines (e.g. serotonin and noradrenalin) as neurotransmitters.

monochromats   Individuals who possess only one class of cone photoreceptor and cannot perform any colour discrimination. They perceive the world only in shades of grey. Monochromats are extremely rare in the human population.

motion sickness   A phenomenon in which the brain detects inconsistencies between vision and vestibular systems and this provokes a pattern of symptoms that include lethargy, light-headedness, sweating, nausea and vomiting.

mucocutaneous skin   One of three skin types; it is mucus producing and lines the entrances to the body.

multipolar cells   *See* stellate cells.

Munsell colour-order system   The Munsell colour-order system describes a collection of coloured chips or patches that are arranged in a three-dimensional manner and used for colour communication. This system was designed by the artist Albert Munsell.

muscle receptors   *See* muscle spindles.

muscle spindles   Proprioceptors in the form of specialized muscle fibres connected in parallel to the ordinary muscle fibres; sensitive to stretch.

myopia   A defect of vision commonly known as short-sightedness in which the far point of the eye is considerably closer than normal. The eyeball is too long, or the refracting power of the eye is too great to focus on distant objects, and light from such an object would be focused in front of the retina.

nares   Another name for the nostrils.

nasal   The half of the retina that is closer to the nose.

neural network   A network of neurons, or more often a computer representation of such a network, implemented to test connectionist ideas. *See also* connectionism.

neural noise   The random element of neural firing, which may be exhibited as firing in the absence of a signal, or variations in firing rate which are not correlated with signal intensity. This gives rise to misses and false alarms.

neurite   An axon or dendrite. This is a term (like fibre) that can be used for any neuronal process. It is especially useful when it is not clear whether the process is an axon or dendrite.

neuropathic pain   *See* neuropathy.

neuropathy   Damage to nerves or abnormal activity in the nervous system.

neuropsychology   The branch of psychology that seeks to deduce how the normal brain functions by observing the nature and degree of dysfunction in brain-damaged patients.

neurotransmitter   A chemical messenger released at a synapse by a presynaptic nerve terminal that interacts with receptor molecules on the postsynaptic membrane. In the case of rods and cones, for example, this is glutamate (an amino acid).

nociceptor   Mechanical, thermal or chemical receptor involved in the detection of harmful stimuli.

Obscure Auditory Dysfunction (OAD)   *See* Central Auditory Processing Disorder (CAPD).

occipital lobe   One of the four lobes of the cerebral cortex situated at the rear of the brain. It is responsible for visual processing.

octopus cells   Neurons with thick dendrites and axons which are found in the ventral cochlear nucleus, and which only respond to the onset of a signal.

oculomotor nuclei   Nuclei found in the brainstem, which are involved in the vestibulo-ocular reflex.

odorant binding proteins (OBPs)   Proteins present in the mucus surrounding the cilia of olfactory neurons that can bind to odorant molecules. They are thought to act as carriers for odorants, transporting what are essentially hydrophobic molecules through a hydrophilic medium to the olfactory neurons.

OFF-centre   Cells, such as bipolar and ganglion cells in the retina, whose receptive field centres are inhibited by stimulation.

olfactory mucus   The secretion that coats the olfactory epithelium, containing mucopolysaccharides, immunoglobulins, enzymes and other proteins.

olfactory receptor gene   The sequence of chromosomal DNA that codes for an olfactory receptor protein. There are about one thousand olfactory receptor genes in the human genome, of which about a third are functional – that is, the corresponding olfactory receptor is actually synthesised.

olfactory tubercule   A structure, otherwise called the anterior perforated substance, found at the base of the olfactory tract.

olivocochlear bundle   Efferent nerve fibres carried by the cochlear nerve from the brainstem to the cochlea. The fibres come from nerve cells around the outside of the superior olivary complex.

ON-centre   Cells, such as bipolar and ganglion cells in the retina, whose receptive field centres are excited by stimulation.

operant conditioning   A form of conditioning whereby the experimenter uses reinforcement or punishment to select, strengthen or weaken a behaviour pattern shown spontaneously.

opponent processing   Opponent processing refers to the fact that the visual system combines the responses of the L, M and S cones to generate three new signals that encode luminance, redness–greenness, and yellowness–blueness.

opsin   The protein part of a visual pigment molecule consisting of a chain of about 350 amino acid residues.

optic chiasm   The point in the visual pathway where the two optic nerves meet and half the fibres in each optic nerve cross over to the other side of the brain. This ensures that the images of the same object in the left and right eyes are processed in the same hemisphere.

optic disc   The area in each eye, commonly called the blind spot, where the axons of the retinal ganglion cells forming the optic nerve come together and leave the eye. There are no photoreceptors in this area.

optic nerve   The nerve that carries all the visual signals from the retina to the lateral geniculate nucleus in the brain. It consists of the axons of retinal ganglion cells, of which there about 1 000 000.

optic radiation   Pathway carrying visual signals from the lateral geniculate nucleus to the primary visual cortex.

optic tract   Formed from half the fibres in each optic nerve, each optic tract carries all the visual information relating to the opposite (contralateral) side of the visual field. Nerve fibres from the nasal side of the retina of each eye cross over to join fibres from the temporal side of the retina of the opposite eye.

organ of Corti   The auditory receptor organ, which contains a series of neuro-epithelial hair cells (receptor cells for hearing) and their supporting structures lying on top of the basilar membrane and beneath the tectorial membrane. It is located within the scala media of the cochlea and extends from the base of the cochlea to the apex.

ossicles   The three small bones found in the middle ear.

otitis media with effusion   A condition arising when the Eustachian tube malfunctions and causes the middle ear to fill up with fluid that is produced by the lining of the cavity itself. (If the fluid is thick and viscid, the condition is given the colloquial name 'glue ear'.) Otitis media with effusion is the commonest cause of conductive hearing loss in the UK.

otoacoustic emissions   Small amounts of sound emitted by the ears in response to sound input and used as the basis of a hearing test for neonates.

otolithic membrane   A delicate acellular structure covering the macula.

otolithic organs   The saccule and the utricle of the inner ear which detect the force of gravity and linear acceleration.

otoliths   Calcium carbonate crystals which cover the surface of the otolithic membrane.

otosclerosis   A condition resulting from the formation of new bone around the footplate of the stapes that fuses the bone rigidly with the bone of the inner ear. This reduces the ear's ability to conduct sound from the ossicular chain to the sensory receptors of the cochlea.

outer ear   Consists of the pinna, the external auditory canal (meatus), and the tympanum (eardrum).

outer hair cells   *See* hair cells.

outer nuclear layer   A layer of the retina consisting of the cell bodies of rods and cones.

outer plexiform layer   A layer of the retina composed of the synaptic connections of rods and cones with bipolar and horizontal cells.

outer spiral fibres   Dendrites of Type II ganglion cells which contact the outer hair cells. Each outer spiral fibre contacts up to ten outer hair cells.

oval window   An opening through the bone that separates the middle ear from the scala vestibuli of the cochlea. It is closed by a membrane to which is connected the footplate of the stapes.

overt orienting   Shift of attention by movement of receptors (e.g. as in eye, head or hand movements). *See also* covert orienting.

P cell   See midget ganglion cell.

Pacinian corpuscle   A type of cutaneous receptor cell that responds to heavy pressure and vibration.

parasol ganglion cell   Ganglion cell (M cell) with a relatively large dendritic field connecting to a relatively large number of diffuse bipolar cells. Their axons connect to the magnocellular layers of the lateral geniculate nucleus.

parietal cortex   The outer cortical layer of the parietal lobes; involved in specialized spatial processing and activated by sounds containing spatial and motion cues.

parietal lobe   Region of the brain lying like a saddle across the top, forward of the occipital region, but behind the frontal lobes.

parvocellular (P) layers   The four upper or dorsal layers of the six main layers of the lateral geniculate nucleus, composed of neurons with relatively small cell bodies. This region receives input from the retina primarily from midget ganglion cells (P cells). The term is also used to describe the retinal ganglion cells that project to the parvocellular layers of the LGN.

passive touch   Being touched.

pattern theory   The theory that taste neurons do not carry exclusive information but cooperate with other neurons in the pathway to provide a pattern of activity.

pentachromats   Pentachromats are creatures whose colour vision is based upon five basic types of receptor. Some pigeons and ducks are pentachromats.

perfect pitch (absolute pitch)   The ability to recognize the pitch of a note in isolation, without an external reference.

periaqueductal gray (PAG)   The region of grey matter in the brainstem that surrounds the cerebral aqueduct of the midbrain.

perilymph   The fluid that fills the scala vestibuli and scala tympani in the cochlea in the inner ear, containing low K^+ and high Na^+ concentrations.

peripheral auditory system   The sound processing components consisting of the outer, middle and inner ear, and the auditory nerve.

peripheral neuropathy   A clinical condition where the sensory afferent fibres have been damaged or destroyed.

phagocytosis   The uptake by a cell of particles or cells into cytoplasmic vacuoles.

phantom limb pain   The perception of pain from a part of the body that does not exist (usually from a limb that has been amputated).

phase ambiguity   Caused when the wavelength of a sound is shorter than the distance between the ears (i.e. high frequencies). Differences in the time at which the same phase of a sound wave reaches each ear can no longer be resolved by the auditory system.

phase locking   The consistent firing of an auditory neuron at the same phase of a sound wave.

phoneme   A unit of speech sound, corresponding approximately with the sound represented by one letter.

phonological dyslexia   A form of dyslexia that renders a patient unable to derive the pronunciations of words (or nonwords) from their spelling, although words can potentially be recognized via the visual route.

phonological route   An information processing pathway that accesses a word's meaning by first deriving its pronunciation from the spelling.

phosphodiesterase (PDE)   A cytoplasmic enzyme that hydrolyses (degrades) a cyclic nucleotide. In visual transduction PDE hydrolyses cyclic guanosine monophosphate (cGMP) to guanosine monophosphate.

photopic   The type of vision that occurs when the level of illumination is high, which is usually mediated by cones. In humans, photopic vision is trichromatic because of the three spectral classes of cone.

photopigments   The light-sensitive pigments found in the retina of humans and other animals. The human retina contains two main classes of photopigment: rhodopsin (in rods) and iodopsin (in cones).

photoreceptors   Sensory cells specialized for the detection of light. The principal photoreceptors of the retina are rods and cones.

photorefractive keratectomy (PRK)   A surgical technique whereby the surface of the corneal stroma is reshaped using a laser to effect a change in the refractive power of the cornea.

pinna   The pinna is the most visible part of the ear. It is a fibrocartilaginous plate that is attached to the head and is useful in the localization of sounds in both the front–back and in the vertical dimensions.

pitch   The psychological attribute of sound most closely associated with the frequency of the sound.

place principle   The idea that the frequency of a tone is signalled by the particular cochlear location that is maximally stimulated.

planum temporale   An area of the auditory cortex, lateral to Heschl's gyrus, involved in movement processing.

polyene chain   A carbon chain consisting of alternating single and double bonds.

polypeptide   A linked sequence of amino acids, the units that form the basic building blocks of all proteins.

population code   The way that certain visual stimulus attributes (e.g. orientation) are encoded not by individual cortical cells but by the pattern of activity across a whole ensemble or population.

positron emission tomography (PET)   An indirect functional imaging technique in which functionally-induced changes in brain metabolism are monitored by the preferential take up of a radioactive isotope that decays by positron emission.

posteroventral cochlear nucleus   The posteroventral division of the cochlear nucleus.

prepyriform cortex   A small nucleus adjacent to the pyriform cortex with axons projecting into the pyriform area and amygdala. The area is part of the olfactory pathway and is known to show a high degree of electrophysiological coherence with the olfactory bulb. Recent evidence suggests that activity from this nucleus may project back to the bulb.

presbyacusis   The hearing loss associated with a decrease in cochlear sensitivity with age.

primaries   A primary is a component of an additive or subtractive colour mixing system. The commonly used additive primaries are red, green and blue (RGB), but for precise colour specification, the CIE XYZ colour-matching functions derived from the RGB primaries are used instead. The subtractive primaries are cyan, magenta and yellow.

primary auditory cortex (A1)   Located in the lateral fissure, along the upper surface of the temporal lobe, the primary auditory cortex is surrounded by the secondary auditory cortex, which is subdivided into six distinct areas.

primary gustatory cortex   The area of cortex responsible for the conscious perception of taste (Brodmann's area 43).

primary somatosensory cortex (S1)   The topographically organized area of the cerebral cortex that receives and processes sensory information from the body's surface.

primary visual cortex   The part of the cortex that receives the most direct projection of visual information from the eyes via the lateral geniculate nucleus; it is also called the striate cortex, area 17, and (in primates only) V1.

priming   The activation by the breathing cycle of brain regions that process olfactory information.

primitive grouping mechanisms   The way in which the listener uses generally useful unlearned cues to separate sound into different sources.

principle of univariance   Absorption of a quantum of short wavelength (e.g. 400 nm) light by a photoreceptor causes the same qualitative response as the absorption of a quantum of long wavelength (e.g. 700 nm) light despite the fact that the former is of higher energy. Consequently, any single photopigment does not encode any information about the relative spectral composition of the light, only its rate of absorption.

proprioception   The sense that provides information about the position and movement of individual body parts.

proprioceptor   *See* proprioception.

protanopia   A form of dichromatic vision where the normal L-cone pigment is absent.

Proust effect   The phenomenon occurring when an odour prompts an emotional recollection of a personal memory.

pseudohomophone   A nonword, with pronunciation identical to that of a real word (e.g. brane).

psychometric function   A plot of response versus the intensity of a stimulus.

pupil   The circular opening in the centre of the iris, the size of which regulates the amount of light that reaches the retina. In a typical human eye, the pupil diameter can vary from about 2 mm (in bright light conditions) to about 8 mm.

pyriform cortex   The rostral region of the layered cortex that is curled up rostrally and medially in the parahippocampal gyrus. This is the primary olfactory cortex, one of three regions (the other two being the anterior olfactory nucleus and the olfactory tubercule) where the axons of the olfactory tract terminate.

radial fibres   Dendrites of Type I ganglion cells, which contact the inner hair cells. Each inner hair cell synapses with up to twenty radial fibres.

ramp-and-hold stimulus   An applied stimulus, the magnitude of which is increased from zero to some maximum value, and then held at that level.

Rayleigh scattering   Scattering of light from particles very much smaller than its wavelength (e.g. molecules). The scattering intensity is proportional to the fourth power of the frequency, so blue light scatters about ten times as much as red light. This accounts for the blue colour of the sky and the red colour of sunsets.

reality monitoring   The normal process underlying conscious awareness of the surroundings, in which current interpretations of sensory input are continually re-checked by further stimulus sampling.

receptive field   A fundamental property of sensory neurons; the region of sensory space which, when stimulated, evokes a response from the neuron. In the visual system, the area of visual space within which patterns of light will elicit a response.

receptor potential   A stimulus-induced change in the membrane potential of a sensory receptor.

referred (pain)   The type of pain experienced when the location of the pain is not at the site of the actual injury or pathology.

refractive index   The refractive index of a medium is the ratio of the speed of light in a vacuum to the speed of light in the medium. Refractive index varies with wavelength and is always greater than one.

refractive power   The ability of a curved surface to refract light. It can be calculated using the equation $P = (n_2 - n_1)/r$ where P is the refractive power in dioptres, n_1 and n_2 are the refractive indices of the first and second media, and r is the radius of curvature of the surface (in metres).

resonant frequency   The value of the frequency of an oscillation that creates the condition of resonance in which the amplitude is a maximum.

reticular formation   Part of the midbrain containing interconnected networks of neurons associated with control of alertness and receiving inputs from several sensory systems.

retina   The neural layer lining the back of the eye, specialized for the detection and transduction of light. Neural information from the retina is transmitted to the brain via the optic nerve.

retinal   The aldehyde derived from vitamin A (retinol) which combines with opsin to form a visual pigment.

11-*cis*-retinal   The substance that, when attached to one of the opsin proteins, forms one of the four types of visual pigment molecules in rods and cones. It is formed by a series of transformations from vitamin A.

retinal pigment epithelium (RPE)   Black pigmented layer lining the back of the eye behind the retina. The cells of the RPE interdigitate with the rods and cones and serve a number of functions including the absorption of stray light, the photoisomerization of retinal and the phagocytosis of the tips of the photoreceptor outer segments.

retinotopic flatmap   Retinotopic data obtained from imaging the visual cortex (using fMRI, for example) can be difficult to interpret. This difficulty arises because the grey matter of the cortex is a two-dimensional sheet which is folded in a highly convoluted way. Using software, this can be unfolded to form what is known as a 'flatmap', making it much easier to interpret retinotopic data.

retinotopic mapping   Determining the boundaries of the visual areas by systematically and sequentially stimulating the different parts of the visual field while imaging the brain using fMRI.

retinotopic organization   *See* visuotopic representation.

retinotopic representation   *See* visuotopic representation.

retrocochlear   Relating to the neural pathway beyond the cochlea, the auditory nerve.

rhodopsin   The visual pigment of rods consisting of a protein, opsin, to which is attached a molecule of 11-*cis*-retinal. Opsin is a member of the 7-transmembrane family, so called because the protein chain traverses the lipid bilayer of the membrane seven times. The 11-*cis*-retinal portion is the chromophore of rhodopsin.

rods   Highly sensitive visual photoreceptors specialized for the type of vision that occurs in dim light (scotopic or 'night vision'). In humans there is one spectral class so that rod vision is monochromatic.

rod spherule   Specialized synaptic terminal of rods composed of an invagination or infolding of the membrane that is occupied by the processes of two horizontal cells and two or more rod bipolar cells associated with a synaptic ribbon.

round window   An opening through the bone that separates the middle ear from the scala tympani of the cochlea. It is located behind and below the oval window and is closed by the round window membrane.

Ruffini ending   A type of cutaneous sensory receptor cell that responds to self-imposed skin stretching such as that caused by moving limbs or digits.

saccades   Brief rapid movements of the eye between fixation points.

saccule   One of the two otolithic organs located in the inner ear; it detects changes in head angle and linear acceleration.

sapid   Having a perceptible taste or flavour, not insipid.

saturation   *See* chroma.

scala media   The cavity of the cochlear duct filled with endolymph and also containing the tectorial membrane. The scala media is separated from the scala vestibuli by Reissner's membrane and from the scala tympani by the basilar membrane. The scala media has a closed end at the cochlear apex.

scala tympani   The perilymph-filled passage of the cochlear canal that extends from the round window at the base to the helicotrema at the apex. It is separated from the scala media by the basilar membrane and the cellular structures attached to it.

scala vestibuli   The perilymph-filled passage of the cochlear canal that extends from the oval window at the base to the helicotrema at the apex.

Scarpa's ganglion   Also known as the vestibular ganglion. It consists of the cell bodies of the vestibular neurons which leave the hair cells of the vestibular labyrinth and travel to the vestibular nuclei in the brainstem.

schema-based mechanisms   The way in which the listener uses detailed knowledge about what specific sounds are like to select a relevant subset of the total sound.

sclera   Colloquially called the 'white' of the eye, the sclera forms most of the outer coat of the eyeball. Its function is to protect the internal contents and maintain the shape of the eyeball.

scotopic   The type of vision that occurs in dim light ('night vision'), which is mediated by rods. Since there is only one spectral class of rod photoreceptors, scotopic vision is monochromatic.

secretory otitis media   *See* otitis media with effusion.

semicircular canals   Part of the inner ear. They detect turning movements of the head (angular acceleration).

signal detection   The discrimination of one signal of interest from a number of other signals. It is believed that the descending auditory pathway plays a role in this.

signal detection theory (SDT)   The theory which accounts for hits and misses in terms of neural noise and the setting of an internal threshold or criterion.

simple cells   A type of cell in the primary visual cortex with a receptive field that responds to a stimulus at a specific position with an appropriate orientation.

sine-wave grating   A grating whose intensity varies from white to black in the form of a sine wave. The rate of change is determined by the spatial frequency.

sine-wave speech   A transformation of natural speech that consists of three (frequency-modulated) sine waves on which the speech frequencies are superimposed.

somatosensation   The bodily or general senses of touch, pain, temperature, proprioception and kinesthesis.

somatosensory cortex   The topographically organized area of the cerebral cortex that receives and processes sensory information from the body's surface (Brodmann's areas 3a, 3b, 1 and 2).

sound pressure level (SPL)   The ratio (in decibels) of the pressure of a sound wave to the reference pressure of $20\,\mu Pa$. $20\,\mu Pa$ is the average minimum pressure the human ear can detect. The corresponding value for intensity is the ratio (in decibels) of the intensity of a sound wave to the reference intensity of $10^{-12}\,W\,m^{-2}$.

source attribution error   A mistake in identifying the source of a piece of information, as when a hypnotized person is taken through an imagined experience, which they subsequently believe to have happened in reality.

spatial antagonism   The phenomenon that the firing of one cell in the human visual system can be inhibited by the firing of a neighbouring cell.

spectral antagonism   The phenomenon that the responses of cells responding primarily to one part of the visible spectrum can be combined with opposite sign with the responses of cells responding to another part of the visible spectrum. This phenomenon results in opponent processing.

spectral power distribution   The amount of light emitted by a source expressed as a function of wavelength.

spectral reflectance   The property of a surface that gives rise to its colour, this is the fraction of light reflected as a function of wavelength in the visible spectrum.

specular reflection   Mirror-like reflection from shiny surfaces. The opposite of diffuse reflection (from matt surfaces), where the light is reflected in all directions evenly.

spelling-to-sound correspondence rules The phonetic rules that govern the relationship between individual letters or small groups of letters and their sound when pronounced. Words that conform to these rules are called regular, and those that do not are termed irregular.

spherical bushy cells Found in the ventral cochlear nuclei and so named because each has a single, stout, modestly-branched primary dendrite that is adorned with numerous fine branchlets. Electrical stimulation of a bushy cell characteristically elicits only one action potential. They provide information about the timing of acoustical stimuli. Also called simply bushy cells.

spinothalamic tract (STT) The neural pathway followed by axons through the spinal cord to the level of the thalamus and beyond.

spiral (cochlear) ganglion Located within the modiolus, it is composed of cell bodies of the neurons of the cochlear nerve. The dendritic processes of these bipolar neurons make synaptic contact with the hair cells. The axons terminate in the cochlear nucleus in the medulla.

stapedius muscle The intra-aural muscle attached to the neck of the stapes. Its reflex response to an intense sound stimulus is to swing the footplate of the stapes outwards and backwards from the oval window. The joint action of the stapedius muscle and the tensor tympani muscle is to limit the motion of the auditory ossicles and thereby help protect the inner ear from damage by intense sound, especially at low frequencies.

stapes The innermost and smallest of the three auditory ossicles which are located in the middle ear. Its shape resembles a stirrup. The head of the stapes is attached to the incus, and the footplate nearly fills the oval window to which it is attached by the annular ligament.

stellate cells Found in the ventral cochlear nuclei, stellate cells have many symmetrical dendrites and respond to a stimulus with a train of regularly-spaced action potentials. They encode frequencies present in a given auditory input.

stereocilia A bundle of hair-like processes attached to the top of the hair cells of the inner ear. Each stereocilium is a rigid cylinder consisting of actin filaments cross-linked to the protein fibrin.

stimulus frequency (principle) The most distinctive organizing principle in the auditory pathway. The component frequencies associated with each auditory stimulus stimulate specific areas of the basilar membrane.

Each auditory nucleus has a tonotopic organization, replicating the progressive change in frequency that occurs along the length of the basilar membrane.

stratum corneum The relatively hard surface of the skin formed by a layer of dead epithelial cells.

stria vascularis An epithelium located on the lateral wall of the cochlear duct which transports endolymph to the scala media.

striate cortex An alternative name for the primary visual cortex, derived from the characteristically striped appearance when examined microscopically.

striola A curved zone in the maculae of the utricle and saccule which contains a large proportion of small hair bundles. It delineates the reversal in orientation of the hair cells of the maculae.

stroma The corneal stroma is the central layer and the main framework of the cornea, which gives the tissue its strength and rigidity.

Stroop effect The effect of confusion, and hence slowness, which occurs when a person attempts rapidly to name the ink colours used to print incompatible colour words (e.g. the word 'blue' printed in red ink).

structural imaging techniques Techniques such as CT and MRI that provide high resolution images of the internal structure of the body, particularly the brain. These techniques have important clinical applications, for example in the detection of tumours and other abnormalities.

substantia gelatinosa (SG) A region of the dorsal horn of the spinal cord (also known as Rexed's lamina II). There are many interneurons that are believed to be important in modulating pain sensations in this area.

subtractive colour mixing Subtractive colour mixing describes the process by which dyes and pigments are physically mixed together to generate a subtractive mixture colour. Examples of subtractive colour mixing can be seen in paint systems and most printers.

summating potential The sustained depolarization of hair cells caused by a sound stimulus at frequencies above 1000 Hz.

superior colliculi The front pair of four bumps located on the dorsal surface of the midbrain. The superior colliculi are involved with vision; the rear pair, the inferior colliculi, are involved with hearing. Region of the midbrain specialized for multisensory integration, in particular the shifting of attention, such as reflexive eye and head movements.

superior nucleus   One of the four vestibular nuclei, it is located in the caudal pons and contains small to medium-sized neurons.

superior olivary complex   The first place in the ascending auditory pathway where information from both ears is combined. It is mainly involved with sound localization.

superior temporal gyrus   The area within the temporal lobe containing the auditory cortex. This region is one of the most highly folded areas of the human brain; gyrus (pl. gyri) is the name given to the crests.

superior temporal sulcus   The area within the temporal lobe associated with higher-level processing of acoustic information. This region is one of the most highly folded areas of the human brain; sulcus (pl. sulci) is the name given to the valleys.

superior turbinate   One of the three structures that arise from the lateral wall of the nasal cavity, the function of which is to create turbulent air flow and to clean, moisten and warm the inhaled air. The superior turbinate is a projection of the ethmoid bone, and is the uppermost and smallest of the three.

supratemporal plane   The upper surface of the superior temporal gyrus.

surface dyslexia   A form of dyslexia in which the sufferer is unable to recognize words via the visual route, resulting in an ability only to read regular words (and nonwords), but not irregular words, such as 'colonel'.

surface spectral reflectance function   The function describing the proportion of incident light at each wavelength that a particular surface reflects. This is a constant property of a surface, determined by the material from which it is made.

sylvian fissure   A deep fold constituting the uppermost boundary of the temporal lobe. Also called the lateral fissure.

synaptic cleft   The space separating nerve cells at a synapse, across which neurotransmitter must diffuse. In rods and cones the synaptic clefts are modified into the invaginations and triads of rod spherules and cone pedicles.

tachistoscope   A device for presenting visual stimuli for brief, controlled lengths of time.

taction   The mechanical aspects of somatosensation.

tectorial membrane   A soft semi-gelatinous ribbon-like structure attached along one edge to the spiral limbus and along the other edge to the outer border of the organ of Corti. It is in intimate contact with the cilia of the hair cells.

temporal   The half of the retina that is further from the nose.

temporal lobe   Located on the side of the brain, above the ears. It functions in hearing, memory, vision and the categorization of objects.

TENS (transcutaneous electrical nerve stimulation)   A technique for pain reduction using electrical stimuli directed through the skin. The stimuli preferentially excite myelinated nerve fibres and may activate inhibitory neurons or stimulate the release of endorphins within the brain.

tensor tympani muscle   The intra-aural muscle attached to the handle of the malleus. Its reflex contraction, in response to intense sound or tactile stimulation to parts of the face, draws the malleus inwards, which increases the tension on the tympanic membrane. The joint action of the tensor tympani muscle and the stapedius muscle is to limit the motion of the auditory ossicles and thereby help protect the inner ear from damage by intense sound, especially at low frequencies.

tetrachromats   Tetrachromats are creatures whose colour vision is based upon four types of cone photoreceptor. There is some evidence that a small proportion of the female human population is tetrachromatic.

thalamus   The part of the forebrain, formed from a collection of about 30 different nuclei, that relays sensory information to the cerebral cortex.

threshold   The smallest value of a stimulus that can be detected. A measure of sensitivity.

tilt after-effect (TAE)   The perception that, following adaptation by a grating tilted slightly away from the vertical, a vertical grating appears tilted in the opposite direction. This is the result of fatiguing the population of cells coding for the original grating orientation.

timbre   A characteristic quality of sounds produced by a particular voice or instrument that depends on the number and quality of the overtones; partly determined by the relative amplitudes of the different harmonics.

time-to-contact (TTC)   The time needed for a moving entity (e.g. a car) to reach a particular goal.

tinnitus   A condition often colloquially described as 'a ringing in the ears'. Formally acknowledged to be the perception of short-lived or persistent episodes of sound that originate in the head; it may represent phantom auditory perception but effective treatments remain elusive.

tip link   A filamentous connection between two hair cell stereocilia.

tonotopic mapping   The coding of sound frequency to position of excitation.

tonotopic organization   A systematic organization within an auditory structure on the basis of characteristic frequency.

top-down   A form of information processing in which the outcome is strongly influenced by previously held concepts or experience. Synonymous with concept driven, this is the converse of bottom-up or data driven.

transducin   A G-protein (GDP-binding protein) found in the outer segments of rods and cones and involved in transduction.

transduction   A general term for the conversion of one form of energy into another. In vision, for example, the process by which light energy in the form of absorbed photons is converted into a neural signal.

transformer action   The mechanism by which sound waves travelling in air in the outer ear are converted to sound waves travelling in fluid in the inner ear without being reflected at the interface. The transformer action is provided by a combination of the difference in area between the tympanic membrane and the stapes footplate and the lever action of the ossicles in the middle ear.

travelling wave   A wave that propagates energy is known as a travelling wave (as opposed to a standing or stationary wave which does not).

trichromatic vision   The normal colour vision that is experienced by humans. The term is sometimes used more generally to refer to the vision experienced by any creature with three types of cone photoreceptors.

trigeminal neuralgia   Episodes of intense facial pain caused by a disorder of the trigeminal nerve.

trigeminal system   The neural system that senses mechanical and other somatosensory stimuli on the face.

tristimulus values   The amounts of the additive primaries required to match a particular stimulus. The primaries may be R, G and B or the CIE colour matching functions X, Y and Z.

two-interval forced choice technique (2IFC)   A psychophysical technique widely used in vision science. A single trial consists of two brief stimulus presentations separated in time, each signalled by an auditory beep. One of the intervals, chosen at random, contains the test stimulus and the other contains no stimulus. The observer has to decide which interval contains the test stimulus and indicate their response by pressing one of two buttons. By performing many trials it is possible to generate a psychometric function.

tympanic membrane   Also known as the eardrum or tympanum. A conically-shaped semi-transparent membrane that separates the external auditory canal (meatus) from the middle ear cavity. The handle of the malleus is attached to it in the middle ear.

tympanosclerosis   Scarring of the eardrum as a result of infection.

umami   One of the main taste categories; a Japanese word meaning 'delicious savoury taste'. It is common in oriental foods and is the taste of amino acids, particularly glutamate and aspartate.

unimodal   Operating in one modality, i.e. associated with one sense only.

utricle   One of two otolithic organs found in the inner ear; it detects changes in head angle and linear acceleration.

utricular cavity   The part of the vestibule, in the inner ear, with which the semicircular canals communicate.

vagus (Xth cranial nerve)   A parasympathetic nerve that supplies structures in the head, neck, thorax and abdomen. In the head it is cranial nerve X and it innervates taste buds in the lining of the mouth.

vallate (papillae)   *See* circumvallate papillae.

value   One of the three variables used to specify a colour in the Munsell system (the others being hue and chroma), it denotes brightness or lightness. The scale of value ranges from 0 (black) to 10 (white).

vestibular apparatus   Also called the vestibular system, a part of the inner ear specialized for the detection of head motion. It consists of the otolithic organs and the semicircular canals.

vestibular labyrinth   The group of structures which constitute the balance organs.

vestibular nerve   Part of the VIIIth cranial nerve that carries information from the vestibular system to the brain (via afferent neurons) and from the brain to the vestibular system (via efferent neurons).

vestibular schwannoma   Benign tumours arising on the vestibular nerve and derived from the Schwann cells that surround and insulate the nerve fibres. They usually cause unilateral hearing loss and tinnitus.

vestibule   A perilymph-filled oval-shaped central cavity of the osseous labyrinth. It contains the oval window, which is located in its wall facing the middle ear cavity (tympanic wall), as well as the utricle and the saccule.

vestibulocochlear nerve   The VIIIth cranial nerve that carries information from the inner ear (cochlea and vestibular system) to the brain (via afferent neurons) and from the brain to the inner ear (via efferent neurons).

vestibulocollic reflex (VCR)   A reflex movement of the head which arises as a result of information from the vestibular system, and serves to stabilize the head against forces which would move it.

vestibulocollic reflex pathway   The pathway through which the VCR is activated.

vestibulo-ocular reflex (VOR)   A reflex movement of the eyes which is stimulated by rotational movements of the head. It stabilizes the visual image on the retina.

vestibulo-ocular reflex pathway   The pathway through which the VOR is activated.

vestibulospinal tract   Part of the medial brainstem pathway that runs from the vestibular nuclear complex along the spinal cord, and is involved in the control of posture in response to information from the vestibular system.

virtual reality headset   A helmet-like device, with built-in displays for each eye, and often with stereo headphones, which presents computer-generated stimuli so that the wearer feels as if they are in a real world.

visual psychophysics   The study and measurement of the performance of the human visual system. This is done by showing subjects visual stimuli (usually close to the limits of detectability) and measuring how well they can perceive those stimuli.

visual pursuit reflex   The tracking action of the eyes, produced when an object being observed is moving across the field of view.

visual route   The information processing path used in reading that accesses a word's meaning by recognizing the overall pattern of its printed form.

visuotopic representation   Neurons within the visual cortex with a defined map of a visual attribute.

voice onset time   A temporal feature that helps to distinguish between two classes of stop consonants, voiced (e.g. 'ba'), and voiceless (e.g. 'pa').

vomeronasal organ   A chemosensory organ, also known as Jacobson's organ, part of an accessory olfactory system specialized for the detection of pheromones and located in the nasal septum or roof of the mouth in vertebrates. In humans, the organ is present but appears to be vestigial (i.e. not functional).

Wernicke's area   The temporoparietal cortex, part of the network of brain areas concerned with linguistic analysis, particularly the analyis of lexical, semantic and syntactic information.

wide-field bipolar cell   A bipolar cell located towards the periphery of the retina with a wide dendritic tree that makes contact with a large number of cones (greater than 15–20).

word superiority effect   A phenomenon in which tachistoscopically-presented letters are more accurately reported when they form part of a word, rather than being displayed individually.

X-ray diffraction pattern   The pattern produced on an X-ray sensitive detector when a beam of X-rays is scattered (diffracted) by regular atomic-scale structures within a substance. Constructive and destructive interference give rise to light regions (diffraction maxima) and dark regions (diffraction minima) respectively on the detector. The relative positions of the diffraction maxima allow the detailed molecular structure of the substance to be determined.

Index

Entries and page numbers in **bold type** refer to key words which are printed in **bold** in the text and which are defined in the Glossary.